Hunter S. Thompson was a humble man who wrote books for a living and spent the rest of his time bogged down in strange and crazy wars. He was the author of many violent books and brilliant political essays, which his friends and henchmen in the international media have managed for many years to pass off as "Gonzo Journalism".

The reasons for this are myriad, and we will speak of them later. In the meantime, Dr. Thompson lived the life of a freelance country gentleman in Woody Creek, Colorado, and existed in a profoundly active Balance of Terror with the local police authorities. He died in 2005.

HUNTER S. THOMPSON

THE GREAT SHARK HUNT

STRANGE TALES FROM A STRANGE TIME

PICADOR

This collection first published 1979 by Summit Books Inc.

First published in Great Britain 1980 by Picador
an imprint of Pan Macmillan, a division of Macmillan Publishers Limited
Pan Macmillan, 20 New Wharf Road, London N1 9RR
Basingstoke and Oxford
Associated companies throughout the world
www.panmacmillan.com

ISBN 978-0-330-26117-3

49 48 47 46 45

A CIP catalogue record for this book is available from
the British Library.

Printed and bound by
CPI Group (UK) Ltd, Croydon, CR0 4YY

Visit **www.picador.com** to read more about all our books and to buy
them. You will also find features, author interviews and news of any author
events, and you can sign up for e-newsletters so that you're always first to hear
about our new releases.

Grateful acknowledgement is made to the following for permission to reprint the articles and excerpts listed:

Boston Globe
'Memoirs of a Wretched Weekend in Washington' by Hunter S. Thompson, 23 February 1969; reprinted by permission of the *Boston Globe*.

Dow Jones & Company, Inc.
'A Footloose American in a Smugglers' Den' by Hunter S. Thompson; reprinted by permission of the *National Observer*, © Dow Jones & Company, Inc. 1962; all rights reserved.

'Chatty Letters During a Journey from Aruba to Rio' by Hunter S. Thompson; reprinted by permission of the *National Observer*, © Dow Jones & Company, Inc. 1962; all rights reserved.

'Democracy Dies in Peru, But Few Seem to Mourn Its Passing' by Hunter S. Thompson; reprinted by permission of the *National Observer*, © Dow Jones & Company, Inc. 1962; all rights reserved.

'Living in the Time of Alger, Greeley, Debs' by Hunter S. Thompson; reprinted by permission of the *National Observer*, © Dow Jones & Company, Inc. 1964; all rights reserved.

'The Catch Is Limited in Indians' "Fish-in" ' by Hunter S. Thompson; reprinted by permission of the *National Observer*, © Dow Jones & Company, Inc. 1964; all rights reserved.

'The Inca of the Andes' by Hunter S. Thompson; reprinted by permission of the *National Observer*, © Dow Jones & Company, Inc. 1963; all rights reserved.

'What Lured Hemingway to Ketchum' by Hunter S. Thompson; reprinted by permission of the *National Observer*, © Dow Jones & Company, Inc. 1964; all rights reserved.

'When the Beatniks Were Social Lions' by Hunter S. Thompson; reprinted by permission of the *National Observer*, © Dow Jones & Company, Inc. 1964; all rights reserved.

'Why Anti-Gringo Winds Often Blow South of the Border' by Hunter S. Thompson; reprinted by permission of the *National Observer*, © Dow Jones & Company, Inc. 1963; all rights reserved.

Granada Publishing Ltd
Fear and Loathing in Las Vegas by Hunter S. Thompson; first published in Great Britain in 1972 by Paladin Books, Granada Publishing Ltd.

*'To Richard Milhous Nixon,
who never let me down.'*

H.S.T.

'To Juan and . . .'

*'When the going gets weird
the weird turn pro.'*

RAOUL DUKE

CONTENTS

PART ONE

PART TWO

PART THREE

PART FOUR

NEWS RELEASE

AIR PROVING GROUND COMMAND
EGLIN AIR FORCE BASE, FLORIDA

"Proof by Test"

OFFICE OF INFORMATION SERVICES
Telephone 26111 - 2622

EGLIN AFB, FLORIDA-(Nov8)-S/Sgt Manmountain Dense, a novice Air Policeman, was severely injured here today, when a wine bottle exploded inside the AP gatehouse at the west entrance to the base. Dense was incoherent for several hours after the disaster, but managed to make a statement which led investigators to believe the bottle was hurled from a speeding car which approached the gatehouse on the wrong side of the road, coming from the general direction of the SEPARATION CENTER.

Further investigation revealed that, only minutes before the incident at the gatehouse, a reportedly ''fanatical'' airman had received his separation papers and was rumored to have set out in the direction of the gatehouse at a high speed in a muffler-less car with no brakes. An immediate search was begun for Hunter S. Thompson, one-time sports editor of the base newspaper and well-known ''morale problem''. Thompson was known to have a sometimes over-powering affinity for wine and was described by a recent arrival in the base sanatorium as ''just the type of bastard who would do a thing like that''.

An apparently uncontrolable iconoclast, Thompson was discharged today after one of the most hectic and unusual Air Force careers in recent history. According to Captain Munnington Thurd, who was relieved of his duties as base classification officer yesterday and admitted to the neuropsychological section of the base hospital, Thompson was ''totally unclassifiable'' and ''one of the most savage and unnatural airmen I've ever come up against.''

''I'll never understand how he got this discharge'', Thurd went on to say. ''I almost had a stroke yesterday when I heard he was being given an honorable discharge. It's terrifying-simply terrifying.''

And then Thurd sank into a delerium.

-30-

ADDRESS REPLY
ATTN: Base Staff Personnel Officer
Personnel Report: A/2C Hunter S. Thompson   23 Aug 57

1. A/2C Hunter S. Thompson, AF 15546879, has worked in the Internal Information Section, OIS, for nearly one year. During this time he has done some outstanding sports writing, but ignored APGC-OIS policy.

2. Airman Thompson possesses outstanding talent in writing. He has imagination, good use of English, and can express his thoughts in a manner that makes interesting reading.

3. However, in spite of frequent counselling with explanation of the reasons for the conservative policy on an AF Base newspaper, Airman Thompson has consistently written controversial material and leans so strongly to critical editorializing that it was necessary to require that all his writing be thoroughly edited before release.

4. The first article that called attention to the writing noted above was a story very critical of Base Special Services. Others that were stopped before they were printed were pieces that severely criticized Arthur Godfrey and Ted Williams that Airman Thompson extracted from national media releases and added his flair for the inuendo and exaggeration.

5. This Airman has indicated poor judgement from other standpoints by releasing Air Force information to the Playground News himself, with no consideration for other papers in the area, or the fact that only <u>official</u> releases, carefully censored by competent OIS staff members, are allowed.

6. In summary, this Airman, although talented, will not be guided by policy or personal advice and guidance. Sometimes his rebel and superior attitude seems to rub off on other airmen staff members. He has little consideration for military bearing or dress and seems to dislike the service and want out as soon as possible.

7. Consequently, it is requested that Airman Thompson be assigned to other duties immediately, and it is recommended that he be earnestly considered under the early release program.

8. It is also requested that Airman Thompson be officially advised that he is to do no writing of any kind for internal or external publication unless such writing is edited by the OIS staff, and that he is not to accept outside employment with any of the local media.

W.S. EVANS, Colonel, USAF
Chief, Office of Information
Services

PART ONE

AUTHOR'S NOTE

'Art is long and life is short,
and success is very far off.'
                    J. Conrad

Well ... yes, and here we go again.

But before we get to the work, as it were, I want to make sure I know how to cope with this elegant typewriter – (and, yes, it appears that I do) – so why not make this quick list of my life's work and then get the hell out of town on the 11:05 to Denver? Indeed. Why not?

But for just a moment I'd like to say, for the permanent record, that it is a very strange feeling to be a forty-year-old American writer in this century and sitting alone in this huge building on Fifth Avenue in New York at one o'clock in the morning on the night before Christmas Eve, 2000 miles from home, and compiling a table of contents for a book of my own Collected Works in an office with a tall glass door that leads out to a big terrace looking down on the Plaza Fountain.

Very strange.

I feel like I might as well be sitting up here carving the words for my own tombstone ... and when I finish, the only fitting exit will be right straight off this fucking terrace and into the Fountain, twenty-eight storeys below and at least 200 yards out in the air and across Fifth Avenue.

Nobody could follow that act.

Not even me ... and in fact the only way I can deal with this eerie situation at all is to make a conscious decision that I have already lived and finished the life I planned to live – (thirteen years longer, in fact) – and everything from now on will be A New Life, a different thing, a gig that ends tonight and starts tomorrow morning.

So if I decide to leap for the Fountain when I finish this memo, I want to make one thing perfectly clear – I would genuinely love to make that leap, and if I don't I will always consider it a mistake and a failed opportunity, one of the very few serious mistakes of my First Life that is now ending.

But what the hell? I probably won't do it (for all the wrong reasons), and I'll probably finish this table of contents and go home for Christmas and then have to live for a hundred more years with all this goddamn gibberish I'm lashing together.

But, Jesus, it would be a wonderful way to go out ... and if I do it

21

you bastards are going to owe me a king-hell forty-four-gun salutr (that word is 'salute', goddamnit – and I guess I can't work this elegant typewriter as well as I thought I could) ...

But you know I *could*, if I had just a little more time.

Right?

Yes.

H.S.T. #1, R.I.P.
23/12/77

FEAR AND LOATHING IN THE BUNKER

The milkman left me a note yesterday.
Get out of this town by noon,
You're coming on way too soon
And besides that
we never liked you anyway ...
John Prine

Woody Creek, Col. – Strange epitaph for a strange year and no real
point in explaining it either. I haven't had a milkman since I was ten
years old. I used to ride around on the route with him, back in Louisville. It was one of those open-door, stand-up vans that you could jump
in and run out of on the run. He would creep that rancid-smelling truck
along the street from house to house while I ran back and forth with
the goods.

I was the runner, the mule, and occasionally the bagman when some
poor wretch behind on her milk bill had to either pay up or drink water
for breakfast that morning.

Those scenes were always unsettling – some half-awake, middle-aged
housewife yelling at me in her bathrobe through the screen door. But I
was a cold-hearted little bastard in those days. 'Sorry ma'am, but my
boss out there in the truck says I can't leave these bottles here unless you
give me $21.16 ...'

No argument ever fazed me. I doubt that I even heard the words. I
was there to collect, not to listen and I didn't give a hoot in hell if they
paid or not; all I really cared about was the adrenalin rush that came
with sprinting across people's front lawns, jumping hedges, and hitting
that slow-rolling truck before it had to stop and wait for me.

There is some kind of heavy connection between that memory and the
way I feel right now about this stinking year that just ended. Everybody
I talk to seems very excited about it. 'God damn, man! it was a fantastic
year,' they say. 'Maybe the most incredible year in our history.'

Which is probably true. I remember thinking that way, myself, back
on those hot summer mornings when John Dean's face lit my tube day
after day ... incredible. Here was this crafty little ferret going down the
pipe right in front of our eyes, and taking the President of the United
States along with him.

It was almost too good to be true. Richard Milhous Nixon, the main
villain of my political consciousness for as long as I can remember, was

finally biting that bullet he's been talking about all those years. The man that not even Goldwater or Eisenhower could tolerate had finally gone too far – and now he was walking the plank, on national TV, six hours a day – with the whole world watching, as it were.

That phrase is permanently etched on some grey rim on the back of my brain. Nobody who was at the corner of Michigan and Balboa on that Wednesday night in August of 1968 will ever forget it.

Richard Nixon is living in the White House today because of what happened that night in Chicago. Hubert Humphrey lost that election by a handful of votes – mine among them – and if I had to do it again I would still vote for Dick Gregory.

If nothing else, I take a certain pride in knowing that I helped spare the nation eight years of President Humphrey – an Administration that would have been equally corrupt and wrongheaded as Richard Nixon's, far more devious, and probably just competent enough to keep the ship of state from sinking until 1976. Then with the boiler about to explode from eight years of blather and neglect, Humphrey's cold-war liberals could have fled down the ratlines and left the disaster to whoever inherited it.

Nixon, at least, was blessed with a mixture of arrogance and stupidity that caused him to blow the boilers almost immediately after taking command. By bringing in hundreds of thugs, fixers and fascists to run the Government, he was able to crank almost every problem he touched into a mindbending crisis. About the only disaster he hasn't brought down on us yet is a nuclear war with either Russia or China or both ... but he still has time, and the odds on his actually doing it are not all that long. But we will get to that point in a moment.

For now, we should make every effort to look at the bright side of the Nixon Administration. It has been a failure of such monumental proportions that political apathy is no longer considered fashionable, or even safe, among millions of people who only two years ago thought that anybody who disagreed openly with 'the Government' was either paranoid or subversive. Political candidates in 1974, at least, are going to have to deal with an angry, disillusioned electorate that is not likely to settle for flag-waving and pompous bullshit. The Watergate spectacle was a shock, but the fact of a millionaire President paying less income tax than most construction workers while gasoline costs a dollar in Brooklyn and the threat of mass unemployment by spring tends to personalize Mr Nixon's failures in a very visceral way. Even Senators and Congressmen have been shaken out of their slothful ruts, and the possibility of impeachment is beginning to look very real.

Given all this, it is hard to shed anything but crocodile tears over White House speechwriter Patrick Buchanan's tragic analysis of the Nixon débâcle. 'It's like Sisyphus,' he said. 'We rolled the rock all the way up the mountain ... and it rolled right back down on us.'

Well ... shucks. It makes a man's eyes damp, for sure. But I have a lot of confidence in Pat, and I suspect he won't have much trouble finding other rocks to roll.

I have not read 'The Myth of Sisyphus' for a while, but if memory serves there is nothing in that story to indicate that the poor bugger ever gave any thought to the real nature or specific gravity of that rock that would eventually roll back on him – which is understandable, perhaps, because when you're locked into that kind of do-or-die gig, you keep pushing and ask questions later.

If any of those six hundred valiant fools who rode in the Charge of the Light Brigade had any doubts about what they were doing, they kept it to themselves. There is no room in Crusades, especially at the command level, for people who ask 'Why?' Neither Sisyphus nor the commander of the Light Brigade nor Pat Buchanan had the time or any real inclination to question what they were doing. They were Good Soldiers, True Believers ... and when the orders came down from above they did what had to be done: Execute.

Which is admirable in a queer kind of way ... except that Sisyphus got mashed, the Light Brigade slaughtered, and Pat Buchanan will survive in the footnotes of history as a kind of half-mad Davy Crockett on the walls of Nixon's Alamo – a martyr, to the bitter end, to a 'flawed' cause and a narrow, atavistic concept of conservative politics that has done more damage to itself and the country in less than six years than its liberal enemies could have done in two or three decades.

When the cold eye of history looks back on Richard Nixon's five years of unrestrained power in the White House, it will show that he had the same effect on conservative/Republican politics as Charles Manson and the Hell's Angels had on hippies and flower power ... and the ultimate damage, on both fronts, will prove out to be just about equal.

Or maybe not – at least not on the scale of sheer numbers of people affected. In retrospect, the grisly violence of the Manson/Angels trips affected very few people directly, while the greedy, fascistic incompetence of Richard Nixon's Presidency will leave scars on the minds and lives of a whole generation – his supporters and political allies no less than his opponents.

Maybe that's why the end of this incredible, frantic year feels so hollow. Looking back on the sixties, and even back to the fifties, the facts of President Nixon and everything that has happened to him – and to us –

seem so queerly fated and inevitable that it is hard to reflect on those years and see them unfolding in any other way.

One of the strangest things about these five downhill years of the Nixon Presidency is that despite all the savage excesses committed by the people he chose to run the country, no real opposition or realistic alternative to Richard Nixon's cheap and mean-hearted view of the American Dream has ever developed. It is almost as if that sour 1968 election rang down the curtain on career politicians.

This is the horror of American politics today – not that Richard Nixon and his fixers have been crippled, convicted, indicted, disgraced and even jailed – but that the only available alternatives are not much better; the same dim collection of burned-out hacks who have been fouling our air with their gibberish for the last twenty years.

How long, oh Lord, how long? And how much longer will we have to wait before some high-powered shark with a fistful of answers will finally bring us face-to-face with the ugly question that is already so close to the surface in this country, that sooner or later even politicians will have to cope with it?

Is the democracy worth all the risks and problems that necessarily go with it? Or, would we all be happier by admitting that the whole thing was a lark from the start and now that it hasn't worked out, to hell with it.

That milkman who made me his bagman was no fool. I took my orders from him and it never occurred to me to wonder where his came from. It was enough for me to cruise those elm-lined streets in a big, bright-coloured van and deliver the goods. But I was ten years old then and I didn't know much ... or at least not as much as I know now.

But every once in a while, on humourless nights like these, I think about how sharp and sure I felt when I was sprinting across those manicured lawns, jumping the finely trimmed hedges and hitting the running board of that slow-cruising truck.

If the milkman had given me a pistol and told me to put a bullet in the stomach of any slob who haggled about the bill, I would probably have done that, too. Because the milkman was my boss and my benefactor. He drove the truck – and as far as I was concerned he might as well have been the Pope or the President. On a 'need to know' basis, the milkman understood that I was not among the needy. Nor was he, for that matter. We were both a lot happier just doing what we were told.

George Orwell had a phrase for it. Neither he nor Aldous Huxley had much faith in the future of participatory democracy. Orwell even set a date: 1984 – and the most disturbing revelation that emerged from last year's Watergate hearings was not so much the arrogance and criminality of Nixon's henchmen, but the aggressively totalitarian character of his whole Administration. It is ugly to know just how close we came to meeting Orwell's deadline.

Meanwhile, it is tempting to dismiss the ominous fact that Richard Nixon is still the President. The spectre of impeachment lends more and more weight to the probability of his resignation. If I were a gambling person – which I am, whenever possible – I would bet that Nixon will resign for 'reasons of health' within the next six months.

It will be a nasty gig when it happens; a maudlin spectacle in prime time on all four TV networks. He will kick out the jams in a desperate bid for martyrdom, and then he will fly off, forever, to a life of brooding isolation – perhaps on one of Robert Abplanalp's private islands in the Bahamas.

There will be all-night poker games on the palm-screened patio, with other wealthy exiles like Howard Hughes and Robert Vesco and occasionally Bebe Rebozo ... and Nixon, the doomed exile, will spend the daylight hours dictating his memoirs in a permanent state of high fever and vengefulness to his faithful secretary and companion, Rose Mary Woods. The only other residents on the island will be Secret Service guards assigned on a six-month rotation basis by Acting President Gerald Ford.

That is one scenario, and the odds would seem to favour it. But there are quite a few others – all based on the grim possibility that Richard Nixon might have no intention at all of resigning. He just may have already sketched out a last-ditch, D-Day style battle plan that would turn the tide with one stroke and scuttle any move for impeachment.

Which brings us back to the question of nuclear war, or at least a quick nuclear zap against China, with the full and formal support of our old ally, Russia.

There is a fiendish simplicity in this plan, a Hitleresque logic so awful that I would not even think about printing it unless I were absolutely certain that Nixon was at least a year ahead of me in the plan and all its details. Even now, I suspect, he spends the last half hour of each day keeping it constantly up to date on one of his yellow legal pads.

So here it is – the Final Solution to Almost All Our Problems:
1 A long-term treaty with Russia, arranged by Henry Kissinger, securing Moscow's support of an American invasion, seizure and terminal occupation of all oil-producing countries in the Middle East. This would not only solve the 'energy crisis' and end unemployment immediately by pressing all idle and able-bodied males into service for the invasion/occupation forces ... but it would also crank up the economy to a war-

time level and give the Federal Government unlimited 'emergency powers'.

2 In exchange for Russian support for our violent seizure of all Middle East oil reserves, the United States would agree to support the USSR in a 'pre-emptive nuclear strike' against targets in China, destroying at least ninety per cent of that nation's industrial capacity and reducing the population to a state of chaos, panic and famine for the next hundred years. This would end the Kremlin's worries about China, guarantee peace in Indochina for the foreseeable future; and ensure a strong and friendly ally, in Japan, as kingpin of the East.

These are merely the highlights of the Final Solution. No doubt there are other and uglier aspects, but my time and space are too limited for any long screeds on the subject. The only real question is whether Mr Nixon is mad enough to run the risk of paralysing both the Congress and the people by resorting to such drastic measures.

There is no doubt at all, in my own mind, that he is capable of it. But it will not be quite as easy for him now as it would have been last year.

Six months ago I was getting a daily rush out of watching the nightmare unfold. There was a warm sense of poetic justice in seeing 'fate' drive these money-changers out of the temple they had worked so hard to steal from its rightful owners. The word 'paranoia' was no longer mentioned, except as a joke or by yahoos, in serious conversations about national politics. The truth was turning out to be even worse than my most 'paranoid ravings' during that painful 1972 election.

But that high is beginning to fade, tailing down to a vague sense of *angst*. Whatever happens to Richard Nixon when the wolves finally trip down his door seems almost beside the point, now. He has been down in his bunker for so long, that even his friends will feel nervous if he tries to re-emerge. All we can really ask of him, at this point, is a semblance of self-restraint until some way can be found to get rid of him gracefully.

This is not a cheerful prospect, for Mr Nixon or anyone else – but it would be a hell of a lot easier to cope with if we could pick up a glimmer of light at the end of this foul tunnel of a year that only mad dogs and milkmen can claim to have survived without serious brain damage.

Or maybe it's just me. It is ten below zero outside and the snow hasn't stopped for two days. The sun has apparently been sucked into orbit behind the comet Kohoutek. Is this really a new year? Are we bottoming out? Or are we into the Age of the Fear?

New York Times, 1 January 1974

THE KENTUCKY DERBY IS DECADENT
AND DEPRAVED

I got off the plane around midnight and no one spoke as I crossed the dark runway to the terminal. The air was thick and hot, like wandering into a steam bath. Inside, people hugged each other and shook hands ... big grins and a whoop here and there: 'By God! You old *bastard*! *Good* to see you, boy! *Damn* good ... and I *mean* it!'

In the air-conditioned lounge I met a man from Houston who said his name was something or other – 'but just call me Jimbo' – and he was here to get it on. 'I'm ready for *anything*, by God! Anything at all. Yeah, what are you drinkin'?' I ordered a Margarita with ice, but he wouldn't hear of it: 'Naw, naw ... what the hell kind of drink is that for Kentucky Derby time? What's *wrong* with you, boy?' He grinned and winked at the bartender. 'Goddamn, we gotta educate this boy. Get him some good *whisky* ...'

I shrugged. 'Okay, a double Old Fitz on ice.' Jimbo nodded his approval.

'Look.' He tapped me on the arm to make sure I was listening. 'I know this Derby crowd, I come here every year, and let me tell you one thing I've learned – this is no town to be giving people the impression you're some kind of faggot. Not in public, anyway. Shit, they'll roll you in a minute, knock you in the head and take every goddamn cent you have.'

I thanked him and fitted a Marlboro into my cigarette holder. 'Say,' he said, 'you look like you might be in the horse business ... am I right?'

'No,' I said. 'I'm a photographer.'

'Oh yeah?' He eyed my ragged leather bag with new interest. 'Is that what you got there – cameras? Who you work for?'

'*Playboy*,' I said.

He laughed. 'Well, goddamn! What are you gonna take pictures of – nekkid horses? Haw! I guess you'll be workin' pretty hard when they run the Kentucky Oaks. That's a race just for fillies.' He was laughing wildly. 'Hell yes! And they'll all be nekkid too!'

I shook my head and said nothing; just stared at him for a moment, trying to look grim. 'There's going to be trouble,' I said. 'My assignment is to take pictures of the riot.'

'What riot?'

I hesitated, twirling the ice in my drink. 'At the track. On Derby Day.

The Black Panthers.' I stared at him again. 'Don't you read the news-papers?'

The grin on his face had collapsed. 'What the *hell* are you talkin' about?'

'Well ... maybe I shouldn't be telling you ...' I shrugged. 'But hell, everybody else seems to know. The cops and the National Guard have been getting ready for six weeks. They have 20,000 troops on alert at Fort Knox. They've warned us – all the press and photographers – to wear helmets and special vests like flak jackets. We were told to expect shooting ...'

'No!' he shouted; his hands flew up and hovered momentarily be-tween us, as if to ward off the words he was hearing. Then he whacked his fist on the bar. 'Those sons of bitches! God Almighty! The Ken-tucky Derby!' He kept shaking his head. 'No! *Jesus!* That's almost too bad to believe!' Now he seemed to be sagging on the stool, and when he looked up his eyes were misty. 'Why? Why *here*? Don't they respect *anything*?'

I shrugged again. 'It's not just the Panthers. The FBI say busloads of white crazies are coming in from all over the country – to mix with the crowd and attack all at once, from every direction. They'll be dressed like everybody else. You know – coats and ties and all that. But when the trouble starts ... well, that's why the cops are so worried.'

He sat for a moment, looking hurt and confused and not quite able to digest all this terrible news. Then he cried out: 'Oh ... Jesus! What in the name of God is happening in this country? Where can you get *away* from it?'

'Not here,' I said, picking up my bag. 'Thanks for the drink ... and good luck.'

He grabbed my arm, urging me to have another, but I said I was overdue at the Press Club and hustled off to get my act together for the awful spectacle. At the airport newsstand I picked up a *Courier-Journal* and scanned the front page headlines: 'Nixon Sends GIs into Cambodia to Hit Reds' ... 'B-52s Raid, then 2,000 GIs Advance 20 Miles' ... '4,000 US Troops Deployed Near Yale as Tension Grows Over Panther Protest.' At the bottom of the page was a photo of Diane Crump, soon to become the first woman jockey ever to ride in the Kentucky Derby. The photographer had snapped her 'stopping in the barn area to fondle her mount, Fathom'. The rest of the paper was spotted with ugly war news and stories of 'student unrest'. There was no mention of any trouble brewing at a university in Ohio called Kent State.

I went to the Hertz desk to pick up my car, but the moon-faced young swinger in charge said they didn't have any. 'You can't rent one any-where,' he assured me. 'Our Derby reservations have been booked for six weeks.' I explained that my agent had confirmed a white Chrysler convertible for me that very afternoon but he shook his head. 'Maybe we'll have a cancellation. Where are you staying?'

I shrugged. 'Where's the Texas crowd staying? I want to be with my people.'

He sighed. 'My friend, you're in trouble. This town is flat *full*. Always is, for the Derby.'

I leaned closer to him, half-whispering: 'Look, I'm from *Playboy*. How would you like a job?'

He backed off quickly. 'What? Come on, now. What kind of a job?'

'Never mind,' I said. 'You just blew it.' I swept my bag off the counter and went to find a cab. The bag is a valuable prop in this kind of work; mine has a lot of baggage tags on it – SF, LA, NY, Lima, Rome, Bangkok, that sort of thing – and the most prominent tag of all is a very official, plastic-coated thing that says 'Photog. Playboy Mag'. I bought it from a pimp in Vail, Colorado, and he told me how to use it. 'Never mention *Playboy* until you're sure they've seen this thing first,' he said. 'Then, when you see them notice it, that's the time to strike. They'll go belly up every time. This thing is magic, I tell you. Pure magic.'

Well ... maybe so. I'd used it on the poor geek in the bar, and now, humming along in a Yellow Cab towards town, I felt a little guilty about jangling the poor bugger's brains with that evil fantasy. But what the hell? Anybody who wanders around the world saying, 'Hell yes, I'm from Texas', deserves whatever happens to him. And he had, after all, come here once again to make a nineteenth-century ass of himself in the midst of some jaded, atavistic freakout with nothing to recommend it except a very saleable 'tradition'. Early in our chat, Jimbo had told me that he hasn't missed a Derby since 1954. 'The little lady won't come any more,' he said. 'She just grits her teeth and turns me loose for this one. And when I say "loose" I do mean *loose*! I toss ten-dollar bills around like they were goin' outa style! Horses, whisky, women ... shit, there's women in this town that'll do *anything* for money.'

Why not? Money is a good thing to have in these twisted times. Even Richard Nixon is hungry for it. Only a few days before the Derby he said, 'If I had any money I'd invest it in the stock market.' And the market, meanwhile, continued its grim slide.

The next day was heavy. With only thirty hours until post time I had no press credentials and – according to the sports editor of the Louisville *Courier-Journal* – no hope at all of getting any. Worse, I needed *two* sets; one for myself and another for Ralph Steadman, the English illustrator who was coming from London to do some Derby drawings. All I knew about him was that this was his first visit to the United States. And the more I pondered that fact, the more it gave me the fear. How would he bear up under the heinous culture shock of being lifted out of London and plunged into a drunken mob scene at the Kentucky Derby? There was no way of knowing. Hopefully, he would arrive at least a day or so ahead, and give himself time to get acclimated. Maybe a few hours of peaceful sightseeing in the Bluegrass country around Lexington. My plan was to pick him up at the airport in the huge Pontiac Ballbuster I'd rented from a used-car salesman named Colonel Quick, then whisk him off to some peaceful setting that might remind him of England.

Colonel Quick had solved the car problem, and money (four times the normal rate) had bought two rooms in a scumbox on the outskirts of town. The only other kink was the task of convincing the moguls at Churchill Downs that *Scanlan's* was such a prestigious sporting journal that common sense compelled them to give us two sets of the best press tickets. This was not easily done. My first call to the publicity office resulted in total failure. The press handler was shocked at the idea that anyone would be stupid enough to apply for press credentials two days before the Derby. 'Hell, you can't be serious,' he said. 'The deadline was two months ago. The press box is full; there's no more room ... and what the hell is *Scanlan's Monthly* anyway?'

I uttered a painful groan. 'Didn't the London office call you? They're flying an artist over to do the paintings. Steadman. He's Irish, I think. Very famous over there. Yes. I just got in from the Coast. The San Francisco office told me we were all set.'

He seemed interested, and even sympathetic, but there was nothing he could do. I flattered him with more gibberish, and finally he offered a compromise: he could get us two passes to the clubhouse grounds but the clubhouse itself and especially the press box were out of the question.

'That sounds a little weird,' I said. 'It's unacceptable. We *must* have access to everything. *All* of it. The spectacle, the people, the pageantry and certainly the race. You don't think we came all this way to watch the damn thing on television, do you? One way or another we'll get inside. Maybe we'll have to bribe a guard – or even Mace somebody.' (I had picked up a spray can of Mace in a downtown drugstore for $5.98 and suddenly, in the midst of that phone talk, I was struck by the hideous possibilities of using it out at the track. Macing ushers at the narrow gates to the clubhouse inner sanctum, then slipping quickly inside, firing a huge load of Mace into the governor's box, just as the race starts. Or Macing helpless drunks in the clubhouse restroom, for their own good ...)

By noon on Friday I was still without credentials and still unable to locate Steadman. For all I knew he'd changed his mind and gone back to London. Finally, after giving up on Steadman and trying unsuccessfully to reach my man in the press office, I decided my only hope for credentials was to go out to the track and confront the man in person, with no warning – demanding only one pass now, instead of two, and talking very fast with a strange lilt in my voice, like a man trying hard to control some inner frenzy. On the way out, I stopped at the motel desk to cash a cheque. Then, as a useless afterthought, I asked if by any wild chance a Mr Steadman had checked in.

The lady on the desk was about fifty years old and very peculiar-looking; when I mentioned Steadman's name she nodded, without looking up from whatever she was writing, and said in a low voice, 'You bet he did.' Then she favoured me with a big smile. 'Yes, indeed. Mr Steadman left for the racetrack. Is he a friend of yours?'

I shook my head. 'I'm supposed to be working with him, but I don't even know what he looks like. Now, goddammit, I'll have to find him in that mob at the track.'

She chuckled. 'You won't have any trouble finding him. You could pick *that* man out of any crowd.'

'Why?' I asked. 'What's wrong with him? What does he look like?'

'Well ...' she said, still grinning, 'he's the funniest looking thing I've seen in a long time. He has this ... ah ... this *growth* all over his face. As a matter of fact it's all over his *head*.' She nodded. 'You'll know him when you see him; don't worry about that.'

Creeping Jesus, I thought. That screws the press credentials. I had a vision of some nerve-rattling geek all covered with matted hair and string-warts showing up in the press office and demanding *Scanlan's* press packet. Well ... what the hell? We could always load up on acid and spend the day roaming around the clubhouse grounds with big sketch pads, laughing hysterically at the natives and swilling mint juleps so the cops wouldn't think we're abnormal. Perhaps even make the act pay: set up an easel with a big sign saying, 'Let a Foreign Artist Paint Your Portrait, $10 Each. Do It NOW!'

I took the expressway out to the track, driving very fast and jumping the monster car back and forth between lanes, driving with a beer in one hand and my mind so muddled that I almost crushed a Volkswagen full of nuns when I swerved to catch the right exit. There was a slim chance, I thought, that I might be able to catch the ugly Britisher before he checked in.

But Steadman was already in the press box when I got there, a bearded young Englishman wearing a tweed coat and RAF sunglasses. There was nothing particularly odd about him. No facial veins or clumps of bristly warts. I told him about the motel woman's description and he seemed puzzled. 'Don't let it bother you,' I said. 'Just keep in mind for the next few days that we're in Louisville, Kentucky. Not London. Not even New York. This is a weird place. You're lucky that mental defective at the motel didn't jerk a pistol out of the cash register and blow a big hole in you.' I laughed, but he looked worried.

'Just pretend you're visiting a huge outdoor loony bin,' I said. 'If the inmates get out of control we'll soak them down with Mace.' I showed him the can of 'Chemical Billy', resisting the urge to fire it across the room at a rat-faced man typing diligently in the Associated Press section. We were standing at the bar, sipping the management's Scotch and congratulating each other on our sudden, unexplained luck in picking up two sets of fine press credentials. The lady at the desk had been very friendly to him, he said. 'I just told her my name and she gave me the whole works.'

By midafternoon we had everything under control. We had seats looking down on the finish line, colour TV and a free bar in the press room, and a selection of passes that would take us anywhere from the clubhouse roof to the jockey room. The only thing we lacked was unlimited access to the clubhouse inner sanctum in sections 'F&G' ... and I felt we needed that, to see the whisky gentry in action. The governor, a swinish neo-Nazi hack named Louie Nunn, would be in 'G', along with Barry Goldwater and Colonel Sanders. I felt we'd be legal in a box in 'G' where we could rest and sip juleps, soak up a bit of atmosphere and the Derby's special vibrations.

The bars and dining rooms are also in 'F&G', and the clubhouse bars on Derby Day are a very special kind of scene. Along with the politicians, society belles and local captains of commerce, every half-mad dingbat who ever had any pretensions to anything at all within five hundred miles of Louisville will show up there to get strutting drunk and slap a lot of backs and generally make himself obvious. The Paddock bar is probably the best place in the track to sit and watch faces. Nobody minds being stared at; that's what they're in there for. Some people spend most of their time in the Paddock; they can hunker down at one of the many wooden tables, lean back in a comfortable chair and watch the ever-changing odds flash up and down on the big tote board outside the window. Black waiters in white serving jackets move through the crowd with trays of drinks, while the experts ponder their racing forms and the hunch betters pick lucky numbers or scan the line-up for rightsounding names. There is a constant flow of traffic to and from the parimutuel windows outside in the wooden corridors. Then, as post time nears, the crowd thins out as people go back to their boxes.

Clearly, we were going to have to figure out some way to spend more time in the clubhouse tomorrow. But the 'walkaround' press passes to F&G were only good for thirty minutes at a time, presumably to allow the newspaper types to rush in and out for photos or quick interviews, but to prevent drifters like Steadman and me from spending all day in the clubhouse, harassing the gentry and rifling the odd handbag or two while cruising around the boxes. Or Macing the governor. The time limit was no problem on Friday, but on Derby Day the walkaround passes would be in heavy demand. And since it took about ten minutes to get from the press box to the Paddock, and ten more minutes to get back, that didn't leave much time for serious people-watching. And unlike most of the others in the press box, we didn't give a hoot in hell what was happening on the track. We had come there to watch the *real* beasts perform.

Later Friday afternoon, we went out on the balcony of the press box and I tried to describe the difference between what we were seeing today and what would be happening tomorrow. This was the first time I'd been to a Derby in ten years, but before that, when I lived in Louisville, I used to go every year. Now, looking down from the press box, I pointed to the huge grassy meadow enclosed by the track. 'That whole thing,' I said, 'will be jammed with people; fifty thousand or so, and most of them staggering drunk. It's a fantastic scene – thousands of people fainting, crying, copulating, trampling each other and fighting with broken whisky bottles. We'll have to spend some time out there, but it's hard to move around, too many bodies.'

'Is it safe out there? Will we *ever* come back?'

'Sure,' I said. 'We'll just have to be careful not to step on anybody's stomach and start a fight.' I shrugged. 'Hell, this clubhouse scene right below us will be almost as bad as the infield. Thousands of raving, stumbling drunks, getting angrier and angrier as they lose more and more money. By midafternoon they'll be guzzling mint juleps with both hands and vomiting on each other between races. The whole place will be jammed with bodies, shoulder to shoulder. It's hard to move around. The aisles will be slick with vomit; people falling down and grabbing at your legs to keep from being stomped. Drunks pissing on themselves in the betting lines. Dropping handfuls of money and fighting to stoop over and pick it up.'

He looked so nervous that I laughed. 'I'm just kidding,' I said. 'Don't worry. At the first hint of trouble I'll start pumping this "Chemical Billy" into the crowd.'

He had done a few good sketches, but so far we hadn't seen that special kind of face that I felt we would need for the lead drawing. It was a face I'd seen a thousand times at every Derby I'd ever been to. I saw it, in my head, as the mask of the whisky gentry – a pretentious mix of booze, failed dreams and a terminal identity crisis; the inevitable result of too much inbreeding in a closed and ignorant culture. One of the key genetic rules in breeding dogs, horses or any other kind of thoroughbred is that close inbreeding tends to magnify the weak points in a bloodline as well as the strong points. In horse breeding, for instance, there is a definite risk in breeding two fast horses who are both a little crazy. The offspring will likely be very fast and also very crazy. So the trick in breeding thoroughbreds is to retain the good traits and filter out the bad. But the breeding of humans is not so wisely supervised, particularly in a narrow Southern society where the closest kind of inbreeding is not only stylish and acceptable, but far more convenient – to the parents – than setting their offspring free to find their own mates, for their own reasons and in their own ways. ('Goddamn, did you hear about Smitty's daughter? She went crazy in Boston last week and married a nigger!')

So the face I was trying to find in Churchill Downs that weekend was a symbol, in my own mind, of the whole doomed atavistic culture that makes the Kentucky Derby what it is.

On our way back to the motel after Friday's races I warned Steadman about some of the other problems we'd have to cope with. Neither of us had brought any strange illegal drugs, so we would have to get by on booze. 'You should keep in mind,' I said, 'that almost everybody you talk to from now on will be drunk. People who seem very pleasant at first might suddenly swing at you for no reason at all.' He nodded, staring straight ahead. He seemed to be getting a little numb and I tried to cheer him up by inviting him to dinner that night, with my brother.

Back at the motel we talked for a while about America, the South, England – just relaxing a bit before dinner. There was no way either of us could have known, at that time, that it would be the last normal conversation we would have. From that point on, the weekend became a vicious, drunken nightmare. We both went completely to pieces. The main problem was my prior attachment to Louisville, which naturally led to meetings with old friends, relatives, etc., many of whom were in the process of falling apart, going mad, plotting divorces, cracking up under the strain of terrible debts or recovering from bad accidents. Right in the middle of the whole frenzied Derby action, a member of my own family had to be institutionalized. This added a certain amount of strain to the situation, and since poor Steadman had no choice but to take whatever came his way, he was subjected to shock after shock.

Another problem was his habit of sketching people he met in the various social situations I dragged him into – then giving them the sketches. The results were always unfortunate. I warned him several times about letting the subjects see his foul renderings, but for some perverse reason he kept doing it. Consequently, he was regarded with fear and loathing by nearly everyone who'd seen or even heard about his work. He couldn't understand it. 'It's sort of a joke,' he kept saying. 'Why, in England it's quite normal. People don't take offence. They understand that I'm just putting them on a bit.'

'Fuck England,' I said. 'This is Middle America. These people regard what you're doing to them as a brutal, bilious insult. Look what happened last night. I thought my brother was going to tear your head off.'

Steadman shook his head sadly. 'But I liked him. He struck me as a very decent, straightforward sort.'

'Look, Ralph,' I said. 'Let's not kid ourselves. That was a very horrible drawing you gave him. It was the face of a monster. It got on his nerves very badly.' I shrugged. 'Why in hell do you think we left the restaurant so fast?'

'I thought it was because of the Mace,' he said.

'What Mace?'

He grinned. 'When you shot it at the headwaiter, don't you remember?'

'Hell, that was nothing,' I said. 'I missed him ... and we were leaving, anyway.'

'But it got all over us,' he said. 'The room was full of that damn gas. Your brother was sneezing and his wife was crying. My eyes hurt for two hours. I couldn't see to draw when we got back to the motel.'

'That's right,' I said. 'The stuff got on her leg, didn't it?'

'She was angry,' he said.

'Yeah ... well, okay ... Let's just figure we fucked up about equally on that one,' I said. 'But from now on let's try to be careful when we're around people I know. You won't sketch them and I won't Mace them. We'll just try to relax and get drunk.'

'Right,' he said. 'We'll go native.'

It was Saturday morning, the day of the Big Race, and we were having breakfast in a plastic hamburger palace called the Fish-Meat Village. Our rooms were just across the road in the Brown Suburban Hotel. They had a dining room, but the food was so bad that we couldn't handle it any more. The waitresses seemed to be suffering from shin splints; they moved around very slowly, moaning and cursing the 'darkies' in the kitchen.

Steadman liked the Fish-Meat place because it had fish and chips. I preferred the 'French toast', which was really pancake batter, fried to the proper thickness and then chopped out with a sort of cookie cutter to resemble pieces of toast.

Beyond drink and lack of sleep, our only real problem at that point was the question of access to the clubhouse. Finally we decided to go ahead and steal two passes, if necessary, rather than miss that part of the action. This was the last coherent decision we were able to make for the next forty-eight hours. From that point on – almost from the very moment we started out to the track – we lost all control of events and spent the rest of the weekend churning around in a sea of drunken horrors. My notes and recollections from Derby Day are somewhat scrambled.

But now, looking at the big red notebook I carried all through that scene, I see more or less what happened. The book itself is somewhat mangled and bent; some of the pages are torn, others are shrivelled and stained by what appears to be whisky, but taken as a whole, with sporadic memory flashes, the notes seem to tell the story. To wit:

Rain all nite until dawn. No sleep. Christ, here we go, a nightmare of mud and madness ... But no. By noon the sun burns through – perfect day, not even humid.

Steadman is now worried about fire. Somebody told him about the clubhouse catching on fire two years ago. Could it happen again? Horrible. Trapped in the press box. Holocaust. A hundred thousand people fighting to get out. Drunks screaming in the flames and the mud, crazed horses running wild. Blind in the smoke. Grandstand collapsing into the flames with us on the roof. Poor Ralph is about to crack. Drinking heavily, into the Haig & Haig.

Out to the track in a cab, avoid that terrible parking in people's front yards, $25 each, toothless old men on the street with big signs: PARK HERE, flagging cars in the yard. 'That's fine, boy, never mind the tulips.' Wild hair on his head, straight up like a clump of reeds.

Sidewalks full of people all moving in the same direction, towards Churchill Downs. Kids hauling coolers and blankets, teenyboppers in tight pink shorts, many blacks ... black dudes in white felt hats with leopard-skin bands, cops waving traffic along.

The mob was thick for many blocks around the track; very slow going in the crowd, very hot. On the way to the press box elevator, just inside the clubhouse, we came on a row of soldiers all carrying long white riot sticks. About two platoons, with helmets. A man walking next to us said they were waiting for the governor and his party. Steadman eyed them nervously. 'Why do they have those clubs?'

'Black Panthers,' I said. Then I remembered good old 'Jimbo' at the airport and I wondered what he was thinking right now. Probably very nervous; the place was teeming with cops and soldiers. We pressed on through the crowd, through many gates, past the paddock where the jockeys bring the horses out and parade around for a while before each race so the betters can get a good look. Five million dollars will be bet today. Many winners, more losers. What the hell. The press gate was jammed up with people trying to get in, shouting at the guards, waving strange press badges: Chicago Sporting Times, Pittsburgh Police Athletic League ... they were all turned away. 'Move on, fella, make way for the working press.' We shoved through the crowd and into the elevator, then quickly up to the free bar. Why not? Get it on. Very hot today, not feeling well, must be this rotten climate. The press box was cool and airy, plenty of room to walk around and balcony seats for watching the race or looking down at the crowd. We got a betting sheet and went outside.

Pink faces with a stylish Southern sag, old Ivy styles, seersucker coats and buttondown collars. 'Mayblossom senility' (Steadman's phrase) ... burnt out early or maybe just not much to burn in the first place. Not much energy in these faces, not much *curiosity*. Suffering in silence, nowhere to go after thirty in this life, just hang on and humour the children. Let the young enjoy themselves while they can. Why not?

The grim reaper comes early in this league ... banshees on the lawn at night, screaming out there beside that little iron nigger in jockey clothes. Maybe he's the one who's screaming. Bad DTs and too many snarls at the bridge club. Going down with the stock market. Oh Jesus the kid has wrecked the new car, wrapped it around the big stone pilla at the bottom of the driveway. Broken leg? Twisted eye? Send him o' to Yale, they can cure anything up there.

Yale? Did you see today's paper? New Haven is under siege. Yale : swarming with Black Panthers ... I tell you, Colonel, the world has gon mad, stone mad. Why, they tell me a goddamn woman jockey migh ride in the Derby today.

I left Steadman sketching in the Paddock bar and went off to place our bets on the fourth race. When I came back he was staring intently at a group of young men around a table not far away. 'Jesus, look at the corruption in that face!' he whispered. 'Look at the madness, the fear, the greed!' I looked, then quickly turned my back on the table he was sketching. The face he'd picked out to draw was the face of an old friend of mine, a prep school football star in the good old days with a sleek red Chevy convertible and a very quick hand, it was said, with the snaps of a 32 B brassiere. They called him 'Cat Man'.

But now, a dozen years later, I wouldn't have recognized him anywhere but here, where I should have expected to find him, in the Paddock bar on Derby Day ... fat slanted eyes and a pimp's smile, blue silk suit and his friends looking like crooked bank tellers on a binge ...

Steadman wanted to see some Kentucky Colonels, but he wasn't sure what they looked like. I told him to go back to the clubhouse men's rooms and look for men in white linen suits vomiting in the urinals. 'They'll usually have large brown whisky stains on the fronts of their suits,' I said. 'But watch the shoes, that's the tip-off. Most of them manage to avoid vomiting on their own clothes, but they never miss their shoes.'

In a box not far from ours was Colonel Anna Friedman Goldman, *Chairman and Keeper of the Great Seal of the Honorable Order of Kentucky Colonels.* Not all the seventy million or so Kentucky Colonels could make it to the Derby this year, but many had kept the faith, and several days prior to the Derby they gathered for their annual dinner at the Seelbach Hotel.

The Derby, the actual race, was scheduled for late afternoon, and as the magic hour approached I suggested to Steadman that we should probably spend some time in the infield, that boiling sea of people across the track from the clubhouse. He seemed a little nervous about it, but since none of the awful things I'd warned him about had happened so far – no race riots, firestorms or savage drunken attacks – he shrugged and said, 'Right, let's do it.'

To get there we had to pass through many gates, each one a step down in status, then through a tunnel under the track. Emerging from the tunnel was such a culture shock that it took a while to adjust. 'God almighty!' Steadman muttered. 'This is a ... Jesus!' He plunged ahead with his tiny camera, stepping over bodies, and I followed, trying to take notes.

Total chaos, no way to see the race, not even the track ... nobody cares. Big lines at the outdoor betting windows, then stand back to watch winning numbers flash on the big board, like a giant bingo game.

Old blacks arguing about bets; 'Hold on there, I'll handle this' (waving pint of whisky, fistful of dollar bills); girl riding piggyback, T-shirt says, 'Stolen from Fort Lauderdale Jail'. Thousands of teenagers, group singing 'Let the Sun Shine In', ten soldiers guarding the American flag with a huge fat drunk wearing a blue football jersey (No. 80) reeling around with quart of beer in hand.

No booze sold out here, too dangerous ... no bathrooms either. Muscle Beach ... Woodstock ... many cops with riot sticks, but no sign of a riot. Far across the track the clubhouse looks like a postcard from the Kentucky Derby.

We went back to the clubhouse to watch the big race. When the crowd stood to face the flag and sing 'My Old Kentucky Home', Steadman faced the crowd and sketched frantically. Somewhere up in the boxes a voice screeched, 'Turn around, you hairy freak!' The race itself was only two minutes long, and even from our super-status seats and using 12-power glasses, there was no way to see what was really happening. Later, watching a TV rerun in the press box, we saw what happened to our horses. Holy Land, Ralph's choice, stumbled and lost his jockey in the final turn. Mine, Silent Screen, had the lead coming into the stretch, but faded to fifth at the finish. The winner was a 16–1 shot named Dust Commander.

Moments after the race was over, the crowd surged wildly for the exits, rushing for cabs and buses. The next day's *Courier* told of violence in the parking lot; people were punched and trampled, pockets were picked, children lost, bottles hurled. But we missed all this, having retired to the press box for a bit of post-race drinking. By this time we were both half-crazy from too much whisky, sun fatigue, culture shock, lack of sleep and general dissolution. We hung around the press box long enough to watch a mass interview with the winning owner, a dapper little man named Lehmann who said he had just flown into Louisville that morning from Nepal, where he'd 'bagged a record tiger'. The sportswriters murmured their admiration and a waiter filled Lehmann's glass with Chivas Regal. He had just won $127,000 with a horse that cost him $6,500 two years ago. His occupation, he said, was 'retired contractor'. And then he added, with a big grin, 'I just retired.'

The rest of that day blurs into madness. The rest of that night too. And all the next day and night. Such horrible things occurred that I can't bring myself even to think about them now, much less put them down in print. Steadman was lucky to get out of Louisville without serious injuries, and I was lucky to get out at all. One of my clearest memories of that vicious time is Ralph being attacked by one of my old friends in the billiard room of the Pendennis Club in downtown Louisville on Saturday night. The man had ripped his own shirt open to the waist before deciding that Ralph was after his wife. No blows were struck, but the emotional effects were massive. Then, as a sort of final horror, Steadman put his fiendish pen to work and tried to patch things up by doing a little sketch of the girl he'd been accused of hustling. That finished us in the Pendennis.

Sometime around ten-thirty Monday morning I was awakened by a scratching sound at my door. I leaned out of bed and pulled the curtain back just far enough to see Steadman outside. 'What the fuck do you want?' I shouted.

'What about having breakfast?' he said.

I lunged out of bed and tried to open the door, but it caught on the night-chain and banged shut again. I couldn't cope with the chain! The thing wouldn't come out of the track – so I ripped it out of the wall with a vicious jerk on the door. Ralph didn't blink. 'Bad luck,' he muttered.

I could barely see him. My eyes were swollen almost shut and the sudden burst of sunlight through the door left me stunned and helpless like a sick mole. Steadman was mumbling about sickness and terrible heat; I fell back on the bed and tried to focus on him as he moved around the room in a very distracted way for a few moments, then suddenly darted over to the beer bucket and seized a Colt 45. 'Christ,' I said. 'You're getting out of control.'

He nodded and ripped the cap off, taking a long drink. 'You know, this is really awful,' he said finally. 'I *must* get out of this place ...' he shook his head nervously. 'The plane leaves at three-thirty, but I don't know if I'll make it.'

I barely heard him. My eyes had finally opened enough for me to focus on the mirror across the room and I was stunned at the shock of recognition. For a confused instant I thought that Ralph had brought somebody with him – a model for that one special face we'd been looking for. There he was, by God – a puffy, drink-ravaged, disease-ridden caricature ... like an awful cartoon version of an old snapshot in some once-proud mother's family photo album. It was the face we'd been looking for – and it was, of course, my own. Horrible, horrible ...

'Maybe I should sleep a while longer,' I said. 'Why don't you go on over to the Fish-Meat place and eat some of those rotten fish and chips? Then come back and get me around noon. I feel too near death to hit the streets at this hour.'

He shook his head. 'No ... no ... I think I'll go back upstairs and work on those drawings for a while.' He leaned down to fetch two more cans out of the beer bucket. 'I tried to work earlier,' he said, 'but my hands keep trembling ... It's teddible, teddible.'

'You've got to stop drinking,' I said.

He nodded. 'I know. This is no good, no good at all. But for some reason it makes me feel better ...'

'Not for long,' I said. 'You'll probably collapse into some kind of hysterical DTs tonight – probably just about the time you get off the plane at Kennedy. They'll zip you up in a straitjacket and drag you down to the Tombs, then beat you on the kidneys with big sticks until you straighten out.'

He shrugged and wandered out, pulling the door shut behind him. I went back to bed for another hour or so, and later – after the daily grapefruit juice run to the Nite Owl Food Mart – we had our last meal at Fish-Meat Village: a fine lunch of dough and butcher's offal, fried in heavy grease.

By this time Ralph wouldn't even order coffee; he kept asking for more water. 'It's the only thing they have that's fit for human consumption,' he explained. Then, with an hour or so to kill before he had to catch the plane, we spread his drawings out on the table and pondered them for a while, wondering if he'd caught the proper spirit of the thing ... but we couldn't make up our minds. His hands were shaking so badly that he had trouble holding the paper, and my vision was so blurred that I could barely see what he'd drawn. 'Shit,' I said. 'We both look worse than anything you've drawn here.'

He smiled. 'You know – I've been thinking about that,' he said. 'We came down here to see this teddible scene: people all pissed out of their minds and vomiting on themselves and all that ... and now, you know what? It's us ...'

Huge Pontiac Ballbuster blowing through traffic on the expressway.

A radio news bulletin says the National Guard is massacring students at Kent State and Nixon is still bombing Cambodia. The journalist is driving, ignoring his passenger who is now nearly naked after taking off most of his clothing, which he holds out the window, trying to wind-wash the Mace out of it. His eyes are bright red and his face and chest are soaked with the beer he's been using to rinse the awful chemical off his flesh. The front of his woollen trousers is soaked with vomit; his body is racked with fits of coughing and wild choking sobs. The journalist rams the big car through traffic and into a spot in front of the terminal, then he reaches over to open the door on the passenger's side and shoves the Englishman out, snarling: 'Bug off, you worthless faggot! You twisted pigfucker! [Crazed laughter.] If I weren't sick I'd kick your ass all the way to Bowling Green – you scumsucking foreign geek. Mace is too good for you ... We can do without your kind in Kentucky.'

Scanlan's Monthly, vol. 1, no. 4, June 1970

A SOUTHERN CITY WITH NORTHERN PROBLEMS

Quino's Cafe is on Market Street, two blocks up the hill from the river in the heart of Louisville's legal and financial district, and often in the long, damp Ohio Valley afternoons a lot of people who might ordinarily avoid such a place will find themselves standing at Quino's white formica counter, drinking a Fehrs or a Falls City beer, and eating a 'genuine twenty cent beercheese sandwich' while they skim through an early edition of the Louisville *Times*. If you stand at the counter and watch the street you will see off-duty cops and courthouse loafers, visiting farmers with five children and a pregnant wife in the cab of a pickup truck, and a well-fed collection of lawyers and brokers in two-button suits and cordovan shoes. You will also see quite a few Negroes, some of them also wearing business suits and cordovan shoes. Louisville takes pride in its race relations, and the appearance of well-dressed Negroes in the Courthouse-City Hall district does not raise any eyebrows.

This city, known as 'Derbytown', and the 'Gateway to the South', has done an admirable job in breaking down the huge and traditional barriers between the black man and the white. Here in the mint julep country, where the Negro used to be viewed with all the proprietary concern that men lavish on a good coon hound ('Treat him fine when he works good – but when he acts lazy and no-count, beat him till he hollers'), the integration of the races has made encouraging headway.

Racial segregation has been abolished in nearly all white public places. Negroes entered the public schools in 1956 with so little trouble that the superintendent of schools was moved to write a book about it, called *The Louisville Story*. Since then, restaurants, hotels, parks, movie theatres, stores, swimming pools, bowling alleys, and even business schools have been opened to Negroes. As a clincher, the city recently passed an ordinance that outlaws racial discrimination in any public accommodation. This has just about done the deed; out of ninety-nine establishments 'tested' by NAACP workers, there were only four complaints – two from the same East End bar. Mayor William Cowger, whose progressive Republican administration has caused even Democrats to mutter with admiration, spoke for most of his fellow citizens recently when he said, 'The stories of violence in other cities should make us proud to live in Louisville. We enjoy national prestige for sane and sensible race relations.'

All this is true – and so it is all the more surprising to visit Louisville and find so much evidence to the contrary. Why, for instance, does a local Negro leader say, 'Integration here is a farce'? Why, also, has a local Negro minister urged his congregation to arm themselves? Why do Louisville Negroes bitterly accuse the Federal urban-renewal project of creating '*de facto* segregation'? Why can't a Negro take out a mortgage to buy a home in most white neighbourhoods? And why is there so much bitterness in the remarks of Louisvillians both black and white? 'Integration is for poor people,' one hears; 'they can't afford to buy their way out of it.' Or, 'In ten years, downtown Louisville will be as black as Harlem.'

What is apparent in Louisville is that the Negro has won a few crucial battles, but instead of making the breakthrough he expected, he has come up against segregation's second front, where the problems are not mobs and unjust laws but customs and traditions. The Louisville Negro, having taken the first basic steps, now faces a far more subtle thing than the simple 'yes' or 'no' that his brothers are still dealing with in most parts of the South. To this extent, Louisville has integrated itself right out of the South, and now faces problems more like those of a Northern or Midwestern city.

The white power structure has given way in the public sector, only to entrench itself more firmly in the private. And the Negro – especially the educated Negro – feels that his victories are hollow and his 'progress' is something he reads about in the newspapers. The outlook for Louisville's Negroes may have improved from 'separate but equal' to 'equal but separate'. But it still leaves a good deal to be desired.

The white power structure, as defined by local Negroes, means the men who run the town, the men who control banking and industry and insurance, who pay big taxes and lend big money and head important civic committees. Their names are not well known to the average citizen, and when they get publicity at all it is likely to be in the society sections of the one-owner local press. During the day, their headquarters is the Pendennis Club on downtown Walnut Street, where they meet for lunch, squash, steam baths, and cocktails. 'If you want to get things done in this town,' according to a young lawyer very much on the way up, 'you'd better belong to the Pendennis.' On evenings and weekends the scene shifts to the Louisville Country Club far out in the East End, or clear across the county line to Harmony Landing, where good polo and good whisky push business out of sight if not out of mind.

Anybody who pays dues to at least two of these clubs can consider himself a member in good standing of the white power structure. This is the group that determines by quiet pressure, direct action, and sometimes even default just how far and fast Louisville will move towards integration. Among themselves, it is clear, they are no more integrated now than they were ten years ago, and they are not likely to be at any time in the near future. They have for the most part taken their sons and daughters out of the public schools or moved to suburban areas where the absence of Negroes makes integration an abstract question. The only time they deal actively with Negroes is when they give the maid a ride to the bus stop, get their shoes shined, or attend some necessary but unpleasant confrontation with a local Negro spokesman. Despite an ancient conditioning to prejudice, however, they are, in the main, a far more progressive and enlightened lot than their counterparts in Birmingham or even in a lot of cases than their own sons and daughters.

There is a feeling in liberal circles, especially in New York and Washington, that the banner of racial segregation has little appeal to the younger generation. And Murray Kempton has written that the special challenge of the 1960s 'is how to appease the Negro without telling the poor white'. But neither theory appears to apply in Louisville. Some of the bitterest racists in town belong to the best families, and no Mississippi dirt farmer rants more often against the 'niggers' than do some of Louisville's young up-and-coming executives just a few years out of college. At Bauer's, a fashionable pine-panelled tavern much frequented by the young bucks of the social set, the sentiment is overwhelmingly anti-Negro. Late in the evening some of the habitués may find themselves carried along in the confusion of drink and good-fellowship towards Magazine Street in the heart of the coloured section. There, at Oliver's and Big John's and the Diamond Horseshoe, the action goes on until dawn and a carload of jovial racists are as welcome as anybody else, black or white. The Negroes suspend their resentment, the whites suspend their prejudice, and everybody enjoys the music and the entertainment. But there is little or no mingling, and the activities of the night are quite separate from those of the day.

You get a feeling, after a while, that the young are not really serious either about denouncing the 'nigger' for 'not knowing his place' or about ignoring the colour line for nocturnal visits to Magazine Street. Both are luxuries that will not last, and the young are simply enjoying them while they can. Mayor Cowger likes to say: 'People are different here. We get along with each other because we don't like trouble.' Others will tell you that Louisville has no overt racial problem because the greatest commitment of the majority of white citizens is simply to maintain the *status quo*, whatever it happens to be.

In such a society, of course, it might be argued that almost anything can happen as long as it happens slowly and inconspicuously without getting people stirred up. All of which naturally frustrates the Negro, who has said that he wants freedom now. If the Negro were patient – and who can tell him he should be? – he would have no problem. But 'freedom now' is not in the white Louisville vocabulary.

A good example of the majority viewpoint shows up in the housing situation, which at the moment is inextricably linked with urban renewal. As it happens, the urban-renewal project centres mainly in the downtown Negro district, and most of the people who have to be relocated are black. It also happens that the only part of town to which Negroes can move is the West End, an old and tree-shaded neighbourhood bypassed by progress and now in the throes of a selling panic because of the Negro influx. There is a growing fear, shared by whites and Negroes alike, that the West End is becoming a black ghetto.

Frank Stanley Jr, the Negro leader who said 'Integration here is a farce', blames urban renewal for the problem. 'All they're doing is moving the ghetto, intact, from the middle of town to the West End.' Urban-renewal officials reply to this by claiming the obvious: that their job is not to desegregate Louisville but to relocate people as quickly and advantageously as possible. 'Sure they move to the West End,' says one official. 'Where else can they go?'

It is a fact that whites are moving out of the West End as fast as they can. A vocal minority is trying to stem the tide, but there is hardly a block without a 'for sale' sign, and some blocks show as many as ten. Yet there is 'hardly any' race prejudice in the West End. Talk to a man with his house for sale and you'll be given to understand that he is not moving because of any reluctance to live near Negroes. Far from it; he is proud of Louisville's progress towards integration. But he is worried about the value of his property; and you know, of course, what happens to property values when a Negro family moves into an all-white block. So he's selling now to get his price while the getting is good.

Depending on the neighbourhood, he may or may not be willing to sell to Negroes. The choice is all his, and will be until Louisville passes an 'open housing' ordinance to eliminate skin colour as a factor in the buying and selling of homes. Such an ordinance is already in the planning stage.

Meanwhile, the homeowner who will sell to Negroes is a rare bird – except in the West End. And arguments are presented with great feeling that those who will show their homes only to whites are not prejudiced, merely considerate of their neighbours. 'Personally, I have nothing against coloured people,' a seller will explain. 'But I don't want to hurt the neighbours. If I sold my house to a Negro it would knock several thousand dollars off the value of every house on the block.'

Most Negro realtors deny this, citing the law of supply and demand. Good housing for Negroes is scarce, they point out, and prices are consequently higher than those on the white market, where demand is not so heavy. There are, however, both white and Negro real-estate speculators who engage in 'block busting'. They will work to place a Negro in an all-white block, then try to scare the other residents into selling cheap. Quite often they succeed – then resell to Negroes at a big profit.

According to Jesse P. Warders, a real-estate agent and a long-time leader in Louisville's Negro community, 'What this town needs is a single market for housing – not two, like we have now.' Warders is counting on an 'open housing' ordinance, and he maintains that the biggest obstacle to open housing without an ordinance is the lack of Negroes on Louisville's Real Estate board.

In order to be a 'realtor' in Louisville, a real-estate agent has to be a member of 'the board', which does not accept Negroes. Warders is a member of the Washington-based National Institute of Real Estate Brokers, which has about as much influence here as the French Foreign Legion.

Louisville, like other cities faced with urban decay, has turned to the building of midtown apartments as a means of luring suburbanites back to the city centre. In the newest and biggest of these, called 'The 800', Warders tried to place a Negro client. The reaction was a good indicator of the problems facing Negroes after they break the barrier of outright racism.

'Do me a favour,' the builder of The 800 told Warders. 'Let me get the place fifty per cent full – that's my break-even point – then I'll rent to your client.'

Warders was unhappy with the rebuff, but he believes the builder will eventually rent to Negroes; and that, he thinks, is real progress. 'What should I say to the man?' he asked. 'I know for a fact that he's refused some white people, too. What the man wants is prestige tenants; he'd like to have the mayor living in his place, he'd like to have the president of the board of aldermen. Hell, I'm in business, too. I might not like what he says, but I see his point.'

Warders has been on the firing line long enough to know the score. He is convinced that fear of change and the reluctance of most whites to act in any way that might be frowned on by the neighbours is the Negroes' biggest problem in Louisville. 'I know how they feel, and so do most of my clients. But do you think it's right?'

The 800 was built with the considerable help of an FHA-guaranteed loan, which places the building automatically in the open housing category. Furthermore, the owner insists that he is colour-blind on the subject of tenants. But he assumes none the less that the prestige tenants he wants would not consider living in the same building with Negroes.

It is the same assumption that motivates a homeowner to sell to whites only – not because of race prejudice but out of concern for property values. In other words, almost nobody has anything against Negroes, but everybody's neighbour does.

This is galling to the Negroes. Simple racism is an easy thing to confront, but a mixture of guilty prejudice, economic worries and threatened social standing is much harder to fight. 'If all the white people I've talked to had the courage of their convictions,' one Negro leader has said, 'we wouldn't have a problem here.'

Louisville's lending institutions frustrate Negroes in the same way. Frank Stanley Jr claims that there's a gentleman's agreement among bankers to prevent Negroes from getting mortgages to buy homes in white neighbourhoods. The complaint would seem to have a certain validity, although once again less sinister explanations are offered. The lending agencies cite business reasons, not race prejudice, as the reason for their stand. Concern for the reaction of their depositors seems to be a big factor, and another is the allegation that such loans would be a poor risk – especially if the institution holds mortgages on other homes in the neighbourhood. Here again is the fear of falling property values.

There is also the question whether a Negro would have any more difficulty getting a mortgage to buy a home in a white upper-class neighbourhood than would a member of another minority group – say, a plumber named Luciano, proud possessor of six children, a dirty spitz that barks at night, and a ten-year-old pickup truck with 'Luciano Plumbing' painted on the side.

Mayor Cowger, a mortgage banker himself, insists that a Negro would have no more trouble than the hypothetical Mr Luciano. Another high-ranking occupant of City Hall disagrees: 'That's what the mayor would like to think, but it just isn't true. Nobody in Rolling Fields, for instance, would want an Italian plumber for a neighbour, but at least they could live with him, whereas a Negro would be unthinkable because he's too obvious. It wouldn't matter if he were a doctor or a lawyer or anything else. The whites in the neighbourhood would fear for the value of their property and try to sell it before it dropped.'

Another common contention is that Negroes 'don't want to move into an all-white neighbourhood'. The East End, for instance, remains solidly white except for alley dwellings and isolated shacks. The mayor, who lives in the East End, has said, 'Negroes don't want to live here. It wouldn't be congenial for them. There are some fine Negro neighbourhoods in the West End – beautiful homes. They don't try to buy homes where they won't be happy. People just don't do things like that.' Some people do, however, and it appears that almost without exception they get turned down flat. One Negro executive with adequate funds called a white realtor and made an appointment to look at a house for sale in the East End. Things went smoothly on the telephone, but when the Negro arrived at the realtor's office the man was incensed. 'What are you trying to do?' he demanded. 'You know I can't sell you that house. What are you up to, anyway?'

No realtor, however, admits to racial prejudice, at least while talking to strangers. They are, they point out, not selling their own homes but those of their clients. In the same fashion, mortgage bankers are quick to explain that they do not lend their own money. A man making inquiries soon gets the impression that all clients, investors, and depositors are vicious racists and dangerous people to cross. Which is entirely untrue in Louisville – although it is hard to see how a Negro, after making the rounds of 'very sympathetic' realtors, could be expected to believe anything else.

Housing ranks right at the top among Louisville's racial problems. According to Frank Stanley Jr, 'Housing is basic; once we have whites and Negroes living together, the rest will be a lot easier.' Jesse P. Warders, the real-estate agent, however, rates unemployment as the number one problem area, because 'Without money you can't enjoy the other things.'

The Louisville Human Relations Commission, one of the first of its kind in the nation, agrees that although the city has made vast strides in the areas of education and public accommodations, the problems of housing and employment are still largely unsolved because 'These areas are much more complex and confront long-established customs based on a heritage of prejudice.' Of the two, however, the commission sees housing as a bigger problem. J. Mansir Tydings, executive director of the commission, is optimistic about the willingness of merchants and other employers to hire Negroes: 'Already – and much sooner than we expected – our problem is training unemployed Negroes to fill positions that are open.'

Yet there is still another big hurdle, less tangible than such factors as housing and employment but perhaps more basic when it comes to finding an ultimate solution. This is the pervasive distrust among the white power structure of the Negro leadership's motives. Out in the dove-shooting country, in the suburbs beyond the East End, Stanley is viewed as an 'opportunist politician' and a 'black troublemaker'. Bishop Ewbank Tucker, the minister who urged his congregation to arm themselves, is called an extremist and a Black Muslim. The possibility that some of the Negro leaders do sometimes agitate for the sake of agitation often cramps the avenues of communication between white and Negro leaders.

Even among Negroes, Stanley is sometimes viewed with uneasiness and Bishop Tucker called a racist. A former president of the Louisville NAACP, on hearing the statement that local Negroes 'resent the national publicity concerning Louisville's progress in race relations,' laughed and dismissed Stanley as a 'very nice, very smart young fella with a lot to learn'. (Stanley is twenty-six.)

'He wants things to go *properly*,' said the NAACP man. 'But difficult things never go properly – life isn't that way.' He smiled nervously. 'Forty years ago I came back here thinking I could be a Black Moses – I thought I was going to set my people free. But I couldn't do it then and it can't be done now. It's not a thing you can do overnight – it's going to take years and years and years.'

Nearly everyone agrees with that, and even with all its problems, Louisville looks to be a lot further along the road to facing and solving the 'Negro problem' than many other cities. Even Stanley, who appears to make a cult of militant noncompromise, will eventually admit to a visitor that he threatens far more demonstrations than he ever intends to produce.

'The white power structure here tries to cling to the *status quo*. They keep telling me not to rock the boat, but I rock it anyway because it's the only way to make them move. We have to keep the pressure on them every minute, or we dissipate our strength.

'Louisville isn't like Birmingham,' he adds. 'I think there's a conviction here that this thing is morally wrong – without that, we'd have real trouble.'

Reporter, vol. 29, 19 December 1963

FEAR AND LOATHING AT THE SUPER BOWL

Grim Notes of a Failed Fan ... *Mano a Mano* with the Oakland Raiders ... Down and Out in Houston ... Is Pro Football over the Hump? ... A Vague & Vengeful Screed on Texas, Jesus, and the Political Realities of the NFL ... Will Ron Ziegler Be the Next Commissioner?

ONE

... and whosoever was not found written into the book of life was cast into the lake of fire ...

Revelations xx, 15

This was the theme of the sermon I delivered off the twentieth-floor balcony of the Hyatt Regency in Houston on the morning of Super Bowl

VIII. It was just before dawn, as I recall, when the urge to speak came on me. Earlier that day I had found – on the tile floor of the men's room on the hotel mezzanine – a religious comic book titled *A Demon's Nightmare*, and it was from the text of this sleazy tract that I chose the words of my sermon.

The Houston Hyatt Regency – like others designed by architect John Portman in Atlanta and San Francisco – is a stack of 1000 rooms, built around a vast lobby at least thirty storeys high, with a revolving 'spindletop' bar on the roof. The whole centre of the building is a tower of acoustical space. You can walk out of any room and look over the indoor balcony (twenty floors down, in my case) at the palm-shrouded, wood and naugahyde maze of the bar/lounge on the lobby floor.

Closing time in Houston is 2:00 a.m. There are after-hours bars, but the Hyatt Regency is not one of them. So – when I was seized by the urge to deliver my sermon at dawn – there were only about twenty ant-sized people moving around in the lobby far below.

Earlier, before the bar closed, the whole ground floor had been jammed with drunken sportswriters, hard-eyed hookers, wandering geeks and hustlers (of almost every persuasion), and a legion of big and small gamblers from all over the country who roamed through the drunken, randy crowd – as casually as possible – with an eye to picking up a last-minute sucker bet from some poor bastard half-mad on booze and willing to put some money, preferably four or five big ones, on 'his boys'.

The spread, in Houston, was Miami by six, but by midnight on Saturday almost every one of the two thousand or so drunks in the lobby of the Regency – official headquarters and media vortex for this eighth annual Super Bowl – was absolutely sure about what was going to happen when the deal went down on Sunday, about two miles east of the hotel on the fog-soaked artificial turf of Rice University stadium.

Ah ... but wait! Why are we talking about gamblers here? Or thousands of hookers and drunken sportswriters jammed together in a seething mob in the lobby of a Houston hotel?

And what kind of sick and twisted impulse would cause a professional sportswriter to deliver a sermon from the Book of Revelations off his hotel balcony on the dawn of Super Sunday?

I had not planned a sermon for that morning. I had not even planned to be in Houston, for that matter ... But now, looking back on that outburst, I see a certain inevitability about it. Probably it was a crazed and futile effort to somehow explain the extremely twisted nature of my relationship with God, Nixon and the National Football League: The three had long since become inseparable in my mind, a sort of unholy trinity that had caused me more trouble and personal anguish in the past few months than Ron Ziegler, Hubert Humphrey and Peter Sheridan all together had caused me in a year on the campaign trail.

Or perhaps it had something to do with my admittedly deep-seated need to have public revenge on Al Davis, general manager of the Oakland Raiders ... Or maybe an overweening desire to confess that I had been wrong, from the start, to have ever agreed with Richard Nixon about *anything*, and especially pro football.

In any case, it was apparently something I'd been cranking myself up to deliver for quite a while ... and, for reasons I still can't be sure of, the eruption finally occurred on the dawn of Super Sunday.

I howled at the top of my lungs for almost thirty minutes, raving and screeching about all those who would soon be cast into the lake of fire, for a variety of low crimes, misdemeanours and general ugliness that amounted to a sweeping indictment of almost everybody in the hotel at that hour.

Most of them were asleep when I began speaking, but as a Doctor of Divinity and an ordained minister in the Church of the New Truth, I knew in my heart that I was merely a vessel – a tool, as it were – of some higher and more powerful voice.

For eight long and degrading days I had skulked around Houston with all the other professionals, doing our jobs – which was actually to do nothing at all except drink all the free booze we could pour into our bodies, courtesy of the National Football League, and listen to an endless barrage of some of the lamest and silliest swill ever uttered by man or beast ... and finally, on Sunday morning about six hours before the opening kickoff, I was racked to the point of hysteria by a hellish interior conflict.

I was sitting by myself in the room, watching the wind & weather clocks on the TV set, when I felt a sudden and extremely powerful movement at the base of my spine. Mother of Sweating Jesus! I thought. What is it – a leech? Are there leeches in this goddamn hotel, along with everything else? I jumped off the bed and began clawing at the small of my back with both hands. The thing felt huge, maybe eight or nine pounds, moving slowly up my spine towards the base of my neck.

I'd been wondering, all week, why I was feeling so low and out of sorts ... but it never occurred to me that a giant leech had been sucking blood out of the base of my spine all that time; and now the goddamn thing was moving up towards the base of my brain, going straight for the medulla ... and as a professional sportswriter I knew that if the bugger ever reached my medulla I was done for.

It was at this point that serious conflict set in, because I realized – given the nature of what was coming up my spine and the drastic effect

I knew it would have, very soon, on my sense of journalistic responsibility – that I would have to do two things immediately: first, deliver the sermon that had been brewing in my brain all week long, and then rush back into the room and write my lead for the Super Bowl story ...

Or maybe write my lead first, and then deliver the sermon. In any case, there was no time to lose. The thing was about a third of the way up my spine now, and still moving at good speed. I jerked on a pair of L. L. Bean stalking shorts and ran out on the balcony to a nearby ice machine.

Back in the room I filled a glass full of ice and Wild Turkey, then began flipping through the pages of *A Demon's Nightmare* for some kind of spiritual springboard to get the sermon moving. I had already decided – about midway in the ice-run – that I had adequate time to address the sleeping crowd and also crank out a lead before that goddamn bloodsucking slug reached the base of my brain – or, even worse, if a sharp dose of Wild Turkey happened to slow the thing down long enough to rob me of my final excuse for missing the game entirely, like last year ...

What? Did my tongue slip there? My fingers? Or did I just get a fine professional hint from my old buddy, Mr Natural?

Indeed. When the going gets tough, the tough get going. John Mitchell said that – shortly before he quit his job and left Washington at ninety miles an hour in a chauffeur-driven limousine.

I have never felt close to John Mitchell, but on that rotten morning in Houston I came as close as I ever will; because he was, after all, a pro ... and so, alas, was I. Or at least I had a fistful of press badges that said I was.

And it was this bedrock sense of professionalism, I think, that quickly solved my problem ... which, until that moment when I recalled the foul spectre of Mitchell, had seemed to require a frantic decision between either delivering my sermon or writing my lead, in the space of an impossibly short time.

When the going gets weird, the weird turn pro.

Who said that?

I suspect it was somebody from the *Columbia Journalism Review*, but I have no proof ... and it makes no difference anyway. There is a bond, among pros, that needs no definition. Or at least it didn't on that Sunday morning in Houston, for reasons that require no further discussion at this point in time ... because it suddenly occurred to me that *I had already written the lead* for this year's Super Bowl game; I wrote it last year in Los Angeles, and a quick rip through my fat manila folder of clips labelled 'Football 73' turned it up as if by magic.

I jerked it out of the file, and retyped it on a fresh page slugged:

'Super Bowl/Houston 74'. The only change necessary was the substitution of 'Minnesota Vikings' for 'Washington Redskins'. Except for that, the lead seemed just as adequate for the game that would begin in about six hours as it was for the one that I missed in Los Angeles in January of 73.

'The precision-jackhammer attack of the Miami Dolphins stomped the balls off the Minnesota Vikings today by stomping and hammering with one precise jack-thrust after another up the middle, mixed with pinpoint-precision passes into the flat and numerous hammer-jack stops around both ends ...'

The jangling of the telephone caused me to interrupt my work. I jerked it off the hook, saying nothing to whoever was on the other end, and began flashing the hotel operator. When she finally cut in I spoke very calmly. 'Look,' I said. 'I'm a very friendly person and a minister of the gospel, to boot – but I thought I left instructions down there to put no calls – NO CALLS, GODDAMNIT! – through to this room, and especially not *now* in the middle of this orgy ... I've been here eight days and nobody's called me yet. Why in hell would they start now? ... What? Well, I simply can't accept that kind of flimsy reasoning, operator. Do you believe in *Hell*? Are you ready to speak with Saint Peter? ... Wait a minute now, calm down ... I want to be sure you understand *one thing* before I get back to my business; I have some people here who *need help* ... But I want you to know that God is Holy! He will *not allow* sin in his presence! The Bible says: "There is none righteous. *No, not one* ... For all have sinned and come short of the glory of God." That's from the book of Romans, young lady ...'

The silence at the other end of the line was beginning to make me nervous. But I could feel the sap rising, so I decided to continue my sermon from the balcony ... and I suddenly realized that somebody was beating on my door. Jesus god, I thought, it's the manager; they've come for me at last.

But it was a TV reporter from Pittsburgh, raving drunk and demanding to take a shower. I jerked him into the room. 'Nevermind the goddamn shower,' I said. 'Do you realize what I have on my spine?' He stared at me, unable to speak. 'A giant leech,' I said. 'It's been there for eight days, getting fatter and fatter with blood.'

He nodded slowly as I led him over to the phone. 'I hate leeches,' he muttered.

'That's the least of our problems,' I said. 'Room service won't send any beer up until noon, and all the bars are closed ... I have this Wild Turkey, but I think it's too heavy for the situation we're in.'

'You're right,' he said. 'I got work to do. The goddamn game's about to start. I need a shower.'

'Me too,' I said. 'But I have some work to do first, so you'll have to make the call.'

'Call?' He slumped into a chair in front of the window, staring out at the thick grey mist that had hung on the town for eight days – except now, as Super Sunday dawned, it was thicker and wetter than ever.

I gave him the phone: 'Call the manager,' I said. 'Tell him you're Howard Cosell and you're visiting up here with a minister in 2003; we're having a private prayer breakfast and we need two fifths of his best red wine, with a box of saltine crackers.'

He nodded unhappily. 'Hell, I came here for a shower. Who needs the wine?'

'It's important,' I said. 'You make the call while I go outside and get started.'

He shrugged and dialled 'O' while I hurried out to the balcony, clearing my throat for an opening run at James ii, 19:

'Beware!' I shouted, 'for the Devils also believe, and tremble!'

I waited for a moment, but there was no reply from the lobby, twenty floors down – so I tried Ephesians vi, 12, which seemed more appropriate:

'For we wrestle not,' I screamed, 'against flesh and blood – but against principalities, against powers, against the rulers of the darkness of this world – and, yes – against spiritual wickedness in high places!'

Still there was no response except the booming echoes of my own voice ... but the thing on my spine was moving with new vigour now, and I sensed there was not much time. All movement in the lobby had ceased. They were all standing still down there – maybe twenty or thirty people ... but were they *listening*? Could they *hear*?

I couldn't be sure. The acoustics of these massive lobbies are not predictable. I knew, for instance, that a person sitting in a room on the eleventh floor, with the door open, could hear – with unnerving clarity – the sound of a cocktail glass shattering on the floor of the lobby. It was also true that almost every word of Gregg Allman's 'Multi-Coloured Lady' played at top volume on a dual-speaker Sony TC-126 in an open-door room on the twentieth floor could be heard in the NFL press room on the hotel mezzanine ... but it was hard to be sure of the timbre and carrying-power of my own voice in this cavern; it sounded, to me, like the deep screaming of a bull elk in the rut ... but there was no way to know, for sure, if I was really getting through.

'Discipline!' I bellowed. 'Remember Vince Lombardi!' I paused to let that one sink in – waiting for applause, but none came. 'Remember George Metesky!' I shouted. 'He had discipline!'

Nobody down in the lobby seemed to catch that one, although I sensed the first stirrings of action on the balconies just below me. It was almost time for the free breakfast in the Imperial Ballroom downstairs, and some of the early-rising sportswriters seemed to be up and about. Somewhere behind me a phone was ringing, but I paid no attention. It was time, I felt, to bring it all together ... my voice was giving out, but despite the occasional dead spots and bursts of high-pitched wavering, I grasped the railing of the balcony and got braced for some flat-out raving:

'Revelations, twenty-fifteen!' I screamed. 'Say Hallelujah! Yes! Say Hallelujah!'

People were definitely responding now. I could hear their voices, full of excitement – but the acoustics of the place made it impossible to get a good fix on the cries that were bounding back and forth across the lobby. Were they saying 'Hallelujah'?

'Four more years!' I shouted. 'My friend General Haig has told us that the forces of darkness are now in control of the nation – and they will rule for four more years!' I paused to sip my drink, then I hit it again: 'And Al Davis has told us that whosoever was not found written in the book of life was cast into the lake of fire!'

I reached around behind me with my free hand, slapping at a spot between my shoulder blades to slow the thing down.

'How many of you will be cast into the lake of fire in the next four years? *How many will survive?* I have spoken with General Haig, and—'

At this point I was seized by both arms and jerked backwards, spilling my drink and interrupting the climax of my sermon. 'You crazy bastard!' a voice screamed. 'Look what you've done! The manager just called. Get back in the room and lock the fucking door! He's going to bust us!'

It was the TV man from Pittsburgh, trying to drag me back from my pulpit. I slipped out of his grasp and returned to the balcony. 'This is Super Sunday!' I screamed. 'I want every one of you worthless bastards down in the lobby in ten minutes so we can praise God and sing the national anthem!'

At this point I noticed the TV man sprinting down the hall towards the elevators, and the sight of him running caused something to snap in my brain. 'There he goes!' I shouted. 'He's headed for the lobby! Watch out! It's Al Davis. He has a knife!'

I could see people moving on all the balconies now, and also down in the lobby. Then, just before I ducked back in my room, I saw one of the glass-walled elevators starting down, with a single figure inside it ... he was the most visible man in the building; a trapped and crazy animal descending slowly – in full view of everybody from the busboys in the ground-floor coffee-shop to Jimmy the Greek on the balcony above me

– to certain captivity by that ugly crowd at the bottom.

I watched for a moment, then hung the DO NOT DISTURB sign on my doorknob and double-locked the door. That elevator, I knew, would be empty when it got to the lobby. There were at least five floors, on the way down, where he could jump out and bang on a friendly door for safe refuge ... and the crowd in the lobby had not seen him clearly enough, through the tinted-glass wall of the elevator, to recognize him later on.

And there was not much time for vengeance, anyway, on the odd chance that anyone cared.

It had been a dull week, even by sportswriters' standards, and now the day of the Big Game was finally on us. Just one more free breakfast, one more ride, and by nightfall the thing would be over.

The first media-bus was scheduled to leave the hotel for the stadium at 10:30, four hours before kickoff, so I figured that gave me some time to relax and act human. I filled the bathtub with hot water, plugged the tape recorder with both speakers into a socket right next to the tub, and spent the next two hours in a steam-stupor, listening to Rosalie Sorrels and Doug Sahm, chewing idly on a small slice of Mr Natural, and reading the *Cocaine Papers* of Sigmund Freud.

Around noon I went downstairs to the Imperial Ballroom to read the morning papers over the limp dregs of NFL's free breakfast, then I stopped at the free bar for a few bloody marys before wandering outside to catch the last bus for the stadium – the CBS special – complete with more bloody marys, screwdrivers and a roving wagon-meister who seemed to have everything under control.

On the bus to the stadium I made a few more bets on Miami. At that point I was picking up everything I could get, regardless of the points. It had been a long and jangled night, but the two things that needed to be done before game-time – my sermon and my lead – were already done, and the rest of the day looked easy: just try to keep out of trouble and stay straight enough to collect on all my bets.

The consensus among the 1600 or so sportswriters in town favoured Miami by almost two to one ... but there are only a handful of sportswriters in this country with enough sense to pour piss out of their own boots, and by Saturday night there was an obvious drift among the few 'smart' ones to Minnesota, with a seven-point cushion. Paul Zimmerman of the New York *Post*, author of *A Thinking Man's Guide to Pro Football* and the sportswriting fraternity's scaled-down answer to the Washington *Post*'s political guru David Broder, had organized his traditional pressroom betting pool – where any sportswriter who felt up to it could put a dollar in the pot and predict the final score (in writing, on the pressroom bulletin board, for all the world to see) ... and whoever came closest would pick up a thousand or so dollars.

Or at least that was the theory. But in reality there were only about 400 writers willing to risk a public prediction on the outcome of a game that – even to an amateur like me – was so obvious that I took every bet I could get against the Vikings, regardless of the spread. As late as 10:30 on Sunday morning I was calling bookies on both coasts, doubling and tripling my bets with every point I could get from five to seven ... and by 2:35 on Sunday afternoon, five minutes after the kickoff, I knew I was home free.

Moments later, when the Dolphins drove the length of the field for another touchdown, I began collecting money. The final outcome was painfully clear less than halfway through the first quarter – and shortly after that, *Sport Magazine* editor Dick Schapp reached over my shoulder in the press section and dropped two bills – a five and a twenty – in my lap.

I smiled back at him. 'Jesus,' I said. 'Are you giving up *already*? This game is far from over, my man. Your people are only twenty-one points down, and we still have a whole half to go.'

He shook his head sadly.

'You're not counting on a second-half rally?' I asked, pocketing his money.

He stared at me, saying nothing ... then he rolled his eyes up towards the soupy mist above the stadium where the Goodyear blimp was hovering, almost invisible in the fog.

When I began this doom-struck story many months ago, the idea was to follow one team all the way to the Super Bowl and, in the process, try to document the alleged – or at least Nixonian – similarities between pro football and politics. The problem, at that time, was to decide which team to follow. It had to be one with a good chance of going all the way, and also a team I could get along with over an extended period of time.

That was in early November, and the list of possibilities included about half the League, but I narrowed it down to the four teams where I already knew some of the players: Los Angeles, Miami, Washington and Oakland ... and after many days of brooding I chose Oakland.

There were two main factors involved: 1) I had already made a large bet, at 8–1 odds, on Oakland to go all the way – as opposed to a 4–1 bet on the Redskins and 2–1 *against* Minnesota ... and 2) When I checked with Dave Burgin, a former San Francisco *Examiner* and Washington *Star-News* sports editor, he said there were only two teams in the whole League flakey enough for me to identify with in any kind of personal or human way: One was Pittsburgh and the other was Oakland.

Well ... it is three months later now, and the question that still haunts me is which jail, morgue or asylum would I be in today if I'd happened to pick one of the *other* teams.

Even now – almost 2000 miles and two months removed from the Raider headquarters in Oakland – I still want to reach for an icepick every time I see a football ... and my only consolation, looking back on that nightmare, is that I might have decided to 'cover' the Dallas Cowboys. Just before talking to Burgin, in fact, I read a savage novel called *North Dallas Forty*, by ex-Cowboy flanker Pete Gent, and it had cranked up my interest in both Dallas and the Cowboys enough so that I was right on the brink of dumping Oakland and heading for Texas ...

Fortunately, I was shrewd enough to choose Oakland – a decision that resulted, less than three weeks after I made it, in a series of personal and professional disasters ranging from massive slander and a beating by stadium-cops outside the Raider dressing room, to total banishment from the field, locker room, press box, and for all practical purposes – because of the dark assumptions that would inevitably be made about any player seen with me in public – from any bar, restaurant, zoo or shotgun store in the Bay Area frequented by any Raider players.

The reasons for all this are still not entirely clear – or maybe they are, and I still can't grasp the real meaning of what happened. Perhaps it was merely a case of the chickens coming home to roost, accompanied by three giant condors.

TWO

The Raiders kicked you out? For what? Drug rumours? [Laughter]
Well, it's nice to know they're starting to give writers the same kind of underhanded chickenshit they've been laying on players for ten years ...
Yeah, it varies from team to team: Like, for me, getting traded to Pittsburgh after all that time in Oakland was like finally coming up for air. As a matter of general philosophy, though, the National Football League is the last bastion of fascism in America.
                Tom Keating, defensive tackle for the Pittsburgh Steelers

To reach the Oakland Raiders' practice field you drive from San Francisco across the Bay Ridge and then south on US 17 to Exit 98 at Hegenberger Road at the south end of Alameda Bay ... turn right at the off-ramp that leads to the Oakland International Airport; glance back at the Edgewater Inn and the squat-white concrete-block building right next to the Edgewater that says 'Oakland Raiders' and then swing north again.

About six miles past the airport entrance, the Oakland Hilton and a speedboat raceway – the road gets narrow and seems to be heading downhill, through a wet desert of stunted jack-pines (or scrub-oaks, or whatever they call those useless little trees that grow on the edge of swamplands all over the country, near places like Pensacola and Portland) ... but this is Oakland, or at least San Leandro, and when you drive twenty miles out of San Francisco to a lonesome place like this, you want a pretty good reason.

... Or at least a decent excuse.

The only people who make this run regularly, in the autumn months between late August and December, are Bay Area sportswriters and people on the payroll of the Oakland Raiders – players, trainers, coaches, owners, etc. – and the only reason they make this grim trip day after day is the nervous fact that the Raiders' practice field and daily headquarters is located, for good or ill, out here on this stinking estuary across the bay from San Francisco.

It is a hard place to find unless you know exactly where to look. The only sure giveaway sign, from the highway, is a sudden rise of thin steel scaffolding looming out of the jack-pines about 200 yards west of the road – and two men in cheap plastic ski jackets on a platform at the top of the tower, aiming big grey movie cameras down at whatever's happening on the other side of that tree-fence.

Turn left just beyond the film-tower, park in a muddy lot full of new Cadillacs and flashy sports cars, and walk up a grassy bank to a one-storey concrete-block building that looks like a dog-kennel or a Pepsi-Cola warehouse in St Louis ... push through a big metal fire-door and along a naked corridor decorated on both sides with black and grey helmets, sharp-edged footballs, red-white-and-blue NFL stickers ... and finally around a corner into the weight-room, a maze of fantastically-complicated machinery with signs all round warning 'unauthorized persons' to keep their goddamn hands off of *everything*. One of the weight-machines costs $6500 and is designed to do nothing but stretch knots out of trapezius muscles; another, costing $8800, is a maze of steel cables, weights and ankle-hooks that will – if used properly – cure kinks, rips and contusions out of every muscle from the hip to the achilles tendon. There are other machines for problems of the feet, neck and elbows.

I was tempted to get physically involved with every machine in the building – just to know how it felt to get jerked around by all that fantastic machinery. I was also tempted to speak with the trainers and sample whatever medications they had to offer – but pro football locker rooms are no longer the wholesale drug dispensaries that they were in the past. National Football League Commissioner 'Pete' Rozelle – along with 'President' Nixon and the network TV moguls – have determined that drugs and pro football won't mix; at least not in public.

On my first visit to the locker room – and on all other visits, for that matter – I avoided both the weight machines and the trainers. There was no point, I felt, in compromising the story early on; although if I'd known what kind of shitrain I was heading into I would have sprung every machine in the building and gobbled every pill I could get my hands on.

But I felt a certain obligation, back then, to act in a 'professional' manner ... and, besides, for my first look at the Raider practice field I was accompanied by a friendly little fellow named Al LoCasale, who had told me when I called on the phone that he was 'executive assistant' to the Raiders' general manager and would-be owner, Al Davis.

LoCasale led me through the locker room, past the weights and the trainers, and out through another small door that opened on to a long green pasture enclosing two football fields, four goal posts, many blocking sleds and tackling dummies, and about sixty men moving around very actively, gathered in four separate groups on both fields.

I recognized John Madden, the head coach, running the offensive unit through short-pass drills on the field to my right ... and on the other field, about fifty yards to my left, another coach was running the defensive unit through some kind of drill I couldn't recognize.

Far down at the other end of the field where the defensive unit was working, I could see George Blanda, the Raiders' forty-six-year-old reserve quarterback and premier place-kicker, working with his own set of handlers and banging one kick after another 'through the uprights' – from the thirty or thirty-five yard line. Blanda and his small crew were paying no attention to what was happening on the offensive and defensive fields. Their job was to keep George sharp on field-goals, and during the two hours I was there, that afternoon, he kicked at least forty or fifty, and I never saw him miss one.

There were two other solitary figures moving around on the field(s) beyond the small enclosure near the locker-room door where LoCasale and several assistants made sure the half-dozen local sportswriters stayed. One was Ray Guy, the rookie punter and number one draft choice from Mississippi, who spent all afternoon kicking one ball after another in tall spiralling arcs above the offensive unit to a brace of ball-boys just in front of the sportswriters' huddle ... and the other was a small wiry man in a tan golf jacket with a greasy duck-tail haircut who paced along the sidelines of both fields with a speedy kind of intensity that I never really noticed until he suddenly appeared very close to me and I heard him ask a sportswriter from the San Francisco *Chronicle* who I was and what I was doing there ...

The conversation took place within ten yards of me, and I heard most of it.

'Who's the big guy over there with the ball in his hand?' asked the man with the DA.

'His name's Thompson,' replied *Chronicle* sportswriter Jack Smith. 'He's a writer for *Rolling Stone*.'

'The Rolling Stones? Jesus Christ! What's he *doing* here? Did *you* bring him?'

'No, he's writing a big article. *Rolling Stone* is a magazine, Al. It's different from the Rolling Stones; they're a rock music group ... Thompson's a buddy of George Plimpton's, I think ... and he's also a friend of Dave Burgin's – you remember Burgin?'

'Holy shit! Burgin! We ran him out of here with a cattle prod!'

I saw Smith laugh at that point, then he was talking again: 'Don't worry, Al. Thompson's okay. He wrote a good book about Las Vegas.'

Good God! I thought. That's it ... If they read that book I'm finished. By this time I'd realized that this strange-looking bugger named 'Al', who looked like a pimp or a track-out, was in fact the infamous Al Davis – general manager and *de facto* owner (pending settlement of a nasty lawsuit scheduled for court-action early this year) of the whole Oakland Raider operation.

Davis glanced over his shoulder at me, then spoke back to Smith: 'Get the bastard out of here. I don't trust him.'

I heard that very clearly – and if I'd had any sense I'd have abandoned the whole story right then, for reasons of extreme and unnatural prejudice; call the office and say I couldn't handle the bad vibes, then jump the next plane to Colorado ... I was watching Davis very closely now, and it occurred to me that the fiendish intensity of his speech and mannerisms reminded me very strongly of another Oakland badass I'd spent some time with, several years earlier – ex-Hell's Angels president Ralph 'Sonny' Barger, who had just beaten a multiple-murder rap and then copped out, they said, to some kind of minor charge like 'Aggravated Assault with Intent to Commit Murder', or 'Possession of Automatic Weapons' (submachine-guns), 'Possession of Heroin (four pounds) with Intent to Sell, and Sexual Assault on Two Minors with Intent to Commit Forcible Sodomy' ...

I had read these things in the *Chronicle* ... but ... What the hell? Why compound these libels? Any society that will put Barger in jail and make Al Davis a respectable millionaire at the same time is not a society to be trifled with.

In any case, the story of my strange and officially ugly relationship with Al Davis is too complicated for any long explanations at this point. I spent several days pacing the sidelines of the Raider practice field with him – prior to the Pittsburgh, Cleveland and Kansas City games – and the only thing I remember him talking about it 'environmental determinism'. He spoke at considerable length on that subject, as I recall, but there is nothing in my notes to indicate precisely what he said about it.

Shortly after I heard him tell Smith to get rid of me on that first afternoon, I walked over to him and somehow got wound up in a conversation about how he was having trouble buying property in Aspen because 'some people out there' thought his money was 'dirty' because of his known connections in Las Vegas. 'Hell, that's no problem,' I told him. 'I once ran for sheriff in Aspen; I know the place pretty well, and I can tell you for sure that at least half the money out there is dirtier than any you're likely to come up with.'

He stopped and eyed me curiously. 'You ran for sheriff?' he said. 'In Aspen, Colorado?'

I nodded. 'Yeah, but I'd rather not talk about it. We didn't lose by much, but losing in politics is like losing in football, right? One vote, one point—'

He smiled crookedly, then began pacing again. 'I don't give a damn about politics,' he said as I hurried along the white-lime sideline to keep up with him. 'The only things that interest me are economics and foreign affairs.'

Jesus Christ! I thought. Economics, foreign affairs, environmental determinism – this bastard is sand-bagging me.

We paced back and forth a while longer, then he suddenly turned on me: 'What are you after?' he snapped. 'Why are you out here?'

'Well ...' I said. 'It would take me a while to explain it. Why don't we have a beer after practice tomorrow and I'll—'

'Not tomorrow,' he said quickly. 'I only come out here on Wednesdays and Thursdays. They get nervous when I'm around, so I try to stay away most of the time.'

I nodded – but I didn't really understand what he meant until an hour or so later, when Coach Madden signalled the end of that day's practice and Davis suddenly rushed on to the field and grabbed the quarterback, Ken Stabler, along with a receiver and a defensive back I didn't recognize, and made them run the same pass pattern – a quick shot from about fifteen yards out with the receiver getting the ball *precisely* at the corner of the goal line and the out-of-bounds line – at least twelve consecutive times until they had it down exactly the way he wanted it.

That is my last real memory of Al Davis: It was getting dark in Oakland, the rest of the team had already gone into the showers, the coach was inside speaking sagely with a gaggle of local sportwriters, somewhere beyond the field-fence a big jet was cranking up its afterburners on the airport runway ... and here was the *owner* of the flakiest team in pro football, running around on a half-dark practice field like a king-hell speed freak with his quarterback and two other key players, insisting that they run the same goddamn play over and over again until they had it *right*.

That was the only time I ever felt that I really understood Davis ... We talked on other days, sort of loosely and usually about football, whenever I would show up at the practice field and pace around the sidelines with him ... and it was somewhere around the third week of my random appearances, as I recall, that he began to act very nervous whenever he saw me.

I never asked why, but it was clear that something had changed, if only back to normal ... After one of the mid-week practices I was sitting with one of the Raider players in the tavern down the road from the fieldhouse and he said: 'Jesus, you know I was walking back to the huddle and I looked over and, god damn, I almost flipped when I saw you and Davis standing together on the sideline. I thought, man, the world really *is* changing when you see a thing like that – Hunter Thompson and Al Davis – Christ, you know that's the first time I ever saw *anybody* with Davis during practice; the bastard's always *alone* out there, just pacing back and forth like a goddamn beast ...'

In the meantime, blissfully unaware of what was about to happen, I was trying to learn as much as possible about the real underbelly of pro football by watching a film of the Denver–Dallas game with several Raider players who provided a running commentary on the action – trying to explain, in language as close as they could cut it for the layman's slow eye, what was happening on the screen and how it might or might not relate to the Denver–Oakland game coming up next Sunday.

The purpose of the film-session was to show me some of the things – in slow motion and repeated instant replay – that nobody in the stands or the press box will ever understand. It was done as a personal favour, at a time when neither I nor any of the Oakland players realized that I was about to be banished. If I'd been writing a story on Evel Knievel at the time, I would have asked him to do the same thing – sit down for an evening with some films of his jumps, and explain each one step-by-step, along with whatever was going through his head at any given moment.

What follows, then, is a random commentary by some pro football players just a few games away from the Super Bowl, watching a film of a game between two teams – one of which they will have to beat on Sunday, to make the playoffs, and another they might have to beat in the Super Bowl itself. The film we were watching was the Denver–Dallas game on 2 December. Dallas won, 22–10 – which hardly matters, because pro football players don't watch game-films to see who won or lost. They watch for patterns, tendencies and individual strengths or weaknesses ... and in this case they were trying to translate their re-actions into language I could get a personal grip on, which accounts for some of the awkward moments.

Under normal circumstances I'd identify all of the voices in this heavily edited tape transcript – but for reasons that will soon become obvious if they aren't already, I decided that it would probably be more comfortable for all of us if I lumped all the player voices under one name: 'Raider'. This takes a bit of an edge off the talk, but it also makes it harder for the NFL security watchdogs to hassle some good people and red-line their names for hanging around with a dope fiend.

THREE

DO NOT MISTAKE ME FOR ANY OTHER READER
I have come here to help to save the suffering. You know God works in a mysterious way. If you have faith in God, don't fail to see:

MOTHER Roberts
PSYCHIC READER AND ADVISER
THE ONE & ONLY GIFTED HEALER

was born with the God-given powers to help humanity and has devoted her life to this work. Tells your friends' and enemies' names without asking a single word. She will tell you what you wish to know regarding health, marriage, love, divorce, courtship, speculations and business transactions of all kinds.

She will tell you of any changes you should or shouldn't make, good or bad. She removes evil influences and bad luck of all kinds. She never fails to reunite the separated, cause speedy and happy marriages. She lifts you out of sorrow and darkness and starts you on the way to success, and happiness. She will give sound and important advice on all affairs of life, whatever they may be. You will find her superior to any other reader you have consulted in the past. A place to bring your friends and feel no embarrassment.

66

Ah yes, Mother Roberts ... I found her card on the bus and jammed it into one of my pockets, thinking that maybe I would give her a call on Monday and make an appointment. I had a lot of heavy questions to lay on her like 'Why am I here, Mother Roberts? What does it all mean? Have I finally turned pro? Can this really be the end? Down and out in Houston with—

'No, I was just kidding, Mother Roberts, just putting you on – just working a bit of the test on you, right? Yes, because what I was really leading up to is this extremely central question ... No, I'm not shy; it's just that I come from way up north where people's lips are frozen about ten months every year, so we don't get used to talking until very late in life ... what? Old? Well, I think you just put your finger or your wand or whatever, right smack on the head of the nail, Mother Roberts, because the godawful truth of the whole matter is that I've been feeling *extremely old* this past week, and ... What? Wait a minute now, goddamnit, I'm still getting up to the main question, which is ... What? No, I *never* curse, Mother Roberts; that was a cry of anguish, a silent scream from the soul, because I feel in serious trouble down here in this goddamn town, and ... Yes, I *am* a white person, Mother Roberts, and we both know there's not a damn thing I can do about it. Are you prejudiced? ... No, let's not get into that. Just let me ask you this question, and if you can give me a straight and reasonable answer I promise I won't come out to your place ... because what I want you to tell me, Mother Roberts – and I mean this very seriously – is why have I been in Houston for eight days without anybody offering me some cocaine? ... Yes, cocaine, that's what I said, and just between you and me I'm damn serious about wanting some ... What? Drugs? *Of course* I'm talking about drugs! Your ad said you could answer my questions and lift me out of sorrow and darkness ... Okay, okay, I'm listening ... Yeah, yeah ... But let me tell you something, Mother Roberts: My name is Al Davis and I'm the editor of *Reader's Digest* ... Right, and I can have you busted right *now* for false advertising ... Yeah, well I think I might pick up some of my people and come out to see you later on to-day; we want some explanations for this kind of anti-christ bullshit. This country's in enough trouble, goddamnit, without people like you running around selling drugs like cocaine to people in serious trouble ...'

Mother Roberts hung up on me at that point. Christ only knows what she thought was about to come down on her when dusk fell on Houston ... Here was the editor of the *Reader's Digest* coming out to her house with a goon squad, and all of them apparently stone mad for cocaine and vengeance ... a terrible situation.

It was not until Monday afternoon that I actually spoke with Mother Roberts on the telephone, but the idea of going over to Galveston and dealing with the whole super scene story from some rotten motel on the edge of the seawall had been wandering around in my head almost from the first hour after I checked into my coveted press-room at the Hyatt Regency.

And in dull retrospect now, I wish I had done that. Almost anything would have been better than that useless week I spent in Houston waiting for the Big Game. The only place in town where I felt at home was a sort of sporadically violent strip joint called the Blue Fox, far out in the country on South Main. Nobody I talked to in Houston had ever heard of it, and the only two sportswriters who went out there with me got involved in a wild riot that ended up with all of us getting maced by undercover vice-squad cops who just happened to be in the middle of the action when it erupted.

Ah ... but that is another story, and we don't have time for it here. Maybe next time. There are two untold sagas that will not fit into this story: One has to do with Big Al's Cactus Room in Oakland, and the other concerns the Blue Fox in Houston.

There is also – at least in the minds of at least two dozen gullible sportswriters at the Super Bowl – the ugly story of how I spent three or four days prior to Super Week shooting smack in a $7 a night motel room on the seawall in Galveston.

I remember telling that story one night in the press lounge at the Hyatt Regency, just babbling it off the top of my head out of sheer boredom ... Then I forgot about it completely until one of the local sportswriters approached me a day or so later and said: 'Say man, I hear you spent some time in Galveston last week.'

'Galveston?'

'Yeah,' he said. 'I hear you locked yourself in a motel over there and shot heroin for three days.'

I looked around me to see who was listening, then grinned kind of stupidly and said, 'Shucks, there wasn't much else to do, you know – so why not get loaded in Galveston?'

He shrugged uncontrollably and looked down at his Old Crow and water. I glanced at my watch and turned to leave. 'Time to hit it,' I said with a smile. 'See you later, when I'm feeling back on my rails.'

He nodded glumly as I moved away in the crowd ... and although I saw him three or four times a day for the rest of that week, he never spoke to me again.

Most sportswriters are so blank on the subject of drugs that you can only talk to them about it at your own risk – which is easy enough, for me, because I get a boot out of seeing their eyes bulge; but it can be disastrous to a professional football player who makes the casual mistake of assuming that a sportswriter knows what he's talking about when he uses a word like 'crank'. Any professional athlete who talks to a sportswriter about 'drugs' – even with the best and most constructive intentions – is taking a very heavy risk. There is a definite element of hysteria about drugs of any kind in pro football today, and a casual remark – even a *meaningless* remark – across the table in a friendly hometown bar can lead, very quickly, to a seat in the witness chair in front of a congressional committee.

Ah ... drugs; that word again. It was a hard word to avoid in NFL circles last year – like the 'missile gap' in the 1960 Kennedy–Nixon election, or 'law and order' in 1968.

1973 was a pretty dull press-year for congressmen. The Senate's Watergate Committee had managed, somehow, to pre-empt most of the ink and air-time ... and one of the few congressmen who managed to lash his own special gig past that barrier was an apparently senile sixty-seven-year-old ex-sheriff and football coach from West Virginia named Harley Staggers.

Somewhere in the spastic interim between John Dean and 'Bob' Haldeman, Congressman Staggers managed to collar some story-starved sportswriter from the New York *Times* long enough to announce that his committee – the House Subcommittee on Investigations – had stumbled on such a king-hell wasps' nest of evidence in the course of their probe into 'the use of drugs by athletes' that the committee was prepared – or *almost* prepared, pending further evidence – to come to grips with their natural human duty and offer up a law, very soon, that would require individual urinalysis tests on all professional athletes and especially pro football players.

These tests would be administered by professional urinalysists – paid by the federal government, out of tax-moneys – and if any one of these evil bastards passed urine that turned red (or green, or blue, or whatever), they would be ... ah ... well ... the Staggers Committee is still mulling on the question of penalties.

Maybe *studying* is a better word. Or *pondering* ... That's right, they're still *pondering* it ... and God's mercy on any muscle-bound degenerate whose piss turns red if Harley ever passes his law. The rumour on Capitol Hill is that Rep. Staggers is even now in the process of arranging for the construction of a model, medium security JOCK/DRUG PENI-

TENTIARY AND REHABILITATION CENTRE on the site of an abandoned missile base near Tonopah, Nevada.

Meanwhile, the Vice-President of the United States has been lashed out of office and disbarred in his home state of Maryland, the President himself is teetering on the brink of a Burglary/Conspiracy indictment that will mean certain impeachment, and the whole structure of our government has become a stagnant mockery of itself and everybody who ever had faith in it.

What all this means to Harley Staggers is hard to say. I am tempted to call him: It is 7:02 in Washington and I suspect he's wide awake, administering the daily beating to his pit-bulls in the backyard garage and waiting for calls from reporters:

'What's up Harley? Who's gonna get it?'

'Well ... let me say this: We know, for a fact, that the situation is out of control and I mean to put a stop to it or fall down trying ...'

'A stop to *what*, Harley?'

'Nevermind that. You know what I mean.' (pause) 'Let me ask you something: Does a phrase like "The playing fields of West Virginia" mean anything to you?' (pause) 'Wait a minute – where were you raised? What's wrong with—' (click) ...

Ah, Jesus ... another bad tangent. Somewhere in the back of my mind I recall signing a contract that said I would never do this kind of thing again; one of the conditions of my turning pro was a clause about swearing off gibberish ...

But, like Gregg Allman says: 'I've wasted so much time ... feelin' guilty ...'

There is some kind of back-door connection in my head between Super Bowls and the Allman Brothers – a strange kind of theme-sound that haunts these goddamn stories no matter where I'm finally forced into a corner to write them. The Allman sound, and rain. There was heavy rain, last year, on the balcony of my dim-lit hotel room just down from the Sunset Strip in Hollywood ... and more rain through the windows of the San Francisco office building where I finally typed out 'the story'.

And now, almost exactly a year later, my main memory of Super Bowl VIII in Houston is rain and grey mist outside another hotel window, with the same strung-out sound of the Allman Brothers booming out of the same portable speakers that I had, last year, in Los Angeles.

There was not much else worth remembering from either game – or at least not much that needs writing about, and the clock on the wall reminds me, once again, that final deadline looms and there is hungry space to fill out there in San Francisco ... Which means no more thinking about rain and music, but a quick and nasty regression to 'professionalism'.

Which is what it's all about.

Indeed, I tend, more and more, to forget these things. Or maybe just to ignore them.

But what the hell? Retirement is just around the corner, so why not wander a bit?

You grow up fast in Texas
and you got to lay it down
Or you'll be working for somebody
way cross town.
                    Doug Sahm

The floor of the Hyatt Regency men's room was always covered, about three inches deep, with discarded newspapers – all apparently complete and unread, except on closer examination you realized that every one of them was missing its sports section. This bathroom was right next to the hotel newsstand and just across the mezzanine from the crowded NFL 'press lounge', a big room full of telephones and free booze, where most of the 1600 or so sportswriters assigned to cover the Big Game seemed to spend about sixteen hours of each day, during Super Week.

After the first day or so, when it became balefully clear that there was no point in anybody except the local reporters going out on the press-bus each day for the carefully staged 'player interviews', that Dolphin tackle Manny Fernandez described as 'like going to the dentist every day to have the same tooth filled', the out-of-town writers began using the local types as a sort of involuntary 'pool' ... which was more like an old British Navy press gang, in fact, because the locals had no choice. They would go out, each morning, to the Miami and Minnesota team hotels, and dutifully conduct the daily interviews ... and about two hours later this mass of useless gibberish would appear, word for word, in the early editions of either the *Post* or the *Chronicle*.

You could see the front door of the hotel from the balcony of the press lounge, and whenever the newsboy came in with his stack of fresh papers, the national writers would make the long forty-eight-yard walk across to the newsstand and cough up fifteen cents each for their copies. Then, on the way back to the press lounge, they would stop for a piss and dump the whole paper – except for the crucial sports section – on the floor of the men's room. The place was so deep, all week, in fresh newsprint, that it was sometimes hard to push the door open.

Forty yards away, on comfortable couches surrounding the free bar, the national gents would spend about two hours each day scanning the local sports sections – along with a never-ending mass of almost psychotically detailed information churned out by the NFL publicity office – on the dim chance of finding something worth writing about that day.

There never was, of course. But nobody seemed really disturbed about it. The only thing most of the sportswriters in Houston seemed to care about was having *something* to write about ... anything at all, boss: a peg, an angle, a quote, even a goddamn rumour.

I remember being shocked at the sloth and moral degeneracy of the Nixon press corps during the 1972 presidential campaign – but they were like a pack of wolverines on speed compared to the relatively élite sportswriters who showed up in Houston to cover the Super Bowl.

On the other hand, there really *was no story*. As the week wore on, it became increasingly obvious that we were all 'just working here'. Nobody knew who to blame for it, and although at least a third of the sportswriters who showed up for that super-expensive shuck knew exactly what was happening, I doubt if more than five or six of them ever actually wrote the cynical and contemptuous appraisals of Super Bowl VIII that dominated about half the conversations around the bar in the press lounge.

Whatever was happening in Houston that week had little or nothing to do with the hundreds of stories that were sent out on the news-wires each day. Most of the stories, in fact, were unabashed rewrites of the dozens of official NFL press releases churned out each day by the League publicity office. Most of the stories about 'fantastic parties' given by Chrysler, American Express and Jimmy the Greek were taken from press releases and rewritten by people who had spent the previous evening at least five miles from the scenes described in their stories.

The NFL's official Super Bowl party – the 'incredible Texas Hoe-Down' on Friday night in the Astrodome – was as wild, glamorous and exciting as an Elks Club picnic on Tuesday in Salina, Kansas. The official NFL press release on the Hoe-Down said it was an unprecedented extravaganza that cost the League more than $100,000 and attracted people like Gene McCarthy and Ethel Kennedy ... Which might have been true, but I spent about five hours skulking around in that grim concrete barn and the only people I recognized were a dozen or so sportswriters from the press lounge.

Anybody with access to a mimeograph machine and a little imagination could have generated at least a thousand articles on 'an orgy of indescribable proportions' at John Connally's house, with Allen Ginsberg as the guest of honour and thirteen thoroughbred horses slaughtered by drug-crazed guests with magnesium butcher knives. Most of the press people would have simply picked the story off the big table in the 'work-room', rewritten it just enough to make it sound genuine, and sent it off on the wire without a second thought.

The bus-ride to the stadium for the game on Sunday took more than an hour, due to heavy traffic. I had made the same six-mile drive the night before in just under five minutes ... but that was under very different circumstances; Rice Stadium is on South Main Street, along the same route that led from the Hyatt Regency to the Dolphin headquarters at the Marriott, and also to the Blue Fox.

There was not much to do on the bus except drink, smoke and maintain a keen ear on the babble of conversations behind me for any talk that might signal the presence of some late-blooming Viking fan with money to waste. It is hard to stay calm and casual in a crowd of potential betters when you feel absolutely certain of winning any bet you can make. At that point, anybody with even a hint of partisan enthusiasm in his voice becomes a possible mark – a doomed and ignorant creature to be lured, as carefully as possible, into some disastrous last-minute wager that could cost him every dollar he owns.

There is no room for mercy or the milk of human kindness in football betting – at least not when you're prepared to get up on the edge with every dollar you own. One-in-one betting is a lot more interesting than dealing with bookies, because it involves strong elements of personality and psychic leverage. Betting against the point spread is a relatively mechanical trip, but betting against another individual can be very complex, if you're serious about it – because you want to know, for starters, whether you're betting against a fool or a wizard, or maybe against somebody who's just *playing* the fool.

Making a large bet on a bus full of sportswriters on the way to the Super Bowl, for instance, can be a very dangerous thing: because you might be dealing with somebody who was in the same fraternity at Penn State with one of the team doctors, and who learned the night before – while drinking heavily with his old buddy – that the quarterback you're basing your bet on has four cracked ribs and can barely raise his passing arm to shoulder level.

Situations like these are not common. Unreported injuries can lead to heavy fines against any team that fails to report one – especially in a Super Bowl – but what is a $10,000 fine, compared to the amount of money that kind of crucial knowledge is worth against a big-time bookie?

The other side of that coin is a situation where a shrewd coach turns the League's 'report all injuries' rule into a psychological advantage for his own team – and coincidentally for any better who knows what's happening – by scrupulously reporting an injury to a star player just before a big game, then calling a press conference to explain that the just-reported injury is of such a nature – a pulled muscle, for instance – that it might or might not heal entirely by game time.

This was what happened in Houston with the Dolphins' Paul Warfield, widely regarded as 'the most dangerous pass receiver in pro football'. Warfield is a game-breaker, a man who commands double-coverage at all times because of his antelope running style, twin magnets for hands, and a weird kind of adrenalin instinct that feeds on tension and high pressure. There is no more beautiful sight in football than watching Paul Warfield float out of the backfield on a sort of angle-streak pattern right into the heart of a 'perfect' zone defence and take a softly thrown pass on his hip, without even seeming to notice the arrival of the ball, and then float another sixty yards into the end zone, with none of the frustrated defensive back ever touching him.

There is an eerie kind of *certainty* about Warfield's style that is far more demoralizing than just another six points on the scoreboard. About half the time he looks bored and lazy – but even the best pass defenders in the league *know*, in some nervous corner of their hearts, that when the deal goes down Warfield is capable of streaking right past them like they didn't exist ...

Unless he's hurt; playing with some kind of injury that might or might not be serious enough to either slow him down or gimp the fiendish concentration that makes him so dangerous ... and this was the possibility that Dolphin coach Don Shula raised on Wednesday when he announced that Warfield had pulled a leg muscle in practice that afternoon and *might* not play on Sunday.

This news caused instant action in gambling circles. Even big-time bookies, whose underground information on these things is usually as good as Pete Rozelle's, took Shula's announcement seriously enough to cut the spread down from seven to six – a decision worth many millions of betting dollars if the game turned out to be close.

Even the *rumour* of an injury to Warfield was worth one point (and even two, with some bookies I was never able to locate) ... and if Shula had announced on Saturday that Paul was definitely not going to play, the spread would probably have dropped to four, or even three ... Because the guaranteed absence of Warfield would have taken a great psychological load off the minds of Minnesota's defensive backs.

Without the ever-present likelihood of a game-breaking 'bomb' at any moment, they could focus down much tighter on stopping Miami's brutal running game – which eventually destroyed them, just as it had destroyed Oakland's nut-cutting defence two weeks earlier, and one of the main reasons why the Vikings failed to stop the Dolphins on the ground was the constant presence of Paul Warfield in his customary wide-receiver's spot.

He played almost the whole game, never showing any sign of injury; and although he caught only one pass, he neutralized two Minnesota defensive backs on every play ... and two extra tacklers on the line of scrimmage might have made a hell of a difference in that embarrassingly decisive first quarter when Miami twice drove what might as well have been the whole length of the field to score fourteen quick points and crack the Vikings' confidence just as harshly as they had cracked the Redskins out in Los Angeles a year earlier.

It is hard to say, even now, exactly why I was so certain of an easy Dolphin victory. The only reason I didn't get extremely rich on the game was my inability to overcome the logistical problems of betting heavily, on credit, by means of frantic long-distance phone calls from a hotel room in Houston. None of the people I met in that violent, water-logged town were inclined to introduce me to a reliable bookmaker – and the people I called on both coasts, several hours before the game on Sunday morning, seemed unnaturally nervous when I asked them to use their own credit to guarantee my bets with their local bookies.

Looking back on it now, after talking with some of these people and cursing them savagely, I see that the problem had something to do with my frenzied speech-pattern that morning. I was still in the grip of what-ever fiery syndrome had caused me to deliver that sermon off the bal-cony a few hours earlier – and the hint of mad tremor in my voice, despite my attempts to disguise it, was apparently communicated very clearly to all those I spoke with on the long-distance telephone.

How long, O Lord, how long? This is the second year in a row that I have gone to the Super Bowl and been absolutely certain – at least forty-eight hours before gametime – of the outcome. It is also the second year in a row that I have failed to capitalize, financially, on this certainty. Last year, betting mainly with wealthy cocaine addicts, I switched all my bets from Washington to Miami on Friday night – and in the resulting confusion my net winnings were almost entirely cancelled by wide-spread rancour and personal bitterness.

This year, in order to side-step that problem, I waited until the last moment to make my bets – despite the fact that I knew the Vikings were doomed after watching them perform for the press at the star-crossed practice field on Monday afternoon before the game. It was clear, even then, that they were spooked and very uncertain about what they were getting into – but it was not until I drove about twenty miles around the belt-way to the other side of town for a look at the Dolphins that I knew, for sure, how to bet.

There are a lot of factors intrinsic to the nature of the Super Bowl that make it far more predictable than regular season games, or even play-offs – but they are not the kind of factors that can be sensed or understood at a distance of 2000 or even twenty miles, on the basis of any wisdom or information that filters out from the site through the rose-coloured, booze-bent media-filter that passes for 'world-wide coverage' at these spectacles.

There is a progression of understanding *vis-à-vis* pro football that varies drastically with the factor of *distance* – physical, emotional, intellectual and every other way ... Which is exactly the way it should be, in the eyes of the amazingly small number of people who own and control the game, because it is this finely managed distance factor that accounts for the high-profit *mystique* that blew the sacred institution of baseball off its 'national pastime' pedestal in less than fifteen years.

There were other reasons for baseball's precipitous loss of popularity among everybody except old men and middle-aged sportswriters between 1959 and now – just as there will be a variety of reasons to explain the certain decline of pro football between now and 1984 – but if sporting historians ever look back on all this and try to explain it, there will be no avoiding the argument that pro football's meteoric success in the 1960s was directly attributable to its early marriage with network TV and a huge, coast-to-coast audience of armchair fans who 'grew up' – in terms of their personal relationships to the Game – with the idea that pro football was something that happened every Sunday on the tube. The notion of driving eight miles along a crowded freeway and then paying $3 to park the car in order to pay another $10 to watch the game from the vantage point of a damp redwood bench fifty-five rows above the nineteen-yard line in a crowd of noisy drunks was entirely repugnant to them.

And they were absolutely right. After ten years of trying it both ways – and especially after watching this last wretched Super Bowl game from a choice seat in the 'press section' very high above the fifty-yard line – I hope to Christ I never again succumb to whatever kind of weakness or madness it is that causes a person to endure the incoherent hell that comes with going out to a cold and rainy stadium for three hours on a Sunday afternoon and trying to get involved with whatever seems to be happening down there on that far-below field.

At the Super Bowl I had the benefit of my usual game-day aids: powerful binoculars, a tiny portable radio for the blizzard of audio-details that nobody ever thinks to mention on TV, and a seat on the good left arm of my friend, Mr Natural ... But even with all these aids and a seat on the fifty-yard line, I would rather have stayed in my hotel room and watched the goddamn thing on TV; or maybe in some howling-drunk bar full of heavy betters – the kind of people who like to bet on every play: pass or run, three to one against a first down, twenty to one on a turnover ...

This is a very fast and active style of betting, because you have to make a decision about every twenty-five seconds. The only thing more intense is betting yes or no on the next shot in something like a pro basketball game between the Celtics and the Knicks, where you might get five or six shots every twenty-four seconds ... or maybe only one, but in any case the betting is almost as exhausting as being out there on the floor.

I stayed in Houston for two days after the game, but even with things calmed down I had no luck in finding the people who'd caused me all my trouble. Both Tom Keating and Al LoCasale were rumoured to be in the vicinity, but – according to some of the New York sportswriters who'd seen them – neither one was eager to either see or be seen with me.

When I finally fled Houston it was a cold Tuesday afternoon with big lakes of standing water on the road to the airport. I almost missed my plane to Denver because of a hassle with Jimmy the Greek about who was going to drive us to the airport and another hassle with the hotel garage-man about who was going to pay for eight days of tending my bogus 'official Super Bowl car' in the hotel garage ... and I probably wouldn't have made it at all if I hadn't run into a NFL publicity man who gave me enough speed to jerk me awake and lash the little white Mercury Cougar out along the Dallas freeway to the airport in time to abandon it in the 'departures/taxis only' area and hire a man for five dollars to rush my bags and sound equipment up to the Continental Airlines desk just in time to make the flight.

Twenty-four hours later I was back in Woody Creek and finally, by sheer accident, making contact with that twisted bastard Keating – who bent my balance a bit by calmly admitting his role in my problem and explaining it with one of the highest left-handed compliments anybody ever aimed at me ...

'I got nothing personal against Thompson,' he told another NFL player who happened to be skiing in Aspen at the time: 'But let's face it, we've got nothing to gain by talking to him. I've read all his stuff and I know how he is; he's a goddamn lunatic – and you've got to be careful with a bastard like that, because no matter how hard he tries, he just can't help but tell the truth.'

When I heard that I just sort of slumped down on my bar-stool and stared at myself in the mirror ... wishing, on one level, that Keating's harsh judgement was right ... but knowing, on another, that the treacherous realities of the worlds I especially work in forced me to abandon the purist stance a long time ago. If I'd written all the truth I knew for the past ten years, about 600 people – including me – would be rotting in prison cells from Rio to Seattle today. Absolute truth is a very rare and dangerous commodity in the context of professional journalism.

What was easily the most provocative quote of that whole dreary week came on the Monday after the game from Miami linebacker Doug Swift. He was talking in his usual loose 'What? Me Worry?' kind of way with two or three sportswriters in the crowded lobby of the Marriott. Buses were leaving for the airport, Dolphin supporters and their wives were checking out, the lobby was full of stranded luggage, and off in one of the corners, Don Shula was talking with another clutch of sportswriters and ridiculing the notion that he would ever get rid of Jim Kiick, despite Kiick's obvious unhappiness at the prospect of riding the bench again next year behind all-pro running back Mercury Morris.

Meanwhile, on the other side of the lobby, Doug Swift was going along with a conversation that had turned, along with Shula's, to money and next year's contracts. Swift listened for a while, then looked up at whoever was talking to him and said:

'You can expect to see a lot of new faces on next year's [Miami] team. A lot of important contracts are coming up for renewal, and you can bet that the guys will be asking for more than management is willing to pay.'

Nobody paid much attention to the decidedly unnatural timing of Swift's matter-of-fact prediction about 'a lot of new faces next year', but it was not the kind of talk designed to tickle either Shula's or Joe Robbie's rampant humours that morning. Jesus, here was the team's player representative – a star linebacker and one of the sharpest and most politically conscious people in the League – telling anyone who cared to listen, not even twelve hours after the victory party, that the embryo 'Dolphin dynasty' was already in a very different kind of trouble than anything the Vikings or the Redskins had been able to lay on them in two straight Super Bowls.

*

Swift's comment was all the more ominous because of his stature as the team's spokesman in the NFL Players' Association – a long-dormant poker club, of sorts, that in recent years has developed genuine muscle. Even in the face of what most of the player reps call a 'legalized and unregulated monopoly' with the power of what amounts to 'life or death' over their individual fates and financial futures in the tight little world of the National Football Leagues, the Players' Association since 1970 has managed to challenge the owners on a few carefully chosen issues ... The two most obvious, or at least most frequently mentioned by players, are the pension fund (which the owners now contribute to about twice as heavily as they did before the threatened strike in 1970) and the players' unilateral rejection, last year, of the 'urinalysis proposal' which the owners and Rozelle were apparently ready and willing to arrange for them, rather than risk any more public fights with Congress about things like TV blackouts and antitrust exemptions.

According to Pittsburgh tackle Tom Keating, an articulate maverick who seems to enjoy a universal affection and respect from almost everybody in the League except the owners and owner-bent coaches, the Players' Association croaked the idea of mass-urinalysis with one quick snarl. 'We just told them to fuck it,' he says. 'The whole concept of mass urine tests is degrading! Jesus, can you imagine what would happen if one of those stadium cops showed up in the press box at half-time with a hundred test tubes and told all the writers to piss in the damn things or turn in their credentials for the rest of the season? I'd like to film that goddamn scene.'

I agreed with Keating that mass-urinalysis in the press box at half-time would undoubtedly cause violence and a blizzard of vicious assaults on the NFL in the next morning's papers ... but, after thinking about it for a while, the idea struck me as having definite possibilities if applied on a broad enough basis:

Mandatory urine-tests for all congressmen and senators at the end of each session, for instance. Who could predict what kind of screaming hell might erupt if Rep. Harley Staggers was suddenly grabbed by two Pinkerton men in a hallway of the US Capitol and dragged – in full view of tourists, newsmen and several dozen of his shocked and frightened colleagues – into a nearby corner and forced to piss in a test tube?

Would Staggers scream for help? Would he struggle in the grip of his captors? Or would he meekly submit, in the interest of national security?

We will probably never know, because the present Congress does not seem to be in a mood to start passing 'forced urinalysis' laws – although the Agnew-style Supreme Court that Nixon has saddled us with would probably look with favour on such a law.

In any case, the threat of mandatory urinalysis for professional athletes will probably be hooted out of Congress as some kind of stupid hillbilly joke if Staggers ever gets serious about it. He is not viewed, in Washington, as a heavy shaker and mover.

When Doug Swift made that comment about 'a lot of new faces on next year's team', he was not thinking in terms of a player-revolt against forced urinalysis. What he had in mind, I think, was the fact that among the Dolphin contracts coming up for renewal this year are those of Larry Csonka, Jake Scott, Paul Warfield, Dick Anderson and Mercury Morris – all established stars earning between $30,000 and $55,000 a year right now, and all apparently in the mood to double their salaries next time around.

Which might seem a bit pushy, to some people – until you start comparing average salary figures in the National Football League against salaries in other pro sports. The average NFL salary (according to figures provided by Players' Association general counsel, Ed Garvey) is $28,500, almost five grand less than the $33,000 average for major league baseball players, and about *half* the average salary (between $50,000 and $55,000) in the National Hockey League ... But when you start talking about salaries in the National Basketball Association, it's time to kick out the jams: The *average* NBA salary is $92,500 a year. (The NBA Players' Association claims that the average salary is $100,000.)

Against this steep-green background, it's a little easier to see why Larry Csonka wants a raise from his current salary of $55,000 – to $100,000 or so, a figure that he'd probably scale down pretty calmly if Joe Robbie offered him the average NBA salary of $92,500.

(A quick little sidelight on all the figures has to do with the price TV advertisers paid to push their products during time-outs and penalty-squabbles at the Super Bowl: The figure announced by the NFL and whatever TV network carried the goddamn thing was $200,000 per minute. I missed the telecast, due to factors beyond my control – which is why I don't know which network sucked up all that gravy, or whether it was Schlitz, Budweiser, Gillette or even King Kong Amyl Nitrites that coughed up $200,000 for every sixty seconds of TV exposure on that grim afternoon.)

But that was just a sidelight ... and the longer I look at all these figures, my watch, and this goddamn stinking mojo wire that's been beeping steadily out here in the snow for two days, the more I tend to see this whole thing about a pending labour-management crunch in the NFL as a story with a spine of its own that we should probably leave for later.

The only other thing – or maybe two things – that I want to hit, lashing the final pages of this bastard into the mojo, has to do with the sudden and apparently serious formation of the 'World Football League' by the same people whose record, so far, has been pretty good when it comes to taking on big-time monopolies. Los Angeles lawyer Gary Davidson is the same man who put both the American Basketball Association and the World Hockey League together – two extremely presumptuous trips that appear to have worked out very nicely, and which also provided the competition factor that caused the huge salary jumps in both basketball and hockey.

Perhaps the best example of how the competition factor affects player salaries comes from the ledger-books of the NFL. In 1959, the average salary in pro football was $9500 a year. But in 1960, when the newly formed AFL began its big-money bidding war against pro football's old guard, the average NFL salary suddenly jumped to $27,500 – and in the thirteen years since then it has crept up another $1000 to the current figure of $28,500.

The explanation for all this – according to Garvey and all the players I've talked to about it – is rooted entirely in the owner-arranged merger between the NFL and the AFL in 1966. 'Ever since then,' says Garvey, 'it's been a buyer's market, and that's why the NFL's average salary figure has remained so stagnant, compared to the other sports.'

Garvey said he'd just as soon not make any public comment on the possibility of a players' strike next summer – but there is a lot of private talk about it among individual players, and especially among the player reps and some of the politically oriented hard rockers life Swift, Keating, and Kansas City's Ed Podolak.

The only person talking *publicly* about a players' strike is Gary Davidson, president of the new World Football League – who called a press conference in New York on 22 January to announce that the WFL was not only going after the top college players and the thirty-five or so NFL veterans who played out their options last year – but, in a sudden reversal of policy that must have sent cold shots of fear through every one of the twenty-six plush boardrooms in the NFL, Davidson announced that the WFL will also draft 'all pro football players, even those under contract', and then begin draining talent out of the NFL by a simple device called 'future contracts'.

If the Boston Bulls of the WFL, for instance, decided to draft Dolphin quarterback Bob Griese this year and sign him to a future contract for 1975, Griese would play the entire 74 season for Miami, and then – after getting a certified deposit slip for something like $2 million in gold bullion from his bank in Zurich – he would have a round of farewell beers with Robbie and Shula before catching the plane for Boston, where he would open the 1976 season as quarterback for the Bulls.

This is only one of several hundred weird scenarios that could start unfolding in the next few months if the WFL franchise-owners have enough real money to take advantage of the NFL players' strike that Gary Davidson says he's waiting for this summer.

Why not? Total madness on the money front: huge bonuses, brutal money raids on NFL teams like the Dolphins and the Raiders; wild-eyed WFL agents flying around the country in private Lear jets with huge sacks of cash and mind-bending contracts for any player willing to switch ...

The only sure loser, in the end, will be the poor bastard who buys a season ticket for the Dolphins 76 season and then picks up the Miami *Herald* the next day to find a red banner headline saying: GRIESE, KIICK, CSONKA, SCOTT, ANDERSON JUMP TO WFL.

Which is sad, but what the hell? None of this tortured bullshit about the future of pro football means anything, anyway. If the Red Chinese invaded tomorrow and banned the game entirely, nobody would really miss it after two or three months. Even now, most of the games are so fucking dull that it's hard to understand how anybody can even watch them on TV unless they have some money hanging on the point spread, instead of the final score.

Pro football in America is over the hump. Ten years ago it was a very hip and private kind of vice to be into. I remember going to my first 49er game in 1965 with fifteen beers in a plastic cooler and a Dr Grabow pipe full of bad hash. The 49ers were still playing in Kezar stadium then, an old grey hulk at the western end of Haight Street in Golden Gate Park. There were never any sellouts, but the 30,000 or so regulars were extremely heavy drinkers, and at least 10,000 of them were out there for no other reason except to get involved in serious violence ... By half time the place was a drunken madhouse, and anybody who couldn't get it on anywhere else could always go underneath the stands and try to get into the long trough of a 'men's room' through the 'out' door; there were always a few mean drunks lurking around to punch anybody who tried that ... and by the end of the third quarter of any game, regardless of the score, there were always two or three huge brawls that would require the cops to clear out whole sections of the grandstand.

But all that changed when the 49ers moved out to Candlestick Park. The prices doubled and a whole new crowd took the seats. It was the same kind of crowd I saw, last season, in the four games I went to at the Oakland Coliseum: a sort of half-rich mob of nervous doctors, lawyers and bank officers who would sit through a whole game without ever making a sound – not even when some freak with a head full of acid spilled a whole beer down the neck of their grey-plastic ski jackets.

Towards the end of the season, when the Raiders were battling every week for a spot in the playoffs, some of the players got so pissed off at the stuporous nature of their 'fans' that they began making public appeals for 'cheering' and 'noise'.

It was a bad joke if you didn't have to live with it – and as far as I'm concerned I hope to hell I never see the inside of another football stadium. Not even a free seat with free booze in the press box.

That gig is over now, and I blame it on Vince Lombardi. The success of his Green Bay approach in the 60s restructured the game entirely. Lombardi never really thought about *winning*; his trip was *not losing* ... Which worked, and because it worked the rest of the NFL bought Lombardi's whole style: avoid mistakes, don't fuck up, hang tough and take no chances ... Because sooner or later the enemy will make a mistake and then you start grinding him down, and if you play the defensive percentage you'll get inside his thirty-yard line at least three times in each half, and once you're inside the thirty you want to be sure to get at least three points ...

Wonderful. Who can argue with a battle-plan like that? And it is worth remembering that Richard Nixon spent many Sundays, during all those long and lonely autumns between 1962 and 68, shuffling around on the field with Vince Lombardi at Green Bay Packer games.

Nixon still speaks of Lombardi as if he might suddenly appear, at any moment, from underneath one of the larger rocks on the White House lawn ... And Don Shula, despite his fairly obvious distaste for Nixon, has adopted the Lombardi style of football so effectively that the Dolphins are now one of the dullest teams to watch in the history of pro football.

But most of the others are just as dull – and if you need any proof, find a TV set some weekend that has pro football, basketball and hockey games on three different channels. In terms of pure action and movement, the NFL is a molasses farm compared to the fine sense of crank that comes on when you get locked into watching a team like the Montreal Canadiens or the Boston Celtics.

One of the few sharp memories I still have from that soggy week in Houston is the sight of the trophy that would go to the team that won the Big Game on Sunday. It was appropriately named after Vince Lombardi: the 'Lombardi Trophy', a thick silver fist rising out of a block of black granite.

The trophy has all the style and grace of an ice floe in the North Atlantic. There is a silver plaque on one side of the base that says something about Vince Lombardi and the Super Bowl ... but the most interesting thing about it is a word that is carved, for no apparent or at least no aesthetic reason, in the top of the black marble base:

'DISCIPLINE'

That's all it says, and all it needs to say.

The 73 Dolphins, I suspect, will be to pro football what the 64 Yankees were to baseball, the final flower of an era whose time has come and gone. The long and ham-fisted shadow of Vince Lombardi will be on us for many more years ... But the crank is gone ...

Should we end the bugger with that?

Why not? Let the sportswriters take it from here. And when things get nervous, there's always that smack-filled $7-a-night motel room down on the seawall in Galveston.

Rolling Stone no. 128, 15 February 1973

THE TEMPTATIONS OF JEAN-CLAUDE KILLY

Grey day in Boston. Piles of dirty snow around the airport ... My cocktail flight from Denver was right on time, but Jean-Claude Killy was not there to meet me.

Bill Cardoso lurked near the gate, grinning through elegant rimless glasses, commenting on our way to the bar that I looked like a candidate for a serious dope bust. Sheepskin vests are not big in Boston these days.

'But look at these fine wing-tips,' I said, pointing down at my shoes.

He chuckled. 'All I can see is that goddamn necklace. Being seen with you could jeopardize my career. Do you have anything illegal in that bag?'

'Never,' I said. 'A man can't travel around on airplanes wearing a Condor Legion neckpiece unless he's totally clean. I'm not even armed ... This whole situation makes me feel nervous and weird and thirsty.' I lifted my sunglasses to look for the bar, but the light was too harsh.

'What about Killy?' he said. 'I thought you were supposed to meet him.'

'I can't handle it tonight,' I said. 'I've been chasing all over the country for ten days on this thing: Chicago, Denver, Aspen, Salt Lake City, Sun Valley, Baltimore. Now Boston and tomorrow New Hampshire. I'm supposed to ride up there with them tonight on the Head Ski bus, but I'm not up to it; all those hired geeks with their rib-ticklers. Let's have a drink, then I'll cancel out on the bus trip.'

It seemed like the only decent thing to do. So we drove around to the airport hotel and went inside, where the desk clerk said the Head Ski people were gathered in Room 247. Which was true; they were in there, perhaps thirty in all, standing around a cloth-covered table loaded with beer and diced hotdogs. It looked like a cocktail party for the local Patrolmen's Benevolent Association. These were the Head Ski dealers, presumably from around the New England area. And right in their midst, looking fatigued and wretchedly uncomfortable – yes, I couldn't quite believe it, but there he was: Jean-Claude Killy, the world's greatest skier, now retired at age twenty-six with three Olympic gold medals, a fistful of golden contracts, a personal manager and ranking-celebrity status on three continents . . .

Cardoso nudged me, whispering, 'Jesus, there's Killy.'

I hadn't expected to find him here; not in a dim little windowless room in the bowels of a plastic motel. I stopped just inside the door . . . and a dead silence fell on the room. They stared, saying nothing, and Cardoso said later that he thought we were going to be attacked.

I hadn't expected a party. I thought we were looking for a private room, containing either 'Bud' Stanner, Head's marketing director, or Jack Rose, the PR man. But neither one was there. The only person I recognized was Jean-Claude, so I waded through the silence to where he was standing, near the hotdog table. We shook hands, both of us vibrating discomfort in this strange atmosphere. I was never quite sure about Killy, never knowing if he understood why I was embarrassed *for him* in those scenes.

A week earlier he'd seemed insulted when I smiled at his pitchman's performance at the Chicago Auto Show, where he and O. J. Simpson had spent two days selling Chevrolets. Killy had seen no humour in his act, and he couldn't understand why I did. Now, standing around in this grim, beer-flavoured sales meeting, it occurred to me that maybe he thought I felt uncomfortable because I wasn't wearing a red tie and a Robert Hall blazer with brass buttons like most of the others. Maybe he was embarrassed to be seen with me, a weird person of some sort . . . and with Cardoso, wearing granny glasses and a big grin, wandering around the room mumbling, 'Jesus, where are we? This must be Nixon headquarters.'

We didn't stay long. I introduced Cardoso as an editor of the Boston *Globe* and that stirred a bit of interest in the dealer-salesmen ranks – they are wise in the ways of publicity – but my neckpiece was obviously more than they could handle. Their faces tensed when I reached into the beer tub; nothing had been offered and my thirst was becoming acute. Jean-Claude just stood there in his blazer, smiling nervously. Outside in the hallway, Cardoso erupted with laughter. 'What an incredible scene! What was he *doing* with those bums?'

I shook my head. Killy's hard-sell scenes no longer surprised me, but finding him trapped in a beer and hotdog gig was like wandering into some housing-project kaffeeklatsch and finding Jacqueline Kennedy Onassis making a straight-faced pitch for Folger's instant-brewed.

My head was not straight at that stage of the investigation. Two weeks of guerrilla warfare with Jean-Claude Killy's publicity juggernaut had driven me to the brink of hysteria. What had begun in Chicago as a simple sketch of a French athlete turned American culture-hero had developed, by the time I got to Boston, into a series of maddening skirmishes with an interlocking directorate of public relations people.

I was past the point of needing any more private time with Jean-Claude. We had already done our thing – a four-hour head-on clash that ended with him yelling: 'You and me, we are completely different. We are not the same kind of people! You don't understand! You could never do what I'm doing! You sit there and smile, but you don't know what it is! I am tired. Tired! I don't care any more – not on the inside or the outside! I don't care what I say, what I think, *but I have to keep doing it*. And two weeks from now I can go back home to rest, and spend all my money.'

There was a hint of decency – perhaps even humour – about him, but the high-powered realities of the world he lives in now make it hard to deal with him on any terms except those of pure commerce. His handlers rush him from one scheduled appearance to the next; his time and priorities are parcelled out according to their dollar/publicity value; everything he says is screened and programmed. He often sounds like a prisoner of war, dutifully repeating his name, rank and serial number . . . and smiling, just as dutifully, fixing his interrogator with that wistful, distracted sort of half-grin that he *knows* is deadly effective because his handlers have showed him the evidence in a hundred press-clippings. The smile has become a trademark. It combines James Dean, Porfiro Rubirosa and a teenage bank clerk with a foolproof embezzlement scheme.

Killy projects an innocence and a shy vulnerability that he is working very hard to overcome. He likes the carefree, hell-for-leather image that he earned as the world's best ski racer, but nostalgia is not his bag, and his real interest now is his new commercial scene, the high-rolling world of the money game, where nothing is free and amateurs are called losers. The wistful smile is still there, and Killy is shrewd enough to value it, but it will be a hard thing to retain through three years of auto shows, even for $100,000 a year.

We began in Chicago, at some awful hour of the morning, when I was roused out of a hotel stupor and hustled around a corner on Michigan

Avenue to where Chevrolet's general manager John Z. DeLorean was addressing an audience of seventy-five 'automotive writers' at a breakfast press conference on the mezzanine of the Continental Plaza. The room looked like a bingo parlour in Tulsa – narrow, full of long formica tables with a makeshift bar at one end serving coffee, bloody marys and sweet rolls. It was the morning of the first big weekend of the Chicago Auto Show, and Chevrolet was going whole-hog. Sitting next to DeLorean at the head table were Jean-Claude Killy and O. J. Simpson, the football hero.

Killy's manager was there – a tall, thick fellow named Mark McCormack, from Cleveland, a specialist in rich athletes and probably the only man alive who knows what Killy is worth. Figures ranging from $100,000 to $500,000 a year are meaningless in the context of today's long-term high finance. A good tax lawyer can work miracles with a six-figure income ... and with all the fine machinery available to a man who can hire the best money-managers, Killy's finances are so skilfully tangled that he can't understand them himself.

In some cases, a big contract – say, $500,000 – is really a five-year annual salary of $20,000 with a $400,000 interest-free loan, deposited in the star's account, paying anywhere from five per cent to twenty per cent annually, depending on how he uses it. He can't touch the principal, but a $400,000 nut will yield $30,000 a year by accident – and a money-man working for thirty per cent can easily triple that figure.

With that kind of property to protect, McCormack has assumed veto power over anyone assigned to write about it for the public prints. This is compounded in its foulness by the fact that he usually gets away with it. Just prior to my introduction he had vetoed a writer from one of the big-selling men's magazines – who eventually wrote a very good Killy article anyway but without ever talking to the subject.

'Naturally, you'll be discreet,' he told me.

'About what?'

'You know what I mean.' He smiled. 'Jean-Claude has his private life and I'm sure you won't want to embarrass him or anyone else – including yourself, I might add – by violating confidence.'

'Well ... certainly not,' I replied, flashing him a fine eyebrow shrug to cover my puzzlement. He seemed pleased, and I glanced over at Killy, who was chatting amiably with DeLorean, saying, 'I hope you can ski with me sometime at Val d'Isère.'

Was there something depraved in that face? Could the innocent smile mask a twisted mind? What was McCormack hinting at? Nothing in Killy's manner seemed weird or degenerate. He spoke earnestly – not comfortable with English, but handling it well enough. If anything, he seemed overly polite, very concerned with saying the right thing, like an

Ivy League business school grad doing well on his first job interview – confident, but not quite sure. It was hard to imagine him as a sex freak, hurrying back to his hotel room and calling room service for a cattle prod and two female iguanas.

I shrugged and mixed myself another bloody mary. McCormack seemed satisfied that I was giddy and malleable enough for the task at hand, so he switched his attention to a small, wavy-haired fellow named Leonard Roller, a representative of one of Chevrolet's numerous public relations firms.

I drifted over to introduce myself. Jean-Claude laid his famous smile on me and we talked briefly about nothing at all. I took it for granted that he was tired of dealing with writers, reporters, gossip-hustlers and that ilk, so I explained that I was more interested in his new role as salesman-celebrity – and his reactions to it – than I was in the standard, question/answer game. He seemed to understand, smiling sympathetically at my complaints about lack of sleep and early-morning press conferences.

Killy is smaller than he looks on television, but larger than most ski racers, who are usually short and beefy, like weight-lifting jockeys and human cannonballs. He is almost six feet tall and claims to weigh 175 pounds – which is easy enough to believe when you meet him head-on, but his profile looks nearly weightless. Viewed from the side, his frame is so flat that he seems like a life-size cardboard cut-out. Then, when he turns to face you again, he looks like a scaled-down Joe Palooka, perfectly built. In swimming trunks he is almost delicate, except for his thighs – huge chunks of muscle, the thighs of an Olympic sprinter or a pro basketball guard ... or a man who has spent a lifetime on skis.

Jean-Claude, like Jay Gatsby, has 'one of those rare smiles with a quality of eternal reassurance in it, that you may come across four or five times in life. It faced – or seemed to face – the whole external world for an instant, and then concentrated on *you* with an irresistible prejudice in your favour. It understood you just as far as you would like to believe in yourself, and assured you that it had precisely the impression of you that, at your best, you hoped to convey.' That description of Gatsby by Nick Carraway – of Scott, by Fitzgerald – might just as well be of J.-C. Killy, who also fits the rest of it: 'Precisely at that point [Gatsby's smile] vanished – and I was looking at an elegant young roughneck, whose elaborate formality of speech just missed being absurd ...'

The point is not to knock Killy's English, which is far better than my French, but to emphasize his careful, finely coached choice of words. 'He's an amazing boy,' I was told later by Len Roller. 'He works at this [selling Chevrolets] just as hard as he used to work at winning races. He *attacks* it with the same concentration you remember from watching him ski.' The assumption that I remembered Killy on skis came naturally to Roller. Jean-Claude is on TV so often, skiing at selected resorts all over the world, that it is nearly impossible to miss seeing him. This is the Exposure that makes him so valuable; every TV appearance adds dollars to his price. People *recognize* Killy, and they like his image – a sexy daredevil, booming downhill towards a cushion of naked snowbunnies. This is why Chevrolet pays him a salary far larger than Nixon's to say, over and over again, 'For me, zee Camaro is a fine foreign sports car. I own one, you know. I keep it in my garage at Val d'Isère' (Killy's hometown in the French Alps).

Jean-Claude emerged from the 1968 Winter Olympics with an incredible three gold medals and then he retired, ending his 'amateur' career like a human skyrocket. There was nothing left to win; after two World Cups (the equivalent of two straight Heisman Trophies in US collegiate football) and an unprecedented sweep of all three Olympic skiing events (the equivalent of a sprinter winning the 100, 200 and 440), Killy's career reads as if his press agent had written the script for it – a series of spectacular personal victories, climaxed by the first triple-crown triumph in the history of skiing while the whole world watched on TV.

The nervous tedium of forced retirement obviously bothers Killy, but it comes as no surprise to him. He was looking over the hump even before his final triumph in the 68 Olympics. Between training sessions at Grenoble he talked like a character out of some early Hemingway sketch, shrugging blankly at the knowledge that he was coming to the end of the only thing he knew: 'Soon skiing will be worn out for me,' he said. 'For the last ten years I have prepared myself to become the world champion. My thoughts were only to better my control and my style in order to become the best. Then last year [1967] I became the world champion. I was given a small medal and for two days after that it was hell. I discovered that I was still eating like everybody else, sleeping like everybody else – that I hadn't become the superman I thought my title would make me. The discovery actually destroyed me for two days. So when people speak to me about the excitement of becoming an Olympic champion this year – should it happen – I know it will be the same thing all over again. I know that after the races at Grenoble the best thing for me is to stop.'

For Killy, the Olympics were the end of the road. The wave of the future crashed down on him within hours after his disputed grand slalom victory over Karl Schranz of Austria. Suddenly they were on him – a chattering greenback swarm of agents, money-mongers and would-be 'personal reps' of every shape and description. Mark McCormack's persistence lent weight to his glittering claim that he could do for Killy what he had already done for Arnold Palmer. Jean-Claude listened, shrugged, then ducked out for a while – to Paris, the Riviera, back home to Val d'Isère – and finally, after weeks of half-heartedly dodging the inevitable, signed with McCormack. The only sure thing in the deal was a hell of a lot of money, both sooner and later. Beyond that, Killy had no idea what he was getting into.

Now he was showing us how much he'd learned. The Chevvy press breakfast was breaking up and Len Roller suggested that the three of us go downstairs to the dining room. J.-C. nodded brightly and I smiled the calm smile of a man about to be rescued from a honkers' convention. We drifted downstairs, where Roller found us a corner table in the dining room before excusing himself to make a phone call. The waitress brought menus, but Killy waved her off, saying he wanted only prune juice. I was on the verge of ordering *huevos rancheros* with a double side of bacon, but in deference to J.-C.'s apparent illness I settled for grapefruit and coffee.

Killy was studying a mimeographed news release that I'd grabbed off a table at the press conference in lieu of notepaper. He nudged me and pointed at something in the lead paragraph. 'Isn't this amazing?' he asked. I looked: The used side of my notepaper was headed: NEWS ... from Chevrolet Motor Division ... CHICAGO – Chevrolet began its 'spring selling season' as early as January first this year, John Z. DeLorean, general manager, said here today. He told newsmen attending the opening of the Chicago Auto Show that Chevrolet sales are off to the fastest start since its record year of 1965. 'We sold 352,000 cars in January and February,' DeLorean said. 'That's 22 per cent ahead of last year. It gave us 26.9 per cent of the industry, compared to 23 per cent a year ago ...'

Killy said it again: 'Isn't this amazing?' I looked to see if he was smiling but his face was deadly serious and his voice was pure snake oil. I called for more coffee, nodding distractedly at Killy's awkward hustle, and cursing the greedy instinct that had brought me into this thing ... sleepless and ill-fed, trapped in a strange food-cellar with a French auto salesman.

But I stayed to play the game, gnawing on my grapefruit and soon following Roller out to the street, where we were scooped up by a large nondescript car that must have been a Chevrolet. I asked where we were going and somebody said, 'First to the Merchandise Mart, where he'll do a tape for Kup's show, and then to the Auto Show – at the Stockyards.'

That last note hung for a moment, not registering ... Kup's show was bad enough. I had been on it once, and caused a nasty scene by calling Adlai Stevenson a professional liar when all the other guests were there to publicize some kind of Stevenson memorial. Now nearly two years later, I saw no point in introducing myself. Kup was taking it easy this time, joking with athletes. Killy was overshadowed by Bart Starr, representing Lincoln-Mercury, and Fran Tarkenton, wearing a Dodge blazer ... but with Killy in eclipse the Chevrolet team still made the nut with O. J. Simpson, modestly admitting that he probably wouldn't tear the National Football League apart in his first year as a pro. It was a dull, low-level discussion, liberally spotted with promo mentions for the Auto Show.

Jean-Claude's only breakthrough came when Kup, cued by a story in that morning's *Tribune*, asked what Killy *really* thought about the whole question of 'amateur' athletic status. 'Is it safe to assume,' Kup asked, 'that you were paid for using certain skis in the Olympics?'

'Safe?' Killy asked ...

Kup checked his notes for a new question and Killy looked relieved. The hypocrisy inherent in the whole concept of 'amateurism' has always annoyed Killy, and now, with the immunity of graduate status, he doesn't mind admitting that he views the whole game as a fraud and a folly. During most of his career on the French ski team he was listed, for publicity reasons, as a government-employed Customs inspector. Nobody believed it, not even officials of the Fédération Internationale de Ski (FIS), the governing body for world-class amateur ski competition. The whole idea was absurd. Who, after all, could believe that the reigning world ski champion – a hero/celebrity whose arrival in any airport from Paris to Tokyo drew crowds and TV cameras – was actually supporting himself on a salary gleaned from his off-season efforts in some dreary customs shed at Marseilles?

He spoke with a definite humility, as if he felt slightly embarrassed by all the advantages he'd had. Then, about two hours later when our talk had turned to contemporary things – the high-style realities of his new jet-set life – he suddenly blurted: 'Before, I could only dream about these things. When I was young I had *nothing*, I was poor ... Now I can have anything I want!'

Jean-Claude seems to understand, without really resenting it, that he is being weaned away from the frank unvarnished style of his amateur days. One afternoon at Vail, for instance, he listened to a sportscaster telling him what a great run he'd just made, and then, fully aware that he was talking for a live broadcast, Jean-Claude laughed at the commentary and said he'd just made one of the worst runs of his life – a complete disaster, doing everything wrong. Now, with the help of his professional advisers, he has learned to be patient and polite – especially in America, with the press. In France he is more secure, and far more recognizable to the people who knew him before he became a salesman.

He was in Paris last spring when Avery Brundage, eighty-two-year-old president of the International Olympic Committee, called on Jean-Claude and several other winners of gold medals at the 1968 Winter Olympics to return them. Brundage, a tunnel-visioned purist of the old school, was shocked by disclosures that many of the winners – including Killy – didn't even know what the word 'amateur' meant. For years, said Brundage, these faithless *poseurs* had been accepting money from 'commercial interests' ranging from equipment manufacturers to magazine publishers.

One of these gimmicks made headlines just prior to the start of the games, if memory serves, and was awkwardly resolved by a quick ruling that none of the winners could either mention or display their skis (or any other equipment) during any TV interview or press exposure. Until then, it had been standard practice for the winner of any major race to make the brand-name on his skis as prominent as possible during all camera sessions. The 'no-show' ruling worked a hardship on a lot of skiers at Grenoble, but it failed to satisfy Avery Brundage. His demand that the medals be returned called up memories of Jim Thorpe, who was stripped of everything he won in the 1912 Olympics because he had once been paid to play in a semi-pro baseball game. Thorpe went along with the madness, returning his medals and living the rest of his life with the taint of 'disgrace' on his name. Even now, the nasty Olympics scandal is the main feature of Thorpe's biographical sketch in the new *Columbia Encyclopedia*.

But when a Montreal *Star* reporter asked Jean-Claude how he felt about turning in his Olympic medals, he replied: 'Let Brundage come over here himself and take them from me.'

It was a rare public display of 'the old Jean-Claude'. His American personality has been carefully manicured to avoid such outbursts. Chevrolet doesn't pay him to say what he thinks, but to sell Chevrolets – and you don't do that by telling self-righteous old men to fuck off. You don't even admit that the French Government paid you to be a skier because things are done that way in France and most other countries, and nobody born after 1900 calls it anything but natural ... when you sell Chevrolets in America you honour the myths and mentality of the marketplace: You smile like Horatio Alger and give all the credit to Mom and Dad, who never lost faith in you and even mortgaged their ingots when things got tough.

Anyone watching our departure from the Kup show must have assumed that J.-C. travelled with five or six bodyguards. I'm still not sure who the others were. Len Roller was always around, and a hostile, burr-haired little bugger from whichever of Chevvy's PR agencies was running the

Auto Show, who took me aside early on to warn me that Roller was 'only a guest – I'm running this show'. Roller laughed at the slur, saying, 'He only *thinks* he's running it.' The others were never introduced; they did things like drive cars and open doors. They were large, unconfident men, very polite in the style of armed gas-station attendants.

We left the Merchandise Mart and zapped off on a freeway to the Auto Show – and suddenly it registered: the Stockyards Amphitheatre. I was banging along the freeway in that big car, listening to the others trade bull/fuck jokes, trapped in the back seat between Killy and Roller, heading for that rotten slaughterhouse where Mayor Daley had buried the Democratic party.

I had been there before, and I remembered it well. Chicago – this vicious, stinking zoo, this mean-grinning, Mace-smelling boneyard of a city; an elegant rockpile monument to everything cruel and stupid and corrupt in the human spirit.

The public is out in force to view the new models. Jean-Claude makes his pitch for Chevrolet every two hours on the button: 1–3–5–7–9. The even numbered hours are reserved for O. J. Simpson.

Barker: 'Tell me, O. J., are you faster than that car over there?'

O. J.: 'You mean that groovy Chevrolet? Naw, man, that's the only thing I know that's faster than me ... ho, ho ...'

Meanwhile, slumped in a folding chair near the Killy exhibit, smoking a pipe and brooding on the spooks in this place, I am suddenly confronted by three young boys wearing Bass Weejuns and Pendleton shirts, junior-high types, and one of them asks me: 'Are you Jean-Claude Killy?'

'That's right,' I said.

'What are you doing?' they asked.

Well, you goddamn silly little waterhead, what the hell does it *look* like I'm doing? But I didn't say that. I gave the question some thought. 'Well,' I said finally, 'I'm just sitting here smoking marijuana.' I held up my pipe. 'This is what makes me ski so fast.' Their eyes swelled up like young grapefruits. They stared at me – waiting for a laugh, I think – then backed away. Five minutes later I looked up and found them still watching me, huddled about twenty feet away behind the sky-blue Z-28 Chevvy on its slow-moving turntable. I waved my pipe at them and smiled like Hubert Humphrey ... but they didn't wave back.

Killy's Auto Show act was a combination interview/autograph thing, with the questions coming from Roller and a silver-blonde model in rubberized stretch pants. The Chevvy people had set up a plywood podium next to the Z-28 – which they said was a new and special model, but which looked like any other Camaro with a (Head) ski rack on top.

Not far away, on another platform, O. J. Simpson fielded questions from a ripe little black girl, also dressed in tight ski pants. The acts remained segregated except in moments of unexpected crowd pressure, when the black model would occasionally have to interview Killy. The blonde girl was never cast with O. J. – at least not while I was there. Which hardly matters, except as casual evidence that Chevvy's image-makers still see racial separatism as good business, particularly in Chicago.

On the way in, Roller had rehearsed Jean-Claude on the Q and A sequence: 'Okay, then I'll say, "I see an interesting looking car over there, Jean-Claude – can you tell us something about it?" And then you say ... what?'

J.-C.: 'Oh, yes, that is my car, the new Z-28. It has seat covers made of Austrian ski sweaters. And you notice my special licence plate, JCK ...'

Roller: 'That's fine. The important thing is to be spontaneous.'

J.-C. (puzzled): 'Spuen-tan-EUS?'

Roller (grinning): 'Don't worry – you'll do fine.'

And he did. Killy's public pitch is very low-key, a vivid contrast to O. J. Simpson, whose sales technique has all the subtlety of a power-slant on third and one ... O. J. *likes* this scene. His booming self-confidence suggests Alfred E. Neuman in blackface or Rap Brown selling watermelons at the Mississippi State Fair. O. J.'s mind is not complicated; he has had God on his side for so long that it never occurs to him that selling Chevrolets is any less holy than making touchdowns. Like Frank Gifford, whose shoes he finally filled in the USC backfield, he understands that football is only the beginning of his TV career. O. J. is a black capitalist in the most basic sense of that term; his business sense is so powerful that he is able to view his blackness as a mere sales factor – a natural intro to the black marketplace, where a honky showboat like Killy is doomed from the start.

There are some people in 'the trade', in fact, who can't understand why the Chevrolet wizards consider Killy as valuable – on the image-selling scale – as a hotdog American folk hero like O. J. Simpson.

'What the hell were they thinking about when they signed that guy for three hundred grand a year?' muttered a ranking 'automotive journalist' as he watched Killy's act on Saturday afternoon.

I shook my head and wondered, remembering DeLorean's owlish confidence that morning at the press breakfast. Then I looked at the crowd surrounding Killy. They were white and apparently solvent, their average age around thirty – the kind of people who could obviously afford to buy skis and make payments on new cars. O. J. Simpson drew bigger crowds, but most of his admirers were around twelve years old. Two-thirds of them were black and many looked like fugitives from the Credit Bureau's garnishee file.

Mark McCormack signed to manage Arnold Palmer a decade ago – just prior to the great golf boom. His reasons for betting on Killy are just as obvious. Skiing is no longer an esoteric sport for the idle rich, but a fantastically popular new winter status-game for anyone who can afford $500 for equipment. Five years ago the figure would have been three times that, plus another loose $1000 for a week at Stowe or Sun Valley, but now, with the advent of snow-making machines, even Chattanooga is a 'ski-town'. The Midwest is dotted with icy 'week-night' slalom hills, lit up like the miniature golf courses of the Eisenhower age.

The origins of the ski boom were based entirely on economics and the appeal of the sport itself ... no freaky hypes or shoestring promotion campaigns ... the money boom of the 1960s produced a sassy middle class with time on its hands, and suddenly there was a mushrooming demand for things like golf clubs, motorboats and skis. In retrospect, the wonder of it is that it took people like McCormack so long to grab a good thing. Or maybe the problem was a lack of ski heroes. Does anyone remember, for instance, who won gold medals at the 64 Winter Olympics? It was the prominence of Jean-Claude Killy (as a hot racer in 1966 and as a press hero in 67 and 68) that suddenly gave skiing an image. Jean-Claude emerged from the 68 Olympics as a sort of suave Joe Namath, a 'swinging Frenchman' with the style of a jet-set maverick and the mind of a Paris bartender.

The result was inevitable: a super-priced French import, tailored strictly for the fast-growing US leisure market, the same people who suddenly found themselves able to afford Porsches, Mercedes and Jaguars ... along with MGs and Volkswagens.

But not Fords or Chevvys. 'Detroit iron' didn't make it in that league ... mainly because there is no room in the brass ranks of the US auto industry for the kind of executive who understands why a man who can afford a Cadillac will buy a Porsche instead. There was simply no status in owning a $10,000 car with no back seat and a hood only five feet long.

So now we have a DeLorean-style blitz for Chevrolet, and it's doing beautifully. Booming Chevvy sales are mainly responsible for GM's spurt to a plus-fifty per cent of the whole auto market. The strategy has been simple enough: a heavy focus on speed, sporty styling and the 'youth market'. This explains Chevvy's taste for such image-makers as Simpson, Glen Campbell and Killy. (Speculation that DeLorean was about to sign Allen Ginsberg proved to be false: General Motors doesn't need poets.)

*

Killy has spent his entire adult life in the finely disciplined cocoon that is part of the price one pays for membership of the French ski team. As a life style, it is every bit as demanding as that of a pro football quarterback. In a sport where the difference between fame and total obscurity is measured in tenths of a second, the discipline of constant, rigid training is all important. Championship skiers, like karate masters, need muscles that most men never develop. The karate parallel extends, beyond muscles, to the necessity for an almost superhuman concentration – the ability to see and remember every bump and twist on a race course, and then to run it without a single mistake: no mental lapses, no distractions, no wasted effort. The only way to win is to come down that hill with maximum efficiency, like a cannonball down a one-rail track. A skier who thinks too much might make points in conversation, but he seldom wins races.

Killy has been accused, by experts, of 'lacking style'. He skis, they say, with the graceless desperation of a man about to crash, fighting to keep his balance. Yet it's obvious, even to a rank amateur, that Killy's whole secret is his feverish concentration. He attacks a hill like Sonny Liston used to attack Floyd Patterson – and with the same kind of awesome results. He wants to *beat* the hill, not just ski it. He whips through a slalom course like O. J. Simpson through a jammed secondary – the same impossible moves; sliding, half-falling, then suddenly free and pumping crazily for the finish line to beat that awful clock, the only judge in the world with the power to send him home a loser.

Shortly after I met him, I told Killy he should see some films of O. J. Simpson running with a football. Jean-Claude didn't know the game, he said, but I insisted that wouldn't matter. 'It's like watching a drunk run through traffic on a freeway,' I said. 'You don't have to know the game to appreciate O. J.'s act – it's a spectacle, a thing to see ...'

That was before I understood the boundaries of Killy's curiosity. Like Calvin Coolidge, he seems to feel that 'the business of America is business'. He comes here to make money, and aesthetics be damned. He wasn't interested in anything about O. J. Simpson except the size of his Chevrolet contract – and only vaguely in that.

Throughout our numerous, distracted conversations, he was puzzled and dimly annoyed with the rambling style of my talk. He seemed to feel that any journalist worthy of his profession would submit ten very precise questions, write down ten scripted Killy answers and then leave. No doubt this reflected the thinking of his PR advisers, who favour such concepts as 'input', 'exposure' and the 'Barnum imperative'.

My decision to quit the Killy story came suddenly, for no special reason .. an irrational outburst of red-eyed temper and festering *angst* with the supplicant's role I'd been playing for two days, dealing with a gang of cheap-jack footmen whose sense of personal importance seemed to depend entirely on the glitter of their hired French property.

Some time later, when I had calmed down enough to consider another attempt at cracking the PR barrier, I talked to Jean-Claude on the telephone. He was in Sun Valley, allowing himself to be photographed for a magazine feature on the 'Killy style'. I called to explain why I hadn't made the flight with him, as planned, from Chicago to Sun Valley. 'You've made some funny friends in the past year,' I said. 'Doesn't it make you nervous to travel around with a bunch of cops?'

He laughed quietly. 'That's right,' he said. 'They are just like cops, aren't they? I don't like it, but what can I do? I am never alone ... This is my life, you know.'

I have a tape of that conversation, and I play it now and then for laughs. It is a weird classic of sorts – forty-five minutes of failed communication, despite heroic efforts on both ends. The over-all effect is that of a career speedfreak jacked up like the great hummingbird, trying to talk his way through a cordon of bemused ushers and into a free, front-row seat at a sold-out Bob Dylan concert.

I had made the call, half-grudgingly, after being assured by Millie Wiggins Solheim, the style queen of Sun Valley, that she had learned through the Head Ski hierarchy that Jean-Claude was eager for a soul-talk with me. What the hell? I thought. Why not? But this time on my terms – in the midnight style of the great hummingbird. The tape is full of laughter and disjointed ravings. Killy first suggested that I meet him again at the Auto Show in Chicago, where he was scheduled for a second weekend of Chevvy gigs on the same 1–3–5–7–9 schedule.

'Never in hell,' I replied. 'You're paid to hang around with those pigs, but I'm not. They acted like they expected me to sneak up and steal the battery out of that goddamn ugly car you were selling.'

He laughed again. 'It's true that they pay me for being there ... but you get paid for writing the article.'

'What article?' I said. 'As far as I know, you don't exist. You're a life-size dummy made of plastic foam. I can't write much of an article about how I once saw Jean-Claude Killy across a crowded room at the Stockyards Amphitheatre.'

There was a pause, another quiet chuckle, then: 'Well, maybe you could write about how hard it is to write about me.'

Oh ho, I thought. You sneaky bugger – there's something in your head, after all. It was the only time I ever felt we were on the same wavelength – and then for only an instant. The conversation deteriorated rapidly after that.

We talked a while longer and I finally said, 'Well, to hell with it. You don't need publicity and I sure as hell don't need this kind of fuck-around ... They should have assigned this story to an ambitious dwarf hooker with gold teeth ...'

There was a long pause at the other end of the line. Then: 'Why don't you call Bud Stanner, the manager from Head Ski. He is here in the Lodge tonight. I think he can arrange something.'

Why not? I thought. By the time I got hold of Stanner it was 1 a.m.

I assured him that all I needed was a bit of casual conversation and some time to watch Killy in action.

'I'm not surprised Jean-Claude wouldn't talk to you tonight,' he said with a knowing chuckle. 'I happen to know he's being ... ah ... *entertained* at the moment.'

'That's weird,' I said, 'I just finished a forty-five-minute talk with him.'

'Oh...?' Stanner pondered my words for a moment, then, like a skilled politician, he ignored them. 'It's the damndest thing you ever saw,' he continued cheerfully. 'Goddamn broads won't give him any peace. It's embarrassing sometimes, the way they come on him ...'

'Yeah,' I said. 'I've heard.' Actually, I'd heard it so often that I recognized it now as part of the programme. Killy has a very obvious, natural kind of sex appeal – so obvious that I was getting a little tired of hustlers nudging me to make sure I noticed. McCormack had set the tone at our first encounter, with his odd warning about 'discretion'. Moments later, replying to somebody who'd asked him if Killy had any plans for a film career, McCormack had grinned and said, 'Oh, we're not in any hurry; he's had plenty of offers. And every time he says no, the price goes up.'

Killy himself says nothing. Straight interviews bore him anyway, but he usually tries to be civil, even smiling, despite the brain-curdling tedium of answering the same questions over and over again. He will cope with almost any kind of giddy ignorance, but his smile snaps off like a dead lightbulb when he senses a carnal drift in the conversation. If the interviewer persists, or launches a direct question like, 'Is there any truth in this rumour about you and Winnie Ruth Judd?' Killy will invariably change the subject with an angry shrug.

His reluctance to talk about women seems genuine, leaving disappointed reporters no choice but to hunker down in misty speculation. 'Killy has a reputation as a skiing Romeo,' wrote the author of a recent magazine article. 'Typically French, though, he remains discreet about his swinging love life, saying little more than, yes, he has a girl friend, a model.'

Which was true. He had spent a quiet vacation with her in the Bahamas the week before I met him in Chicago, and at first I got the impression that he was fairly serious about her ... Then, after listening to his pitch-men for a while, I wasn't sure what I thought. The 'discretion' that would have been the despair of any old-style, low-level press agent has become, in the hands of McCormack's cool futurists, a mysterious and half-sinister cover story, using Killy's awkward 'no comment' behaviour to enhance whatever rumour he refuses to talk about.

Jean-Claude understands that his sex-life has a certain publicity value, but he hasn't learned to like it. At one point I asked him how he felt about that aspect of his image. 'What can I say?' he shrugged. 'They keep talking about it. I am normal. I like girls. But what I do is really my own business, I think ...'

(Shortly after that phone talk with him in Sun Valley, I learned that he really *was* being 'entertained' when I called, and I've never quite understood why he spent forty-five minutes on the phone in those circumstances. What a terrible scene for the girl ...)

I tried to be frank with Stanner. Early on, in our talk, he said: 'Look, I'll give you all the help I can on this thing, and I think I'm in a position to give you the kind of help you need. Naturally, I'd expect some play for Head Skis in your photo coverage and of course that's my job ...'

'Fuck the skis,' I replied. 'I couldn't give a hoot in hell if he skis on metal bowls; all I want to do is talk to the man, in a decent human manner, and find out what he thinks about things.'

This was not the kind of thing Stanner wanted to hear, but under the circumstances he handled it pretty well. 'OK,' he said, after a brief pause. 'I think we understand each other. You're looking for input that's kind of offbeat, right?'

'Input?' I said. He had used the term several times and I thought I'd better clarify it.

'You know what I mean,' he snapped, 'and I'll try to set it up for you.'

I started making plans to go up to Sun Valley anyway but then Stanner disrupted everything by suddenly offering to arrange for me – instead of *Ski* magazine's editor – to accompany J.-C. on that eastbound flight. 'You'll have a whole day with him,' Stanner said, 'and if you want to come to Boston next week I'll save you a seat on the company bus for the ride to Waterville Valley in New Hampshire. Jean-Claude will be along, and as far as I'm concerned you can have him all to yourself for the whole trip. It takes about two hours. Hell, maybe you'd rather do that, instead of working your ass off to make that cross-country flight with him ...'

'No,' I said. 'I'll do it both ways – first the flight, then the bus ride; that should give me all the offbeat input I need.'

He sighed.

*

Killy was there in Salt Lake, red-eyed and jittery with a coke and a ham sandwich in the airport café. A man from United Airlines was sitting with him, a waitress stopped to ask for his autograph, people who had no idea who he was paused to nod and stare at 'the celebrity'.

The local TV station had sent out a camera crew, which caused a crowd to gather around the gate where our plane was waiting. 'How do these people know when I'm here?' he muttered angrily as we hurried down the corridor towards the mob.

I smiled at him. 'Come on,' I said, 'you know damn well who called them. Do we have to keep playing this game?'

He smiled faintly, then lined it out like a veteran. 'You go ahead,' he said. 'Get our seats on the plane while I talk to these camera people.'

Which he did, while I boarded the plane and instantly found myself involved in a game of musical chairs with the couple who were being moved back to the tourist compartment so Jean-Claude and I could have their first class seats. 'I've blocked these two off for you,' the man in the blue uniform told me.

The dowdy little stewardess told the victims how sorry she was – over and over again, while the man howled in the aisle. I hunkered down in the seat and stared straight ahead, wishing him well. Killy arrived, ignoring the ruckus and slumping into his seat with a weary groan. There was no doubt in his mind that the seat was being saved for Jean-Claude Killy. The man in the aisle seemed to recognize that his protest was doomed: his seats had been seized by forces beyond his control. 'You sons of bitches!' he yelled, shaking his fist at the crewmen who were pushing him back towards the tourist section. I was hoping he would whack one of them or at least refuse to stay on the plane but he caved in, allowing himself to be hustled off like a noisy beggar.

'What was that about?' Killy asked me.

I told him. 'Bad scene, eh?' he said. Then he pulled a car racing magazine out of his briefcase and focused on that. I thought of going back and advising the man that he could get a full refund on his ticket if he kept yelling, but the flight was delayed for at least an hour on the runway and I was afraid to leave my seat for fear it might be grabbed by some late-arriving celebrity.

Within moments, a new hassle developed. I asked the stewardess for a drink and was told that it was against the rules to serve booze until the plane was airborne. Thirty minutes later, still sitting on the runway, I got the same answer. There is something in the corporate manner of United Airlines that reminds me of the California Highway Patrol, the exaggerated politeness of people who would be a hell of a lot happier if all their customers were in jail – and especially *you*, sir.

Flying United, to me, is like crossing the Andes in a prison bus. There is no question in my mind that somebody like Pat Nixon personally approves every United stewardess. Nowhere in the Western world is there anything to equal the collection of self-righteous shrews who staff the 'friendly skies of United'. I do everything possible to avoid that airline, often at considerable cost and personal inconvenience. But I rarely make my own reservations and United seems to be a habit – like Yellow Cabs – with secretaries and PR men. And maybe they're right ...

My constant requests for a drink to ease the delay were rebuked with increasing severity by the same stewardess who had earlier defended my right to preempt a first class seat. Killy tried to ignore the argument but finally abandoned his magazine to view the whole scene with nervous alarm. He lifted his dark glasses to wipe his eyes – red-veined balls in a face that looked much older than twenty-six. Then a man in a blue blazer confronted us, shoving a little girl ahead of him. 'Probably you don't remember me, Jean-Claude,' he was saying. 'We met about two years ago at a cocktail party in Vail.'

Killy nodded, saying nothing. The man shoved an airline ticket envelope at him, grinning self-consciously: 'Could you autograph this for my little girl, please? She's all excited about being on the same plane with you.'

Killy scrawled an illegible signature on the paper, then stared blankly at the cheap camera the girl was aiming at him. The man backed away, unnerved by Killy's failure to remember him. 'Sorry to bother you,' he said. 'But my little girl, you know ... since we seem to be delayed here ... well, thanks very much.'

Killy shrugged as the man backed off. He hadn't said a word and I felt a little sorry for the reject, who appeared to be a broker of some kind.

The moppet came back with the camera, wanting a second shot; 'in case the first one doesn't come out'. She took one very quickly, then asked J.-C. to remove his glasses. 'No!' he snapped. 'The light hurts my eyes.' There was a raw, wavering note in his voice, and the child, a shade more perceptive than her father, took her picture and left without apologies.

Now, less than a year later, Killy is making very expensive and elaborate commercials for United Airlines. He was in Aspen recently 'secretly' filming a ski race for showing, months later, on national TV. He didn't ring me up ...

Killy refused both the drink and the meal. He was clearly on edge and I was pleased to find that anger made him talkative. By this time I had disabused myself of the notion that we had any basic rapport; his habit-smiles were for people who asked habit-questions – fan-magazine bull-shit and pulp philosophy: How do you like America? (It is truly wonderful. I would like to see it all in a Camaro.) How did it feel to win three gold medals in the Olympics? (It felt truly wonderful. I plan to have them mounted on the dashboard of my Camaro.)

Somewhere in the middle of the flight, with our conversation lagging badly, I reverted to a Hollywood-style of journalism that Killy instantly picked up on. 'Tell me,' I said. 'What's the best place you know? If you were free to go anyplace in the world right now – no work, no obligation, just to enjoy yourself – where would it be?'

His first answer was 'home', and after that came Paris and a clutch of French resort areas – until I had to revise the question and eliminate France altogether.

Finally he settled on Hong Kong. 'Why?' I asked. His face relaxed in a broad, mischievous grin. 'Because a friend of mine is head of the police there,' he said, 'and when I go to Hong Kong I can do anything I want.'

I laughed, seeing it all on film – the adventures of a filthy-rich French cowboy, turned loose in Hong Kong with total police protection. With J.-C. Killy as the hellion and maybe Rod Steiger as his cop-friend. A sure winner . . .

Looking back, I think that Hong Kong note was the truest thing Jean-Claude ever said to me. Certainly it was the most definitive – and it was also the only one of my questions he obviously enjoyed answering.

By the time we got to Chicago I'd decided to spare us both the agony of prolonging the 'interview' all the way to Baltimore. 'I think I'll get off here,' I said as we left the plane. He nodded, too tired to care. Just then we were confronted by a heavy blonde girl with a clipboard. 'Mister Killy?' she said. J.-C. nodded. The girl mumbled her name and said she was there to help him make connections to Baltimore. 'How was Sun Valley?' she asked. 'Was it good skiing?' Killy shook his head, still walking very fast up the corridor. The girl was half trotting beside us. 'Well, I hope *the other activities* were satisfactory,' she said with a smile. Her emphasis was so heavy, so abysmally raw, that I glanced over to see if she was drooling.

'Who are you?' she asked suddenly.

'Never mind,' I said. 'I'm leaving.'

Now, many months later, my clearest memory of that whole Killy scene is a momentary expression on the face of a man who had nothing to do with it. He was a drummer and lead singer in a local jazz-rock band I heard one night at a New Hampshire ski resort where Killy was making a sales appearance. I was killing time in a dull midnight bistro when this nondescript little bugger kicked off on his own version of a thing called 'Proud Mary' – a heavy blues shot from Creedence Clearwater. He was getting right into it, and somewhere around the third chorus I recognized the weird smile of a man who had found his own rhythm, that rumoured echo of a high white sound that most men never hear. I sat there in the dark smoke of that place and watched him climb ... far up on some private mountain to that point where you look in the mirror and see a bright bold streaker, blowing all the fuses and eating them like popcorn on the way up.

That image had to remind me of Killy, streaking down the hills at Grenoble for the first, second and third of those incredible three gold medals. Jean-Claude had *been there* – to that rare high place where only the snow leopards live; and now, twenty-six-years-old with more dollars than he can use or count, there is nothing else to match those peaks he has already beaten. Now it is all downhill for the world's richest ski bum. He was good enough – and lucky – for a while, to live in that win-lose, black-white, do-or-die world of the international super TV athlete. It was a beautiful show while it lasted, and Killy did his thing better than anyone else has ever done it before.

But now, with nothing else to win, he is down on the killing floor with the rest of us – sucked into strange and senseless wars on unfamiliar terms; haunted by a sense of loss that no amount of money can ever replace; mocked by the cotton-candy rules of a mean game that still awes him ... locked into a gilded life-style where winning means keeping his mouth shut and reciting, on cue, from other men's scripts. This is Jean-Claude Killy's new world: He is a handsome middle-class French boy who trained hard and learned to ski so well that now his name is immensely saleable on the marketplace of a crazily inflated culture-economy that eats its heroes like hotdogs and honours them on about the same level.

His TV-hero image probably surprises him more than it does the rest of us. We take whatever heroes come our way, and we're not inclined to haggle. Killy seems to understand this, too. He is taking advantage of a money-scene that never existed before and might never work again – at least not in his lifetime or ours, and maybe not even next year.

On balance, it seems unfair to dismiss him as a witless greedhead, despite all the evidence. Somewhere behind that wistful programmed smile I suspect there is something akin to what Norman Mailer once called (speaking of James Jones) 'an animal sense of who has the power'. There is also a brooding contempt for the *American* system that has made him what he is. Killy doesn't understand this country; he doesn't even like it – but there is no question in his mind about his own proper role in a scene that is making him rich. He is his manager's creature, and if Mark McCormack wants him to star in a geek film or endorse some kind of skin-grease he's never heard of ... well, that's the way it is. Jean-Claude is a good soldier; he takes orders well and he learns quickly. He would rise through the ranks in any army.

Killy reacts; thinking is not his gig. So it is hard to honour him for whatever straight instincts he still cultivates in private – while he mocks them in public, for huge amounts of money. The echo of Gatsby's style recalls the truth that Jimmy Gatz was really just a rich crook and a booze salesman. But Killy is not Gatsby: He is a bright young Frenchman with a completely original act ... and a pragmatic frame of reference that is better grounded, I suspect, than my own. He is doing pretty well for himself, and nothing in his narrow, high-powered experience can allow him to understand how I can watch his act and say that it looks, to me, like a very hard dollar – maybe the hardest.

A FINAL NOTE FROM THE AUTHOR

OWL FARM

Please insert this quote at beginning or end of Killy piece. – Thompson.

'No eunuch flatters his own noise more shamefully nor seeks by more infamous means to stimulate his jaded appetite, in order to gain some favour, than does the eunuch of industry.'

– The quote, as I have it, is attributed to one Billy Lee Burroughs ... but if memory serves, I think it comes from the writings of K. Marx. In any case, I can trace it down if need be ...

Scanlan's Monthly, vol. 1, no. 1, March 1970

THE ULTIMATE FREE LANCER

You asked me for an article on whatever I wanted to write about and since you don't pay I figure that gives me *carte blanche*. I started out tonight on an incoherent bitch about the record business ... I was looking at the jacket copy on the *Blues Project* album ... but the 'producer's' name was in huge script on the back, and underneath it were four or five other names ... punks and narks and other ten-percenters who apparently had more leverage than the musicians who made the album, and so managed to get their names on the record jacket.

I was brooding about this – which I'll write about sometime later – when I picked up the latest *Free Press* and read an obituary for a three-year-old kid named 'Godot' ... which was nice, but as I read it I was reminded again of Lionel Olay and how the *Free Press* commemorated his death with a small block of unsold advertising space that had to be used anyway, so why not for Lionel? I'm also reminded that I've asked you twice for a copy of his article on Lenny Bruce (in which Lionel wrote his own obituary), and that you've disregarded both queries. Maybe there's no connection between this and the fact that the *Blues Project* people were fucked out of any mention except photos on their own album, but I think there is. I see it as two more good examples of the cheap, mean, grinning-hippie capitalism that pervades the whole new scene ... a scene which provides the Underground Press Syndicate with most of its copy and income. Frank Zappa's comments on rock joints and light shows (*FP* 12-30) was a welcome piece of heresy in an atmosphere that is already rigid with pre-public senility. The concept of the UPS is too right to argue with, but the reality is something else. As Frank Zappa indicated, if only in a roundabout way, there are a lot of people trying to stay alive and working WITHIN the UPS spectrum, and not on the ten per cent fringes. That's where *Time* magazine lives ... way out there on the puzzled, masturbating edge, peering through the keyhole and selling what they see to the big wide world of chamber of commerce voyeurs who support the public prints.

Which brings us back to Lionel, who lived and died as walking proof that all heads exist alone and at their own risk. Maybe I'm wrong; maybe his funeral procession on the Sunset Strip was enough to bring even cops to their knees ... but since I didn't hear anything about that action, I have to doubt it. I suspect Lionel died pretty much as he lived: as a freelance writer hustler, grass-runner and general free spirit. I'm sure a lot of people knew him better than I did, but I think I knew him pretty well. I first met him in Big Sur in 1960, when we were both broke and grubbing for rent money. After that we did a lot of writing back and forth, but we'd only meet (usually at the Hot Springs in Big Sur) after long months of different action in very different worlds (he was broke somewhere in New England when I was in Peru, and later in Rio I got a letter from him with a Chicago postmark ... when I got back to New York he wrote from LA, saying he'd decided to settle there because it was the 'only home we had'.

I've never been sure if he included me in that definition, but I know he was talking about a lot of people beyond himself and his wife, Beverly. Lionel saw the West Coast of the 1960s as Malcolm Cowley saw New York after World War One – as 'the homeland of the uprooted'. He saw his own orbit as something that included Topanga, Big Sur, Tijuana, the Strip and occasional runs up north to the Bay Area.

He wrote for *Cavalier*, and the *Free Press* and anyone who would send him a cheque. When the cheques didn't come he ran grass to New York and paid his rent with LSD. And when he had something that needed a long run of writing time he would take off in his Porsche or his Plymouth or any one of a dozen other cars that came his way, and cadge a room from Mike Murphy at Hot Springs, or in brother Dennis' house across the canyon. Lionel and Dennis were old friends, but Lionel knew too much – and insisted on saying it – to use that friendly leverage as a wedge to the screen-writing business, where Dennis Murphy was making it big. Lionel had already published two novels and he was a far better plot-maker than most of the Hollywood hacks, but every time he got a shot at the big cop-out money he blew it with a vengeance. Now and then one of the New York editors would give him enough lee-way to write what he wanted, and a few of his articles are gems. He did one for *Cavalier* on the soul of San Francisco that is probably the best thing ever written on that lovely, gutless town. Later he wrote a profile on Lenny Bruce (for the *Free Press*) that – if I ran a newspaper – I'd reprint every year in boldface type, as an epitaph for free lancers everywhere.

Lionel was the ultimate free lancer. In the nearly ten years I knew him, the only steady work he did was as a columnist for the Monterey *Herald* ... and even then he wrote on his own terms on his own subjects, and was inevitably fired. Less than a year before he died his willful ignorance of literary politics led him to blow a very rich assignment from *Life* magazine, which asked him for a profile on Marty Ransahoff, a big name Hollywood producer then fresh from a gold-plated bomb called *The Sandpiper*. Lionel went to London with Ransahoff ('first-cabin all the way', as he wrote me from the SS *United States*) and after two months in the great man's company he went back to Topanga and wrote a piece that resembled nothing so much as Mencken's brutal obituary on William Jennings Bryan. Ransahoff was described as a 'pompous toad' – which was not exactly what *Life* was looking for. The article naturally bombed, and Lionel was back on the bricks where he'd spent the last half of his forty-odd years. I'm not sure how old he was when he died, but it wasn't much over forty ... according to Beverly he suffered a mild stroke that sent him to the hospital, and then a serious stroke that finished him.

Word of his death was a shock to me, but not particularly surprising since I'd called him a week or so before and heard from Beverly that he was right on the edge. More than anything else, it came as a harsh confirmation of the ethic that Lionel had always lived but never talked about ... the dead end loneliness of a man who makes his own rules.

Like his Basque anarchist father in Chicago, he died without making much of a dent. I don't even know where he's buried, but what the hell? The important thing is where he lived.

Now, what? While the new wave flowered, Lenny Bruce was hounded to death by the cops. For 'obscenity'. Thirty thousand people (according to Paul Krassner) are serving time in the jails of this vast democracy on marijuana charges, and the world we have to live in is controlled by a stupid thug from Texas. A vicious liar, with the ugliest family in Christendom ... mean Okies feeling honoured by the cheap indulgence of a George Hamilton, a stinking animal ridiculed even in Hollywood. And California, 'the most progressive state', elects a governor straight out of a George Grosz painting, a political freak in every sense of the word except California politics ... Ronnie Reagan, the White Hope of the West.

Jesus, no wonder Lionel had a stroke. What a nightmare it must have been for him to see the honest rebellion that came out of World War Two taken over by a witless phoney like Warhol ... the Exploding Plastic Inevitable, lights, noise, love the bomb! And then to see a bedrock madman like Ginsberg copping out with tolerance poems and the same sort of swill that normally comes from the Vatican. Kerouac hiding out with his 'mère' on Long Island or maybe St Petersburg ... Kennedy with his head blown off and Nixon back from the dead, running wild in the power vacuum of Lyndon's hopeless bullshit ... and of course Reagan, the new dean of Berkeley. Progress marches on, courtesy, as always, of General Electric ... with sporadic assists from Ford, GM, ATT, Lockheed and Hoover's FBI.

And there's the chill of it. Lionel was one of the original anarchist-head-beatnik-free lancers of the 1950s ... a bruised fore-runner of Leary's would-be 'drop-out generation' of the 1960s. The head generation ... a loud, cannibalistic gig where the best are fucked for the worst reasons, and the worst make a pile by feeding off the best. Promoters, hustlers, narks, con men – all selling the new scene to *Time* magazine and the Elks Club. The handlers get rich while the animals either get busted or screwed to the floor with bad contracts. Who's making money off the *Blues Project*? Is it Verve (a division of MGM), or the five ignorant bastards who thought they were getting a break when Verve said they'd make them a record? And who the fuck is 'Tom Wilson', the 'producer' whose name rides so high on the record jacket? By any other name he's a vicious ten-percenter who sold 'army surplus commodities' in the late 1940s, 'special-guaranteed used cars' in the 1950s, thirty-cent thumb-prints of John Kennedy in the 1960s ... until he figured out

that the really big money was in drop-out revolution. Ride the big
wave: folk-rock, pot symbols, long hair, and $2.50 minimum at the
door. Light shows! Tim Leary! Warhol! NOW!

Distant Drummer, vol. 1, no. 1, November 1967

COLLECT TELEGRAM FROM A MAD DOG

Not being a poet, and drunk as well,
leaning into the diner and dawn
and hearing a juke box mockery of some better
human sound
I wanted rhetoric
but could only howl the rotten truth
Norman Luboff
should have his nuts ripped off with a plastic fork.
Then howled around like a man with the
final *angst*,
not knowing what I wanted there
Probably the waitress, bend her double
like a safety pin,
Deposit the mad seed before they
tie off my tubes
or run me down with Dingo dogs
for not voting
at all.

Suddenly a man with wild eyes rushed
out from the wooden toilet
Foam on his face and waving a razor
like a flag, shouting
It's Starkweather god damn I know
that voice
We'll take our vengeance now!
McConn, *en route* from LA to some
rumoured home,
killing the hours till the bars opened
stranded on Point Richmond when they closed
the night before,

thinking finally he had come among friends
or at least one.

We rang for Luboff
on the pay phone, but there was
no contact
Some tortured beast of a bad loser has already
croaked him, said McConn
We'll have a drink.
But the Mariners' Tavern was not open
for twenty minutes, so we read
a newspaper
and saw where just about everybody
had been fucked in the face
or some other orifice
or opening, or possibility
for one good reason or another
by the time the *Chronicle* went to press
before last midnight.

We rang for the editor
but the switchboard clamped him off.
Get a lawyer, I said. These swine have gone
far enough.
But the lawyers were all in bed
Finally we found one, limp from an orgy and
too much sleep
Eating cheese blintzes with sour cream and gin
on a redwood balcony with a
fine exposure.
Get your ass up, I said. It's Sunday and
the folks are in church. Now is the time to
lay a writ on them,
Cease and desist
Specifically Luboff and the big mongers,
the slumfeeders, the perverts
and the pious.

The legal man agreed
We had a case and indeed a duty to
Right these wrongs, as it were
The price would be four thousand in front and
ten for the nut.

I wrote him a check on the Sawtooth
National Bank,
but he hooted at it
While rubbing a special oil on
his palms
To keep the chancres from itching
beyond endurance
On this sabbath.
McConn broke his face with a running
Cambodian chop, then we
drank his gin, ate his blintzes
But failed to find anyone
to rape
and went back to the Mariners' Tavern
to drink in the sun.
Later, from jail
I sent a brace of telegrams
to the right people,
explaining my position.

Spider Magazine, vol. 1, no. 7, 13 October 1965

'GENIUS 'ROUND THE WORLD STANDS HAND IN HAND, AND ONE SHOCK OF RECOGNITION RUNS THE WHOLE CIRCLE 'ROUND'

ART LINKLETTER

I live in a quiet place, where any sound at night means something is about to happen: You come awake fast – thinking, what does *that* mean?

Usually nothing. But sometimes ... it's hard to adjust to a city gig where the night is full of sounds, all of them comfortably routine. Cars, horns, footsteps ... no way to relax; so drown it all out with the fine white drone of a cross-eyed TV set. Jam the bugger between channels and doze off nicely ...

Ignore that nightmare in the bathroom. Just another ugly refugee from the love generation, some doom-struck gimp who couldn't handle the pressure. My attorney has never been able to accept the notion – often espoused by reformed drug abusers and especially popular among those on probation – that you can get a lot higher without drugs than with them.

And neither have I, for that matter. But I once lived down the hill from Dr — on — Road,* a former acid guru who later claimed to have made that long jump from chemical frenzy to preternatural consciousness. One fine afternoon in the first rising curl of what would soon become the great San Francisco acid wave I stopped by the Good Doctor's house with the idea of asking him (since he was even then a known drug authority) what sort of advice he might have for a neighbour with a healthy curiosity about LSD.

I parked on the road and lumbered up his gravel driveway, pausing *en route* to wave pleasantly at his wife, who was working in the garden under the brim of a huge seeding hat ... a good scene, I thought: The old man is inside brewing up one of his fantastic drug-stews, and here we see his woman out in the garden, pruning carrots, or whatever ... humming while she works, some tune I failed to recognize.

Humming. Yes ... but it would be nearly ten years before I would recognize that sound for what it was: Like Ginsberg far gone in the Om, — was trying to *humm me off*. That was no old lady out there in that garden; it was the good doctor *himself* – and his humming was a frantic attempt to block me out of his higher consciousness.

I made several attempts to make myself clear: just a neighbour come to call and ask the doctor's advice about gobbling some LSD in my shack just down the hill from his house. I did, after all, have weapons. And I liked to shoot them – especially at night, when the great blue flame would leap out, along with all that noise ... and, yes, the bullets, too. We couldn't ignore that. Big balls of lead/alloy flying around the valley at speeds up to 3700 feet per second ...

But I always fired into the nearest hill or, failing that, into blackness. I meant no harm; I just liked the explosions. And I was careful never to kill more than I could eat.

'Kill'? I realized I could never properly explain that word to this creature toiling here in its garden. Had it ever eaten meat? Could it conjugate the verb 'hunt'? Did it understand hunger? Or grasp the awful fact that my income averaged around $32 a week that year?

No ... no hope of communication in this place. I recognized that – but not soon enough to keep the drug doctor from humming me all the way down his driveway and into my car and down the mountain road. Forget LSD, I thought. Look what it's done to *that* poor bastard.

So I stuck with hash and rum for another six months or so, until I

* Names deleted at insistence of publisher's lawyer.

moved into San Francisco and found myself one night in a place called the Fillmore Auditorium. And that was that. One grey lump of sugar and BOOM. In my mind I was right back there in the doctor's garden. Not on the surface, but *underneath* – poking up through that finely cultivated earth like some kind of mutant mushroom. A victim of the drug explosion. A natural street freak, just eating whatever came by. I recall one night in the Matrix, when a road-person came in with a big pack on his back, shouting: 'Anybody want some L ... S ... D ...? I got all the makin's right here. All I need is a place to cook.'

The manager was on him at once, mumbling, 'Cool it, cool it, come on back to the office.' I never saw him after that night, but before he was taken away, the road-person distributed his samples. Huge white spansules. I went into the men's room to eat mine. But only *half* at first, I thought. Good thinking, but a hard thing to accomplish under the circumstances. I ate the first half, but spilled the rest on the sleeve of my red Pendleton shirt ... And then, wondering what to do with it, I saw one of the musicians come in. 'What's the trouble,' he said.

'Well,' I said. 'All this white stuff on my sleeve is LSD.'

He said nothing. Merely grabbed my arm and began sucking on it. A very gross tableau. I wondered what would happen if some Kingston Trio/young stockbroker type might wander in and catch us in the act. Fuck him, I thought. With a bit of luck, it'll ruin his life – forever thinking that just behind some narrow door in all his favourite bars, men in red Pendleton shirts are getting incredible kicks from things he'll never know. Would he dare to suck a sleeve? Probably not. Play it safe. Pretend you never saw it ...

Strange memories on this nervous night in Las Vegas. Five years later? Six? It seems like a lifetime, or at least a main era – the kind of peak that never comes again. San Francisco in the middle sixties was a very special time and place to be a part of. Maybe it *meant something*. Maybe not, in the long run ... but no explanation, no mix of words or music or memories can touch that sense of knowing that you were there and alive in that corner of time and the world. Whatever it meant ...

History is hard to know, because of all the hired bullshit, but even without being sure of 'history' it seems entirely reasonable to think that every now and then the energy of a whole generation comes to a head in a long fine flash, for reasons that nobody really understands at the time – and which never explain, in retrospect, what actually happened.

My central memory of that time seems to hang on one or five or maybe forty nights – or very early mornings – when I left the Fillmore half-crazy and, instead of going home, aimed the big 650 Lightning across the Bay Bridge at a hundred miles an hour wearing L. L. Bean shorts and a Butte sheepherder's jacket ... booming through the Treasure Island tunnel at the lights of Oakland and Berkeley and Richmond, not quite sure which turn-off to take when I got to the other end (always stalling at the tollgate, too twisted to find neutral while I fumbled for change) ... but being absolutely certain that no matter which way I went I would come to a place where people were just as high and wild as I was: no doubt at all about that ...

There was madness in any direction, at any hour. If not across the Bay, then up the Golden Gate or down 101 to Los Altos or La Honda ... You could strike sparks anywhere. There was a fantastic universal sense that whatever we were doing was *right*, that we were winning ...

And that, I think, was the handle – that sense of inevitable victory over the forces of old and evil. Not in any mean or military sense; we didn't need that. Our energy would simply *prevail*. There was no point in fighting – on our side or theirs. We had all the momentum; we were riding the crest of a high and beautiful wave ...

So now, less than five years later, you can go up on a steep hill in Las Vegas and look west, and with the right kind of eyes you can almost *see* the high-water mark – that place where the wave finally broke and rolled back.

Fear and Loathing in Las Vegas, New York, Random House, 1972

JACKET COPY FOR FEAR & LOATHING IN LAS VEGAS: A SAVAGE JOURNEY TO THE HEART OF THE AMERICAN DREAM

The book began as a 250-word caption for *Sports Illustrated*. I was down in LA, working on a very tense and depressing investigation of the allegedly accidental killing of a journalist named Ruben Salazar by the Los Angeles County Sheriff's Dept – and after a week or so on the story I was a ball of nerves & sleepless paranoia (figuring that *I* might be next) ... and I needed some excuse to *get away* from the angry vortex of that story & try to make sense of it without people shaking butcher knives in my face all the time.

My main contact on that story was the infamous Chicano lawyer Oscar Acosta – an old friend, who was under bad pressure at the time, from his super-militant constituents, for even *talking* to a gringo/

gabacho journalist. The pressure was so heavy, in fact, that I found it impossible to talk to Oscar alone. We were always in the midst of a crowd of heavy streetfighters who didn't mind letting me know that they wouldn't need much of an excuse to chop me into hamburger.

This is no way to work on a very volatile & very complex story. So one afternoon I got Oscar in my rented car and drove him over to the Beverly Hills Hotel – away from his bodyguards, etc. – and told him I was getting a bit wiggy from the pressure; it was like being on stage all the time, or maybe in the midst of a prison riot. He agreed, but the nature of his position as 'leader of the militants' made it impossible for him to be openly friendly with a *gabacho*.

I understood this ... and just about then, I remembered that another old friend, now working for *Sports Illustrated*, had asked me if I felt like going out to Vegas for the weekend, at their expense, and writing a few words about a motorcycle race. This seemed like a good excuse to get out of LA for a few days, and if I took Oscar along it would also give us time to talk and sort out the evil realities of the Salazar/murder story.

So I called *Sports Illustrated* – from the patio of the Polo Lounge – and said I was ready to do the 'Vegas thing'. They agreed ... and from here on in there is no point in running down details, because they're all in the book.

More or less ... and this qualifier is the essence of what, for no particular reason, I've decided to call *gonzo* journalism. It is a style of 'reporting' based on William Faulkner's idea that the best fiction is far more *true* than any kind of journalism – and the best journalists have always known this.

Which is not to say that fiction is necessarily 'more true' than journalism – or vice versa – but that both 'fiction' and 'journalism' are artificial categories; and that both forms, at their best, are only two different means to the same end. This is getting pretty heavy ... so I should cut back and explain, at this point, that *Fear & Loathing in Las Vegas* is a *failed experiment* in *gonzo* journalism. My idea was to buy a fat notebook and record the whole thing, *as it happened*, then send in the notebook for publication – without editing. That way, I felt, the eye & mind of the journalist would be functioning as a camera. The writing would be selective & necessarily interpretive – but once the image was written, the words would be final; in the same way that a Cartier-Bresson photograph is always (he says) the full-frame negative. No alterations in the darkroom, no cutting or cropping, no spotting ... no editing.

But this is a hard thing to do, and in the end I found myself imposing an essentially fictional framework on what began as a piece of straight/crazy journalism. True *gonzo* reporting needs the talents of a master journalist, the eye of an artist/photographer and the heavy balls of an actor. Because the writer *must* be a participant in the scene, while he's writing it – or at least taping it, or even sketching it. Or all three. Probably the closest analogy to the ideal would be a film director/producer who writes his own scripts, does his own camera work and somehow manages to film himself in action, as the protagonist or at least a main character.

The American print media are not ready for this kind of thing, yet. *Rolling Stone* was probably the only magazine in America where I could get the Vegas book published. I sent *Sports Illustrated* 2500 words – instead of the 250 they asked for – and my manuscript was aggressively rejected. They refused to even pay my minimum expenses ...

But to hell with all that. I seem to be drifting away from the point – that *Fear & Loathing* is not what I thought it would be. I began writing it during a week of hard typewriter nights in a room at the Ramada Inn – in a place called Arcadia, California – up the road from Pasadena & right across the street from the Santa Anita racetrack. I was there during the first week of the spring racing – and the rooms all around me were jammed with people I couldn't quite believe.

Heavy track buffs, horse trainers, ranch owners, jockeys & their women ... I was lost in that swarm, sleeping most of each day and writing all night on the Salazar article. But each night, around dawn, I would knock off the Salazar work and spend an hour or so, cooling out, by letting my head unwind and my fingers run wild on the big black Selectric ... jotting down notes about the weird trip to Vegas. It had worked out nicely, in terms of the Salazar piece – plenty of hard straight talk about who was lying and who wasn't, and Oscar had finally relaxed enough to talk to me straight. Flashing across the desert at 110 in a big red convertible with the top down, there is not much danger of being bugged or overheard.

But we stayed in Vegas a bit longer than we'd planned to. Or at least *I* did. Oscar had to get back for a nine o'clock court appearance on Monday. So he took a plane and I was left alone out there – just me and a massive hotel bill that I knew I couldn't pay, and the treacherous reality of that scene caused me to spend about thirty-six straight hours in my room at the Mint Hotel ... writing feverishly in a notebook about a nasty situation that I thought I might *not* get away from.

These notes were the genesis of *Fear & Loathing*. After my escape from Nevada and all through the tense work week that followed (spending all my afternoons on the grim streets of East LA and my nights at the typewriter in that Ramada Inn hideout) ... my only loose & human moments would come around dawn when I could relax and fuck around with this slow-building, stone-crazy Vegas story.

By the time I got back to the *Rolling Stone* hq. in San Francisco, the Salazar story was winding out at around 19,000 words, and the strange Vegas 'fantasy' was running on its own spaced energy and pushing 5000 words – with no end in sight and no real reason to continue working on it, except the pure pleasure of unwinding on paper. It was sort of an exercise – like *Bolero* – and it might have stayed that way if Jann Wenner, the editor of *Rolling Stone*, hadn't liked the first twenty or so jangled pages enough to take it seriously on its own terms and tentatively schedule it for publication – which gave me the push I needed to keep working on it.

So now, six months later, the ugly bastard is finished. And I like it – despite the fact that I failed at what I was trying to do. As true *gonzo* journalism, this doesn't work at all – and even if it did, I couldn't possibly admit it. Only a goddamn lunatic would write a thing like this and then claim it was true. The week the first section of *Fear & Loathing* appeared in *Rolling Stone* I found myself applying for White House press credentials – a plastic pass that would give me the run of the White House, along with at least theoretical access to the big oval room where Nixon hangs out, pacing back & forth on those fine thick taxpayers' carpets and pondering Sunday's pointspread. (Nixon is a *serious* pro football freak. He and I are old buddies on this front: We once spent a long night together on the thruway from Boston to Manchester, dissecting the pro & con strategy of the Oakland-Green Bay Super Bowl game. It was the only time I've ever seen the bugger relaxed – laughing, whacking me on the knee as he recalled Max McGee's one-handed catch for the back-breaking touchdown. I was *impressed*. It was like talking to Owsley about acid.)

The trouble with Nixon is that he's a serious *politics junkie*. He's totally hooked ... and like any other junkie, he's a bummer to have around: especially as President.

And so much for all that ... I have all of 1972 to fuck around with Nixon, so why hassle it here?

Anyway, the main point I wanted to make about *Fear & Loathing* is that although it's not what I meant it to be, it's still so *complex* in its failure that I feel I can take the risk of defending it as a first, gimped effort in a direction that what Tom Wolfe calls 'the new journalism' has been flirting with for almost a decade.

Wolfe's problem is that he's too crusty to *participate* in his stories. The people he feels comfortable with are dull as stale dogshit, and the people who seem to fascinate him as a writer are so weird that they make him nervous. The only thing new and unusual about Wolfe's journalism is that he's an abnormally *good* reporter; he has a fine sense of echo and at least a peripheral understanding of what John Keats was talking about when he said that thing about truth & beauty. The only reason Wolfe seems 'new' is because William Randolph Hearst bent the spine of American journalism very badly when it was just getting started. All Tom Wolfe did – after he couldn't make it on the *Washington Post* and couldn't even get hired by the *National Observer* – was to figure out that there was really not much percentage in playing the old *Colliers'* game, and that if he was ever going to make it in 'journalism', his only hope was to make it on his own terms: by being *good* in the classical – rather than the contemporary – sense, and by being the kind of journalist that the American print media honour mainly in the breach. Or, failing that, at the funeral. Like Stephen Crane, who couldn't even get a copy-boy's job on today's *New York Times*. The only difference between working for the *Times* and *Time* magazine is the difference between being a third-string all-American fullback at Yale instead of Ohio State.

And again, yes, we seem to be rambling – so perhaps I should close this off.

The only other important thing to be said about *Fear & Loathing* at this time is that it was *fun* to write, and that's rare – for me, at least, because I've always considered writing the most hateful kind of work. I suspect it's a bit like fucking, which is only fun for amateurs. Old whores don't do much giggling.

Nothing is fun when you *have to do it* – over & over, again & again – or else you'll be evicted, and that gets old. So it's a rare goddamn trip for a locked-in, rent-paying writer to get into a gig that, even in retrospect, was a kinghell, highlife fuckaround from start to finish ... and then to actually get *paid* for writing this kind of manic gibberish seems genuinely weird; like getting paid for kicking Agnew in the balls.

So maybe there's hope. Or maybe I'm going mad. These are not easy things to be sure of, either way ... and in the meantime we have this failed experiment in *gonzo* journalism, the certain truth of which will never be established. That much is definite. *Fear & Loathing in Las Vegas* will have to be chalked off as a frenzied experiment, a fine idea that went crazy about halfway through ... a victim of its own conceptual schizophrenia, caught & finally crippled in that vain, academic limbo between 'journalism' & 'fiction'. And then hoist on its own petard of multiple felonies and enough flat-out crime to put anybody who'd admit to this kind of stinking behaviour in the Nevada State Prison until 1984.

So now, in closing, I want to thank everybody who helped me put this happy work of fiction together. Names are not necessary here; they know who they are – and in this foul era of Nixon, that knowledge and private laughter is probably the best we can hope for. The line between martyrdom and stupidity depends on a certain kind of tension in the body politic – but that line disappeared, in America, at the trial of the 'Chicago 7/8', and there is no point in kidding ourselves, now, about who has the power.

In a nation ruled by swine, all pigs are upward-mobile – and the rest of us are fucked until we can put our acts together: not necessarily to win, but mainly to keep from losing completely. We owe that to ourselves and our crippled self-image as something better than a nation of panicked sheep ... but we owe it especially to our children, who will have to live with our loss and all its long-term consequences. I don't want my son asking me, in 1984, why his friends are calling me a 'good German'.

Which gets down to a final point about *Fear & Loathing in Las Vegas*. I have called it, only half sarcastically, 'a vile epitaph for the drug culture of the sixties', and I think it is. This whole twisted saga is a sort of atavistic endeavour, a dream-trip into the past – however recent – that was only half successful. I think we both understood, all along, that we were running a hell of a risk by laying a sixties trip on Las Vegas in 1971 ... and that neither one of us would ever pass this way again.

So we pushed it as far as we could, and we survived – which means something, I guess, but not much beyond a good story ... and now, having done it, written it, and humping a reluctant salute to that decade that started so high and then went so brutally sour, I don't see much choice but to lash down the screws and get on with what has to be done. Either that or do nothing at all – fall back on the good German, panicked sheep syndrome, and I don't think *I'm* ready for that. At least not right now.

Because it was nice to be loose and crazy with a good credit card in a time when it was *possible* to run totally wild in Las Vegas and then get paid for writing a book about it ... and it occurs to me that I probably just made it, just under the wire and the deadline. Nobody will dare admit this kind of behaviour in print if Nixon wins again in 72.

The swine are gearing down for a serious workout this time around. Four more years of Nixon means four more years of John Mitchell – and four more years of Mitchell means another decade or more of bureaucratic fascism that will be so entrenched, by 1976, that nobody will feel up to fighting it. We will feel too old by then, too beaten, and by then even the myth of the road will be dead – if only for lack of exercise. There will not be any wild-eyed, dope-sucking anarchists driving around the country in fireapple red convertibles if Nixon wins again in 72.

There will not even be any convertibles, much less any dope. And all the anarchists will be locked up in rehabilitation pens. The international hotel-chain lobby will ram a bill thru congress, setting mandatory death penalties for anyone jumping a hotel bill – and death by castration & whipping if the deed is done in Vegas. The only legal high will be supervised Chinese acupuncture, in government hospitals at $200 a day – with Martha Mitchell as Secretary of Health, Education and Welfare, operating out of a luxurious penthouse on top of the Walter Reed Army Hospital.

So much, then, for the road – and for the last possibilities of running amok in Las Vegas & living to tell the tale. But maybe we won't really miss it. Maybe law & order is really the best way to go, after all.

Yeah ... maybe so, and if that's the way it happens ... well, at least I'll know I was *there*, neck deep in the madness, before the deal went down, and I got so high and wild that I felt like a two-ton Manta Ray jumping all the way across the Bay of Bengal.

It was a good way to go, and I recommend it highly – at least for those who can stand the trip. And for those who can't, or won't, there is not much else to say. Not now, and certainly not by me, or Raoul Duke either. *Fear & Loathing in Las Vegas* marks the end of an era ... and now, on this fantastic Indian summer morning in the Rockies, I want to leave this noisy black machine and sit naked on my porch for a while, in the sun.

Previously unpublished

A CONVERSATION ON RALPH STEADMAN AND HIS BOOK, *AMERICA*, WITH DR HUNTER S. THOMPSON

HST: I'm sitting here looking at Ralph's book. It's terrible, a really rotten thing to publish ...

ED.: What's wrong with it?

HST: It's embarrassing. I hate to go into the details. This scatological scene here, with sex organs and things ...

ED.: You've worked with Ralph Steadman quite a bit, Dr Thompson. Some of the material in this book came out of assignments and trips you made together. How did you two hook up in the first place?

HST: Ah, let's see ... I ran into him at the Kentucky Derby in May of 1969. I had been looking around for an artist to go to the Derby with me. I called Warren Hinckle, the editor at *Scanlan's*, and said, 'We need somebody with a really peculiar sense of humour, because this is going to be a very twisted story. It'll require somebody with a serious kink in his brain.' So Hinckle thought for a while and said, 'I know just the person for you. He's never been published over here before. His name is Ralph Steadman, he works for *Private Eye* in London and we'll get him over there right away.' So I went down there thinking that whatever showed up would be pretty hard to cope with.

Ralph was a day late; he checked into the wrong room, at the wrong hotel ... this was his first visit to this country, by the way, the Kentucky Derby. He's had four basic reasons for coming to this country, which might explain something about the nature of the drawings in this book. His first visit was for the Kentucky Derby in 1969 ... he hadn't been here before that. His second gig – also for *Scanlan's* – was the America's Cup yacht race at Newport, Rhode Island, in 1970. The third was the 1972 Democratic Convention in Miami for *Rolling Stone*. And the fourth was the Watergate hearings in Washington in the summer of 73. He went to a few other places in conjunction with those trips – places like Dallas, Disneyland, Santa Fé – but those were mainly side trips. The assignments that set the psychological tone for his reaction to this country were the Kentucky Derby, the America's Cup, Miami Beach for the Convention and Watergate. That's a pretty heavy series of shocks, I think, for an artist in his late twenties who never wanted to work over here in the first place.

ED.: Why not?

HST: I don't think he ever even liked the idea of this country, much less the reality.

ED.: That shows. He seems to be horrified by America.

HST: Yeah. That's one of the reasons he's fun to work with – he has a really fine, raw sense of horror.

ED.: What is it about America that horrifies him?

HST: Everything. The only time I've ever seen him relaxed and peaceful in this country was when he and his wife came out to my place in Colorado for a while ... But, of course, that's total isolation; Ralph is very sensitive about his privacy.

ED.: How does he behave in public when you've been with him?

HST: He's deceptively mild in public, although every once in a while he'll run amok. He behaved pretty well at the Derby, even though he was drunk the whole time.

ED.: Drunk?

HST: He's constantly drunk, in public—

ED.: Does he draw on the spot?

HST: Well he *sketches* on the spot, he takes a lot of photographs. He uses a little sort of Minox-type camera. I didn't see him taking that many photos in Miami and Washington. He used to do more of that in the old days. Now he sketches on the spot, but then he goes back to the hotel and has the whole assignment finished that same night.

ED.: So he's very fast?

HST: Yes, it's shocking to work with him. Just about the time I'm starting to sit down and get to work, he's finished. It's depressing. It took me three weeks to write that Kentucky Derby story, but Steadman did his drawings in three days. He's not really a serious boozer, you know, but when he comes over here and gets involved in these horrible scenes, it causes him to drink heavily.

ED.: What happened at the America's Cup?

HST: Well we met in New York, flew to Newport, and on the way I ... uh ... I had a whole bunch of these little purple pills somebody had given me. I knew it was going to be a beastly goddamn assignment and I had definite plans for keeping it as unhinged as possible ... kind of off-balance, off-centre. I had no intention of getting a serious story out of it. Our idea was to drive this boat we'd chartered right into the race, right into the course. It was a fifty-foot sloop – not a racing boat, but a pretty big sailing yacht. Unfortunately, the weather was so horrible that the bastards only raced one day out of three and the scene was still going on when we had to leave ... for a very specific reason.

On the way up, I took one of these purple pills, which turned out to be psilocybin I think. They were just about right. I ended up taking two or three a day, for general research purposes ... Steadman doesn't get at all into drugs usually – he smokes a little now and then, but he's horrified of anything psychedelic. He had a kind of personal drug crisis up there in Newport. We spent the first two days just waiting for the weather to lift so the boats could go out. It was intolerably dull, and on the third day he said, 'You seem to be having a wonderful time in this nightmare. I can't figure it out.' And I said, 'Well, I rely on my medicine to keep totally twisted. Otherwise, I couldn't stand this bullshit.' And he said, 'Well, maybe I'll try one.' At this point, I was up to about four a day ... So he tried one – I think he got it down about six o'clock at night in one of those bars in town, a yachting crowd bar on the pier. And by midnight he was completely berserk. He stayed that way for about ninety-six hours, during which time we had to leave, had to charter a plane and flee because the police were looking for us.

ED.: Why?

HST: Well, at some point the morning after we took that first pill – or it might have been the next morning, I'm not sure – Ralph was in an insane condition for three or four straight days – but at one point I decided that, in order to get things moving a bit, we'd sneak over to the

Australian yacht, the challenger *Gretel*, and paint 'Fuck the Pope' on the side in huge letters, as big as we could make them. So that when *Gretel* boomed out of the harbour in the morning, this brutal graffiti would be painted in such a way that people on board, the crew members, couldn't see it because 'Fuck the Pope' would be below the deck on the water line ... whereas everybody *else* would see it immediately from the press and spectator boats.

But there was no way to get *in* there, to do the paint job. It was like trying to get into Fort Knox. The boats were guarded so well that the only way to get near them was to come in from the sea. Even that was sort of guarded, because it was all lit up, and no boat of any size or any reason to be out there at night could have made it by sea.

So we got a dinghy off the boat we were chartering. I hadn't rowed a boat at all for about ten years, and I don't think Ralph had *ever* rowed one. I ended up rowing. The boat was just about big enough for the two of us to fit in – a very small dinghy. And we came in kind of around the pilings on the sea-side. We were sneaking from piling to piling. We'd bought these six cans of red spray paint from the hardware store in the town and – no, I actually bought them in New York, come to think of it. So I guess I *knew* what we were going to do. Ralph was going to be the artist and I was just rowing the boat.

Somehow we managed to get right next to the Australian yacht. It looked like a huge, silver knife in the water; just a giant blade, a racing machine – not good for anything else, absolutely stark and menacing. Particularly when you find yourself down at the water line right next to the hull – with all the spotlights and guards around it, up above.

We could hear people talking further back, at the entrance to the dock. It never occurred to them that anyone would come in from the sea. I was trying to hold the dinghy against the side without making any noise, while Ralph stood and painted. And you know those spray-paint cans have a little ball in them, and in order to mix the paint up, you have to shake it – the little ball bangs around inside, and it hisses just before the paint catches and it starts to work.

It was the goddamn little ball that got us. Because it was so quiet in the harbour – the sound of that ball bouncing around inside as Ralph shook the can up ... And then when he started cursing as the hissing got going, this really alarmed whoever was up there, and they began to shout.

Somebody looked over the side and yelled. 'What are you guys doing down there?' And I said something like 'Nothing, nothing at all,' and told Ralph to keep going. And then they began to shout and a Land-Rover came speeding down the length of the dock, lights went on everywhere, all over the damn slip. It was a pretty tough stretch to row across with all these lights on us. But we realized we were going to have to do it – or get jailed immediately – so Ralph just hung on and we took off towards the darkness and the open sea in this dinghy with all these people yelling at us – and Ralph still in a terrible psychological condition ...

Because this was *real fear* that came on top of everything else. When the spotlights hit us, I thought they might start shooting. They were almost insanely serious about the security.

We got away by heading out to sea, then doubling back into the darkness of the piling across the harbour. But we knew we had only gotten away temporarily, because by this time they'd seen us ... We were in a yellow dinghy belonging to a yellow boat, and by dawn there would be no question as to where we'd come from.

We were fucked; there was no doubt about it. Steadman was raving incoherently as we rowed back to our boat; he hates violence of any kind ... But I figured he'd hate jail even worse, so when we got to our boat I told him to pack his gear while I took a big flare-gun up on deck and fired three huge parachute flares up into the night – these brutes that cost about ten dollars apiece; they go up about 100 yards, then explode into four falling fireballs ... the kind of things you're never suppose to use except for serious emergencies at sea. Anyway, I fired three of these while Ralph was packing – twelve orange fireballs that went off like twelve shotgun blasts and lit up the whole harbour ... Some of them fell on boats and started fires, people were shouting, leaping out of their bunks and grabbing fire extinguishers ... There was total chaos in the harbour.

I went below and got my own stuff together, then we hailed a passing motor launch – it was almost dawn by this time – and whoever was running that launch agreed to give us a ride into the shore for twenty dollars.

From there we got a cab straight to the airport and chartered a small plane to Boston. Ralph was still in a really fiendish condition. He was barefooted, out of his mind and his only refuge was New York. I called down there and found out that *Scanlan's* had folded yesterday, but a friend of Steadman's would meet him at the airport. I said, 'Now look, you *have* to meet him, because he's in terrible condition ... I have to be back in Colorado today in order to file to run for sheriff' ... that was the deadline. So this guy agreed to meet Ralph at La Guardia. He went into a raving frenzy, cursing me, cursing America ...

ED.: Cursing?

HST: Oh yes. He was very bitter about it – having lost his shoes, his dignity, his sanity – all that sort of thing ... I put him on the plane to

New York, then flew off to Colorado ... and the next time I heard from him was about a month later, when I got a letter saying he'd never come to this country again, and certainly not as long as *I* was here.

What had happened was – I found out later – there was nobody at the airport in New York City. Nobody met him. He had no shoes, no money, he didn't know anything about New York. The *Scanlan's* office was closed, he couldn't even get in there, nobody answered the phone. He borrowed ten dollars for the cab from a bartender on Forty-fifth Street ... By this time his mind was coming apart. I talked to one of the people in the hotel that *Scanlan's* used and they remembered this strange, wild-eyed Britisher pacing around the lobby, kicking the walls with his bare feet and cursing everybody who came near him. Finally, he remembered some editor – a friend of a friend, I think – that he had some connection with. By this time his face and head had turned completely purple, his feet were bleeding. It was about twenty-four hours after he arrived that he finally got to this editor's apartment somehow, in a state of shattered nervous hysteria. She sort of nursed him back to health, and I think he had a return ticket – he never leaves home unless the money and a ticket are all brought to the house and handed to him. He has no faith in expense reimbursement, which I think is very wise.

ED.: Have all his experiences in America been like that?

HST: Well, he fled Miami after two days. He came over to cover the Democratic Convention, but he couldn't handle Miami.

ED.: He also covered the Republican Convention ...

HST: No, he watched that on television in London. He refused to come back to Miami, for any reason.

ED.: Why?

HST: He couldn't stand Miami Beach. The shock was too great. There's a drawing in the book that explains why ...

ED.: Why does he submit himself to this kind of rape?

HST: I think he gets a perverse kind of kick out of it. His best drawings come out of situations where he's been most anguished. So I deliberately put him into shocking situations when I work with him. I've always found that that's when he does his best stuff ... I took him into the Watergate hearings completely drunk. And then we had to sit down at a press table in an aisle where the senators came in and out during the voting breaks. Ralph leaped up during one of the intermissions with a beer in his hand and knocked Sam Ervin off his feet. He almost got my press pass pulled, almost got us thrown out of the hearings permanently. Sometimes he seems unconscious of the things he's doing. People think he doesn't quite know what's going on. The real trouble he generates comes later, when people realize what he's done.

ED.: When they look at his drawings.

124

HST: Yes. When they realize they were very nice to him, and then they see themselves horribly caricatured ... He did that to my brother once.

ED.: Your brother?

HST: Yeah, we were down there at the Derby. Davison went to college on a football scholarship as a linebacker – he encouraged Ralph to do a sketch of him, sitting in a restaurant in Louisville – and Ralph did it. I thought we were in serious trouble. At that point, I Maced the waiter at the restaurant and we had to leave.

ED.: Mace? You *Maced* him?

HST: Yeah, I Maced the waiter. He was a surly bastard, and I figured a shot of Mace would be good for him – and for us, too.

ED.: What provoked you?

HST: It was just an argument we got into with the waiter. I'm not sure how it developed. I Maced him right after Ralph had done this drawing of my brother. All of a sudden we had something new to cope with. In fact, we had to leave the restaurant immediately.

ED.: Ralph's kinda like Clark Kent, you know. He has that mild-mannered disguise.

HST: Yes. I wonder what would show on his chest if we could do a drawing of him ripping back the shirt ... maybe an adder or an iguana or a Gila monster ...

ED.: Yes. The kind that sits for hours and then kills you.

HST: With a flip of the tongue ... yes, I think a Gila monster would be appropriate. A Gila monster with a ball-point pen for a tongue.

ED.: Ralph works in ball-point?

HST: I'm not sure ... As I recall, he uses chalk and big, bright pencils; and when he's carrying those big pads around with him, it sets him off from almost anybody he's near.

ED.: Do people go up and look at what he's doing?

HST: No, because he works so fast and he concentrates so intensely. It would be like harassing a TV cameraman. There's something about Steadman that warns people not to interfere with him when he's working.

ED.: Why do you like to work with him? Would you rather work with Ralph than a photographer?

HST: Definitely. Photographers generally get in the way of stories. Steadman has a way of becoming part of the story. And I like to see things through his eyes. He gives me a perspective that I wouldn't normally have because he's shocked at things I tend to take for granted. Photographers just run around sucking up anything they can focus on and don't talk much about what they're doing. Photographers don't participate in the story. They all can act, but very few of them think.

Steadman thinks more like a writer; I can communicate with him. He comes to grips with a story sort of the same way I do ... I don't mean that we always agree on what somebody *looks* like. But we can go to the Watergate hearings, for instance, and he'll be shaken and repulsed by something that happens and once he points it out to me, I'll agree with him.

ED.: What is it about America that you think shocks him most?

HST: I think it's the lack of subtlety and the lack of the traditional British attempt to cover up the warts, or explain them away somehow. In America, we decorate the warts, sell them, cultivate them ... I'm looking at this drawing he did in Vegas of all those cops standing in the lobby.

ED.: Is it the people who shock him?

HST: Yeah. The extreme types – cowboys and burr-haired cops, horrible Southern drunkards at the Kentucky Derby and gross degenerates in Miami beach. Of course that's all he's seen on these experiences.

ED.: He's had a one-sided look at things, travelling with you.

HST: That's true. It's been pretty hard for him ...

ED.: Couldn't be worse.

HST: Only if he'd travelled with Charlie Manson, somebody like that ... Ralph seems to work much better when he's genuinely offended. And I've learned now I can just kinda chuckle when I see something, and even if it's not worth writing, I'll think, 'Ah-hah, this'll really give the bastard a jolt ...' So I'll make sure he has to confront it.

ED.: He needs to be in jeopardy?

HST: I think that's part of the reason the Vegas book worked so well. That sense of being in jeopardy ran all through it. I think he identified very strongly with it. There's no substitute for that horrible adrenalin rush.

There's a paranoid flash in a lot of his works too. He has a paranoid side to him: 'People are lying to me; that can't be true ... if Thompson says I should turn right here, probably I should turn left ...' He gets very confused about things like that. But he's fun to work with. I think he deliberately gets himself in situations that I have to get him out of, so I have to worry about him. That thing at the Watergate is a perfect example, although I didn't rescue him then, I knew what was going to happen.

ED.: You didn't rescue him?

HST: Well, I pulled him out after a while – but not when he jumped up and crashed through a line of marshals around Ervin and knocked him into the TV cameras. It was a narrow aisle between the press table and the TV ... it was all their machinery really, all the hardware.

ED.: Who would you compare him to in the history of art? What do you think of him, objectively?

HST: George Grosz, I guess. That's who I think of right away. And ... Hogarth ... or maybe Pat Oliphant today ...

ED.: Do you think he's given us an accurate portrait of America?

HST: Well, I'm not sure Hogarth was entirely objective – but, yes, there's an element of reality, even in Ralph's most grotesque drawings. He catches things. Using a sort of venomous, satirical approach, he exaggerates the two or three things that horrify him in a scene or situation ... And you can say that these people didn't look *exactly* like that, but when you can look at them again it seems pretty damn close. All the cops in the Vegas hotel lobby are wearing the same plaid Bermuda shorts, and they're uglier than any group of mutants you'd see at a bad insane asylum – you know, for the criminally insane. But I look back on that scene and I know they weren't much different, really. They had on different coloured shirts and they weren't *all* crazy and dangerous-looking – but he caught the one or two distinguishing characteristics among them: the beady eyes, burr haircuts, weasel teeth, beer bellies. If you exaggerate those four characteristics, you get a pretty grizzly drawing ...

ED.: He is a realist, then ...

HST: Oh yes. By way of exaggeration and selective grotesquery. His view of reality is not entirely normal. Ralph sees through the glass very darkly. He doesn't merely render a scene, he *interprets* it, from his own point of view. For instance, he felt the senators should be on trial at the Watergate hearings. He was convinced that they were totally corrupt. Corruption in its broadest sense seems to be the thing that shocks him and gets him cranked more than anything else ... congenital corruption ... on a level far beyond police payoffs or political bribery ... deeply corrupt people, performing essentially corrupt actions, in the name of law and order.

ED.: Do you plan any further projects together?

HST: The trial of Nixon would be a nice trip for Steadman.

ED.: In the Senate?

HST: Yes. Nixon doesn't have to be in the dock – according to law – but it's possible that he might be ... and I think that would be an ideal story for Ralph. Or maybe a very expensive wedding in the South – old, incestuous families, things like that – or a carnival scene, like a travelling carnival, with sideshows at country fairs ... and I think he could get off pretty harshly on an LA gang rape or a sex orgy on Beekman Place in New York ... There's a kind of wild theme in his drawings: decadence, corruption, immorality ... like these horrible people in plastic hats standing outside the Kennedy Memorial in Dallas. Obscenity in its broadest sense is another hallmark of the things that shock him ... I think he sees all of Dallas and Texas and even all of America as obscene, or at least a mockery of what it should be – the way it claims to be, from his point of view. He probably thinks it was doomed from the start. He has that King-George-III notion of America.

ED.: Yes, as an Englishman ... We fucked up from the beginning. We should have stayed with those guys.

HST: Right. A bunch of crude upstarts – couldn't make it work. Maybe Ralph should spend more time at Shriners conventions. I notice he caught one of those in Dallas. We should lock him in a hotel at the National Shriners Convention in Duluth for a whole week ... Jesus, that might be a terminal shock ... or he'd come up with some fantastic drawings. He works best when you put him in a situation where he's bordering on flipping out, but not quite, you know – where he can still function.

ED.: It's the old edge.

HST: Why not? It's a nice place to work ... When he's comfortable and not stunned or appalled at what he's seeing, then he doesn't do his best stuff ... it's not bad, but it doesn't have that ...

ED.: Doesn't have the bite.

HST: Well, that's probably true, but you can't expect a mind like Ralph's to stay up on the wire *all the time*; it's too fucking painful, even when you do it in short doses. But Steadman has pretty good sense about that, so I figure he'll keep his edge for a while ... which is a good thing for me, because there's nobody I'd rather work with.

June 1974

America by Ralph Steadman, San Francisco, Straight Arrow Press, 1974

STRANGE RUMBLINGS IN AZTLAN

The ... Murder ... and Resurrection of Ruben Salazar by the Los
Angeles County Sheriff's Department ... Savage Polarization & the
Making of a Martyr ... Bad News for the Mexican-American ... Worse
News for the Pig ... And Now the New Chicano ... Riding a Grim
New Wave ... The Rise of the *Batos Locos* ... Brown Power and a
Fistful of Reds ... Rude Politics in the *Barrio* ... Which Side Are You
On ... Brother? ... There Is No More Middleground ... No Place to
Hide on Whittier Boulevard ... No Refuge from the Helicopters ... No
Hope in the Courts ... No Peace with the Man ... No Leverage
Anywhere ... and No Light at the End of This Tunnel ... *Nada* ...

Morning comes hard to the Hotel Ashmun; this is not a place where
the guests spring eagerly out of bed to greet the fresh new day. But on
this particular morning everybody in the place is awake at the crack of
dawn: There is a terrible pounding and shrieking in the hallway, near
room no. 267. Some junkie has ripped the doorknob off the communal
bathroom, and now the others can't get in – so they are trying to kick
the door down. The voice of the manager wavers hysterically above the
din: 'Come on now, fellas – do I have to call the sheriff?' The reply
comes hard and fast: 'You filthy *gabacho* pig! You call the fuckin'
sheriff and I'll cut your fuckin' throat.' And now the sound of wood
cracking, more screaming, the sound of running feet outside my door,
no. 267.

The door is locked, thank Christ – but how can you say for sure in a
place like the Hotel Ashmun? Especially on a morning like this with a
mob of wild junkies locked out of the hall bathroom and maybe knowing that no. 267 is the only room within lunging distance that has a
private bath. It is the best in the house, at $5.80 a night, and the lock
on the door is brand new. The old one was ripped out about twelve
hours earlier, just before I checked in.

The desk clerk had gone to a lot of trouble to get me into this room.
His key wouldn't fit the new lock. 'Jesus Christ!' he kept muttering.
'This key *has* to fit! This is a brand new *Yale lock*.' He stared balefully
at the bright new key in his hand.

'Yeah,' I said. 'But that key is for a *Webster* lock.'

'By God you're *right*!' he exclaimed. And he rushed off, leaving us
standing there in the hallway with big chunks of ice in our hands.
'What's wrong with that guy?' I asked. 'He seems out of control – all
this sweating and grappling and jabbering ...'

Benny Luna laughed. 'Man, he's nervous! You think it's *normal* for him to be lettin' four nasty lookin' Chicanos into his best room at three in the morning? With all of us carryin' chunks of ice and funny-lookin' leather bags?' He was staggering around the hall, convulsed with laughter. 'Man, this guy is *freaked*! He doesn't know *what's* goin' on!'

'*Three* Chicanos,' said Oscar. 'And one hillbilly.'

'You didn't tell him I was a writer, did you?' I asked. I'd noticed Oscar talking to the man, a tall sort of defeated looking Germanic type, but I hadn't paid much attention.

'No, but he recognized *me*,' Oscar replied. 'He said, "You're the lawyer, aren't you?" So I said, "That's right, and I want your best room for this *gabacho* friend of mine." ' He grinned, 'Yeah, he knows *something's* wrong with this scene, but he doesn't know what. These guys are scared of *everything* now. Every merchant on Whittier Boulevard is sure he's living on borrowed time, so they go all to pieces at the first sign of anything strange going on. It's been this way ever since Salazar.'

The room clerk/manager/keeper/etc. suddenly rounded the hallway corner with the right key, and let us into the room. It was a winner – a rundown echo of a place I stayed in a few years ago in the slums of Lima, Peru. I can't recall the name of that place, but I remember that all the room keys were attached to big wooden knobs about the size of grapefruits, too big to fit in a pocket. I thought about suggesting this to our man in the Hotel Ashmun, but he didn't wait around for tips or small-talk. He was gone in a flash, leaving us alone to deal with a quart of rum and God only knows what else ... We put the ice in a basin next to the bed and chopped it up with a huge rigging knife. The only music was a tape cassette of *Let It Bleed*.

What better music for a hot night on Whittier Boulevard in 1971? This has not been a peaceful street, of late. And in truth it was *never* peaceful. Whittier is to the vast Chicano *barrio* in East Los Angeles what the Sunset Strip is to Hollywood. This is where the street action lives: the bars, the hustlers, the drug market, the whores – and also the riots, the trashings, killings, gassings, the sporadic bloody clashes with the hated, common enemy: the cops, the Pigs, the Man, that blue-crusted army of fearsome *gabacho* troops from the East LA Sheriff's Department.

The Hotel Ashmun is a good place to stay if you want to get next to whatever's happening on Whittier Boulevard. The window of no. 267 is about fifteen feet above the sidewalk and just a few blocks west of the Silver Dollar Café, a nondescript tavern that is not much different from any of the others nearby. There is a pool table in the rear, a pitcher of beers sells for a dollar, and the faded Chicano barmaid rolls dice with the patrons to keep the jukebox going. Low number pays, and nobody seems to care who selects the music.

We had been in there earlier, when not much was happening. It was my first visit in six months, since early September when the place was still rancid with the stench of CS gas and fresh varnish. But now, six months later, the Silver Dollar had aired out nicely. No blood on the floor, no ominous holes in the ceiling. The only reminder of my other visit was a thing hanging over the cash register that we all noticed immediately. It was a black gas mask, staring blindly out at the room – and below the gas mask was a stark handprinted sign that said: 'In memory of 29 August 1970.'

Nothing else, no explanation. But no explanation was necessary – at least not to anybody likely to be found drinking in the Silver Dollar. The customers are locals: Chicanos and *barrio* people – and every one of them is acutely aware of what happened in the Silver Dollar Café on 29 August 1970.

That was the day that Ruben Salazar, the prominent 'Mexican-American' columnist for the Los Angeles *Times* and news director for bilingual KMEX-TV, walked into the place and sat down on a stool near the doorway to order a beer he would never drink. Because just about the time the barmaid was sliding his beer across the bar a Los Angeles County sheriff's deputy named Tom Wilson fired a tear gas bomb through the front door and blew half of Ruben Salazar's head off. All the other customers escaped out the back exit to the alley, but Salazar never emerged. He died on the floor in a cloud of CS gas – and when his body was finally carried out, hours later, his name was already launched into martyrdom. Within twenty-four hours, the very mention of the name 'Ruben Salazar' was enough to provoke tears and fist-shaking tirades not only along Whittier Boulevard but all over East LA.

Middle-aged housewives who had never thought of themselves as anything but lame-status 'Mexican-Americans' just trying to get by in a mean gringo world they never made suddenly found themselves shouting '*Viva la raza*' *in public.* And their husbands – quiet Safeway clerks and lawn-care salesmen, the lowest and most expendable cadres in the great *gabacho* economic machine – were volunteering to *testify*; yes, to stand up in court, or wherever, and calling themselves Chicanos. The term 'Mexican-American' fell massively out of favour with all but the old and conservative – and the rich. It suddenly came to mean 'Uncle Tom'. Or in the argot of East LA – '*Tio Taco*'. The difference between a Mexican-American and a Chicano was the difference between a Negro and a black.

All this has happened very suddenly. Too suddenly for most people.

One of the basic laws of politics is that action moves away from the centre. The middle of the road is only popular when nothing is happening. And nothing serious has been happening politically in East LA for longer than most people can remember. Until six months ago the whole place was a colourful tomb, a vast slum full of noise and cheap labour, a rifle shot away from the heart of downtown Los Angeles. The *barrio*, like Watts, is actually a part of the city core – while places like Hollywood and Santa Monica are separate entities. The Silver Dollar Café is a ten-minute drive from City Hall. The Sunset Strip is a thirty-minute sprint on the Hollywood Freeway.

Whittier Boulevard is a hell of a long way from Hollywood, by any measure. There is no psychic connection at all. After a week in the bowels of East LA I felt vaguely guilty about walking into the bar in the Beverly Hills Hotel and ordering a drink – as if I didn't quite belong there, and the waiters all knew it. I had been there before, under different circumstances, and felt totally comfortable. Or almost. There is no way to . . . well, to hell with that. The point is that this time I felt *different*. I was oriented to a completely different world – fifteen miles away.

MARCHA POR LA JUSTICIA

THERE ARE NO POLICE COMMUNITY RELATIONS IN THE CHICANO COMMUNITIES. NO, EVER SINCE THE POLICE RIOT ON 29 AUGUST IT HAS BECOME TOO OBVIOUS TO IGNORE THE FACT THAT THE LAPD, THE SHERIFFS, AND THE HIGHWAY PATROL HAVE FOR YEARS BEEN SYSTEMATICALLY TRYING TO DESTROY THE TRUE SPIRIT OF OUR PEOPLE. IN THE PAST, POLICE HAVE BROKEN UP EVERY ATTEMPT OF OUR PEOPLE TO GET JUSTICE, THEY HAVE BEATEN YOUNG STUDENTS PROTESTING POOR EDUCATION, RAIDED OFFICES, ARRESTED LEADERS, CALLED US COMMUNISTS AND GANGSTERS IN THE PRESS, AND EVERYTHING ELSE ON THE STREETS WHEN THE PRESS WAS GONE.

EVEN MORE INSIDIOUS THAN THE DIRECT POLITICAL REPRESSION AGAINST LEADERS AND DEMONSTRATIONS IS THE CONTINUOUS ATTACKS ON THE EVERYDAY LIFE OF PEOPLE IN THE BARRIOS. ALMOST EVERY MONTH EACH BARRIO HAS SUFFERED THROUGH AT LEAST ONE CASE OF SEVERE BRUTALITY OR MURDER AND THEN STRUGGLED TO DEFEND FRIENDS AND WITNESSES WHO FACE BUM RAPS. ONE WEEK IT'S SAN FERNANDO, THEN LINCOLN HEIGHTS, EAST LA, VENICE, THE HARBOR AND POMONA . . . THEY HIT ONE BARRIO AT A TIME, TRYING TO BREAK OUR UNITY AND OUR SPIRIT.

ON 29 AUGUST, THROUGH ALL OF OUR BARRIOS WERE DEMONSTRATIONS FOR PEACE AND JUSTICE AND THE POLICE RIOTED AND ATTACKED. OUT OF FEAR, THEY INSTALLED MARTIAL LAW, ARRESTING AND ABUSING HUNDREDS OF COMMUNITY PEOPLE. THEY KILLED GILBERTO DIAZ, LYNN

WARD, AND RUBEN SALAZAR, THE MAN WHO COULD TELL OUR STORY TO THE NATION AND THE WORLD.

WE MUST NOT FORGET THE LESSON OF 29 AUGUST, THAT THE MAJOR SOCIAL AND POLITICAL ISSUE WE FACE IS POLICE BRUTALITY. SINCE THE 29TH POLICE ATTACKS HAVE BEEN WORSE, EITHER THE PEOPLE CONTROL THE POLICE, OR WE ARE LIVING IN A POLICE STATE.

WE MUST NOT ALLOW THE POLICE TO BREAK OUR UNITY. WE MUST CARRY ON THE SPIRIT OF RUBEN SALAZAR AND EXPOSE THIS BRUTALITY TO THE NATION AND THE WORLD. THE CHICANO MORATORIUM COMMITTEE CALLS UPON YOU TO SUPPORT OUR NON-VIOLENT MARCH FOR JUSTICE THROUGH THE BARRIOS OF THE GREATER LOS ANGELES AREA.

CARAVANS WILL BE COMING FROM DOZENS OF CITIES AND AROUND OUR BARRIOS. WE WILL ALL MEET AT THE ELA SHERIFF'S SUB-STATION ON 3RD STREET BETWEEN FETTERLY AND WOODS. AT 11:00 A.M., 31 JANUARY 1971. JOIN YOUR LOCAL CARAVAN. FOR FURTHER INFORMATION CALL 268-6745.

Handbill from the National Chicano Moratorium Committee

My first night in the Hotel Ashmun was not restful. The others had left around five, then there was the junkie eruption at seven ... followed an hour later by a thundering, low-fidelity outburst of wailing Norteno music from the jukebox in the Boulevard Café across the street ... and then, about nine-thirty, I was jerked up again by a series of loud whistles from the sidewalk right under my window, and a voice calling, 'Hunter! Wake-up, man! Let's get moving.'

Holy Jesus! I thought. Only three people in the world know where I am right now, and they're all asleep. Who else could have tracked me to this place? I bent the metal slats of the venetian blind apart just enough to look down at the street and see Rudy Sanchez, Oscar's quiet little bodyguard, looking up at my window and waving urgently: 'Come on out, man, it's time. Oscar and Benny are up the street at the Sweetheart. That's the bar on the corner where you see all those people in front. We'll wait for you there, OK? You awake?'

'Sure I'm awake,' I said. 'I've been sitting here *waiting* for you lazy criminal bastards. Why do Mexicans need so much fucking sleep?'

Rudy smiled and turned away. 'We'll be *waiting* for you, man. We're gonna be drinkin' a hell of a lot of bloody marys and you know the rule. We'll wait for you there, OK? You awake?'

'Never mind that,' I muttered. 'I need a shower.'

But my room had no shower. And somebody, that night, had managed to string a naked copper wire across the bathtub and plug it into a socket underneath the basin outside the bathroom door. For what reason? Demon rum, I had no idea. Here I was in the best room in the house, looking for the shower and finding only an electrified bathtub. And no place to righteously shave – in the best hotel on the strip. Finally I scrubbed my face with a hot towel and went across the street to the Sweetheart Lounge.

Oscar Acosta, the Chicano lawyer, was there; leaning on the bar, talking idly with some of the patrons. Of the four people around him – all in their late twenties – two were ex-cons, two were part-time dynamite freaks and known fire-bombers, and three of the four were veteran acid-eaters. Yet none of this surfaced in the conversation. The talk was political, but only in terms of the courtroom. Oscar was dealing with two hyperpolitical trials at the same time.

In one, the trial of the 'Biltmore Six', he was defending six young Chicanos who'd been arrested for trying to burn down the Biltmore Hotel one night about a year ago, while Governor Ronald Reagan was delivering a speech there in the ballroom. Their guilt or innocence was immaterial at this point, because the trial had developed into a spectacular attempt to overturn the entire Grand Jury selection system. In the preceding months, Acosta had subpoenaed every Superior Court Judge in Los Angeles County and cross-examined all 109 of them at length, under oath, on the subject of their 'racism'. It was a wretched affront to the whole court system, and Acosta was working overtime to make it as wretched as possible. Here were these hundred and nine old men, these *judges*, compelled to take time out from whatever they were doing and go into another courtroom to take the stand and deny charges of 'racism' from an attorney they all loathed.

Oscar's contention, throughout, was that all Grand Juries are racist, since all grand jurors have to be recommended by Superior Court Judges – who naturally tend to recommend people they know personally or professionally. And that therefore no ratbastard Chicano street crazy, for instance, could possibly be indicted by 'a jury of his peers'. The implications of a victory in this case were so obvious, so clearly menacing to the court system, that interest in the verdict had filtered all the way down to places like the Boulevard, the Silver Dollar and the Sweetheart. The level of political consciousness is not normally high in these places – especially on Saturday mornings – but Acosta's very presence, no matter where he goes or what he seems to be doing, is so grossly political that anybody who wants to talk to him has to figure out some way to deal on a meaningful political level.

'The thing is to never talk down,' he says. 'We're not trying to win votes out here. Hell, that trip's been done, it's over. The idea now is to make people *think*. Force them to think. And you can't do that by walking around slapping strangers on the back and buying them beers.' Then grinning. 'Unless you happen to be babbling drunk or stoned. Which is certainly not my style; I want to make that one thing very clear.'

But today the talk was easy, with no ulterior politics. 'Say, Oscar,' somebody asked. 'How do we stand on that Grand Jury thing? What's our chances?'

Acosta shrugged. 'We'll win. Maybe not on this level, but we'll win on appeal.'

'That's good, man. I hear you're really workin' on the bastards.'

'Yeah, we're fuckin' em over. But that one might take another year. Right now we have to think about Corky's trial. It starts Tuesday.'

'Corky's in town?' The interest is obvious. Heads turn to listen. Rudy eases back a few feet so he can watch the whole bar, scanning the faces for any that might be *too* interested. Paranoia is rampant in the *barrio*: Informers. Narcs. Assassins – who knows? And Rudolfo 'Corky' Gonzales is a definite heavy, prime target for a frame or a set-up. A scholarly, soft-spoken ex-boxer, his Denver-based 'Crusade for Justice' is one of the few *viable* Chicano political organizations in the country. Gonzales is a poet, a street-fighter, a theorist, an organizer, and the most influential 'Chicano leader' in the country next to César Chavez.

Whenever Corky Gonzales appears in East LA – if only to stand trial on a misdemeanour weapons bust – the level of political tension rises noticeably. Gonzales has a very intense following in the *barrio*. Most of his supporters are young: students, dropouts, artists, poets, crazies – the people who *respect* César Chavez, but who can't really *relate* t church-going farmworkers.

'This weekend is going to be hell,' Oscar had told me the night befor. 'Whenever Corky's in town, my apartment turns into a fucking zoo. have to go to a motel to get any sleep. Shit, I can't stay up all nigl arguing radical politics when I have to be in court the next mornin These wild-eyed fuckers show up at all hours; they bring wine, joint acid, mescaline, guns ... Jesus, Corky wouldn't dare take that kind c risk. He's already here, but I don't know where he's staying. He checked into some kind of goddamn Holiday Inn or something, abou five miles out on Rosemeade, but he won't tell anybody where it is – not even me, his lawyer.' He smiled. 'And that's pretty shrewd, because if I knew where he was I might go over there some night all twisted and crazy about calling a general strike at dawn, or some other dangerous bullshit that would freak him.'

He nodded, smiling lazily down at his drink. 'As a matter of fact, I *have* been thinking about calling a general strike. The movement is so goddamn splintered right now that almost anything would help. Yeah, maybe I should write Corky a speech along those lines, then call a press conference for tomorrow afternoon in the Silver Dollar.' He laughed bitterly and called for another bloody mary.

Acosta has been practising law in the *barrio* for three years. I met him a bit earlier than that, in another era – which hardly matters here, except that it might be a trifle less than fair to run this story all the way out to the end without saying at least once, for the record, that Oscar is an old friend and occasional antagonist. I first met him, as I recall, in a bar called the 'Daisy Duck' in Aspen, when he lumbered up to me and started raving about 'ripping the system apart like a pile of cheap hay', or something like that ... and I remembered thinking, 'Well, here's another one of those fucked-up, guilt-crazed dropout lawyers from San Francisco – some dingbat who ate one too many *tacos* and decided he was really Emiliano Zapata.'

Which was OK, I felt, but it was a hard act to handle in Aspen in that high white summer of 1967. That was the era of *Sergeant Pepper*, the *Surrealistic Pillow* and original Buffalo Springfield. It was a good year for everybody – or for *most* people, anyway. There were exceptions, as always. Lyndon Johnson was one, and Oscar Acosta was another. For entirely different reasons. That was not a good summer to be either the President of the United States or an angry Mexican lawyer in Aspen.

Oscar didn't hang around long. He washed dishes for a while, did a bit of construction work, bent the County Judge out of shape a few times, then took off for Mexico to 'get serious'. The next thing I heard, he was working for the public defender's office in LA. That was sometime around Christmas of 1968, which was not a good year for anybody – except Richard Nixon, and perhaps Oscar Acosta. Because by that time Oscar was beginning to find his own track. He was America's only 'Chicano lawyer', he explained in a letter, and he liked it. His clients were all Chicanos and most were 'political criminals', he said. And if they were guilty it was only because they were 'doing what had to be done'.

That's fine, I said. But I couldn't really get into it. I was all *for it*, you understand, but only on the basis of a personal friendship. *Most* of my friends are into strange things I don't totally understand – and with a few shameful exceptions I wish them all well. Who am I, after all, to tell some friend he shouldn't change his name to Oliver High, get rid of his family and join a Satanism cult in Seattle? Or to argue with another friend who wants to buy a single-shot Remington Fireball so he can go out and shoot cops from a safe distance?

Whatever's right, I say. Never fuck with a friend's head by accident. And if their private trips get out of control now and then – well, you do what has to be done.

Which more or less explains how I suddenly found myself involved in the murder of Ruben Salazar. I was up in Portland, Oregon, at the time.

trying to cover the National American Legion Convention and the Sky River Rock Festival at the same time ... and I came back to my secret room in the Hilton one night to find an 'urgent message' to call Mr Acosta in Los Angeles.

I wondered how he had managed to track me down in Portland. But I knew, somehow, what he was calling about. I had seen the LA *Times* that morning, with the story of Salazar's death, and even at a distance of 2000 miles it gave off a powerful stench. The problem was not just a gimp or a hole in the story; the whole goddamn thing was wrong. It made no sense at all.

The Salazar case had a very special hook in it: not that he was a Mexican or a Chicano, and not even Acosta's angry insistence that the cops had killed him in cold blood and that nobody was going to do anything about it. These were all proper ingredients for an outrage, but from my own point of view the most ominous aspect of Oscar's story was his charge that the police had deliberately gone out on the streets and killed a reporter who'd been giving them trouble. If this was true, it meant the ante was being upped drastically. When the cops declare open season on journalists, when they feel free to declare any scene of 'unlawful protest' a free fire zone, that will be a very ugly day – and not just for journalists.

For thirteen devastated blocks, darkened stores stood gaping, show windows smashed. Traffic signs, spent shotgun shells, chunks of brick and concrete littered the pavement. A pair of sofas, gutted by fire, smouldered at a kerbside splashed with blood. In the hot blaze of police flares, three Chicano youths swaggered down the ruined street. 'Hey brother,' one yelled to a black reporter, 'was this better than Watts?'
                                                                    Newsweek, 15 Feb. 71

Ruben Salazar is a bona fide martyr now – not only in East LA, but in Denver and Santa Fé and San Antonio, throughout the Southwest. The length and breadth of Aztlán – the 'conquered territories' that came under the yoke of gringo occupation troops more than 100 years ago, when '*vendido* politicians in Mexico City sold out to the US' in order to call off the invasion that gringo history books refer to as the 'Mexican-American War'. (Davy Crockett, Remember the Alamo, etc.)

As a result of this war, the US government was ceded about half of what was then the Mexican nation. This territory was eventually broken up into what is now the states of Texas, New Mexico, Arizona and the southern half of California. This is Aztlán, more a concept than a real definition. But even as a concept it has galvanized a whole generation of young Chicanos to a style of political action that literally terrifies their

Mexican-American parents. Between 1968 and 1970 the 'Mexican-American Movement' went through the same drastic changes and heavy trauma that had earlier afflicted the Negro Civil Rights Movement in the early sixties. The split was mainly along generational lines, and the first 'young radicals' were overwhelmingly the sons and daughters of middle-class Mexican-Americans who had learned to live with 'their problem'.

At this stage, the movement was basically intellectual. The word 'Chicano' was forged as a necessary identity for the people of Aztlán – neither Mexicans nor Americans, but a conquered Indian/*mestizo* nation sold out like slaves by its leaders and treated like indentured servants by its conquerers. Not even their language was definable, much less their identity. The language of East LA is a speedy sort of *cholo* mixture of Mexican Spanish and California English. You can sit in the Boulevard Café on Whittier on a Saturday morning and hear a young Chicano ex-con explaining to his friends: 'This goddamn *gabacho* parole officer tells me I have to get the sewing machine back. I talked to that goddamn *vendido* and the *vieja tambien*, and they tell me don't worry, we won't say nothing that would send you back to the joint. But the *gabacho* keeps pushin' me. What can I do?' And then, suddenly noticing a vagrant gringo nearby, he finishes the whole story in rapid, angry Spanish.

There are a lot of ex-cons in the movement now, along with a whole new element – the '*batos locos*'. And the only difference, really, is that the ex-cons are old enough to have done time for the same things the *batos locos* haven't been arrested for, yet. Another difference is that the ex-cons are old enough to frequent the action bars along Whittier, while most of the *batos locos* are still teenagers. They drink heavily, but not in the Boulevard or the Silver Dollar. On Friday night you will find them sharing quarts of sweet Key Largo in the darkness of some playground in the housing project. And along with the wine, they eat seconal – which is massively available in the *barrio*, and also cheap: a buck or so for a rack of five reds, enough to fuck *anybody* up. Seconal is one of the few drugs on the market (legal or otherwise) that is flat guaranteed to turn you *mean*. Especially with wine on the side and a few 'whites', bennies, for a chaser. This is the kind of diet that makes a man want to go out and stomp people ... the only other people I've ever seen heavily into the red/white/wine diet were the Hell's Angels.

The results are about the same. The Angels would get loaded and then snarl around looking for somebody to chainwhip. The *batos locos* get loaded and start looking for their own kind of action (burning a store, rat-packing a nigger, or stealing some cars for a night of high-speed cruising on the freeways). The action is almost always illegal, usually violent – but only recently has it become 'political'.

Perhaps the main movement/focus in the *barrio* these days is the politicalization of the *batos locos*. The term translates literally as 'crazy guys', but in harsh political terms it translates as 'street crazies', teenage wildmen who have nothing to lose except their hostility and a vast sense of doom and boredom with the world as they know it. 'These guys aren't afraid of the pigs,' a Chicano activist told me. 'Hell, they *like* a fight with the pigs. They *want* it. And there's a hell of a lot of 'em, man. Maybe two hundred thousand. If we can organize these guys, man, we can move on *anybody*.'

But the *batos locos* are not easily organized. For one thing, they're hopelessly ignorant about politics. They hate politicians – even Chicano politicians. They are also very young, very hostile, and when you get them excited they are likely to do almost anything – especially when they're full of wine and reds. One of the first overt attempts to bring the *batos locos* into the new Chicano politics was the mass rally against police brutality last 31 January. The organizers took great care to make sure the thing would be peaceful. The word went out all over the *barrio* that 'this one has to be cool – no riot, no violence'. A truce was arranged with the East LA sheriff's department; the cops agreed to 'keep a low profile', but they nonetheless sand-bagged and barricaded the sheriff's sub-station right next to the site of the rally in Belvedere Park.

Writing in the *Nation*, a Chicago priest named David F. Gomez described the scene as the rally gathered steam: 'Despite the tension, a fiesta atmosphere prevailed as Chicanos sat on the scarred grass of the park's soccer field and listened while *barrio* speakers aired grievances of police brutality and the gringo occupation of Aztlán. Oscar Acosta gave the most rousing talk of the afternoon. '*Ya es tiempo*. The time is now! There's only one issue. Not police abuse. We are going to be clubbed over the head for as long as we live because we're Chicanos! The real issue is *nuestra tierra*, our land. Some people call us rebels and revolutionaries. Don't believe it. Emiliano Zapata was a revolutionary because he fought against other Mexicans. But we are not fighting our own people but gringos! We are not trying to overturn our own government. We don't have a government! Do you think there would be police helicopters patrolling our communities day and night if anybody considered us real citizens with rights!'

The rally *was* peaceful – all the way to the end. But then, when fighting broke out between a handful of Chicanos and jittery cops, nearly a thousand young *batos locos* reacted by making a frontal assault on the cop headquarters with rocks, bottles, clubs, bricks and everything else they could find. The cops withstood the attack for about an hour, then swarmed out of the place with a stunning show of force that included firing deadly buckshot balls out of 12-gauge shotguns straight into the crowd. The attackers fled through the backstreets to Whittier Boulevard, and trashed the street again. The cops pursued, firing shotguns and pistols at point blank range. After two hours of street warfare, the toll was one dead, thirty serious injuries and a little less than a half million dollars' worth of .damage – including seventy-eight burned and battered police cars.

The entire LA power structure was outraged. And the Chicano Moratorium Committee was aghast. The rally's main organizer – twenty-four-year-old Rosalio Munoz, a former president of the UCLA student body – was so shocked by the outburst that he reluctantly agreed – with the sheriff – that any further mass rallies would be too dangerous. 'We will have to find a new way of expressing grievances,' said a spokesman for the more moderate Congress of Mexican-American Unity. 'From now on the course will be to play a low profile.'

But nobody spoke for the *batos locos* – except maybe the sheriff. 'This violence was not caused by outsiders,' he said, 'but by members of the Chicano community! They can't say we provoked them this time.' This was a definite switch from the standard-brand cop-analysis of 'Mexican violence'. In the past they had always blamed it on 'communists and outside agitators'. But now, it seemed, the sheriff was finally catching on. The real enemy was the same people his men had to deal with every goddamn day of the week, in all kinds of routine situations – on streetcorners, in bars, domestic brawls and car accidents. The *gente*, the street people, the ones who *live* there. So in the end, being a sheriff's deputy in East LA was not much different from being a point man for the Americal Division in Vietnam. 'Even the kids and old women are VC.'

This is the new drift, and everybody in East LA who's willing to talk about it uses the term 'since Salazar'. In the six months since the murder and the unsettling coroner's inquest that followed it up, the Chicano community has been harshly sundered by a completely new kind of polarization, another painful amoeba-trip. But the split this time was not between the young militants and the old *Tio Tacos*; this time it was between student-type militants and this whole new breed of supermilitant street crazies. The argument was no longer *whether* to fight – but when, and how, and with what weapons.

Another awkward aspect of the new split was that it was no longer a simple matter of 'the generation gap' – which had been painful, but essentially simple; now it was more than a conflict of life-styles and attitudes; the division this time was more along economic, or *class* lines.

And this was painfully complex. The original student activists had been militant, but also reasonable – in their own eyes, if not in the eyes of the law.

But the *batos locos* never even pretended to be reasonable. They wanted to get it on, and the sooner the better. Anytime, anywhere: Just give us a reason to work out on the pig, and we're ready.

This attitude created definite problems within the movement. The street people had right instincts, said the leadership, but they were not wise. They had no programme; only violence and vengeance – which was wholly understandable, of course, but how could it *work*? How could the traditionally stable Mexican-American community gain anything, in the long run, by declaring total war on the *gabacho* power structure and meanwhile purging its own native *vendidos*?

AZTLAN! Love it or leave it.
    Sign at Chicano rally

Ruben Salazar was killed in the wake of a Watts-style riot that erupted when hundreds of cops attacked a peaceful rally in Laguna Park, where 5000 or so liberal/student/activist type Chicanos had gathered to protest the drafting of 'Aztlán citizens' to fight for the US in Vietnam. The police suddenly appeared in Laguna Park, with no warning, and 'dispersed the crowd' with a blanket of tear gas, followed up by a Chicago-style mop-up with billyclubs. The crowd fled in panic and anger, inflaming hundreds of young spectators who ran the few blocks to Whittier Boulevard and began trashing every store in sight. Several buildings were burned to the ground; damage was estimated at somewhere around a million dollars. Three people were killed, sixty injured – but the central incident of that 29 August 1970 rally was the killing of Ruben Salazar.

And six months later, when the National Chicano Moratorium Committee felt it was time for another mass rally, they called it to 'carry on the spirit of Ruben Salazar'.

There is irony in this, because Salazar was nobody's militant. He was a professional journalist with ten years of experience on a variety of assignments for the neo-liberal Los Angeles *Times*. He was a nationally known reporter, winning prizes for his work in places like Vietnam, Mexico City and the Dominican Republic. Ruben Salazar was a veteran war correspondent, but he had never shed blood under fire. He was good, and he seemed to like the work. So he must have been slightly bored when the *Times* called him back from the war zones, for a raise and a well-deserved rest covering 'local affairs'.

He focused on the huge *barrio* just east of city hall. This was a scene he had never really known, despite his Mexican-American heritage. But he locked into it almost instantly. Within months, he had narrowed his work for the *Times* down to a once-a-week column for the newspaper, and signed on as news director for KMEX-TV – the 'Mexican-American station', which he quickly transformed into an energetic, aggressively political voice for the whole Chicano community. His coverage of police activities made the East Los Angeles sheriff's department so unhappy that they soon found themselves in a sort of running private argument with this man Salazar, this spic who refused to be reasonable. When Salazar got on to a routine story like some worthless kid named Ramirez getting beaten to death in a jail-fight, he was likely to come up with almost anything – including a series of hard-hitting news commentaries strongly suggesting that the victim had been beaten to death by the jailers. In the summer of 1970 Ruben Salazar was warned three times, by the cops, to 'tone down his coverage'. And each time he told them to fuck off.

This was not common knowledge in the community until after he was murdered. When he went out to cover the rally that August afternoon he was still a 'Mexican-American journalist'. But by the time his body was carried out of the Silver Dollar, he was a stone Chicano martyr. Salazar would have smiled at this irony, but he would not have seen much humour in the way the story of his death was handled by the cops and the politicians. Nor would he have been pleased to know that almost immediately after his death his name would become a battle cry, prodding thousands of young Chicanos who had always disdained 'protest' into an undeclared war with the hated gringo police.

His paper, the LA *Times*, carried the account of its former foreign correspondent's death on its Monday front page: 'Mexican-American newsman Ruben Salazar was killed by a bullet-like tear gas shell fired by a sheriff's deputy into a bar during rioting Saturday in East Los Angeles.' The details were hazy, but the new, hastily revised police version was clearly constructed to show that Salazar was the victim of a regrettable accident which the cops were not aware of until many hours later. Sheriff's deputies had cornered an armed man in a bar, they said, and when he refused to come out – even after 'loud warnings' (with a bull horn) 'to evacuate' – 'the tear gas shells were fired and several persons ran out the back door'.

At that time, according to the sheriff's nervous mouthpiece, Lt Norman Hamilton, a woman and two men – one carrying a 7.65 automatic pistol – were met by deputies, who questioned them. 'I don't know whether the man with the gun was arrested on a weapons violation or not,' Hamilton added.

Ruben Salazar was not among those persons who ran out the back door. He was lying on the floor, inside, with a huge hole in his head. But the police didn't know this, Lieutenant Hamilton explained, because, 'they didn't enter the bar until approximately 8 p.m., when rumours began circulating that Salazar was missing', and 'an unidentified man across the street from the bar' told a deputy, 'I think there's an injured man in there.' 'At this point,' said Hamilton, 'deputies knocked down the door and found the body.' Two and a half hours later at 10.40 p.m., the sheriff's office admitted that 'the body' was Ruben Salazar.

'Hamilton could not explain,' said the *Times*, 'why two accounts of the incident given to the *Times* by avowed eyewitnesses differed from the sheriff's accounts.'

For about twenty-four hours Hamilton clung grimly to his original story – a composite, he said, of first-hand police accounts. According to this version, Ruben Salazar had been 'killed by errant gunfire . . . during the height of a sweep of more than 7000 people in [Laguna] Park when police ordered everyone to disperse'. Local TV and radio newscasts offered sporadic variations on this theme – citing reports 'still under investigation' that Salazar had been shot accidentally by careless streetsnipers. It was tragic, of course, but tragedies like this are inevitable when crowds of innocent people allow themselves to be manipulated by a handful of violent, cop-hating anarchists.

By late Sunday, however, the sheriff's story had collapsed completely – in the face of sworn testimony from four men who were standing within ten feet of Ruben Salazar when he died in the Silver Dollar Café at 4045 Whittier Boulevard, at least a mile from Laguna Park. But the real shocker came when these men testified that Salazar had been killed – not by snipers or errant gunfire – but by a cop with a deadly tear gas bazooka.

Acosta had no trouble explaining the discrepancy. 'They're lying,' he said. 'They *murdered* Salazar and now they're trying to cover it up. The sheriff already panicked. All he can say is, "No comment." He's ordered every cop in the county to *say nothing* to anybody – especially the press. They've turned the East LA sheriff's station into a fortress. Armed guard all around it.' He laughed. 'Shit, the place looks like a prison – but with all the cops *inside*!'

Sheriff Peter J. Pitchess refused to talk to me when I called. The rude aftermath of the Salazar killing had apparently unhinged him completely. On Monday he called off a scheduled press conference and instead issued a statement, saying: 'There are just too many conflicting stories, some from our own officers, as to what happened. The sheriff wants an opportunity to digest them before meeting with newsmen.'

*

Indeed. Sheriff Pitchess was not alone in his inability to digest the garbled swill that his office was doling out. The official version of the Salazar killing was so crude and illogical – even after revisions – that not even the sheriff seemed surprised when it began to fall apart even before Chicano partisans had a chance to attack it. Which they would, of course. The sheriff had already got wind of what was coming: many eyewitnesses, sworn statements, first-hand accounts – all of them hostile.

The history of Chicano complaints against cops in East LA is not a happy one. 'The cops never lose,' Acosta told me, 'and they won't lose this one either. They just murdered the only guy in the community they were really afraid of, and I guarantee you no cop will ever stand trial for it. Not even for manslaughter.'

I could accept that. But it was difficult, even for me, to believe that the cops had killed him deliberately. I knew they were capable of it, but I was not quite ready to believe they had actually done it ... because once I believed that, I also had to accept the idea that they are prepared to kill anybody who seems to be annoying them. Even me.

As for Acosta's charge of murder, I knew him well enough to understand how he could make that charge *publicly* ... I also knew him well enough to be sure he wouldn't try to hang that kind of monstrous bullshit on me. So our phone talk naturally disturbed me ... and I fell to brooding about it, hung on my own dark suspicions that Oscar had told me the truth.

On the plane to LA I tried to make some kind of a case – either pro or con – from my bundle of notes and newsclips relating to Salazar's death. By that time at least six reportedly reliable witnesses had made sworn statements that differed drastically, on several crucial points, with the original police version – which nobody believed anyway. There was something very disturbing about the sheriff's account of that accident; it wasn't even a good *lie*.

Within hours after the *Times* hit the streets with the news that Ruben Salazar had in fact been killed by cops -- rather than street-snipers – the sheriff unleashed a furious assault on 'known dissidents' who had flocked into East Los Angeles that weekend, he said, to provoke a disastrous riot in the Mexican-American community. He praised his deputies for the skilful zeal they displayed in restoring order to the area within two and a half hours, 'thus averting a major holocaust of much greater proportions'.

Pitchess did not identify any 'known dissidents', but he insisted that they had committed 'hundreds of provocative acts'. For some reason the sheriff failed to mention that his deputies had already jailed one of the most prominent Chicano militants in the nation. 'Corky' Gonzales had been arrested during Saturday's riot on a variety of charges that the police never really explained. Gonzales, fleeing the combat zone on a flatbed truck with twenty-eight others, was arrested first for a traffic violation, then on a concealed weapons charge and finally for 'suspicion of robbery' when police found $300 in his pocket. Police Inspector John Kinsling said it was a 'routine' booking. 'Any time we stop a traffic case and find that there is a weapon in the car and that its occupants have a sizeable amount of money,' he said, 'we always book them for suspicion of robbery.'

Gonzales ridiculed the charge, saying, 'Anytime a Mexican is found with more than $100 he's charged with a felony.' The police had originally claimed he was carrying a loaded pistol and more than 1000 rounds of ammunition, along with many spent cartridges – but by Wednesday all felony charges had been dropped. As for 'robbery', Gonzales said, 'Only a lunatic or a fool could believe that twenty-nine people would rob a place and then jump on a flatbed truck to make their getaway.' He had climbed aboard the truck with his two children, he said, to get them away from the cops who were gassing the rally, to which he'd been invited as one of the main speakers. The $300, he said, was expense money for himself and his children – for meals in LA and three round-trip bus tickets from Denver to LA.

That was the extent of Corky Gonzales' involvement in the Salazar incident, and at a glance it seems hardly worth mentioning – except for a rumour in the Los Angeles lawyers' grapevine that the robbery charge was only a ruse, a necessary holding action, to set Gonzales up for a 'Chicano Seven' conspiracy bust – charging that he came from Denver to Los Angeles with the intention of causing a riot.

Both Sheriff Pitchess and Los Angeles Police Chief Edward Davis were quick to seize on this theory. It was the perfect tool for this problem: not only would it frighten the local Chicanos and hamstring nationally known militants like Gonzales, but it could also be used to create a sort of 'red menace' smokescreen to obscure the nasty realities of the Ruben Salazar killing.

The sheriff fired the first salvo, which earned him a giant banner headline in Tuesday's LA *Times* and a heavy pro-police editorial in Wednesday's *Herald-Examiner*. Meanwhile, Chief Davis launched a second blast from his listening post in Portland, where he had gone to vent his wisdom at the American Legion convention. Davis blamed all the violence, that Saturday, on a 'hard core group of subversives who infiltrated the anti-war rally and turned it into a mob', which soon ran wild in a frenzy of burning and looting. 'Ten months ago,' he explained, 'the Communist Party in California said it was giving up on the blacks to concentrate on the Mexican-Americans.'

Nowhere in the *Herald* editorial – and nowhere in either statement by the sheriff and the police chief – was there any mention of the name Ruben Salazar. The *Herald*, in fact, had been trying to ignore the Salazar story from the very beginning. Even in Sunday's first story on the riot – long before any 'complications' developed – the classic Hearst mentality was evident in the paper's full-page headline: 'East Los Angeles Peace Rally Explodes in Bloody Violence ... Man Shot to Death; Buildings Looted, Burned.' Salazar's name appeared briefly, in a statement by a spokesman for the LA County sheriff's department – a calm and confident assertion that the 'veteran reporter' had been shot in Laguna Park, by persons unknown, in the midst of a bloody clash between police and militants. So much for Ruben Salazar.

And so much for the Los Angeles *Herald-Examiner* – a genuinely rotten newspaper that claims the largest circulation of any afternoon daily in America. As one of the few remaining Hearst organs, it serves a perverted purpose in its role as a monument to everything cheap, corrupt and vicious in the realm of journalistic possibility. It is hard to understand, in fact, how the shrivelled Hearst management can still find enough gimps, bigots and deranged Papists to staff a rotten paper like the *Herald*. But they manage, somehow ... and they also manage to sell a lot of advertising in the monster. Which means the thing is actually being read, and perhaps taken seriously, by hundreds of thousands of people in America's second largest city. At the top of Wednesday's editorial page – right next to the red menace warning – was a large cartoon titled 'At the Bottom of it All'. It showed a flaming Molotov cocktail crashing through a window, and on the bottom (*bottom*, get it?) of the bottle is a hammer and sickle emblem. The editorial itself was a faithful echo of the Davis-Pitchess charges: 'Many of the dissidents came here from other cities and states to join agitators in Los Angeles to set off for a major riot, which was planned in advance ... That the holocaust did not erupt into greater proportions is due to the bravery and tactics of the sheriff's deputies ... Those arrested should be prosecuted to the fullest extent of the law. Precautions must be doubled to prevent a recurrence of such criminal irresponsibility.' The continued existence of the Hearst *Examiner* explains a lot about the mentality of Los Angeles – and also, perhaps, about the murder of Ruben Salazar.

So the only way to go was to reconstruct the whole thing on the basis of available eyewitness testimony. The police refused to say anything at all – especially to the press. The sheriff said he was saving 'the truth' for the official coroner's inquest.

Meanwhile, evidence was building up that Ruben Salazar had been murdered – either deliberately or for no reason at all. The most damaging anti-cop testimony thus far had come from Guillermo Restrepo, a twenty-eight-year-old reporter and newscaster for KMEX-TV, who was covering the 'riot' with Salazar that afternoon, and who had gone with him into the Silver Dollar Café 'to take a leak and drink a quick beer before we went back to the station to put the story together'. Restrepo's testimony was solid enough on its own to cast a filthy shadow on the original police version, but when he produced two *more* eyewitnesses who told exactly the same story, the sheriff abandoned all hope and sent his scriptwriters back to the sty.

Guillermo Restrepo is well known in East LA – a familiar figure to every Chicano who owns a TV set. Restrepo is the out-front public face of KMEX-TV news ... and Ruben Salazar, until 29 August 1970, was the man behind the news – the editor.

They worked well together, and on that Saturday when the Chicano 'peace rally' turned into a Watts-style street riot, both Salazar and Restrepo decided that it might be wise if Restrepo – a native Colombian – brought two of his friends (also Colombians) to help out as spotters and *de facto* bodyguards.

Their names were Gustavo Garcia, age thirty, and Hector Fabio Franco, also thirty. Both men appear in a photograph (taken seconds before Salazar was killed) of a sheriff's deputy pointing a shotgun at the front door of the Silver Dollar Café. Garcia is the man right in front of the gun. When the picture was taken he had just asked the cop what was going on, and the cop had just told him to get back inside the bar if he didn't want to be shot.

The sheriff's office was not aware of this photo until three days after it was taken – along with a dozen others – by two *more* eyewitnesses, who also happened to be editors of *La Raza*, a militant Chicano newspaper that calls itself 'the voice of the East LA *barrio*'. (Actually, it is one of several. The Brown Berets publish a monthly tabloid called *La Causa*. The National La Raza Law Students' Association has its own monthly – *Justicia O!* The Socialist Workers Party covers the *barrio* with the *Militant* and the East LA Welfare Rights Organization has its own tabloid – *La Causa de los Pobres*. There is also *Con Safos* – a quarterly review of Chicano art and literature.)

The photographs were taken by Raul Ruiz, a twenty-eight-year-old teacher of Latin American studies at San Fernando Valley State College. Ruiz was on assignment for *La Raza* that day when the rally turned into a street war with police. He and Joe Razo – a thirty-three-year-old law student with an MA in psychology – were following the action along Whittier Boulevard when they noticed a task force of sheriff's deputies preparing to assault the Silver Dollar Café.

Their accounts of what happened there – along with Ruiz' photos –

were published in *La Raza* three days after the sheriff's office said Salazar had been killed a mile away in Laguna Park, by snipers and/or 'errant gunfire'.

The *La Raza* spread was a bombshell. The photos weren't much individually, but together – along with Ruiz/Razo testimony – they showed that the cops were still lying when they came up with their second (revised) version of the Salazar killing.

It also verified the Restrepo-Garcia-Franco testimony, which had already shot down the original police version by establishing, beyond any doubt, that Ruben Salazar had been killed, by a deputy sheriff, in the Silver Dollar Café. They were certain of *that*, but no more. They were puzzled, they said, when the cops appeared with guns and began threatening them. But they decided to leave anyway – by the back door, since the cops wouldn't let anybody out of the front – and that was when the shooting started, less than thirty seconds after Garcia was photographed in front of that shotgun barrel on the sidewalk.

The weakness in the Restrepo-Garcia-Franco testimony was so obvious that not even the cops could miss it. They knew nothing beyond what had happened *inside* the Silver Dollar at the time of Salazar's death. There was no way they could have known what was happening *outside*, or *why* the cops started shooting.

The explanation came almost instantly from the sheriff's office – once again from Lt Hamilton. The police had received an 'anonymous report', he said, that 'a man with a gun' was inside the Silver Dollar Café. This was the extent of their 'probable cause', their reason for doing what they did. These actions, according to Hamilton, consisted of 'sending several deputies' to deal with the problem ... and they did so by stationing themselves in front of the Silver Dollar and issuing 'a loud warning' with a bullhorn calling all those inside to come outside with their hands above their heads.

There was no response, Hamilton said, so a deputy then fired two tear gas projectiles into the bar through the front door. At this point two men and a woman fled out the back and one of the men was relieved by waiting deputies of a 7.65 calibre pistol. He was not arrested – not even detained – and at that point a deputy fired two more tear gas projectiles through the front door of the place.

Again there was no response, and after a fifteen-minute wait one of the braver deputies crept up and skilfully slammed the front door – *without entering*, Hamilton added. The only person who actually entered the bar, according to the police version, was the owner, Pete Hernandez, who showed up about half an hour after the shooting and asked if he could go inside and get his rifle.

Why not? said the cops, so Hernandez went in the *back door* and got his rifle out of the rear storeroom – about fifty feet away from where Ruben Salazar's body lay in a fog of rancid CS gas.

Then, for the next two hours, some two dozen sheriff's deputies cordoned off the street in front of the Silver Dollar's front door. This naturally attracted a crowd of curious Chicanos, not all of them friendly – and one, an eighteen-year-old girl, was shot in the leg with the same kind of tear gas bazooka that had blown Ruben Salazar's head apart.

This is a fascinating tale ... and perhaps the most interesting thing about it is that it makes no sense at all, not even to a person willing to accept it as the absolute truth. But who could possibly believe it? Here, in the middle of a terrible riot in a hostile ghetto with a Chicano population of more than a million, the Los Angeles sheriff's department had put every available man on the streets in a vain attempt to control the mass looting and arson by angry mobs ... but somehow, with the riots still running in high gear, at least a dozen deputies from the élite Special Enforcement Bureau (read TAC Squad) are instantly available in response to an 'anonymous report' that 'a man with a gun' is holed up, for some reason, in an otherwise quiet café more than ten blocks away from the vortex of the actual rioting.

They swoop down on the place and confront several men trying to leave. They threaten to kill these men – but make no attempt to either arrest or search them – and force them all back inside. Then they use a bullhorn to warn everybody inside to come out with their hands up. And then, almost instantly after giving the warning, they fire – through the open front door of the place and from a distance of no more than ten feet – two highpowered tear gas projectiles designed 'for use against barricaded criminals' and capable of piercing a one-inch pine board at 300 feet.

Then, when a man carrying an automatic pistol tries to flee out the back door, they take his gun and tell him to get lost. Finally, after firing two more gas bombs through the front door, they seal the place up – without ever entering it – and stand around outside for the next two hours, blocking a main boulevard and attracting a large crowd. After two hours of this madness, they 'hear a rumour' – again from an anonymous source – that there might be an injured man inside the bar they sealed off two hours ago. So they 'break down the door' and find the body of an eminent journalist – 'The only Chicano in East LA', according to Acosta, 'that the cops were really afraid of.'

Incredible as it seems, the sheriff decided to stick with this story – despite a growing body of eyewitness accounts that contradict the police version of 'probably cause'. The police say they went to the Silver Dollar Café to arrest that 'man with a gun'. But eight days after the killing they were still trying to locate the source of this fatal tip.

Two weeks later at the coroner's inquest, the sheriff's key witness on this critical point mysteriously appeared. He was a fifty-year-old man named Manuel Lopez who claimed all credit for the tip with his tale of having seen two armed men – one with a revolver and one carrying a rifle in the port arms position – go into the Silver Dollar shortly before Salazar was killed. Lopez quickly 'motioned to' the sheriff's officers stationed nearby, he said, and they responded by parking a patrol car directly across the six-lane boulevard from the Silver Dollar's front door. Then using a loud bullhorn, the deputies gave two distinct warnings for everybody in the bar to 'throw out their weapons and come out with their hands over their heads'.

Then, after a five- or ten-minute wait, Lopez said, three rounds of tear gas were fired at the bar, with one projectile glancing off the front doorway and two whooshing through a black curtain that was hanging a couple of feet back from the open doorway. It was too dark to see what was happening inside the bar, Lopez added.

By his own admission at the inquest, Lopez' behaviour on the afternoon of Saturday 29 August was something singular. When the riot broke out and mobs began looting and burning, Mr Lopez took off his shirt, donned a fluorescent red hunting vest and stationed himself in the middle of Whittier Boulevard as a volunteer cop. He played the role with such zeal and fanatic energy that by nightfall he found himself famous. At the height of the violence he was seen dragging a bus bench into the middle of the boulevard in order to block all traffic and divert it off to side streets. He was also seen herding bystanders away from a burning furniture store ... and later, when the riot-action seemed over, he was observed directing a group of sheriff's deputies towards the Silver Dollar Café.

Indeed, there was no arguing with his claim two weeks later that he had been right in the middle of things. His testimony at the inquest sounded perfectly logical and so finely informed that it was hard to understand how such a prominent extroverted witness could possibly have escaped being quoted – or at least mentioned – by the dozens of newsmen, investigators and assorted tipsters with access to the Salazar story. Lopez' name had not even been mentioned by the sheriff's office, which could have saved itself a lot of unnecessary public grief by even *hinting* that they had a witness as valuable as Manuel Lopez. They had not been reluctant to display their other two 'friendly' witnesses – neither of whom had seen any 'men with guns', but they both backed the Lopez version of the actual shooting sequence. Or at least they backed it until the cops produced Lopez. Then the other two witnesses refused to testify at the coroner's inquest and one of them admitted that his real name was David Ross Ricci, although the police had introduced him originally as 'Rick Ward'.

The Salazar inquest rumbled on for sixteen days, attracting large crowds and live TV coverage from start to finish. (In a rare demonstration of non-profit unity, all seven local TV stations formed a combine of sorts, assigning the coverage on a rotating basis, so that each day's proceedings appeared on a different channel.) The LA *Times* coverage – by Paul Houston and Dave Smith – was so complete and often so rife with personal intensity that the collected Smith/Houston file reads like a finely-detailed non-fiction novel. Read separately, the articles are merely good journalism. But as a document, arranged chronologically, the file is more than the sum of its parts. The main theme seems to emerge almost reluctantly, as both reporters are driven to the obvious conclusion that the sheriff, along with his deputies and all his official allies, have been *lying* all along. This is never actually stated, but the evidence is overwhelming.

A coroner's inquest is not a trial. Its purpose is to determine the circumstances surrounding a person's death – not who might have killed him, or why. If the circumstances indicate foul play, the next step is up to the DA. In California a coroner's jury can reach only two possible verdicts: that the death was 'accidental', or that it was 'at the hands of another'. And in the Salazar case, the sheriff and his allies *needed* a verdict of 'accidental'. Anything else would leave the case open – not only to the possibility of a murder or manslaughter trial for the deputy, Tom Wilson, who finally admitted firing the death weapon; but also to the threat of a million-dollar negligence lawsuit against the County by Salazar's widow.

The verdict finally hinged on whether or not the jury could believe Wilson's testimony that he fired into the Silver Dollar – at the *ceiling* – in order to ricochet a tear gas shell into the rear of the bar and force the armed stranger inside to come out the front door. But somehow Ruben Salazar had managed to get his head in the way of that carefully aimed shell. Wilson had never been able to figure out, he said, what went wrong.

Nor could he figure out how Raul Ruiz had managed to 'doctor' those photographs that made it look like he and at least one other deputy were aiming their weapons straight into the Silver Dollar, pointing them directly at people's heads. Ruiz had no trouble explaining it. His testimony at the inquest was no different from the story he had told me just a few days after the murder. And when the inquest was over there was nothing in the 2025 pages of testimony – from 61 witnesses and 204 exhibits – to cast any serious doubt on the 'Chicano eyewitness report' that Ruiz wrote for *La Raza* when the sheriff was still maintaining that Salazar had been killed by 'errant gunfire' during the violence in Laguna Park.

The inquest ended with a split verdict. Smith's lead paragraph in the 6 October *Times* read like an obituary: 'Monday the inquest into the death of newsman Ruben Salazar ended. The sixteen-day inquiry, by far the longest and costliest such affair in county history, concluded with a verdict that confuses many, satisfies few and means little. The coroner's jury came up with two verdicts: death was "at the hands of another person" (four jurors) and death was by "accident" (three jurors). Thus, inquests might appear to be a waste of time.'

A week later, District Attorney Evelle Younger – a staunch law & order man – announced that he had reviewed the case and decided that 'no criminal charge is justified', despite the unsettling fact two of the three jurors who had voted for the 'death by accident' verdict were now saying they had made a mistake.

But by that time nobody really gave a damn. The Chicano community had lost faith in the inquest about midway through the second day, and all the rest of the testimony only reinforced their anger at what most considered an evil whitewash. When the DA announced that no charges would be filed against Wilson, several of the more moderate Chicano spokesmen called for a federal investigation. The militants called for an uprising. And the cops said nothing at all.

There was one crucial question, however, that the inquest settled beyond any reasonable doubt. Ruben Salazar couldn't possibly have been the victim of a conscious, high-level cop conspiracy to get rid of him by staging an 'accidental death'. The incredible tale of half-mad stupidity and dangerous incompetence on every level of the law enforcement establishment was perhaps the most valuable thing to come out of the inquest. Nobody who heard that testimony could believe that the Los Angeles County sheriff's department is capable of pulling off a delicate job like killing a newsman *on purpose*. Their handling of the Salazar case – from the day of his death all the way to the end of the inquest – raised serious doubts about the wisdom of allowing cops to walk around loose on the street. A geek who can't hit a twenty foot wide ceiling is not what you need, these days, to pull off a nice clean first-degree murder.

But premeditation is only necessary to a charge of *first degree* murder. The Salazar killing was a second-degree job. In the terms of section

187 of the California Penal Code and in the political context of East Los Angeles in 1970, Ruben Salazar was killed 'unlawfully' and 'with malice aforethought'. These are treacherous concepts, and no doubt there are courts in this country where it might be argued successfully that a cop has a 'lawful' right to fire a deadly tear gas bazooka point-blank into a crowd of innocent people on the basis of some unfounded suspicion that one of them *might* be armed. It might also be argued that this kind of crazed and murderous assault can be accomplished without 'malice aforethought'.

Maybe so. Maybe Ruben Salazar's death can be legally dismissed as a 'police accident', or as the result of 'official negligence'. Most middle-class, white-dominated juries would probably accept the idea. Why, after all, would a clean-cut young police officer deliberately kill an innocent bystander? Not even Ruben Salazar – ten seconds before his death – could believe that he was about to have his head blown off by a cop for no reason at all. When Gustavo Garcia warned him that the cops outside were about to shoot, Salazar said, 'That's impossible; we're not doing anything.' Then he stood up and caught a tear gas bomb in his left temple.

The malignant reality of Ruben Salazar's death is that he was murdered by angry cops for no reason at all – and that the LA sheriff's department was and still is prepared to defend that murder on grounds that it was entirely justified. Salazar was killed, they say, because he happened to be in a bar where police thought there was also a 'man with a gun'. They gave him a chance, they say, by means of a bullhorn warning ... and when he didn't come out with his hands up, they had no choice but to fire a tear gas bazooka into the bar ... and his head got in the way. Tough luck. But what was he doing in that place, anyway? Lounging around a noisy Chicano bar in the middle of a communist riot?

What the cops are saying is that Salazar got what he deserved – for a lot of reasons, but mainly because he happened to be in their way when they had to do their duty. His death was unfortunate, but if they had to do it all over again they wouldn't change a note.

This is the point they want to make. It is a local variation on the standard Mitchell-Agnew theme: Don't fuck around, boy – and if you want to hang around with people who do, don't be surprised when the bill comes due – whistling in through the curtains of some darkened barroom on a sunny afternoon when the cops decide to make an example of somebody.

The night before I left town I stopped by Acosta's place with Guillermo Restrepo. I had been there earlier, but the air was extremely heavy. As always, on stories like this, some of the troops were getting nervous about the stranger hanging around. I was standing in the kitchen watching Frank put some *tacos* together and wondering when he was going to start waving the butcher knife in my face and yelling about the time I Maced him on my porch in Colorado (that had been six months earlier, at the end of a very long night during which we had all consumed a large quantity of cactus products; and when he started waving a hatchet around I'd figured Mace was the only answer ... which turned him to jelly for about forty-five minutes, and when he finally came around he said, 'If I ever see you in East Los Angeles, man, you're gonna wish you never heard the word "Mace", because I'm gonna carve it all over your fuckin' body.')

So I was not entirely at ease watching Frank chop hamburger on a meat block in the middle of East LA. He hadn't mentioned the Mace, not yet, but I knew we would get to it sooner or later ... and I'm sure we would have, except that suddenly out in the living room some geek was screaming: 'What the hell is this goddamn *gabacho* pig writer doing here? Are was fuckin' *crazy* to be letting him hear all this shit? Jesus, he's heard enough to put every one of us away for five years!'

Longer than that, I thought. And at that point I stopped worrying about Frank. A firestorm was brewing in the main room – between me and the door – so I decided it was about time to drift around the corner and meet Restrepo at the Carioca. Frank gave me a big smile as I left.

A man police say preyed on elderly women was charged Tuesday with one count of murder and 12 of robbery. Frazier DeWayne Brown, 44, a 6-foot, 2-inch, 230-pound former Los Angeles county sheriff's deputy, was arraigned in the same Hall of Justice courtroom where he once worked as a bailiff. Police had long been seeking a man who befriended elderly women at bus stops and later attacked and robbed them. Evidence against Brown included possessions taken from victims of strong-arm robberies and found in his home.

LA Times 31 March 1971

Several hours later we came back. Guillermo wanted to talk to Oscar about putting pressure on the KMEX-TV management to keep him (Restrepo) on the air. 'They want to get *rid* of me,' he explained. 'They started the pressure the day after Ruben was killed – the next fuckin' day!'

We were sitting on the floor in the living room. Outside, overhead, the police helicopter was looping around in the sky above Whittier Boulevard, sweeping the neighbourhood with a giant searchlight beam that revealed nothing – and served no purpose except to drive the Chicanos below into a seething rage. 'Those sons of bitches!' Acosta muttered. '*Look* at that goddamn thing!' We had all gone out in the yard to stare up at the monster. There was no way to ignore it. The noise was bad enough, but the probing searchlight was such an obvious, outrageous harassment that it was hard to understand how even a cop could explain it away as anything but deliberate mockery and provocation.

'Now *tell* me,' said Acosta. '*Why* are they doing a thing like this? Why? You think they don't *know* what effect it has on us?'

'They know,' said Restrepo. He lit a cigarette as we went back inside. 'Listen,' he said, 'I get about fifteen telephone calls every day from people who want to tell me stories about what the police have done to them – *terrible* stories. I've been hearing them for a year and a half, every goddamn day – and the funny thing is, I never used to believe these people. Not completely. I didn't think they were *lying*, just exaggerating.' He paused, glancing around the room, but nobody spoke. Restrepo is not entirely trusted in these quarters; he is part of the establishment – like his friend, Ruben Salazar, who bridged that gap the hard way.

'But ever since Ruben,' Restrepo continued, 'I *believe* these stories. They're true! I realize that, now – but what can I do?' He shrugged, nervously aware that he was talking to people who had made that discovery a long time ago. 'Just the other night,' he said, 'I got a call from a man who said the cops killed his cousin in the yail. He was a homosexual, a young Chicano, nobody political – and the police report said he hung himself in his cell. Suicide. So I checked it out. And, man, it made me sick. This guy's body was *all bruises*, black and blue marks all over him – and right across his forehead he had sixteen fresh stitches.

'The police report said he tried to escape so they had to dominate him. They got him sewed up at the hospital, but when they took him to yail, the warden or yailer or whatever they call the bastard wouldn't *accept* him, because he was bleeding so bad. So they took him back to the hospital and got a doctor to sign some paper saying he was OK to be put in the yail. But they had to *carry* him. And the next day they took a picture of him hanging from the end of the top bunk with his own shirt tied around his neck.

'You *believe* that? Not me. But you tell me – what can I *do*? Where do I look for the truth? Who can I ask? The sheriff? Goddamn, I can't go on the air with a story about how the cops killed a guy in the yail unless I *know* something for proof! Jesus Christ, we all *know*. But just to know is not enough. You understand that? You see why I never made that story on TV?'

Acosta nodded. As a lawyer, he understood perfectly that evidence is *necessary* – on the air and in print, as well as in the courtroom. But

Frank was not convinced. He was sipping from a quart of sweet Key Largo wine, and in fact he didn't even know who Restrepo was. 'Sorry, man,' he'd said earlier. 'But I don't watch the news on TV.'

Acosta winced. *He* watches and reads *everything*. But most of the people around him think the news – on the TV or radio or newspapers or whatever – is just another rotten *gabacho* trick. Just another bad shuck, like the others. 'The news', to them, is pure propaganda – paid for by the advertisers. 'Who pays the bill for that bullshit?' they ask. 'Who's behind it?'

Who indeed? Both sides seem convinced that the 'real enemy' is a vicious conspiracy of some kind. The Anglo power structure keeps telling itself that 'the Mexican problem' is really the work of a small organization of well-trained Communist agitators, working twenty-five hours a day to transform East LA into a wasteland of constant violence – mobs of drug-crazed Chicanos prowling the streets at all times, terrorizing the merchants, hurling firebombs into banks, looting stores, sacking offices and massing now and then, armed with Chinese sten pistols, for all-out assaults on the local sheriff's fortress.

A year ago this grim vision would have been a bad joke, the crude ravings of some paranoid hysterical Bircher. But things are different now; the mood of the *barrio* is changing so fast that not even the most militant of the young Chicano activists claim to know what's really happening. The only thing everybody agrees on is that the mood is getting ugly, the level of tension is still escalating. The *direction* of the drift is obvious. Even Gov. Reagen is worried about it. He recently named Danny Villaneuva, one-time kicking specialist for the Los Angeles Rams and now general manager of KMEX-TV, as the Governor's personal ambassador to the whole Chicano community. But, as usual, Reagan's solution is part of the problem. Villanueva is overwhelmingly despised by the very people Reagan says he's 'trying to reach'. He is the classic *vendido*. 'Let's face it,' says a Chicano journalist not usually identified with the militants, 'Danny is a goddamn pig. Ruben Salazar told me that. You know KMEX used to be a good news station for Chicanos. Ruben was the one who did that, and Danny was afraid to interfere. But within twenty-four hours after Ruben was murdered, Villaneuva started tearing up the news department. He wouldn't even let Restrepo show films of the cops gassing people in Laguna Park, the day after Ruben died! Now he's trying to get rid of Restrepo, cut the balls off the news and turn KMEX-TV back into a *safe Tio Taco* station. Shit! And he's getting away with it.'

The total castration of KMEX-TV would be a crippling blow to the movement. A major media voice can be an invaluable mobilizing tool, particularly in the vast urban sprawl of Los Angeles. All it takes is a sympathetic news director with enough leverage and personal integrity to deal with the news on his own terms. The man who hired Ruben Salazar, former station director Joe Rank, considered him valuable enough to out-bid the blue-chip Los Angeles *Times* for the services of one of that paper's ranking stars – so nobody argued when Salazar demanded absolute independence for his KMEX news operation. But with Salazar dead, the station's Anglo ownership moved swiftly to regain control of the leaderless news operation.

Guillermo Restrepo, Salazar's heir apparent, suddenly discovered that he had no leverage at all. He was muscled into a straight newscaster's role. He was no longer free to investigate any story that he felt was important ... If the Chicano Moratorium Committee called a press conference to explain why they were organizing a mass rally against 'police brutality', for instance, Restrepo had to get permission to cover it. And Chicano activists soon learned that a two-minute news feature on KMEX was crucial to the success of a mass rally, because TV was the only way to reach a mass Chicano audience in a hurry. And no other TV station in LA was interested in any kind of Chicano news except riots.

'Losing Ruben was a goddamn disaster for the movement,' Acosta said recently. 'He wasn't really *with* us, but at least he was interested. Hell, the truth is I never really liked the guy. But he was the only journalist in LA with real influence who would come to a press conference in the *barrio*. That's the truth. Hell, the only way we can get those bastards to listen to us is by renting a fancy hotel lounge over there in West Hollywood or some bullshit place like that – where *they* can feel comfortable – and hold our press conference there. With free coffee and snacks for the press. But even then, about half the shitheads won't come unless we serve free booze, too. Shit! Do you know what that *costs*?'

This was the tone of our conversation that night when Guillermo and I went over to Oscar's pad for a beer and some talk about politics. The place was unnaturally quiet. No music, no grass, no bad-mouth *bato loco* types hunkered down on the pallets in the front room. It was the first time I'd seen the place when it didn't look like a staging area for some kind of hellish confrontation that might erupt at any moment.

But tonight it was deadly quiet. The only interruption was a sudden pounding on the door and voices shouting: 'Hey, man, open up. I got some *brothers* with me!' Rudy hurried to the door and peered out through the tiny eyewindow. Then he stepped back and shook his head emphatically. 'It's some guys from the project,' he told Oscar. 'I know them, but they're all fucked up.'

'God *damn* it,' Acosta muttered. 'That's the last thing I need tonight. Get rid of them. Tell them I have to be in court tomorrow. Jesus! I *have* to get some sleep!'

Rudy and Frank went outside to deal with the brothers. Oscar and Guillermo went back to politics – while I listened, sensing a downhill drift on all fronts. *Nothing* was going right. The jury was still out on Corky's case, but Acosta was not optimistic. He was also expecting a decision on his Grand Jury challenge in the 'Biltmore Six' case. 'We'll probably lose that one, too,' he said. 'The bastards think they have us on the run now; they think we're demoralized – so they'll keep the pressure on, keep pushing.' He shrugged. 'And maybe they're right. Shit. I'm tired of arguing with them. How long do they expect me to keep coming down to their goddamn courthouse and begging for justice? I'm *tired* of that shit. We're *all* tired.' He shook his head slowly then ripped the pop-top out of a Budweiser that Rudy brought in from the kitchen. 'This legal bullshit ain't makin' it,' he went on. 'The way it looks now, I think we're just about finished with that game. You know at the noon recess today I had to keep a bunch of these goddamn *batos locos* from stomping the DA. Christ! That would fuck me for good. They'll send me to the goddamn pen for hiring thugs to assault the prosecutor!' He shook his head again. 'Frankly, I think the whole thing is out of control. God only knows where it's heading, but I know it's going to be heavy, I think maybe the real shit is about to come down.'

There was no need to ask what he meant by 'heavy shit'. The *barrio* is already plagued by sporadic fire-bombings, explosions, shootings and minor violence of all kinds. But the cops see nothing 'political' in these incidents. Just before I left town I talked on the phone with a lieutenant at the East LA sheriff's office. He was anxious to assure me that the area was totally pacified. 'You have to remember,' he said, 'that this has always been a high-crime area. We have a lot of trouble with teenage gangs, and it's getting worse. Now they're all running around with .22 rifles and handguns, looking for fights with each other. I guess you could say they're sort of like the Blackstone Rangers in Chicago, except that our gangs are younger.'

'But they're not into politics like the black gangs in Chicago?' I asked.

'Are you kidding?' he replied. 'The only political thing the Blackstone Rangers ever did was con somebody out of a federal grant for a lot of money.'

I asked him about some of the stories I'd heard about bombings, etc. But he quickly dismissed them as rumours. Then, during the next half hour of random talking about things that had happened in the past few weeks, he mentioned one dynamiting and a building burned down at East Los Angeles College, and also the firebombing of a local *vendido* politician's real estate office. 'But they hit the wrong guy,' the Lt said with a chuckle. 'They bombed another realtor who happened to have the same name as the guy they were after.'

'*Que malo*,' I mumbled, lapsing into my own dialect. 'But aside from all that, you people don't see real trouble brewing? What about these rallies that keep turning into riots?'

'It's always the same bunch of troublemakers,' he explained. 'They take a crowd that's gathered for other reasons, and then they subvert it.'

'But that last rally was called to protest *police brutality*,' I said. 'And then it turned into a riot. I saw the films – fifty or sixty police cars lined up bumper to bumper on Whittier Boulevard, deputies firing shotguns into the crowd ...'

'That was *necessary*,' he replied. 'That mob was out of control. They *attacked* us.'

'I know,' I said.

'And let me tell you something else,' he went on. 'That rally wasn't *really* about "police brutality". The guy who organized it, Rosalio Munoz, told me he was just using that slogan to get people out to the park.'

'Well, you know how they are,' I said. Then I asked him if he could give me the names of any Chicano leaders I should talk to if I decided to write an article about the scene in East LA.

'Well, there's Congressman Roybal,' he said. 'And that real estate man I told you about ...'

'The one who got fire-bombed?'

'Oh no,' he replied. 'The other guy – the one they *intended* to fire-bomb.'

'OK,' I said. 'I'll write those names down. And I guess if I decide to look around the *barrio* you guys could help me out, right? Is it safe to walk around out there, with all these gangs running around shooting at each other?'

'No problem,' he said. 'We'll even let you ride around in a radio car with some of the officers.'

I said that would be fine. What better way, after all, to get the inside story? Just spend a few days touring the *barrio* in a cop car. Particularly right now, with everything calm and peaceful.

'We see no evidence of any political tension,' the Lt had told me. 'We have a great deal of community support.' He chuckled. 'And we also have a very active intelligence bureau.'

'That's good,' I said. 'Well, I have to hang up now, or I'll miss my plane.'

'Oh, then you've decided to do the story? When will you be in town?'

'I've been here for two weeks,' I said. 'My plane leaves in ten minutes.'

'But I thought you said you were calling from San Francisco,' he said.

'I did,' I said. 'But I was lying.' (click)

It was definitely time to leave. The last loose end in the Salazar case had been knotted up that morning when the jury came back with a 'guilty' verdict for Corky Gonzales. He was sentenced to '40 days and 40 nights' in the LA County jail for possession of a loaded revolver on the day of Salazar's death. 'We'll appeal,' said Acosta, 'but for political purposes this case is finished. Nobody's worried about Corky surviving forty days in jail. We wanted to confront the *gabacho* court system with a man the whole Chicano community knew was technically innocent, then let them draw their own conclusions about the verdict.

'Hell, we never denied that *somebody* had a loaded pistol in that truck. But it wasn't Corky. He wouldn't dare carry a goddamn gun around with him. He's a *leader*. He doesn't have to carry a gun for the same goddamn reason Nixon doesn't.'

Acosta had not stressed that point in the courtroom, for fear of alarming the jury and inflaming the gringo press. Not to mention the cops. Why give them the same kind of flimsy excuse to shoot at Gonzales that they already used to justify shooting Ruben Salazar?

Corky merely shrugged at the verdict. At forty-two, he has spent half his life gouging justice out of the man, and now he views the Anglo court system with the quiet sort of fatalistic humour that Acosta hasn't learned yet. But Oscar is getting there fast. The week of April Fools Day 1971 was a colossal bummer for him; a series of bad jolts and setbacks that seemed to confirm all his worst suspicions.

Two days after Corky's conviction, Superior Court Judge Arthur Alarcon – a prominent Mexican-American jurist – rejected Acosta's carefully constructed motion to quash the 'Biltmore Six' indictments because of 'sub-conscious, institutional racism' in the Grand Jury system. This effort had taken almost a year of hard work, much of it done by Chicano law students who reacted to the verdict with a bitterness matching Acosta's.

Then, later that same week, the Los Angeles Board of Supervisors voted to use public funds to pay all legal expenses for several policemen recently indicted 'for accidentally' killing two Mexican nationals – a case known in East LA as 'the murder of the Sanchez brothers'. It was a case of mistaken identity, the cops explained. They had somehow been given the wrong address of an apartment where they thought 'two Mexican fugitives' were holed up, so they hammered on the door and shouted a warning to 'come out of there with your hands over your head or we'll come in shooting'. Nobody came out, so the cops went in shooting to kill.

But how could they have known that they'd attacked the wrong apartment? And how could they have known that neither one of the Sanchez brothers understood English? Even Mayor Sam Yorty and Police Chief Ed Davis admitted that the killings had been very unfortunate. But when the Federal DA brought charges against the cops, both Yorty and Davis were publicly outraged. They both called press conferences and went on the air to denounce the indictments – in language that strangely echoed the American Legion outcry when Lt Calley was charged with murdering women and children at My Lai.

The Yorty/Davis tirades were so gross that a District Court judge finally issued a 'gag order' to keep them quiet until the case comes to trial. But they had already said enough to whip the whole *barrio* into a rage at the idea that Chicano tax dollars might be used to defend some 'mad dog cops' who frankly admitted killing two Mexican nationals. It sounded like a replay of the Salazar bullshit: same style, same excuse, same result – but this time with different names, and blood on a different floor. 'They'll put me in jail if I won't pay taxes,' said a young Chicano watching a soccer game at a local playground, 'then they take my tax money and use it defend some killer pig. Hell, what if they had come to my address by mistake? I'd be dead as hell right now.'

There was a lot of talk in the *barrio* about 'drawing some pig blood for a change' if the Supervisors actually voted to use tax funds to defend the accused cops. A few people actually called City Hall and mumbled anonymous threats in the name of the 'Chicano Liberation Front'. But the Supervisors hung tough. They voted on Thursday, and by noon the news was out: The city would pick up the tab.

At 5:15 p.m. on Thursday afternoon the Los Angeles City Hall was rocked by a dynamite blast. A bomb had been planted in one of the downstairs restrooms. Nobody was hurt, and the damage was officially described as 'minor'. About $5000 worth, they said – small potatoes, compared to the bomb that blew a wall out of the District Attorney's office last fall after Salazar died.

When I called the sheriff's office to ask about the explosion they said they couldn't talk about it. City Hall was out of their jurisdiction. But they were more than willing to talk when I asked if it was true that the bomb had been the work of the Chicano Liberation Front.

'Where'd you hear that?'

'From the City News Service.'

'Yeah, it's true,' he said. 'Some woman called up and said it was done in memory of the Sanchez brothers, by the Chicano Liberation Front. We've heard about those guys. What do *you* know about them?'

'Nothing,' I said. 'That's why I called the sheriff. I thought your intelligence network might know something.'

'Sure they do,' he said quickly. 'But all that information is confidential.'

Rolling Stone no. 81, 29 April 1971

FREAK POWER IN THE ROCKIES

A Memoir and Rambling Discussion (with Rude Slogans) of Freak Power in the Rockies ... on the Weird Mechanics of Running a Takeover Bid on a Small Town ... and a Vulgar Argument for Seizing Political Power and Using It like a Gun Ripped Away from a Cop ... with Jangled Comments on the Uncertain Role of the Head and the Awful Stupor Factor ... and Other Disorganized Notes on 'How to Punish the Fatbacks', How to Make Sure that Today's Pig Is Tomorrow's Offal ... and Why This Crazed New World Can Only Be Dealt with by ... A New *Posse*!

– or –

Just how weird can you stand it, brother – before your love will crack?
Mike Lydon in Ramparts, March 1970

Two hours before the polls closed we realized that we had no headquarters – no hole or great hall where the faithful could gather for the awful election-night deathwatch. Or to celebrate the great victory that suddenly seemed very possible.

We had run the whole campaign from a long oaken table in the Jerome Tavern on Main Street, working flat out in public so anyone could see or even join if they felt ready ... but now, in these final hours, we wanted a bit of privacy; some clean, well-lighted place, as it were, to hunker down and wait ...

We also needed vast quantities of ice and rum – and a satchel of brain-rattling drugs for those who wanted to finish the campaign on the highest possible note, regardless of the outcome. But the main thing we needed, with dusk coming down and the polls due to close at 7 p.m., was an office with several phone lines, for a blizzard of last-minute calls to those who hadn't yet voted. We'd collected the voting lists just before 5:00 – from our poll-watcher teams who'd been checking them off since dawn – and it was obvious, from a very quick count, that the critical freak power vote had turned out in force.

Joe Edwards a twenty-nine-year-old head, lawyer and bike-racer from Texas, looked like he might, in the waning hours of election day in November 1969, be the next Mayor of Aspen, Colorado.

The retiring mayor, Dr Robert 'Buggsy' Barnard, had been broadcasting vicious radio warnings for the previous forty-eight hours, raving about long prison terms for vote-fraud and threatening violent harassment by 'phalanxes of poll-watchers' for any strange or freaky-looking scum who might dare to show up at the polls. We checked the laws and found that Barnard's radio warnings were a violation of the 'voter intimidation' statutes, so I called the District Attorney and tried to have the mayor arrested at once ... but the DA said, 'Leave me out of it; police your own elections.'

Which we did, with finely organized teams of poll-watchers: two inside each polling place at all times, with six more just outside in vans or trucks full of beef, coffee, propaganda, check lists and bound Xerox copies of all Colorado voting laws.

The idea was to keep massive assistance available, at all times, to our point men *inside* the official voting places. And the reasoning behind this rather heavy public act – which jolted a lot of people who wouldn't have voted for Edwards anyway – was our concern that the mayor and his cops would create some kind of ugly scene, early on, and rattle the underground grapevine with fear-rumours that would scare off a lot of our voters. Most of our people were fearful of *any* kind of legal hassle at the polls, regardless of their rights. So it seemed important that we should make it very clear, from the start, that we knew the laws and we weren't going to tolerate *any* harassment of our people. None.

Each poll-watcher on the dawn shift was given a portable tape-recorder with a microphone that he was instructed to stick in the face of any opposition poll-watcher who asked anything beyond the legally-allowable questions regarding name, age and residence. Nothing else could be asked, under penalty of an obscure election law relating to 'frivolous challenge', a little brother to the far more serious charge of 'voter intimidation'.

And since the only person who had actually threatened to intimidate voters was the mayor, we decided to force the confrontation as soon as possible in Ward 1, where Buggsy had announced that he would personally stand the first poll-watching shift for the opposition. If the buggers wanted a confrontation, we decided to give it to them.

163

The polling place in Ward 1 was a lodge called the Cresthaus, owned by an old and infamous Swiss/Nazi who calls himself Guido Meyer. Martin Bormann went to Brazil, but Guido came to Aspen – arriving here several years after the Great War ... and ever since then he has spent most of his energy (including two complete terms as city magistrate) getting even with this country by milking the tourists and having young (or poor) people arrested.

So Guido was watching eagerly when the Mayor arrived in his parking lot at ten minutes to seven, creeping his Porsche through a gauntlet of silent Edwards people. We had mustered a half-dozen of the scurviest looking *legal* voters we could find – and when the Mayor arrived at the polls these freaks were waiting to vote. Behind them, lounging around a coffee-dispenser in an old VW van, were at least a dozen others, most of them large and bearded, and several so eager for violence that they had spent the whole night making chain-whips and loading up on speed to stay crazy.

Buggsy looked horrified. It was the first time in his long drug experience that he had ever laid eyes on a group of non-passive, super-aggressive heads. What had got into them? Why were their eyes so wild? And why were they yelling: 'You're fucked, Buggsy ... We're going to croak you ... Your whole act is doomed ... We're going to beat your ass like a gong.'

Who were they? All strangers? Some gang of ugly bikers or speed-freaks from San Francisco? Yes ... of course ... that bastard Edwards had brought in a bunch of ringers. But then he looked again ... and recognized, at the head of the group, his ex-drinkalong bar-buddy Brad Reed, the potter and known gun freak, 6 feet 4 inches and 220, grinning down through his beard and black hair-flag ... saying nothing, just smiling ...

Great God, he knew the others, too ... there was Don Davidson, the accountant, smooth shaven and quite normal-looking in a sleek maroon ski parka, but not smiling at all ... and who were those girls, those ripe blonde bodies whose names he knew from chance meetings in friendlier times? What were they doing out here at dawn, in the midst of this menacing mob?

What indeed? He scurried inside to meet Guido, but instead ran into Tom Benton, the hairy artist and known radical ... Benton was grinning like a crocodile and waving a small black microphone, saying: 'Welcome, Buggsy. You're late. The voters are waiting outside ... Yes, did you see them out there? Were they friendly? And if you wonder what *I'm* doing here, I'm Joe Edwards' poll-watcher ... and the reason I have this little black machine here is that I want to tape every word you say when you start committing felonies by harassing our voters ...'

The Mayor lost his first confrontation almost instantly. One of the first obvious Edwards-voters of the day was a blond kid who looked about seventeen. Buggsy began to jabber at him and Benton moved in with the microphone, ready to intervene ... but before Benton could utter a word the kid began snarling at the Mayor, yelling: 'Go fuck yourself, Buggsy! *You* figure out how old I am. I know the goddamn law! I don't have to show you proof of *anything*! You're a *dying man*, Buggsy! Get out of my way. I'm ready to vote!'

The Mayor's next bad encounter was with a heavy young girl with no front teeth, wearing a baggy grey T-shirt and no bra. Somebody had brought her to the polls, but when she got there she was crying – actually shaking with fear – and she refused to go inside. We weren't allowed within 100 feet of the door, but we got word to Benton and he came out to escort the girl in. She voted, despite Buggsy's protests, and when she came outside again she was grinning like she'd just clinched Edwards' victory all by herself.

After that, we stopped worrying about the Mayor. No goons had shown up with blackjacks, no cops were in evidence, and Benton had established full control of his turf around the ballot box. Elsewhere, in Wards 2 and 3, the freak-vote was not so heavy and things were going smoothly. In Ward 2, in fact, our official poll-watcher (a drug person with a beard about two feet long) had caused a panic by challenging dozens of *straight* voters. The city attorney called Edwards and complained that some ugly lunatic in Ward 2 was refusing to let a seventy-five-year-old woman cast her ballot until she produced a birth certificate. We were forced to replace the man; his zeal was inspiring, but we feared he might spark a backlash.

This had been a problem all along. We had tried to mobilize a huge underground vote, without frightening the burghers into a counterattack. But it didn't work – primarily because most of our best people were also hairy, and very obvious. Our opening shot – the midnight registration campaign – had been ramrodded by bearded heads: Mike Solheim and Pierre Landry, who worked the streets and bars for head voters like wild junkies, in the face of near-total apathy.

Aspen is full of freaks, heads, fun-hogs and weird night-people of every description ... but most of them would prefer jail or the bastinado to the horror of actually registering to vote. Unlike the main bulk of burghers and businessmen, the dropout has to *make an effort* to use his long-dormant vote. There is not much to it, no risk and no more than ten minutes of small talk and time ¬ but to the average dropout the idea of registering to vote is a very heavy thing. The psychic implications, 'copping back into the system', etc., are fierce ... and we learned, in Aspen, that there is no point even trying to convince people to take that step unless you can give them a very good reason. Like a very unusual candidate ... or a fireball pitch of some kind.

The central problem that we grappled with last fall is the gap that separates the head culture from activist politics. Somewhere in the nightmare of failure that gripped America between 1965 and 1970, the old Berkeley-born notion of beating the system by fighting it gave way to a sort of numb conviction that it made more sense in the long run to flee, or even to simply hide, than to fight the bastards on anything even vaguely resembling their own terms.

Our ten-day registration campaign had focused almost entirely on the head/dropout culture; they wanted no part of activist politics and it had been a hellish effort to convince them to register at all. Many had lived in Aspen for five or six years, and they weren't at all concerned with being *convicted* of vote-fraud – they simply didn't want to be hassled. Most of us are living here because we like the idea of being able to walk out our front doors and smile at what we see. On my own front porch I have a palm tree growing in a blue toilet bowl ... and on occasion I like to wander outside, stark naked, and fire my .44 magnum at various gongs I've mounted on the nearby hillside. I like to load up on mescaline and turn my amplifier up to 110 decibels for a taste of 'White Rabbit' while the sun comes up on the snow-peaks along the continental divide.

Which is not entirely the point. The world is full of places where a man can run wild on drugs and loud music and fire power – but not for long. I lived a block above Haight Street for two years but by the end of 66 the whole neighbourhood had become a cop-magnet and a bad sideshow. Between the narcs and the psychedelic hustlers, there was not much room to live.

What happened in the Haight echoed earlier scenes in North Beach and the Village ... and it proved, once again, the basic futility of seizing turf you can't control. The pattern never varies: a low-rent area suddenly blooms new and loose and human – and then fashionable, which attracts the press and the cops at about the same time. Cop problems attract more publicity, which then attracts fad-salesmen and hustlers – which means money, and that attracts junkies and jack-rollers. Their bad action causes publicity and – for some perverse reason – an influx of bored, upward mobile types who dig the menace of 'white ghetto' life and whose expense-account tastes drive local rents and street prices out of reach of the original settlers ... who are forced, once again, to move on.

One of the most hopeful developments of the failed Haight-Ashbury scene was the exodus to rural communes. Most of the communes failed – for reasons that everybody can seen now, in retrospect (like that scene in *Easy Rider* where all those poor freaks were trying to grow their crops in dry sand) – but the few that succeeded, like the Hog Farm in New Mexico, kept a whole generation of heads believing that the future lay somewhere outside the cities.

In Aspen, hundreds of Haight-Ashbury refugees tried to settle in the wake of that ill-fated 'summer of love' in 1967. The summer was a wild and incredible dope orgy here, but when winter came the crest of that wave broke and drifted on the shoals of local problems such as jobs, housing and deep snow on the roads to shacks that, a few months earlier, had been easily accessible. Many of the West Coast refugees moved on, but several hundred stayed; they hired on as carpenters, waiters, bartenders, dish-washers ... and a year later they were part of the permanent population. By mid-69 they occupied most of Aspen's so-called 'low-cost housing' – first the tiny mid-town apartments, then outlying shacks, and finally the trailer courts.

So most of the freaks felt that voting wasn't worth the kind of bullshit that went with it, and the mayor's illegal threats only reinforced their notion that politics in America was something to be avoided. Getting busted for grass was one thing, because the 'crime' was worth the risk ... but they saw no sense in going to court for a 'political technicality', even if they weren't guilty.

(This sense of 'reality' is a hallmark of the drug culture, which values the instant reward – a pleasant four-hour high – over anything involving a time lag between the effort and the end. On this scale of values, politics is too difficult, too 'complex' and too 'abstract' to justify any risk or initial action. It is the flip side of the 'good German' syndrome.)

The idea of asking young heads to 'go clean' never occurred to us. They could go dirty, or even naked, for all we cared ... all we asked them to do was first *register* and then *vote*. A year earlier these same people had seen no difference between Nixon and Humphrey. They were against the war in Vietnam, but the McCarthy crusade had never reached them. At the grass-roots of the dropout culture, the idea of going Clean for Gene was a bad joke. Both Dick Gregory and George Wallace drew unnaturally large chunks of the vote in Aspen. Robert Kennedy would probably have carried the town, if he hadn't been killed, but he wouldn't have won by much. The town is essentially Republican: GOP registrations outnumber Democrats by more than two to one ... but the combined total of both major parties just about equals the number of registered independents, most of whom pride themselves on being totally unpredictable. They are a jangled mix of left/crazies and Birchers; cheap bigots, dope dealers, nazi ski instructors and spaced-off 'psychedelic farmers' with no politics at all beyond self-preservation.

At the end of that frenzied ten-day hustle (since we kept no count, no lists or records) we had no way of knowing how many half-stirred dropouts had actually registered, or how many of those would vote. So it was a bit of a shock all around when, towards the end of that election day, our poll-watchers' tallies showed that Joe Edwards had already cashed more than 300 of the 486 *new* registrations that had just gone into the books.

The race was going to be very close. The voting lists showed roughly 100 pro-Edward voters who hadn't showed up at the polls, and we figured that 100 phone calls might raise at least twenty-five of these laggards. At that point it looked like twenty-five might make the nut, particularly in a sharply divided three-way mayor's race in a town with only 1623 registered voters.

So we needed those phones. But where? Nobody knew ... until a girl who'd been working on the phone network suddenly came up with a key to a spacious two-room office in the old Elks Club building. She had once worked there, for a local businessman and ex-hipster named Craig, who had gone to Chicago on business.

We seized Craig's office at once, ignoring the howls and curses of the mob in the Elks bar – where the outgoing mayor's troops were already gathering to celebrate the victory of his hand-picked successor. (Legally, there was nothing they could do to keep us out of the place, although later that night they voted to have Craig evicted ... and he is now running for the state legislature on a Crush the Elks platform.) By six o'clock we had the new headquarters working nicely. The phone calls were extremely brief and direct: 'Get off your ass, you bastard! We *need* you! Get out and vote!'

About six people worked the lists and the phones. Others went off to hustle the various shacks, lodges, hovels and communes where we knew there were voters but no phones. The place filled up rapidly, as the word went out that we finally had a headquarters. Soon the whole second-floor of the Elks Club was full of bearded freaks yelling frantically at each other; strange-looking people rushing up and down the stairs with lists, notebooks, radios, and cases of Budweiser ...

Somebody stuck a purple spansule in my hand, saying, 'Goddamn, you look tired! What you need is a hit of this excellent mescaline.' I nodded absently and stuck the thing in one of the twenty-two pockets in my red campaign parka. Save this drug for later, I thought. No point getting crazy until the polls close ... keep checking these stinking lists, squeeze every last vote out of them ... keep calling, pushing, shouting at the bastards, threaten them ...

There was something weird in the room, some kind of electric madness that I'd never noticed before. I stood against a wall with a beer in my hand and watched the machinery working. And after a while I realized what the difference was. For the first time in the campaign, these people really believed we were going to win – or at least that we had a good chance. And now, with less than an hour to go, they were working like a gang of coal-miners sent down to rescue the survivors of a cave-in. At that point – with my own role ended – I was probably the most pessimistic person in the room; the others seemed entirely convinced that Joe Edwards would be the next Mayor of Aspen ... that our wild-eyed experiment with freak power was about to carry the day and establish a nationwide precedent.

We were in for a very long night – waiting for the ballots to be counted by hand – but even before the polls closed we knew we had changed the whole structure of Aspen's politics. The old guard was doomed, the liberals were terrorized and the underground had emerged, with terrible suddenness, on a very serious power trip. Throughout the campaign I'd been promising, on the streets and in the bars, that if Edwards won this Mayor's race I would run for Sheriff next year (November 1970) ... but it never occurred to me that I would actually have to run; no more than I'd ever seriously believed we could mount a 'takeover bid' in Aspen.

But now it was happening. Even Edwards, a sceptic from the start, had said on election eve that he thought we were going to 'win big'. When he said it we were in his office, sorting out Xerox copies of the Colorado election laws for our poll-watching teams, and I recall being stunned at his optimism.

'Never in hell,' I said. 'If we win at all it's going to be damn close – like twenty-five votes.' But his comment had jangled me badly. God damn! I thought. Maybe we *will* win ... and what then?

Finally, at around 6:30, I felt so useless and self-conscious just hanging around the action that I said what the hell, and left. I felt like Dagwood Bumstead pacing back and forth in some comic-strip version of a maternity-ward waiting room. Fuck this, I thought. I'd been awake and moving around like a cannonball for the last fifty hours, and now – with nothing else to confront – I felt the adrenalin sinking. Go home, I thought, eat this mescaline and put on the earphones, get away from this public agony ...

At the bottom of the long wooden stairway from Craig's office to the street I paused for a quick look into the Elks Club bar. It was crowded and loud and happy ... a bar full of winners, like always. They had never backed a loser. They were the backbone of Aspen: shop-owners, cowboys, firemen, cops, construction workers ... and their leader was the most popular mayor in the town's history, a two-term winner now backing his own hand-picked successor, a half-bright young lawyer. I flashed the Elks a big smile and a quick V-fingered 'victory' sign. Nobody smiled ... but it was hard to know if they realized that their man was already croaked; in a sudden three-way race he had bombed early, when the local Contractors' Association and all their real estate allies had made the painful decision to abandon Oates, their natural gut-choice, and devote all their weight and leverage to stopping the 'hippie candidate', Joe Edwards. By the weekend before election day it was no longer a three-way campaign ... and by Monday the only question left was how many mean-spirited, right-bent shitheads could be mustered to vote *against* Joe Edwards.

The other alternative was a fifty-five-year-old lady shopkeeper backed by author Leon Uris and the local Republican majority ... Eve Homeyer, a longtime functionary in the Colorado GOP, had spent thousands of dollars on a super-chintzy campaign to re-create herself in the boneless image of Mamie Eisenhower. She hated stray dogs and motorcycles made her ears ring. Progress was nice and development was good for the local economy. Aspen should be made safe for the annual big-spending visits of the Atlanta Ski Club and the Texas Cavaliers – which meant building a four-lane highway through the middle of town and more blockhouse condominiums to humour more tourists.

She played Nixon to Oates' Agnew. If the sight of naked hippies made her sick, she wasn't quite ready to cut their heads off. She was old and cranky, but not quite as mean as Oates' vigilante backers who wanted a mayor who would give them free rein to go out and beat the living shit out of anybody who didn't look like natural material for the Elks' and Eagles' membership drives. And where Oates wanted to turn Aspen into a Rocky Mountain version of Atlantic City ... Eve Homeyer only wanted to make it a sort of St Petersburg with a Disneyland overlay. She agreed *halfway*, with everything Lennie Oates stood for ... but she wanted it made damn clear that she viewed Joe Edwards' candidacy as pure demented lunacy – a form of surly madness so wrong and rotten that only the wretched and the scum of the earth could give it a moment's thought.

We had already beaten Oates, but I was too tired to hassle the Elks right then, and in some strange way I felt sorry for them. They were about to be stomped very badly by a candidate who agreed with them more than they knew. The people who had reason to fear the Edwards campaign were the sub-dividers, ski-pimps and city-based land-developers who had come like a plague of poison roaches to buy and sell the whole valley out from under the people who still valued it as a good place to live, not just a good investment.

Our programme, basically, was to drive the real estate goons completely out of the valley: to prevent the State Highway Department from bringing a four-lane highway into the town and in fact *to ban all auto traffic from every downtown street.* Turn them all into grassy malls where everybody, even freaks, could do whatever's right. The cops would become trash collectors and maintenance men for a fleet of municipal bicycles, for anybody to use. No more huge, space-killing apartment buildings to block the view, from any downtown street, of anybody who might want to look up and see the mountains. No more land-rapes, no more busts for 'flute-playing' or 'blocking the sidewalk' ... fuck the tourists, dead-end the highway, zone the greedheads out of existence, and in general create a town where people could live like human beings, instead of slaves to some bogus sense of progress that is driving us all mad.

Joe Edwards' platform was against the developers, not the old-timers and ranchers – and it was hard to see, from their arguments, how they could disagree in substance with anything we said ... unless what they were really worried about was the very good chance that a win by Edwards would put an end to their options of selling out to the highest bidder. With Edwards, they said, would come horrors like zoning and ecology, which would cramp their fine western style, the buy low, sell high ethic ... free enterprise, as it were, and the few people who bothered to argue with them soon found that their nostalgic talk about 'the good old days' and 'the tradition of this peaceful valley' was only an awkward cover for their fears about 'socialist-thinking newcomers'.

Whatever else the Edwards campaign may or may not have accomplished, we had croaked that stupid sentimental garbage about the 'land-loving old-timers'.

I left the Elks Club building and stopped on Ayman Street for a moment to look up at the tall hills around the town. There was already snow on Smuggler, to the north ... and on Bell, behind Little Nell, the ski trails were dim white tracks ... steep toll-roads, waiting for Christmas and the blizzard of fat-wallet skiers who keep Aspen rich: eight dollars a day to ski on those hills, $150 for a pair of good skis, $120 for the right-boots, $65 for a Meggi sweater, $75 for a goose-down parka ... and $200 more for poles, gloves, goggles, hat, socks, and another $70 for a pair of ski pants ...

Indeed. The ski industry is big business. And '*après*-ski' is bigger: $90 a day for an apartment in the Aspen Alps, $25 apiece for a good meal & wine in the Paragon ... and don't forget the Bates Floaters (official *après*-ski boot of the US Olympic team – the worst kind of flimsy shit imaginable for $30 a pair).

It adds up to something like an average figure of $500 a week for the typical midwest dingbat who buys both his gear and his style out of *Playboy*. Then you multiply $100 a day by the many skier days logged in 1969–70 by the Aspen Ski Corp, and what you get is a staggering winter gross for a Rocky Mountain village with a real population of just over 2000.

Which is only half the story: The other half is an annual 30–35 per cent growth/profit jump on all money fronts ... and what you see here (or *saw*, prior to Nixon's economic adjustments) is/was a king-hell gold-mine with no end in sight. For the past ten years Aspen has been the showpiece/money-hub of a gold rush that has made millionaires. In the wake of World War Two, they flocked in from Austria and Switzerland (never from Germany, they said) to staff the embryo nerve/resort centres of a sport that would soon be bigger than golf or bowling ... and now, with skiing firmly established in America, the original German hustlers are wealthy burghers. They own restaurants, hotels, ski shops and especially vast chunks of real estate in places like Aspen.

After a savage, fire-sucking campaign we lost by only six votes, out of 1200. Actually we lost by one vote, but five of our absentee ballots didn't get here in time – primarily because they were mailed (to places like Mexico and Nepal and Guatemala) five days before the election.

We came very close to winning control of the town, and that was the crucial difference between our action in Aspen and, say, Norman Mailer's campaign in New York – which was clearly doomed from the start. At the time of Edwards campaign we were not conscious of any precedent ... and even now, in calm retrospect, the only similar effort that comes to mind is Bob Scheer's 1966 run for a US Congress seat in Berkeley/Oakland – when he challenged liberal Jeffrey Cohelan and lost by something like two per cent of the vote. Other than that, most radical attempts to get into electoral politics have been colourful, fore-doomed efforts in the style of the Mailer-Breslin gig.

This same essential difference is already evident in 1970, with the sudden rash of assaults on various sheriffs' fiefs. Stew Albert got 65,000 votes in Berkeley, running on a neo-hippie platform, but there was never any question of his winning. Another notable exception was David Pierce, a thirty-year-old lawyer who was actually elected mayor of Richmond (pop. 100,000 plus), California, in 1964. Pierce mustered a huge black ghetto vote – mainly on the basis of his lifestyle and his promise to 'bust Standard Oil'. He served, and in fact ran, the city for three years – but in 1967 he suddenly abandoned everything to move to a monastery in Nepal. He is now in Turkey, *en route* to Aspen and then California, where he plans to run for governor.

Another was Oscar Acosta, a brown power candidate for sheriff of Los Angeles County, who pulled 110,000 votes out of something like two million.

Meanwhile in Lawrence, Kansas, George Kimball (defence minister for the local White Panther party) has already won the Democratic primary – running unopposed – but he expects to lose the general election by at least ten to one.

On the strength of the Edwards showing, I had decided to surpass my pledge and run for sheriff, and when both Kimball and Acosta visited Aspen recently, they were amazed to find that I actually expect to *win* my race. A preliminary canvass shows me running well ahead of the Democratic incumbent, and only slightly behind the Republican challenger.

The root point is that Aspen's political situation is so volatile – as a result of the Joe Edwards campaign – that *any* freak power candidate is now a possible winner.

In my case, for instance, I will have to work very hard – and spew out some really heinous ideas during my campaign – to get *less* than thirty per cent of the vote in a three-way race. And an underground candidate who really wanted to win could assume, from the start, a working nut of about forty per cent of the electorate – with his chances of victory riding almost entirely on his backlash potential; or how much active fear and loathing his candidacy might provoke among the burghers who have controlled local candidates for so long.

The possibility of victory can be a heavy millstone around the neck of any political candidate who might prefer, in his heart, to spend his main energies on a series of terrifying, whiplash assaults on everything the voters hold dear. There are harsh echoes of the *Magic Christian* in this technique: The candidate first creates an impossible psychic maze, then he drags the voters into it and flails them constantly with gibberish and rude shocks. This was Mailer's technique, and it got him 55,000 votes in a city of ten million people – but in truth it is more a form of vengeance than electoral politics. Which is not to say that it can't be effective, in Aspen or anywhere else, but as a political strategy it is tainted by a series of disastrous defeats.

In any event, the *Magic Christian* concept is one side of the 'new politics' coin. It doesn't work, but it's fun ... unlike that coin's other face that emerged in the presidential campaign of Gene McCarthy and Bobby Kennedy in 1968. In both cases, we saw establishment candidates *claiming conversion* to some newer and younger state of mind (or political reality) that would make them more in tune with a newer, younger and weirder electorate that had previously called them both useless.

And it worked. Both conversions were hugely successful, for a while

... and if the tactic itself seemed cynical, it is still hard to know, in either case, whether the tactic was father to the conversion, or vice-versa. Which hardly matters, for now. We are talking about political-action formats: if the *Magic Christian* concept is one, then the Kennedy/McCarthy format has to qualify as another ... particularly as the national Democratic Party is already working desperately to make it work again in 1972, when the Demos' only hope of unseating Nixon will again be some shrewd establishment candidate on the brink of menopause who will suddenly start dropping acid in late 71 and then hit the rock-festival trail in the summer of 72. He will doff his shirt at every opportunity and his wife will burn her bra ... and millions of the young will vote for him, against Nixon.

Or will they? There is still another format, and this is the one we stumbled on in Aspen. Why not challenge the establishment with a candidate they've never heard of? Who has never been primed or prepped or greased for public office? And whose lifestyle is already so weird that the idea of 'conversion' would never occur to him?

In other words, why not run an honest freak and turn him loose, on *their* turf, to show up all the 'normal' candidates for the worthless losers they are and always have been? Why defer to the bastards? Why assume they're intelligent? Why believe they won't crack and fold in a crunch? (When the Japs went into Olympic volleyball they ran a blitz on everybody using strange but maddeningly legal techniques like the 'Jap roll', the 'dink spike' and the 'lightning belly pass' that reduced their taller opponents to screaming jelly.)

This is the essence of what some people call 'the Aspen technique' in politics: neither opting out of the system, nor working within it ... but calling its bluff, by using its strength to turn it back on itself ... and by always assuming that the people in power are not smart. By the end of the Edwards campaign, I was convinced, despite my lifelong bias to the contrary, that the law was actually on our side. Not the cops, or the judges or the politicians – but the actual law, itself, as printed in the dull and musty lawbooks that we constantly had to consult because we had no other choice.

But in November of 69 we had no time for this kind of theory-talk or thinking. I remember a list of books I wanted to get and read, in order to learn something about politics, but I barely had time to sleep, much less to do any reading. As the *de facto* campaign manager, I felt like a man who had started some kind of bloody gang-fight by accident ... and as the Edwards campaign grew crazier and more vicious, my only real concern was to save my own ass by warding off a disaster. I didn't know Edwards at all, but by mid-October I felt personally responsible for his future – and his prospects, at that point, were not good. Bill Dunaway, the 'liberal' publisher of the Aspen *Times*, told me on the morning of election that I had 'singlehandedly destroyed Joe Edwards' legal career in Aspen' by 'forcing him into politics'.

This was the liberal myth – that some drug-addled egomaniac writer from Woody Creek had run amok on horse-tranquillizers, and then laid his bad trip on the local head population ... who were normally quite peaceful and harmless, as long as they had enough drugs. But now, for some goddamn reason, they had gone completely wild – and they were dragging poor Edwards down with them.

Right ... poor Edwards: He was recently divorced and living with his girlfriend in a local garret, half-starving for income in a town full of lame dilettante lawyers, and his name was completely unknown except as 'that bastard who sued the city' a year earlier, on behalf of two long-hairs who claimed the cops were discriminating against them. Which was true, and the lawsuit had a terrible effect on the local police. The Chief (now a candidate for sheriff) had quit or been fired in a rage, leaving his patrolmen on probation to a federal judge in Denver – who put the suit in limbo, while warning the Aspen cops that he would bust the city severely at the first sign of 'discriminatory law enforcement' against hippies.

This lawsuit had severe repercussions in Aspen: The mayor was shackled, the City Council lost its will to live, the City Magistrate, Guido Meyer, was fired instantly – even before the Police Chief – and the local cops suddenly stopped busting longhairs for things like 'blocking the sidewalk', which carried a ninety-day jail sentence that summer, along with a $200 fine.

That bullshit stopped at once, and it has stayed stopped – thanks entirely to Edwards' lawsuit; the local liberals called an ACLU meeting, and let it go at that. So only a waterhead could have been surprised when, a year later, a handful of us in search of a mayor candidate decided to call on Joe Edwards. Why not? It made perfect sense – except to the liberals, who were not quite comfortable with a freak power candidate. They didn't mind Edwards, they said, and they even agreed with his platform – which we had carefully carved to their tastes – but there was something very ominous, they felt, about the 'rabble' support he was getting: not the kind of people one really wanted to sip vichyssoise with – wild heads, bikers and anarchists who didn't know Stevenson and hated Hubert Humphrey. Who were these people? What did they want?

What indeed? The local businessmen's bund was not puzzled. Joe Edwards, to them, was the leader of a Communist drug plot to destroy their way of life, sell LSD to their children and Spanish fly to their wives. Never mind that many of their children were already selling LSD to each other, and that most of their wives couldn't get humped on a bad night in Juarez ... that was all beside the point. The *point* was that a gang of freaks was about to take over the town.

And why not? We had never denied it. Not even in the platform – which was public, and quite mild. But somewhere around the middle of the Edwards campaign even the liberals got a whiff of what his platform really meant. They could see a storm gathering behind it, that our carefully reasoned words were only an opening wedge for drastic action. They knew, from long experience, that a word like 'ecology' can mean almost anything – and to most of them it meant spending one day a year with a neighbourhood clean-up crew, picking up beer cans and sending them back to Coors for a refund that would be sent, of course, to their favourite charity.

But 'ecology', to us, meant something else entirely: We had in mind a deluge of brutally restrictive actions that would permanently cripple not only the obvious landrapers but also that quiet cabal of tweedy / liberal speculators who insist on dealing in private, so as not to foul the image ... Like Armand Bartos, the New York 'art patron' and jet-set fashion-pacer often hummed in *Women's Wear Daily* ... who is also the owner/builder and oft-cursed landlord of Aspen's biggest and ugliest trailer court. The place is called 'Gerbazdale', and some of the tenants insist that Bartos raises their rents every time he decides to buy another pop art original.

'I'm tired of financing that asshole's art collection,' said one. 'He's one of the most blatant goddamn slumlords in the western world. He milks us out here, then gives our rent money to shitheads like Warhol.'

Bartos is in the same league with Wilton 'Wink' Jaffee Jr – a New York stockbroker recently suspended for unethical manipulation of the market. Jaffee has taken great pains to cultivate his image, in Aspen, as that of an arty-progressive Eastern aesthete. But when the SEC zapped him, he responded by quickly leasing a chunk of his vast ranch – between Aspen and Woods Creek – to a high-powered gravel-crushing operation from Grand Junction, which immediately began grinding up the earth and selling it, by the ton, to the State Highway Department. And now, after destroying the earth and fouling the Roaring Fork River, the swine are demanding a zoning variance so they can build an asphalt plant ... on the elegant Aspen estate that Wink Jaffee no doubt describes quite often to his progressive friends on Wall Street.

These, and others like them, are the kind of shysters and horsey hypocrites who pass for 'liberals' in Aspen. So we were not surprised when many of them made a point of withdrawing their support about halfway through Edwards' campaign. At first they had liked our words and our fiery underdog stance (fighting the good fight in another hopeless cause, etc.), but when Edwards began looking like a winner, our liberal allies panicked.

By noon on election day, the only real question was how many liberals had hung on. A few had come over, as it were, but those few were not enough to form the other half of the nervous power base we had counted on from the start. The original idea had been to lash together a one-shot coalition and demoralize the local money/politics establishment by winning a major election before the enemy knew what was happening. Aspen's liberals are a permanent minority who have never won *anything*, despite their constant struggles ... and Aspen's fabled 'underground' is a far larger minority that has never even *tried* to win anything.

So *power* was our first priority. The platform – or at least our public version of it – was too intentionally vague to be anything but a flexible, secondary tool for wooing the liberals and holding our coalition. On the other hand, not even the handful of people in the power nexus of Joe Edwards' campaign could guarantee that he could start sodding the streets and flaying the sheriff just as soon as he got elected. He was, after all, a lawyer – an evil trade, at best – and I think we all knew, although nobody ever said it, that we really had no idea what the bastard might do if he got elected. For all we knew he could turn into a vicious monster and have us all jailed for sedition.

None of us even *knew* Joe Edwards. For weeks we had joked about our 'ghost candidate' who emerged from time to time to insist that he was the helpless creature of some mysterious political machine that had caused his phone to ring one Saturday at midnight, and told him he was running for Mayor.

Which was more or less true. I had called him in a frenzy, full of booze and resentment at a rumour that a gaggle of local powermongers had already met and decided who Aspen's next mayor would be – a giddy old lady would run unopposed behind some kind of lunatic obscenity they called a 'united front', or 'progressive solidarity' – endorsed by Leon Uris, who is Aspen's leading stag movie fan, and who writes books, like *Exodus*, to pay his bills. I was sitting in Peggy Clifford's living room when I heard about it, and, as I recall, we both agreed that the fuckers had gone too far this time.

Someone suggested Ross Griffin, a retired ski-bum and lifelong mountain beatnik who was going half-straight at the time and talking about running for the City Council ... but a dozen or so trial-balloon calls convinced us that Ross wasn't quite weird enough to galvanize the street vote, which we felt would be absolutely necessary. (As it turned out, we were wrong: Griffin ran for the council and won by a huge margin in a ward full of heads.)

But at the time it seemed necessary to come up with a candidate whose strange tastes and para-legal behaviour were absolutely beyond question ... a man whose candidacy would torture the outer limits of political gall, whose name would strike fear and shock in the heart of every burgher, and whose massive unsuitability for the job would cause even the most apolitical drug-child in the town's most degenerate commune to shout, 'Yes! I must *vote* for that man!'

Joe Edwards didn't quite fill that bill. He was a bit too straight for the acid-people, and a little too strange for the liberals – but he was the only candidate even marginally acceptable on both ends of our un-tried coalition spectrum. And twenty-four hours after our first jangled phone talk about 'running for Mayor' he said, 'Fuck it, why not?'

The next day was Sunday and *The Battle of Algiers* was playing at the Wheeler Opera House. We agreed to meet afterwards, on the street, but the hook-up was difficult, because I didn't know what he looked like. So we ended up milling around for a while, casting sidelong glances at each other, and I remember thinking, Jesus, could that be *him* over there? That scurvy-looking geek with the shifty eyes? Shit, he'll never win anything ...

Finally after awkward introductions, we walked down to the old Jerome Hotel and ordered some beers sent out to the lobby, where we could talk privately. Our campaign juggernaut, that night, consisted of me, Jim Salter and Mike Solheim – but we all assured Edwards that we were only the tip of the iceberg that was going to float him straight into the sea-lanes of big-time power politics. In fact, I sensed that both Solheim and Salter were embarrassed to find themselves there – assuring some total stranger that all he had to do was say the word and we would make him Mayor of Aspen.

None of us had even a beginner's knowledge of how to run a political campaign. Salter writes screenplays (*Downhill Racer*) and books (*A Sport and a Pastime*). Solheim used to own an elegant bar called Leadville, in Ketchum, Idaho, and his Aspen gig is housepainting. For my part, I had lived about ten miles out of town for two years, doing everything possible to avoid Aspen's feverish reality. My lifestyle, I felt, was not entirely suited for doing battle with any small-town political establishment. They had left me alone, not hassled my friends (with two unavoidable exceptions – both lawyers), and consistently ignored all rumours of madness and violence in my area. In return, I had consciously avoided writing about Aspen ... and in my very limited congress with the local authorities I was treated like some kind of half-mad cross between a hermit and a wolverine, a thing best left alone as long as possible.

So the 69 campaign was perhaps a longer step for me than it was for Joe Edwards. He had already tasted political conflict and he seemed to dig it. But my own involvement amounted to the wilful shattering of what had been, until then, a very comfortable truce ... and looking back I'm still not sure what launched me. Probably it was Chicago – that brain-raping week in August of 68. I went to the Democratic Convention as a journalist, and returned a raving beast.

For me, that week in Chicago was far worse than the worst bad acid trip I'd even heard rumours about. It permanently altered my brain chemistry, and my first new idea – when I finally calmed down – was an absolute conviction there was no possibility for any personal truce, for me, in a nation that could hatch and be proud of a malignant monster like Chicago. Suddenly, it seemed imperative to get a grip on those who had somehow slipped into power and caused the thing to happen.

But who were they? Was Mayor Daley a cause, or a symptom? Lyndon Johnson was finished, Hubert Humphrey was doomed, McCarthy was broken, Kennedy was dead, and that left only Nixon, that pompous, plastic little fart who would soon be our President. I went to Washington for his inauguration, hoping for a terrible shitrain that would pound the White House to splinters. But it didn't happen; no shitrain, no justice ... and Nixon was finally in charge.

So in truth it was probably a sense of impending doom, of horror at politics in general, that goaded me into my role in the Edwards campaign. The reasons came later, and even now they seem hazy. Some people call politics fun, and maybe it is when you're winning. But even then it's a mean kind of fun, and more like the rising edge of a speed trip than anything peaceful or pleasant. Real happiness, in politics, is a wide-open hammer shot on some poor bastard who knows he's been trapped, but can't flee.

The Edwards campaign was more an uprising than a movement. We had nothing to lose: we were like a bunch of wild-eyed amateur mechanics rolling a homemade racing car on to the track at Indianapolis and watching it overtake a brace of big Offenhausers at the 450 pole. There were two distinct phases in the month-long Edwards campaign. For the first two weeks we made a lot of radical noise and embarrassed our friends and discovered that most of the people we had counted on were absolutely useless.

So nobody was ready for the second phase, when the thing began coming together like a conquered jigsaw puzzle. Our evening strategy meetings in the Jerome Bar were suddenly crowded with people demanding a piece of the action. We were inundated with $5 and $10 contributions from people whom none of us knew. From Bob Krueger's tiny darkroom and Bill Noonan's angry efforts to collect enough money to pay for a full-page ad in Dunaway's liberal *Times*, we suddenly inherited all the facilities of the 'Center of the Eye' Photography School and an unlimited credit-line (after Dunaway fled to the Bahamas) from Steve Herron at the *Times*-owned radio station, then the only one in town. (Several months after the election a twenty-four-hour FM station began broadcasting – with daytime Muzak balanced off against a late-night freak-rock gig as heavy as anything in SF or LA.) With no local television, the radio was our equivalent of a high-powered TV campaign. And it provoked the same kind of surly reaction that has been shrugged off, on both coasts, by US Senate candidates such as Ottinger (NY) and Tunney (Calif.).

That comparison is purely technical. The radio spots we ran in Aspen would have terrified political eunuchs like Tunney and Ottinger. Our theme song was Herbie Mann's 'Battle Hymn of the Republic', which we ran over and over again – as a doleful background to very heavy raps and evil mockery of the retrograde opposition. They bitched and groaned, accusing us in their ignorance of 'using Madison Avenue techniques', while in truth it was pure Lenny Bruce. But they didn't know Lenny; their humour was still Bob Hope, with a tangent taste for Don Rickles here and there among the handful of swingers who didn't mind admitting that they dug the stag movies, on weekends, at Leon Uris' home on Red Mountain.

We enjoyed skewering those bastards. Our radio wizard, an ex-nightclub comic, Phil Clark, made several spots that caused people to foam at the mouth and chase their tails in impotent rage. There was a thread of high, wild humour in the Edwards campaign, and that was what kept us all sane. There was a definite satisfaction in knowing that, even if we lost, whoever beat us would never get rid of the scars. It was necessary, we felt, to thoroughly terrify our opponents, so that even in hollow victory, they would learn to fear every sunrise until the next election.

This worked out nicely – or at least effectively, and by the spring of 1970 it was clear on all fronts, that Aspen's traditional power structure was no longer in command of the town. The new City Council quickly broke down to a permanent 3–4 split, with Ned Vare as the spokesman for one side and a Bircher-style dentist named Comcowich taking care of the other. This left Eve Homeyer, who had campaigned with the idea that the mayor was 'only a figurehead', in the nasty position of having to cast a tie-breaking vote on every controversial issue. The first few were minor, and she voted her Agnew-style convictions in each case ... but the public reaction was ugly, and after a while the council lapsed into a kind of nervous stalemate, with neither side anxious to bring *anything* to a vote. The realities of a small-town politics are so close to the bone that there is no way to avoid getting cursed in the streets, by somebody, for any vote you cast. An alderman in Chicago can insulate himself almost completely from the people he votes against, but there is no escape in a place the size of Aspen.

The same kind of tension began popping up on other fronts: The local high school principal tried to fire a young teacher for voicing a left-wing political bias in the classroom, but her students went on strike and not only forced the teacher's reinstatement but very nearly got the principal fired. Shortly after that, Ned Vare and a local lawyer named Shellman savaged the State Highway Department so badly that all plans to bring the four-lane highway through town were completely de-funded. This drove the County Commissioners into a filthy funk; the highway had been their pet project, but suddenly it was screwed, doomed ... by the same gang of bastards who had caused all the trouble last fall.

The Aspen Medical Center was filled with cries of rage and anguish. Comcowich the twisted dentist rushed out of his office in that building and punched a young freak off his bicycle, screeching: 'You dirty little motherfucker we're going to run you all out of town!' Then he fled back inside, to his office across the hall from that of the good Dr Barnard (Buggsy) and his like-minded cohort Dr J. Sterling Baxter.

For five years these two had controlled Aspen's affairs with a swagger that mixed sports cars and speed with mistresses and teenyboppers and a cavalier disdain for the amenities of the medical profession. Buggsy handled the municipal action, while Baxter ran the county, and for five fairly placid years the Aspen Medical Center was Aspen's Tammany Hall. Buggsy dug his Mayor's act immensely. From time to time he would run amok and abuse his power disgracefully, but in general he handled it well. His friends were many and varied – ranging from dope dealers and outlaw bikers to district judges and horse-traders ... even me, and in fact it never crossed my mind that Buggsy would be anything but a tremendous help when we kicked off the Edwards campaign. It seemed entirely logical that an *old* freak would want to pass the torch to a *young* freak ...

Instead, he refused to go gracefully, and rather than helping Edwards he tried to destroy him. At one point Barnard actually tried to get back into the race himself, and when that didn't work he shoved in a last-minute dummy. This was poor Oates, who went down – along with Buggsy – to an ignominious defeat. We beat them stupid, and Barnard couldn't believe it. Shortly after the polls closed, he went down to City Hall and stared balefully at the blackboard when the clerk started posting the returns. The first figures stunned him visibly, they said, and by ten o'clock he was raving incoherently about 'fraud' and 'recounts' and 'those dirty bastards who turned on me'.

One of his friends who was there recalls it as a very heavy scene ... although Dylan Thomas might have dug it, for the Mayor is said to have raged horribly against the dying of the light.

And so much for what might have been a very sad story ... except that Buggsy went home that night and began laying feverish plans to become Mayor of Aspen again. His new power base is a thing called the Taxpayers' League, a sort of reverse-élite corps of the booziest Elks and Eagles, whose only real point of agreement is that every animal in this world that has walked on two legs for less than fifty years is evil, queer and dangerous. The Taxpayers' League is a really classic example of what anthropologists call an 'atavistic endeavour'. On the scale of political development, they are still flirting with Senator Bilbo's dangerously progressive proposal to send all the niggers back to Africa on a fleet of iron barges.

This is Buggsy's new constituency. They are not *all* vicious drunks, and not *all* mental defectives either. Some are genuinely confused and frightened at what seems to be the end of the world as they know it. And this is sad, too ... but the saddest thing of all is that, in the context of this article, the Taxpayers' League is not irrelevant. In the past six months this group has emerged as the most consistently effective voting bloc in the valley. They have beaten the liberals handily in every recent encounter (none crucial) that came down, in the end, to a matter of who had the muscle.

Who indeed? The liberals simply can't get it up ... and since the end of the Edwards campaign we have deliberately avoided any effort to mobilize the freak power bloc. The political attention span of the average dropout is too short, we felt, to blow it on anything minor. Nearly everyone who worked on the Edwards gig last year was convinced that he would have won easily if the election had been held on 14 November instead of 4 November ... or if we'd started whipping our act together even a week earlier.

Maybe so, but I doubt it. The idea assumes that we had *control* of the thing – but we didn't. The campaign was out of control from beginning to end and the fact that it peaked on election day was a perfect accident, a piece of luck that we couldn't have planned. By the time the polls opened we had fired just about every shot we had. There was nothing left to do, on election day, except deal with Buggsy's threats – and that was done before noon. Beyond that, I don't recall that we did much – until just before the polls closed – except drive around town at high speed and drink vast amounts of beer.

There is no point even hoping for that kind of luck again this year. We began organizing in mid-August – six weeks earlier than last time – and unless we can pace the thing perfectly we might find ourselves limp and burned out two weeks before the election. I have a nightmare vision of our whole act coming to a massive orgiastic climax on 25 October: two thousand costumed freaks doing the schottische, in perfect unison, in front of the County Courthouse ... sweating, weeping, chanting ... 'Vote NOW! Vote NOW.' Demanding the ballot *at once*, completely stoned on politics, too high and strung out to even recognize their candidate, Ned Vare, when he appears on the courthouse steps and shouts for them all to back off: 'Go back to your homes! You can't vote for ten more days!' The mob responds with a terrible roar, then surges forward ... Vare disappears ...

I turn to flee, but the Sheriff is there with a huge rubber sack that he quickly flips over my head and places me under arrest for felony conspiracy. The elections are cancelled and J. Sterling Baxter places the town under martial law, with himself in total command ...

Baxter is both the symbol and the reality of the old/ugly/corrupt political machine that we hope to crack in November. He will be working from a formidable power base: a coalition of Buggsy's 'Taxpayers' and Comcowich's right-wing suburbanites – along with heavy institutional support from both banks, the Contractors' Association and the all-powerful Aspen Ski Corporation. He will also have the financing and organizing resources of the local GOP, which outnumbers the Democrats more than two to one in registrations.

The Democrats, with an eye on the probability of another Edwards-style uprising on the left, are running a political transvestite, a middle-aged realtor whom they will try to promote as a 'sensible alternative' to the menacing 'extremes' posed by Baxter and Ned Vare. The incumbent Sheriff is also a Democrat.

Vare is running as an Independent and his campaign symbol, he says, will be 'a tree'. For the Sheriff's campaign, my symbol will be either a horribly deformed cyclops owl, or a double-thumbed fist, clutching a peyote button, which is also the symbol of our general strategy and organizing cabal, the Meat Possum Athletic Club. At the moment I am registered as an Independent, but there is still the possibility – pending the outcome of current negotiations for campaign financing – that I may file for office as a Communist. It will make no difference which label I adopt; the die is already cast in my race – and the only remaining question is how many Freaks, heads, criminals, anarchists, beatniks, poachers, wobblies, bikers and persons of weird persuasion will come out of their holes and vote for me. The alternatives are depressingly obvious: my opponents are hopeless bums who would be more at home on the Mississippi State Highway Patrol ... and, if elected, I promise to recommend them both for the kind of jobs they deserve.

Ned Vare's race is both more complex and far more important than mine. He is going after the dragon. Jay Baxter is the most powerful political figure in the county. He is *the* County Commissioner; the other two are echoes. If Vare can beat Baxter that will snap the spine of the local/money/politics establishment ... and if freak power can do that in Aspen, it can also do it in other places. But if it *can't* be done here, one of the few places in America where we can work off a proven power base – then it is hard to imagine it working in any other place with fewer natural advantages. Last fall we came within six votes, and it will probably be close again this time. Memories of the Edwards campaign will guarantee a heavy turnout, with a dangerous backlash factor that could wipe us out completely unless the head population can get itself together and actually *vote*. Last year perhaps the heads voted; this year we will need them all. The ramifications of this election go far beyond any local issues or candidates. It is an experiment with a totally new kind of political muscle ... and the results, either way, will definitely be worth pondering.

TENTATIVE PLATFORM
THOMPSON FOR SHERIFF
ASPEN, COLORADO, 1970

1 Sod the streets at once. Rip up all city streets with jackhammers and use the junkasphalt (after melting) to create a huge parking and auto-storage lot on the outskirts of town – preferably somewhere out of sight, like between the new sewage plant and McBride's new shopping centre. All refuse and other garbage could be centralized in this area – in memory of Mrs Walter Paepke, who sold the land for development. The only automobiles allowed into town would be limited to a network of 'delivery-alleys', as shown in the very detailed plan drawn by architect/planner Fritz Benedict in 1969. All public movement would be by foot and a fleet of bicycles, maintained by the city police force.
2 Change the name 'Aspen', by public referendum, to 'Fat City'. This would prevent greedheads, land-rapers and other human jackals from capitalizing on the name 'Aspen'. Thus, Snowmass-at-Aspen – recently sold to Kaiser/Aetna of Oakland – would become 'Snowmass-at-Fat City'. Aspen Wildcat – whose main backers include the First National City Bank of New York and the First Boston Capital Corp. – would-

have to be called 'Fat City Wildcat'. All roadsigns and roadmaps would have to be changed from Aspen to 'Fat City'. The local post office and chamber of commerce would have to honour the new name. 'Aspen', Colo. would no longer exist – and the psychic alterations of this change would be massive in the world of commerce: Fat City Ski Fashions, the Fat City Slalom Cup, Fat City Music Festival, Fat City Institute for Humanistic Studies ... etc. And the main advantage here is that changing the name of the town would have no major effect on the town itself, or on those people who came here because it's a good place to *live*. What effect the name-change might have on those who came here to buy low, sell high and then move on is fairly obvious ... and eminently desirable. These swine should be fucked, broken and driven across the land.

3 Drug sales must be controlled. My first act as sheriff will be to install, on the courthouse lawn, a bastinado platform and a set of stocks – in order to punish dishonest dope dealers in a proper public fashion. Each year these dealers cheat millions of people out of millions of dollars. As a breed, they rank with sub-dividers and used car salesmen and the Sheriff's Dept will gladly hear complaints against dealers at any hour of the day or night, with immunity from prosecution guaranteed to the complaining party – provided the complaint is valid. (It should be noted, on this point in the platform, that any sheriff of any county in Colorado is legally responsible for enforcing *all* state laws regarding drugs – even those few he might personally disagree with. The statutes provide for malfeasance penalties up to $100 in each instance, in cases of wilful nonenforcement ... but it should also be noted that the statutes provide for many other penalties, in many other strange and unlikely circumstances, and as sheriff I shall make myself aware of *all* of them, without exception. So any vengeful, ill-advised dingbat who might presume to bring malfeasance charges against my office should be quite sure of his/her facts ...) And in the meantime, it will be the general philosophy of the sheriff's office that *no* drug worth taking should be sold for money. Non-profit sales will be viewed as borderline cases, and judged on their merits. But *all* sales for money-profit will be punished severely. This approach, we feel, will establish a unique and very human *ambiance* in the Aspen (or Fat City) drug culture – which is already so much a part of our local reality that only a falangist lunatic would talk about trying to 'eliminate it'. The only realistic approach is to make life in this town very ugly for *all* profiteers – in drugs and all other fields.

4 Hunting and fishing should be forbidden to *all* non-residents, with the exception of those who can obtain the signed endorsement of a resident – who will then be legally responsible for any violation or abuse committed by the non-resident he has 'signed for'. Fines will be heavy and the general policy will be merciless prosecution of all offenders. But – as in the case of the proposed city name-change – this 'local endorsement' plan should have no effect on anyone except greedy, dangerous kill-freaks who are a menace wherever they go. This new plan would have no effect on residents – except those who chose to *endorse* visiting 'sportsmen'. By this approach – making hundreds or even thousands of individuals personally responsible for protecting the animals, fish and birds who live here – we would create a sort of *de facto* game preserve, without the harsh restrictions that will necessarily be forced on us if these bloodthirsty geeks keep swarming in here each autumn to shoot everything they see.

5 The sheriff and his deputies should *never* be armed in public. Every urban riot, shoot-out and blood-bath (involving guns) in recent memory has been set off by some trigger-happy cop in a fear frenzy. And no cop in Aspen has had to use a gun for so many years that I feel safe in offering a $12 cash award to anybody who can recall such an incident in writing. (Box K-3, Aspen.) Under normal circumstances a pistol-grip Mace-bomb, such as the MK-V made by Gen. Ordnance, is more than enough to quickly wilt any violence problem that is likely to emerge in Aspen. And anything the MK-V can't handle would require reinforcements anyway ... in which case the response would be geared at all times to massive retaliation: a brutal attack with guns, bombs, pepperfoggers, wolverines and all other weapons deemed necessary to restore the civic peace. The whole notion of disarming the police is to *lower* the level of violence – while guaranteeing, at the same time, a terrible punishment to anyone stupid enough to attempt violence on an unarmed cop.

6 It will be the policy of the sheriff's office savagely to harass all those engaged in any form of land-rape. This will be done by acting, with utmost dispatch, on any and all righteous complaints. My first act in office – after setting up the machinery for punishing dope-dealers – will be to establish a research bureau to provide facts on which any citizen can file a writ of seizure, a writ of stoppage, a writ of fear, of horror ... yes ... even a writ of assumption ... against any greedhead who has managed to get around our antiquated laws and set up a tar-vat, scum-drain or gravel-pit. These writs will be pursued with overweening zeal ... and always within the letter of the law. Selah.

Rolling Stone no. 67, 1 October 1970

MEMO FROM THE SPORTS DESK:
THE SO-CALLED 'JESUS FREAK' SCARE

A recent emergency survey of our field-sources indicates a firestorm of lunacy brewing on the neo-religious front. Failure to prepare for this madness could tax our resources severely – perhaps to the breaking point. During the next few months we will almost certainly be inundated, even swamped, by a nightmare-blizzard of schlock, gibberish, swill & pseudo-religious bullshit of every type and description. We can expect no relief until after Christmas. This problem will manifest itself in many treacherous forms – and we will have to deal with them all. To wit:

1 The mailroom will be paralysed by wave after wave of pamphlets, records, warnings and half-mad screeds from persons and/or commercial organizations attempting to cash in on this grisly shuck. So we have already made arrangements to establish an alternative mailroom, to handle our serious business.

2 We expect the main elevators to be jammed up, day and night, by a never-ending swarm of crazies attempting to drag huge wooden crosses and other over-sized gimcracks into the building. To circumvent this, we are even now in the process of installing a powerful glass/cube electric lift on the *exterior* of the building for employee/business & general editorial use. The ingress/egress door will be cut in the east wall, behind Dave Felton's cubicle. The ground-floor door will be disguised as a huge packing crate in the parking lot. An armed guard will be on duty at all times.

3 We expect the phone lines to be tied up almost constantly by hired and/or rabid *Jesus freaks* attempting to get things like 'Today's Prayer Message', etc., into our editorial columns. Our policy will be *not* to reject these things: No, we will *accept* them. They will all be switched to a special automated phone-extension in the basement of the building. Yail Bloor, the eminent theologist, has prepared a series of recorded replies for calls of this nature. Any callers who resist automation can leave their names & numbers, so Inspector Bloor can return their calls and deal with them personally between the hours of 2 and 6 a.m.

These are only a few of the specific horrors that we will have to come to grips with between now and September. There will, of course, be others – less tangible and far more sensitive – such as subversion of key personnel. As always, there will be a few brainless scumbags going under

– succumbing, as it were – to the lure of this latest cult. We expect this, and when these organizational blow-holes appear, they will be *plugged* with extreme speed & savagery.

It is the view of the Sports Desk that a generation of failed dingbats and closet-junkies should under no circumstances be allowed to foul our lines of communication at a time when anybody with access to a thinking/nationwide audience has an almost desperate obligation to speak *coherently*. This is not the year for a mass reversion to atavistic bullshit – and particularly not in the pages of *Rolling Stone*.

We expect the pressure to mount in geometric progressions from now until December, & then to peak around Christmas. Meanwhile, it is well to remember the words of Dr Heem, one of the few modern-day wizards who has never been wrong. Dr Heem was cursed by Eisenhower, mocked by Kennedy, jeered by Tim Leary and threatened by Eldridge Cleaver. But he is still on the stump . . . still hustling.

'The future of Christianity is far too fragile,' he said recently, 'to be left in the hands of the Christians – especially *pros*.'

The Sports Desk feels very strongly about this. Further warnings will issue, as special problems arise. Which they will. We are absolutely certain of this, if nothing else. What we are faced with today is the same old rising tide that's been coming for the past five years or more . . . the same old evil, menacing, frog-eyed trip of a whole generation run amok from too many failures.

Which is fine. It was long overdue. And once again in the words of Dr Heem, 'Sometimes the old walls are so cock-eyed that you can't even fit a new window.' But the trouble with the *Jesus freak* outburst is that it is less a window than a gigantic Spanish Inquisition, the Salem Witch Trials, the Rape of the Congo and the Conquest of the Incas, the Mayans, and the Aztecs. Entire civilizations have been done in by vengeful monsters claiming a special relationship with 'God'.

What we are dealing with now is nothing less than another empire on the brink of collapse – more than likely of its own bad weight & twisted priorities. This process is already well underway. Everything Nixon stands for is doomed, now or later.

But it will sure as hell be *later* if the best alternative we can mount is a generation of loonies who've given up on everything except a revival of the same old primitive bullshit that caused all our troubles from the start. What a *horror* to think that all the fine, high action of the sixties would somehow come down – ten years later – to a gross & mindless echo of Billy Sunday.

This is why the Sports Desk insists that these waterheads must be kept out of the building at all costs. We have serious business to deal with, and these fuckers will only be in the way.

Sincerely,
Raoul Duke

Rolling Stone no. 90, 2 September 1971

MEMOIRS OF A WRETCHED WEEKEND IN WASHINGTON

One of my clearest memories of that wretched weekend is the sight of Jerry Rubin standing forlornly on the steps of a marble building near the Capitol, watching a gang fight at the base of a flagpole. The 'counter-inaugural' parade had just ended and some of the marchers had decided to finish the show by raping the American flag. Other marchers protested, and soon the two factions were slugging it out.

The flag slipped down the pole a few feet, then went back up as a group of anti-war patriots formed a sort of human anchor on the main pulley-rope. These defenders of the flag were part of the Mobilization Committee to End the War in Vietnam (MOBE), organizers of the 'counter-inaugural' ... the liberal, pacifist collegiate wing of the protest. The attackers, screaming 'Tear the damn thing down,' were a wild and disorganized hellbroth of young streetfighters, ranging from local SDS militants to a motorcycle gang called the 'Huns'. There were blacks on both sides of the argument, but most of the fist-action involved young whites.

As I backed away from the brawl, two dogs began fighting behind me and a march leader shouting 'Peace!' into his bullhorn was attacked by a freak wearing a Prussian helmet. The anti-war parade had turned savagely on itself.

Rubin, a Yippie organizer and veteran of every major protest since the first Berkeley uprising in 1964, was staring at the chaos around the flagpole. 'Awful,' he muttered: 'This whole thing is depressing ... no life, no direction ... this may be the last demonstration.'

His words echoed a notion I'd just scribbled in my notebook: 'No more singing, no more speeches, farewell to all that ...'. I understood what Rubin meant; our paths had crossed constantly in the past four years, from the Bay Area to Chicago ... always on different levels of

189

involvement, he as a central figure and I as a journalist ... but now, in 1969, it was obvious to both of us that the scene had changed drastically.

Violence and confrontation are the themes now. The whole concept of 'peaceful protest' died in Chicago, at the Democratic Convention. Nobody invited Joan Baez to Washington; nobody sang 'We Shall Overcome'. There were other, newer slogans here, like 'Kill the Pigs!' '—— the War', and 'Two-Four-Six-Eight ... Organize to Smash the State!' Vicious dissidence is the style. Nobody goes limp. They throw rocks at the cops, then run ... and two minutes later they pop up somewhere else and throw more rocks.

We have come a long way from Berkeley and the Free Speech Movement. There is a new meanness on both sides ... and no more humour.

For Rubin, the change is bitterly personal. As a result of the police riot in Chicago, he is now free on $25,000 bail, charged with solicitation to commit mob action, a felony carrying a possible five-year prison sentence. In the good old days, three months in jail was considered harsh punishment for a protest leader. Now, in the Nixon era, people like Rubin are candidates for the bastinado.

As for me ... well, the change is not yet physical. With press credentials, I usually manage to avoid arrest ... although I suspect that, too, will change in the new era. A press badge or even a notebook is coming to be a liability in the increasingly polarized atmosphere of these civil conflicts. Neutrality is obsolete. The question now, even for a journalist, is 'Which side are you on?' In Chicago I was clubbed by police: In Washington I was menaced by demonstrators.

The inauguration weekend was a king-hell bummer in almost every way. The sight of Nixon taking the oath, the doomed and vicious tone of the protest, constant rain, rivers of mud, an army of rich swineherds jamming the hotel bars, old ladies with blue hair clogging the restaurants ... a horror-show, for sure. Very late one night, listening to the radio in my room I heard a song by The Byrds, with a refrain that went: *'Nobody knows ... what trouble they're in; Nobody thinks ... it might happen again.'* It echoed in my head all weekend, like a theme song for a bad movie ... the Nixon movie.

My first idea was to load up on LSD and cover the inauguration that way, but the possibilities were ominous: a scene that bad could only be compounded to the realm of mega-horrors by something as powerful as acid. No ... it had to be done straight, or at least with a few joints in calm moments ... like fast-stepping across the Mall, bearing down on the Smithsonian Institution with a frenzied crowd chanting obscenities about Spiro Agnew ... mounted police shouting 'Back! Back!' ... and the man next to me, an accredited New York journalist, hands me a weird cigarette, saying, 'Why not? It's all over anyway ...'

Indeed. He was right. From my point of view – and presumably from his – it was all over. Richard Nixon had finally become President. All around us these eighteen- and nineteen-year-old loonies were throwing firecrackers and garbage at the mounted police. From inside the Smithsonian, Agnew's people were looking out, crowded against the doorway glass, watching the mob as it menaced late-arriving guests. A cop lost his temper and rushed into the crowd to seize an agitator ... and that was the last we saw of him for about three minutes. When he emerged, after a dozen others had rushed in to save him, he looked like some ragged hippie ... the mob had stripped him of everything except his pants, one boot, and part of his coat. His hat was gone, his gun and gunbelt, all his badges and police decorations ... he was a beaten man and his name was Lennox. I know this because I was standing beside the big plainclothes police boss who was shouting, 'Get Lennox in the van!'

Lennox was not in full control of himself; he was screaming around like a guinea hen just worked over by a pack of wild dogs. The supervisor bore down on him, raging at the spectacle of a chewed-up cop running around in full view of the press and the mob ... adding insult to injury. They put Lennox in the van and we never saw him again.

How could this happen? With Spiro Agnew and his guests looking out from the elegant museum on the eve of his inauguration as Vice-President of the US, a mob of dissident 'pacifists' mauls a cop assigned to protect the party. This man Lennox had read too many old newspapers, too many reports about 'cowardly, non-violent demonstrators'. So he rushed in to grab one of them – to enforce the law – and they nearly did him in. A man standing next to the action said: 'They took turns kicking him in the head.' They tore everything off of him – thirty more seconds and they'd have stripped him completely naked.'

Rotten behaviour, no doubt about it. Several hours later, riding in a cab in another part of Washington, I told the black cabbie what had happened. 'Beautiful, beautiful,' he said. 'I used to be on the force and I was ready to go back ... but not now; hell, I don't want to be a public enemy.'

I went to the inauguration for several reasons, but mainly to be sure it wasn't a TV trick. It seemed impossible that it could actually happen: President Nixon. *En route* to Washington, crossing the Rockies in a big jet with a drink in my hand I wrote in my notebook: 'One year later, flying east again to cover Nixon ... last time it was to New York and then on the Yellowbird Special to Manchester, New Hampshire ... to Nixon headquarters at the Holiday Inn, greeted by speechwriter Pat Buchanan who didn't approve of my garb ... Mistah Nixon, he doan like ski jackets, boy – and where's yore tie? Buchanan, a rude suspicious geek, liberty-lobby type ... but now he's in Washington, and so is the boss.'

All the staffers called him 'the boss'. His speeches and campaign appearances were called 'drills'. I'm not sure what they called me, but it must have been ugly. Here is an excerpt from the article I wrote after following him around New Hampshire for ten days:

Richard Nixon has never been one of my favourite people. He was ... a man with no soul, no inner convictions ... The 'old Nixon' didn't make it. Neither did earlier models of the 'new Nixon'. So now we have 'Nixon mark IV', and as a journalist I suppose it's only fair to say that this latest model might be different and maybe even better in some ways. But as a customer, I wouldn't touch it – except with a long cattle prod.

So now, a year later, I was going to Washington to see my President inaugurated. 'Bring us together again.' Well ... good luck, old sport ... but I think I'll just drop out for a while. Give me a ring when you get the others together ... I'll come over and take a group photo with my snorkel camera.

At the Baltimore airport I ran into Bob Gover, arriving from New Orleans with a new wife and a big movie camera. Gover is a writer (*One Hundred Dollar Misunderstanding*, among others), but he's into a film gig now, making a movie of the impending revolution that he thinks will be out in the open before 1970. Not everyone involved in 'the movement' is that optimistic; the timetable varies from six months to four years, but there is near-unanimous agreement that some kind of shattering upheaval will occur before 1972 ... not just riots, or closing down universities, but a violent revolution.

This ominous prospect has already cracked the fragile solidarity of the 'new left'. Until now, the war in Vietnam has been a sort of umbrella-issue, providing a semblance of unity to a mixed bag of anti-war groups with little else in common. The 'counter-inaugural' in Washington showed, very clearly, that this alliance is breaking down.

Indeed, the whole scene is polarizing. With Nixon and John Mitchell on the right, drumming for law and order ... and with the blacks and the student left gearing down for revolution ... the centre is almost up for grabs. The only centrist-style heavyweight these days is Senator Ted Kennedy, who seems to be playing the same kind of build and consolidate game that Richard Nixon perfected in 1966.

Kennedy began to haunt Nixon even before he was sworn in. On Saturday, two days before the Inauguration, Teddy dominated local newscasts by unveiling a bust of his murdered brother, Robert, in the courtyard of the Justice Department. Then, two days after the inaugural, Teddy was the star of a big-name fund raising rally at the Washington Hilton. The idea was to pay off Robert's campaign debts, but a local newspaper columnist said it 'looked like the kickoff of Teddy's campaign'. The senator, ever-cautious, was quoted in the Washington *Post* as saying he hadn't picked a Vice President yet, for 1972. Nixon's reaction to this boffo was not reported in the press. The only public comment came from Raoul Duke, a visiting dignitary, who said: 'Well ... nobody laughed when Banquo's ghost came to the party ... and remember the Baltimore Colts.'

In any case, the battle is joined ... Revolution versus the wave of the past. Rumours persist that Mr Nixon remains confident – for reasons not apparent to anyone under fifty, except cops, evangelists and members of the liberty lobby. The rest of us will have to start reading fiction again, or maybe build boats. The demands of this growing polarization – this banshee screaming 'Which side are you on?' – are going to make the Johnson years seem like a peace festival. Anybody who thinks Nixon wrote that soothing inaugural speech should remember the name, Ray Price. He is Nixon's Bill Moyers, and – like Moyers – a good man to watch for signs of a sinking ship. Price is Nixon's house liberal, and when he quits we can look for that era of bloody chaos and streetfighting ... and perhaps even that revolution the wild turks on the new left are waiting for. President Nixon has moved into a vacuum that neither he nor his creatures understand. They are setting up, right now, in the calm eye of a hurricane ... and if they think the winds have died, they are in for a bad shock.

And so are the rest of us, for we are all in that eye – even the young militants of the new left, who are now more disorganized than even the liberal Democrats, who at least have a figurehead. The Washington protest was a bust, despite the claims of the organizers ... and for reasons beyond mud and rain. Jerry Rubin was right: it was probably 'the last demonstration' – or at least the last one in that older, gentler and once-hopeful context.

On Monday night, around dusk, I went back to the big circus tent that had been the scene, just twenty hours earlier of MOBE's counter-inaugural ball. On Sunday night the tent had been a mob scene, with thousands of laughing young dissidents smoking grass and bouncing balloons around in the flashing glare of strobe lights and rock music. Phil Ochs was there, and Paul Krassner ... and Judy Collins sent a telegram saying she couldn't make it but 'keep up the fight' ... the crowd dug it all, and passed the hat for a lot of dollars to pay for the tent rental. A casual observer might have thought it was a victory prank.

Then, after Nixon's parade, I went back to the tent to see what was happening ... and it was gone, or at least going. A six-man crew from the Norfolk Tent Co. had taken down everything but the poles and cables. Thick rolls of blue and white canvas lay around in the mud, waiting to be put on a truck and taken back to the warehouse.

As the tent disappeared, piece by piece, young girls with long hair and boys carrying rucksacks drifted by and stopped to watch. They had come back, like me, half-expecting to find something happening. We stood there for a while, next to the Washington Monument ... nobody talking, not even the tent-company crew ... and then we drifted off in different directions. It was cold, and getting colder. I zipped up my ski jacket and walked fast across the Mall. To my left, at the base of the monument, a group of hippies was passing a joint around ... and off to the right a mile or so away, I could see the bright dome of the Capitol ... Mr Nixon's Capitol.

Suddenly I felt cold, and vaguely defeated. More than eight years ago, in San Francisco, I had stayed up all night to watch the election returns ... and when Nixon went down I felt like a winner.

Now, on this Monday night in 1969, President Nixon was being honoured with no less than six inaugural balls. I brooded on this for a while, then decided I would go over to the Hilton, later on, and punch somebody. Almost anybody would do ... but hopefully I could find a police chief from Nashville or some other mean geek. In the meantime, there was nothing to do but go back to the hotel and watch the news on TV ... maybe something funny, like film clips of the bastinado.

Boston *Globe*, 23 February 1969

PART TWO

PRESENTING: THE RICHARD NIXON DOLL (OVERHAULED 1968 MODEL)

No interview with Richard Nixon will end until he refers to himself, at least once, as a 'political man'. His opponents, by implication, are mere 'politicians'. Especially the man Nixon plans to defeat this November ... for the Presidency of the United States. Selah.

The major polls and surveys in the country suggest that Nixon may be right, despite the outraged howls of all those voters who insist that a choice between Nixon and Johnson is no choice at all. Sen. Eugene McCarthy has called it 'a choice between obscenity and vulgarity'. Yet McCarthy is the political heir of Aldai Stevenson, who said that 'People get the kind of government they deserve.' If this is true, then 1968 is probably the year in which the great American chicken will come home to roost ... either for good or for ill.

So it was with a sense of morbid curiosity that I went to New England not long ago to check on 'the real Richard Nixon'. Not necessarily the 'new Nixon', or even the newest model of the old 'new Nixon', who is known to the press corps that follows him as 'Nixon Mark IV'. My assignment was to find the man behind all these masks, or maybe to find that there was no mask at all – that Richard Milhous Nixon, at age fifty-five, was neither more nor less than what he appeared to be – a plastic man in a plastic bag, surrounded by hired wizards so cautious as to seem almost plastic themselves ... These political handlers were chosen this time for their coolness and skill for only one job: to see that Richard Nixon is the next President of the United States.

One of the handlers, Henry Hyde, presumably felt I was a threat to the Nixon camp. He called *Pageant* to check me out. This was after he got into my room somehow – while I was away, eating breakfast – and read my typewritten notes. The Nixon people, who wore baggy, dark-coloured suits and plenty of greasy kid stuff (they looked like models at an Elks Club style show), seemed to feel I was disrespectful because I was dressed like a ski bum. *Pageant* reassured Mr Hyde as to the purity of my mission and intentions in spite of my appearance.

Richard Nixon has never been one of my favourite people, anyway. For years I've regarded his very existence as a monument to all the rancid genes and broken chromosomes that corrupt the possibilities of the American Dream; he was a foul caricature of himself, a man with no soul, no inner convictions, with the integrity of a hyena and the style of a poison toad. The Nixon I remembered was absolutely humourless;

I couldn't imagine him laughing at anything except maybe a paraplegic who wanted to vote Democratic but couldn't quite reach the lever on the voting machine.

After 1960, though, I no longer took him seriously. Two years later he blew his bid for the governorship of California and made it overwhelmingly clear that he no longer took *himself* seriously – at least not as a politician. He made a national ass of himself by blaming his defeats on the 'biased press'. He called a press conference and snarled into the microphone: 'You won't have Dick Nixon to kick around any more, because, gentlemen, this is my final press conference.'

There is no avoiding the fact that Richard Nixon would not be running for President in 1968 if John Kennedy hadn't been assassinated five years earlier ... and if the GOP hadn't nominated Barry Goldwater in 1964 ... which guaranteed the election of Lyndon Johnson, who has since done nearly everything wrong and botched the job so that now even Nixon looks good beside him.

The situation is so obvious that Nixon, 'the political man', can't resist it. And who can blame him for taking his luck where he finds it? He's back on the 'fast track' that he likes to talk about, with the Presidency to gain and nothing at all to lose. He's obviously enjoying this campaign. It's a bonus, a free shot, his last chance to stand eyeball to eyeball again with the high rollers.

Richard Nixon has been in politics all his life; for twenty-one years he has rolled about as high as a politician can in this country, and his luck has been pretty good. His instincts are those of a professional gambler who wins more often than he loses; his 'skill' is nine parts experience to one part natural talent, and his concept of politics is entirely mechanical.

Nixon is a political technician, and he has hired technicians to help him win this time. As a campaign team, they are formidable. They have old pros, young turks, crippled opponents, and a candidate who once came within an eyelash of beating the late John F. Kennedy.

The 'new Nixon' is above anger, and he rarely has time for casual conversation. His staffers explain to the grumbling press that 'Mr Nixon is busy writing tonight's speech'. He is grappling in private, as it were, with the subtle contradictions of the Asian mind. (He slipped once in public during a late February trip to Wisconsin. 'This country cannot tolerate a long war,' he said. 'The Asians have no respect for human lives. They don't care about body counts.' The implied racial slur was a departure from his carefully conceived campaign oratory.)

At one point I asked Ray Price, one of Nixon's chief braintrusters, why the candidate was having such difficulty finding words to echo Dean Rusk's views on Vietnam. Nixon's speeches for the past four nights had been straight out of the Johnson-Rusk handbook on the 'domino theory'.

Price looked hurt. 'Well,' he said slowly, 'I really wish you'd done your homework on this. Mr Nixon has gone to a lot of trouble to clarify his views on Vietnam, and I'm only sorry that – well ...' He shook his head sadly, as if he couldn't bring himself to chastise me any further on the hallowed premises of a Howard Johnson's motel.

We went to his room, where he dug up a reprint of an article from the October 1967 issue of *Foreign Affairs*. The title was 'Asia After Vietnam', and the author was Richard M. Nixon. I was hoping for something more current, but Price was suddenly called off on other business. So I took the article to the bar and went through it several times without finding anything to clear my head. It was thoughtful, articulate, and entirely consistent with the thinking of John Foster Dulles.

I was disappointed with Price – for the same reason I'd been disappointed all week with Nixon. In various ways they both assumed that I – and all the other reporters – would fail to understand that Nixon was not only being evasive with regard to Vietnam that week but that he was doing it deliberately and for good reason. George Romney's campaign was obviously on its last legs; New Hampshire was sewn up for Nixon, and the best way to maintain that lead was to stay visible and say nothing more controversial than 'God Bless America'. Romney tried desperately to provoke an argument, but Nixon ignored every challenge.

Nixon did confess that he had a way to end the war, but he wouldn't tell how. Patriotically he explained why: 'No one with this responsibility who is seeking office should give away any of his bargaining positions in advance.' (Nixon's wife, Pat, has confidence in his ability to cope with Vietnam. 'Dick would never have let Vietnam drag on like this,' she says.)

Both Romney and McCarthy had their Manchester headquarters at the Wayfarer, an elegant, woodsy motel with a comfortable bar and the best dining room in the area. Nixon's Holiday Inn command post was on the other side of town, a grim-looking concrete structure. I asked one of Nixon's advisers why they had chosen such a dreary place. 'Well,' he replied with a smile, 'our only other choice was the Wayfarer – but we left that for Romney when we found out that it's owned by one of the most prominent political operators in the state – a Democrat, of course.' He chuckled. 'Yeah, poor George really stepped into that one.'

Nixon's pros had won another point; there was nothing newsworthy about it, but those who mattered in the state political hierarchy understood, and they were the people Nixon needed to win New Hampshire. Small victories like this add up to delegates. Even before the votes were counted in New Hampshire, GOP strategists said Nixon had already gathered more than 600 of the 667 votes he would need to win the nomination.

There is no denying his fine understanding of the American political process. I went to New Hampshire expecting to find a braying ass, and I came away convinced that Richard Nixon has one of the best minds in politics. He understands problems very quickly; you can almost hear his brain working when he's faced with a difficult question. He concentrates so visibly that it looks like he's posing, and his answer, when it flows, will nearly always be *right, for the situation* – because Nixon's mind is programmed, from long experience, to *cope* with difficult situations. The fact that he often distorts the question – and then either answers it dishonestly or uses it to change the subject – is usually lost in the rhetoric. 'I'm really better at dialogue,' he says. 'The question-and-answer format is good for me. I like it on TV. The set speech is one of those things like the Rotary Club luncheon. I can do it, but if I had my druthers, I'd make it all Q and A.' The 'old Nixon' would argue in public; the 'new Nixon' won't. He has learned this lesson well, even if painfully.

The 'new Nixon' is a very careful man when it comes to publicity; he smiles constantly for the cameras, talks always in friendly platitudes, and turns the other cheek to any sign of hostility. His press relations are 'just fine', he says, and if anyone mentions that 'final press conference' he held in 1962, Nixon just smiles and changes the subject. He is making a conscious effort to avoid antagonizing reporters this time, but he is still very leery of them. Nixon takes all his meals in his room, which he never leaves except to rush off to one of his 'drills' – the term he and his staffers use to mean any speech or public appearance. His staffers sometimes join reporters in the bar, but never Nixon. He neither drinks nor smokes, they say, and bars make him nervous. Humphrey Bogart would have taken a dim view of Nixon. It was Bogart who said, 'You can't trust a man who doesn't drink.' And it was Raoul Duke who said, 'I'd never buy a used car from Nixon unless he was drunk.'

People who talk like that are not the sort that Nixon likes to have around, especially when he's engaged in something else and can't keep an eye on them. Perhaps this explains why his staffers got so upset when I tried to attend a taping session one afternoon at a TV station in Manchester. Nixon was scheduled to make some television commercials, featuring himself and a group of citizens in a question-and-answer session. The press had not been invited; I wanted to watch Nixon, however, in a relaxed and informal setting.

My request to sit in on the tape session was flatly denied. 'This is a *commercial* taping,' said Henry Hyde. 'Would Procter & Gamble let you into their studios? Or Ford?' Hyde was a gear and sprocket sales-man in Chicago before he became Nixon's press aide, so I wasn't sur-prised at his weird analogy. I merely shrugged and took a cab that afternoon down to the TV station – half expecting to be thrown out the moment I showed up. This didn't happen, perhaps because a CBS camera crew was already there and muttering darkly about Nixon's re-fusal to see them. They left shortly after I arrived, but I hung around to see what would happen.

The atmosphere was very sinister. Nixon was off in another room, as usual, rehearsing with his cast. They spent an hour getting all the ques-tions right. Meanwhile Hyde and other staffers took turns watching me. None of them knew who the 'citizens' who were to appear on the pro-gramme were, or who had chosen them. 'They're just people who want to ask him questions,' said Hyde.

Whoever they were, they were shrouded in great secrecy – despite the fact that their faces would soon be appearing on local TV screens with monotonous regularity. At one point I was making notes near the studio door when it suddenly flew open and two of Nixon's staffers came at me in a very menacing way. 'What are you writing?' snapped one.

'Notes,' I said.

'Well, write them on the other side of the room,' said the other. 'Don't stand around this door.'

So I went to the other side of the room and made some more notes about the strange, paranoid behaviour that had puzzled me for the past few days. And then I went back to the Holiday Inn and waited for the next 'drill'.

Nixon's speeches that week are hardly worth mentioning – except as indisputable proof that the 'old Nixon' is still with us. On Vietnam he echoes Johnson: on domestic issues he talks like Ronald Reagan. He is a champion of 'free enterprise' at home and 'peace with honour' abroad. People with short memories say he sounds in speeches like a 'milder version of Goldwater', or a 'Johnson without a drawl'. But those who recall the 1960 campaign know exactly whom he sounds like: Richard Milhous Nixon.

And why shouldn't he? Nixon's political philosophy was formed and tested by the time he became Vice-President of the United States at age forty. It served him well enough for the next eight years, and in 1960 nearly half the voters in the country wanted him to be the next Presi-dent. This is not the background of a man who would find any serious reason, at age fifty-five, to change his political philosophy.

He has said it himself: 'All this talk about "the new Nixon". Maybe it's there, but perhaps many people didn't know the old one.' He under-standably dislikes the implications of the term: The necessity for a 'new Nixon' means there must have been something wrong with the old one, and he strongly disputes that notion.

There is probably some truth in what he says, if only to the extent that he will now talk candidly with individual reporters – especially those from influential papers and magazines. Some of them have discovered to their amazement, that the 'private Nixon' is not the monster they'd always assumed him to be. In private he can be friendly and surprisingly frank, even about himself. This was never the case with the 'old Nixon'.

So there is no way of knowing if the 'private Nixon' was always so different from the public version. We have only his word, and – well, he is, after all, a politician running for office, and a very shrewd man. After several days of watching his performance in New Hampshire I suspected that he'd taken a hint from Ronald Reagan and hired a public relations firm to give him a new image. Henry Hyde denied this emphatically. 'That's not his style,' he said. 'Mr Nixon runs his own campaigns. You'd find that out pretty quick if you worked for him.'

'That's a good idea,' I said. 'How about it?'

'What?' he asked humourlessly.

'A job. I could write him a speech that would change his image in twenty-four hours.'

Henry didn't think much of the idea. Humour is scarce in the Nixon camp. The staffers tell jokes now and then, but they're not very funny. Only Charley McWhorter, the resident political expert, seems to have a sense of the absurd.

Oddly enough, Nixon himself shows traces of humour. Not often in public, despite his awkward attempts to joke about how bad he looks on television and that sort of thing. ('I understand the skiing is great here,' he told one audience. 'I've never skied, but' – he touched his nose – 'I have a personal feeling about it.') Every now and then he will smile spontaneously at something, and it's not the same smile that he beams at photographers.

At one point I had a long conversation with him about pro football. I'd heard he was a fan, and earlier that night in a speech at a chamber of commerce banquet he'd said that he'd bet on Oakland in the Super Bowl. I was curious, and since Ray Price had arranged for me to ride back to Manchester in Nixon's car, I took the opportunity to ask him about it. Actually, I suspected that he didn't know football from pig-hustling and that he mentioned it from time to time only because his wizards had told him it would make him seem like a regular guy.

But I was wrong. Nixon *knows* pro football. He'd taken Oakland and six points in the Super Bowl, he said, because Vince Lombardi had told him up in Green Bay that the AFL was much stronger than the sports-writers claimed. Nixon cited Oakland's sustained drive in the second half as evidence of their superiority over the Kansas City team that had challenged the Packers in 1967 and had totally collapsed in the second half. 'Oakland didn't fold up,' he said. 'That second-half drive had Lombardi worried.'

I remembered it, and mentioned the scoring play – a sideline pass to an unknown receiver named Bill Miller.

Nixon hesitated for a moment, then smiled broadly and slapped me on the leg. 'That's right,' he said. 'Yes, the Miami boy.' I couldn't believe it; he not only knew Miller, but he knew what college he'd played for. It wasn't his factual knowledge of football that stunned me; it was his genuine interest in the game. 'You know,' he said, 'the worst thing about campaigning, for me, is that it ruins my whole football season. I'm a sports buff, you know. If I had another career, I'd be a sportscaster – or a sportswriter.'

I smiled and lit a cigarette. The scene was so unreal that I felt like laughing out loud – to find myself zipping along a New England freeway in a big yellow car, being chauffeured around by a detective while I relaxed in the back seat and talked about football with my old buddy Dick Nixon, the man who came within 100,000 votes of causing me to flee the country in 1960. I was on the verge of mentioning this to him, but just then we came to the airport and drove out on the runway, where his chartered Lear Jet was waiting to zap him off to the wild blue yonder of Miami for a 'think session' with his staff. (There he rises early and works a twenty-hour day. He skimps on food – breakfast is juice, cereal, and milk; lunch is a sandwich, and dinner might be roast beef or steak, which he often doesn't finish – and keeps his weight at a constant 175 pounds. He swims some, suns a lot, yet rarely seems to stop working. 'I'll say this – he has enough stamina to be President,' says William P. Rogers, an old friend. 'He has the most stamina of any man I have ever known.')

We talked for a while beside the plane, but by that time I'd thought better of saying anything rude or startling. It had been exceptionally decent of him to give me a ride and an hour of his time, so I controlled the almost irresistible urge to gig him on his embryonic sense of humour.

It was almost midnight when the sleek little plane boomed down the runway and lifted off towards Florida. I went back to the Holiday Inn and drank for a while with Nick Ruwe, the chief advance man for New Hampshire.

'I almost had a heart attack tonight when I looked over and saw you poking around that jet engine with a cigarette in your mouth,' Ruwe said. He shook his head in disbelief. 'My God, what a nightmare!'

'Sorry,' I said. 'I didn't realize I was smoking.'

But I remembered leaning on the wing of the plane, an arm's length away from the fully loaded fuel tank. Somebody should have mentioned the cigarette, I thought, and the fact that nobody did makes me wonder now if Nixon's human machinery is really as foolproof as it seems to be. Or perhaps they all noticed I was smoking and – like Ruwe – said nothing at all.

Or perhaps that's beside the point. Senator McCarthy's success in New Hampshire can hardly be attributed to the hard-nosed professionalism of his staff ... and in this broader context the Nixon campaign seems flawed. There is a cynicism at the core of it, the confident assumption that success in politics depends more on shrewd technique than on the quality of the product. The 'old Nixon' didn't make it. Neither did earlier models of the 'new Nixon'. So now we have 'Nixon Mark IV', and as a journalist I suppose it's only fair to say that this latest model might be different and maybe even better in some ways. But as a customer, I wouldn't touch it – except with a long cattle prod.

Granted, the 'new Nixon' is more relaxed, wiser, more mellow. But I recognize the man who told a student audience at the University of New Hampshire that one of his biggest problems in politics has always been 'that I'm not a good actor, I can't be phony about it, I still refuse to wear make-up ...' Three weeks later this same man, after winning the New Hampshire primary, laughingly attributed his victory to the new make-up he'd been wearing. He thought he was being funny – at least on one level – but on another level he was telling the absolute truth.

Pageant, July 1968

AUTHOR'S NOTE

Dawn is coming up in San Francisco now: 6:09 a.m. I can hear the rumble of early morning buses under my window at the Seal Rock Inn ... out here at the far end of Geary Street: this is the end of the line, for buses and everything else, the western edge of America. From my desk I can see the dark jagged hump of Seal Rock looming out of the ocean in the grey morning light. About two hundred seals have been barking out there most of the night. Staying in this place with the windows open is like living next to a dog pound. Last night we had a huge paranoid poodle up here in the room, and the dumb bastard went totally out of control when the seals started barking – racing around the room like a chicken hearing a pack of wolves outside the window, howling & whining, leaping up on the bed & scattering my book-galley pages all over the floor, knocking the phone off the hook, upsetting the gin bottles, trashing my carefully organized stacks of campaign photographs ... off to the right of this typewriter, on the floor between the beds. I can see an 8x10 print of Frank Mankiewicz yelling into a telephone at the Democratic Convention in Miami; but that one will never be used, because the goddamn hound put five big claw-holes in the middle of Frank's chest.

That dog will not enter this room again. He came in with the book-editor, who went away about six hours ago with thirteen finished chapters – the bloody product of fifty-five consecutive hours of sleepless, foodless, high-speed editing. But there was no other way to get the thing done. I am not an easy person to work with, in terms of deadlines. When I arrived in San Francisco to put this book together, they had a work-hole set up for me downtown at the *Rolling Stone* office ... but I have a powerful aversion to working in offices, and when I didn't show up for three or four days they decided to do the only logical thing: move the office out here to the Seal Rock Inn.

One afternoon about three days ago they showed up at my door, with no warning, and loaded about forty pounds of supplies into the room: two cases of Mexican beer, four quarts of gin, a dozen grapefruits, and enough speed to alter the outcome of six Super Bowls. There was also a big Selectric typewriter, two reams of paper, a face-cord of oak firewood and three tape recorders – in case the situation got so desperate that I might finally have to resort to verbal composition.

We came to this point sometime around the thirty-third hour, when I developed an insoluble writer's block and began dictating big chunks of the book straight into the microphone – pacing around the room at the end of an eighteen-foot cord and saying anything that came into my head. When we reached the end of a tape the editor would jerk it out of the machine and drop it into a satchel ... and every twelve hours or so a messenger would stop by to pick up the tape satchel and take it downtown to the office, where unknown persons transcribed it on to manuscript paper and sent it straight to the printer in Reno.

There is a comfortable kind of consistency in this kind of finish, because that's the way all the rest of the book was written. From December 71 to January 73 – in airport bars, all-nite coffee shops and dreary hotel rooms all over the country – there is hardly a paragraph in this jangled saga that wasn't produced in a last-minute, teeth-grinding frenzy. There was never enough time. Every deadline was a crisis. All around me were experienced professional journalists meeting deadlines far more frequent than mine, but I was never able to learn from their example.

Reporters like Bill Greider from the Washington *Post* and Jim Naughton of the New York *Times*, for instance, had to file long, detailed, and relatively complex stories *every day* – while my own deadline fell every two weeks – but neither one of them ever seemed in a hurry about getting their work done, and from time to time they would try to console me about the terrible pressure I always seemed to be labouring under.

Any $100-an-hour psychiatrist could probably explain this problem to me, in thirteen or fourteen sessions, but I don't have time for that. No doubt it has something to do with a deep-seated personality defect, or maybe a kink in whatever blood vessel leads into the pineal gland ... On the other hand, it might easily be something as simple & basically perverse as whatever instinct it is that causes a jackrabbit to wait until the last possible second to dart across the road in front of a speeding car.

People who claim to know jackrabbits will tell you they are primarily motivated by fear, stupidity, and craziness. But I have spent enough time in jackrabbit country to know that most of them lead pretty dull lives; they are bored with their daily routines: eat, fuck, sleep, hop around a bush now & then ... No wonder some of them drift over the line into cheap thrills once in a while; there has to be a powerful adrenalin rush in crouching by the side of a road, waiting for the next set of headlights to come along, then streaking out of the bushes with split-second timing and making it across to the other side just inches in front of the speeding front wheels.

Why not? Anything that gets the adrenalin moving like a 440 volt blast in a copper bathtub is good for the reflexes and keeps the veins free of cholesterol ... but too many adrenalin rushes in any given time-span have the same bad effect on the nervous system as too many electroshock treatments are said to have on the brain: after a while you start burning out the circuits.

When a jackrabbit gets addicted to road-running, it is only a matter of time before he gets smashed – and when a journalist turns into a politics junkie he will sooner or later start raving and babbling in print about things that only a person who has been there can possibly understand.

Some of the scenes in this book will not make much sense to anybody except the people who were involved in them. Politics has its own language, which is often so complex that it borders on being a code, and the main trick in political journalism is learning how to translate – to make sense of the partisan bullshit that even your friends will lay on you – without crippling your access to the kind of information that allows you to keep functioning. Covering a presidential campaign is not a hell of a lot different from getting a long-term assignment to cover a newly elected District Attorney who made a campaign promise to 'crack down on organized crime'. In both cases, you find unexpected friends on both sides, and in order to protect them – and to keep them as sources of private information – you wind up knowing a lot of things you can't print, or which you can only say without even hinting at where they came from.

This was one of the traditional barriers I tried to ignore when I moved to Washington and began covering the 72 presidential campaign. As far as I was concerned, there was no such thing as 'off the record'. The most consistent and ultimately damaging failure of political journalism in America has its roots in the clubby/cocktail personal relationships that inevitably develop between politicians and journalists – in Washington or anywhere else where they meet on a day-to-day basis. When professional antagonists become after-hours drinking buddies, they are not likely to turn each other in ... especially not for 'minor infractions' of rules that neither side takes seriously; and on the rare occasions when minor infractions suddenly become major, there is panic on both ends.

A classic example of this syndrome was the disastrous 'Eagleton affair'. Half of the political journalists in St Louis and at least a dozen in the Washington press corps knew Eagleton was a serious boozer with a history of mental breakdowns – but none of them had ever written about it, and the few who were known to have mentioned it privately clammed up 1000 per cent when McGovern's harried staffers began making inquiries on that fateful Thursday afternoon in Miami. Any Washington political reporter who blows a senator's chance for the vice-presidency might as well start looking for another beat to cover – because his name will be instant mud on Capitol Hill.

When I went to Washington I was determined to avoid this kind of trap. Unlike most other correspondents, I could afford to burn all my bridges behind me – because I was only there for a year, and the last thing I cared about was establishing long-term connections on Capitol Hill. I went there for two reasons: (1) to learn as much as possible about the mechanics and realities of a presidential campaign, and (2) to write about it the same way I'd write about anything else – as close to the bone as I could get, and to hell with the consequences.

It was a fine idea, and on balance I think it worked out pretty well – but in retrospect I see two serious problems in that kind of merciless, ballbusting approach. The most obvious and least serious of these was the fact that even the few people I considered my friends in Washington treated me like a walking bomb; some were reluctant to even drink with me, for fear that their tongues might get loose and utter words that would almost certainly turn up on the newsstands two weeks later. The other, more complex, problem had to do with my natural out-front bias in favour of the McGovern candidacy – which was not a problem at first, when George was such a hopeless underdog that his staffers saw no harm in talking frankly with any journalist who seemed friendly and interested – but when he miraculously emerged as the front-runner I found myself in a very uncomfortable position. Some of the friends I'd made earlier, during the months when the idea of McGovern winning the Democratic nomination seemed almost as weird as the appearance of a full-time *Rolling Stone* correspondent on the campaign trail, were no longer just a handful of hopeless idealists I'd been hanging around with for entirely personal reasons, but key people in a fast-rising movement that suddenly seemed capable not only of winning the party nomination but driving Nixon out of the White House.

McGovern's success in the primaries had a lasting effect on my relationship with the people who were running his campaign – especially those who had come to know me well enough to sense that my contempt for the time-honoured double standard in political journalism might not be entirely compatible with the increasingly pragmatic style of politics that George was getting into. And their apprehension increased measurably as it became obvious that dope fiends, anarchists, and big-beat dropouts were not the only people who read the political coverage in *Rolling Stone*. Not long after McGovern's breakthrough victory in the Wisconsin primary, arch-establishment mouthpiece Stewart Alsop went out of his way to quote some of my more venomous comments on Muskie and Humphrey in his *Newsweek* column, thus raising me to the level of at least neo-respectability at about the same time McGovern began to look like a winner.

Things were never the same after that. A cloud of hellish intensity had come down on the McGovern campaign by the time it rolled into California. Mandates came down from the top, warning staffers to beware of the press. The only exceptions were reporters who were known to have a decent respect for things said 'in confidence', and I didn't fit that description.

And so much for all that. The point I meant to make here – before we wandered off on that tangent about jackrabbits – is that everything in this book except the footnotes was written under savage deadline pressure in the travelling vortex of a campaign so confusing and unpredictable that not even the participants claimed to know what was happening.

I had never covered a presidential campaign before I got into this one, but I quickly got so hooked on it that I began betting on the outcome of each primary – and, by combining aggressive ignorance with a natural instinct to mock the conventional wisdom, I managed to win all but two of the fifty or sixty bets I made between February and November. My first loss came in New Hampshire, where I felt guilty for taking advantage of one of McGovern's staffers who wanted to bet that George would get more than 35 per cent of the vote; and I lost when he wound up with 37.5 per cent. But from that point on, I won steadily – until 7 November, when I made the invariably fatal mistake of betting my emotions instead of my instinct.

The final result was embarrassing, but what the hell? I blew that one, along with a lot of other people who should have known better, and since I haven't changed anything else in this mass of first-draft screeds that I wrote during the campaign, I can't find any excuse for changing my final prediction. Any re-writing now would cheat the basic concept of the book, which – in addition to the publisher's desperate idea that it might sell enough copies to cover the fantastic expense bills I ran up in the course of those twelve frantic months – was to lash the whole thing together and essentially *record the reality of an incredibly volatile presidential campaign while it was happening*: from an eye in the eye of the hurricane, as it were, and there is no way to do that without rejecting the luxury of hindsight.

So this is more a jangled campaign diary than a record or reasoned analysis of the 72 presidential campaign. Whatever I wrote in the midnight hours on rented typewriters in all those cluttered hotel rooms along the campaign trail – from the Wayfarer Inn outside Manchester to the Neil House in Columbus to the Wilshire Hyatt House in LA and the Fontainebleau in Miami – is no different now than it was back in March and May and July when I was cranking it out of the typewriter one page at a time and feeding it into the plastic maw of that goddamn mojo wire to some hash-addled freak of an editor at the *Rolling Stone* news-desk in San Francisco.

What I would like to preserve here is a kind of high-speed cinematic reel-record of what the campaign was like *at the time*, not what the whole thing boiled down to or how it fits into history. There will be no shortage of books covering that end. The last count I got was just before Christmas in 72, when ex-McGovern speech writer Sandy Berger said at least nineteen people who'd been involved in the campaign were writing books about it – so we'll eventually get the whole story, for good or ill.

Meanwhile, my room at the Seal Rock Inn is filling up with people who seem on the verge of hysteria at the sight of me still sitting here wasting time on a rambling introduction, with the final chapter still unwritten and the presses scheduled to start rolling in twenty-four hours ... but unless somebody shows up pretty soon with extremely powerful speed, there might not *be* any final chapter. About four fingers of king-hell crank would do the trick, but I am not optimistic. There is a definite scarcity of genuine, high-voltage crank on the market these days – and according to recent statements by official spokesmen for the

Justice Department in Washington, that's solid evidence of progress in our war against dangerous drugs.

Well ... thank Jesus for that. I was beginning to think we were never going to put the arm on that crowd. But the people in Washington say we're finally making progress. And if anybody should know, it's them. So maybe this country's about to get back on the right track.

                                                    H.S.T.
                                    Sunday, 28 January 1973
                                    San Francisco, Seal Rock Inn

                        Fear and Loathing: On the Campaign Trail,
                        San Francisco, Straight Arrow Books, 1973

JUNE 1972: THE McGOVERN JUGGERNAUT ROLLS ON

The press room was crowded – two dozen or so ranking media wizards, all wearing little egg-shaped ID tags from the Secret Service: Leo Sauvage/*Le Figaro*, Jack Perkins/NBC, R. W. Apple/NY *Times* ... the McGovern campaign went big-time, for real, in California. No more of that part-time, secondary coverage. McGovern was suddenly the front-runner, perhaps the next President, and virtually every room in the hotel was filled with either staff or media people ... twelve new typewriters in the press suite, ten phones, four colour TV sets, a well-stocked free bar, even a goddamn mojo wire.*

The gossip in the press room was heavier than usual that night: Gary Hart was about to be fired as McGovern's campaign manager; Fred Dutton would replace him ... Humphrey's sister had just been arrested in San Diego on a warrant connected with Hubert's campaign debts ... Muskie was offering to support McGovern if George would agree to take over $800,000 of his (Muskie's) campaign debt ... But Crouse was

* Aka Xerox Telecopier. We have had many inquiries about this. 'Mojo wire' was the name originally given the machine by its inventor, Raoul Duke. But he signed away the patent, in the throes of a drug frenzy, to Xerox board chairman Max Palevsky, who claimed the invention for himself and re-named it the 'Xerox Telecopier'. Patent royalties now total $100 million annually, but Duke receives none of it. At Palevsky's insistence he remains on the *Rolling Stone* payroll, earning $50 each week, but his 'sports column' is rarely printed and he is formally barred by court order, along with a writ of permanent constraint, from Pavlevsky's house & grounds.

nowhere in sight. I stood around for a while, trying to piece together a few grisly unsubstantiated rumours about 'heavy pols preparing to take over the whole McGovern campaign' ... Several people had chunks of the story, but nobody had a real key; so I left to go back down to my room to think for a while.

That was when I ran into Mankiewicz, picking a handful of thumb-tacked messages off the bulletin board outside the door.

'I have a very weird story for you,' I said.

He eyed me cautiously. 'What is it?'

'Come over here,' I said motioning him to follow me down the corridor to a quiet place ... Then I told him what I had heard about Humphrey's midnight air-courier to Vegas. He stared down at the carpet, not seeming particularly interested – but when I finished he looked up and said, 'Where'd you *hear* that?'

I shrugged, sensing definite interest now. 'Well, I was talking to some people over at a place called the Losers, and—'

'With Kirby?' he snapped.

'No,' I said. 'I went over there looking for him, but he wasn't around.' Which was true. Earlier that day Kirby Jones, McGovern's press secretary, had told me he planned to stop by the Losers Club later on, because Warren Beatty had recommended it highly ... but when I stopped by around midnight there was no sign of him.

Mankiewicz was not satisfied. 'Who was there?' he asked. 'Some of *our* people? Who was it?'

'Nobody you'd know,' I said. 'But what about this Humphrey story? What can you tell me about it?'

'Nothing,' he said, glancing over his shoulder at a burst of yelling from the press room. Then: 'When's your next issue coming out?'

'Thursday.'

'Before the election?'

'Yeah, and so far I don't have anything worth a shit to write about – but this thing sounds interesting.'

He nodded, staring down at the floor again, then shook his head. 'Listen,' he said. 'You could cause a lot of trouble for us by printing a thing like that. They'd know where it came from, and they'd jerk our man right out.'

'What man?'

He stared at me, smiling faintly.

At this point the story becomes very slippery, with many loose ends and dark shadows – but the nut was very simple: I had blundered almost completely by accident on a flat-out byzantine spook story. There was nothing timely or particularly newsworthy about it, but when your deadline is every two weeks you don't tend to worry about things like scoops and newsbreaks. If Mankiewicz had broken down and admitted to me that night that he was actually a red Chinese agent and that McGovern had no pulse, I wouldn't have known how to handle it – and the tension of trying to keep that kind of heinous news to myself for the next four days until *Rolling Stone* went to press would almost certainly have caused me to lock myself in my hotel room wtih eight quarts of Wild Turkey and all the Ibogaine I could get my hands on.

So this strange tale about Humphrey & Vegas was not especially *newsworthy*, by my standards. Its only real value, in fact, was the rare flash of contrast it provided to the insane tedium of the surface campaign. Important or not, this was something very different: midnight flights to Vegas, mob money funnelled in from casinos to pay for Hubert's TV spots; spies, runners, counterspies; cryptic phone calls from airport phone booths ... Indeed; the dark underbelly of big-time politics. A useless story, no doubt, but it sure beat the hell out of getting back on that goddamn press bus and being hauled out to some shopping centre in Gardena and watching McGovern shake hands for two hours with lumpy housewives.

Unfortunately, all I really knew about what I called the U-13 story was the general outline and just enough key points to convince Mankiewicz that I might be irresponsible enough to go ahead and try to write the thing anyway. All I knew – or *thought* I knew – at that point was that somebody very close to the top of the Humphrey campaign had made secret arrangements for a night flight to Vegas in order to pick up a large bundle of money from unidentified persons presumed to be sinister, and that this money would be used by Humphrey's managers to finance another one of Hubert's eleventh-hour fast-finish blitzkriegs.

Even then, a week before the vote, he was thought to be running ten points and maybe more behind McGovern – and since the average daily media expenditure for each candidate in the California primary was roughly $30,000 a day, Humphrey would need at least twice that amount to pay for the orgy of exposure he would need to overcome a ten-point lead. No less than a quick $500,000.

The people in Vegas were apparently willing to spring for it, because the plane was already chartered and ready to go when McGovern's headquarters got word of the flight from their executive-level spy in the Humphrey campaign. His identity remains a mystery – in the public prints, at least – but the handful of people aware of him say he performed invaluable services for many months.

His function in the U-13 gig was merely to call McGovern headquarters and tell them about the Vegas plane. At this point, my second- or third-hand source was not sure what happened next. According to the story, two McGovern operatives were instantly dispatched to keep around-the-clock watch on the plane for the next seventy-two hours, and somebody from McGovern headquarters called Humphrey and warned him that they knew what he was up to.

In any case, the plane never took off and there was no evidence in the last week of the campaign to suggest that Hubert got a last-minute influx of money, from Vegas or anywhere else.

That is as much of the U-13 story as I could piece together without help from somebody who knew the details – and Mankiewicz finally agreed, insisting the whole time that he knew nothing about the story except that he didn't want to see it in print before election day, that if I wanted to hold off until the next issue he would put me in touch with somebody who would tell me the whole story, for good or ill.

'Call Miles Rubin,' he said, 'and tell him I told you to ask him about this. He'll fill you in.'

That was fine, I said. I was in no special hurry for the story, anyway. So I let it ride for a few days, missing my deadline for that issue ... and on Wednesday I began trying to get hold of Miles Rubin, one of McGovern's top managers for California. All I knew about Rubin before I called was that several days earlier he had thrown Washington *Post* correspondent David Broder out of his office for asking too many questions – less than twenty-four hours before Broder appeared on Rubin's TV screen as one of the three interrogators on the first Humphrey/McGovern debate.

My own experience with Rubin turned out to be just about par for the course. I finally got through to him by telephone on Friday, and explained that Mankiewicz had told me to call him and find out the details of the U-13 story. I started to say we could meet for a beer or two sometime later that afternoon and he could—

'Are you kidding?' he cut in. 'That's one story you're never going to hear.'

'What?'

'There's no point even talking about it,' he said flatly. Then he launched into a three-minute spiel about the fantastic honesty and integrity that characterized the McGovern campaign from top to bottom, and why was it that people like me didn't spend more time writing about the truth and the decency and the integrity, instead of picking around the edge for minor things that weren't important anyway?

'Jesus Christ!' I muttered. Why argue? Getting anything but pompous bullshit and gibberish out of Rubin would be like trying to steal meat from a hammerhead shark.

'Thanks,' I said, and hung up.

That night I found Mankiewicz in the press room and told him what had happened.

He couldn't understand it, he said. But he would talk to Miles tomorrow and straighten it out.

I was not optimistic; and by that time I was beginning to agree that the U-13 story was not worth the effort. The big story in California, after all, was that McGovern was on the brink of locking up a first-ballot nomination in Miami – and that Hubert Humphrey was about to get stomped so badly at the polls that he might have to be carried out of the state in a rubber sack.

The next time I saw Mankiewicz was on the night before the election and he seemed very tense, very strong into the gila monster trip ... and when I started to ask him about Rubin he began ridiculing the story in a VERY LOUD VOICE, so I figured it was time to forget it.

Several days later I learned the reason for Frank's bad nerves that night. McGovern's fat lead over Humphrey, which had hovered between fourteen and twenty percentage points for more than a week, had gone into a sudden and apparently uncontrollable dive in the final days of the campaign. By election eve it had shrunk to five points, and perhaps even less.

The shrinkage crisis was a closely guarded secret among McGovern's top command. Any leak to the press could have led to disastrous headlines on Tuesday morning: Election Day ... McGovern Falters; Humphrey Closing Gap ... a headline like that in either the Los Angeles *Times* or the San Francisco *Chronicle* might have thrown the election to Humphrey by generating a last minute sympathy/underdog turnout and whipping Hubert's field workers into a frenzied 'get out the vote' effort.

But the grim word never leaked, and by noon on Tuesday an almost visible wave of relief rolled through the McGovern camp. The dike would hold, they felt, at roughly five per cent.

The coolest man in the whole McGovern entourage on Tuesday was George McGovern himself – who had spent all day Monday on airplanes, racing from one critical situation to another. On Monday morning he flew down to San Diego for a major rally; then to New Mexico for another final-hour rally on the eve of the New Mexico primary (which he won the next day – along with New Jersey and South Dakota) ... and finally on Monday night to Houston for a brief, unscheduled

214

appearance at the National Governors' Conference, which was rumoured to be brewing up a 'stop McGovern' movement.

After defusing the crisis in Houston he got a few hours' sleep before racing back to Los Angeles to deal with another emergency: His twenty-two-year-old daughter was having a premature baby and first reports from the hospital hinted at serious complications.

But by noon the crisis had passed, and somewhere sometime around one he arrived with his praetorian guard of eight Secret Service agents at Max Palevsky's house in Bel Air, where he immediately changed into swimming trunks and drove into the pool. The day was grey and cool, no hint of sun, and none of the other guests seemed to feel like swimming.

For a variety of tangled reasons – primarily because my wife was one of the guests in the house that weekend – I was there when McGovern arrived. So we talked for a while, mainly about the possibility of either Muskie or Humphrey dropping out of the race and joining forces with George if the price was right ... and it occurred to me afterwards that it was the first time he'd ever seen me without a beer can in my hand or babbling like a loon about freak power, election bets, or some other twisted subject ... but he was kind enough not to mention this.

It was a very relaxed afternoon. The only tense moment occurred when I noticed a sort of narrow-looking man with a distinctly predatory appearance standing off by himself and glowering down at the white telephone as if he planned to jerk it out by the root if it didn't ring within ten seconds and tell him everything he wanted to know.

'Who the hell is *that*?' I asked, pointing across the pool at him.

'That's Miles Rubin,' somebody replied.

'Jesus,' I said. 'I should have guessed.'

Moments later my curiosity got the better of me and I walked over to Rubin and introduced myself. 'I understand they're going to put you in charge of press relations after Miami,' I said as we shook hands.

He said something I didn't understand, then hurried away. For a moment I was tempted to call him back and ask if I could feel his pulse. But the moment passed and I jumped into the pool, instead.*

The rest of the day disintegrated into chaos, drunkenness, and the kind of hysterical fatigue that comes from spending too much time rac-

---

* Later in the campaign, when Rubin and I became reasonably good friends, he told me that the true story of the 'U-13' was essentially the same as the version I'd pieced together in California. The only thing I didn't know, he said, was that Humphrey eventually got the money anyway. For some reason, the story as I originally wrote it was almost universally dismissed as 'just another one of Thompson's Mankiewicz fables'.

ing from one place to another and being shoved around in crowds. McGovern won the Democratic primary by exactly five per cent – 45 to 40 – and Nixon came from behind in the GOP race to nip Ashbrook by 87 to 13.

She was gonna be an actress and I was gonna learn to fly
She took off to find the footlights and I took off to find the sky.
'Taxi' by Harry Chapin

George McGovern's queer idea that he could get himself elected President on the Democratic ticket by dancing a muted whipsong on the corpse of the Democratic Party is suddenly beginning to look very sane, and very possible. For the last five or six days in California, McGovern's campaign was covered from dawn to midnight by fifteen or twenty camera crews, seventy-five to a hundred still photographers, and anywhere from fifty to two hundred linear/writing press types.

The media crowd descended on McGovern like a swarm of wild bees, and there was not one of them who doubted that he/she was covering the winner. The sense of impending victory around the pool at the Wilshire Hyatt House was as sharp and all-pervasive as the gloom and desperation in Hubert Humphrey's national staff headquarters about ten miles west at the far more chic and fashionable Beverly Hilton.

In the McGovern press suite the big-time reporters were playing stud poker – six or eight of them, hunkered down in their shirt-sleeves and loose ties around a long white-cloth-covered table with a pile of dollar bills in the middle and the bar about three feet behind Tom Wicker's chair at the far end. At the other end of the room, to Wicker's left, there were three more long white tables, with four identical big typewriters on each one and a pile of white legal-size paper stacked neatly beside each typewriter. At the other end of the room, to Wicker's right, was a comfortable couch and a giant floor-model twenty-four-inch Motorola colour TV set ... the screen was so large that Dick Cavett's head looked almost as big as Wicker's, but the sound was turned off and nobody at the poker table was watching the TV set anyway. Mort Sahl was dominating the screen with a seemingly endless, borderline-hysteria monologue about a bunch of politicians he didn't have much use for – (Muskie, Humphrey, McGovern) – and two others (Shirley Chisholm and former New Orleans DA Jim Garrison) that he liked.

I knew this, because I had just come up the outside stairway from my room one floor below to get some typing paper, and I'd been watching the Cavett show on my own twenty-one-inch Motorola colour TV.

I paused at the door for a moment, then edged around to the poker table towards the nearest stack of paper. 'Ah, decadence, decadence ...'

I muttered. 'Sooner or later it was bound to come to this.'

Kirby Jones looked up and grinned. 'What are you bitching about this time, Hunter? Why are you always bitching?'

'Never mind that,' I said. 'You owe me $20 & I want it now.'

'What?' he looked shocked. 'Twenty dollars for what?'

I nodded solemnly. 'I knew you'd try to welsh. Don't tell me you don't remember that bet.'

'What bet?'

'The one we made on the train in Nebraska,' I said. 'You said Wallace wouldn't get more than 300 delegates ... But he already has 317, and I want that $20.'

He shook his head. 'Who *says* he has that many? You've been reading the New York *Times* again.' He chuckled and glanced at Wicker, who was dealing. 'Let's wait until the convention, Hunter, things might be different then.'

'You pig,' I muttered, easing towards the door with my paper. 'I've been hearing a lot about how the McGovern campaign is finally turning dishonest, but I didn't believe it until now.'

He laughed and turned his attention back to the game. 'All bets are payable in Miami, Hunter. That's when we'll count the marbles.'

I shook my head sadly and left the room. Jesus, I thought, these bastards are getting out of hand. Here we were still a week away from D-day in California, and the McGovern press suite was already beginning to look like some kind of Jefferson-Jackson Day stag dinner. I glanced back at the crowd around the table and realized that not one of them had been in New Hampshire. This was a totally different crowd, for good or ill. Looking back on the first few weeks of the New Hampshire campaign, it seemed so different from what was happening in California that it was hard to adjust to the idea that it was still the same campaign. The difference between a sleek front-runner's act in Los Angeles and the spartan, almost skeletal machinery of an underdog operation in Manchester was almost more than the mind could deal with all at once.*

Four months ago on a frozen grey afternoon in New Hampshire the McGovern 'press bus' rolled into the empty parking lot of a motel on the outskirts of Portsmouth. It was 3:30 or so, and we had an hour or so to kill before the Senator would arrive by air from Washington and lead us downtown for a hand-shaking gig at the Booth fishworks.

* California was the first primary where the McGovern campaign was obviously well-financed. In Wisconsin, where McGovern's money men had told him privately that they would withdraw their support if he didn't finish first or a very close second, the press had to pay fifty cents a beer in the hospitality suite.

The bar was closed, but one of McGovern's advance men had arranged a sort of beer/booze and sandwich meat smorgasbord for the press in a lounge just off the lobby ... so all six of us climbed out of the bus, which was actually an old three-seater airport limousine, and I went inside to kill time.

Of the six passengers in the 'press bus', three were local McGovern volunteers. The other three were Ham Davis from the Providence *Journal*, Tim Crouse from the *Rolling Stone* Boston bureau, and me. Two more media/press people were already inside: Don Bruckner from the Los Angeles *Times*, and Michelle Clark from CBS.*

There was also Dick Dougherty, who had just quit his job as chief of the LA *Times* New York bureau to become George McGovern's press secretary, speechwriter, main fixer, advance man, and all-purpose travelling wizard. Dougherty and Bruckner were sitting off by themselves at a corner table when the rest of us straggled into the lounge and filled our plates at the smorgasbord table: olives, carrots, celery stalks, salami, devilled eggs ... but when I asked for beer, the middle-aged waitress who was also the desk clerk said beer 'wasn't included' in 'the arrangements', and that if I wanted any I would have to pay cash for it.

'That's fine,' I said. 'Bring me three Budweisers.'

She nodded. 'With three glasses?'

'No. One glass.'

She hesitated, then wrote the order down and lumbered off towards wherever she kept the beer. I carried my plate over to an empty table and sat down to eat and read the local paper ... but there was no salt and pepper on the table, so I went back up to the smorgasbord to look for it & bumped into somebody in a tan gabardine suit who was quietly loading his plate with carrots & salami.

'Sorry.' I said.

'Pardon *me*,' he replied.

I shrugged and went back to my table with the salt and pepper. The only noise in the room was coming from the LA *Times* corner. Everybody else was either reading or eating, or both. The only person in the room not sitting down was the man in the tan suit at the smorgasbord

---

* The New Hampshire primary was Michelle's first assignment in national politics. 'I don't have the vaguest idea what I'm doing,' she told me. 'I think they're just letting me get my feet wet.' Three months later, when McGovern miraculously emerged as the front-runner, Michelle was still covering him. By that time her star was rising almost as fast as McGovern's. At the Democratic Convention in Miami, Walter Cronkite announced on the air that she had been officially named 'correspondent'. On 8 December 1972, Michelle Clark died in a plane crash at Midway Airport in Chicago – the same plane crash that killed the wife of Watergate defendant Howard Hunt.

table. He was still fumbling with the food, keeping his back to the room ...

There was something familiar about him. Nothing special – but enough to make me glance up again from my newspaper; a subliminal recognition-flash of some kind, or maybe just the idle journalistic curiosity that gets to be a habit after a while when you find yourself drifting around in the nervous murk of some story with no apparent meaning or spine to it. I had come up to New Hampshire to write a long thing on the McGovern campaign – but after twelve hours in Manchester I hadn't seen much to indicate that it actually existed, and I was beginning to wonder what the fuck I was going to write about for that issue.

There was no sign of communication in the room. The press people, as usual, were going out of their way to ignore each other's existence. Ham Davis was brooding over the New York *Times*, Crouse was re-arranging the contents of his knapsack, Michelle Clark was staring at her fingernails, Bruckner and Dougherty were trading Sam Yorty jokes ... and the man in the tan suit was still shuffling back and forth at the smorgasbord table – totally absorbed in it, studying the carrots ...

Jesus Christ! I thought. The candidate! That crouching figure up there at the food table is George McGovern.

But where was his entourage? And why hadn't anybody else noticed him? Was he actually *alone*?

No, that was impossible. I had never seen a presidential candidate moving around in public without at least ten speedy 'aides' surrounding him at all times. So I watched him for a while, expecting to see his aides flocking in from the lobby at any moment ... but it slowly dawned on me that the candidate was by *himself*: there were no aides, no entourage, and nobody else in the room had even noticed his arrival.

This made me very nervous. McGovern was obviously waiting for somebody to greet him, keeping his back to the room, not even looking around – so there was no way for him to know that nobody in the room even knew he was there.

Finally I got up and walked across to the food table, watching McGovern out of the corner of one eye while I picked up some olives, fetched another beer out of the ice bucket ... and finally reached over to tap the candidate on the arm and introduce myself:

'Hello, Senator. We met a few weeks ago at Tom Braden's house in Washington.'

He smiled and reached out to shake hands. 'Of course, of course,' he said. 'What are you doing up *here*?'

'Not much, so far,' I said. 'We've been waiting for *you*.'

He nodded, still poking around with the cold cuts. I felt very uneasy.

Our last encounter had been somewhat jangled. He had just come back from New Hampshire, very tired and depressed, and when he arrived at Braden's house we had already finished dinner and I was getting heavily into drink. My memory of that evening is somewhat dim, but even in dimness I recall beating my gums at top speed for about two hours about how he was doing everything wrong and how helpless it was for him to think he could ever accomplish anything with that goddamn albatross of a Democratic Party on his neck, and that if he had any *real* sense he would make drastic alterations in the whole style & tone of his campaign and re-model it along the lines of the Aspen freak power uprising, specifically, along the lines of my own extremely weird and nerve-rattling campaign for Sheriff of Pitkin County, Colorado.

McGovern had listened politely, but two weeks later in New Hampshire there was no evidence to suggest that he had taken my advice very seriously. He was still plodding along in the passive/underdog role, still driving back & forth across the state in his lonely one-car motorcade to talk with small groups of people in rural living rooms. Nothing heavy, nothing wild or electric. All he was offering, he said, was a rare and admittedly longshot opportunity to vote for an honest and intelligent presidential candidate.

A very strange option, in any year – but in mid-February of 1972 there were no visible signs, in New Hampshire, that the citizenry was about to rise up and drive the swine out of the temple. Beyond that, it was absolutely clear – according to the wizards, gurus, and gentlemen journalists in Washington – that Big Ed Muskie, the man from Maine, had the Democratic nomination so deep in the bag that it was hardly worth arguing about.

Nobody argued with the things McGovern said. He was right, of course – but nobody took him very seriously, either ...

7:45 a.m.... The sun is fighting through the smog now, a hot grey glow on the street below my window. Friday morning business-worker traffic is beginning to clog Wilshire Boulevard and the Glendale Federal Savings parking lot across the street is filling up with cars. Slump-shouldered girls are scurrying into the big Title Insurance & Trust Company and Crocker National Bank buildings, rushing to punch in on the time clock before 8:00.

I can look down from my window and see the two McGovern press buses loading. Kirby Jones, the press secretary, is standing by the door of the no. 1 bus and herding two groggy CBS cameramen aboard like some kind of latter-day Noah getting goats aboard the ark. Kirby is responsible for keeping the McGovern press/media crowd happy – or at least happy enough to make sure they have the time and facilities to report whatever McGovern, Mankiewicz, and the other main boys want to see and read on tonight's TV news and in tomorrow's newspapers. Like any other good press secretary, Kirby doesn't mind admitting – off the record – that his love of pure truth is often tempered by circumstances. His job is to convince the press that everything the candidate says is even now being carved on stone tablets.

The truth is whatever George says; this is all ye know and all ye need to know. If McGovern says today that the most important issue in the California primary is abolition of the sodomy statutes, Kirby will do everything in his power to convince everybody on the press bus that the sodomy statutes *must* be abolished ... and if George decides tomorrow that his pro-sodomy gig isn't making it with the voters, Kirby will get behind a quick press release to the effect that 'new evidence from previously obscure sources' has convinced the Senator that what he really meant to say was that sodomy itself should be abolished.

This kind of fancy footwork was executed a lot easier back there in the early primaries than it is now. Since Wisconsin, McGovern's words have been watched very carefully. Both his mushrooming media entourage and his dwindling number of opponents have pounced on anything even vaguely controversial or potentially damaging in his speeches, press conferences, position papers, or even idle comments.

McGovern is very sensitive about this sort of thing, and for excellent reason. In three of the last four big primaries (Ohio, Nebraska & California) he has spent an alarmingly big chunk of his campaign time *denying* that behind his calm and decent façade he is really a sort of Trojan Horse candidate – coming on in public as a bucolic Jeffersonian Democrat while secretly plotting to seize the reins of power and turn them over at midnight on inauguration day to a red-bent hellbroth of radicals, dopers, traitors, sex fiends, anarchists, winos, and 'extremists' of every description.

The assault began in Ohio, when the Senator from Boeing (Henry Jackson, D-Wash.) began telling everybody his advance man could round up to listen to him that McGovern was not only a marijuana sympathizer, but also a fellow traveller ... Not *exactly* a dope-sucker and a card-carrying red, but almost.

In Nebraska it was Humphrey, and although he dropped the fellow traveller slur, he added amnesty and abortion to the marijuana charge and caused McGovern considerable grief. By election day the situation was so grim in traditionally conservative, Catholic Omaha that it looked like McGovern might actually *lose* the Nebraska primary, one of the kingpins in his overall strategy. Several hours after the polls closed the mood in the Omaha Hilton situation room was extremely glum. The

221

first returns showed Humphrey well ahead, and just before I was thrown out I heard Bill Dougherty – Lt Gov. of South Dakota and one of McGovern's close friends and personal advisers – saying: 'We're gonna get zinged tonight, folks.'

It was almost midnight before the out-state returns began offsetting Hubert's big lead in Omaha, and by 2:00 a.m. on Wednesday it was clear that McGovern would win – although the final six per cent margin was about half of what had been expected ten days earlier, before Humphrey's local allies had fouled the air with alarums about amnesty, abortion, and Marijuana.

Sometime around 11:30 I was readmitted to the situation room – because they wanted to use my portable radio to get the final results – and I remember seeing Gene Pokorny slumped in a chair with his shoes off and a look of great relief on his face. Pokorny, the architect of McGovern's breakthrough victory in Wisconsin, was also the campaign manager of Nebraska, his home state, and a loss there would have badly affected his future. Earlier that day in the hotel coffee shop I'd heard him asking Gary Hart which state he would be assigned to after Nebraska.

'Well, Gene,' Hart replied with a thin smile. 'That depends on what happens tonight, doesn't it?' Pokorny stared at him, but said nothing. Like almost all the other key people on the staff, he was eager to move on to California.

'Yeah,' Hart continued. 'We were planning on sending you out to California from here, but recently I've been thinking more and more about that slot we have open in the Butte, Montana office.'

Again, Pokorny said nothing ... but two weeks later, with Nebraska safely in the bag, he turned up in Fresno and hammered out another McGovern victory in the critically important Central Valley. And that slot in Butte is still open ...

Which is getting a bit off the point here. Indeed. We are drifting badly – from motorcycles to Mankiewicz to Omaha, Butte, Fresno ... where will it end?

The point, I think, was that in both the Ohio and Nebraska primaries, back to back, McGovern was confronted for the first time with the politics of the rabbit-punch and the groin shot, and in both states he found himself dangerously vulnerable to this kind of thing. Dirty politics confused him. He was not ready for it – and especially not from his fine old friend and neighbour, Hubert Humphrey. Towards the end of the Nebraska campaign he was spending most of his public time explaining that he was *not* for abortion on demand, *not* for legalized marijuana, *not* for unconditional amnesty ... and his staff was becoming more and more concerned that their man had been put completely on the defensive.

This is one of the oldest and most effective tricks in politics. Every hack in the business has used it in times of trouble, and it has even been elevated to the level of political mythology in a story about one of Lyndon Johnson's early campaigns in Texas. The race was close and Johnson was getting worried. Finally he told his campaign manager to start a massive rumour campaign about his opponent's life-long habit of enjoying carnal knowledge of his own barnyard sows.

'Christ, we can't get away with calling him a pig-fucker,' the campaign manager protested. 'Nobody's going to believe a thing like that.'

'I know,' Johnson replied. 'But let's make the sonofabitch *deny* it.'

McGovern has not learned to cope with this tactic yet. Humphrey used it again in California, with different issues, and once again George found himself working overtime to deny wild, baseless charges that he was: (1) planning to scuttle both the Navy and the Air Force, along with the whole aerospace industry, and (2) he was a sworn foe of all Jews, and if he ever got to the White House he would immediately cut off all military aid to Israel and sit on his hands while Russian-equipped Arab legions drove the Jews into the sea.

McGovern scoffed at these charges, dismissing them as 'ridiculous lies', and repeatedly explained his positions on both issues – but when they counted the votes on election night it was obvious that both the Jews and the aerospace workers in Southern California had taken Humphrey's bait. All that saved McGovern in California was a long-overdue success among black voters, strong support from Chicanos, and a massive pro-McGovern youth vote.

This is a very healthy power base, if he can keep it together – but it is not enough to beat Nixon in November unless McGovern can figure out some way to articulate his tax and welfare positions a hell of a lot more effectively than he did in California. Even Hubert Humphrey managed to get McGovern tangled up in his own economic proposals from time to time during their TV debates in California – despite the fact that towards the end of that campaign Humphrey's senile condition was so obvious that even I began feeling sorry for him.

Indeed. Sorry. Senile. Sick. Tangled ... That's exactly how I'm beginning to feel. All those words and many others, but my brain is too numb to spit them out of the memory bank at this time. No person in my condition has any business talking about Hubert Humphrey's behaviour. My brain has slowed down to the point of almost helpless stupor. I no longer even have the energy to grind my own teeth.

So this article is not going to end the way I thought it would ... and looking back at the lead I see that it didn't even start that way either. As for the middle, I can barely remember it. There was something about making a deal with Mankiewicz and then seizing power in American Samoa, but I don't feel ready right now. Maybe later ...

Way out on the far left corner of this desk I see a note that says 'Call Mankiewicz – Miami Hotel rooms.'

That's right. He was holding three rooms for us at the convention. Probably I should call him right away and firm that up ... or maybe not.

But what the hell? These things can wait. Before my arms go numb there were one or two points I wanted to make. This is certainly no time for any heavy speculation or long-range analysis – on any subject at all, but especially not on anything as volatile and complex as the immediate future of George McGovern *vis-à-vis* the Democratic Party.

Yet it is hard to avoid the idea that McGovern has put the party through some very drastic changes in the last few months. The good ole boys are not pleased with him. But they can't get a grip on him either – and now, less than three weeks before the convention, he is so close to a first-ballot victory that the old hacks and ward-heelers who thought they had total control of the party less than six months ago find themselves skulking around like old winos in the side alleys of presidential politics – first stripped of their power to select and control delegations, then rejected as delegates themselves when Big Ed took his overcrowded bandwagon over the high side on the first lap ... and now, incredible as it still seems to most of them, they will not even be allowed into the party convention next month.

One of the first people I plan to speak with when I get to Miami is Larry O'Brien: shake both of his hands and extend powerful congratulations to him for the job he has done on the party. In January of 1968 the Democratic Party was so fat and confident that it looked like they might keep control of the White House, the Congress, and in fact the whole US Government almost indefinitely. Now, four and a half years later, it is a useless bankrupt hulk. Even if McGovern wins the Democratic nomination, the party machinery won't be of much use to him, except as a vehicle.

'Traditional politics with a vengeance' is Gary Hart's phrase – a nutshell concept that pretty well describes the theory behind McGovern's amazingly effective organization.

The 'politics of vengeance' is a very different thing – an essentially psychotic concept that Hart would probably not go out of his way to endorse.

Vehicle ... vehicle ... vehicle – a very strange looking word, if you stare at it for eight or nine minutes ... 'Skulking' is another interesting-looking word.

And so much for that.

The morning news says Wilbur Mills is running for President again. He has scorned all invitations to accept the number two spot with anyone else – especially George McGovern. A very depressing bulletin. But Mills must know what he's doing. His name is said to be magic in certain areas. If the party rejects McGovern, I hope they give it to Mills. That would just about make the nut.

Another depressing news item – out of Miami Beach this time – says an unnatural number of ravens have been seen in the city recently. Tourists have complained of being kept awake all night by 'horrible croaking sounds' outside their hotel windows. 'At first there were only a few,' one local businessman explained. 'But more and more keep coming. They're building big nests in the trees along Collins Avenue. They're killing the trees and their droppings smell like dead flesh.'

Many residents say they can no longer leave their windows open at night, because of the croaking. 'I've always loved birds,' said another resident. 'But these goddamn ravens are something else!'

LATER IN JUNE

Mass Burial for Political Bosses in New York ... McGovern over the Hump ... The Death by Beating of a Six-Foot Blue-Black Serpent ... What Next for the Good Ole Boys? ... Anatomy of a Fixer ... Treachery Looms in Miami ...

It is now clear that this once small devoted band has become a great surging multitude all across this country – and it will not be denied.
George McGovern, on the night of the New York primary

The day after the New York primary I woke up in a suite on the twenty-fourth floor of Delmonico's Hotel on Park Avenue with a hellish wind tearing both rooms apart and rain coming in through all the open windows ... and I thought: Yes, wonderful, only a lunatic would get out of bed on a day like this; call room service for grapefruit and coffee, along with a New York *Times* for brain food, and one of those portable brickdome fireplaces full of oil-soaked sawdust logs that they can roll right into the suite and fire up at the foot of the bed.

Indeed. Get some heat in the room, but keep the windows open – for the sounds of the wind and the rain and the far-off honking of all those taxi horns down on Park Avenue.

Then fill a hot bath and get something like *Memphis Underground* on the tape machine. Relax, relax. Enjoy this fine rainy day, and send the bill to Random House. The budget boys won't like it, but to hell with them. Random House still owes me a lot of money from that time when the night watchman beat my snake to death on the white marble steps leading up to the main reception desk.

I had left it overnight in the editor's office, sealed up in a cardboard box with a sacrificial mouse ... but the mouse understood what was happening, and terror gave him strength to gnaw a hole straight through the side of the box and escape into the bowels of the building.

The snake followed, of course – through the same hole – and some-where around dawn, when the night watchman went out to check the main door, he was confronted with a six-foot blue-black serpent slither-ing rapidly up the stairs, flicking its tongue at him and hissing a warning that he was sure – according to his own account of the incident – was the last sound he would ever hear.

The snake was a harmless Blue Indigo that I'd just brought back from a reptile farm in Florida ... but the watchman had no way of knowing; he had never seen a snake. Most natives of Manhattan Island are terri-fied of all animals except cockroaches and poodles ... so when this poor ignorant bastard of a watchman suddenly found himself menaced by a hissing, six-foot serpent coming fast up the stairs at him from the general direction of Cardinal Spellman's quarters just across the courtyard ... he said the sight of it made him almost crazy with fear, and at first he was totally paralysed.

Then, as the snake kept on coming, some primal instinct shocked the man out of his trance and gave him the strength to attack the thing with the first weapon he could get his hands on – which he first described as a 'steel broom handle', but which further investigation revealed to have been a metal tube jerked out of a nearby vacuum cleaner.

The battle apparently lasted some twenty minutes: a terrible clang-ing and screaming in the empty marble entranceway, and finally the watchman prevailed. Both the serpent and the vacuum tube were beaten beyond recognition, and later that morning a copy editor found the watchman slumped on a stool in the basement next to the xerox machine, still gripping the mangled tube and unable to say what was wrong with him except that something horrible had tried to get him, but he finally managed to kill it.

The man has since retired, they say. Cardinal Spellman died and Random House moved to a new building. But the psychic scars remain, a dim memory of corporate guilt that is rarely mentioned except in times of stress or in arguments over money. Every time I start feeling a bit uneasy about running up huge bills on the Random House tab, I think about that snake – and then I call room service again.

STATE VOTE AIDS MCGOVERN:
SENATOR'S SLATES WIN BY LARGE MARGIN
IN THE SUBURBS

That was the *Times*'s big headline on Wednesday morning. The three a's candidate (acid, abortion, amnesty) had definitely improved his position by carrying the suburbs. The bulk of the political coverage on page one had to do with local races – 'Ryan, Badillo, Rangel win: Coller is in close battle' ... 'delegates named' ... Bingham defeats Scheuer; Rooney apparent winner'.

Down at the bottom of the page was a block of wire-photos from the National Mayors' Conference in New Orleans – also on Tuesday – and the choice shot from down there showed a smiling Hubert Humphrey sitting next to Mayor Daley of Chicago with the Mayor of Miami Beach leaning into the scene with one of his arms around Daley and the other around Hubert.

The caption said, 'Ex-mayor is hit with mayors'. The 'details, page 28' said Humphrey had definitely emerged as the star of the mayors' conference. The two losers were shown in smaller photos underneath the Daley/Humphrey thing. Muskie 'received polite applause', the caption said, and the camera had apparently caught him somewhere near the beginning of a delayed Ibogaine rush: his eyes are clouding over, his jaw has gone slack, his hair appears to be combed back in a DA.

The caption under the McGovern photo says, 'He, too, received moderate response.' But McGovern at least looked human, while the other four looked like they had just been trucked over on short notice from some third-rate wax museum in the French Quarter. The only genuinely ugly face of the five is that of Mayor Daley: He looks like a potato with mange – it is the face of a man who would see nothing wrong with telling his son to go out and round up a gang of thugs with bullhorns and kick the shit out of anybody stupid enough to challenge the Mayor of Chicago's right to name the next Democratic candidate for President of the United States.

I stared at the front page for a long time; there was something wrong with it, but I couldn't quite fix on the problem until ... yes ... I realized that the whole front page of the 21 June New York *Times* could just as easily have been dated 8 March, the day after the New Hampshire primary.

'Pacification' was failing again in Vietnam; Defense Secretary Melvin Laird was demanding more bombers; ITT was beating another illegal stock-sales rap ... but the most striking similarity was in the overall impression of what was happening in the fight for the Democratic presidential nomination.

Apparently nothing had changed. Muskie looked just as sick and confused as he had on that cold Wednesday morning in Manchester four months ago. McGovern looked like the same tough but hopeless underdog – and there was nothing in the face of either Daley or Humphrey to indicate that either one of those corrupt and vicious old screws had any doubt at all about what was going to happen in Miami in July. They appeared to be very pleased with whatever the Mayor of Miami Beach was saying to them ...

An extremely depressing front page, at first glance – almost rancid with a sense of *déjà vu*. There was even a Kennedy story: Will he or won't he?

This was the most interesting story on the page, if only because of the timing. Teddy had been out of the campaign news for a few months, but now – according to the *Times*'s R. W. Apple Jr – he was about to make his move:

'City Councilman Matthew J. Troy Jr will announce today that he is supporting Senator Edward M. Kennedy for the Democratic vice-presidential nomination, informed sources said last night. Mr Troy, a long-time political ally of the Kennedy family, was one of the earliest supporters of Senator George McGovern for the Presidency. As such, he would be unlikely to propose a running mate for the South Dakotan unless both men had indicated their approval.'

Unlikely.

Right. The logic was hard to deny. A McGovern/Kennedy ticket was probably the only sure winner available to the Democrats this year, but beyond that it might solve all of Kennedy's problems with one stroke. It would give him at least four and probably eight years in the spotlight; an unnaturally powerful and popular vice-president with all the advantages of the office and very few of the risks. If McGovern ran wild and called for the abolition of free enterprise, for instance, Kennedy could back off and shake his head sadly ... but if McGovern did everything right and won a second term as the most revered and successful President in the nation's history, Teddy would be right there beside him – the other half of the team; so clearly the heir apparent that he would hardly have to bother about campaigning in public in 1980.

Don't worry, boys, we'll weather this storm of approval and come out as
hated as ever.

Saul Alinsky to his staff shortly before his death, June 1972

The primaries are finally over now: twenty-three of the goddamn things
– and the deal is about to go down. New York was the last big spectacle
before Miami Beach, and this time McGovern's people really kicked
out the jams. They stomped every hack, ward-heeler, and 'old-line party
boss' from Buffalo to Brooklyn. The Democratic Party in New York
State was left in a frightened shambles.

Not even the state party leader, Joe Crangle, survived the McGovern
blitz. He tried to pass for 'uncommitted' – hoping to go down to Miami
with at least a small remnant of the big-time bargaining power he'd
planned on when he originally backed Muskie – but McGovern's merciless young streetfighters chopped Crangle down with the others. He will
watch the convention on TV, along with Brooklyn party boss Meade
Esposito and once-powerful Bronx leader Patrick Cunningham.

Former New York Governor Averell Harriman also wound up on the
list of ex-heavies who will not attend the convention. He too was an
early Muskie supporter. The last time I saw Averell he was addressing
a small crowd in the West Palm Beach railroad station – framed in a
halo of spotlights on the caboose platform of Big Ed's 'Sunshine Special'
... and the man from Maine was standing tall beside him, smiling
broadly, looking every inch the winner that all those half-bright party
bosses had assured him he was definitely going to be.

It was just about dusk when Harriman began speaking, as I recall,
and Muskie might have looked a little less pleased if he'd had any way
of knowing that – ten blocks away, while Ave was still talking – a
human threshing machine named Peter Sheridan was eagerly hitting the
bricks after two weeks in the Palm Beach jail on a vagrancy rap.

Unknown to either Big Ed or Peter, their paths were soon destined to
cross. Twelve hours later, Sheridan – the infamous wandering boohoo
for the Neo-American church – would board the 'Sunshine Special' for
the last leg of the trip into Miami.

That encounter is already legend. I am not especially proud of my
role in it – mainly because the nightmare developed entirely by accident
– but if I could go back and try it all over again I wouldn't change a
note.

At the time I felt a bit guilty about it: having been, however inno-
cently, responsible for putting the Demo front-runner on a collision
course with a gin-crazed acid freak – but that was before I realized what
kind of a beast I was dealing with.

It was not until his campaign collapsed and his ex-staffers felt free to talk that I learned that working for Big Ed was something like being locked in a rolling boxcar with a vicious 200-pound water rat. Some of his top staff people considered him dangerously unstable. He had several identities, they said, and there was no way to be sure on any given day if they would have to deal with Abe Lincoln, Hamlet, Captain Queeg, or Bobo the Simpleminded ...

Many strange Muskie stories, but this is not the time for them. Perhaps after the convention, when the pressure lets off a bit – although not even that is certain, now: Things are getting weird.

The only 'Muskie story' that interests me right now is the one about how he managed to con those poor bastards into making him the *de facto* party leader and also the bosses' choice to carry the party colours against Nixon in November. I want to know that story, and if anybody who reads this can fill me in on the details, by all means call at once c/o *Rolling Stone*, San Francisco.

The Muskie nightmare is beginning to look more and more like a major political watershed for the Democratic Party. When Big Ed went down he took about half of the national power structure with him. In one state after another – each time he lost a primary – Muskie crippled and humiliated the local Democratic power-mongers: governors, mayors, senators, congressmen ... Big Ed was supposed to be their ticket to Miami, where they planned to do business as usual once again, and keep the party at least livable, if not entirely healthy. All Muskie had to do, they said, was keep his mouth shut and act like Abe Lincoln.

The bosses would do the rest. As for that hare-brained bastard McGovern, he could take those reformist ideas he'd been working on, and jam them straight up his ass. A convention packed wall to wall with Muskie delegates – the rancid cream of the party, as it were – would make short work of McGovern's Boy Scout bullshit.

That was four months ago, before Muskie began crashing around the country in a stupid rage and destroying everything he touched. First it was booze, then reds, and finally over the brink into ibogaine ... and it was right about that time that most of the good ole boys decided to take another long look at Hubert Humphrey. He wasn't much; they all agreed on that – but by May he was all they had left.

Not much, for sure. Any political party that can't cough up anything better than a treacherous brain-damaged old vulture like Hubert Humphrey deserves every beating it gets. They don't hardly make 'em like Hubert any more – but just to be on the safe side, he should be castrated anyway.

Castrated? Jesus! Is nothing sacred? Four years ago Hubert Humphrey ran for President of the United States on the Democratic ticket – and he almost won.

It was a very narrow escape. I voted for Dick Gregory in 68, and if somehow Humphrey manages to slither on to the ticket again this year I will vote for Richard Nixon.

But Humphrey will not be on the ticket this year – at least not on the Democratic ticket. He may end up running with Nixon, but the odds are against him there, too. Not even Nixon could stoop to Hubert's level.

So what will Humphrey do with himself this year? Is there no room at the top for a totally dishonest person? *A United States senator?* A loyal party man?

Well ... as much as I hate to get away from objective journalism, even briefly, there is no other way to explain what that treacherous bastard appears to be cranking himself up for this time around, except by slipping momentarily into the realm of speculation.

But first, a few realities: (1) George McGovern is so close to a first-ballot nomination in Miami that everybody except Hubert Humphrey, Gene McCarthy, Shirley Chisholm, and Ed Muskie seems ready to accept it as a foregone conclusion ... (2) The national Democratic Party is no longer controlled by the old guard, boss-style hacks like George Meany and Mayor Daley – or even by the old guard liberal-*manqué* types like Larry O'Brien, who thought they had things firmly under control as recently as six months ago ... (3) McGovern has made it painfully clear that he wants more than just the nomination; he has every intention of tearing the Democratic Party completely. apart and rebuilding it according to his own blueprint ... (4) If McGovern beats Nixon in November he will be in a position to do anything he wants either to or with the party structure ... (5) But if McGovern loses in November, control of the Democratic Party will instantly revert to the ole boys, and McGovern himself will be labelled 'another Goldwater' and stripped of any power in the party.

The pattern is already there, from 1964, when the Nixon/Mitchell brain-trust – already laying plans for 1968 – sat back and let the GOP machinery fall into the hands of the Birchers and the right-wing crazies for a few months ... and when Goldwater got stomped, the Nixon/ Mitchell crowd moved in and took over the party with no argument from anybody ... and four years later Nixon moved into the White House.

There have already been a few rumblings and muted threats along these lines from the Daley/Meany faction. Daley has privately threatened to dump Illinois to Nixon in November if McGovern persists in challenging Daley's eighty-five-man slave delegation to the convention in Miami ... and Meany is prone to muttering out loud from time to time that maybe organized labour would be better off in the long run by enduring another four years under Nixon, rather than running the risk of whatever radical madness he fears McGovern might bring down on him.

The only other person who has said anything about taking a dive for Nixon in November is Hubert Humphrey, who has already threatened in public – at the party's credentials committee hearings in Washington last week – to let his friend Joe Alioto, the Mayor of San Francisco, throw the whole state of California to Nixon unless the party gives Hubert 151 California delegates – on the basis of his losing show of strength in that state's winner-take-all primary.

Hubert understood all along that California was all or nothing. He continually referred to it is the 'big one', and 'the Super Bowl of the primaries' ... but he changed his mind when he lost. One of the finest flashes of TV journalism in many months appeared on the CBS evening news the same day Humphrey formally filed his claim to almost half the California delegation. It was a Walter Cronkite interview with Hubert in California, a week or so prior to election day. Cronkite asked him if he had any objections to the winner-take-all aspect of the California primary, and Humphrey replied that he thought it was absolutely wonderful.

'So even if you lose out here – if you lose all 271 delegates – you wouldn't challenge the winner-take-all rule?' Cronkite asked.

'Oh, my goodness, no,' Hubert said. 'That would make me sort of a spoilsport, wouldn't it?'

On the face of it, McGovern seems to have everything under control now. Less than twenty-four hours after the New York results were final, chief delegate-meister Rick Stearns announced that George was over the hump. The New York blitz was the clincher, pushing him over the 1350 mark and mashing all but the flimsiest chance that anybody would continue to talk seriously about a 'Stop McGovern' movement in Miami. The Humphrey/Muskie axis had been desperately trying to put something together with ageing diehards like Wilbur Mills, George Meany, and Mayor Daley – hoping to stop McGovern just short of 1400 – but on the weekend after the New York sweep George picked up another fifty or so from the last of the non-primary state caucuses and by Sunday, 25 June, he was only a hundred votes away from the 1509 that would zip it all up on the first ballot.

At that point the number of officially 'uncommitted' delegates was still hovering around 450, but there had already been some small-scale defections to McGovern, and the others were getting nervous. The whole purpose of getting yourself elected as an uncommitted delegate is to be able to arrive at the convention with bargaining power. Ideology has nothing to do with it.

If you're a lawyer from St Louis, for instance, and you manage to get yourself elected as an uncommitted delegate for Missouri, you will hustle down to Miami and start scouting around for somebody to make a deal with ... which won't take long, because every candidate still in the running for anything at all will have dozens of his own personal fixers roaming around the hotel bars and buttonholing uncommitted delegates to find out what they want.

If your price is a lifetime appointment as a judge on the US Circuit Court, your only hope is to deal with a candidate who is so close to that magic 1509 figure that he can no longer function in public because of uncontrollable drooling. If he is stuck around 1400 you will probably not have much luck getting that bench appointment ... but if he's already up to 1499 he won't hesitate to offer you the first opening on the US Supreme Court ... and if you catch him peaked at 1505 or so, you can squeeze him for almost anything you want.

The game will get heavy sometimes. You don't want to go around putting the squeeze on people unless you're absolutely clean. *No skeletons in the closet*: no secret vices ... because if your vote is important and your price is high, the fixer-man will have already checked you out by the time he offers to buy you a drink. If you bribed a traffic-court clerk two years ago to bury a drunk driving charge, the fixer might suddenly confront you with a photostat of the citation you thought had been burned.

When that happens, you're fucked. Your price just went down to zero, and you are no longer an uncommitted delegate.

There are several other versions of the reverse-squeeze: the fake hit-and-run; glassine bags found in your hotel room by a maid; grabbed off the street by phoney cops for statutory rape of a teenage girl you never saw before ...

Every once in a while you might hit on something with real style, like this one: On Monday afternoon, the first day of the convention, you – the ambitious young lawyer from St Louis with no skeletons in the closet and no secret vices worth worrying about – are spending the afternoon by the pool at the Playboy Plaza, soaking up sun and gin/tonics when you hear somebody calling your name. You look up and see a smiling, rotund chap about thirty-five years old coming at you, ready to shake hands.

'Hi there, Virgil,' he says. 'My name's J. D. Squane. I work for Senator Bilbo and we'd sure like to count on your vote. How about it?'

You smile, but say nothing – waiting for Squane to continue. He will want to know your price.

But Squane is staring out to sea, squinting at something on the horizon ... then he suddenly turns back to you and starts talking very fast about how he always wanted to be a riverboat pilot on the Mississippi, but politics got in the way ... 'And now, goddamnit, we *must* get these last few votes ...'

You smile again, itching to get serious. But Squane suddenly yells at somebody across the pool, then turns back to you and says: 'Jesus, Virgil, I'm really sorry about this, but I have to run. That guy over there is delivering my new Jensen Interceptor.' He grins and extends his hand again. Then: 'Say, maybe we can talk later on, eh? What room are you in?'

'1909.'

He nods. 'How about seven, for dinner? Are you free?'

'Sure.'

'Wonderful,' he replies. 'We can take my new Jensen for a run up to Palm Beach ... It's one of my favourite towns.'

'Mine too,' you say. 'I've heard a lot about it.'

He nods. 'I spent some time there last February ... but we had a bad act, dropped about twenty-five grand.'

Jesus! Jensen Interceptor; twenty-five grand ... Squane is definitely big-time.

'See you at seven,' he says, moving away.

The knock comes at 7:02 – but instead of Squane it's a beautiful silver-haired young girl who says J. D. sent her to pick you up. 'He's having a business dinner with the Senator and he'll join us later at the Crab House.'

'Wonderful, wonderful – shall we have a drink?'

She nods. 'Sure, but not here. We'll drive over to North Miami and pick up my girlfriend ... but let's smoke this before we go.'

'Jesus! That looks like a cigar!'

'It is!' she laughs. 'And it'll make us both crazy.'

Many hours later, 4:30 a.m. Soaking wet, falling into the lobby, begging for help: no wallet, no money, no ID. Blood on both hands and one shoe missing, dragged up to the room by two bellboys ...

Breakfast at noon the next day, half sick in the coffee shop – waiting for a Western Union money order from the wife in St Louis. Very spotty memories from last night.

'Hi there, Virgil.'

J. D. Squane, still grinning. 'Where were you last night, Virgil? I came by right on the dot, but you weren't in.'

'I got mugged – by your girlfriend.'

'Oh? Too bad. I wanted to nail down that ugly little vote of yours.'

'Ugly? Wait a minute ... That girl you sent; we went someplace to *meet you.*'

'Bullshit! You double-crossed me, Virgil! If we weren't on the same team I might be tempted to lean on you.'

Rising anger now, painful throbbing in the head. 'Fuck you, Squane! I'm on *nobody's* team! If you want my vote you know damn well how to get it – and that goddamn dope-addict girlfriend of yours didn't help any.'

Squane smiles heavily. 'Tell me, Virgil – what was it you wanted for the vote of yours? A seat on the federal bench?'

'You're goddamn fuckin'-a right! You got me in bad trouble last night, J. D. When I got back there my wallet was gone and there was blood on my hands.'

'I know. You beat the shit out of her.'

'What?'

'Look at these photographs, Virgil. It's some of the most disgusting stuff I've ever seen.'

'Photographs?'

Squane hands them across the table.

'Oh my God!'

'Yeah, that's what *I* said, Virgil.'

'No! This can't be *me*! I never saw that girl! Christ, she's only a child!'

'That's why the pictures are so disgusting, Virgil. You're lucky we didn't take them straight to the cops and have you locked up.' Pounding the table with his fist. 'That's *rape*, Virgil! That's *sodomy*! With a *child*!'

'No!'

'*Yes*, Virgil – and now you're going to pay for it.'

'How? What are you talking about?'

Squane smiling again. 'Votes, my friend. Yours and five others. Six votes for six negatives. Are you ready?'

Tears of rage in the eyes now. 'You evil sonofabitch! You're blackmailing me!'

'Ridiculous, Virgil. Ridiculous. I'm talking about coalition politics.'

'I don't even *know* six delegates. Not personally, anyway. And besides, they all *want* something.'

Squane shakes his head. 'Don't *tell* me about it, Virgil. I'd rather not hear. Just bring me six names off this list by noon tomorrow. If they all vote right, you'll never hear another word about what happened last night.'

'What if I can't?'

Squane smiles, then shakes his head sadly. 'Your life will take a turn for the worse, Virgil.'

Ah, bad craziness ... a scene like that could run on forever. Sick dialogue comes easy after five months on the campaign trail. A sense of humour is not considered mandatory for those who want to get heavy into presidential politics. Junkies don't laugh much; their gig is too serious – and the politics junkie is not much different on that score than a smack junkie.

The high is very real in both worlds, for those who are into it – but anybody who has ever tried to live with a smack junkie will tell you it can't be done without coming to grips with the spike and shooting up, yourself.

Politics is no different. There is a fantastic adrenalin high that comes with total involvement in almost any kind of fast-moving political campaign – especially when you're running against big odds and starting to feel like a winner.

As far as I know, I am the only journalist covering the 72 presidential campaign who has done any time on the other side of that gap – both as a candidate and a backroom pol, on the local level – and despite all the obvious differences between running on the freak power ticket for Sheriff of Aspen and running as a well-behaved Democrat for President of the United States, the roots are surprisingly similar ... and whatever real differences exist are hardly worth talking about, compared to the massive, unbridgeable gap between the cranked-up reality of living day after day in the vortex of a rolling campaign – and the fiendish rat-bastard tedium of covering that same campaign as a journalist, from the outside looking in.

For the same reason that nobody who has never come to grips with the spike can ever understand how far away it really is across that gap to the place where the smack junkie lives ... there is no way for even the best and most talented journalist to know what is really going on inside a political campaign unless he has been there himself.

Very few of the press people assigned to the McGovern campaign, for instance, have anything more than a surface understanding of what is really going on in the vortex ... or if they do, they don't mention it, in print or on the air: And after spending half a year following this god-damn zoo around the country and watching the machinery at work I'd be willing to bet pretty heavily that not even the most privileged ranking insiders among the campaign press corps are telling much less than they know.

Fear and Loathing: On the Campaign Trail,
San Francisco, Straight Arrow Books, 1973

SEPTEMBER

Fat City Blues ... Fear and Loathing on the White House Press Plane ... Bad *Angst* at McGovern Headquarters ... Nixon Tightens the Screws ... 'Many Appeared to Be in the Terminal Stages of Campaign Bloat' ...

Hear me, people: We have now to deal with another race – small and feeble when our fathers first met them, but now great and overbearing. Strangely enough they have a mind to till the soil and the love of possession is a disease with them. These people have made many rules that the rich may break but the poor may not. They take their tithes from the poor and weak to support the rich and those who rule.

Chief Sitting Bull, speaking at the Powder River Conference in 1877

If George McGovern had a speech writer half as eloquent as Sitting Bull, he would be home free today – instead of twenty-two points behind and racing around the country with both feet in his mouth. The Powder River Conference ended ninety-five years ago, but the old chief's baleful analysis of the white man's rape of the American continent was just as accurate then as it would be today if he came back from the dead and said it for the microphones on prime-time TV. The ugly fallout from the American Dream has been coming down on us at a pretty consistent rate since Sitting Bull's time – and the only real difference now, with election day 72 only a few weeks away, is that we seem to be on the verge of *ratifying* the fallout and forgetting the dream itself.

Sitting Bull made no distinction between Democrats and Republicans – which was probably just as well, in 1877 or any other year – but it's also true that Sitting Bull never knew the degradation of travelling on Richard Nixon's press plane; he never had the bilious pleasure of dealing with Ron Ziegler, and he never met John Mitchell, Nixon's king fixer.

If the old Sioux chief had ever done these things, I think – despite his angry contempt for the white man and everything he stands for – he'd be working overtime for George McGovern today.

These past two weeks have been relatively calm ones for me. Immediately after the Republican Convention in Miami, I dragged myself back to the Rockies and tried to forget about politics for a while – just lie naked on the porch in the cool afternoon sun and watch the aspen trees turning gold on the hills around my house; mix up a huge canister of gin and grapefruit juice, watch the horses nuzzling each other in the pasture across the road, big logs in the fireplace at night; Herbie Mann, John Prine, and Jesse Colin Young booming out of the speakers ... zip off every once in a while for a fast run into town along a back road above the river: to the health-centre gym for some volleyball, then over to Benton's gallery to get caught up on whatever treacheries the local greedheads rammed through while I was gone, watch the late TV news and curse McGovern for poking another hole in his own boat, then stop by the Jerome on the way out of town for a midnight beer with Solheim.

After two weeks on that peaceful human schedule, the last thing I wanted to think about was the grim, inescapable spectre of two more frenzied months on the campaign trail. Especially when it meant coming back here to Washington, to start laying the groundwork for a long and painful autopsy job on the McGovern campaign. What went wrong? Why had it failed? Who was to blame? And, finally, what next?

That was one project. The other was to somehow pass through the fine eye of the White House security camel and go out on the campaign trail with Richard Nixon, to watch him waltz in – if only to get the drift of his thinking, to watch the moves, his eyes. It is a nervous thing to consider: not just four more years of Nixon, but Nixon's *last four years in politics* – completely unshackled, for the first time in his life, from any need to worry about who might or might not vote for him the next time around.

If he wins in November, he will finally be free to do whatever he wants ... or maybe 'wants' is too strong a word for right now. It conjures up images of Papa Doc, Batista, Somoza; jails full of bewildered 'political prisoners' and the constant cold-sweat fear of jackboots suddenly kicking your door off its hinges at four a.m.

There is no point in kidding ourselves about what Richard Nixon really *wants* for America. When he stands at his White House window and looks out on an anti-war demonstration, he doesn't see 'dissenters', he sees *criminals*. Dangerous parasites, preparing to strike at the heart of the great American system that put him where he is today.

There may not be much difference between Democrats and Republicans; I have made that argument myself – with considerable venom, as I recall – over the past ten months ... But only a blind geek or a waterhead could miss the difference between McGovern and Richard Nixon. Granted, they are both white men; and both are politicians – but the similarity ends right there, and from that point on the difference is so vast that anybody who can't see it deserves whatever happens to them if Nixon gets re-elected due to apathy, stupidity, and laziness on the part of potential McGovern voters.

The tragedy of this campaign is that McGovern and his staff wizards have not been able to dramatize what is really at stake on 7 November. We are not looking at just another dim rerun of the 68 Nixon/Humphrey trip, or the LBJ/Goldwater fiasco in 64. Those were both useless drills. I voted for Dick Gregory in 68, and for 'No' in 64 ... but this one is different, and since McGovern is so goddamn maddeningly inept with the kind of words he needs to make people understand what he's up to, it will save a lot of time here – and strain on my own weary head – to remember Bobby Kennedy's ultimate characterization of Richard Nixon, in a speech at Vanderbilt University in the spring of 1968, not long before he was murdered.

'Richard Nixon,' he said, 'represents the dark side of the American spirit.'

I don't remember what else he said that day. I guess I could look it up in the New York *Times* speech morgue, but why bother? That one line says it all.

The mood at McGovern's grim headquarters building at 1910 K Street, NW, in Washington is oddly schizoid these days: a jangled mix of defiance and despair – tempered, now and then, by quick flashes of a lingering conviction that George can still win.

McGovern's young staffers, after all, have *never lost an election they expected to win, at the outset* – and they definitely expected to win this one. They are accustomed to being far behind in the public opinion polls. McGovern has almost always been the underdog, and – except for California – he has usually been able to close the gap with a last-minute stretch run.

Even in the primaries he lost – New Hampshire, Ohio, Pennsylvania – he did well enough to embarrass the pollsters, humiliate the pols, and crank up his staff morale another few notches.

But that boundless blind faith is beginning to fade now. The curse of Eagleton is beginning to make itself felt in the ranks. And not even Frank Mankiewicz, the wizard of Chevy Chase, can properly explain why McGovern is now being sneered at from coast to coast as 'just another politician'. Mankiewicz is still the main drivewheel in this hamstrung campaign; he has been the central intelligence from the very beginning – which was fine all around, while it worked, but there is not a hell of a lot of evidence to suggest that it's working real well these days, and it is hard to avoid the idea that Frank is just as responsible for whatever is happening now as he was six months ago, when McGovern came wheeling out of New Hampshire like the abominable snowman on a speed trip.

If George gets stomped in November, it will not be because of anything Richard Nixon did to him. The blame will trace straight back to his brain-trust, to whoever had his ear tight enough to convince him that all that bullshit about 'new politics' was fine for the primaries, but it would never work against Nixon – so he would have to abandon his original power base, after Miami, and swiftly move to consolidate the one he'd just shattered: the Meany/Daley/Humphrey/Muskie axis, the senile remnants of the Democratic Party's once-powerful 'Roosevelt coalition'.

McGovern agreed. He went to Texas and praised LBJ; he revised his economic programme to make it more palatable on Wall Street; he went to Chicago and endorsed the whole Daley/Democratic ticket, including State's Attorney Ed Hanrahan, who is still under indictment on felony/conspiracy (obstruction of justice) charges for his role in a police raid on local Black Panther headquarters three years ago that resulted in the murder of Fred Hampton.

In the speedy weeks between March and July, the atmosphere in McGovern's cramped headquarters building on Capitol Hill was so high that you could get bent by just hanging around and watching the human machinery at work.

The headquarters building itself was not much bigger than McGovern's personal command post in the Senate Office Building, five blocks away. It was one big room about the size of an Olympic swimming pool – with a grocery store on one side, a liquor store on the other, and a tree-shaded sidewalk out front. The last time I was there, about two weeks before the California primary, I drove my blue Volvo up on the sidewalk and parked right in front of the door. Crouse went inside to find Mankiewicz while I picked up some Ballantine ale.

'Is this a charge?' the booze-clerk asked.

'Right,' I said. 'Charge it to George McGovern.'

He nodded, and began to write it down.

'Hey, wait a minute!' I said. 'I was just kidding. Here – here's the cash.'

He shrugged and accepted the three bills ... and when I got to Frank's office and told him what had happened, he didn't seem surprised. 'Yeah, our credit's pretty good,' he said, 'in a lot of places where we never even asked for it.'

That was back in May, when the tide was still rising. But things are different now, and the credit is not so easy. The new K Street headquarters is an eight-storey tomb once occupied by the 'Muskie for President' juggernaut. Big Ed abandoned it when he dropped out of the race for the Democratic nomination, and it stood empty for a month or so after that – but when McGovern croaked Humphrey in California and became the nominee-apparent, his wizards decided to get a new and larger headquarters.

The Muskie building was an obvious choice – if only because it was available very cheap, and already wired for the fantastic maze of phone lines necessary for a presidential campaign headquarters. The man from Maine and his army of big-time backers had already taken care of that aspect; they had plenty of phone lines, along with all those endorsements.

Not everybody on the McGovern staff was happy with the idea of moving out of the original headquarters. The decision was made in California, several days before the primary, and I remember arguing with Gary Hart about it. He insisted the move was necessary, for space reasons ... and even in retrospect my argument for keeping the original headquarters seems irrational. It was a matter of karma, I said, psychic continuity. And besides, I had spent some time in the Muskie building on the night of the New Hampshire primary, when the atmosphere of the place was strongly reminiscent of Death Row at Sing Sing. So my memories of that building were not pleasant – but my reasons, as usual, had a noticeably mystic flavour to them. And Gary, as usual, was thinking in terms of hard lawyer's logic and political pragmatism.

So the McGovern headquarters was moved, after Miami, from the original base between the liquor store and the grocery store on Capitol Hill to the Muskie tomb on K Street, in the fashionable downtown area. It was a central location, they said, with a big parking lot next door. It also had two elevators and sixteen bathrooms.

The original headquarters had only one bathroom, with a cardboard arrow on the door that could be moved, like a one-armed clock, to three different positions: MEN, WOMEN or EMPTY.

There was also a refrigerator. It was small, but somehow there were always a few cans of beer in it, even for visiting journalists. Nobody was in charge of stocking it, but nobody drank the last beer without replacing it, either ... (or maybe it was all a shuck from the start; maybe they had a huge stash outside the back door, but they only kept two or three cans in the refrigerator, so that anybody who drank one would feel so guilty that he/she would bring six to replace it, the next time they came around ... but I doubt it; not even that devious Arab bastard Rick Stearns would plot things that carefully).

*

But what the hell? All that is history now, and after roaming around the new McGovern headquarters building for a week or so, the only refrigerator I found was up in finance director Henry Kimmelman's office on the sixth floor. I went up there with Pat Caddell one afternoon last week to watch the Cronkite/Chancellor TV news (every afternoon at 6:30, all activity in the building is suspended for an hour while the staff people gather around TV sets to watch 'the daily bummer', as some of them call it) and Kimmelman has the only accessible colour set in the building, so his office is usually crowded for the news hour.

But his set is fucked, unfortunately. One of the colour tubes is blown, so everything that appears on the screen has a wet purple tint on it. When McGovern comes on, rapping out lines from a speech that somebody watching one of the headquarters' TV sets just wrote for him a few hours earlier, his face appears on the set in Kimmelman's office as if he were speaking up from the bottom of a swimming pool full of cheap purple dye.

It is not a reassuring thing to see, and most of the staffers prefer to watch the news on the black & white sets downstairs in the political section ...

What? We seem to be off the track here. I was talking about my first encounter with the refrigerator in Henry Kimmelman's office – when I was looking for beer, and found none. The only thing in the icebox was a canned martini that tasted like brake fluid.

One canned martini. No beer. A purple TV screen. Both elevators jammed in the basement; fifteen empty bathrooms. Seventy-five cents an hour to park in the lot next door. Chaos and madness in the telephone switchboard. Fear in the back rooms, confusion up front, and a spooky vacuum on top – the eighth floor – where Larry O'Brien is supposed to be holding the gig together ... what is he doing up there? Nobody knows. They never see him.

'Larry travels a lot,' one of the speech writers told me. 'He's number one, you know – and when you're number one you don't have to try so hard, right?'

The McGovern campaign appears to be fucked at this time. A spectacular come-from-behind win is still possible – on paper and given the right circumstances – but the underlying realities of the campaign itself would seem to preclude this. A cohesive, determined campaign with the same kind of multi-level morale that characterized the McGovern effort in the months preceding the Wisconsin primary might be a good bet to close a twenty-point gap on Nixon in the last month of this grim presidential campaign.

As usual, Nixon has peaked too early – and now he is locked into what is essentially a holding action. Which would be disastrous in a close race, but – even by Pat Caddell's partisan estimate – Nixon could blow twenty points off his lead in the next six weeks and still win. (Caddell's figures seem in general agreement with those of the most recent Gallup Poll, ten days ago, which showed that Nixon could blow *thirty* points off his lead and still win.)

My own rude estimate is that McGovern will steadily close the gap between now and 7 November, but not enough. If I had to make book right now, I would try to get McGovern with seven or eight points, but I'd probably go with five or six, if necessary. In other words, my guess at the moment is that McGovern will lose by a popular vote margin of 5.5 per cent – and probably far worse in the electoral college.*

The tragedy of this is that McGovern appeared to have a sure lock on the White House when the sun came up on Miami Beach on the morning of Thursday 13 July. Since then he has crippled himself with a series of almost unbelievable blunders – Eagleton, Salinger, O'Brien, etc. – that have understandably convinced huge chunks of the electorate, including at least half of his own hard-core supporters, that the candidate is a gibbering dingbat. His behaviour since Miami has made a piecemeal mockery of everything he seemed to stand for during the primaries.

Possibly I'm wrong on all this. It is still conceivable – to me at least – that McGovern might actually win. In which case I won't have to worry about my PO Box at the Woody Creek general store getting jammed up with dinner invitations from the White House. But what the hell? Mr Nixon never invited me, and neither did Kennedy or LBJ.

I survived those years of shame, and I'm not especially worried about enduring four more. I have a feeling that my time is getting short, anyway, and I can think of a hell of a lot of things I'd rather find in my mailbox than an invitation to dinner in the servants' quarters.

Let those treacherous bastards eat by themselves. They deserve each other.

Ah, Jesus! The situation is out of hand again. The sun is up, the deal is down, and that evil bastard Mankiewicz just jerked the kingpin out of

---

* I was somewhat off on this prediction. The final margin was almost 23%. At this point in the campaign I was no longer functioning with my ruthless objectivity. Back in May and June, when my head was still clear, I won vast amounts of money with a consistency that baffled the experts. David Broder still owes me $500 as a result of his ill-advised bet on Hubert Humphrey in the California primary. But he still refuses to pay on the grounds that I lost the 500 back to him as a result of a forfeited foot-race between Jim Naughton and Jack Germond in Miami Beach.

my finely crafted saga for this issue. My brain has gone numb from this madness. After squatting for thirteen days in this scum-crusted room on the top floor of the Washington Hilton – writing feverishly, night after night, on the home-stretch realities of this goddamn wretched campaign – I am beginning to wonder what in the name of twisted Jesus ever possessed me to come here in the first place. What kind of madness lured me back to this stinking swamp of a town?

Am I turning into a politics junkie? It is not a happy thought – particularly when I see what it's done to all the others. After two weeks in Woody Creek, getting back on the press plane was like going back to the cancer ward. Some of the best people in the press corps looked so physically ravaged that it was painful to even see them, much less stand around and make small talk.

Many appeared to be in the terminal stages of campaign bloat, a gruesome kind of false-fat condition that is said to be connected somehow with failing adrenal glands. The swelling begins within twenty-four hours of that moment when the victim first begins to suspect that the campaign is essentially meaningless. At that point, the body's entire adrenalin supply is sucked back into the gizzard, and nothing either candidate says, does, or generates will cause it to rise again ... and without adrenalin, the flesh begins to swell; the eyes fill with blood and grow smaller in the face, the jowls puff out from the cheekbones, the neck-flesh droops, and the belly swells up like a frog's throat ... The brain fills with noxious waste fluids, the tongue is rubbed raw on the molars, and the basic perception antennae begin dying like hairs in a bonfire.

I would like to think – or at least *claim* to think, out of charity if nothing else – that campaign bloat is at the root of this hellish *angst* that boils up to obscure my vision every time I try to write anything serious about presidential politics.

But I don't think that's it. The real reason, I suspect, is the problem of coming to grips with the idea that Richard Nixon will almost certainly be re-elected for another four years as President of the United States. If the current polls are reliable – and even if they aren't, the sheer size of the margin makes the numbers themselves unimportant – Nixon will be re-elected by a huge majority of Americans who feel he is not only more honest and more trustworthy than George McGovern, but also more likely to end the war in Vietnam.

The polls also indicate that Nixon will get a comfortable majority of the youth vote. And that he might carry all fifty states.

Well ... maybe so. This may be the year when we finally come face to face with ourselves; finally just lay back and say it – that we are really just a nation of 220 million used car salesmen with all the money we need to buy guns, and no qualms at all about killing anybody else in the world who tries to make us uncomfortable.

The tragedy of all this is that George McGovern, for all his mistakes and all his imprecise talk about 'new politics' and 'honesty in government', is one of the few men who've run for President of the United States in this century who really understands what a fantastic monument to all the best instincts of the human race this country might have been, if we could have kept it out of the hands of greedy little hustlers like Richard Nixon.

McGovern made some stupid mistakes, but in context they seem almost frivolous compared to the things Richard Nixon does every day of his life, on purpose, as a matter of policy and a perfect expression of everything he stands for.

Jesus! Where will it end? How low do you have to stoop in this country to be President?

Fear and Loathing: On the Campaign Trail,
San Francisco, Straight Arrow Books, 1973

OCTOBER

'Ask Not for Whom the Bell Tolls ...'

Due to circumstances beyond my control, I would rather not write anything about the 1972 presidential campaign at this time. On Tuesday 7 November, I will get out of bed long enough to go down to the polling place and vote for George McGovern. Afterwards, I will drive back to the house, lock the front door, get back in bed, and watch television as long as necessary. It will probably be a while before the *angst* lifts – but whenever it happens I will get out of bed again and start writing the mean, cold-blooded bummer that I was not quite ready for today. Until then, I think Tom Benton's 're-elect the President' poster says everything that needs to be said right now about this malignant election. In any other year I might be tempted to embellish the death's head with a few angry flashes of my own. But not in 1972. At least not in the sullen numbness of these final hours before the deal goes down – because words are no longer important at this stage of the campaign; all the best ones were said a long time ago, and all the right ideas were bouncing around in public long before Labor Day.

That is the one grim truth of this election most likely to come back and haunt us: The options were clearly defined, and all the major candidates except Nixon were publicly grilled, by experts who demanded to know exactly where they stood on every issue from gun control and abortion to the ad valorem tax. By mid-September both candidates had staked out their own separate turf and if not everybody could tell you what each candidate stood for *specifically*, almost everyone likely to vote in November understood that Richard Nixon and George McGovern were two very different men: not only in the context of politics, but also in their personalities, temperaments, guiding principles, and even their basic lifestyles ...

There is almost a yin/yang clarity in the difference between the two men, a contrast so stark that it would be hard to find any two better models in the national politics arena for the legendary *duality* – the congenital split personality and polarized instincts – that almost everybody except Americans has long since taken for granted as the key to our national character. This was not what Richard Nixon had in mind when he said, last August, that the 1972 presidential election would offer voters 'the clearest choice of this century', but on a level he will never understand he was probably right ... and it is Nixon himself who represents that dark, venal, and incurably violent side of the American character almost every other country in the world has learned to fear and despise. Our Barbie doll President, with his Barbie doll wife and his boxful of Barbie doll children is also America's answer to the monstrous Mr Hyde. He speaks for the werewolf in us; the bully, the predatory shyster who turns into something unspeakable, full of claws and bleeding string-warts, on nights when the moon comes too close ...

At the stroke of midnight in Washington, a drooling red-eyed beast with the legs of a man and a head of a giant hyena crawls out of its bedroom window in the south wing of the White House and leaps fifty feet down to the lawn ... pauses briefly to strangle the Chow watchdog, then races off into the darkness ... towards the Watergate, snarling with lust, loping through the alleys behind Pennsylvania Avenue, and trying desperately to remember which one of those four hundred identical balconies is the one outside Martha Mitchell's apartment ...

Ah ... nightmares, nightmares. But I was only kidding. The President of the United States would never act that weird. At least not during football season. But how would the voters react if they knew the President of the United States was presiding over 'a complex, far-reaching and sinister operation on the part of White House aides and the Nixon campaign organization ... involving sabotage, forgery, theft of confidential files, surveillance of Democratic candidates and their families and persistent efforts to lay the basis for possible blackmail and intimidation.'

That ugly description of Nixon's staff operations comes from a New York *Times* editorial on Thursday 12 October. But neither Nixon nor anyone else felt it would have much effect on his steady two-to-one lead over McGovern in all the national polls. Four days later the *Times*/Yankelovich poll showed Nixon ahead by an incredible twenty points (57 per cent to 37 per cent, with 16 per cent undecided) over the man Bobby Kennedy described as 'the most decent man in the Senate'.

'Ominous' is not quite the right word for a situation where one of the most consistently unpopular politicians in American history suddenly skyrockets to folk hero status while his closest advisers are being caught almost daily in nazi-style gigs that would have embarrassed Martin Bormann.

How long will it be before 'demented extremists' in Germany or maybe Japan, start calling us a nation of pigs? How would Nixon react? 'No comment'? And how would the popularity polls react if he just came right out and admitted it?

> *Fear and Loathing: On the Campaign Trail,*
> San Francisco, Straight Arrow Books, 1973

EPITAPH

Four More Years ... Nixon *Über Alles* ... Fear and Loathing at the Super Bowl ...

President Nixon will be sworn into office for a second term today, emboldened by his sweeping electoral triumph of last November and a Vietnam peace settlement apparently within his grasp ... In the most expensive inauguration in American history – the cost is officially estimated at more than $4 million – Mr Nixon will once again take the oath on a temporary stand outside the east front of the Capitol, then ride in a parade expected to draw 200,000 people to Pennsylvania Avenue and its environs, and millions more to their television sets ... It will be the President's first statement to the American people since his television appearance on 6 November, election eve. Since then the peace talks have collapsed, massive bombing of North Vietnam has been

instituted and then called off, and the talks have resumed without
extended public comment from Mr Nixon ...

San Francisco *Chronicle*, 20 January 1973

When the Great Scorer comes to write
against your name – he marks –
Not that you won or lost –
But how you played the game.

Grantland Rice

Who was known – prior to his death in the late fifties
– as 'the dean of American sportswriters', and one
of Richard Nixon's favourite authors.

They came together on a hot afternoon in Los Angeles, howling and
clawing at each other like wild beasts in heat.

Under a brown California sky, the fierceness of their struggle brought
tears to the eyes of 90,000 God-fearing fans.

They were twenty-two men who were somehow more than men.

They were giants, idols, titans ...

Behemoths.

They stood for everything good and true and right in the American
spirit.

Because they had guts.

And they yearned for the ultimate glory, the great prize, the final
fruits of a long and vicious campaign.

Victory in the Super Bowl : $15,000 each.

They were hungry for it. They were thirsty. For twenty long weeks,
from August through December, they had struggled to reach the pinnacle ... and when dawn lit the beaches of Southern California on that
fateful Sunday morning in January, they were ready.

To seize the final fruit.

They could almost taste it. The smell was stronger than a ton of rotten
mangoes. Their nerves burned like open sores on a dog's neck. White
knuckles. Wild eyes. Strange fluid welled up in their throats, with a taste
far sharper than bile.

Behemoths.

Those who went early said the pre-game tension was almost unbearable. By noon, many fans were weeping openly, for no apparent reason.
Others wrung their hands or gnawed on the necks of pop bottles, trying
to stay calm. Many fist-fights were reported in the public urinals. Nervous ushers roamed up and down the aisles, confiscating alcoholic

beverages and occasionally grappling with drunkards. Gangs of seconal-crazed teenagers prowled through the parking lot outside the stadium, beating the mortal shit out of luckless stragglers ...

What? No ... Grantland Rice would never have written weird stuff like that: His prose was spare & lean; his descriptions came straight from the gut ... and on the rare and ill-advised occasions when he wanted to do a 'think piece', he called on the analytical powers of his medulla. Like all great sportswriters, Rice understood that his world might go all to pieces if he ever dared to doubt that his eyes were wired straight to his lower brain – a sort of *de facto* lobotomy, which enables the grinning victim to operate entirely on the level of sensory perception ...

Green grass, hot sun, sharp cleats in the turf, thundering cheers from the crowd, the menacing scowl on the face of a $30,000-a-year pulling guard as he leans around the corner on a Lombardi-style power sweep and cracks a sharp plastic shoulder into the line-backer's groin ...

Ah yes, the simple life: back to the roots, the basics – first a mouse-trap, then a Crackback & a buttonhook off a fake triple-severse fly pattern, and finally the bomb ...

Indeed. There is a dangerous kind of simple-minded power/precision worship at the root of the massive fascination with pro football in this country, and sportswriters are mainly responsible for it. With a few rare exceptions like Bob Lypsyte of the New York *Times* and Tom Quinn of the (now-defunct) Washington *Daily News*, sportswriters are a kind of rude and brainless subculture of fascist drunks whose only real function is to publicize & sell whatever the sports editor sends them out to cover ...

Which is a nice way to make a living, because it keeps a man busy and requires no thought at all. The two keys to success as a sportswriter are: (1) a blind willingness to believe anything you're told by the coaches, flacks, hustlers, and other 'official spokesmen' for the team-owners who provide the free booze ... and: (2) a *Roget's Thesaurus*, in order to avoid using the same verbs and adjectives twice in the same paragraph.

Even a sports editor, for instance, might notice something wrong with a lead that said: 'The precision-jackhammer attack of the Miami Dolphins stomped the balls off the Washington Redskins today by stomping and hammering with one precise jackthrust after another up the middle, mixed with pinpoint precision passes into the flat and numerous hammer-jack stomps around both ends ...'

Right. And there was the genius of Grantland Rice. He carried a pocket thesaurus, so that 'the thundering hoofbeats of the four horsemen' never echoed more than once in the same paragraph, and the 'granite-grey sky' in his lead was a 'cold dark dusk' in the last lonely line of his heart-rending, nerve-ripping stories ...

There was a time, about ten years ago, when I could write like Grantland Rice. Not necessarily because I believed all that sporty bullshit, but because sportswriting was the only thing I could do that anybody was willing to pay for. And none of the people I wrote about seemed to give a hoot in hell what kind of lunatic gibberish I wrote about them, just as long as it *moved*. They wanted action, colour, speed, violence ... At one point, in Florida, I was writing variations on the same demented themes for three competing papers at the same time, under three different names. I was a sports columnist for one paper in the morning, sports editor for another in the afternoon, and at night I worked for a pro wrestling promoter, writing incredibly twisted 'press releases' that I would plant, the next day, in both papers.

It was a wonderful gig, in retrospect, and at times I wish I could go back to it – just punch a big hatpin through my frontal lobes and maybe regain that happy lost innocence that enabled me to write, without the slightest twinge of conscience, things like: 'The entire Fort Walton Beach police force is gripped in a state of fear this week; all leaves have been cancelled and Chief Bloor is said to be drilling his men for an emergency alert situation on Friday and Saturday night – because those are the nights when "Kazika, the Mad Jap", a 440-pound sadist from the vile slums of Hiroshima, is scheduled to make his first – and no doubt his last – appearance in Fish-head Auditorium. Local wrestling impresario Lionel Olay is known to have spoken privately with Chief Bloor, urging him to have "every available officer" on duty at ringside this weekend, because of the Mad Jap's legendary temper and his invariably savage reaction to racial insults. Last week, in Detroit, Kazika ran amok and tore the spleens out of three ringside spectators, one of whom allegedly called him a "yellow devil".'

'Kazika', as I recall, was a big half-bright Cuban who once played third-string tackle for Florida State University in Tallahassee, about 100 miles away – but on the fish-head circuit he had no trouble passing for a dangerous Jap strangler, and I soon learned that pro wrestling fans don't give a fuck anyway.

Ah, memories, memories ... and here we go again, back on the same old trip: digressions, tangents, crude flashbacks ... When the 72 presidential campaign ended I planned to give up this kind of thing ...

But what the hell? Why not? It's almost dawn in San Francisco now, the parking lot outside this building is flooded about three inches deep with another drenching rain, and I've been here all night drinking coffee

& Wild Turkey, smoking short Jamaican cigars and getting more & more wired on the Allman Brothers' 'Mountain Jam', howling out of four big speakers hung in all four corners of the room.

Where is the MDA? With the windows wide open and the curtains blowing into the room and the booze and the coffee and the smoke and the music beating heavy in my ears, I feel the first rising edge of a hunger for something with a bit of the crank in it.

Where is Mankiewicz tonight?

Sleeping peacefully?

No ... probably not. After two years on the edge, involuntary retirement is a hard thing to cope with. I tried it for a while, in Woody Creek, but three weeks without even a hint of crisis left me so nervous that I began gobbling speed and babbling distractedly about running for the US Senate in 74. Finally, on the verge of desperation, I took the bushplane over to Denver for a visit with Gary Hart, McGovern's ex-campaign manager, telling him I couldn't actually put him on the payroll right now, but that I was counting on him to organize Denver for me.

He smiled crookedly but refused to commit himself ... and later that night I heard, from an extremely reliable source, that Hart was planning to run for the Senate himself in 1974.

Why? I wondered. Was it some kind of subliminal, un-focused need to take vengeance on the press?

On *me*? The first journalist in Christendom to go on record comparing Nixon to Adolf Hitler?

Was Gary so blinded with bile that he would actually run against me in the primary? Would he risk splitting the 'three a's' vote and maybe sink us both?

I spent about twenty-four hours thinking about it, then flew to Los Angeles to cover the Super Bowl – but the first person I ran into down there was Ed Muskie. He was wandering around in the vortex of a big party on the main deck of the *Queen Mary*, telling anybody who would listen that he was having a hell of a hard time deciding whether he was for the Dolphins or the Redskins. I introduced myself as Peter Sheridan, 'a friend of Donald Segretti's'. 'We met on the "Sunshine Special" in Florida,' I said. 'I was out of my head ...' But his brain was too clouded to pick up on it ... so I went up to the crow's nest and split a cap of black acid with John Chancellor.

He was reluctant to bet on the game, even when I offered to take Miami with no points. A week earlier I'd been locked into the idea that the Redskins would win easily – but when Nixon came out for them and George Allen began televising his prayer meetings I decided that any team with both God and Nixon on their side was fucked from the start.

So I began betting heavily on Miami – which worked out nicely, on paper, but some of my heaviest bets were with cocaine addicts, and they are known to be very bad risks when it comes to paying off. Most coke freaks have already blown their memories by years of over-indulgence on marijuana, and by the time they get serious about coke they have a hard time remembering what day it is, much less what kind of ill-considered bets they might or might not have made yesterday.

Consequently – although I won all my bets – I made no money.

The game itself was hopelessly dull – like all other Super Bowls – and by half time Miami was so clearly in command that I decided to watch the rest of the drill on TV at Cardoso's Hollywood Classic / Day of the Locust-style apartment behind the Troubadour ... but it was impossible to keep a fix on it there, because everybody in the room was so stoned that they kept asking each other things like 'How did Miami get the ball? Did we miss a kick? Who's ahead now? Jesus, how did they get fourteen points? How many points is ... ah ... *touchdown?*'

Immediately after the game I received an urgent call from my attorney, who claimed to be having a terminal drug experience in his private bungalow at the Chateau Marmont ... but by the time I got there he had finished the whole jar.

Later, when the big rain started, I got heavily into the gin and read the Sunday papers. On page thirty-nine of *California Living* magazine I found a hand-lettered ad from the McDonald's Hamburger Corporation, one of Nixon's big contributors in the 72 presidential campaign:

PRESS ON, it said. NOTHING IN THE WORLD CAN TAKE THE PLACE OF PERSISTENCE. TALENT WILL NOT: NOTHING IS MORE COMMON THAN UNSUCCESSFUL MEN WITH TALENT, GENIUS WILL NOT: UNREWARDED GENIUS IS ALMOST A PROVERB. EDUCATION ALONE WILL NOT: THE WORLD IS FULL OF EDUCATED DERELICTS. PERSISTENCE AND DETERMINATION ALONE ARE OMNIPOTENT.

I read it several times before I grasped the full meaning. Then, when it came to me, I called Mankiewicz immediately.

'Keep your own counsel,' he said. 'Don't draw any conclusions from anything you see or hear.'

I hung up and drank some more gin. Then I put a Dolly Parton album on the tape machine and watched the trees outside my balcony getting lashed around in the wind. Around midnight, when the rain stopped, I put on my special Miami Beach nightshirt and walked several blocks down La Cienega Boulevard to the Losers Club.

Fear and Loathing: On the Campaign Trail,
San Francisco, Straight Arrow Books, 1973

MEMO FROM THE SPORTS DESK & RUDE NOTES FROM A DECOMPRESSION CHAMBER IN MIAMI

There is no joy in Woody Creek tonight – at least not in the twisted bowels of this sink-hole of political iniquity called the Owl Farm – because, 2000 miles away in the swampy heat of Washington, DC, my old football buddy, Dick Nixon, is lashing around in bad trouble ... The vultures are coming home to roost – like he always feared they would, in the end – and it hurts me in a way nobody would publish if I properly described it, to know that I can't be with him on the sweaty ramparts today, stomping those dirty buzzards like Davy Crockett bashing spics off the walls of the Alamo.

> *Delta Dawn ... What's that*
> *flower you have on?*

Fine music on my radio as dawn comes up on the Rockies ... But suddenly the music ends and ABC (American Entertainment Network) News interrupts: Martha Mitchell is demanding that 'Mister President' either resign or be impeached, for reasons her addled tongue can only hint at ... and Charles 'Tex' Colson, the President's erstwhile *special counsel*, is denying all statements & sworn testimony, by anybody, linking him to burglaries, fire-bombings, wire-tappings, perjuries, payoffs and other routine felonies in connection with his job at the White House ... and President Nixon is relaxing, as it were, in his personal beachfront mansion at San Clemente, California, surrounded by the scuzzy remnants of his once imperial guard ... Indeed, you can almost hear the rattle of martini-cups along the airwaves as Gerald Warren – Ron Ziegler's doomed replacement – cranks another hastily rewritten paragraph (amendment no. 67 to paragraph no. 13 of President Nixon's original statement denying everything ...) into the overheated Dex machine to the White House, for immediate release to the national media ... and the White House press room is boiling with guilt-crazed journalists, ready to pounce on any new statement like a pack of wild African dogs, to atone for all things they knew but never wrote when Nixon was riding high ...

Why does Nixon use the clumsy Dex, instead of the mojo? Why does he drink martinis, instead of Wild Turkey? Why does he wear boxer shorts? Why is his life a grim monument to everything plastic, de-sexed and non-sensual? When I look at Nixon's White House I have a sense of *absolute* personal alienation. The President and I seem to disagree on almost *everything* – except pro football, and Nixon's addiction to that has caused me to view it with a freshly jaundiced eye, or what the late John Foster Dulles called 'an agonizing reappraisal'. Anything Nixon likes *must* be suspect. Like cottage cheese and catsup ...

'The Dex machine'. Jesus! Learning that Nixon and his people use *this* – instead of the smaller, quicker, more versatile (and portable) mojo wire – was almost the final insult: coming on the heels of the gross sense of injury I felt when I saw that my name was not included on the infamous 'enemies of the White House' list.

I would almost have preferred a vindictive tax audit to that kind of crippling exclusion. Christ! What kind of waterheads compiled that list? How can I show my face in the Jerome Bar, when word finally reaches Aspen that I wasn't on it?

Fortunately, the list was drawn up in the summer of 71 – which partially explains why my name was missing. It was not until the autumn of 72 that I began referring to the President, in nationally circulated print, as a cheapjack punk and a lust-maddened werewolf, whose very existence was (and remains) a bad cancer on the American political tradition. Every ad the publishers prepared for my book on the 1972 campaign led off with a savage slur on all that Richard Nixon ever hoped to represent or stand for. The man is a walking embarrassment to the human race – and especially, as Bobby Kennedy once noted, to that high, optimistic potential that fuelled men like Jefferson and Madison, and which Abe Lincoln once described as 'the last, best hope of man'.

There is slim satisfaction in the knowledge that my exclusion from the (1971) list of 'White House enemies' has more to do with timing and Ron Ziegler's refusal to read *Rolling Stone* than with the validity of all the things I've said and written about that evil bastard.

I was, after all, the only accredited journalist covering the 1972 presidential campaign to compare Nixon with Adolf Hitler ... I was the only one to describe him as a congenital thug, a fixer with the personal principles of a used-car salesman. And when these distasteful excesses were privately censured by the docile White House press corps, I compounded my flirtation with bad taste by describing the White House correspondents as a gang of lame whores & sheep without the balls to even argue with Ron Ziegler – who kept them all dancing to Nixon's bogus tune, until it became suddenly fashionable to see him for the hired liar he was and has been all along.

The nut of my complaint here – in addition to being left off the list – is rooted in a powerful resentment at not being recognized (not even by Ziegler) for the insults I heaped on Nixon *before* he was laid low. This is a matter of journalistic ethics – or perhaps even 'sportsmanship' – and I take a certain pride in knowing that I kicked Nixon before he went down. Not afterwards – though I plan to do *that*, too, as soon as possible.

And I feel no more guilt about it than I would about setting a rat trap in my kitchen, if it ever seemed necessary – and certainly no more guilt than I know Nixon would feel about hiring some thug like Gordon Liddy to set me up for a felony charge, if my name turned up on his list.

When they update the bugger, I plan to be on it. My attorney is even now preparing my tax records, with an eye to confrontation. When the next list of 'White House enemies' comes out, I want to be on it. My son will never forgive me – ten years from now – if I fail to clear my name and get grouped, for the record, with those whom Richard Milhous Nixon considered dangerous.

Dick Tuck feels the same way. He was sitting in my kitchen, watching the TV set, when Sam Donaldson began reading the list on ABC-TV.

'Holy shit!' Tuck muttered. 'We're not *on* it.'

'Don't worry,' I said grimly. 'We *will* be.'

'What can we *do*?' he asked.

'Kick out the jams,' I said. 'Don't worry, Dick. When the next list comes out, we'll *be there*. I guarantee that.'

Dr Hunter S. Thompson
'Rude Notes from a Decompression Chamber in Miami' ... June 73

FROM: Raoul Duke, Sports Editor

TO: Main/Edit Control

C.C.: Legal, Finance, Security, et al.

SUBJECT: Imminent emergence of Dr Thompson from the decompression chamber in Miami, and probable inability of the Sports Desk or anyone else to control his movements at that time ... especially in connection with his ill-conceived plan to move the National Affairs Desk back to Washington and bring Ralph Steadman over from England to cause trouble at the Watergate hearings ...

EDITORS' NOTE

The following intra-corporate memo arrived by mojo wire from Colorado shortly before deadline time for this issue. It was greeted with mixed emotions by all those potentially afflicted ... and because of the implications, we felt a certain obligation to lash up a quick, last-minute explanation ... primarily for those who have never understood the real function of Raoul Duke (whose official title is 'sports editor'), and also for the many readers whose attempts to reach Dr Thompson by mail, phone & other means have not borne fruit.

The circumstances of Dr Thompson's removal from the public world have been a carefully guarded secret for the past several months. During the last week of March – after a strange encounter with Henry Kissinger while on 'vacation' in Acapulco – Dr Thompson almost drowned when his SCUBA tanks unexplainably ran out of air while diving for black coral off the Yucatan Coast of Mexico, at a depth of some 300 feet. His rapid emergence from these depths – according to witnesses – resulted in a near-fatal case of the bends, and an emergency-chartered/night-flight to the nearest decompression chamber, which happened to be in Miami.

Dr Thompson was unconscious in the decompression chamber – a round steel cell about twelve feet in diameter – for almost three weeks. When he finally regained his wits it was impossible to speak with him, except by means of a cracked loudspeaker tube & brief handwritten notes held up to the window. A television set was introduced into the chamber at his insistence and, by extremely complicated manoeuvring, he was able to watch the Watergate hearings ... but, due to the dangerous differences in pressurization, he was unable to communicate anything but garbled notes on his impressions to Duke, his long-time friend and associate who flew to Miami immediately, at his own expense.

When it became apparent that Dr Thompson would be in the chamber indefinitely, Duke left him in Miami – breathing easily in the chamber with a TV set & several notebooks – and returned to Colorado, where he spent the past three months handling the Doktor's personal & business affairs, in addition to organizing the skeletal framework for his 1974 senate race.

It was a familiar role for Duke, who has been Dr Thompson's close friend & adviser since 1968 – after fourteen years of distinguished service in the CIA, the FBI and the Pittsburgh (Pa.) Police Intelligence Unit. His duties, since hiring on with Dr Thompson, have been understandably varied. He has been described as 'a weapons expert', a 'ghost-writer', a 'bodyguard', a 'wizard' and a 'brutal fixer'.

'Compared to the things I've done for Thompson,' Duke says, 'both Gordon and Liddy and Howard Hunt were stone *punks*.'

It is clear, from this memo, that Duke has spent a good bit of his time in Colorado watching the Watergate hearings on TV – but it is also clear that his tentative conclusions are very different from the ones Dr Thompson reached, from his admittedly singular vantage point in that decompression chamber in downtown Miami.

The editors of *Rolling Stone* would prefer not to comment on *either* of these viewpoints at this time, nor to comment on the nightmare/blizzard of expense vouchers submitted, by Duke, in connection with this dubious memo. In accordance with our long tradition, however, we are placing the public interest (publication of Duke's memo, in this case) on a plane far above and beyond our inevitably mundane haggling about the cost of breakfast and lunch.

What follows, then, is a jangled mix of Duke's official communications with this office, and Thompson's 'Watergate Notes' (forwarded to us, by Duke) from his decompression chamber in Miami. The chronology is not entirely consistent. Duke's opening note, for instance, reflects his concern & alarm with Dr Thompson's decision to go directly to Miami – once the doctors have confirmed his ability to function in normal air-pressures – to the harsh & politically volatile atmosphere in Washington, DC. Unlike Duke, he seems blindly obsessed with the day-to-day details of the Watergate hearings ... and what is also clear from this memo is that Dr Thompson has maintained regular contact (despite all medical and physical realities, according to the doctors in charge of his chamber in Miami) with his familiar campaign trail allies, Tim Crouse and Ralph Steadman. An invoice received only yesterday, from the manager of the Watergate Hotel, indicates that somebody has reserved a top-floor river-view suite, under the names of 'Thompson, Steadman & Crouse' ... four adjoining rooms at $277 a day, with a long list of special equipment and an unlimited in-house expense authorization.

Needless to say, we will ... but, why mention that now? The dumb buggers are already into it, and *something* is bound to emerge. We can save the bargaining for later ...

The Editors

DUKE MEMO NO. 9, 2 JULY 1973

Gentlemen:
This will confirm my previous warnings in re: the dangerously unstable condition of Dr Thompson, whose most recent communications leave no doubt in my mind that he still considers himself the national affairs editor of *Rolling Stone* – and in that capacity he has somehow made arrangements to fly immediately from Miami to Washington, upon his release, to 'cover' the remaining episodes of the Watergate hearings. I have no idea what he really means by the word 'cover' – but a phone-talk late last night with his doctors gave me serious pause. He will leave the chamber at the end of this week, and he's talking in terms of 'saturation coverage'. According to the doctors, there is no way to communicate with him in the chamber except by notes held up to the glass

window – but I suspect he has a phone in there, because he has obviously communicated at length with Crouse, Steadman, Mankiewicz and several others. A person resembling Crouse was seen loitering around the chamber last Monday night around 3:30 a.m. ... and a call to Steadman's agent in London confirmed that Ralph has left his hideout in the south of France and is booked on a Paris-Washington flight next Thursday, the day before Thompson's release.

Mankiewicz denies everything, as usual, but I talked to Sam Brown in Denver yesterday and he said the word around Washington is that Frank is 'acting very nervous' and also ordering Wild Turkey 'by the case' from Chevy Chase Liquors. This indicates, to me, that Frank knows something. He has probably been talking to Crouse, but Tim's number in Boston won't answer, so I can't confirm anything there.

Dr Squane, the bends specialist in Miami, says Thompson is 'acceptably rational' – whatever that means – and that they have no reason to keep him in the chamber beyond Friday. My insistence that he be returned at once to Colorado – under guard if necessary – has not been taken seriously in Miami. The bill for his stay in the chamber – as you know – is already over $3000, and they are not anxious to keep him there any longer than absolutely necessary. I got the impression, during my talk with Doc Squane last night, that Thompson's stay in the chamber has been distinctly unpleasant for the staff. 'I'll never understand why he didn't just wither up and die,' Squane told me. 'Only a *monster* could survive that kind of trauma.'

I sensed disappointment in his voice, but I saw no point in arguing. We've been through this before, right? And it's always the same gig. My only concern for right now – as Thompson's *de facto* personal guardian – is to make sure he doesn't get involved in serious trouble, if he's serious about going to Washington.

Which he *is*, I suspect – and that means, if nothing else, that he'll be running up huge bills on the *Rolling Stone* tab. Whether or not he will write anything coherent is a moot point, I think, because *whatever* he writes – if anything – will necessarily be long out of date by the time it appears in print. Not even the Washington *Post* and the New York *Times*, which arrive daily (but three days late) out here in Woody Creek, can compete with the spontaneous, brain-boggling horrors belching constantly out of the TV set.

Last Saturday afternoon, for instance, I was sitting here very peacefully – minding the store, as it were – when the tube suddenly erupted with a genuinely *obscene* conversation between Mike Wallace and John Ehrlichman.

I was sitting on the porch with Gene Johnston – one of Dr Thompson's old friends and ex-general manager of the Aspen Wallposter – when Sandy called us inside to watch the show. Ehrlichman's face was so awful, so obviously mired in a lifetime of lies and lame treachery, that it was just about impossible to watch him in our twisted condition.

'Jesus Christ, *look* at him!' Johnston kept muttering. 'Two months ago, that bastard was *running the country.*' He opened a beer and whacked it down on the table. 'I never want to hear the word "paranoid" again, goddamnit! Not after seeing *that* face!' He reeled towards the front door, shaking his head and mumbling: 'God damn! I can't *stand* it!'

I watched the whole thing, myself, but not without problems. It reminded me of *Last Exit to Brooklyn* – the rape of a bent whore – but I also knew Dr Thompson was watching the show in Miami, and that it would fill him with venom & craziness. Whatever small hope we might have had of keeping him away from Washington during this crisis was burned to a cinder by the Wallace-Ehrlichman show. It had the effect of reinforcing Thompson's conviction that Nixon had cashed his cheque – and that possibility alone is enough to lure him to Washington for the death-watch.

My own prognosis is less drastic, at this point in time [sic], but it's also a fact that I've never been able to share the Doktor's obsessive political visions – for good or ill. My job has to do with nuts & bolts, not terminal vengeance. And it also occurs to me that there is nothing in the Watergate revelations, thus far, to convince anyone but a stone partisan fanatic that we will all be better off when it's finished. As I see it, we have already reaped the *real* benefits of this spectacle – the almost accidental castration of dehumanized power-mongers like Haldeman, Ehrlichman and Tom Charles Huston, that vicious young jackal of a lawyer from Indianapolis that Nixon put in charge of the Special Domestic Intelligence operation.

Dumping thugs like these out of power for the next three years gives us all new room to breathe, for a while – which is just about all we can hope for, given the nature of the entrenched (Democratic) opposition. Nixon himself is no problem, now that all his ranking thugs have been neutralized. Just imagine what those bastards might have done, given three more years on their own terms.

Even a casual reading of White House memorandums in re: domestic subversives & other White House enemies (Bill Cosby, James Reston, Paul Newman, Joe Namath, et al.) is enough to queer the faith of any American less liberal than Mussolini. Here is a paragraph from one of his (21 September 1970) memos to Harry 'Bob' Haldeman:

'What we cannot do in a court room via criminal prosecutions to curtail the activities of some of these groups, IRS [the Internal Revenue

Service] could do by administrative · action. Moreover, valuable intelligence-type information could be turned up by IRS as a result of their field audits ...'

Dr Thompson – if he were with us & certifiably de-pressurized at this point in time – could offer some first-hand testimony about how the IRS and the Treasury Department were used, back in 1970, to work muscle on ideological enemies like himself ... and if Thompson's account might be shrugged off as 'biased', we can always compel the testimony of Aspen police chief, Dick Richey, whose office safe still holds an illegal sawed-off shotgun belonging to a US Treasury Department undercover agent from Denver who fucked up in his efforts to convince Dr Thompson that he should find a quick reason for dropping out of electoral politics. That incident came up the other afternoon at the Jerome Bar in Aspen, when Steve Levine, a young reporter from Denver, observed that 'Thompson was one of the original victims of the Watergate syndrome – but nobody recognized it then; they called it paranoia.'

Right ... But that's another story, and we'll leave it for the Doktor to tell. After three months in the decompression chamber, he will doubtless be cranked up to the fine peaks of frenzy. His 'Watergate notes from the chamber' show a powerful, brain-damaged kind of zeal that will hopefully be brought under control in the near future ... and I'm enclosing some of them here, as crude evidence to show he's still functioning, despite the tragic handicap that comes with a bad case of the bends.

In closing, I remain ... Yrs in fear & loathing:

Raoul Duke, Spts Ed.

EDITOR'S NOTE:
What follows is the unfinished mid-section of Dr Thompson's notes from the decompression chamber. This section was written in his notebook on the day after convicted Watergate burglar James McCord's appearance before the Ervin committee on national TV. It was transcribed by a nurse who copied Dr Thompson's notes as he held them up, page by page, through the pressure-sealed window of his chamber. It is not clear, from the text, whether he deliberately wrote this section with a 'Woody Creek, Colorado' dateline, or whether he planned to be there by the time it was printed.

In either case, he was wrong. His case of the bends was severe, almost fatal. And even upon his release there is no real certainty of recovery. He might have to re-enter the decompression chamber at any time, if he suffers a relapse.

None of which has any bearing on what follows – which was published exactly as he wrote it in the chamber:

Jesus, where will it end? Yesterday I turned on my TV set – hungry for some decent upbeat news – and here was an ex-Army Air Force colonel with nineteen years in the CIA under his belt admitting that he'd wilfully turned himself into a common low-life burglar because he thought the Attorney General and the President of the US had more or less *ordered* him to. Ex-Colonel McCord felt he had a duty to roam around the country burglarizing offices and ransacking private/personal files – because the security of the USA was at stake.

Indeed, we were in serious trouble last year – and for five or six years before that, if you believe the muck those two vicious and irresponsible young punks at the Washington *Post* have raked up.

'Impeachment' is an ugly word, they say, *Newsweek* columnist Shana Alexander says 'all but the vulture-hearted want to believe him ignorant'. A week earlier, Mrs Alexander wrote a 'love letter' to Martha Mitchell: 'You are in the best tradition of American womanhood, defending your country, your flag ... but most of all, defending your man.'

Well ... shucks. I can hardly choke back the tears ... and where does that leave Pat Nixon, who apparently went on a world cruise under a different name the day after McCord pulled the plug and wrote that devastating letter to Judge Sirica.

The public prints – and especially *Newsweek* – are full of senile gibberish these days. Stewart Alsop wakes up in a cold sweat every morning at the idea that Congress might be forced to impeach 'the President'.

For an answer to that, we can look to Hubert Humphrey – from one of the nine speeches he made during his four-and-a-half hour campaign for Democratic candidate George McGovern in the waning weeks of last November's presidential showdown – Humphrey was talking to a crowd of hardhats in SF, as I recall, and he said, 'My friends, we're not talking about re-electing the President – we're talking about re-electing Richard Nixon.'

Even a blind pig finds an acorn now and then. Humphrey's voice just belched out of my radio, demanding that we *get to the bottom of this Watergate mess*, but meanwhile we have to make sure the Ruskies understand that we all stand firmly behind the President.

Right. As far behind him as possible, if GOP standard-bearers like B. Goldwater and Hugh Scott are any measure of the party's allegiance to the frightened unprincipled little shyster they were calling – when they nominated him for re-canonization ten months ago in Miami –

261

'one of the greatest Presidents in American history'. We will want those tapes for posterity because we won't hear their like again – from Scott, Goldwater, Duke Wayne, Martha, Sammy Davis, Senator Percy or any-one else. Not even George Meany will join a foursome with Richard Nixon these days. The hallowed halls of the White House no longer echo with the happy sound of bouncing golf balls. Or footballs either, for that matter ... or any other kind.

The hard-nosed super-executives Nixon chose to run this country for us turned on each other like rats in a slum-fire when the first signs of trouble appeared. What we have seen in the past few weeks is the in-credible spectacle of a President of the United States either firing or being hastily abandoned by all of his hired hands and cronies – all the people who put him where he is today, in fact, and now that they're gone he seems helpless. Some of his closest 'friends' and advisers are headed for prison, his once-helpless Democratic Congress is verging on mutiny, the threat of impeachment looms closer every day, and his coveted 'place in history' is even now being etched out in acid by eager Harvard historians.

Six months ago Richard Nixon was Zeus himself, calling firebombs and shitrains down on friend and foe alike – the most powerful man in the world, for a while – but all that is gone now and nothing he can do will ever bring a hint of it back. Richard Nixon's seventh crisis will be his last. He will go down with Harding and Grant as one of America's classically rotten presidents.

Which is exactly what he deserves – and if saying that makes me 'one of the vulture-hearted', by Ms Alexander's lights ... well ... I think I can live with it. My grandmother was one of those stunned old ladies who cried when the Duke of Windsor quit the big throne to marry an American commoner back in 1936. She didn't know the Duke or any-thing about him. But she knew – along with millions of other old ladies and closest monarchists – that a once and future king had a duty to keep up the act. She wept for her lost illusions – for the same reason Stewart Alsop and Shana Alexander will weep tomorrow if President Richard M. Nixon is impeached and put on trial by the US Senate.

Our congressmen will do everything possible to avoid it, because most of them have a deep and visceral sympathy, however denied and reluc-tant, for the 'tragic circumstances' that led Richard Nixon to what even Evans and Novak call 'the brink of ruin'. The loyal opposition has not distinguished itself in the course of this long-running nightmare. Even Nixon's oldest enemies are lying low, leaving the dirty work to hired lawyers and faceless investigators. Senators Kennedy, McGovern and Fulbright are strangely silent, while Humphrey babbles nonsense and Muskie hoards his energy for beating back personal attacks by Strom

Thurmond. The only politicians talking publicly about the dire implications of the Watergate iceberg are those who can't avoid it – the four carefully selected eunuch/Democrats on the Senate Select Investigating Committee and a handful of panicked Republicans up for re-election in 1974.

The slow-rising central horror of Watergate is not that it might grind down to the reluctant impeachment of a vengeful thug of a president whose entire political career has been a monument to the same kind of cheap shots and treachery he finally got nailed for, but that we might somehow fail to learn something from it.

Already – with the worst news yet to come – there is an ominous tide of public opinion that says whatever Nixon and his small gang of henchmen and hired gunsels might have done, it was probably no worse than what other politicians have been doing all along, and still are.

Anybody who really believes this is a fool – but a lot of people seem to, and that evidence is hard to ignore. What almost happened here – and what was only avoided because the men who made Nixon President and who were running the country in his name knew in their hearts that they were all mean, hollow little bastards who couldn't dare turn their backs on each other – was a takeover and total perversion of the American political process by a gang of cold-blooded fixers so incompetent that they couldn't even pull off a simple burglary ... which tends to explain, among other things, why 25,000 young Americans died for no reason in Vietnam while Nixon and his brain-trust were trying to figure out how to admit the whole things was a mistake from the start.

At press time, the National Affairs Suite in Washington had been re-opened and prepared for 'total coverage'. Thompson arrived there 7 July, and we expect his reports soon.

Rolling Stone no. 140, 2 August 1973

FEAR AND LOATHING AT THE WATERGATE: MR NIXON HAS CASHED HIS CHEQUE

ONE

The Worm Turns in Swamptown ... Violent Talk at the National Affairs Desk ... Narrow Escape for Tex Colson ... Heavy Duty in The Bunker ... No Room for Gonzo? 'Hell, They Already Have This Story Nailed Up and Bleeding from Every Extremity.'

Reflecting on the meaning of the last presidential election, I have decided at this point in time that Mr Nixon's landslide victory and my overwhelming defeat will probably prove to be of greater value to the nation than would the victory my supporters and I worked so hard to achieve. I think history may demonstrate that it was not only important that Mr Nixon win and that I lose, but that the margin should be of stunning proportions ... The shattering Nixon landslide, and the even more shattering exposure of the corruption that surrounded him, have done more than I could have done in victory to awaken the nation ... This is not a comfortable conclusion for a self-confident – some would say self-righteous – politician to reach ...
George McGovern in the *Washington Post*, 12 August 1973

Indeed. But we want to keep in mind that 'comfortable' is a very relative word around Washington these days – with the vicious tentacles of Watergate ready to wrap themselves around almost anybody, at any moment – and when McGovern composed those eminently reasonable words in the study of his stylish home on the woodsy edge of Washington, he had no idea how close he'd just come to being extremely 'uncomfortable'.

I have just finished making out a report addressed to somebody named Charles R. Roach, a claims examiner at the mid-Atlantic regional headquarters of Avis rent-a-car in Arlington, Virginia. It has to do with a minor accident that occurred on Connecticut Avenue, in downtown Washington, shortly after George and his wife had bade farewell to the last staggering guests at the party he'd given on a hot summer night in July commemorating the first anniversary of his seizure of the presidential nomination in Miami.

The atmosphere of the party itself had been amazingly loose and pleasant. Two hundred people had been invited – twice that many showed up – to celebrate what history will record, with at least a few asterisks, as one of the most disastrous presidential campaigns in American history. Midway in the evening I was standing on the patio, talking to Carl Wagner and Holly Mankiewicz, when the phone began ringing and whoever answered it came back with the news that President Nixon had just been admitted to the nearby Bethesda Naval Hospital with what was officially announced as 'viral pneumonia'.

Nobody believed it, of course. High-powered journalists like Jack Germond and Jules Witcover immediately seized the phones to find out what was *really* wrong with Nixon ... but the rest of us, no longer locked into deadlines or the fast-rising terrors of some tomorrow's election day, merely shrugged at the news and kept on drinking. There was nothing unusual, we felt, about Nixon caving in to some real or even psychosomatic illness. And if the truth was worse than the news ... well ... there would be nothing unusual about that either.

One of the smallest and noisiest contingents among the 200 invited guests was the handful of big-time journalists who'd spent most of last autumn dogging McGovern's every lame footstep along the campaign trail, while two third-string police reporters from the *Washington Post* were quietly putting together the biggest political story of 1972 or any other year – a story that had already exploded, by the time of McGovern's 'anniversary' party, into a scandal that has even now burned a big hole for itself in every American history textbook written from 1973 till infinity.

One of the most extraordinary aspects of the Watergate story has been the way the press has handled it: What began in the summer of 1972 as one of the great media-bungles of the century has developed, by now, into what is probably the most thoroughly and most professionally covered story in the history of American journalism.

When I boomed into Washington last month to meet Steadman and set up the National Affairs Desk once again, I expected – or in retrospect I *think* I expected – to find the high-rolling *news-meisters* of the capital press corps jabbering blindly among themselves, once again, in some stylish sector of reality far-removed from the Main Nerve of 'the story' ... like climbing aboard Ed Muskie's 'Sunshine Special' in the Florida primary and finding every media star in the nation sipping bloody marys and convinced they were riding the rails to Miami with 'the candidate' ... or sitting down to lunch at the Sioux Falls Holiday Inn on election day with a half-dozen of the heaviest press wizards and coming away convinced that McGovern couldn't possibly lose by more than ten points.

My experience on the campaign trail in 1972 had not filled me with a real sense of awe, *vis-à-vis* the wisdom of the national press corps ... so

I was seriously jolted, when I arrived in Washington, to find that the bastards had this Watergate story nailed up and bleeding from every extremity – from Watergate and all its twisted details, to ITT, the Vesco case, Nixon's lies about the financing for his San Clemente beach-mansion, and even the long-dormant 'Agnew scandal'.

There was not a hell of a lot of room for a gonzo journalist to operate in that high-tuned atmosphere. For the first time in memory, the Washington press corps was working very close to the peak of its awesome but normally dormant potential. The *Washington Post* has a half-dozen of the best reporters in America working every tangent of the Watergate story like wild-eyed junkies set adrift, with no warning, to find their next connection. The *New York Times*, badly blitzed on the story at first, called in hotrods from its bureaux all over the country to overcome the *Post*'s early lead. Both *Time*'s and *Newsweek*'s Washington bureaux began scrambling feverishly to find new angles, new connections, new leaks and leads in this story that was unravelling so fast that *nobody* could stay on top of it ... And especially not the three (or four) TV networks, whose whole machinery was geared to visual/action stories, rather than skilfully planted tips from faceless lawyers who called on private phones and then refused to say anything at all in front of the cameras.

The only standard-brand visual 'action' in the Watergate story had happened at the very beginning – when the burglars were caught in the act by a squad of plain-clothes cops with drawn guns – and that happened so fast that there was not even a still photographer on hand, much less a TV camera.

The network news moguls are not hungry for stories involving weeks of dreary investigation and minimum camera possibilities – particularly at a time when almost every ranking TV correspondent in the country was assigned to one aspect or another of a presidential campaign that was still boiling feverishly when the Watergate break-in occurred on 17 June. The Miami conventions and the Eagleton fiasco kept the Watergate story backstage all that summer. Both the networks and the press had their 'first teams' out on the campaign trail until long after the initial indictments – Liddy, Hunt, McCord, et al. – on 15 September. And by election day in November, the Watergate story seemed like old news.

It was rarely if ever mentioned among the press people following the campaign. A burglary at the Democratic national headquarters seemed relatively minor, compared to the action in Miami. It was a 'local' (Washington) story, and the 'local staff' was handling it ... but I *had* no local staff, so I made the obvious choice.

Except on two occasions, and the first of these still haunts me. On the night of 17 June I spent most of the evening in the Watergate Hotel: From about eight o'clock until ten I was swimming laps in the indoor pool, and from 10:30 until a bit after 1:00 a.m. I was drinking tequila in the Watergate bar with Tom Quinn, a sports columnist for the now-defunct *Washington Daily News*.

Meanwhile, upstairs in room 214, Hunt and Liddy were already monitoring the break-in, by walkie-talkie, with ex-FBI agent Alfred Baldwin in his well-equipped spy-nest across Virginia Avenue in room 419 of the Howard Johnson Motor Lodge. Jim McCord had already taped the locks on two doors just underneath the bar in the Watergate garage, and it was probably just about the time that Quinn and I called for our last round of tequila that McCord and his team of Cubans moved into action – and got busted less than an hour later.

All this was happening less than 100 yards from where we were sitting in the bar, sucking limes and salt with our Sauza Gold and muttering darkly about the fate of Duane Thomas and the pigs who run the National Football League.

Neither Bob Woodward nor Carl Bernstein from the *Post* were invited to McGovern's party that night – which was fitting, because the guest list was limited to those who had lived through the day-to-day nightmare of the 72 campaign ... People like Frank Mankiewicz, Miles Rubin, Rick Stearns, Gary Hart and even *Newsweek* correspondent Dick Stout, whose final dispatch on the doomed McGovern campaign very nearly got him thrown out of the *Dakota Queen II* at 30,000 feet over Lincoln, Nebraska, on the day before the election.

This was the crowd that had gathered that night in July to celebrate his last victory before the great disaster – the slide that began with Eagleton and ended, incredibly, with Watergate. The events of the past six months had so badly jangled the nerves of the invited guests – the staffers and journalists who had been with McGovern from New Hampshire all the way to Sioux Falls on election day – that nobody really wanted to go to the party, for fear that it might be a funeral and a serious bummer.

By the end of the evening, when the two dozen bitter-enders had forced McGovern to break out his own private stock – ignoring the departure of the caterers and the dousing of the patio lights – the bulk of the conversation was focused on which one or ones of the Secret Service men assigned to protect McGovern had been reporting daily to Jeb Magruder at CREEP, and which one of the ten or twelve journalists with access to the innards of George's strategy had been on CREEP's payroll at $1500 a month. This journalist – still publicly unknown and undenounced – was referred to in White House memos as 'Chapman's friend', a mysterious designation that puzzled the whole Washington press corps until one of the President's beleaguered ex-aides explained privately that 'Chapman' is a name Nixon used, from time to time, in the good old days when he was able to travel around obscure Holiday Inns under phoney names ...

R. Chapman, Pepsi-Cola salesman, New York City ... with a handful of friends carrying walkie-talkies and wearing white leather shoulder-holsters ... But what the hell? Just send a case of Pepsi up to the suite, my man, and don't ask questions; your reward will come later – call the White House and ask for Howard Hunt or Jim McCord; they'll take care of you.

Right. Or maybe Tex Colson, who is slowly and surely emerging as the guiding light behind Nixon's whole arsenal of illegal, immoral and un-ethical 'black advance' or 'dirty tricks' department. It was Colson who once remarked that he would 'walk over his grandmother for Richard Nixon' ... and it was Colson who hired head 'plumber' Egil 'Bud' Krogh, who in 1969 told Daniel X. Friedman, chairman of the psy-chiatry department at the University of Chicago: 'Anyone who opposes us, we'll destroy. As a matter of fact, anyone who doesn't support us, we'll destroy.'

Colson, the only one of Nixon's top command to so far evade Water-gate's legal noose, is the man who once told White House cop Jack Caulfield to put a firebomb in the offices of the staid/liberal Brookings Institution, in order to either steal or destroy some documents he con-sidered incriminating. Colson now says he was 'only joking' about the firebomb plan, but Caulfield took it so seriously that he went to then White House counsel John Dean and said he refused to work with Colson any longer, because he was 'crazy'.

Crazy? Tex Colson?

Never in hell. 'He's the meanest man in American politics,' says Nixon's speechwriter Pat Buchanan, smiling lazily over the edge of a beer can beside the pool outside his Watergate apartment. Buchanan is one of the few people in the Nixon administration with a sense of humour. He is so far to the right that he dismisses Tex Colson as a 'Massachusetts liberal'. But for some reason, Buchanan is also one of the few people – perhaps the only one – on Nixon's staff, who has friends at the other end of the political spectrum. At one point during the campaign I mentioned Buchanan at McGovern headquarters, for some reason, and Rick Stearns, perhaps the most hardline left-bent ideologue on McGovern's staff, sort of chuckled and said, 'Oh yeah, we're pretty good friends. Pat's the only one of those bastards over there with any principles.' When I mentioned this to another McGovern staffer, he snapped: 'Yeah, maybe so ... like Josef Goebbels had principles.'

My own relationship with Buchanan goes back to the New Hampshire primary in 1968 when Nixon was still on the dim fringes of his political comeback. We spent about eight hours one night in a Boston hotel room, finishing off a half gallon of Old Crow and arguing savagely about politics: As I recall, I kept asking him why a person who seemed to have good sense would be hanging around with Nixon. It was clear even then that Buchanan considered me stone crazy, and my dismissal of Nixon as a hopeless bum with no chance of winning anything seemed to amuse him more than anything else.

About eight months later, after one of the strangest and most brutal years in American history, Richard Nixon was President and Pat Buchanan was one of his top two speechwriters along with Ray Price, the house moderate. I didn't see Pat again until the McGovern campaign in 72 when Ron Ziegler refused to have me on the Nixon press plane and Buchanan intervened to get me past the White House guard and into what turned out to be a dull and useless seat on the plane with the rest of the White House press corps. It was also Buchanan who inter-viewed Garry Wills, introducing him into the Nixon campaign of 1968 – an act of principle that resulted in an extremely unfriendly book called *Nixon Agonistes*.

So it seemed entirely logical, I thought – going back to Washington in the midst of this stinking Watergate summer – to call Buchanan and see if he felt like having thirteen or fourteen drinks on some afternoon when he wasn't at the White House working feverishly in what he calls 'the bunker'. Price and Buchanan write almost everything Nixon says and they are busier than usual these days, primarily figuring out what *not* to say. I spent most of one Saturday afternoon with Pat lounging around a tin umbrella table beside the Watergate pool and talking lazily about politics in general. When I called him at the White House the day be-fore, the first thing he said was, 'Yeah, I just finished your book.'

'Oh Jesus,' I replied, thinking this naturally meant the end of any relationship we'd ever have. But he laughed. 'Yeah, it's one of the funniest things I've ever read.'

One of the first things I asked him that afternoon was something that had been simmering in my head for at least a year or so and that was how he could feel comfortable with strange friends like me and Rick Stearns, and particularly how he could possibly feel comfortable sitting out in the open – in plain sight of the whole Watergate crowd – with a known monster whose affection for Richard Nixon was a matter of fairly brutal common knowledge – or how he felt comfortable playing poker once or twice a week sometimes with Rick Stearns, whose political views are almost as diametrically opposed to Buchanan's as mine are. He shrugged it off with a grin, opening another beer. 'Oh, well, we ideologues seem to get along better than the others. I don't agree with Rick on anything at all that I can think of, but I like him and I respect his honesty.'

A strange notion, the far left and far right finding some kind of odd common ground beside the Watergate pool and particularly when one of them is a top Nixon speechwriter, spending most of his time trying to keep the boss from sinking like a stone in foul water, yet now and then laughingly referring to the White House as the Bunker.

After the sixth or seventh beer, I told him about our abortive plot several nights earlier to seize Colson out of his house and drag him down Pennsylvania Avenue tied behind a huge gold Oldsmobile Cutlass. He laughed and said something to the effect that 'Colson's so tough, he might like it.' And then, talking further about Colson, he said, 'But you know he's not really a conservative.'

And that's what seems to separate the two GOP camps, like it separates Barry Goldwater from Richard Nixon. Very much like the difference between the Humphrey Democrats and the McGovern Democrats. The ideological wing versus the pragmatists, and by Buchanan's standards it's doubtful that he even considers Richard Nixon a conservative.

My strange and violent reference to Colson seemed to amuse him more than anything else. 'I want to be very clear on one thing,' I assured him. 'If you're thinking about having me busted for conspiracy on this, remember that I've already deliberately dragged you into it.' He laughed again and then mentioned something about the 'one overt act' necessary for a conspiracy charge, and I quickly said that I had no idea where Tex Colson even lived and didn't really want to know, so that even if we'd wanted to drag the vicious bastard down Pennsylvania Avenue at sixty miles per hour behind a gold Oldsmobile Cutlass we had no idea, that night, where to find him, and about halfway into the plot we crashed into a black and gold Cadillac on Connecticut Avenue and drew a huge mob of angry blacks who ended all thought of taking vengeance on Colson. It was all I could do to get out of that scene without getting beaten like a gong for the small creases our rented Cutlass had put in the fender of the Cadillac.

Which brings us back to that accident report I just wrote and sent off to Mr Roach at Avis mid-Atlantic headquarters in Arlington. The accident occurred about 3:30 in the morning when either Warren Beatty or Pat Caddell opened the door of a gold Oldsmobile Cutlass I'd rented at Dulles airport earlier that day, and banged the door against the fender of a massive black & gold Cadillac roadster parked in front of a latenight restaurant on Connecticut Avenue called Anna Maria's. It seemed like a small thing at the time, but in retrospect it might have spared us all – including McGovern – an extremely nasty episode.

Because somewhere in the late hours of that evening, when the drink had taken hold and people were jabbering loosely about anything that came into their heads, somebody mentioned that 'the worst and most vicious' of Nixon's backstairs White House hit men – Charles 'Tex' Colson – was probably the only one of the dozen or more Nixon/CRP functionaries thus far sucked into the Watergate scandal who was not likely to do any time, or even be indicted.

It was a long, free-falling conversation, with people wandering in and out, over a time-span of an hour or so – journalists, pols, spectators – and the focus of it, as I recall, was a question that I was trying to get some bets on: How many of the primary Watergate figures would actually serve time in prison?

The reactions ranged from my own guess that only Magruder and Dean would live long enough to serve time in prison, to Mankiewicz's flat assertion that 'everybody except Colson' would be indicted, convicted, sentenced and actually hauled off to prison.

(Everybody involved in this conversation will no doubt deny any connection with it – or even hearing about it, for that matter – but what the hell? It did, in fact, take place over the course of some two or three days, in several locations, but the seed of speculation took root in the final early-morning hours of McGovern's party ... although I don't remember that George himself was involved or even within earshot at any time. He has finally come around to the point where his friends don't mind calling him 'George' in the friendly privacy of his own home, but that is not quite the same thing as getting him involved in a felony-conspiracy/attempted murder charge that some wild-eyed, Nixon-appointed geek in the Justice Department might try to crank up on the basis of a series of boozy conversations among journalists, politicians and other half-drunk cynics. Anybody who has spent any time around late-night motel bars with the press corps on a presidential campaign knows better than to take their talk seriously ... but after reading reviews of my book on the 72 campaign, it occurs to me that some people will believe almost *anything* that fits their preconceived notions.)

And so much for all that.

2 August Patio Bar beside the Washington Hilton swimming pool
Steadman and his wife had just arrived from England. Sandy had flown in the day before from Colorado and I had come up from Miami after a long vacation in the decompression chamber. It was a Tuesday or Wednesday afternoon, I think, and the Watergate hearings were in progress but we'd decided to take the first day off and get ourselves under control.

One of the first things I had to do was make out a long overdue accident report for that night, two weeks earlier, when the door of my rented car smacked into the Cadillac at four in the morning. The Avis people were threatening to cut off my coverage for 'non-cooperation' so I'd brought the insanely complicated accident report down to the patio table by the pool, thinking to fill it out with the help of eight or nine Carlsbergs.

Steadman was already sketching distractedly, swilling beers at a feverish rate and muttering darkly to himself about the terrible conditions in the hotel and how earlier that morning while passing thru the coffee shop, a huge ceiling lamp had fallen from the ceiling and nearly killed him.

It was 'teddible teddible', he said, 'the damn thing came so close that it knocked my briefcase full of drawings out of my hand. Six inches closer and it would have caved in my head!'

I nodded sympathetically, thinking it was just another one of those ugly twists of luck that always seem to afflict Ralph in this country, and I kept on grappling with the accident report.

Steadman was still babbling. 'God, it's hot ... Ah, this teddible thirst ... what's that you've got there?'

'The goddamn accident report. I've got to make it out.'

'Accident report?'

'Yeah, I had a small wreck the last time I was here about two weeks ago ...'

'Alright, alright ... Yes, two more Carlsbergs.'

'... And the car blew up the next night and I had to abandon it in Rock Creek Park at four in the morning. I think they're still billing me for it.'

'Who?'

'The Avis people.'

'My God, that's teddible.'

'I only had it two nights. The first night I had this wreck, and the next night it blew up.'

'What were you doing in this wretched city at four in the morning?'

'Well, actually we were thinking about going out to Tex Colson's house and jerking him out of bed, tying him behind the car with a big rope and dragging him down Pennsylvania Avenue ... then cutting him loose in front of the White House guard gate.'

'You're kidding ... You don't really mean that. You wouldn't do a thing like that, would you?'

'Of course not. That would be a conspiracy to commit either murder or aggravated assault, plus kidnapping ... and you know me, Ralph; that's not my style at all.'

'That's what I mean. You were drunk perhaps, eh?'

'Ah, we were drunk yes. We'd been to a party at McGovern's.'

'McGovern's? Drinking? Who was with you?'

'Drinking heavily, yes. It was Warren Beatty and Pat Caddell, McGovern's poll wizard, and myself and for some reason it occurred to me that the thing to do at that hour of the morning was to go out and get Colson.'

'My God, that's crazy! You must have been stoned and drunk – especially by four in the morning.'

'Well, we left McGovern's at about 2:30 and we were supposed to meet Crouse at this restaurant downtown ... McGovern lives somewhere in the northwest part of town and it had taken me two hours to find the damn house and I figured it would take me another two hours to get out again unless I could follow somebody. Crouse was about a block ahead of me when we left. I could see his taillights but there was another car between me and Crouse and I was afraid I'd lose him in that maze of narrow little streets, almost like country lanes.

' "We can't let Crouse get away," I said. So I slammed it into passing gear and passed the car right in front of me in order to get behind Crouse, and all of a sudden here was a car coming the other direction on this street about fifteen feet wide – just barely enough room for two cars to pass and certainly not enough room for three cars to pass, one of them going about seventy miles an hour with a drunk at the wheel.

'I thought, hmmmm, well ... I can either slow down or stomp on it and squeeze in there, so I stomped on it and forced the oncoming car up over the kerb and on to the grass in order to avoid me as I came hurtling back into my own lane, and just as I flashed past him I happened to look over and saw that it was a police car. Well, I thought, this is not the time to stop and apologize; I could see him in my rear view mirror, stopping and beginning to turn around ... So instead of following Crouse, I took the first left I could, turned the lights off and drove like a bastard – assuming the cop would probably chase Crouse and run him down and arrest him, but as it happened he didn't get either one of us.'

'What a rotten thing to do.'

'Well, it was him or me, Ralph ... as a matter of fact I worried about it when we didn't see Tim at the restaurant later on. But we were late because we did some high-speed driving exercises in the southeast area of Washington – flashing along those big empty streets going into corners at eighty miles an hour and doing 180s ... it was a sort of thunder road driving trip, screwing it on with that big Cutlass.'

'Enormous car?'

'A real monster, extremely overpowered ...'

'How big is it? The size of a bus?'

'No, normal size for a big car, but extremely powerful – much more, say, than a Mustang or something like that. We did about an hour's worth of crazed driving on these deserted streets, and it was during this time that I mentioned that we should probably go out and have a word with Mr Colson – because during a conversation earlier in the evening, the consensus among the reporters at McGovern's party was that Colson was probably the only one of Nixon's first-rank henchmen who would probably not even be indicted.'

'Why's that?'

'He had managed to keep himself clean, somehow – up to that point anyway. Now, he's been dragged into the ITT hassle again, so it looks like he might go down with all the others.

'But at that point, we thought, well, Colson really is the most evil of those bastards, and if he gets off there is really no justice in the world. So we thought we'd go out to his house – luckily none of us knew where he lived – and beat on his door, mumbling something like: "God's mercy on me! My wife's been raped! My foot's been cut off!" Anything to lure him downstairs ... and the minute he opened the door, seize him and drag him out to the car and tie him by the ankles and drag him down to the White House.'

'He could identify you ...'

'Well, he wouldn't have time to know exactly who it was – but we thought about it for a while, still driving around, and figured a beastly thing like that might be the only thing that could get Nixon off the hook, because he could go on television the next afternoon, demanding to make a nationwide emergency statement, saying: "Look what these thugs have done to poor Mr Colson! This is exactly what we were talking about! This is why we had to be so violent in our ways, because these thugs will stop at nothing! They dragged Mr Colson the length of Pennsylvania Avenue at four in the morning, then cut him loose like a piece of meat!" He would call for more savage and stringent security measures against "the kind of animals who would do a thing like this". So we put the plot out of our heads.'

'Well, it would have been a bit risky ... wouldn't have done the Democratic party any good at all, would it?'

'Well, it might have created a bit of an image problem – and it would have given Nixon the one out he desperately needs now, a way to justify the whole Watergate trip by raving about "this brutal attack" ... That's an old Hell's Angels gig, dragging people down the street. Hell's Angels. *Pachucos*, drunken cowboys.

'But I thought more about it later, when I finally got back to the hotel after that stinking accident I'm still trying to explain ... and it occurred to me that those bastards are really mean enough to do that to Colson, themselves – if they only had the wits to think about it. They could go out and drag him down the street in a car with old McGovern stickers on the bumpers or put on false beards and wave a wine bottle out the window as they passed the White House and cut him loose. He'd roll to a stop in front of the guard house and the guard would clearly see the McGovern sticker on the car screeching off around the corner and that's all Nixon would need. If we gave them the idea, they'd probably go out and get Colson tonight.'

'He'd be babbling, I'd think—'

'He'd be hysterical, in very bad shape. And of course he'd claim that McGovern thugs had done it to him – if he were still able to talk. I really believe Nixon would do a thing like that if he thought it would get him out of the hole ... So I thought about it a little more, and it occurred to me what we should do was have these masks made up – you know those rubber masks that fit over the whole head.'

'Ah yes, very convincing ...'

'Yeah, one of them would have to be the face of Haldeman, one the face of Ehrlichman and one the face of Tony Ulasewicz.'

'Yes, the meanest men on the Nixon staff.'

'Well, Colson's the meanest man in politics, according to Pat Buchanan. Ulasewicz is the hit man, a hired thug. I thought if we put these masks on and wore big overcoats or something to disguise ourselves and went out to his house and kind of shouted: "Tex, Tex! It's me, Tony. Come on down. We've got a big problem." And the minute he opens the door, these people with the Haldemann and Ehrlichman masks would jump out from either side and seize him by each arm – so that he sees who has him, but only for two or three seconds, before the person wearing the Ulasewicz mask slaps a huge burlap sack over his head, knots it around his knees and then the three of them carry him out to the car and lash him to the rear bumper and drag him down the street – and just as we passed the White House guard station, slash the rope so that Colson would come to a tumbling bloody stop right in front of the guard ... and after two or three days in the emergency ward, when he was finally able to talk, after coming out of shock, he would swear that the people who got him were Haldeman, Ehrlichman and Ulasewicz – and he would *know* they were mean enough to do it, because that's the way *he* thinks. He's mean enough to do it himself. You'd have to pick a night when they were all in Washington, and Colson would swear that they did it to him, no matter what they said. He would *know* it, because he had *seen* them.'

'Brilliant, brilliant. Yes, he'd be absolutely convinced – having seen the men and the faces.'

'Right. But of course you couldn't talk – just seize him and go. What would you think if you looked out and saw three people you recognized, and suddenly they jerked you up and tied you behind a car and dragged you forty blocks? Hell, you *saw* them. You'd testify, swear under oath ... which would cause Nixon probably to go completely crazy. He wouldn't know *what* to believe! How could he be sure that Haldeman, Ehrlichman and Ulasewicz hadn't done it? Nobody would know, not even by using lie detectors ... But that's a pretty heavy act to get into – dragging people around the street behind rented Avis cars, and we never quite got back to it, anyway, but if we hadn't had that accident we might have given it a little more thought although I still have no idea where Colson lives and I still don't want to know. But you have to admit it was a nice idea.'

'That's a lovely thing, yes.'

'You know Colson had that sign on the wall in his office saying ONCE YOU HAVE THEM BY THE BALLS, THEIR HEARTS AND MINDS WILL FOLLOW.'

'Right.'

'He's an ex-Marine captain. So it would be a definite dose of his own medicine.'

'Do you really think he deserves that kind of treatment?'

'Well, he was going to set off a firebomb in the Brookings Institution, just to recover some papers ... Colson is not one of your friendlier, happier type of persons. He's an evil bastard, and dragging him down the street would certainly strike a note of terror in that crowd; they could use some humility.'

'Poetic justice, no?'

'Well, it's a little rough ... it might not be necessary to drag him forty blocks. Maybe just four. You could put him in the trunk for the first thirty-six blocks, then haul him out and drag him the last four; that would certainly scare the piss out of him, bumping along the street, feeling all his skin being ripped off ...'

'He'd be a bloody mess. They might think he was just some drunk and let him lie there all night.'

'Don't worry about that. They have a guard station in front of the White House that's open twenty-four hours a day. The guards would recognize Colson ... and by that time of course his wife would have called the cops and reported that a bunch of thugs had kidnapped him.'

'Wouldn't it be a little kinder if you drove about four more blocks and stopped at a phone box to ring the hospital and say, "Would you mind going around to the front of the White House? There's a naked man lying outside in the street, bleeding to death ..."'

'... and we think it's Mr Colson.'

'It would be quite a story for the newspapers, wouldn't it?'
'Yeah, I think it's safe to say we'd see some headlines on that one.'

TWO

Flashbacks & Time Warps ... Scrambled Notes and Rude Comments
from the High Country ... Dean vs. Haldeman in the Hearing
Room ... A Question of Perjury ... Ehrlichmann Sandbags an Old
Buddy ... Are the Sharks Deserting the Suckfish?

EDITOR'S NOTE:
Due to circumstances beyond our control, the following section was
lashed together at the last moment from a six-pound bundle of documents, notebooks, memos, recordings and secretly taped phone conversations with Dr Thompson during a month of erratic behaviour in
Washington, New York, Colorado and Miami. His 'long-range plan', he
says, is to 'refine' these nerve-wracking methods, somehow, and eventually 'create an entirely new form of journalism'. In the meantime, we
have suspended his monthly retainer and cancelled his credit card. During one four-day period in Washington he destroyed two cars, cracked
a wall in the Washington Hilton, purchased two French horns at $1100
each and ran through a plate-glass door in a Turkish restaurant.

Compounding the problem was the presence in Washington, for the
first time, of our artist Ralph Steadman – an extremely heavy drinker
with little or no regard for either protocol or normal social amenities.
On Steadman's first visit to the Watergate hearing room he was ejected
by the Capitol Police after spilling beer on a TV monitor and knocking
Sam Ervin off his feet while attempting to seize a microphone to make
a statement about 'the rottenness of American politics'. It was only the
timely intervention of *New York Post* correspondent John Lang that
kept Steadman from being permanently barred from the hearing room.

In any case, the bulk of what follows appears exactly as Dr Thompson wrote it originally in his notebooks. Given the realities of our constant deadline pressure, there was no other way to get this section into
print.

Jesus, this Watergate thing is unbelievable. It's terrible, like finding out your wife is running around but you don't want to hear about it.

> Remark of a fat man from Nashville sharing a taxi with
> Ralph Steadman.

Tuesday morning 26 June 1973, 8:13 a.m. in the Rockies ...
Bright sun on the grass outside my windows behind this junk TV set and long white snowfields, still unmelted, on the peaks across the valley. Every two or three minutes the doleful screech of a half-wild peacock rattles the windows. The bastard is strutting around on the roof, shattering the morning calm with his senseless cries.

His noise is a bad burden on Sandy's nerves. 'God damnit!' she mutters. 'We *have* to get him a hen!'

'Fuck him; we *got* him a hen – and she ran off and got herself killed by coyotes. What the crazy bastard needs now is a bullet through the vocal cords. He's beginning to sound like Herman Talmadge.'

'Talmadge?'

'Watch what's happening, goddamnit! Here's another true son of the South. First it was Thompson ... now Talmadge ... and then we'll get that half-wit pimp from Florida.'

'Gurney?'

I nodded, staring fixedly at the big blueish eye on the permanently malfunctioned 'colour TV' set that I hauled back from Washington last summer, when I finally escaped from the place ... But now I was using it almost feverishly, day after day, to watch what was *happening* in Washington.

The Watergate hearings – my daily fix, on TV. Thousands of people from all over the country are writing the networks to demand that this goddamn tedious nightmare be jerked off the air so they can get back to their favourite soap operas: *As the World Turns*, *The Edge of Night*, *The Price Is Right* and *What Next for Weird Betty?* They are bored by the spectacle of the Watergate hearings. The plot is confusing, they say; the characters are dull, and the dialogue is repulsive.

The President of the United States would never act that way – at least not during baseball season. Like Nixon's new White House chief of staff, Melvin Laird, said shortly before his appointment: 'If the President turns out to be guilty, I don't want to hear about it.'

This is the other end of the attitude-spectrum from the comment I heard, last week, from a man in Denver: 'I've been waiting a long time for this,' he said. 'Maybe not as long as Jerry Voorhis or Helen

Gahagan Douglas ... and I never really thought it would happen, to tell you the truth.' He flashed me a humourless smile and turned back to his TV set. 'But it *is*, by God! And it's almost too good to be true.'

My problem – journalistically, at least – has its roots in the fact that I agree with just about everything that laughing, vengeful bastard said that day. We didn't talk much. There was no need for it. Everything Richard Milhous Nixon ever stood for was going up in smoke right in front of our eyes. And anybody who could understand and appreciate *that*, I felt, didn't need many words to communicate. At least not with me.

(The question is: what did he *stand for*, and what next for *that*? Agnew? Reagan? Rockefeller? Even Percy? Nixon was finally 'successful' for the same reason he was finally brought low. He kept pushing, pushing, pushing – and inevitably he pushed too far.)

Noon – Tuesday 26 June
The TV set is out on the porch now – a move that involved much cursing and staggering.

Weicker has the mike – *mano a mano* on Dean – and after thirteen minutes of apparently aimless blathering he comes off no better than Talmadge. Weicker seemed oddly cautious – a trifle obtuse, perhaps.

What are the connections? Weicker is a personal friend of Pat Gray's. He is also the only member of the Select Committee with after-hours personal access to John Dean.

– Live from Senate Caucus Room –
flash on CBS screen

Live? Rehearsed? In any case, Dean is livelier than most – not only because of what he has to say, but because he – unlike the other witnesses – refused to say it first in executive session to committee staffers before going on TV.

Strange – Dean's obvious credibility comes not from his long-awaited impact (or lack of it) on the American public, but from his obvious ability to deal with the seven senatorial inquisitors. They seem awed.

Dean got his edge, early on, with a mocking lash at the integrity of minority counsel Fred Thompson – and the others fell meekly in line. Dean radiates a certain very narrow kind of authority – nothing *personal*, but the kind of nasal blank-hearted authority you feel in the presence of the taxman or a very polite FBI agent.

Only Baker remains. *His* credibility took a bad beating yesterday. Dean ran straight at him, startling the TV audience with constant references to Baker's personal dealings with the White House, prior to the hearings. There was no need to mention that Baker is the son-in-law of that late and only half-lamented 'Solon' from the great State of Illinois, Sen. Everett Dirksen.

Dean is clearly a shrewd *executive*. He will have no trouble getting a good job when he gets out of prison.

Now Montoya – the flaccid Mex-Am from New Mexico. No problem here for John Dean ... Suddenly Montoya hits Dean head-on with Nixon's bogus quote about Dean's *investigation* clearing all members of White House staff. Dean calmly shrugs it off as a lie – 'I never made any investigation.'

– Montoya continues with entire list of *prior* Nixon statements.

Dean: 'In totality, there are less than accurate statements in that ... ah ... those statements.'

Montoya is *after Nixon's head*! Is this the *first sign*? Over the hump for Tricky Dick?

***Recall lingering memory of Miami Beach plainclothes cop, resting in armoury behind Convention Center on night of Nixon's renomination – ('You tell 'em, Tricky Dick.') – watching Nixon's speech on TV ... with tear gas fumes all around us and demonstrators gagging outside.

4:20 EDT
As usual, the pace picks up at the end. These buggers should be forced to keep at it for fifteen or sixteen straight hours – heavy doses of speed, pots of coffee, Wild Turkey, etc., force them down to the raving hysterical *quick*. Wild accusations, etc. ...

Dean becomes more confident as time goes on – a bit *flip* now, finding his feet.

Friday morning, 29 June ... 8:33 a.m.
Jesus, this waterhead Gurney again! You'd think the poor bugger would have the sense to not talk any more ... but no, Gurney is still blundering along, still hammering blindly at the receding edges of Dean's 'credibility' in his now-obvious role as what Frank Reynolds and Sam Donaldson on ABC-TV both described as 'the waterboy for the White House'.

Gurney appears to be deaf; he has a brain like a cow's udder. He asks his questions – off the typed list apparently furnished him by minority (GOP) counsel, Fred J. Thompson – then his mind seems to wander, his eyes roam lazily around the room while Thompson whispers industriously in his ear, his hands shuffle papers distractedly on the table in front of his microphone ... and meanwhile, Dean meticulously chews up his questions and hands them back to him in shreds; so publicly mangled that their fate might badly embarrass a man with good sense ...

But Gurney seems not to notice: His only job on this committee is to *defend the presidency*, according to his instructions from the White House – or at least whatever third-string hangers-on might still be working there – and what we tend to forget, here, is that it's totally impossible to understand Gurney's real motives without remembering that he's the Republican Senator from Florida, a state where George Wallace swept the *Democratic primary* in 1972 with 78% of the vote, and which went 72% for Nixon in November.

In a state where even Hubert Humphrey is considered a dangerous radical, Ed Gurney's decision to make an ignorant yahoo of himself on national TV makes excellent sense – at least to his own constituency. They are watching TV down in Florida today, along with the rest of the country, and we want to remember that if Gurney appears in Detroit and Sacramento as a hideous caricature of the imbecilic Senator Cornpone – that's not necessarily the way he appears to the voters around Tallahassee and St Petersburg.

Florida is not Miami – contrary to the prevailing national image – and one of the enduring mysteries in American politics is how a humane & relatively enlightened politician like Reubin Askew could have been elected Governor of one of the few states in the country where George Wallace would have easily beaten Richard Nixon – in a head-to-head presidential race – in either 1968 or 1972. Or even 1976, for that matter ...

And so much for all that. Gurney is off the air now – having got himself tangled up in a legal/constitutional argument with Sam Ervin and Dean's attorney. He finally just hunkered down and passed the mike to Senator Inouye, who immediately re-focused the questioning by prodding Dean's memory on the subject of White House efforts to seek vengeance on their 'enemies'.

Which senators – in addition to Teddy Kennedy – were subjects of surveillance by Nixon's gumshoes? Which journalists – in addition to the man from *Newsday* who wrote unfavourable things about Bebe Rebozo – were put on the list to have their tax returns audited? Which athletes and actors – in addition to Joe Namath and Paul Newman – were put on the list to be 'screwed'?

Dean's answers were vague on these things. He's not interested in 'interpreting the motives of others', he says – which is an easy thing to forget, after watching him on the tube for three days, repeatedly incriminating at least half the ranking fixers in Nixon's inner circle: Colson, Haldeman, Ehrlichman, Mitchell, Magruder, Strachan, Ziegler, Moore, LaRue, Kalmbach, Nofziger, Krogh, Liddy, Kleindienst ... and the evidence is 'mind-boggling', in Senator Baker's words, when it comes in the form of verbatim memos and taped phone conversations.

The simple-minded vengefulness of the language seems at least as disturbing as the vengeful plots unveiled.

5:35 p.m.
Sitting out here on the porch, naked in a rocking chair in the half-shade of a dwarf juniper tree – looking out at snow-covered mountains from this hot lizard's perch in the sun with no clouds at 8000 feet – a mile and a half high, as it were – it is hard to grasp that this dim blue tube sitting on an old bullet-pocked tree stump is bringing me every uncensored detail – for five or six hours each day from a musty brown room 2000 miles east – of a story that is beginning to look like it can have only one incredible ending – the downfall of the President of the United States.

Six months ago, Richard Nixon was the most powerful political leader in the history of the world, more powerful than Augustus Caesar when he had his act rolling full bore – six months ago.

Now, with the passing of each sweaty afternoon, into what history will call 'the summer of 73', Richard Nixon is being dragged closer and closer – with all deliberate speed, as it were – to disgrace and merciless infamy. His place in history is already fixed: He will go down with Grant and Harding as one of democracy's classic mutations.

9:22 p.m.
Billy Graham Crusade on both TV channels ... But what? What's happening here? An acid flashback? A time warp? CBS has Graham in Orange County, raving about 'redemption through *blood*'. Yes, God demands *blood*! ... but ABC is running the Graham Crusade in South Africa, a huge all-white Afrikaner pep rally at Johannesburg's Wanderers Stadium. (Did I finally get that right, are these mushrooms deceiving me?)

Strange ... on this eve of Nixon's demise, his private preacher is raving about *blood* in Los Angeles (invoking the actual bloody images of Robert Kennedy's brain on the cold concrete floor of the Ambassador Hotel kitchen and Jack Kennedy's blood 'on his widow's dress that tragic day in Dallas' ... and the blood of Martin Luther King on that motel balcony in Memphis).

But *wait*? Is that a *black* face I see in the crowd at Wanderers Stadium? Yes, a rapt black face, wearing aviator shades and a green army uniform ... stoned on Billy's message, along with all the others: 'Your *soul* is searching for God! [Pause, body crouched, both fists shaking defiantly in the air ...] They tore his flesh! They pulled his *beard* out.' Graham is in a wild Charlton Heston fighting stance now: 'And while they were doing that, seventy-two million avenging angels had to be held back ... yes ... by the bloody arm of the Lord ... from sweeping this planet into *hell*.'

Cazart! Seventy-two million of the fuckers, eh? That threat would never make the nut in LA. It would have to be seventy-two *billion* there. But South Africa is the last of the white nazi bush-leagues, and when you mention seventy-two million of *anything* ready to sweep across the planet, they *know* what you mean in South Africa.

Niggers. The avenging black horde ... and suddenly it occurs to me that Graham's act is extremely subtle; he is actually *threatening* this weeping crowd of white-supremist burghers ... Indeed ... Redemption thru fear! It knocked 'em dead in Houston, so why not here?

10:05

The news, and John Dean again – that fiendish little drone. (Did the president seem *surprised* when you gave him this information?) 'No sir, he did not.'

The junkies are rolling up the tents at Camp David tonight. Mister Nixon has cashed his cheque. Press reports from 'the western White House' in San Clemente say the President has 'no comment' on Dean's almost unbelievably destructive testimony.

No comment. The boss is under sedation. Who is with him out there on that lonely western edge of America tonight. Bebe Rebozo? Robert Abplanalp, W. Clement Stone?

Probably not. They must have seen what Nixon saw today – that the Ervin committee was going to give Dean a *free ride*. His victims will get their shots at him tomorrow – or next week – but it won't make much difference, because the only ones left to question him are the ones he publicly ridiculed yesterday as tools of the White House. Baker's credibility is so crippled – in the wake of Dean's references in his opening statement to Baker's alleged 'willingness to cooperate' with the Nixon brain-trust in the days before these hearings – that anything Baker hits Dean with tomorrow will seem like the angry retaliation of a much-insulted man.

And what can poor Gurney say? Dean contemptuously dismissed him – in front of a nationwide TV audience of seventy million cynics – as such a hopeless yo-yo that he wouldn't even have to be leaned on. Gurney was the only one of the seven senators on the Ervin committee that Nixon's strategists figured was safely in their pocket, before the hearings started. Weicker, the maverick Republican, was considered a lost cause from the start.

'We knew we were in trouble when we looked at that line-up,' Dean testified. There was something almost like a smile on his face when he uttered those words ... the rueful smile of a good loser, perhaps? Or maybe something else. The crazy, half-controlled flicker of a laugh on the face of a man who is just beginning to think he might *survive* this incredible trip. By 4:45 on Tuesday, Dean had the dazed, still hyper-tense look of a man who knows he went all the way out to the edge, with no grip at all for a while, and suddenly feels his balance coming back.

Well ... maybe so. If Dean can survive tomorrow's inevitable counter-attack it's all over. The Harris poll in today's Rocky Mountain *News* – even *before* Dean's testimony – showed Nixon's personal credibility rating on the Watergate 'problem' had slipped to a fantastic new low of 15-70% negative. If the Ervin committee lets even half of Dean's testi-mony stand, Richard Nixon won't be able to give away dollar bills in Times Square on the Fourth of July.

Monday 15 July, 2:10 p.m.
Watergate Hearings
Old Senate Office Building
*Mystery witness – Alex Butterfield. Impossible to see witness' face from periodical seat directly behind him.

*Rufus (pipe) Edmisten, Ervin's man, the face behind Baker and Ervin. 'Politically ambitious – wants to run for Attorney General of North Carolina' – always sits on camera.

Butterfield regales room with tales of elaborate taping machine in Oval Office (see clips). Nixon's official *bugger* – 'liaison to SS'.

BF: – sharp dark blue suit – Yes sir – *it was a great deal more difficult to pick up in the cabinet room.*

Talmadge: Who installed the devices?

BF: SS ? Tech. Security Div. ... To record things for posterity.

T: Why were these devices installed?

BF: Constant taping of all conversations in Oval Office for tran-scriptions for *Nixon library*. Voice activated mikes all over Nixon's office ... With time delay, so as not to cut out during pauses.

Fred Thompson looks like a Tennessee moonshiner who got rich – somebody sent him to a haberdasher when he heard he was going to Washington.

Four 6 x 6 chandeliers – yellow cut glass – hanging from ceiling, but obscured by banks of Colortran TV lites. Stan Tredick and other photogs with cardboard shields taped over lenses to cut out TV lights from above.

•

2:34 – Voting warning signal?

Ah ha! Butterfield will produce Dean-Nixon tape from 15 September?

T: No warning signal?

BF: No sir, not to my knowledge.

T: This taping was solely to serve historical purposes?

BF: Yes sir, as far as I know.

??: Key Biscayne and San Clemente?

BF: No recording device there – at least not by me.

NY Post headline: NIXON BUGS SELF (full page).

*The most obvious difference between being in the hearing room and watching TV is the *scale* – sense of smallness like a football stadium. The players seem human-sized and the grass seems real (in some cases). Room 318 is only about 100 x 100 – unlike the vast theatre it looks on TV.

*Constant stream of students being run in and out behind us.

Kalmbach sitting right in front of me – waiting to testify. $300 grey linen suit – $75 wing tips – lacquered black hair and tailored shirt – thin blue stripes on off-white. Large, rich. Sitting with silver-haired lawyer.

*Ervin reads letter from Buzhardt. Sends buzz through room – says LBJ did some taping.

Interesting – sitting directly behind witness chair – you can look right at Ervin and catch his facial expressions – as if he was looking at *me*. Nodding – fixed stare – occasional quick notes with yellow pencil.

*Kalmbach/Ulasewicz phone calls – from phone booth to phone booth – like Mafia operations. – Check *Honour Thy Father* for similar.

*Kalmbach '... It was about this time that I began to have a *degree of concern about this assignment*.'

4:50: Tedium sets in

Sudden vision of reaching out with Ostrich Lasso and slipping it around Kalmbach's neck then tightening it up and jerking him backwards.

Sudden uproar in gallery

– Cameras clicking feverishly as Kalmbach *struggles* with piano wire noose around his neck

– falling backwards

Unable to control laughter at this image ... forced to leave hearing room, out of control, people staring at me ...

*Ron MacMahon, Baker's press Sec., ex-Tennessee newsman, 'How can they *not* give 'em to us? [Nixon office tapes] Down in Tennessee we used to have a courthouse fire now and then ...'

*

Burnhardt J. Leinan, 27, Jerseyville, Illinois 62052. Came to DC by train – thirteen cars pulled by steam locomotive, coal tender. With 100 people Chi-Wash. Private train – Southern RR Independence Limited ('Watergate Special').

'Most people in Jerseyville only got interested when Dean produced the enemies list.'

– Why?

'Because they couldn't understand why certain names were on it – Newman, Streisand, Channing, Cosby – they couldn't understand why such a list was kept.'

*Carol Arms Bar – like a tavern full of football fans – with the game across the street. Hoots of laughter in bar at La Rue's deadpan account of Liddy's offer to 'be on any street corner at any time – and we could have him assassinated'.

All *Watergate groupies* seem to be anti-Nixon – both in the hearing room and bars around Old Senate Building. Like fans cheering the home team – 'the seven blocks of jelly'.

Tuesday 24 July
Benton's studio, 8:00 p.m.
PBS in Aspen is off again – even worse than PBS in DC.

*Ehrlichman takes the oath with Heil Hitler salute/no laughter from spectators.

– Boredom in hearing room, tedium at press tables.

Ehrlichman's face – ARROGANCE. Keep the fucker on TV – ten hours a day – ten straight days.

E: We saw very little chance of getting FBI to move ... very serious problem.

[Right! The nation's crawling with communists, multiplying like rats.]

Ehrlichman must have seen himself on *Sixty Minutes – so he knows how he looks on TV* – keeps glancing sideways at camera. Ehrlichman's 'faulty memory' ... Brookings – didn't remember who authorized fire-bombing – *didn't remember who he called to cancel Brookings bomb plot.*

(Same backgrounds – Civic Club, Country Club, JCC, USC/UCLA – law school, law firms, ad agencies.)

*Attitudes of Thomp-Baker & Gurney are critical – they related to Nixon's survival chances – rats sneaking off a sinking ship.

*E has insane gall to challenge Ervin on constitutional issues – Nixon's *right* to authorize Ellsberg burglary.

Dan Rather says Nixon wants a *confrontation NOW* – and also wants Cox to resign – Nixon, by withholding tapes, makes conviction of Haldeman, Ehrlichman, Dean, etc. impossible ... thus holding this over their heads – to keep them from talking.

'Hang together or hang separately.'

Ben Franklin

EDITOR'S NOTE
The following conversation between Ehrlichman and Herb Kalmbach arrived as a third generation Xerox in a package with Dr Thompson's notebooks. The transcript was released by Ehrlichman himself – he hadn't told Kalmbach he was taping their phone call for possible use in his defence. This was not one of those documents ferreted out by the Select Committee investigators. According to Thompson, the following transcript is 'the single most revealing chunk of testimony yet in terms of the morality of these people. It's like suddenly being plunged into the middle of the White House.'

CONVERSATION WITH HERB KALMBACH – 19 APRIL 1973, 4:50 P.M.

E: Ehrlichman
K: Kalmbach
E: Hi, how are you?
K: I'm pretty good. I'm scheduled for two tomorrow afternoon.
E: Where – at the jury or the US Attorney?
K: At the jury and I'm scheduled at 5:30 this afternoon with Silver.
E: Oh, are you?
K: Yeah. I just wanted to run through quickly several things, John, in line with our conversation. I got in here last night and there was a call from O'Brien. I returned it, went over there today and he said the reason for the call is LaRue has told him to ask him to call me to say that he had to identify me in connection with this and he wanted me to know that and so on.
E: Did he tell you about Dean?
K: Nope.
E: Well Dean has totally cooperated with the US Attorney in the hopes of getting immunity. Now what he says or how he says nobody seems to be able to divine but he.
K: The whole *enchilada*?
E: He's throwing on on Bob and me heavily.
K: He is?

287

E: Yep.

K: He is.

E: And taking the position that he was a mere agent. Now on your episode he told me before he left, so to speak, he, Dean, told me that really my transaction with him involving you was virtually my only area of liability in this thing and I said, well, John, what in the world are you talking about? He said, well I came to you from Mitchell and I said Mitchell needs money could we call Herb Kalmbach and ask him to raise some. And I said, and Dean says to me, and you said yes.

And I said yep, that's right. And he said well that does it. And I said well that's hard for me to believe. I don't understand the law but I don't think Herb entered into this with any guilty intent and I certainly didn't and so I said I just find that hard to imagine. Now since then I've retained counsel.

K: Oh, you have?

E: ... very good and who agrees with me that it is the remotest kind of nonsense but the point that I think has to be clarified, that I'm going to clarify if I get a chance, is that the reason that Dean had to come to me and to Bob where you were concerned is that we had promised you that you would not be run pillar to post by Maurice Stans.

K: And also that you knew I was your friend and you knew I was the President's attorney.

E: Sure.

K: Never do anything improper, illegal, unethical or whatever.

E: Right.

K: And ...

E: But the point is that rather than Mitchell calling you direct Mitchell knew darn well that you were no longer available.

K: Yep.

E: Now this was post 6 April, was it not?

K: Yep, 7 April.

E: So that Mitchell and Stans both knew that there wasn't any point in calling you direct because we had gotten you out of that on the pretext that you were going to do things for us.

K: That's right.

E: And so it was necessary for Dean to come to me and then in turn to Bob and plead a very urgent case without really getting into any specifics except to say you had to trust me, this is very important, and Mitchell is up his tree, or, you know, I mean is really worked, he didn't use that phrase, but he is really exercised about this. And; John if you tell me it's that important, why yes.

K: You know, when you and I talked and it was after John had given me that word, and I came in to ask you, John is this an assignment I have to take on? You said, yes it is period and move forwards. Then that was all that I needed to be assured that I wasn't putting my family in jeopardy.

E: Sure.

K: And I would just understand that you and I are absolutely together on that.

E: No question about it, Herb, that I would never knowingly have put you in any kind of a spot.

K: Yeah. Well, and when we talked you knew what I was about to do, you know, to go out and get the dough for this purpose; it was humanitarian.

E: It was a defence fund.

K: ... to support the family. Now the thing that was disquieting and this thing with O'Brien was that he said that there is a massive campaign evidently under way to indict all the lawyers including you and me, and I was a little shocked and I guess what I need to get from you, John, is assurance that this is not true.

E: Well, I don't know of any attempt to target you at all. My hunch is that they're trying to get at me, they're trying to corroborate. See what they said to Dean is that he gets no consideration from them unless they can corroborate Haldeman and my liability.

K: God, if I can make it plain that it was humanitarian and nothing else.

E: Yeah, and the point that I undoubtedly never expressed to you that I continually operated on the basis of Dean's representation to me.

K: Yep. It was not improper.

E: Right.

K: And there was nothing illegal about it.

E: See, he's the house lawyer.

K: Yep, exactly and I just couldn't believe that you and Bob and the President, just too good friends to ever put me in the position I would be putting my family on the line.

K: And it's just unbelievable, unthinkable. Now shall I just – I'll just if I'm asked by Silver I'll just lay it out just exactly that way.

E: Yeah, I wouldn't haul the President into it if you can help it.

K: Oh, no, I will not.

E: But I think the point that I will make in the future if I'm given the chance is that you were not under our control in any sort of a slavery sense but that we had agreed that you would not be at the beck and call of the committee.

K: And, of course, too, that I acted only on orders and, you know, on direction and if this is something that you felt sufficiently important and that you were assured it was altogether proper, then I would take it on because I always do it and always have. And you and Bob and the President know that.

E: Yeah, well, as far as propriety is concerned I think we both were relying entirely on Dean.

K: Yep.

E: I made no independent judgement.

K: Yep. Yep.

E: And I'm sure Bob didn't either.

K: Nope and I'm just, I just have the feeling, John, that I don't know if this is a weak reed, is it?

E: Who, Dean?

K: No, I mean are they still going to say well Herb you should have known.

E: I don't know how you could have. You didn't make any inquiries.

K: Never. And the only inquiries I made, John, was to you after I talked to John Dean.

E: And you found that I didn't know just a whole helluva lot.

K: You said this is something I have to do and ...

E: Yeah, and the reason that I said that, as you know, was not from any personal inquiry but was on the basis of what had been represented to me.

K: Yeah, and then on – to provide the defence fund to take care of the families of those fellas who were then ...

E: Indigent.

K: Not then been found guilty or not guilty.

E: And the point being here without attempting to induce them to do a damn thing.

K: Absolutely not and that was never, that was exactly right.

E: OK.

K: Now, can I get in to see you tomorrow before I go in there at two?

E: If you want to. They'll ask you.

K: Will they?

E: Yep.

K: Well, maybe I shouldn't.

E: They'll ask you to whom you've spoken about your testimony and I would appreciate it if you would say you've talked to me in California because at that time I was investigating this thing for the President.

K: And not now?

E: Well, I wouldn't ask you to lie.

K: No, I know.

E: But the point is ...

K: But the testimony was in California.

E: The point is. Well, no, your recollection of facts and so forth.

K: Yes, I agree.

E: See, I don't think we were ever seen together out there but at some point I'm going to have to say that I talked to O'Brien and Dean and Magruder and Mitchell and you and a whole lot of people about this case.

K: Yeah.

E: And so it would be consistent.

K: Do you feel, John, that calling it straight shot here, do you feel assured as you did when we were out there that there's no culpability here?

E: Yes.

K: And nothing to worry about?

E: And Herb, from everything I hear they're not after you.

K: Yes, sir.

E: From everything I hear.

K: Barbara, you know.

E: They're out to get me and they're out to get Bob.

K: My God. All right, well, John, it'll be absolutely clear that there was nothing looking towards any cover-up or anything. It was strictly for the humanitarian and I just want ... when I talked to you I just wanted you to advise me that it was all right on that basis.

E: On that basis.

K: To go forward.

E: That it was necessary.

K: And that'll be precisely the way it is.

E: Yeah, OK. Thanks, Herb. Bye.

5:00 p.m. Monday 30 July
Hearing Room
Old Senate Office Building
  *Haldeman opening statement
 – Terrible heat from TV lights turn back towards press and gallery. Barking (sounds of dog kennel) in press room as Haldeman comes on. Not on Nat. TV, but audible in hallway.

'Nor did I ever suggest ... [The Super Eagle Scout wounded tone of voice –] I had full confidence in Dean as did the President at that time ...'

Haldeman's 1951 burr-cut seems as out of place – even weird – in this room as a bearded Senator would have seemed in 1951. Or a nigger in Beta Theta Phi fraternity in the late 1940s.

Haldeman's head on camera looks like he got bashed on the head with a rake.

Total tedium sets in as Haldeman statement drones on ... his story is totally different from Dean's on crucial points ... definite perjury here ... which one lying?

If the recent speech [15 August] does not produce the results the President wants, he will then do what he has already come to doing. He will use all the awe-inspiring resources of his office to 'come out swinging with both fists'. Divisive will be a mild way of describing the predictable results.

Joe Alsop, *Washington Post*, 17/8/73

The clear warning: Mr Nixon will not do any more to clear himself of the taints of Watergate because he cannot: If the Democrats do not allow him to get back on the job of President, but continue what one high presidential aide called the 'vendetta' against him, his next move will be full retaliation.

Evans and Novak, *Washington Post*, 17/8/73

'When I am attacked,' Richard Nixon once remarked to this writer, 'it is my instinct to strike back.' The President is now clearly in a mood to obey his instinct ... So on Wednesday 18 July, at a White House meeting it was agreed unanimously that the tapes should not be released. This decision, to use the sports clichés to which the President is addicted, meant an entirely new ball game, requiring a new game plan. The new game plan calls for a strategy of striking back, in accord with the presidential instinct, rather than a policy of attempted accommodation ...

Stewart Alsop, *Newsweek*, 6/8/73

Cazart! It is hard to miss the message in those three shots ... even out here in Woody Creek, at a distance of 2000 miles from the source, a joint-statement, as it were, from Evans & Novak and both Alsop brothers hits the nerves like a blast of summer lightning across the mountains. Especially when you read them all in the same afternoon, while sifting through the mail-heap that piled up in my box, for three weeks, while I was wasting all that time back in Washington, once again, trying to get a grip on the thing.

Crouse had warned me, by phone, about the hazards of coming east. 'I know you won't believe this,' he said, 'so you might as well just get on a plane and find out for yourself – but the weird truth is that Washington is the only place in the country where the Watergate story seems *dull*. I can sit up here in Boston and get totally locked into it, on the tube, but when I go down there to that goddamn hearing room I get so bored and depressed I can't think.'

Now, after almost a month in that treacherous swamp of a town, I understand what Crouse was trying to tell me. After a day or so in the hearing room, hunkered down at a press table in the sweaty glare of those blinding TV lights, I discovered a TV set in the bar of the Capitol Hill Hotel just across the street from the old Senate Office Building, about a three-minute sprint from the hearing room itself ... so I could watch the action on TV, sipping a Carlsberg until something looked about to happen, then dash across the street and up the stairs to the hearing room to see whatever it was that seemed interesting.

After three or four days of this scam, however, I realized that there was really no point in going to the hearing room at all. Every time I came speeding down the hall and across the crowded floor of the high-domed, white-marble rotunda where a cordon of cops kept hundreds of waiting spectators penned up behind velvet ropes, I felt guilty ... Here was some ill-dressed geek with a bottle of Carlsberg in his hand, waving a press pass and running right through a whole army of cops, then through the tall oak doors and into a front row seat just behind the witness chair – while this mob of poor bastards who'd been waiting since early morning, in some cases, for a seat to open up in the SRO gallery.

After a few more days of this madness, I closed up the National Affairs Desk and went back home to brood.

THREE

To the Mattresses ... Nixon Faces History, and to Hell with The *Washington Post* ... The Hazy Emergence of a New and Cheaper Strategy ... John Wilson Draws 'The Line' ... Strange Troika & a Balance of Terror ... McGovern Was Right

---

When democracy granted democratic methods to us in times of opposition, this was bound to happen in a democratic system. However, we National Socialists never asserted that we represented a democratic point of view, but we have declared openly that we used the democratic methods only in order to gain power and that, after assuming the power, we would deny to our adversaries without any consideration the means which were granted to us in times of our opposition.
Josef Goebbels

What will Nixon do now? That is the question that has every wizard in Washington hanging by his or her fingernails – from the bar of the

National Press Club to the redwood sauna in the Senate Gymnasium to the hundreds of high-powered cocktail parties in suburbs like Bethesda, MacLean, Arlington, Cabin John and especially in the leafy white ghetto of the district's northwest quadrant. You can wander into Nathan's tavern at the corner of M Street & Wisconsin in Georgetown and get an argument about 'Nixon's strategy' without even mentioning the subject. All you have to do is stand at the bar, order a Bass Ale, and look interested: The hassle will take care of itself; the very air in Washington is electric with the vast implications of Watergate.

Thousands of big-money jobs depend on what Nixon does next; on what Archibald Cox has in mind; on whether 'Uncle Sam's' TV hearings will resume full-bore after Labor Day, or be either telescoped or terminated like Nixon says they should be.

The smart money says the Watergate hearings, as such, are effectively over – not only because Nixon is preparing to mount a popular crusade against them, but because every elected politician in Washington is afraid of what the Ervin committee has already scheduled for the 'third phase' of the hearings.

Phase two, as originally planned, would focus on 'dirty tricks' – a colourful, shocking and essentially minor area of inquiry, but one with plenty of action and a guaranteed audience appeal. A long and serious look at the 'dirty tricks' aspect of national campaigning would be a death-blow to the daily soap-opera syndrome that apparently grips most of the nation's housewives. The cast of characters, and the twisted tales they could tell, would shame every soap-opera scriptwriter in America.

Phase three/campaign financing is the one both the White House and the Senate would prefer to avoid – and, given this mutual distaste for exposing the public to the realities of campaign financing, this is the phase of the Watergate hearings most likely to be cut from the schedule. 'Jesus Christ,' said one Ervin committee investigator, 'we'll have *Fortune*'s 500 in that chair, and every one of those bastards will take at least one Congressman or Senator down with him.'

At the end of phase one – the facts & realities of the Watergate affair itself – the seven Senators on the Ervin committee took an informal vote among themselves, before adjourning to a birthday party for Senator Herman Talmadge, and the tally was 4–3 *against* resuming the hearings in their current format. Talmadge cast the deciding vote, joining the three Republicans – Gurney, Baker and Weicker – in voting to wrap the hearings up as soon as possible. Their reasons were the same ones Nixon gave in his long-awaited TV speech on 15 August, when he said the time had come to end this daily bummer and get back to 'the business of the people'.

Watching Nixon's speech in hazy colour on the Owl Farm tube with New York Mayor John Lindsay, Wisconsin Congressman Les Aspin and former Bobby Kennedy speechwriter Adam Wolinsky, I half expected to hear that fine old Calvin Coolidge quote: 'The business of America is business.'

And it only occurred to me later that Nixon wouldn't have dared to use that one, because no president since Hubert Hoover has been forced to explain away the kind of root-structural damage to the national economy that Nixon is trying to explain today. And Hoover at least had the excuse that he 'inherited his problems' from somebody else – which Nixon can't claim, because he is now in his *fifth* year as president, and when he goes on TV to explain himself he is facing an audience of fifty to sixty million who can't afford steaks or even hamburger in the supermarkets, who can't buy gasoline for their cars, who are paying fifteen and twenty per cent interest rates for bank loans, and who are being told now that there may not be enough fuel oil to heat their homes through the coming winter.

This is not the ideal audience for a second-term president, fresh from a landslide victory, to confront with twenty-nine minutes of lame gibberish about mean nit-pickers in Congress, the good ole American way, and let's get on with business.

Indeed. That's the first thing Richard Nixon and I have ever agreed on, politically – and what we are dealing with now is no longer hard ideology, but a matter of simple competence. What we are looking at on all our TV sets is a man who finally, after twenty-four years of frenzied effort, became the President of the United States with a personal salary of $200,000 a year and an unlimited expense account including a fleet of private helicopters, jetliners, armoured cars, personal mansions and estates on both coasts and control over a budget beyond the wildest dreams of King Midas ... and all the dumb bastard can show us, after five years of total freedom to do anything he wants with all this power, is a shattered national economy, disastrous defeat in a war he could have ended four years ago on far better terms than he finally came around to, and a hand-picked personal staff put together through five years of screening, whose collective criminal record will blow the minds of high-school American history students for the next 100 years. Nixon's hand-picked Vice-President is about to be indicted for extortion and bribery; his former campaign manager and his former secretary of commerce & personal fund-raiser have already been indicted for perjury, two of his ranking campaign managers had already pleaded guilty to obstruction of justice, the White House counsel is headed for prison on more felony counts than I have room to list here, and before the trials are finished ...

*

Sen. Talmadge: *'Now, if the President could authorize a covert break-in and you do not know exactly where that power would be limited, you do not think it could include murder, do you?'*
John Ehrlichman: *'I do not know where the line is, Senator.'*

With the first phase of the Watergate hearings more or less ended, one of the few things now unmistakably clear, as it were, is that nobody in Nixon's White House was willing to 'draw the line' anywhere short of re-electing the President in 1972. Even John Mitchell – whose reputation as a super-shrewd lawyer ran afoul of the Peter Principle just as soon as he became Nixon's first attorney general – lost his temper in an exchange with Sen. Talmadge at the Watergate hearings and said, with the whole world watching, that he considered the re-election of Richard Nixon in 72 'so important' that it outweighed all other considerations.

It was a classic affirmation of the 'attorney-client relationship' – or at least a warped mixture of that and the relationship between an ad agency executive and a client with a product to sell – but when Mitchell uttered those lines in the hearing room, losing control of himself just long enough to fatally confuse 'executive loyalty' with 'executive privilege', it's fair to assume that he knew he was already doomed ... He had already been indicted for perjury in the Vesco case, he was facing almost certain indictment by Archibald Cox,·and previous testimony by John Dean had made it perfectly clear that Nixon was prepared to throw John Mitchell to the wolves, to save his own ass.

This ominous truth was quickly reinforced by the testimony of John Ehrlichman and Harry 'Bob' Haldeman, whose back-to-back testimony told most of the other witnesses (and potential defendants) all they needed to know. By the time Haldeman had finished testifying – under the direction of the same criminal lawyer who had earlier represented Ehrlichman – it was clear that somebody in the White House had finally seen fit to 'draw the line'.

It was not quite the same line Mitchell and Ehrlichman had refused to acknowledge on TV, but in the final analysis it will be far more critical to the fate of Richard Nixon's presidency ... and, given Mitchell's long personal relationship with Nixon, it is hard to believe he didn't understand his role in the 'new strategy' well before he drove down from New York to Washington, by chauffeured limousine, for his gig in the witness chair.

The signs were all there. For one, it had been Haldeman and Ehrlichman – with Nixon's tacit approval – who had eased Mitchell out of his 'number one' role at the White House. John Mitchell, a millionaire Wall Street lawyer until he got into politics, was more responsible than any other single person for the long comeback that landed Nixon in the

White House in 1968. It was Mitchell who rescued Nixon from oblivion in the mid-sixties when Nixon moved east to become a Wall Street lawyer himself – after losing the presidency to John Kennedy in 1960 and then the governorship of California to Pat Brown in 62, a humiliating defeat that ended with his 'You won't have Dick Nixon to kick around any more' outburst at the traditional loser's press conference.

The re-election of Mr Nixon, followed so quickly by the Watergate revelations, has compelled the country to re-examine the reality of our electoral process ...

'The unravelling of the whole White House tangle of involvement has come about largely by a series of fortuitous events, many of them unlikely in a different political context. Without these events, the cover-up might have continued indefinitely, even if a Democratic administration vigorously pursued the truth ...

'In the wake of Watergate may come more honest and thorough campaign reform than in the aftermath of a successful presidential campaign which stood for such reform. I suspect that after viewing the abuses of the past, voters in the future will insist on full and open debate between the candidates and on frequent, no-holds-barred press conferences for all candidates, and especially the President.

'And I suspect the Congress will respond to the fact that Watergate happened with legislation to assure that Watergate never happens again. Today the prospects for further restrictions on private campaign financing, full disclosure of the personal finances of the candidates, and public finance of all federal campaigns seem to me better than ever – and even better than if a new Democratic administration had urged such steps in early 1973. We did urge them in 1972, but it took the Nixon landslide and the Watergate exposé to make the point.

'I believe there were great gains that came from the pain of defeat in 1972. We proved a campaign could be honestly financed. We reaffirmed that a campaign could be open in its conduct and decent in its motivation. We made the Democratic party a place for people as well as politicians. And perhaps in losing we gained the greatest victory of all – that Americans now perceive, far better than a new President could have persuaded them, what is precious about our principles and what we must do to preserve them. The nation now sees itself through the prism of Watergate and the Nixon landslide; at last, perhaps, we see through a glass clearly.

'Because of all this, it is possible that by 1976, the 200th anniversary of America's birth, there will be a true rebirth of patriotism; that we will not only know our ideals but live them; that democracy may once again become a conviction we keep and not just a description we apply to ourselves. And if the McGovern campaign advanced that hope, even in defeat, then, as I said on election night last November, "Every minute and every hour and every bone-crushing effort ... was worth the entire sacrifice." '

George McGovern in the Washington Post, 12 August 1973

Jesus ... Sunday morning in Woody Creek and here's McGovern on the mini-tube beside my typewriter, looking and talking almost exactly like he was in those speedy weeks between the Wisconsin and Ohio primaries, when his star was rising so fast that he could barely hang on to it. The sense of *déjà vu* is almost frightening: Here is McGovern speaking sharply *against the system*, once again, in response to questions from CBS's Connie Chung and Marty Nolan from the Boston *Globe*, two of the most ever-present reporters on the 72 campaign trail ... and McGovern, brought back from the dead by a political miracle of sorts, is hitting the first gong of doom for the man who made him a landslide loser nine months ago: 'When that [judicial] process is complete and the Supreme Court rules that the President must turn over the tapes – and he refuses to do so – I think the Congress will have no recourse but to seriously consider impeachment.'

Cazart! The fat is approaching the fire – very slowly, and in very cautious hands, but there is no ignoring the general drift of things. Sometime between now and the end of 1973, Richard Nixon may have to bite that bullet he's talked about for so long. Seven is a lucky number for gamblers, but not for fixers, and Nixon's seventh crisis is beginning to put his first six in very deep shade. Even the most conservative betting in Washington, these days, has Nixon either resigning or being impeached by the autumn of 74 – if not for reasons directly connected to the 'Watergate scandal', then because of his inability to explain how he paid for his beach mansion at San Clemente, or why Vice-President Agnew – along with most of Nixon's original White House command staff – is under indictment for felonies ranging from extortion and perjury to burglary and obstruction of justice.

Another good bet in Washington – running at odds between two and three to one, these days, is that Nixon will crack both physically and mentally under all this pressure, and develop a serious psychosomatic illness of some kind: maybe another bad case of pneumonia.

This is not so wild a vision as it might sound – not even in the context of my own known taste for fantasy and savage bias in politics. Richard Nixon, a career politician who has rarely failed to crack under genuine pressure, is under more pressure now than most of us will ever understand. His whole life is turning to shit, just as he reached the pinnacle ... and every once in a while, caving in to a weakness that blooms in the cool, thinking hours around dawn, I have to admit that I feel a touch of irrational sympathy for the bastard. Not as the President: a broken little bully who would sacrifice us all to save himself – if he still had the choice – but the same kind of sympathy I might feel, momentarily, for a vicious cheap-shot linebacker whose long career comes to a sudden end one Sunday afternoon when some rookie flanker shatters both his knees with a savage crackback block.

Cheap-shot artists don't last very long in pro football. To cripple another person intentionally is to violate the same kind of code as the legendary 'honour among thieves'.

More linebackers than thieves believe this, but when it comes to politics – to a twenty-eight-year career of cheap shots, lies and thievery – there is no man in America who should understand what is happening to him now better than Richard Milhous Nixon. He is a living monument to the old army rule that says: 'The only *real* crime is getting caught.'

This is not the first time Richard Nixon has been caught. After his failed campaign for the governorship of California in 1962 he was formally convicted – along with H. R. Haldeman, Maurice Stans, Murray Chotiner, Herb Klein and Herb Kalmbach – for almost exactly the same kind of crudely illegal campaign tactics that he stands accused of today.

But this time, in the language of the sergeants who keep military tradition alive, 'he got caught every which way' ... and 'his ass went into the blades'.

Not many people have ever written in the English language better than a Polack with a twisted sense of humour who called himself Joseph Conrad. And if he were with us today I think he'd be getting a fine boot out of this Watergate story. Mr Kurtz, in Conrad's *Heart Of Darkness*, did his thing.

Mr Nixon also did his thing.

And now, just as surely as Kurtz: 'Mistah Nixon, he dead.'

Rolling Stone no. 144, 27 September 1973

FEAR AND LOATHING IN WASHINGTON: THE BOYS IN THE BAG

'It was a nice place. They were principled people, generally.'*

Mr McGovern described the president personally as a 'blob out there' 'of no constant principle except opportunism and political manipulation', a man 'up to his ears in political sabotage', who was 'afraid of the people' and regularly favoured the 'powerful and greedy' over the public interest. The president's defence programmes were 'madness'; he had 'degraded the Supreme Court' and, on three occasions at least, Mr McGovern drew parallels between the president and his government and Adolf Hitler and his Nazi Reich. As for the Nixon administration, it was the 'most morally bankrupt, the most morally corrupt, the trickiest, most deceitful ... in our entire national history'.

White House speechwriter Patrick J. Buchanan, in the *New York Times*, 24 November 1972

'When I am attacked,' Richard Nixon once remarked to this writer, 'it is my instinct to strike back.' The president is now clearly in a mood to obey his instincts ... So on Wednesday 18 July at a White House meeting, it was agreed unanimously that the tapes should not be released. This decision, to use the sports clichés to which the president is addicted, meant an entirely new ball game, requiring a new game plan. The new game plan calls for a strategy of striking back, in accord with the presidential instinct, rather than a policy of attempted accommodation ...

Columnist Stewart Alsop, *Newsweek*, 6 August 1973

The tragedy of all this is that George McGovern, for all his mistakes and all his imprecise talk about 'new politics' and 'honesty in government' is one of the few men who've run for president of the United States in this century who really understands what a fantastic monument to all the best instincts of the human race this country might have been, if we could have kept it out of the hands of greedy little hustlers like Richard Nixon. McGovern made some stupid mistakes, but in context they seem almost frivolous compared to the things

* Quote from Robert C. Odle, office administrator for CREEP.

Richard Nixon does every day of his life, on purpose, as a matter of
policy and a perfect expression of everything he stands for. Jesus! Where
will it end? How low do you have to stoop in this country to be
president?

Rolling Stone *correspondent Hunter S. Thompson, writing on the*
Nixon-McGovern campaign, September 1972

The Third Reich, which was born on 30 January 1933, Hitler boasted
would endure for a thousand years, and in Nazi parlance it was often
referred to as 'The Thousand Year Reich'. It lasted twelve years and
four months ...

Willian Shirer, from *The Rise and Fall of the Third Reich*

For reasons that will never be clear to anyone – and especially not to
the management and other guests in this place – the National Affairs
Desk is operating once again at the Royal Biscayne Hotel, about 900
crooked metres from the Nixon/Rebozo compound on the other side
of the island. The desk itself is a round slab of what appears to be low-
grade jacaranda wood.

The centrepiece is a bright orange electric typewriter that I rented
several days ago from a business-machine store on 125th Street in North
Miami. It is a Swedish 'Facit' – a deceptively sharp-looking machine
about five times slower in both directions than the IBM Selectric and
totally useless for any kind of speed-lashed gonzo work. For all its style
and voltage, the Facit is about as quick in the hands as one of those
1929-model Underwoods that used to be standard equipment in the city
room of the *New York Mirror*. Nobody knows exactly what happened
to all those old Underwoods when the *Mirror* died of bad age, but one
rumour in the trade says they were snapped up at a dime on the dollar
by Norman Cousins and then resold at a tidy profit to the *Columbia
Journalism Review*.

Which is interesting, but it is not the kind of thing you normally want
to develop fully in your classic pyramid lead ... and that's what I was
trying to deal with, when I suddenly realized that my typewriter was as
worthless as tits on a boar hog.

Besides that, there were other mechanical problems: no water, no ice,
no phone service, and finally the discovery of two Secret Service men in
the room right next to me.

I was getting a little paranoid about the phone situation. It followed a
series of unsettling events that caused me to think seriously about going
back to Washington when Nixon left the next day, rather than staying on
in order to open a special account in Bebe Rebozo's bank over in the
shopping centre across Ocean Drive. The Key Biscayne Bank seems like

as good a place as any to do business, primarily because of the unusual investment opportunities available to special clients.

I have applied for 'special' status, but recent developments have made me less than optimistic. Several days ago, on my first visit to the Nixon compound, I got no further than the heavily guarded gatehouse on Harbor Drive. 'Are they expecting you?' the state trooper asked me.

'Probably not,' I said. 'I thought I'd just drop by for a drink or two, then have a look around. I've never seen the place, you know. What goes on in there?'

The trooper seemed to stiffen. His eyes narrowed and he stared intently at the black coral fist hanging on a chain around my neck. 'Say ... ah ... I'd like to see your identification, fella. You carrying any?'

'Of course,' I said. 'But it's out there in the car. I don't have any pockets in these trunks.' I walked across the hot asphalt road, feeling my bare feet stick to the tar with every step, and vaulted into the big bronze convertible without opening the door. Looking back at the gatehouse, I noticed that the trooper had been joined by two gentlemen in dark business suits with wires coming out of their ears. They were all waiting for me to come back with my wallet.

To hell with this, I thought, suddenly starting the engine. I waved to the trooper. 'It's not here,' I shouted. 'I guess I left it back at the hotel.' Without waiting for an answer, I eased the car into gear and drove off very slowly.

Almost immediately, the big railroad-crossing-style gate across Nixon's road swung up in the air and a blue Ford sedan rolled out. I slowed down even more, thinking he was going to pull me over to the side, but instead he stayed about 100 feet behind me – all the way to the hotel, into the parking lot, and around the back almost into the slot behind my room. I got out, thinking he was going to pull up right behind me for a chat – but he stopped about fifty feet away, backed up, and drove away.

Later that afternoon, sitting in the temporary White House press room outside the Four Ambassadors Hotel in downtown Miami about ten miles away, I told *New York Times* correspondent Anthony Ripley about the incident. 'I really expected the bastard to follow me right into my room.'

Ripley laughed. 'That's probably where he is right now – with about three of his friends, going through all your luggage.'

Which may have been true. Anybody who spends much time around the Secret Service and acts a little bent has to assume things like that ... especially when you discover, by sheer accident, that the room right next to yours is occupied by two SS agents.

That was the second unsettling incident. The details are vaguely interesting, but I'd prefer not to go into them at this point – except to say that I thought I was becoming dangerously paranoid until I got hold of a carbon copy of their room-registration receipt. Which made me feel a little better about my own mental health, at least. It is far better to *know* the Secret Service is keeping an eye on you than to suspect it all the time without ever being sure.

It was the third incident, however, that caused me to start thinking about moving the desk back to Washington at once. I was awakened in the early hours of the morning by a telephone call and a strange voice saying, 'The president is going to church. You'll have to hurry if you want to catch him.'

What? My mind was blank. What president? Why should I want to *catch* him? Especially in a church?

'Who the hell *is* this?' I said finally.

'Tony,' said the voice.

I was reaching around in the darkness for a light switch. For a moment I thought I was still in Mexico. Then I found a light switch and recognized the familiar surroundings of the National Affairs Suite. Jesus! I thought. Of course! Key Biscayne. President Nixon. It all made sense now: The bastards were setting me up for a bust on some kind of bogus assassination attempt. The agents next door have probably already planted a high-powered rifle in the trunk of my car, and now they're trying to lure me over to some church where they can grab me in front of all the press cameras as soon as I drive up and park. Then they'll 'find' the rifle in the trunk about two minutes before Nixon arrives to worship – and that'll be it for me. I could already see the headlines: NIXON ASSASSINATION PLOT FOILED; SHARPSHOOTER SEIZED AT KEY BISCAYNE CHURCH. Along with front-page photos of state troopers examining the rifle, me in handcuffs, Nixon smiling bravely at the cameras ...

The whole scene flashed through my head in milliseconds; the voice on the phone was yelling something at me. Panic fused my brain. No! I thought. Never in hell.

'You crazy son of a bitch!' I yelled into the phone. 'I'm not going near that goddamn church!' Then I hung up and went instantly back to sleep.

Later that afternoon, Ripley stopped by the hotel and we had a few beers out by the beach-bar. 'Jesus Christ!' he said. 'You were really out of your mind this morning, weren't you?'

'What?'

He laughed. 'Yeah. You *screamed* at me. Hell, I just thought you might like to catch the scene over at Nixon's church.'

'For Christ's sake don't call me with any more tips for a while.'

'Don't worry,' he replied. 'We're leaving today, anyway. Will you be on the plane?'

'No,' I said. 'I'm going to sleep for two days, then take a boat back to Washington. This has not been a good trip for me. I think I'll give up covering Nixon for a while – at least until I can whip this drinking problem.'

'Maybe what you should do is get into a different line of work, or have yourself committed.'

'No,' I said. 'I think I'll get a job teaching journalism.'

In the context of journalism, here, we are dealing with a new kind of 'lead' – the symbiotic trapezoid quote. The *Columbia Journalism Review* will never sanction it; at least not until the current editor dies of brain syphilis, and probably not even then.

What?

Do we have a libel suit on our hands?

Probably not, I think, because nobody in his right mind would take a thing like that seriously – and especially not that gang of senile hags who run the *Columbia Journalism Review*, who have gone to considerable lengths in every issue during the past year or so to stress, very heavily, that *nothing* I say should be taken seriously.

'Those who can, do. Those who can't, teach.' George Bernard Shaw said that, for good or ill, and I only mention it here because I'm getting goddamn tired of being screeched at by waterheads. Professors are a sour lot, in general, but professors of journalism are especially rancid in their outlook because they have to wake up every morning and be reminded once again of a world they'll never know.

THUMP! Against the door. Another goddamn newspaper, another cruel accusation. THUMP! Day after day, it never ends ... Hiss at the alarm clock, suck up the headlines along with a beaker of warm Drano, then off to the morning class ... To teach journalism: circulation, distribution, headline counting and the classical pyramid lead.

Jesus, let's not forget that last one. Mastery of the pyramid lead has sustained more lame yoyos than either Congress or the peacetime army. Five generations of American journalists have clung to that petrified tit, and when the deal went down in 1972 their ranks were so solid that seventy-one per cent of the newspapers in this country endorsed Richard Nixon for a second term in the White House.

Now, eighteen months later, the journalistic establishment that speaks for Nixon's erstwhile 'silent majority' has turned on him with a wild-eyed, coast-to-coast venom rarely witnessed in the American newspaper trade. The only recent example that comes to mind is Nixon's own blundering pronouncement of Charles Manson's guilt while Manson was still on trial in Los Angeles.

In addition to introducing the symbiotic trapezoid quote as the wave of the future in journalism, I have some other ideas to get into: mainly about Richard Nixon, and some of these are ugly ... or ugly by my standards, at any rate, because most of them revolve around the very distinct possibility that Nixon might survive his seventh crisis – and in surviving leave us a legacy of failure, shame and corruption beyond anything conceivable right now.

This is a grim thing to say, or even think, in the current atmosphere of self-congratulation and renewed professional pride that understandably pervades the press & politics circuit these days. Not only in Washington, but all over the country wherever you find people who are seriously concerned with the health and life expectancy of the American political system.

The baseline is always the same: 'We almost blew it,' they say, 'but somehow we pulled back from the brink.' Names like Sirica, Woodward, Bernstein, Cox, Richardson, Ruckelshaus are mentioned almost reverently in these conversations, but anybody who's been personally involved in the Watergate affair and all its nasty sidebars for any length of time knows that these were only the point men – invaluable for their balls and their instincts and their understanding of what they were doing in that never-ending blizzard of crucial movements when a single cop-out might have brought the whole scene down on top of them all. But there were literally hundreds, maybe thousands, of others who came up to those same kinds of moments and said, 'Well, I wasn't really planning on this, but if that's the way it is, let's get it on.'

There are a lot of people in this country – editors, congressmen and lawyers among others – who like themselves a lot better today for the way they reacted when the Watergate octopus got hold of them.

There are also a lot of people who got dragged down forever by it – which is probably just as well, for the rest of us, because many of them were exposed as either dangerous bunglers, ruthless swine or both. Others – many of them peripherally involved in one aspect or another of 'Watergate' but lucky enough not to get caught – will probably be haunted by a sense of nervous guilt for a while, but in a year or two they will forget all about it. These, in a way, are almost as dangerous as the ones who are going to jail – because they are the 'good Germans' among us, the ones who made it all possible.

I've been trying to finish *The Rise and Fall of the Third Reich* for at least the last three months; hauling the huge bugger along in my baggage to places like Buffalo, Oakland, Ann Arbor, Houston, and finally all the way down to the jungles and lost fishing villages of Mexico's Yucatán peninsula ...

But things have been happening too fast, and there was never enough time or privacy to get seriously into the thing – not even down in the Yucatan, lying around in big hammocks in fifty-peso-a-night hotels where we had to keep the Hong Kong-built ceiling fans cranked up to top speed for enough wind in the room to drive the roaches back into the corners.

At one point, I tried to read it in a hotel room near the ruins of the Mayan civilization at Chichen Itza – thinking to get a certain weird perspective on American politics in the seventies by pondering the collapse of 'The Thousand Year Reich' while sitting on the stone remnants of another and totally different culture that survived for *more* than a thousand years before anybody in Europe even knew that a place called 'America' existed. The Aztec socio-political structure was a fine-tuned élitest democracy that would have embarrassed everybody connected with either the French or American revolutions.

The ancient Greeks and Romans seem like crude punks compared to what the Mayans, Aztecs and Incas put together in Mexico and South America in the twenty or so centuries between 500 BC and the ill-fated 'Spanish conquest' in 1525. The Mayan calendar, devised several centuries before the birth of Christ, is still more precise than the one we use today: They had the solar year broken down to exactly 365.24 days, and 12 lunar months of 29.5 days each. None of this sloppy 'leap year' business, or odd-numbered months.

According to most military experts, Adolf Hitler went over the hump somewhere around the middle of 1942. At that point – even according to Albert Speer, his personal architect and all-round technical wizard – the Reich was spread too thin: militarily, financially, industrially, politically and every other way. Speer had all the blueprints, the plans, the figures, and an almost daily fix on what was happening to boiling Hitler's head. Given all that, Speer says, he knew in his heart they were headed downhill after the summer of 42.

But it was almost three years and at least three million deaths later that Hitler finally admitted what Speer, one of his closest 'friends' and advisers, says he knew all along – or at least during those last three years when Albert and all the others in the Führer's inner circle were working twenty, twenty-two and sometimes twenty-four hours a day, seven days a week, to keep the Reich propped up on an ever-eroding base of conquered slave labour and frenzied schemes to create a 'super-weapon' that would somehow turn the tide.

None of this rotten madness worked out, of course, and as a reward for his stupid loyalty to Hitler, Albert Speer spent twenty years of his life locked up in Spandau Prison as one of Germany's major war criminals. Hitler was consistent to the end. He had no stomach for jail cells or courtrooms – unless they were *his* – so as soon as he got word that Russo-American tanks were rumbling into the suburbs of Berlin, he went down in his private bunker and killed both himself and his faithful mistress, Eva Braun, with what some people say was a very elegant, gold-plated Walther machine-pistol.

Nobody knows for sure, because the bunker was ravaged by fire soon afterwards ... and the only alleged witness to Hitler's death was his personal aide and adviser, Martin Bormann, who either escaped at the last moment or was burned to such an unrecognizable cinder that his body was never found.

Everybody who knew Bormann hated and feared him – even Hitler, who apparently treated him like a pet cobra – and few of the Reich's survivors ever accepted the fact of his death in that fiery bunker. He was too evil and crafty for that, they insisted, and the general assumption was that Bormann had kept his personal escape plan finely organized, on a day-to-day basis, since the winter of 43.

West German military intelligence now lists him as officially dead, but not many people believe it – because he keeps turning up, now and then, in places like Asuncion, Paraguay, the Brazilian Matto Grosso, or high in the Argentine lake country.

Bormann was the Tex Colson of his time, and his strange relationship with Hitler seems not much different from the paranoid fragments of the Nixon-Colson relationship that emerged from the now-infamous 'White House transcripts' of April 1974.

We are drifting into some ugly parallels here, and if I'd written this kind of thing two years ago I'd have expected to pick up the *New York Times* a week later and see myself mangled all over the op-ed page by Pat Buchanan, and then beaten into a bloody coma the next evening by some of Colson's hired thugs in an alley behind the National Press Building – a long stone's throw, as it were, from the White House.

But like Tommy Rush says, 'Times ain't now, but like they used to be ...'

Which is true. There is not much doubt about that. But after watching the TV news on all three networks last night and then reading all the Nixon stories in today's *Washington Post*, I have an eerie feeling that the times ain't now quite like they appear to be, either.

There was something oddly hollow and out of focus about last night's main TV-news story on the US Supreme Court's dramatic and potentially ominous decision to postpone its traditional June recess and stay on through July to render what will clearly be an historic judgment, one way or another, on special prosecutor Leon Jaworski's either bold or desperate leapfrog attempt to force an immediate High Court decision on President Nixon's right to ignore a subpoena – for sixty-four tape recordings and other White House documents – from a special prosecutor appointed under extremely sensitive circumstances by the US Senate with his independence explicity guaranteed by the new US attorney general as a condition of his taking office.

All three networks treated this latest development in the strange and terrible saga of Richard Nixon as a staggering and perhaps even fatal blow to his chances of survival in the White House. The mere fact that the court was willing to stay over and hear Jaworski's argument, they implied, was a sure sign that at least four of the justices (enough, in this case) were prepared to rule, just as soon as the question is formally presented, *against* Nixon's claim of 'executive privilege' with regard to Jaworski's subpoena. The special prosecutor had apparently won a major victory, and the president was in very deep trouble. Only David Schumacher on ABC hinted, very briefly, that there had been no victory celebrations among Jaworski's staff people that afternoon. But he didn't say why ...

And, frankly, I'll be fucked if I can either. I brooded on it for a while, but all that came to mind was some half-remembered snarl from the lips of President Andrew Jackson when the Supreme Court ruled against him on some kind of question involving a federal land grant to the Seminole Indians. Jackson, a veteran Indian-fighter, took the ruling as a personal insult. 'Well,' he said, 'the judges have made their decision – now let them enforce it.'

Josef Stalin, about 100 years later, had similar views with regard to the Roman Catholic Church. He had gone into one of his rages, according to the story as I heard it, and this one had something to do with a notion that seized him, after five days and nights in a brutal vodka orgy, that every Catholic in Moscow should be nailed up on a telephone pole by dawn on Easter Sunday. This announcement caused genuine fear in the Kremlin, because Stalin – like Colson – was known by his staff to be 'capable of almost anything'. When he calmed down a bit, one of his advisers suggested that a mass crucifixion of Russian Catholics – for no reason at all – would almost certainly raise hackles in the Vatican and no doubt anger the pope.

'Fuck the pope,' Stalin mumbled. 'How many divisions does he have?'

These stories are hard to nail down with any real certainty, but there is a mean kind of consistency in the punch lines that makes them hard to forget ... especially when you start pondering the spectacle of a borderline psychotic with the brain of a small-time chiseller and the power to literally blow up the world never more than sixty seconds away from his gnawed-red fingertips, doing everything he can to force a hellish confrontation with the higest judicial and legislative authorities in his own country.

This is what Nixon has been trying to do for at least the past three months – and, if Stewart Alsop was right, since 18 July of last year. That was the Wednesday meeting at the White House, he said, when 'it was agreed unanimously that the tapes should not be released'.

I would like to have talked with Stewart Alsop about that meeting, but he died last month of leukemia – after writing very candidly and even casually, at times, about his impending death from a disease that he had known for at least two years was slowly and steadily killing him. I didn't know him personally and as a journalist I rarely agreed with him, but there was an uncommon sense of integrity and personal commitment in everything he wrote ... and an incredible sense of style, strength and courage in the way he chose to die.

Stewart Alsop, for all his experience in politics and all his friends in every eyrie in Washington, seemed baffled all the way to his grave by the reality of Watergate and its foul implications for some of the ideas and people he believed in. As one of Washington's ranking journalists, he was privy to things like that meeting last July in the White House, where Nixon and a handful of others sat down and gave serious thought to all their possible options with regard to those reels of harmless looking celluloid that had suddenly turned into time bombs. Alsop could understand all the *facts* of a scene like that, but not the reality. Like most of the people he grew up with, Stewart Alsop was *born* a Republican.

It was as much a way of life as a thought-out political philosophy, and along with all the privileges came a certain sense of *noblesse oblige*.

Alsop *understood* these things – which explains probably better than anything else why it was almost genetically impossible for him to come to grips with the idea that the Oval Office of the White House – under a second-term Republican president who had also been a Republican vice-president, senator and congressman – was in fact a den of thieves, fixers and felons.

This kind of savage reality was too much for sixty-year-old élitist Republicans like Stewart Alsop to cope with. It was like showing up at the White House for your monthly chat with the President on some normal afternoon and finding the Oval Office full of drunken Hell's Angels ... and the President so stoned on reds that he can't even recognize you, babbling distractedly and shovelling big mounds of white powder around on his desk with the butt of a sawed-off shotgun.

There are not many senior political columnists in Washington who could handle a scene like that. Their minds would refuse to accept it ...

for the same reason they still can't accept the stark and fearful truth that President Richard Milhous Nixon is not only going to be impeached, but he actually *wants* to be impeached. Immediately.

This is probably the one simple fact, right now, in a story that is going to become so heinously complicated in the next few months that every reporter assigned to it will need both a shrewd criminal lawyer and scholar in the field of constitutional law right next to him or her at all times.

There is no question at all – even now, in these last moments of calm before the shitrain starts – that this 'Nixon impeachment' saga is going to turn some of the best minds in American journalism to mush before it's over ...

And that statement will just have to sit there; I refuse to even try to explain it. There will be plenty of time for that; thousands of hours in God only knows how many courtrooms. And Nixon will eventually be impeached, if only because he has the leverage to put the House of Representatives in a position where it will have no other choice.

Nixon's lawyers – who have already cost the taxpayers nearly $400,000 in legal fees – have now abandoned all pretence in their efforts to insult and provoke Congressman Peter Rodino's House Judiciary Committee into exactly the kind of quick, angry and ill-considered vote *for* impeachment that Rodino and committee counsels John Doar and Albert Jenner have been bending over backwards to avoid ... until they can put together enough evidence – before the hearings are opened to the public and the full House convenes on TV to hear the charges – to build a far more solid and serious case for impeachment than the one they appear to have now. Nixon would like nothing better than to stampede the House of Representatives into a televised yea or nay show-down, based on charges no more serious than contempt of Congress, contempt of court(s) and, by implication, the grossest kind of contempt for everybody in the country with an IQ higher than 50.

But not even Ron Ziegler is counting on a farce of that magnitude. On 27 May, the UPI wire carried an official statement by Ziegler, from Key Biscayne, to the effect that formal impeachment proceedings against the boss would 'come as no surprise' to him. Nor would impeachment itself, he implied. So why don't they just get on with it?

Why indeed?

One of the main reasons has to do with all those tapes that Nixon apparently decided quite a while ago that he would never turn over to anybody, anywhere, for any reason at all. Thus far, he has shrugged off subpoenas for more than 100 of his taped conversations – sixty-four from Jaworski and about fifty from the Rodino committee. Many of these are overlapping, and nobody in Washington seems to know which set of subpoenas would have legal preference – or even who will have to decide that question, if it ever comes up in real life.

If Nixon hangs tough on his 'stonewalling' strategy with regard to the tapes, not even a definitive ruling by the US Supreme Court can force him to give them up. Noncompliance would put him in contempt of the highest court in the land and constitute further grounds for impeachment – but why should that worry him? The court has no more divisions than the pope did in Stalin's time – and no more real power over Nixon than it did over Andrew Jackson.

It is hard to imagine Chief Justice Burger signing a 'no-knock' search warrant and sending a squad of US marshals over to the White House with instructions to kick down the door and tear the place apart until they 'find those goddamn tapes'.

Special Prosecutor Jaworski is aware of all this, but it doesn't seem to bother him. He wants a ruling from the High Court, anyway, and before the end of July he will have one. It may not make any tangible difference, in the end, but at the very least it will be one more nail in Nixon's plastic coffin ... and another piece of sharp, hard-nosed legal work by Jaworski, who must be feeling about nine feet tall today – after replacing Archibald Cox in a cloud of almost universal scorn and suspicion that he was nothing but a hired fixer brought in by Nixon and Connally to 'put the cap on the bottle'.

Jaworski was a definite sleeper, or at least that's the way it looks from outside his amazingly leakless operation. If he's a Nixon-Connally fixer, he's been pretty clever about it so far and he's fooled a lot of people, including some of the most cynical heads in Washington.

But not all. There are still some people around town who remind you that Houston, Jaworski's home, is a breeding ground for some of the most vicious golf-hustlers in the country – the kind who will lose the first fifteen holes to you for $100 each, then whack you for $5000 a hole on the last three.

Which may be true. But if it is, Leon is cutting his margin pretty thin; he will have to play his last three holes all at once on 8 July, when he argues his tape subpoena case in front of what Washington lawyers call a 'bobtailed' US Supreme Court.

Justice William Rehnquist, the fourth and most virulently conservative of the four Nixon appointees, has been either pressured or cajoled by the others to remove himself from the case because of his previous association with the Nixon administration. Rehnquist was an assistant attorney general in John Mitchell's Justice Department before Nixon picked him up by his jackboots and hoisted him on to the court.

This leaves an interesting line-up to decide the (legal) fate of the tapes: the three right-bent Nixon appointees – Burger, Blackmun and Powell – to balance the three-man 'liberal bloc': Douglas, Marshall and Brennan. The two critical swing votes will be Byron White, a closet-fascist appointed by John Kennedy, and Eisenhower nominee Potter Stewart, a sort of libertarian conservative who recently shocked many of his friends and philosophical brethren by publicly denouncing Nixon's blatant 'politicalization' of the court.

Stewart, far more than White, seems genuinely and even personally offended at finding himself grouped with what he plainly considers four half-bright political hacks who don't know the law from a leach-field. If Jaworski can mount a sound enough legal argument to convince Stewart that Nixon has no basic or inalienable right to withhold the tapes, he will probably win the case even if White goes along once again with Nixon's gunsels. Because there will only be three of them, this time – with Rehnquist brooding darkly on the sidelines – and in the case of a 4-4 tie, if Jaworski wins. He has already won a verdict on essentially the same question in the US Court of Appeals, and when a lower court verdict is carried up as high as it can go and results in a tie vote, the lower court verdict stands.

Whatever the verdict, it will almost certainly come before the House of Representatives votes on impeachment ... and if Nixon loses and then decides to defy the Supreme Court, that will give many of the publicly 'undecided' congressmen a hard nudge in the direction of voting against him. The final vote will probably come sometime in late August, and if I had to bet on the outcome now I'd guess the margin will be almost 2-1 against the president, although a simple majority would do it.

Nixon would probably agree with me on that, and also on the idea that betting on the outcome of the House impeachment vote right now is more a matter of the point spread than simple winning or losing.

The real test will come in the Senate, where Nixon can *afford* a 2-1 point spread against him and still win the verdict. Out of 100 votes in the Senate, Nixon will need only thirty-four to beat the whole rap ... which is not a really formidable nut to have to make, given the nature of politicians and the ever-increasing likelihood that the final vote in the Senate – the savage climax to 'the whole *enchilada*' – will happen no earlier than mid-October, about two weeks before election day on the first Tuesday in November.

Exactly one-third of the Senate – just one vote less than Nixon needs for acquittal – will be running for re-election this November, and every one of them (either thirty-three or thirty-four, because three into 100 won't go) is reportedly terrified at the prospect of having to campaign for re-election back home, while at the same time having to participate in a nationally televised trial on one of the heaviest questions in American history, and then being forced to cast a monumentally public vote either for or against President Nixon on the very eve of their own election days.

If it comes down to that, in terms of timing, the public opinion polls will no doubt be a much more potent factor than they have been up to now -- for the same reason that Congress waited until the polls climbed over fifty per cent in favour of impeachment before getting the process underway ... and there is not much Nixon can do now to affect the polls enough to change the House vote on impeachment.

But his ability to affect the outcome of the Senate/conviction vote is a hard thing to argue with. For one thing, he plans to spend most of the summer flashing around Europe, Israel, Egypt, Russia and anywhere else where they'll talk to him, in what will probably be a fairly effective effort to grab enough headlines to keep 'the impeachment story' at least below the fold on most front pages.

Meanwhile, the haggard remnants of his presidential staff will be working about eighteen hours a day to suppress and deflate any new evidence that might affect either his standing in the polls or the outcome of his Senate/conviction trial. Less than half of those thirty-four votes he needs for acquittal are up for re-election in 74, and any incumbent president – even one who's already been impeached – has a massive amount of leverage when it comes to using the political pork barrel.

There is not much doubt, on the numbers question, that at least twenty of the 100 senators will not vote to convict Nixon under *any* circumstances ... unless he violates that old law of Indiana politics about being 'found in bed with either a live man or a dead woman'.

Nixon is not one of your more vulnerable politicians in this area. It is difficult, in fact, to imagine him being in bed at all – and especially not with anything human.

So we can scratch twenty votes, for starters – which means he needs only fourteen more, and we want to remember here that he'll be dealing almost entirely with yahoo Republicans and redneck Southern Democrats. Given the 34/66 cut, he can afford to ignore every man in the Senate who has ever been even remotely suspected of anti-Nixon sympathies ... so he can write off at least fifty votes with one stroke, which means he will not be far off if he assumes a mathematical base of fifty votes definitely against him, twenty definitely for him, and thirty undecided.

Of those thirty, he needs only fourteen – and any man who has spent his entire adult life dealing on the ethical fringes of Washington politics should feel fairly comfortable with those numbers. Any president who can't piece off fourteen senators would never have made it to the White House in the first place.

And Nixon has two extremely heavy hole cards: 1) He has personal control over most of the potentially fatal evidence that might be used against him if he ever comes to trial (the Oval Office tapes, which he retains the option to destroy now or later, if he hasn't already done that ...) and 2) he has become such a personal embarrassment and political millstone around the neck of the Republican party that he could easily buy at least ten of those votes by agreeing, in secret, to resign the presidency in a gesture of splendid martyrdom within forty-eight hours after the Senate votes *not* to convict him on the House impeachment charges.

This solution would get a lot of people off the hook – especially Nixon, who has nothing to gain from hanging on for another two years in the White House. His effectiveness as president was a wasted hope from the very beginning – but it has taken five years, two elections and one mind-bending scandal to make the cheap little bastard understand it.

Even Nixon should understand, now, that the only hope for his salvation in the history books is to somehow become a martyr and the most obvious way to do that, at this point in the saga, is to make some kind of a deal with the heavies in his own party to get him off their backs as quickly as possible by trading the guarantee of a dignified resignation for a vote of acquittal in the Senate.

This is a pretty good bet, I think, and unless the Rodino committee comes up with some unnaturally strong evidence before the House votes on impeachment, I don't have much faith in a Senate vote for conviction. A working figure, for now, would be about 60-40 *against* Nixon ... but 60-40 is not enough; it has to be 67-33 against, and that will be a hard nut to make.

In addition to the leverage it gives Nixon with the gurus of his own party, the 'resignation in exchange for acquittal' strategy has a certain appeal for the Democrats – but only if it can be arranged and finished off before 20 January 1975. If Gerald Ford assumes the presidency before that date, he will only be legally eligible to run for one more term. But if Ford becomes president anytime after January of 75, he'll be eligible for *two* terms, and most Democrats in the Senate would prefer to short-circuit that possibility.

So Nixon is not without options, when it comes down to nut-cutting time. There is very little chance that he will finish his second term, but the odds for a scenario of impeachment in the House, acquittal in the Senate and then a maudlin spectacle of martyred resignation before 20 January of next year are pretty good.

One of the very few drastic developments that could alter that timetable would be an unexpected crunch of some kind that would force Nixon to yield up his tapes. But nothing in the recent behaviour of either the president or his lawyers shows any indication of that. As long as he clings to the tapes, Nixon has a very strong bargaining position *vis-à-vis* both the people who insist on hearing them and those few whose physical freedom depends on *nobody* hearing them.

At least a half-dozen voices on those tapes belong to people who are scheduled to go on trial, very soon, on serious felony charges ... and they are the same ones, presumably, who attended that secret meeting in the White House, last July, when it was decided that the tapes should never be released.

It is safe to assume that there were probably some very strong and pragmatic reasons for that decision – particularly in the cases of 'Bob' Haldeman and John Ehrlichman, whose fate in the courts is considered to be almost entirely dependent on Nixon's resolve to hang on to those tapes at all costs ... Or, failing that, to destroy them if that ever seems necessary.

Nixon understands this. On the basis of his own crudely edited transcripts, there is enough evidence on those tapes to have Nixon impeached, convicted and jailed for his own protection before the first football Sunday in September. For some reason that probably not even Nixon understands now, he gave seven of these tapes to Judge Sirica last winter. Two or three of them at least were found to be unaltered originals, and Sirica eventually turned these over to the House Judiciary Committee as evidence in the impeachment inquiry.

So there are a hundred or more people wandering around Washington today who have heard 'the real stuff', as they put it – and despite their professional caution when the obvious question arises, there is one reaction they all feel free to agree on: that nobody who felt shocked, depressed or angry after reading the edited White House transcripts should ever be allowed to hear the actual tapes, except under heavy sedation or locked in the trunk of a car. Only a terminal cynic, they say, can listen for any length of time to the real stuff without feeling a compulsion to do something like drive down to the White House and throw a bag of live rats over the fence.

Yes ... looking back at that line I just wrote, it occurs to me that almost half the people I know have been feeling that kind of compulsion almost steadily for the last eight or nine years. My friend Yail Bloor, for instance, claims to have thrown a whole garbage can full of live rats, roach and assorted small vermin over the White House fence about a week before Lyndon Johnson announced his retirement in 1968. 'It was a wonderful feeling,' he says, 'but only because it was Johnson. I knew, for some reason, that he would really *hate* the sight of big rats on the White House lawn.' He paused and reached for his snuffbox, taking a huge hit of Dr Johnson's best in each nostril.

'I'm not sure why,' he went on, 'but I wouldn't get any satisfaction out of doing a thing like that to Nixon. He might actually *like* rats.'

Mother of babbling God, I just took a break from this gibberish long enough to watch the evening news ... and there was the face and voice of Tex Colson, jolting a Washington courtroom with a totally unforeseen confession of guilt on one count of obstruction of justice in return – on the basis of an elaborately covered TV statement on the subject of his own guilt and deep involvement in almost every aspect of Watergate – for the opportunity to take whatever punishment he deserves and purge himself once and for all by 'telling everything I know' about 'many things I have not been able to talk freely about until now'.

Colson – of all people! First he converts to Jesus, and now he's copping a plea and holding a press conference on national TV to announce that he intends to confess everything. Which means, apparently, that he is now available to testify for the prosecution in every Watergate-related trial from now until all his old friends and conspirators are either put behind bars with a Gideon Bible in their hands or standing in line at a soup kitchen in Butte, Montana.

What will Nixon make of *this* freak-out? Tex Colson, one of the most unprincipled thugs in the history of American politics, was supposed to be a main link in that unbreakable and fatally interdependent inner circle – along with Haldeman, Ehrlichman and Nixon – who wouldn't think twice about stonewalling God himself. Not even Richard Nixon, at the peak of his power and popularity, felt comfortable with the knowledge that a monster like Colson had an office in the White House. Nixon felt so strongly about Colson's savagery, in fact, that he went out of his way to defame him by deliberately publishing some of his own harsh judgements on Colson's total lack of *any* sense of ethics or morality in the official White House transcripts.

And Nixon speechwriter Pat Buchanan, widely regarded as one of the most aggressive, hardline right-wingers since Josef Goebbels, once described Colson as 'the meanest man in American politics' ... which is no small compliment, coming from Buchanan, who has spent the better part of his last decade working with some of the meanest and most congenitally fascistic bastards ever to work for *any* government.

I will have to call Buchanan tomorrow and ask him what he thinks about Tex Colson now. As a matter of fact, I will have to call a lot of people tomorrow about this thing – because if Colson really is serious about telling everything he knows, Richard Nixon is in very deep trouble. He may as well go out on Pennsylvania Avenue tomorrow and start peddling those tapes to the highest bidder, because Colson knows enough ugly stories about the Nixon regime to make most of the talk on those tapes seem like harmless cocktail gossip.

At a glance, there are two ways to view Colson's breakdown: one is to take his conversion to Jesus seriously, which is difficult ... and the other is to take it as a warning that even the president should have better sense than to cross 'the meanest man in American politics'.

There is another way to interpret it, but that will have to wait for later – along with a lot of other things. This is not the kind of story to try to cope with while roaming back and forth across the country in jet airliners ... although there is nothing in any of the current journalism out of Washington, on the tube or in print, to indicate that it is any easier to cope with there than in Key Biscayne, Calgary, or even Mexico City. The entire Washington Press Corps seems at least temporarily paralysed by the sheer magnitude and complexity of the thing ...

It will be a nasty story to cover, especially in the swamp-like humidity of a Washington summer ... but it is definitely worth watching, and perhaps even being a part of, because whatever kind of judgement and harsh reality finally emerges will be an historical landmark in the calendar of civilizations and a beacon, for good or ill, to all the generations that will inherit this earth – or whatever we leave of it – just as surely as we inherited it from the Greeks and the Romans, the Mayans and the Incas, and even from the 'Thousand Year Reich'.

The impeachment of Richard Nixon will end in a trial that will generate an interminable blizzard of headlines, millions of dollars' worth of media coverage, and a verdict that will not matter nearly as much to the defendant as it will to the jurors. By the time the trial starts – assuming that Nixon can sustain his lifelong appetite for humiliation that has never been properly gratified – the fate of Nixon himself will have shrunk to the dimensions of a freakish little side effect. The short-lived disaster of his presidency is already neutralized, and the outcome of his impeachment ordeal will have very little effect on his role in tomorrow's history texts. He will be grouped, along with presidents like Grant and Harding, as a corrupt and incompetent mockery of the American Dream he praised to long and loud in all his speeches ... not just as a 'crook', but so crooked that he required the help of a personal valet to screw his pants on every morning.

By the time Richard Milhous Nixon goes on trial in the Senate, the only reason for trying him will be to understand how he ever became president of the United States at all ... and the real defendant, at that point, will be the American political system.

The trial of Richard Nixon, if it happens, will amount to a *de facto* trial of the American Dream. The importance of Nixon now is *not* merely to get rid of him; that's a strictly political consideration ... The real question is why we are being forced to impeach a president elected by the largest margin in the history of presidential elections.

So, with the need for sleep coming up very fast now, we want to look at two main considerations: 1) the necessity of actually bringing Nixon to trial, in order to understand our reality in the same way the Nuremberg trials forced Germany to confront itself ... and 2) the absolutely vital necessity of filling the vacuum that the Nixon impeachment will leave, and the hole that will be there in 1976.

Rolling Stone no. 164, 4 July 1974

FEAR AND LOATHING IN LIMBO: THE SCUM ALSO RISES

... before I could come to any conclusion it occurred to me that my speech or my silence, indeed any action of mine, would be a mere futility. What did it matter what anyone knew or ignored? What did it matter who was manager? One gets sometimes such a flash of insight. The essentials of this affair lay deep under the surface, beyond my reach, and beyond my power of meddling.

Joseph Conrad, *Heart of Darkness*

Well ... this is going to be difficult. That sold-out knucklehead refugee from a 1969 'Mister Clean' TV commercial has just done what only the most cynical and paranoid kind of malcontent ever connected with national politics would have dared to predict ...

If I followed my better instincts right now, I would put this typewriter in the Volvo and drive to the home of the nearest politician – *any* politician – and hurl the goddamn machine through his front window ... flush the bugger out with an act of lunatic violence then soak him down with Mace and run him naked down Main Street in Aspen with a bell around his neck and black lumps all over his body from the jolts of a high-powered 'Bull Buster' cattle prod.

But old age has either mellowed me or broken my spirit to the point where I will probably not do that – at least not today, because that blundering dupe in the White House has just plunged me into a deep and vicious hole.

About five hours after I'd sent the final draft of a massive article on the demise of Richard Nixon off on the mojo wire and into the cold maw of the typesetter in San Francisco, Gerald Ford called a press conference in Washington to announce that he had just granted a 'full, free and absolute' presidential pardon, covering any and all crimes Richard Nixon may or may not have committed during the entire five and a half years of his presidency.

Ford sprung his decision with no advance warning at 10:40 on a peaceful Sunday morning in Washington, after emerging from a church service with such a powerful desire to dispense mercy that he rushed back to the White House – a short hump across Lafayette Park – and summoned a weary Sunday-morning skeleton crew of correspondents and cameramen to inform them, speaking in curiously zombielike tones, that he could no longer tolerate the idea of ex-President Nixon suffering in grief-crazed solitude out there on the beach in San Clemente, and that his conscience now compelled him to end both the suffering of Nixon and the national *angst* it was causing by means of a presidential edict of such king-sized breadth and scope as to scourge the poison of Watergate from our national consciousness forever.

Or at least that's how it sounded to me, when I was jolted out of a sweat-soaked coma on Sunday morning by a frantic telephone call from Dick Tuck. 'Ford *pardoned* the bastard!' he screamed. 'I warned you, didn't I? I buried him twice, and he came back from the dead both times ... Now he's done it again; he's running around loose on some private golf course in Palm Desert.'

I fell back on the bed, moaning heavily. No, I thought. I didn't *hear* that. Ford had gone out of his way, during his first White House press conference, to impress both the Washington press corps and the national TV audience with his carefully considered refusal to interfere in any way with Special Prosecutor Leon Jaworski's legal duty to proceed on the basis of evidence and 'prosecute any and all individuals'. Given the context of the question, Ford's reply was widely interpreted as a signal to Jaworski that the former president should not be given any special treatment ... And it also meshed with Ford's answer to a question in the course of his confirmation hearings in the Senate a few months earlier, when he'd said, 'I don't think the public would stand for it,' when asked if an appointed vice-president would have the power to pardon the president who'd appointed him, if the president were removed from office under criminal circumstances.

I recalled these things Ford had said, but I was not so sure I'd heard Dick Tuck correctly – or if I'd really heard him at all. I held my right hand up in front of my eyes, trying to remember if I'd eaten anything the night before that could cause hallucinations. If so, my hand would appear to be transparent, and I would be able to see all the bones and blood vessels very clearly.

But my hand was not transparent. I moaned again, bringing Sandy in from the kitchen to find out what was wrong. 'Did Tuck just call?' I asked.

She nodded: 'He was almost hysterical. Ford just gave Nixon a full pardon.'

I sat up quickly, groping around on the bed for something to smash. 'No!' I shouted. 'That's impossible!'

She shook her head. 'I heard it on the radio, too.'

I stared at my hands again, feeling anger behind my eyes and noise coming up in my throat: 'That stupid, lying bastard! Jesus! Who votes for these treacherous scumbags! You can't even trust the dumb ones! Look at Ford! He's too goddamn stupid to arrange a deal like that! Hell, he's almost too stupid to lie.'

Sandy shrugged. 'He gave Nixon all the tapes, too.'

'Holy shit!' I leaped out of bed and went quickly to the phone. 'What's Goodwin's number in Washington? That bonehead Rotarian sonofabitch made a deal? Maybe Dick knows something.'

But it was twenty-four hours later when I finally got hold of Goodwin, and by that time I had made a huge chart full of dates, names and personal connections – all linked and cross-linked by a maze of arrows and lines. The three names on the list with far more connections than any others were Laird, Kissinger and Rockefeller. I had spent all night working feverishly on the chart, and now I was asking Goodwin to have a researcher check it all out.

'Well,' he replied. 'A lot of people in Washington are thinking along those same lines today. No doubt there was some kind of arrangement, but—' He paused. 'Aren't we pretty damn close to the deadline? Jesus Christ, you'll never be able to check all that stuff before—'

'Mother of babbling God!' I muttered. The word 'deadline' caused my brain to seize up momentarily. Deadline? Yes. Tomorrow morning, about fifteen more hours ... With about ninety per cent of my story already set in type, one of the threads that ran all the way through it was my belief that nothing short of a nuclear war could prevent Richard Nixon's conviction. The only thing wrong with that argument was its tripod construction, and one of the three main pillars was my assumption that Gerald Ford had not been lying when he'd said more than once, for the record, that he had no intention of considering a presidential pardon for Richard Nixon 'until the legal process has run its course'.

Cazart! I hung up the phone and tossed my chart across the room. That rotten, sadistic little thief had done it again. Just one month earlier he had sandbagged me by resigning so close to the deadline that I almost had a nervous breakdown while failing completely ... And now he was doing it again, with this goddamn presidential pardon, leaving me with less than twenty-four hours to revise completely a 15,000 word story that was already set in type.

It was absolutely impossible, no hope at all – except to lash as many last-minute pages as possible into the mojo and hope for the best. Maybe somebody in San Francisco would have time, when the deadline crunch came, to knit the two versions together ... But there was no way at all to be sure, so this will be an interesting article to read when it comes off the press ...

Indeed ... cast your bread on the waters ... why not?

I was brooding on this and cursing Nixon, more out of habit than logic, for his eerie ability to make life difficult for me ... when it suddenly occurred to me that the villain this time was not Nixon, but Gerald Ford. He was the one who decided to pardon Nixon (for reasons we can hopefully deal with later) on 30 August, when he instructed his White House counsel, Philip Buchen, to work out the legal details and consult with Nixon's new defence lawyer, John Miller, one-time campaign aide to Robert Kennedy.

Incredibly, Miller informed Buchen that he would have to make sure a presidential pardon was 'acceptable' to Nixon; and twenty-four hours later he came back with word that the ex-president, whose condition had been publicly described by anonymous 'friends' that week as almost terminally 'disturbed and depressed' at the prospect of his imminent indictment by Jaworski's grand jury – had been able to get a grip on himself long enough to decide that he would not be offended by the offer of a full presidential pardon – just as long as the offer also granted Nixon sole ownership and control of *all* the White House tapes.

Ford quickly agreed, a concession that could mean $5 million or more to Nixon: He can milk them for the bulk of his presidential memoirs, for which his new agent claims already to have been offered a $2 million advance, and after that he has the legal right either to destroy the tapes or sell them to the highest bidder.

Arrangements for the presidential pardon were not completed until Friday 6 September – and only then after President Ford sent his personal emissary, Benton L. Becker, out to San Clemente to make sure things went smoothly. Becker, a vaguely sinister Washington attorney who is currently under investigation by the IRS for alleged tax evasion, describes himself as an 'unpaid legal adviser' to President Ford and also a personal friend.

They first met in 1969, Becker says, when he volunteered to help then Congressman Ford in his ill-advised campaign to persuade the House of

Representatives to impeach US Supreme Court Justice William O. Douglas. That effort failed miserably, and Ford now seems embarrassed at the memory of it, but he still defends Becker as 'a man of the highest professional ethics'.

There is some disagreement on this. According to the *Washington Post*, 'Justice Department sources said they were astounded when they learned that Becker had been used by the White House to negotiate with the former president, "My God, doesn't Ford know about this case?" said one source. "The guy's under investigation." '

Which is not necessarily a bad sign, in this day and age. Most of my friends have been 'under investigation' at one time or another in the past ten years or so, and my own FBI file dates back at least to 1958, when I refused to accept a security clearance from the Air Force, on the grounds that I didn't honestly consider myself a good security risk because I disagreed strongly with the slogan: 'my country, right or wrong'.

My clearance was not granted, but I was never hassled about it – and instead of being sent to a top-secret radar installation near the Arctic Circle, I was passed over for promotion and placed in a job as sports editor of a base newspaper on the Gulf Coast of Florida.

Ah ... but we seem to be wandering here ... I was talking about Benton Becker and his delicate task of negotiating the details of a full presidential pardon for Richard Nixon, whose tragic mental condition was even then being slandered almost daily, at this stage of the pardon, by unnamed friends and advisers. At this point in the pardon negotiations, both Ford and Nixon had learned that Jaworski's grand jury planned to indict the ex-president on as many as ten counts – an ugly prospect that led Ford to suggest that Nixon might temper the grand jury's aggressive attitude by 'volunteering' to admit at least some small measure of guilt for his role in the Watergate cover-up, in exchange for the pardon that would give him total immunity from prosecution anyway, regardless of what he admitted.

This suggestion almost torpedoed the negotiations. Nixon 'angrily rejected' it, says one of Ford's White House advisers, and Becker was hard-pressed to keep the deal on its rails. By Friday evening, however, Nixon's mood had improved to the point where he agreed to accept both the pardon and the tapes. Becker was elated; he flew back to Washington and reported to Ford that his mission had been 100 per cent successful. The new president received the news gratefully, and scheduled a short-notice press conference on Sunday to lay the fine news on his public.

Yeah ... I know: There is something just a little bit weird about that story, but I don't have any time to check on it right now. All the details, however, have appeared in one form or another in either the *Washington Post* or the *Washington Star-News*.

I cite those sources only because the story makes no sense at all, on its face ... But then none of the other stories in the New York or Washington papers on the Monday after the announcement of the Ford/Nixon treaty made much sense, either ... primarily because Sunday is a very hard day to find anybody in Washington who doesn't want to be found; which includes just about everybody with good sense except the kind of man who calls a press conference at 10:30 on Sunday morning and drones out a stone-faced announcement that he knows will have half the nation howling with rage before nightfall ... But by nightfall, Ford's version of the pardon was spread all over the country on the wires, while enraged editors at the *Times*, the *Post* and the *Star* were still trying to pry their hotrod investigative reporters out of weekend cabins in the Virginia mountains and beachhouses on the Maryland shore.

I have very dim memories of Tuck's call. Less than five hours earlier, I had passed out very suddenly in the bathtub, after something like 133 hours of non-stop work on a thing I'd been dragging around with me for two months and revising in ragged notebooks and on rented typewriters in hotels from Key Biscayne to Laguna Beach, bouncing in and out of Washington to check the pressure and keep a fix on the timetable, then off again to Chicago or Colorado ... before heading back to Washington again, where the pressure valves finally blew all at once in early August, catching me in a state of hysterical exhaustion and screeching helplessly for speed when Nixon suddenly caved in and quit, ambushing me on the brink of a deadline and wasted beyond the help of anything but the most extreme kind of chemo-therapy.

It takes about a month to recover physically from a collapse of that magnitude, and at least a year to shake the memory. The only thing I can think of that compares to it is that long, long moment of indescribably intense sadness that comes just before drowning at sea, those last few seconds on the cusp when the body is still struggling but the mind has given up ... a sense of absolute failure and a very clear understanding of it that makes the last few seconds before blackout seem almost peaceful. Getting rescued at that point is far more painful than drowning: Recovery brings back terrifying memories of struggling wildly for breath ...

This is precisely the feeling I had when Tuck woke me up that morning to say that Ford had just granted Nixon 'full, free and absolute' pardon. I had just written a long, sporadically rational brief, of sorts – explaining how Nixon had backed himself into a corner and why it was inevitable that he would soon be indicted and convicted on a felony 'obstruction of justice' charge, and then Ford would pardon him, for a lot of reasons I couldn't agree with, but which Ford had already stated so firmly that there didn't seem to be much point in arguing about it. The logic of sentencing Nixon to a year in the same cell with John Dean was hard to argue with on either legal or ethical grounds, but I understood politics well enough by then to realize that Nixon would have to plead guilty to something like the rape/murder of a Republican senator's son before Gerald Ford would even consider letting him spend any time in jail.

I had accepted this, more or less. Just as I had more or less accepted – after eighteen months of total involvement in the struggle to get rid of Nixon – the idea that Gerald Ford could do just about anything he felt like doing, as long as he left me alone. My interest in national politics withered drastically within hours after Nixon resigned.

After five and a half years of watching a gang of fascist thugs treating the White House and the whole machinery of the federal government like a conquered empire to be used like the spoils of war for any purpose that served either the needs or whims of the victors, the prospect of some harmless, half-bright jock like Gerry Ford running a cautious, caretaker-style government for two or even six years was almost a welcome relief. Not even the ominous sight of Vice-President Nelson Rockefeller hovering a heartbeat away from the presidency had much effect on my head.

After more than ten years of civil war with the White House and all the swine who either lived or worked there, I was ready to give the benefit of the doubt to almost any president who acted half human and had enough sense not to walk around in public wearing a swastika armband.

This is more or less what I wrote, I think, after Nixon resigned and I was faced with the obligation to fill enough space to justify all those expenses I ran up while chasing Nixon around the country and watching him sink deeper and deeper in the quicksand of his own excrement. In the early stages of the deathwatch, there was a definite high in watching the Congress reluctantly gearing up for a titanic battle with Richard Nixon and his private army of fixers who had taken over the whole executive branch of the government by the time he sailed triumphantly into his second term.

By the middle of last summer, the showdown had become inevitable and when Nixon looked at the balance sheet in August and saw both the legislative and judicial branches of the federal government joining forces against him, he knew he was finished.

On 9 August, he quit and was gone from Washington twelve hours later in a cloud of disgrace. He was finished: There was no doubt about it. Even his ranking staffers were muttering about his dangerously irrational state of mind towards the end, and his farewell speech to the Cabinet and White House staff was so clearly deranged that even I felt sorry for him ... And when the helicopter whisked him off to exile in California, an almost visible shudder of relief swept through the crowd on the White House lawn that had gathered for the sad spectacle of his departure.

Nixon was about 30,000 feet over St Louis in Air Force One when his chosen successor, Gerald Ford, took the oath. Ford had been selected, by Nixon, to replace Spiro Agnew, convicted several months earlier of tax fraud and extortion ... and Nixon himself, before quitting, had tacitly admitted his guilt in a felony conspiracy to obstruct justice.

I left Washington the day after Ford was sworn in, too tired to feel anything but a manic sense of relief as I staggered through the lobby at National Airport with about 200 pounds of transcripts of the Senate Watergate and House Judiciary Committee Hearings that had been rendered obsolete as evidence by Nixon's forced resignation two days earlier. I was not quite sure why I wanted them, but evidence of any kind is always reassuring to have, and I felt that after two or three months of sleep I might be able to use them in some way.

Now, almost exactly four weeks later, that suitcase full of transcripts is still lying open beside my desk ... and now that Gerald Ford has granted Nixon a presidential pardon so sweeping that he will never have to stand trial for anything, those books of evidence that would have guaranteed his impeachment if he hadn't resigned are beginning to pique my interest ...

===

Honky-Tonk Tunes and a Long-Remembered Dream ... Constant Haggling, Useless Briefings and a Howling Voice at the Door

===

American politics will never be the same again.
> Senator George McGovern, acceptance speech, 13 July 1972,
> Miami, Florida

Another hot, heavy rain in Washington, at 4:33 on a wet Wednesday morning, falling like balls of sweat against my window ... Twelve feet wide and six feet tall, the high yellow eye of the National Affairs Suite looking out across the rotting roofs of our nation's capital at least a mile away through the haze and the rain to the fine white marble spire of the Washington Monument and the dark dome of the Capitol ...

Hillbilly music howling out of the radios across the room from the typewriter.

And when it's midnight in Dallas, I'll be somewhere on a big jet plane ... If I could only understand you, maybe I could cope with the loneliness I feel ...

Honky-tonk tunes and a quart of Wild Turkey on the sideboard, ripped to the tits on whatever it was in that bag I bought tonight from the bull fruit in Georgetown, looking down from the desk at yesterday's huge *Washington Post* headline:

PRESIDENT ADMITS WITHHOLDING DATA
TAPES SHOW HE APPROVED COVER-UP

Every half-hour on the half-hour, WXRA – the truckers' station over in Alexandria – keps babbling more and more hideous news of 'rapidly dissolving' support in the House and the Senate. All ten members of the House Judiciary Committee who voted *against* the articles of impeachment on national TV last week have now reversed themselves, for the record, and said they plan to vote *for* impeachment when – or if – it comes to a vote in the House on 19 August. Even Barry Goldwater has leaked (and then denied) a UPI report that he thinks Nixon should resign, for the good of the country ... and also for the good of Goldwater and everybody else in the Republican party, such as it is.

Indeed. The rats are deserting the ship at high speed. Even the dingbat senator from Colorado, Peter Dominick – the GOP claghorn who nominated Nixon for the Nobel Peace Prize less than two years ago – has called the president's eleventh-hour admission of complicity in the Watergate cover-up 'sorrowful news'.

We will not have Richard Nixon to kick around much longer – which is not especially 'sorrowful news' to a lot of people, except that the purging of the cheap little bastard is going to have to take place here in Washington and will take up the rest of our summer.

One day at a time, Sweet Jesus ... That's all I'm askin' from you ...

And now the Compton Brothers with a song about '... when the wine ran out and the jukebox ran out of tunes ...'

Jesus, we need more ice and whisky here. Fill the bag with water and suck down the dregs. The rain is still lashing my window, the dawn sky is still black and this room is damp and cold. Where is the goddamn heat switch? Why is my bed covered with newspaper clips and US Government Printing Office evidence books from the Nixon impeachment hearings?

Ah ... madness, madness. On a day like this, not even the prospect of Richard Nixon's downfall can work up the blood. This is stone, flat-out fucking weather.

On another day like this, a long time ago, I was humming across the bridge out of Louisville, Kentucky, in an old Chevy with three or four good ole boys who worked with me at a furniture factory in Jefferson-ville, Indiana ... The tyres were hissing on the wet asphalt, the wind-shield wipers were lashing back and forth in the early morning rain and we were hunkered down in the car with our lunch bags and moaning along with a mean country tune on the radio when somebody said:.

'Jesus Christ: Why are we going to *work* on a day like this? We must be *goddamn crazy.* This is the kind of day when you want to be belly-to-belly with a good woman, in a warm bed under a tin roof with the rain beating down and a bottle of good whisky right next to the bed.'

Let me be there in your mornin', let me be there in your night ... Let me be there when you need me ... and make it right.

Ah, this haunting, honky music ... I am running a serious out-of-control fever for that long-remembered dream of a tin-roof, hard-rain, belly-to-belly day with a big iron bolt on the door and locked away in a deep warm bed from every connection to the outside world except a $14.95 tin radio wailing tunes like 'I Smell a Rat' and 'The Wild Side of Life'.

This is not your ideal flying weather. Both National and Dulles air-ports are 'closed for the rest of the morning', they say ... But despite all that I find myself on the phone demanding plane reservations back to Colorado. Fuck the weather ...

Whoever answered the phone at United Airlines said the weather was 'expected to be clear' by early afternoon and there were plenty of seats open for the 4:40 flight to Denver.

'Wonderful,' I said, 'but I want a first-class seat in the *smokers'* section.'

'I'll check,' she said, and moments later she was back with bad news: 'The smoking seats are all taken, sir, but if it makes no difference to you—'

'It does,' I said. 'I *must* smoke. I insist on it.'

She checked again and this time the news was better: 'I think we can open a smoking seat for you, sir. Could I have your name?'

'Nader,' I said. 'R. Nader.'

'How do you spell that?'

I spelled it for her, then set my alarm for two and fell asleep on the couch, still wearing my wet swimming trunks. After two months on the Nixon impeachment trial, my nerves were worn raw from the constant haggling and frustrated hostility of all those useless, early morning White House press briefings and long, sweaty afternoons pacing aimlessly around the corridors of the Rayburn Office Building on Capitol Hill, waiting for crumbs of wisdom from any two or three of those thirty-eight luckless congressmen on the House Judiciary Committee hearing evidence on the possible impeachment of Richard Nixon.

It was an eerie spectacle: The whole Nixonian empire – seemingly invincible less than two years ago – was falling apart of its own foul weight right in front of our eyes. There was no denying the vast and historic proportions of the story, but covering it on a day-to-day basis was such a dull and degrading experience that it was hard to keep a focus on what was really happening. It was essentially a lawyer's story, not a journalist's.

I never made that plane. Sometime around noon I was jolted awake by a pounding on my door and a voice shouting, 'Wake up, goddamnit, the whole town's gone crazy – the sonofabitch has caved in – he's quitting.'

'No!' I thought. 'Not now! I'm too weak to handle it.' These goddamn rumours had kept me racing frantically around Washington day and night for almost a week – and when the shitrain finally began, I was helpless. My eyes were swollen shut with chlorine poisoning and when I tried to get out of bed to open the door, I almost snapped both ankles. I had fallen asleep wearing rubber-soled basketball shoes, which had wedged themselves between the sheets at the foot of the bed so firmly that my first thought was that somebody had strapped me down on the bed.

The howling voice at my door was Craig Vetter, another *Rolling Stone* writer who had been in town for two weeks trying to make some kind of connection with Nixon's priest ... But the priest was finished now and the town was going wild. A *Washington Post* reporter said he had never seen the newsroom so frantic – not even when John Kennedy was murdered or during the Cuban missile crisis. The prevailing rumours on Capitol Hill had Nixon either addressing a joint session of Congress at 4:30 that afternoon or preparing a final statement for delivery at 7:00 on all three networks ... but a call to the White House pressroom spiked both these rumours, although the place was filling up with reporters who'd picked up an entirely different rumour: that either Ziegler or Nixon himself would soon appear in the pressroom to make a statement of some kind.

Six more calls from the National Affairs Suite churned up at least six more impossible rumours. Every switchboard in town that had any connection with either journalism or politics was jammed and useless. Later that night, even the main White House switchboard jammed up for the first time most reporters could remember, and for the next two days almost everybody who worked in the White House – even private secretaries – kept their home phones off the hook because of the chaos.

It was about 1:30 on Wednesday afternoon when I got through to Marty Nolan in the White House pressroom. We compared rumours and killed both lists very quickly. 'This is all crazy bullshit,' said Nolan. 'We're just being jerked around. He's not going to do anything serious today, but just on the chance that he might, I don't dare leave this goddamn dungeon.'

I had been on the verge of going down there, but after arranging with Nolan and about six other people in strategic positions in different parts of town to call me instantly if anything started to happen, I decided that the best thing to do was to take both the TV set and the FM radio down to a table by the pool and have all my calls transferred down to the lifeguard's telephone ... Which turned out to be the best of all possible solutions: Vetter and I set up a totally efficient communications post beside the pool, and for the next forty-eight hours we were able to monitor the whole craziness from our table beside the pool.

The Suck-Tide Reaches San Clemente ... Ziegler Brings the News to the Boss ... General Haig and the Bag of Dimes ... The Sybaritic Priest and the Mentally Retarded Rabbi ... More Talk of the 'Suicide Option'

Well ... the goddamn thing is over now; it ended on Thursday afternoon with all the grace and meaning of a coke bottle thrown off a third-floor fire escape on the Bowery – exploding on the sidewalk and scaring the shit out of everybody in range, from the ones who got righteously ripped full of glass splinters to the swarm of 'innocent bystanders' who still don't know what happened ...

... And probably never will; there is a weird, unsettled, painfully incomplete quality about the whole thing. All over Washington tonight is the stench of a massive psychic battle that *nobody* really won. Richard Nixon has been broken, whipped and castrated all at once, but even for me there is no real crank or elation in having been a front-row spectator at the final scenes, the deathwatch, the first time in American history that a president has been chased out of the White House and cast down in the ditch with all the other geeks and common criminals ...

Looking back on the final few months of his presidency, it is easy to see that Nixon was doomed all along – or at least from that moment when Archibald Cox first decided to force a showdown on the 'executive privilege' question by sending a US marshal over to the White House with a subpoena for some of the Oval Office tapes.

Nixon naturally defied that subpoena, but not even the crazed firing of Cox, Richardson and Ruckelshaus could make it go away. And when Jaworski challenged Nixon's right to defy that subpoena in the US Supreme Court, the wheels of doom began rolling. And from that point on, it was clear to all the principals except Nixon himself that the unthinkable was suddenly inevitable; it was only a matter of time ... And it was just about then that Richard Nixon began losing his grip on reality.

Within hours after Jaworski and Nixon's 'Watergate lawyer' James St Clair had argued the case in a special session of the court, I talked to Pat Buchanan and was surprised to hear that Nixon and his wizards in the White House were confident that the verdict would be 5-3 in their favour. Even Buchanan, who thinks rationally about seventy-nine per cent of the time, apparently believed – less than two weeks before the court ruled unanimously *against* Nixon – that five of the eight justices who would have to rule on that question would see no legal objection to ratifying Nixon's demented idea that anything discussed in the president's official office – even a patently criminal conspiracy – was the president's personal property, if he chose to have it recorded on his personal tape-recording machinery.

The possibility that even some of the justices the boss himself had appointed to the Court might not cheerfully endorse a concept of presidential immunity that mocked both the US Constitution and the Magna Carta had apparently been considered for a moment and then written off as too farfetched and crazy even to worry about by all of Nixon's personal strategists.

It is still a little difficult to believe, in fact, that some of the closest advisers to the president of a constitutional democracy in the year nineteen hundred and seventy-four might actually expect the highest court in *any* constitutional democracy to crank up what is probably the most discredited precedent in the history of Anglo-American jurisprudence – the 'divine right of kings' – in order to legalize the notion that a president of the United States or any other would-be democracy is above and beyond the law.

That Nixon and his personal gestapo actually believed this could happen is a measure of the insanity quotient of the people Nixon took down in the bunker with him when he knew the time had come to get serious.

But even as they raved, you could hear a hollow kind of paranoid uncertainty in their voices, as if they could already feel the ebb tide sucking around their ankles – just as Nixon must have felt it when he walked alone on the beach at San Clemente a few weeks earlier, trudging slowly along in the surf with his pantlegs rolled up while he waited in angry solitude for the results of the Supreme Court vote on his claim of 'executive privilege'. That rush of sucking water around his ankles must have almost pulled him out to sea when Ziegler called down from the big dune in front of La Casa Pacifica: 'Mister President! Mister President! We just got the news! The vote was unanimous – eight to zero.'

Nixon whoops with delight: He stops in his waterfilled tracks and hurls out both arms in the twin-victory sign. 'Wonderful!' he shouts. 'I *knew* we'd win it, Ron! Even without that clown Renchburg. It wasn't for nothing that I appointed those other dumb farts to the court!'

Ziegler stares down at him, at this doomed scarecrow of a president down there on the edge of the surf. Why is he grinning? Why does he seem so happy at this terrible news?

'No!' Ziegler shouts. 'That is not what I meant. That is not what I meant at all!' He hesitates, choking back a sob. 'The vote was eight to zero, Mister President – *against* you.'

'What?' The scarecrow on the beach goes limp. His arms collapse, his hands flap crazily around the pockets of his wet pants. 'Those dirty bastards!' he screams. 'We'll break their balls!'

'Yes *sir*!' Ziegler shouts. 'They'll wish they'd never been born!' He jerks a notebook out of his inside coat pocket and jots: 'Break their balls.'

By this time the wet president is climbing the dune in front of him. 'What happened?' Nixon snarls. 'Did somebody get to Burger?'

Ziegler nods. 'What else? Probably it was Edward Bennet Williams.'

'Of course,' says Nixon. 'We should never have left that dumb son-ofabitch back there in Washington by himself. We know he'll do business: That's why we put him there.' He kicks savagely at a lone ice plant in the sand. 'Goddamnit! Where was Colson? Burger was *his* assignment, right?'

Ziegler winces. 'Colson's in jail, sir. Don't you remember?'

Nixon stares blankly, then recovers: 'Colson? In jail? What did he do?' He picks up a kelp head and lashes it against his shin. 'Never mind, I remember now – but what about Ehrlichman? He can jerk Burger and those other clowns around like a goddamn Punch and Judy show!'

Ziegler stares out to sea for a moment, his eyes cloud over. 'Well, sir ... John's not much good to us any more. He's going to prison.'

Nixon stiffens, dropping the kelp head in the sand. 'Holy shit, Ron! Why should John go to prison? He's one of the finest public servants I've ever had the privilege of knowing!'

Ziegler is weeping only now, his emaciated body is wracked by deep sobs. 'I *don't know*, sir. I can't explain it.' He stares out to sea again, fighting to gain control of himself. 'These are terrible times, Mister President. Our enemies are closing in. While you were out there on the beach, the Avis agency in Laguna called and cancelled our credit. *They took my car*, Mister President! My gold Cadillac convertible! I was on the phone with Buzhardt – about the Supreme Court business, you know – when I looked out the window and saw this little nigger in an Avis uniform driving my car out the gate. The guards said he had a writ of seizure, signed by the local sheriff.'

'My God!' Nixon exclaims. 'We'll break his balls! Where's a telephone? I'll call Haldeman.'

'It's no use, sir,' Ziegler replies. 'We can't make any outgoing calls until we pay the phone company $33,000. They sent a man down to fix the lines so we can only take incoming calls – for the next eighty-six hours, and then we'll be cut off entirely. If you want to call Washington, we'll have to walk to the San Clemente Inn and use a pay phone. I think General Haig has a bag of dimes in his room.'

Nixon stiffens again; his brain is mired in deep thought. Then his eyes light up and he grabs Ziegler by the arm, dragging him towards the house. 'Come on, Ron,' he snaps, 'I have an idea.'

Ziegler stumbles along behind the president: He feels the energy flowing into him – the boss is on the move.

Nixon is talking as he runs: 'I think I've isolated our problem, Ron. We need credit, right? OK, where's that Jew?'

'Jew?'

'You know who I mean, goddamnit – that rabbi. They can always get credit, can't they? A rabbi? We'll send some of the Secret Service boys up there to Laguna to round him up. He's probably in the bar up there on top of the Surf and Sand; that's where he hangs out.' Nixon laughs wildly now. 'Shit, *nobody* questions a rabbi's credit! You tell the SS boys to pick him up and throw a real scare into him, then bring him down here and I'll *stroke* him.'

Now Ziegler is laughing. His eyes are bright and he is writing fast in his notebook. 'It's a wonderful idea, sir, just wonderful! First we stonewall the bastards, then we outflank them with a Jew!'

Nixon nods happily. 'They'll never know what hit 'em, Ron. You know what I've always said: "When the going gets tough, the tough get going."'

'That's right, sir. I remember when Coach Lombardi—'

Nixon cuts him off with a sudden clap of his wet hands; the sound causes two Secret Service agents in the nearby shrubbery to go for their guns. 'Hold on, Ron! Just hold it right there! You know who taught

Coach Lombardi everything he knew?' He smiles deeply. 'Me! The President!'

Ziegler wrings his hands, his eyeballs bulge, his face is twisted with reverence. 'I *remember* that, sir – I remember!'

'*Good*, Ron, good! Only losers forget ... And you know what Coach Lombardi said about *that*.' Nixon seizes his press secretary by both elbows and comes up close to his face: His breath is foul, his eyeballs are bloodshot, his pupils are dangerously dilated, his words come in short, high-pitched barks like a rabid hyena: 'You show me a good loser, Ron – and I'll show you a *loser*.'

Ziegler is overwhelmed: His eyes are so wide that he can't even blink; his body is rigid but his soul is on fire. His face is a mask of pure zeal: Ron Ziegler – left-hand man to a doomed and criminal president, the political flip side of every burned-out acid freak who voted for Goldwater and then switched to Tim Leary until the pain got too bad and the divine light of either Jesus or Maharaj Ji lured him off in the wake of another perfect master.

Ah, poor Ron. I knew him well enough. It was Ziegler, in fact, who tipped me off many months ago that Nixon was finished. This was back in July, in that lull before the storm when the wizards in Washington were beginning to nod glumly at each other whenever somebody suggested that the impeachment drive seemed to be faltering and that maybe Nixon was bottoming out, that in fact he had already bounced off the bottom and was preparing to take the offensive once again.

These were the salad days of early summer, before the fateful Supreme Court decision, when Nixon's Goebbels – ex-White House 'communications director' Ken Clawson – was creating a false dawn over the White House by momentarily halting Nixon's year-long slide in the public opinion polls with a daily drumbeat of heavy, headline-grabbing attacks on 'professional Nixon haters' in the press, and 'unprincipled, knee-jerk liberals in Congress'. At that point in time, most of Nixon's traditional allies were beginning to hear the death shrieks of the banshee floating over the White House lawns at night, and even Billy Graham had deserted him. So Clawson, in a stroke of cheap genius, put a sybaritic Jesuit priest and a mentally retarded rabbi on the payroll and sent them forth to do battle with the forces of evil.

Father John McLaughlin, the Jesuit, wallowed joyfully in his role as 'Nixon's priest' for a month or so, but his star faded fast when it was learned he was pulling down more than $25,000 a year for his efforts and living in a luxury apartment at the Watergate. His superiors in the church were horrified, but McLaughlin gave them the back of his hand and, instead, merely cranked up his speechmaking act. In the end, however, not even Clawson could live with the insistent rumour that the good Jesuit Father was planning to marry his girlfriend. This was too much, they say, for the rigid sensibilities of General Haig, the White House chief of staff, whose brother was a legitimate priest in Baltimore. McLaughlin disappeared very suddenly, after six giddy weeks on the national stage, and nothing has been heard of him since.

But Clawson was ready for that. No sooner had the priest been deep-sixed than he unveiled another holy man – the Rabbi Baruch Korff, a genuine dingbat with barely enough sense to tie his own shoes, but who eagerly lent his name and his flaky presence to anything Clawson aimed him at. Under the banner of something called the 'National Citizens' Committee for Fairness to the President', he 'organized' rallies, dinner parties and press conferences all over the country. One of his main financial backers was Hamilton Fish Sr, a notorious fascist and the father of New York Congressman Hamilton Fish Jr, one of the Republican swing votes on the House Judiciary Committee who quietly voted for impeachment.

Only a month ago, the storms of destiny seemed to be subsiding for President Nixon. Among the knowledgeable in Washington, the conviction was growing that the impeachment campaign against him had spent its moment ... [But] it is now clear that the Knowledgeable were wrong, that they mistook a break in the clouds for lasting sunshine ...

R. W. Apple Jr, *New York Times*, 28 July 1974

In fact, however, Nixon was already doomed by the time the Rodino committee got around to voting. The unanimous Supreme Court vote on the question of 'executive privilege' with regard to the sixty-four disputed tapes was the beginning of the end. Nixon had known all along that the release of those tapes would finish him – but he had consistently lied about their contents: not only to the press and the public, but also to his wife and his daughters and all the hardcore loyalists on his staff. He lied about the tapes to Barry Goldwater and Gerry Ford, to Hugh Scott and John Rhodes, to Al Haig and Pat Buchanan and even to his own attorney, James St Clair – who was stupid enough, like the others, to have believed him when he swore that the tapes he refused to let anybody listen to would finally prove his innocence.

Both of his lawyers, in fact, had done everything in their power to *avoid* hearing the goddamn things. It finally required a direct order from Judge Sirica, on two separate occasions, to compel Buzhardt and St Clair to listen to the tapes. Buzhardt was first, and within hours after hearing the fatal conversation with Haldeman of 23 June 1972, he was rushed to the intensive care ward of a private hospital in Virginia with a serious 'heart attack' that rendered him incommunicado for almost two months.

I was sitting in a bar called the Class Reunion, about two blocks from the White House, when I heard the tragic news ... And I recall saying to *Boston Globe* correspondent Marty Nolan: 'We'll never see Buzhardt again. They can't afford to let him live. If he survives whatever Ziegler put in his coffee when he was listening to those tapes, Haldeman will go out there and stick a hatpin up his nose while he's wasted on Demerol, jam it straight into his brain when the nurse gets out of the room. Take my word for it, Marty. I know how these people operate. Buzhardt will never leave that hospital alive.'

Nolan nodded, oblivious to Buzhardt's grim fate. At that point, almost every journalist in Washington assigned to the Nixon deathwatch had been averaging about two hours sleep a night since the beginning of summer. Many were weak and confused, succumbing to drink or drugs whenever possible. Others seemed to hover from day to day on the brink of terminal fatigue. Radio and TV reporters in the White House pressroom were reduced to tearing articles out of the nearest newspaper and reading them verbatim straight over the air – while the newspaper and magazine people would tape the live broadcasts and then transcribe them word for word under their own bylines. By the end of July, the prospect of having to cover an impeachment debate in the House and then a trial in the Senate for three or four months without relief was almost unbearable. As August began and Nixon still showed no signs of giving up, there was more and more talk of 'the suicide option'.

Last Breakfast at the White House ... The Scumbag I Passed to a New Generation ... Cold Turkey Swoops Down & Panic for Watergate Junkies

---

Sometime around dawn on the Friday morning of Richard Milhous Nixon's last breakfast in the White House I put on my swimming trunks and a red rain parka, laced my head with some grey Argentine snuff, and took an elevator down to the big pool below my window in the National Affairs Suite at the Washington Hilton. It was still raining, so I carried my portable TV set, a notebook and four bottles of Bass Ale in a waterproof canvas bag.

The lower lobby was empty, except for the night watchman – a meaty black gentleman whose main duty was to keep people like me out of the pool at night, but we had long since come to a friendly understanding on this subject. It was against the rules to swim when the pool was closed but there was no rule to prevent a Doctor of Divinity from going out there to meditate on the end of the diving board.

'Mornin', Doc,' said the watchman. 'Up a little early, ain't you? Especially on a nasty day like this.'

'Nasty?' I replied. 'What are you – some kind of goddamn Uncle Tom Republican? Don't you know who's leaving town today?'

He looked puzzled for a moment, then his face cracked into a grin. 'You're right, by God! I almost forgot. We finally got rid of that man, didn't we, Doc?' He nodded happily. 'Yes sir, we finally got rid of him.'

I reached into my bag and opened two Bass Ales. 'This is a time for celebration,' I said, handing him one of the bottles. I held mine out in front of me: 'To Richard Nixon,' I said, 'may he choke on the money he stole.'

The watchman glanced furtively over his shoulder before lifting his ale for the toast. The clink of the two bottles coming together echoed briefly in the vast, deserted lobby.

'See you later,' I said. 'I have to meditate for a while, then hustle down to the White House to make sure he really leaves. I won't believe it until I see it with my own eyes.'

The flat surface of the pool was pocked with millions of tiny raindrops beating steadily down on the water. There was a chain lock on the gate, so I climbed over the fence and walked down to the deep end, where I located a dry spot under a tree near the diving board. The *CBS Morning News* would be on in about twenty minutes; I turned on the TV set, adjusted the aerial and turned the screen so I could see it from the pool about twenty feet away. It was a system I'd worked out last summer at the Senate Watergate hearings: After every two laps, I could look over the edge of the pool and check the screen to see if Hughes Rudd's face had appeared yet. When it did, I would climb out of the water and lie down on the grass in front of the set – turn up the sound, light a cigarette, open a fresh Bass Ale and take notes while I watched the tiny screen for a general outline of whatever action Sam Ervin's Roman circus might be expected to generate that day.

I stayed out there by the pool for almost two hours, sliding in and out of the water to run a few laps and then back out to stretch out on the grass to make a note now and then on the news. Not much was happening, except for a few kinky interviews down by the White House gate with people who claimed to have been on the deathwatch for three days and nights without sleeping ... But very few of them could even begin to explain why they were doing it. At least half the crowd around the White House during those last few days looked like people who spend every weekend prowling the demolition derby circuit.

The only other action on the news that Friday morning was an occasional rerun of Nixon's official resignation speech from the night before. I had watched it with Vetter in the Watergate bar. It seemed like a good place to be on that night, because I had also been there on the night of 17 June 1972 – while the Watergate burglary was happening five floors above my head.

But after I'd watched Nixon's speech for the third time, a strange feeling of nervousness began working on me and I decided to get out of town as soon as possible. The movie was over – or at least it would be over in two or three hours. Nixon was leaving at 10 : 00, and Ford would be sworn in at noon. I wanted to be there on the White House lawn when Nixon was lifted off. That would be the end of *my* movie.

It was still raining when I left and the pool was still empty. I put the TV set back in the canvas bag and climbed over the gate by the lifeguard shack. Then I stopped and looked back for a moment, knowing I would never come back to this place, and if I did it would not be the same. The pool would be the same, and it would be easy enough to pick up a case of Bass Ale or a battery TV set ... And I could even come down here on rainy summer mornings and watch the morning news ...

But there would not be this kind of morning any more, because the main ingredient for that mix was no longer available in Washington; and if you asked any of the people who were known to have a real taste for it, the hard-core Nixon *aficionados*, they all understood that it would not be available again for a hell of a long time and probably never.

Nobody even talks about substitutes or something almost exactly the same. The mould disappeared about three minutes after they made that evil bastard ... and although there was never any doubt about who stole it, nobody had any proof.

No ... even with the pool and the ale and grass and the portable TV set, the morning news will not be the same without the foul spectre of Richard Nixon glaring out of the tube. But the war is over now and he lost ... Gone but not forgotten, missed but not mourned; we will not see another one like him for quite a while. He was dishonest to a fault, the truth was not in him, and if it can be said that he resembled any other living animal in this world, it could only have been the hyena.

I took a cab down to the White House and pushed through the sullen mob on the sidewalk to the guardhouse window. The cop inside glanced

337

at my card, then looked up – fixing me with a heavy-lidded quaalude stare for just an instant, then nodded and pushed his buzzer to open the gate. The pressroom in the west wing was empty, so I walked outside to the rose garden, where a big olive-drab helicopter was perched on the lawn, about 100 feet out from the stairs. The rain had stopped and a long, red carpet was laid out on the wet grass from the White House door to the helicopter. I eased through the crowd of photographers and walked out, looking back at the White House, where Nixon was giving his final address to a shocked crowd of White House staffers. I examined the aircraft very closely, and I was just about to climb into it when I heard a loud rumbling behind me; I turned around just in time to see Richard and Pat coming towards me, trailing their daughters and followed closely by Gerald Ford and Betty. Their faces were grim and they were walking very slowly; Nixon had a glazed smile on his face, not looking at anybody around him, and walked like a wooden Indian full of thorazine.

His face was a greasy death mask. I stepped back out of his way and nodded hello but he didn't seem to recognize me. I lit a cigarette and watched him climb the steps to the door of the helicopter ... Then he spun around very suddenly and threw his arms straight up in the famous twin-victory signal; his eyes were still glazed, but he seemed to be looking over the heads of the crowd at the White House.

Nobody was talking. A swarm of photographers rushed the plane as Nixon raised his arms – but his body had spun around too fast for his feet, and as his arms went up I saw him losing his balance. The grimace on his face went slack, then he bounced off the door and stumbled into the cockpit. Pat and Ziegler were already inside, Ed Cox and Tricia went in quickly without looking back, and a Marine in dress blues shut the door and jumped away as the big rotor blades began turning and the engine cranked up to a dull, whining roar.

I was so close that the noise hurt my ears. The rotor blades were invisible now, but the wind was getting heavier; I could feel it pressing my eyeballs back into their sockets. For an instant I thought I could see Richard Nixon's face pressed up to the window. Was he smiling? Was it Nixon? I couldn't be sure. And now it made no difference.

The wind blast from the rotors was blowing people off-balance now; photographers were clutching their equipment against their bodies and Gerald Ford was leading his wife back towards the White House with a stony scowl on his face.

I was still very close to the helicopter, watching the tyres. As the beast began rising, the tyres became suddenly fat; there was no more weight on them ... The helicopter went straight up and hovered for a moment, then swooped down towards the Washington Monument and then angled up into the fog. Richard Nixon was gone.

The end came so suddenly and with so little warning that it was almost as if a muffled explosion in the White House had sent up a mushroom cloud to announce that the scumbag had been passed to what will have to pose for now as another generation. The main reaction to Richard Nixon's passing – especially among journalists who had been on the deathwatch for two years – was a wild and wordless orgasm of long-awaited relief that tailed off almost instantly to a dull, post-coital sort of depression that still endures.

Within hours after Nixon's departure, every bar in downtown Washington normally frequented by reporters was a sinkhole of gloom. Several hours after Gerald Ford was sworn in, I found ex-Kennedy speechwriter Dick Goodwin in a bar not far from the *Rolling Stone* office across the street from the White House. He was slumped in a booth by himself, staring blankly into his drink like a man who had just had his teeth ripped out by a savage bill collector.

'I feel totally drained,' he said. 'It's like the circus just left town. This is the end of the longest running continuous entertainment this city ever had.' He waved his arm at the waitress for another drink. 'It's the end of an era. Now I know how all those rock freaks felt when they heard the Beatles were breaking up.'

I felt the same way. All I wanted to do was get the hell out of town as soon as possible. I had just come from the White House pressroom, where a smoglike sense of funk – or 'smunk' as somebody over there might describe it – had settled on the room within minutes after Ford took the oath. The deathwatch was finally over; the evil demon had been purged and the good guys had won – or at least the bad guys had lost, but that was not quite the same thing. Within hours after Richard Nixon left Washington, it was painfully clear that Frank Mankiewicz had spoken too soon when he'd predicted, just a few weeks before the fall, that Washington would be 'the Hollywood of the seventies'. Without Nixon to stir up its thin juices, the Washington of the seventies could look forward to the same grim fate as Cinderella's gilded coach at the stroke of midnight. It would turn back into a pumpkin, and any mysterious shoes left lying around on the deserted ballroom floors of the Watergate era would not interest a genial pragmatist like Gerald Ford. He would not have much time, for a while, to concern himself with anything but the slide into national bankruptcy that Nixon had left him to cope with ... And, despite all its menacing implications, the desperate plight of the national economy was not a story that called up the same kind of journalistic adrenalin that Washington and most of the country had been living on for so long that the prospect of giving it up caused a serious panic in the ranks of all the Watergate junkies who never even knew they were hooked until the cold turkey swooped into their closets.

We all knew it was coming – the press, the Congress, the public, all the backstage handlers in Washington and even Nixon's own henchmen – but we all had our own different timetables, and when his ballon suddenly burst on that fateful Monday in August, it happened so fast that none of us were ready to deal with it. The Nixon presidency never really had time to *crumble*, except in hazy retrospect ... In reality, it *disintegrated*, with all the speed and violence of some flimsy and long-abandoned gazebo suddenly blasted to splinters by chain lightning.

The bolts came so fast that it was hard to keep count. On the Wednesday morning after the House Judiciary Committee voted to recommend his impeachment, Richard Nixon was a beleaguered Republican president with powerful Republican (and Southern Democratic) allies in both the House and the Senate: His impeachment seemed almost certain, but the few people in Washington crass enough to bet money on a thing like this were still calling his chances of conviction in the Senate 'just about even'. This prognosis held for about seventy-two hours, which was time enough for almost everybody in Washington to start gearing down for an endless summer – a humid nightmare of booze, sweat and tension, of debate in the House, delay in the courts and finally a trial in the Senate that might drag on until Christmas.

It was an ugly prospect, even for those of us who openly welcomed the prospect of seeing Richard Nixon in the dock. On the last afternoon of the Judiciary hearings, I found myself leaning against a tree on the grass of the US Capitol lawn, hopelessly stoned, staring up at the huge golden dome (while loud knots of tourists wearing Bermuda shorts and Instamatic cameras climbed the marble steps a hundred yards in front of me) and wondering, 'What in the fuck am I doing here? What kind of sick and twisted life have I fallen into that would cause me to spend some of the best hours of my life in a cryptlike room full of cameras, hot lights and fearful politicians debating the guilt or innocence of Richard Milhous Nixon?'

The Politician and the Pawnbroker ... The *New York Times* Hits the Trenches, The *Washington Post* Opens a Multi-Pronged Panzer Offensive ... Lessons of a Crime Spree in Lexington ... A Compound Tangent Mushrooms Dangerously

Innocence? It is difficult even to type that word on the same page with Nixon's name. The man was *born* guilty – not in the traditional Vatican sense of 'original sin', but in a darker and highly personalized sense that Nixon himself seems to have recognized from the very beginning.

Nixon's entire political career – and in fact his whole life – is a gloomy monument to the notion that not even pure schizophrenia or malignant psychosis can prevent a determined loser from rising to the top of the heap in this strange society we have built for ourselves in the name of 'democracy' and 'free enterprise'. For most of his life, the mainspring of Richard Nixon's energy and ambition seems to have been a deep and unrecognized need to overcome, at all costs, that sense of having been *born guilty* – not for crimes or transgressions *already* committed, but for those he somehow sensed he was fated to commit as he grappled his way to the summit. If Nixon had been born Jewish, instead of black Irish, he would probably have been a pawnbroker instead of a politician, not only because the suburbs of Los Angeles would never have elected a Jewish congressman in 1946, but because running a big-league pawnshop would have fuelled him with the same kind of guilt-driven energy that most of our politicians – from the county assessor level all the way up to the White House – seem to thrive on.

On any given morning, both the politician and the pawnbroker can be sure that by sundown the inescapable realities of their calling will have forced them to do something they would rather not have to explain, not even to themselves. The details might vary, but the base line never changes: 'I will feel more guilty tomorrow than I felt yesterday ... But of course I have no choice: *They* have made me what I am and by God, *they'll* pay for it.'

So the cycle runs on. Both the politician and the pawnbroker are doomed to live like junkies, hooked on the mutant energy of their own unexplainable addictions.

In this baleful sense, Richard Nixon is definitely 'one of us' – as *New York Times* columnist Tom Wicker wrote, in a very different context, back in the early sixties. The phrase was Conrad's, from *Lord Jim*: 'He was one of us ...' – and when I read Wicker's piece more than a decade ago I remember feeling angry that the *New York Times* had the power to hire another one of these goddamn gothic Southern sots and turn him loose to stumble around Washington and spew out this kind of bullshit.

Anybody stupid enough to identify with Richard Nixon the same way Conrad's Marlow identified with Lord Jim was beyond either help or any hope of credibility, I felt, and for the next seven or eight years I dismissed everything Wicker wrote as the mumblings of a hired fool ... And when Wicker's point of view began swinging very noticeably in the direction of my own, in the late 1960s, I was almost as disturbed – for entirely different reasons – as the *Times* editors in New York who also noticed the drift and swiftly deposed him from his heir-apparent role to James Reston as the new chief of the paper's Washington Bureau.

The masthead of the *New York Times*'s Washington Bureau is a reliable weathervane for professional observers of the changing political climate. Control of the bureau is usually in the hands of somebody the magnates in New York believe is more or less on the same wavelength as the men in control of the government. Arthur Krock, for instance, got along fine with Eisenhower, but he couldn't handle the Kennedys and was replaced by Reston, a JFK partisan in 1960 and a 'Roosevelt coalition' neopopulist who also got along well with Lyndon Johnson. But when Johnson quit in 1968 and the future looked very uncertain, Reston was promoted to a management job in New York and was succeeded by Wicker at about the same time Robert Kennedy was deciding to make his move for the presidency; but when Bobby was killed and McCarthy collapsed, the *Times* hedged its bet on Humphrey by deposing Wicker and replacing him with Max Frankel, a smooth and effective diplomat/journalist who could presumably get along with either Hubert *or* Nixon ... But not even Frankel could handle four more years, apparently, and the Nixon/Agnew landslide in 1972 forced the admittedly anti-Nixon *Times* into a stance of agonizing reappraisal. Frankel moved up to New York, and since the most obvious candidates for his job were relatively liberal young turks like Bob Semple, Anthony Lewis or Johnny Apple, who were clearly out of step with the mandate of vengeance that Nixon claimed by virtue of his shattering victory over McGovern, the *Times* management in New York made a fateful policy decision that would soon come back to haunt them.

On the theory that the best offence, at that point, was a good defence, they pulled in their editorial horns for the duration and sent an elderly, conservative mediocrity named Clifton Daniel down from the executive backwaters of New York to keep the aggressive Washington Bureau under control. At almost the same time, they hired one of Nixon's top speechwriters, Bill Safire, and gave him a prominent ranking columnist's spot on the *Times* editorial pages. Both of these moves were thinly veiled concessions to the prospect of a revenge-hungry Nixon/Agnew juggernaut that had already telegraphed its intention to devote as much of its second (and final) term energies to their 'enemies' in the 'national media' as they had already successfully devoted in the first term to scuttling the US Supreme Court.

It was clearly a management decision, safely rooted in the *Times* concept of itself as 'a newspaper of record', not advocacy – and when you're in the busines of recording history, you don't declare war on the people who're making it. 'If you want to get along, go along.' That is an ancient political axiom often attributed to Boss Tweed, the legendary 'pol' and brute fixer who many journalists in Washington insist still sits on the editorial board of the *New York Times*.

Which is probably not true, if only because the *Times* got burned so badly by going along with Tweed's crude logic in the winter of 1972–73 that the whole Washington Bureau – except perhaps Clifton Daniel – is still reeling from the beating they took from the *Washington Post* on the Nixon/Watergate story. While the *Times* was getting down in the trenches and methodically constructing its own journalistic version of a Maginot line against the inevitable Nixon/Agnew offensive, the *Post* was working twenty-five hours a day on a multipronged panzer-style offensive that would soon become one of the most devastating scoops in the history of American journalism.

Rather than be cowed by Nixon and his army of power-crazed thugs, the *Post* elected to meet them head-on, hitting both flanks and the centre all at once – and when the bloody dust began settling, just a few weeks ago, with both Agnew and Nixon having resigned in disgrace, the *Washington Post* had unquestionably replaced the *New York Times* as the nation's premier political newspaper.

To compensate for the loss of what is widely regarded as one of the fattest and heaviest jobs in journalism, the *Times* gave Wicker a column – his own chunk of turf, as it were – and that unexpected burst of freedom seemed to have an almost consciousness-expanding effect on his head. When I met him for the first time in Miami in that star-crossed political summer of 1972, he was writing one of the sanest columns on the market and he talked like a happy man.

We were sitting at a beach table near the surf, outside the Fontainebleau Hotel on Miami Beach, taking a break from the chaos of the Democratic Convention, and I took the opportunity to tell him about my reaction to his long-ago comment on Nixon.

'Yeah,' he said. 'I'm not sure what I was thinking when I wrote that, but—'

'No,' I said. 'You were right.'

He stared at me, looking puzzled.

It was one of those days that we all hit once in a while when everything you mean to say sounds wrong when you hear it coming out of your mouth. I tried briefly to explain what I really meant, but even the explanation came out bent, so I decided to drop the subject ... What I had in mind, I think, was the idea that Nixon really *was* 'one of us' – not in Conrad's sense of that term, or my own, but as an almost perfect expression of 'the American way of life' that I'd been so harshly immersed in for the past eight or nine months of travelling constantly around the country to cover the presidential primaries.

Jesus! This idea seems just as tangled tonight as it did two years ago when I was trying to explain it to Wicker – so I think I'll let it drop, once again, and move on to something else ... But not without a final backward glance at the election results in November of 72, when Richard Nixon was re-elected to the White House by the largest margin of any president since George Washington. There is no way to erase that ominous fact from the record books – any more than Nixon will ever be able to erase from the history books the fact that he was the first American president to be driven out of the White House because of admittedly criminal behaviour while in office.

Looking back on that crippled conversation with Wicker in Miami, it occurs to me that maybe almost everybody in the country – except possibly Wicker – might have been spared what Gerald Ford called 'our national nightmare' if Tom had been kept on as the *New York Times* Washington Bureau chief in 1968, instead of being converted to a columnist. The social and political pressures of the job would have driven him half crazy, but his then emerging sense of outrage at the whole style and content of the Nixon administration might have been contagious enough, within the bureau, to encourage a more aggressive kind of coverage among the *Times* reporters he would have been assigning to look behind Nixon's façade.

As it turned out, however, those fascist bastards had to be given so much rope that they came close to hanging all the rest of us along with themselves, before the *Washington Post* finally filled the power vacuum created by the *New York Times*'s sluggish coverage of those four years when Nixon and his fixers were organizing vengeful plans like John Dean's list of 'our enemies' to be harassed by the IRS, and the Tom Charles Huston 'Domestic Intelligence Plant' that amounted to nothing less than the creation of a White House gestapo.

But the climate of those years was so grim that half the Washington press corps spent more time worrying about having their telephones tapped than they did about risking the wrath of Haldeman, Ehrlichman and Colson by poking at the weak seams of a Mafia-style administration that began cannibalizing the whole government just as soon as it came into power. Nixon's *capos* were never subtle; they swaggered into Washington like a conquering army, and the climate of fear they engendered apparently neutralized the *New York Times* along with all the other pockets of potential resistance. Nixon had to do everything but fall on his own sword before anybody in the Washington socio-political establishment was willing to take him on.

Like the black teenage burglars who are terrorizing chic Georgetown these days, Nixon conquered so easily that he soon lost any fear of being caught. Washington police have noted a strange pattern involving burglaries in Georgetown and other posh neighbourhoods in the white ghetto of the city's northwest sector: A home that has been robbed once is far more likely to be hit again than a home that has never been hit at all. Once they spot an easy mark, the burglars get lazy and prefer to go back for seconds and even thirds, rather than challenge a new target.

The police seem surprised at this pattern but in fact it's fairly traditional among amateurs – or at least among the type I used to hang around with. About fifteen years ago, when I was into that kind of thing, I drifted into Lexington, Kentucky, one evening with two friends who shared my tastes; we moved into an apartment across the street from a gas station which we broke into and robbed on three consecutive nights.

On the morning after the first hit, we stood transfixed at the apartment window, drinking beer and watching the local police 'investigating' the robbery ... And I remember thinking, now that poor fool over there has probably never been hit before, and what he's thinking now is that his odds of being hit again anytime soon are almost off the board. Hell, how many gas stations have ever been robbed two nights in a row?

So we robbed it again that night, and the next morning we stood at the window drinking beer and watched all manner of hell break loose between the station owner and the cops around the gas pumps across the street. We couldn't hear what they were saying, but the proprietor was waving his arms crazily and screaming at the cops, as if he suspected *them* of doing it.

Christ, this is wonderful, I thought. If we hit the bugger again tonight he'll go stark raving mad tomorrow morning when the cops show up ... which was true: On the next morning, after three consecutive robberies, the parking lot of that gas station was like a war zone, but this time the cops showed up with reinforcements. In addition to the two police cruisers, the lot filled up with chromeless, dust-covered Fords and crew-cut men wearing baggy brown suits and shoes with gum-rubber soles. While some of them spoke earnestly with the proprietor, others dusted the doorknobs, window latches and the cash register for fingerprints.

It was hard to know, from our window across the street, if we were watching the FBI, local detectives or insurance agency investigators at work ... But in any case I figured they'd have the whole station ringed with armed guards for the next few nights, so we decided to leave well enough alone.

About six in the evening, however, we stopped there and had the tank filled up with ethyl. There were about six bony-faced men hanging around the office, killing the time until dark by studying road maps and tyre-pressure charts. They paid no attention to us until I tried to put a dime in the coke machine.

'It ain't workin',' one of them said. He shuffled over and pulled the whole front of the machine open, like a broken refrigerator, and lifted a coke bottle out of the circular rack. I gave him the dime and he dropped it into his pocket.

'What's wrong with the machine?' I asked, remembering how hard it had been to rip the bastard open with a crowbar about twelve hours earlier to reach the money box.

'No concern of yours,' he muttered, lighting up a Marvel and staring out at the pump where the attendant was making change for a ten-dollar bill after cleaning our windshield and checking the oil. 'Don't worry,' he said. 'There's some folks gonna be a lot worse off than that there machine before this night's out tonight.' He nodded. 'This time we're *ready* for them sonsabitches.'

And they were. I noticed a double-barrelled shotgun standing in a corner by the rack full of oil cans. Two big coon hounds were asleep on the greasy linoleum floor, with their collar chains looped around the base of the chewing gum machine. I felt a quick flash of greed as I eyed the glass bulb filled with all those red, white, blue and green gum balls. We had looted the place of almost everything else, and I felt a pang of regret at having to leave the gum machine untouched: All those pennies just sitting there with nobody to fondle them ...

But in retrospect I think that moment was the beginning of wisdom for me. We had pushed our luck far enough with that place and the world was full of colourful gum-ball machines. There was a weird and menacing edge in the man's voice that it took me a long time to forget.

We drove downtown and cruised around drinking warm beer for a while, then we robbed a crowded liquor store on Main Street by starting a fight with the clerks and then cleaning out the cash register while they struggled to defend themselves.

We got less than $200 out of that one, as I recall – about the same as we'd picked up from three hits on the gas station – and on the way out of town I remember thinking that maybe I could do something a little better in this life than robbing gas stations and liquor stores. After taking enough crazy risks to put all three of us in prison for at least five years, we had about $135 apiece to show for it and about half of that was already spent on gas, food, beer and hiring winos to buy whisky for us because we were too young to get served and the winos were charging double for anything they bought for us.

That weekend crime spree in Lexington was my last haul, as they say; I even gave up shoplifting, which altered my lifestyle pretty severely for a while because it had taken me several years to master the kind of skill and mental attitude it takes to walk into a jewellery store and come out with six watches, or in the front door of a tavern and hassle the bartender with a false ID long enough to let a friend slip out the back door with a case of Old Forester ... But when I quit that gig, I quit it completely and after fifteen years on the wagon my skills are so hopelessly atrophied that now I can't even steal a newspaper from an open rack on the street.

Ah ... mother of jabbering God, how in the hell did I get off on that tangent about teenage street crime? This is supposed to be a deep and serious political essay about Richard Nixon ...

Although maybe that wasn't such a tangent, after all. The original point, I think, had to do with street-punk mentality that caused Nixon to push his luck so far that it was finally almost impossible *not* to get himself busted. For a while he had the luck and arrogance of a half-smart amateur. From their base in the White House, Nixon and the LA account execs he brought with him treated the old-line Washington power structure with the same kind of contempt that young burglars casing Georgetown seem to have for the forts of the rich and powerful – or that I had for that poor bastard who owned the gas station in Lexington.

This is a very hard thing for professional cops, journalists or investigators to cope with. Like doctors and lawyers, most of the best minds in police work have been trained since puberty to think in terms of patterns and precedents: Anything original tends to have the same kind of effect on their investigative machinery as a casually mutilated punch-card fed into a computer. The immediate result is chaos and false conclusions ... But both cops and computers are programmed to know when they've been jammed by a wild card or a joker, and in both cases there are usually enough competent technicians standing by to locate the problem and get the machinery working again pretty quickly.

Right ... and now we have gone off on a dangerous compound tangent. And it has mushroomed into something unmanageable ... But before we zoom off in whatever direction might come next, it would be unfair not to mention that the *Times* was the first paper to break the Pentagon Papers story, a command decision that forced Nixon and his would-be enforcers to come out in the open with fangs bared, snarling threats to have everybody connected with the publication of the Pentagon Papers either lashed into jail or subpoenaed into so many courtrooms that all their minds would snap before they finally wound up in the poorhouse.

As it turned out, however, the *Times* management strapped on its collective balls and announced that they were prepared to go to the mat with Nixon on that one – a surprisingly tough stance that was almost instantly backed up by influential papers like the *Los Angeles Times*, the *Washington Post* and the *St Louis Post-Dispatch* ... And the appearance of that solid front, however shaky, caused serious turmoil in the White House. Spiro Agnew was pried loose from his kickback racket and sent out on the stump to stir up the silent majority against the 'radic-libs' and 'liberal élitists' of the 'eastern media establishment' – the 'nattering nabobs of negativism'.

Jesus! Those were the days, eh?

STRANGE INTERLUDE: An Aborted Prediction, for the Record ... Grim Dispatches from San Clemente: A Pitiful Basket Case, a Chronic Bed-Wetter ... The Millionaire Felon on the Federal Dole ... The Sudden News from Mister Ford

---

Won't you fly O eagle fly
You better run little cottontail run
I hope you both live long enough
To see the setting sun
          Marshall Tucker Band

6 September 1974

The headline in today's *Washington Post* says Richard Nixon is 'lonely and depressed' down there in his exile hideout in San Clemente. He sucks eggs for breakfast and wanders back and forth on the beach, spitting frequently into the surf and brooding about some vicious Polack whose name he can't remember ... Some low-life friend of John Connally from Houston; the same white-haired little bugger who caused all the trouble with the Supreme Court, and now he has a runaway Grand Jury full of uppity niggers who – in Nixon's own words – 'want to pick the carcass'.

Indeed ... What the hell is a carcass good for anyway, except to pick at? Gnaw the skull, suck the bones, then soak the bastard with gasoline and toss a match on it.

Jesus! How much more of this cheapjack bullshit can we be expected to take from that stupid little gunsel? Who gives a fuck if he's lonely and depressed out there in San Clemente? If there were any such thing as true justice in this world, his rancid carcass would be somewhere down around Easter Island right now, in the belly of a hammerhead shark.

But, no – he is sitting out there in the imitation-leather-lined study of his oceanside estate, still guarded constantly by a detail of Secret Service agents and still communicating with the outside world through an otherwise unemployable $40,000-a-year mouthpiece named Ron Ziegler ... and still tantalizing the national press with the same kind of shrewdly programmed leaks that served him so well in the last months of his doomed presidency ...

'He's terribly depressed, with much to be depressed about,' says a friend. 'Anyone would be depressed in his situation. I don't mean he's going off the deep end. I just mean that everything happened to him, seemingly all at once, and he doesn't know what to do about it.'

Well ... shucks. I'd be tempted to put my mind to the task of helping the poor bastard figure out 'what to do about' this cruel nutcracker that he somehow stumbled into ... but I have a powerful suspicion that probably that gang of mean niggers in Washington has already solved Nixon's problem for him. They are going to indict the bastard and try to put him on trial.

Nixon knows this. He is not the kind of lawyer you'd want to hire for anything serious, but the reality of his situation *vis-à-vis* the Watergate grand jury is so bleak that even *he* has to grasp it ... and this is the reason, I think, for the more or less daily front-page comments on his half-mad and pathetically crippled mental condition. He has devised another one of his famous fourth-down game breakers – the same kind of three-fisted brainstorm that climaxed with his decision to defuse the whole impeachment process by releasing his own version of 'the tapes', or the time he figured out how to put a quick lid on the Watergate burglary investigation by blaming the whole thing on John Dean.

According to one Washington topsider, widely respected as an unimpeachable source and a shrewd judge of presidential character: 'Dick Nixon is in a league all by himself when you're talking about style and grace under pressure. His instincts when the crunch comes are absolutely amazing.'

Nobody will argue with that – although his strategy since leaving the White House has been marked by an unnatural focus on subtlety. The savage warrior of old now confronts us in the guise of a pitiful, frightened old pol – a whipped and broken man, totally at the mercy of his enemies and baffled by the firestorm of disasters that drove him out of the White House.

Which may even be partially true: He will probably go to his grave believing he was not *really* guilty of anything except underestimating the power of his enemies ... But the fact remains that Jaworski will very likely break the news of Nixon's formal indictment before this article appears on the newsstands, and when that happens there will be only one man in the country with the power to arbitrarily short-circuit the legal machinery that in theory could land Richard Nixon in the same cellblock with John Dean.

That man is Gerald Ford, but he will have a hard time justifying a blanket presidential pardon for an admitted felon without at least the *appearance* of a ground swell of public sympathy to back him up.

So we may as well get braced for a daily dose of extremely grim news out of San Clemente, once Nixon is formally indicted. We will hear reports that the ex-president frequently bursts into tears for no reason at all, that he utters heart-rending screams every night in his sleep, and the *Los Angeles Herald-Examiner* will quote an unnamed 'prominent Beverly Hills psychiatrist' who will describe Nixon as a 'pitiful basket case' and 'a chronic bedwetter'. And if Ford still seems reluctant to let Nixon go free, we will start seeing front-page 'exclusive photos' of Nixon alone on the beach, staring soulfully at the sunset with tears drooling out of his eyes.

It will be a carefully orchestrated public relations campaign in the classic Nixon tradition. Ziegler will hold daily press briefings and read finely crafted descriptions of the former president's pitiful condition from the typewriter of Ray Price, Nixon's former chief speechwriter at the White House. Both Price and Pat Buchanan, the left and right forks of Nixon's tongue ever since he decided to make his move on the White House back in 1965, showed up at the San Clemente fortress in early September, both insisting they had just come out to say hello and 'check up on the old man'. As it happened, however, they both appeared about the same time rumours began surfacing in New York about a $2-million advance that Nixon had been offered for his memoirs.

Neither Price nor Buchanan claimed to know anything definite about the book offer, but in New York Spiro Agnew's literary agent was telling everybody who asked that the Nixon deal could be closed momentarily for at least $2 million and maybe more.

That is a hell of a lot of money for *anybody's* memoirs – even people who might reasonably be expected to tell the truth. But even a ridiculously fraudulent version of his five and a half wretched years in the White House and his own twisted view of the scandal that finished him off would be an automatic best seller if the book-buying public could be conned somehow into believing Richard Nixon was actually the author.

Meanwhile, with either Price or Buchanan or both standing ready to write his memoirs for him, Nixon was pondering an offer from *Reader's Digest* to sign on as a 'consulting editor' at a salary of $100,000 a year ... And Thursday of that week, President Ford made headlines by urging the Congress to appropriate $850,000 to cover Nixon's pension, living expenses and other costs of the painful transition from the White House to San Clemente. When the $850,000 runs out, he will have to scrimp until 1 July of next year, when he will pick up another $400,000 that will have to last him until 1 July 1976. For as long as he lives, Richard Nixon will be on the federal dole forever at $400,000 a year – $60,000 pension, $96,000 to cover his personal staff salaries, $40,000 for travel, $21,000 to cover his telephone bills and $100,000 for 'miscellaneous'.

On top of his $400,000 annual expense account, Nixon's twenty-four-hour-a-day Secret Service protection will cost the taxpayers between $500 and $1000 a day for as long as he lives – a conservative figure, considering the daily cost of things like helicopters, patrol boats, walkie-talkies and car telephones, along with salaries and living expenses for ten or twelve full-time agents. There is also the $40,000 a year Ron Ziegler still commands, as a ranking public servant. Add another $30,000 to $50,000 each for personal aides like Stephen Bull and Rose Mary Woods, plus all their living and travel expenses – and the cost of maintaining Richard Nixon in exile adds up to something like $750,000 a year ... and these are merely the *expenses*. His personal income will presumably derive from things like the $2 million advance on his memoirs, his $100,000 a year stipend from *Reader's Digest*, and the $5000 a crack he can average, with no effort at all, on the year-round lecture circuit.

So ... what we are looking at here is a millionaire ex-president and admitted felon; a congenital thief and pathological liar who spent twenty-eight years on the public sugar tit and then quit just in time to avoid the axe. If he had fought to the bitter end, as he'd promised Julie he would 'as long as even one senator believes in me', he risked losing about ninety-five per cent of the $400,000 annual allowance he became qualified for under the 'former presidents act' by resigning ... But a president who gets impeached, convicted and dragged out of the White House by US marshals is not covered by the 'former presidents act'. If Nixon had fought to the end and lost – which had become absolutely inevitable by the time he resigned – he would have forfeited all but about $15,000 a year from the federal dole ... So, in retrospect, the reason he quit is as easy to see as the numbers on his personal balance sheet. The difference between resignation and being kicked out of office was about $385,000 a year for the rest of his life.

Most of this annual largesse will come, one way or another, out of the pockets of the taxpayers. *All* of the taxpayers. Even George and Eleanor McGovern will contribute a slice of their income to Richard Nixon's retirement fund ... And so will I, unless Jaworski can nail the bastard on enough felony counts to strip him not only of his right to vote, like Agnew, but also his key to the back door of the Federal Treasury – which is not very likely now that Ford has done everything but announce the date for when he will grant the pardon.

The White House announced yesterday a negotiated agreement with Richard M. Nixon under which the former president and the US government will have joint custody of White House tapes and presidential documents but with Mr Nixon determining who shall have access to them.

In the letter of agreement making him the 'sole legal owner of the papers and tapes until their future donation to the government', Mr Nixon specifically asserted his legal title to 'all literary rights' accompanying possession of the materials. Mr Nixon has reportedly been told that a book of memoirs would be worth at least $2 million.

Washington Post, 9 September 1974

President Ford virtually made up his mind five days ago to grant a pardon to former-President Richard M. Nixon.

On Wednesday, presidential counsel Philip Buchen met with Herbert Miller, Nixon's attorney, at the White House and disclosed that Ford was considering executive clemency.

Would Nixon accept a pardon? Buchen asked.

Miller responded that he did not know, according to Buchen. But after checking with Nixon by telephone – the ex-president was at his home in San Clemente, California – Miller reported that a pardon was acceptable.

With that, the pardon was set, though Ford was unable to announce the pardon publicly until yesterday morning because it took several days to complete the arrangements.

Washington Star-News, 9 September 1974

Only ten days ago, in the first formal press conference of his administration, Mr Ford had said that it would be 'unwise and untimely' of him to make any commitment to a pardon until legal action was taken.

But the president was aware that political reaction was building in favour of prosecution of Mr Nixon, a point dramatically confirmed by a Gallup Poll last week which showed that 56% of the American people thought that Mr Nixon should be tried while only 37% opposed such action.

Washington Post, 9 September 1974

Powerful Men Brought Weeping to Their Knees ... The Stinking Realities of Richard Nixon's Place in History ... The Mushwit Son-in-Law and the Last Tape

THE EX-PRESIDENT'S GIFTS

To the editor:

The letter of Sylvia Wallace (23 August), warning that 'we may yet see a Nixon renascent', caused me such grave concern that I immediately consulted the ineffable wisdom of the *I Ching* for some clue to the future of Mr Nixon. I was uneeringly directed to the Po Hexagram and the learned commentaries thereon. The book confirmed my worst fears: 'Its strong subject, notwithstanding the attempts against him, survives and acquires fresh vigour. The people again cherish their sovereign and the plotters have wrought to their own overthrow.'

The 'legal steps' that your correspondent suggests to prevent Nixon's rebirth could prove woefully ineffective. I suggest that, after hanging, the body be drawn, quartered and burned and the ashes buried in an unmarked grave in a distant field guarded by an élite corps, lest his hard-core followers come and steal the remains and proclaim: He is risen!

Please! If Mr Nixon regains popular favour, it will not be through any 'revisionism' or reworking of the facts supporting the charges of guilt. It will probably be that coming events will force a careful reevaluation of his contributions to the nation and crystallize an awareness of the misfortune suffered by the nation in the loss of his special gifts in these critical times. We may come to feel like the shepherd who had no sooner been conned by some pointy-eared gentleman into getting rid of his mean, tough sheep dog because of its fleas than the wolves reappeared on the scene.

Theodore P. Daly
Somers, New York
Letters to the editor
New York Times
4 September 1974

*

A prominent San Clemente supporter of Mr Nixon since he went to Congress in 1946, who asked not to be identified, said he had heard that the Lincoln Club of Orange County, made up largely of wealthy industrialists who contributed millions of dollars to Republican campaign coffers, including Mr Nixon's, had invited the former president to become a member of the select and influential group.

'You won't find Mr Nixon living the life of a recluse,' the Republican informant said. 'Now that he is clear of any criminal prosecution, don't be surprised if he comes back into California politics. I think he should. I'd like to see him run for Senator John V. Tunney's seat in 1976.'

New York Times, 9 September 1974

We are still too mired in it now to fit all the pieces together and understand what really happened in these last two frenzied years ... or to grasp that the real meaning of what our new president calls the 'national nightmare' and what historians will forever refer to as 'Watergate' will probably emerge not so much from the day-to-day events of the crisis, or even from its traumatic resolution – but more from what the survivors will eventually understand *was prevented from happening*.

I was out there on the crowded concrete floor of the Miami Beach Convention Center in August of 1972 when that howling mob of Republican delegates confirmed Richard Nixon's lust for another term in the White House with their constant, thunderous chant of 'FOUR MORE YEARS! FOUR MORE YEARS! FOUR MORE YEARS!'

It was bad enough, just listening to that demagogic swill – but I doubt if there were more than a dozen people in Miami that week who really understood what that cheap, demented little fascist punk had in mind for his four more years. It involved the systematic destruction of everything this country claims to stand for, except the rights of the rich to put saddles on the backs of the poor and use public funds to build jails for anybody who complained about it.

The tip of the iceberg began emerging about six months after Nixon took his second oath of office, when Senator Sam Ervin took his initially harmless-looking Watergate Committee act on national TV. It didn't catch on, at first; the networks were deluged with letters from angry housewives, cursing Ervin for depriving them of their daily soap operas – but after two or three weeks the Senate Watergate hearings were the hottest thing on television.

Here, by God, was a *real* soap opera: tragedy, treachery, weird humour and the constant suspense of never knowing who was lying and who was telling the truth ... Which hardly mattered to the vast audience of political innocents who soon found themselves as hooked on the all-day hearings as they'd previously been on the soaps and the quiz shows. Even Hollywood scriptwriters and apolitical actors were fascinated by the dramatic pace and structure of the hearings.

The massive complexities of the evidence, the raw drama of the daily confrontations and the deceptively elfin humour of 'Senator Sam' came together in a multilevelled plot that offered something to almost everybody – from bleeding hearts and Perry Mason fans to S&M freaks and the millions of closet Hell's Angels whose sole interest in watching the hearings was the spectacle of seeing once-powerful men brought weeping to their knees.

Consider John Mitchell, for instance – a millionaire Wall Street lawyer and close friend of the president, an arrogant, triple-chinned Roman who was Nixon's campaign manager in 68 and attorney general of the United States for four years until his old buddy put him in charge of the Committee to Re-elect the President in 1972 ... Here was a sixty-one-year-old man with more money than he could count and so much power that he saw nothing unusual in treating the FBI, the Secret Service and every federal judge in the country like serfs in his private police force ... who could summon limousines, helicopters or even Air Force One to take him anywhere he wanted to go by merely touching a buzzer on his desk ...

And suddenly, at the very pinnacle of his power, he casually puts his initials on a memo proposing one of at least a dozen or so routine election-year bits of 'undercover work' – and several months later while having breakfast in the Polo Lounge of the Beverly Hills Hotel, he gets a phone call from some yoyo named Liddy, whom he barely knows, saying that four Cubans he's never even met have just been caught in the act of burglarizing the office of the Democratic National Committee located in an office building about 200 yards across the plaza below his own balcony in the Watergate apartments ...

Which seems like a bad joke, at first, but when he gets back to Washington and drops by the White House to see his old buddy, he senses that something is wrong. Both Haldeman and Ehrlichman are in the Oval Office with Nixon; the president greets him with a nervous smile but the other two say nothing. The air reeks of tension. What the hell is going on here? Mitchell starts to sit down on the couch and call for a drink but Nixon cuts him off: 'We're working on something, John. I'll call you at home later on, from a pay phone.'

Mitchell stares at him, then picks up his briefcase and quickly says goodbye. Jesus Christ! What *is* this? On the way out to the limousine in the White House driveway, he sees Steve Bull's secretary reading a late edition of the *Washington Star-News* and idly snatches it out of her hands as he walks by ... Moments later, as the big Cadillac rolls out into traffic on Pennsylvania Avenue, he glances at the front page and is startled by a large photo of his wife; she is packing a suitcase in the bedroom of their Watergate apartment. And next to the photo is a headline saying something like 'Martha on the Rampage Again, Denounces "Dirty Business" at White House'.

'Good God!' he mutters. The Secret Service man in the front seat glances back at him for a moment, then looks away. Mitchell scans the story on Martha: She has freaked out again. Where does she keep getting that goddamn speed? he wonders; her eyes in the photo are the size of marbles. According to the story, she called UPI reporter Helen Thomas at four in the morning, cursing incoherently about 'Mister President' and saying she has to get out of Washington at once, go back to the apartment in New York for a few days of rest.

Wonderful, Mitchell thinks. The last thing I need right now is to have her screaming around the apartment all night with a head full of booze and speed. Mitchell hates speed. In the good old days, Martha would just drink herself into a stupor and pass out ... But when they moved down to Washington she began gobbling a pill here and there, just to stay awake at parties, and that's when the trouble started ...

Then his eyes shift up to the lead story and he suddenly feels his balls contract violently, crawling straight up into his belly. 'WATERGATE BURGLARY CONNECTED TO WHITE HOUSE', says the headline, and in the first graph of the story he sees the name of E. Howard Hunt, which he recognizes instantly – and a few graphs lower, goddamnit, is Gordon Liddy's name.

No need to read any further. Suddenly it all makes sense. He hears himself moan and sees the agent glance back at him again, saying nothing. He pulls the paper up in front of his face, but he is no longer reading. His finely tuned lawyer's mind is already racing, flashing back over all the connections: phone calls to Hunt, arguments with Liddy, secret meetings in Key Biscayne, Larry O'Brien, Cuban burglars with CIA connections, Howard Hughes ...

He is fucked. It has taken less than thirty seconds for his brain to connect all the details ... And yes, of course, that's what Nixon was talking about with those bastards, Haldeman and Ehrlichman. They knew. The president knew. Hunt and Liddy knew ... Who else? Dean? Magruder? LaRue? How many others?

The limousine slows down, making the turn off Virginia Avenue and into the Watergate driveway. Instinctively, he glances up at the fifth floor of the office building and sees that all the lights are still on in O'Brien's office. That was where it had happened, right here in his own goddamn fortress ...

His mind is still racing when the agent opens the door. 'Here we are, sir. Your luggage is in the trunk; we'll bring it right up.'

John Mitchell crawls out of the bright black Cadillac limousine and walks like a zombie through the lobby and into the elevator. Dick will be calling soon, he thinks. We'll have to act fast on this goddamn thing, isolate those dumb bastards and make sure they *stay* isolated.

The elevator stops and they walk down the soft, red-carpeted hall to his door. The agent goes in first to check all the rooms. Mitchell glances down the hall and sees another Secret Service man by the door to the fire exit. He smiles hello and the agent nods his head. Jesus Christ! What the hell am I worried about? We'll have this thing wrapped up and buried by ten o'clock tomorrow morning. They can't touch *me*, goddamnit. They wouldn't dare!

The agent inside the apartment is giving him the all-clear sign. 'I put your briefcase on the coffee table, sir, and your luggage is on the way up. We'll be outside by the elevator if you need anything.'

'Thanks,' Mitchell says. 'I'll be fine.' The agent leaves, closing the door softly behind him. John Mitchell walks over to the TV console and flips on the evening news, then pours himself a tall glass of scotch on the rocks and stretches out on the sofa, watching the tube, and waits for Nixon to call – from a pay phone. He knows what that means and it has nothing to do with dimes.

That was John Mitchell's last peaceful night in Washington. We will probably never know exactly what he and Nixon talked about on the telephone, because he was careful to make the call from one of the White House phones that was not wired into the tape-recording system ... Mitchell had not been told, officially, about the president's new tape toy; the only people who knew about it, officially, were Nixon, Haldeman, Larry Higby, Steve Bull, Alex Butterfield and the three Secret Service agents responsible for keeping it in order ... But unofficially almost everybody with personal access to the Oval Office had either been told on the sly or knew Richard Nixon well enough so they didn't need to be told ... In any case, there is enough testimony in the files of the Senate Watergate committee to suggest that most of them had their own recording systems and taped most of what they said to each other, anyway.

Neither John Ehrlichman nor Charles Colson, for instance, were 'officially' aware of the stunningly sophisticated network of hidden bugs that the Technical Security Division of the Secret Service had constructed for President Nixon. According to Alex Butterfield's testimony in closed hearings before the House Judiciary Committee, Nixon told chief SS agent Wong to have his electronics experts wire every room, desk, lamp, phone and mantelpiece inside the White House grounds where the President was likely ever to utter a word of more than one syllable on any subject.

I've been using tape recorders in all kinds of journalistic situations for almost ten years, all kinds of equipment, ranging from ten-inch studio reels to raisin-sized mini-bugs – but I have never even *seen* anything like the system Wong's Secret Service experts rigged up for Nixon in the White House. In addition to dozens of wireless, voice-activated mikes about the size of a pencil eraser that he had built into the woodwork, there were also custom-built sensors, delay mechanisms and 'standby' switches wired into telephones that either Bull or Butterfield could activate.

In the cabinet room, for instance, Nixon had microphones built into the bases of the wall lamps that he could turn on or off with harmless-looking buzzers labelled 'Haldeman' and 'Butterfield' on the rug underneath the cabinet table in front of his chair. The tapes and recording equipment were installed in a locked closet in the basement of the west wing, but Nixon could start the reels rolling by simply pressing on the floor buzzer marked 'Butterfield' with the toe of his shoe – and to stop the reels, putting the machinery back on standby, he could step on the 'Haldeman' button ...

Any serious description of Nixon's awesome tape-recording system would take thousands of words and boggle the minds of most laymen, but even this quick capsule is enough to suggest two fairly obvious but rarely mentioned conclusions: Anybody with this kind of a tape system, installed and maintained twenty-four hours a day by Secret Service electronics experts, is going to consistently produce extremely high quality voice reproductions. And since the White House personnel office can hire the best transcribing typists available, and provide them with the best tape-transcribing machinery on the market, there is only one conceivable reason for those thousands of maddening, strategically spotted 'unintelligibles' in the Nixon version of the White House tapes. Any Kelly Girl agency in the country would have given Nixon his money back if their secretaries had done that kind of damage to his transcripts. Sloppiness of that magnitude can only be deliberate, and Nixon is known to have personally edited most of those tape transcripts before they were typed for the printer ... Which doesn't mean much, now that Nixon's version of the transcripts is no longer potential evidence but sloppy artifacts that are no longer even interesting to read except as an almost criminally inept contrast to the vastly more detailed and coherent transcripts that House Judiciary Committee transcribers produced from the same tapes. The only people with any reason to worry about either the implications of those butchered transcripts or the ham-fisted criminal who did the final editing job are the editors at whichever publishing house decides to pay Richard Nixon $2 million for his presidential memoirs, which will be heavily dependent on that vast haul of Oval Office tapes that Gerald Ford has just decreed are the personal property of Richard Nixon. He will have the final edit on *those* transcripts, too – just before he sends the final draft of his memoirs to the printer. The finished book will probably sell for $15; and a lot of people will be stupid enough to buy it.

The second and more meaningful aspect *vis-à-vis* Nixon's tape system has to do with the way he used it. Most tape freaks see their toys as a means to bug other people, but Nixon had the SS technicians install almost every concealed bug in his system with a keen eye for its proximity to Richard Nixon.

According to Butterfield, Nixon was so obsessed with recording every move and movement of his presidency for the history books that he often seemed to be thinking of nothing else. When he walked from the White House to his office in the EOB, for instance, he would carry a small tape recorder in front of his mouth and maintain a steady conversation with it as he moved in his stiff-legged way across the lawn ... And although we will never hear those tapes, the mere fact that he was constantly making them, for reasons of his own, confirms Alex Butterfield's observation that Richard Nixon was so bewitched with the fact that he really was *the President* that his only sense of himself in that job came from the moments he could somehow record and squirrel away in some safe place, for tomorrow night or the ages.

There is a bleeding kind of irony in this unnatural obsession of Nixon's with his place in history when you realize what must have happened to his mind when he finally realized, probably sometime in those last few days of his doomed presidency, just exactly what kind of place in history was even then being carved out for him.

In the way it is usually offered, the sleazy little argument that 'Nixon has been punished enough' is an ignorant, hack politician cliché ... But that image of him walking awkward and alone across the White House lawn at night, oblivious to everything in front or on either side of him except that little black and silver tape recorder that he is holding up to his lips, talking softly and constantly to 'history', with the brittle intensity of a madman: When you think on that image for a while, remember that the name Nixon will seem to give off a strange odour every time it is mentioned for the next 300 years, and in every history book written from now on, 'Nixon' will be synonymous with shame, corruption and failure.

No other president in American history has been driven out of the White House in a cloud of disgrace. No other president has been forced to preside over the degrading collapse of his own administration or been forced to stand aside and watch helplessly – and also guiltily – while some of his close friends and ranking assistants are led off to jail. And finally, no president of the United States has even been so vulnerable to criminal prosecution, so menaced by the threat of indictment and trial, crouched in the dock of a federal courtroom and so obviously headed for prison that only the sudden grant of presidential pardon from the man he appointed to succeed him could prevent his final humiliation.

These are the stinking realities that will determine Richard Nixon's place in American history ... And in this ugly context, the argument that 'Richard Nixon has been punished enough' takes on a different meaning. He will spend many nights by himself in his study out there in San Clemente, listening over and over to those tapes he made for the ages and half-remembering the feel of thick grass on the rose garden lawn adding a strange new spring to his walk, even making him talk a bit louder as he makes his own knotty, plastic kind of love to his sweet little Japanese bride, telling it over and over again that he really *is* the President, the most powerful man in the world – and goddamnit, you better never forget that!

Richard Nixon is free now. He bargained wisely and well. His arrangement with Ford has worked nicely, despite that week or so of bad feeling when he had to get a little rough with Gerry about the pardon, threatening to call in the *LA Times* man and play that quick little tape of their conversation in the Oval Office – the one where he offered to make Gerry the vice-president, in exchange for a presidential pardon whenever he asked for it – and he had known, by then, that he would probably need it a lot sooner than Gerry realized. Once their arrangement was made (and taped), Nixon just rode for as long as he could, then got off in time to sign up for his lifetime dole as a former president.

He will rest for a while now, then come back to haunt us again. His mushwit son-in-law, David Eisenhower, is urging him to run for the US Senate from California in 1976, and Richard Nixon is shameless enough to do it. Or if not in the Senate, he will turn up somewhere else. The only thing we can be absolutely sure of, at this point in time, is that we are going to have Richard Milhous Nixon to kick around for at least a little while longer.

Rolling Stone no. 171, 10 October 1974

PART THREE

TRAVELLER HEARS MOUNTAIN MUSIC WHERE IT'S SUNG

Renfro Valley, Ky – The Bluegrass country is cold and brown in the winter. Night comes early and the horses are taken inside to sleep in heated barns. The farmers sit around pot bellied stoves and pass the time with a banjo and a jug and sometimes a bit of talk. Not many visitors in the winter. Not much to do, either.

Here in Rock Castle county the biggest event of the week is the Saturday night show in a little spot on the map called Renfro Valley, a big barn and a recording studio on US highway 25, about fifty miles south of Lexington.

Ten years ago they flocked to this place like pilgrims to the shrine – not just from the nearby Bluegrass towns, but from all over the nation. They came for the country music and the all-day sings and to get a look at the old Kentucky barn dance they'd heard so often on their radios at home. It got so big that 15,000 people showed up one summer Saturday night, and a national magazine sent down a team of cameras to record the scene for posterity.

Now perhaps 150 will show up. They come down from Berea and Crab Orchard, and Preachersville, and from places like Egypt and Shoulderblade across the mountains. Not many from out of state. Not even enough to justify using the barn, which is closed until spring, when the crowds will pick up again.

Only the locals show up in the winter. They come with guitars and bass fiddles and old songbooks, and they gather in the studio to do a radio show that you can still hear in some cities, but not in so many as you could a few years back. The show starts around seven and winds up at 9:30 – just about the time the hillbilly singers and the Bluegrass banjo champs are warming up at Gerde's in New York's Greenwich Village.

Folks around here don't have much time for strangers. You ask what goes on at Renfro Valley and they shrug and say, 'Not much.' You want to find a restaurant after 8 p.m. and – if you can find anybody to ask – they'll direct you to Lexington, an hour's drive.

You have a thirst and they tell you, 'This here's a dry county.' Pause. 'Yep, dry county.' Another pause. 'Maybe if you go up the road a piece to where you find a sort of restaurant, maybe somebody there can fix you up.'

So if you want entertainment in these parts, you go to Renfro Valley and you go early. The studio is warm and the music is every bit as real as the people who sing it.

'Well, now, for all you folks out there in radioland, I want to say that we got a little gal visitin' with us this evenin'. Little Brenda Wallen, from up in Winchester, I believe ...'

And little Brenda sings: 'Beeyooteeful lies, beeyooteeful lies ... each one a heartbreak ... in perfect disguise ...'

Then the Hibbard Brothers quartet, lean mountain faces and huge hands poking out of gabardine sleeves – 'O, what a time we will have up in heaven ...'

A murmur of approval from the audience. A flashbulb pops near the back of the room. Things are picking up. The Farmer Sisters take their turn at the mike, with a rippling version of 'You're the Reason'.

A few cheers from the crowd, a quick burst of fiddle music from a man beside the piano, then somebody holds up a hand for silence. Time for the commercial.

'This here's a long one,' says the announcer, glancing at a yellow script in his hand, 'so let's do it all at once and get it over with.' Snickers from the audience. Everybody grins as the commercial is read very earnestly into the mike that will carry it out to the Good Lord only knows where.

The announcer finishes and heaves a sigh of relief, also into the mike. Everybody laughs and the show goes on. Meanwhile, the Greenbriar Boys are tuning their instruments at Gerde's; in a few hours there will be a long, button down line outside the hungry i in San Francisco, waiting to hear the latest hillbilly sensation.

It's 9:30 in Rock Castle county and the old Kentucky barn dance is over until next week. Only a few people remain in the studio. One of them is John Lair, a local boy and a onetime Chicago disc jockey who came back home to put Renfro Valley on the map. Red Foley got his start here. So did the Coon Creek Sisters, from a place back in the hills called Pinch 'Em Tight Holler.

Lair seems genuinely puzzled by the term, 'Bluegrass music'. He thinks it's a misnomer.

'It's plain old mountain music,' he insists. 'Same stuff they've been singing for more than a hundred years.' He chuckles and shakes his head. 'You go up to Lexington and call it Bluegrass music and you'll have a fight on your hands.'

Lair says goodnight and leaves to go home. Outside, the parking lot is almost empty. A visitor has two choices – drive up to Lexington for something to eat and maybe a good fight, or hurry to the nearest motel.

A few miles up the road is a town called Nicholasville, where motel owners won't even answer the door after what they consider a decent hour. When I stopped a man on the street and asked him why this was, he said he was the chief of police and offered to rent me a bed in his house.

I went back to one of the motels, went into the office, turned on the light, picked a key off the desk and located a cabin by myself. The next morning it took me twenty minutes to find somebody to pay – and then I was told I wouldn't be welcome there in the future because my car had a licence plate from Louisville. They don't care much for city boys, specially when they're roamin' around late at night.

If you drive thru Kentucky and plan to spend the night, get your room early and if you like a toddy before bedding down, remember that 86 of the 120 counties are bone dry until you make friends. Grog shops are few and far between, and a man without foresight will usually go to bed thirsty.

Winter mornings are bleak. Almost always you wake up to a grey sky and a good country breakfast: fried sausage or ham, fried eggs, fried potatoes, and a plate of biscuits with butter and apple jelly. Then, after a pot of coffee, you move on.

No matter which way you go you'll drive thru a lot of cold, barren country to get there. North, thru the heart of the Bluegrass, west towards Louisville, east into the mountains, or south to Tennessee.

Not much speed on those narrow highways, plenty of time to look off across the white fences and wonder how the cows find anything to eat in the frozen fields. Time to listen to the sermons on the radio or the lonely thump of a shotgun somewhere back from the road.

Not much to hurry about in the Bluegrass, specially in the winter when the trees are bare and the barns are white with frost and most folks are inside by the stove.

Chicago Tribune, 18 February 1962

A FOOTLOSE AMERICAN IN A SMUGGLERS' DEN

In Puerto Estrella, Colombia, there is little to do but talk. It is difficult to say just what the villagers are talking about, however, because they speak their own language – a tongue called Guajiro, a bit like Arabic, which doesn't ring well in a white man's ear.

Usually they are talking about smuggling, because this tiny village with thatched roof huts and a total population of about 100 South American Indians is a very important port of entry. Not for humans, but for items like whisky and tobacco and jewellery. It is not possible for a man to get there by licensed carrier, because there are no immigration officials and no customs. There is no law at all, in fact, which is precisely why Puerto Estrella is such an important port.

It is far out at the northern tip of a dry and rocky peninsula called La Guajira, on which there are no roads and a great deal of overland truck traffic. The trucks carry contraband, hundreds of thousands of dollars worth of it, bound for the interiors of Colombia and Venezuela. Most of it comes from Aruba, brought over at night on fast trawlers and put ashore at Puerto Estrella for distribution down the peninsula on the trucks.

I arrived at dusk on a fishing sloop from Aruba. And since there is no harbour I was put ashore in a tiny rowboat. Above us, on a sharp cliff, stood the entire population of the village, staring grimly and without much obvious hospitality at Puerto Estrella's first tourist in history.

In Aruba, the Guajiro Indians are described as 'fierce and crazy and drunk all day on coconut whisky'. Also in Aruba you will hear that the men wear 'nothing but neckties, knotted just below the navel'. That sort of information can make a man uneasy, and as I climbed the steep path, staggering under the weight of my luggage, I decided that at the first sign of unpleasantness I would begin handing out neckties like Santa Claus – three fine paisleys to the most menacing of the bunch, then start ripping up shirts.

As I came over the brink of the cliff, a few children laughed, an old hag began screeching, and the men just stared. Here was a white man with twelve Yankee dollars in his pocket and more than $500 worth of camera gear slung over his shoulders, hauling a typewriter, grinning, sweating, no hope of speaking the language, no place to stay – and somehow they were going to have to deal with me.

There was a conference, and then a small man stepped forward and made motions indicating that I should put my gear on an ancient truck which started with a crank. I was taken to an abandoned hospital, where I was given a sort of cell with a filthy mattress and broken windows to let in the air.

There is not much for the tourist in Puerto Estrella, no hotels, restaurants, or souvenirs. Nor is the food palatable. Three times a day I faced it – leaves, maize, and severely salted goat meat, served up with muddy water.

The drinking was a problem too, but in a different way. At the crack of dawn on the day after my arrival I was awakened and taken before a jury of village bigwigs. Its purpose was to determine the meaning of my presence. These gentlemen had gathered in the only concrete-block house in town, and before them on the table was a cellophane-wrapped bottle of Scotch whisky.

After an hour or so of gestures, a few words of Spanish, and nervous demonstrations of my camera equipment, they seemed to feel a drinking bout was in order. The Scotch was opened, five jiggers were filled, and the ceremony began.

It continued all that day and all the next. They tossed it off straight in jiggers, solemnly at first and then with mounting abandon. Now and then one of them would fall asleep in a hammock, only to return a few hours later with new thirst and vigour. At the end of one bottle they would proudly produce another, each one beautifully wrapped in cellophane.

As it turned out, three things made my visit a success. One was my size and drinking capacity (it was fear – a man travelling alone among reportedly savage Indians dares not get drunk); another was the fact that I never turned down a request for a family portrait (fear, again); and the third was my 'lifelong acquaintance' with Jacqueline Kennedy, whom they regard as some sort of goddess.

With the exception of a few sophisticates and local bigwigs, most of the men wore the necktie – a Guajiro version of the time-honoured loin-cloth. The women, again with a few exceptions, wore dull and shapeless long black gowns.

A good many of the men also wore two and three hundred dollar wrist watches, a phenomenon explained by the strategic location of Puerto Estrella and the peculiar nature of its economy. It would not be fair to say that the Indians arbitrarily take a healthy cut of all the contraband that passes through their village, but neither would it be wise to arrive and start asking pointed questions, especially since anyone arriving on his own is wholly dependent on the good will of the Indians to get him out again.

Trying to leave can turn a man's hair white. You are simply stuck until one of the Indians has to run some contraband down the peninsula to Maicao.

There is nothing to do but drink, and after fifty hours of it I began to lose hope. The end seemed to be nowhere in sight; and it is bad enough to drink Scotch all day in any climate, but to come to the tropics and start belting it down for three hours each morning before breakfast can bring on a general failure of health. In the mornings we had Scotch and arm-wrestling; in the afternoons, Scotch and dominoes.

The break came at dusk on the third day, when the owner of a truck called the Power Wagon rose abruptly from the drinking table and said we would leave immediately. We had a last round, shook hands all around, and shoved off. The truck was fully loaded, and I rode in back with my gear and a young Indian girl.

The drive from Puerto Estrella to Maicao is ten to twelve hours, depending on which rut you take, but it seems like forty days on the rack. On top of the heinous discomfort, there is the distinct possibility of being attacked and shot up by either bandits or the law. As far as the *contrabandista* is concerned, one is as bad as the other.

The smugglers travel armed but they put their faith in speed, punishing both truck and passengers unmercifully as they roar through dry river beds and across long veldt-like plains on a dirt track which no conventional car could ever navigate.

We rumbled into Maicao at three in the afternoon. They dropped me at the airport, where my luggage was thoroughly searched by a savage-looking gendarme before I was allowed on the plane for Barranquilla. An hour later, there was another search at the Barranquilla airport. When I asked why, they replied I was coming from an area called Guajira, known to be populated by killers and thieves and men given over to lives of crime and violence.

I had a feeling that nobody really believed I had been there. When I tried to talk about Guajira, people would smile sympathetically and change the subject. And then we would have another beer, because Scotch is so expensive in Barranquilla that only the rich can afford it.

National Observer, 6 August 1962

WHY ANTI-GRINGO WINDS OFTEN BLOW SOUTH OF THE BORDER

One of my most vivid memories of South America is that of a man with a golf club – a five-iron, if memory serves – driving golf balls off a penthouse terrace in Cali, Colombia. He was a tall Britisher, and had what the British call 'a stylish pot' instead of a waistline. Beside him on a small patio table was a long gin-and-tonic, which he refilled from time to time at the nearby bar.

He had a good swing, and each of his shots carried low and long out over the city. Where they fell, neither he nor I nor anyone else on the terrace that day had the vaguest idea. The penthouse, however, was in a residential section on the edge of the Rio Cali, which runs through the middle of town. Somewhere below us, in the narrow streets that are lined by the white adobe blockhouses of the urban peasantry, a strange hail was rattling on the roofs – golf balls, 'old practice duds', so the Britisher told me, that were 'hardly worth driving away'.

In the weeks that followed, when I became more aware of the attitude a good many Colombians have towards that nation's Anglo-Saxon population, I was glad nobody had traced the source of those well-hit mashies. Colombians, along with their Venezuelan neighbours, may well be the most violent people on the continent, and a mixture of insult and injury does not rank high as a national dish.

It is doubtful that the same man would drive golf balls off a rooftop apartment in the middle of London. But it is not really surprising to see it done in South America. There, where the distance between the rich and the poor is so very great, and where Anglo-Saxons are automatically among the élite, the concept of *noblesse oblige* is subject to odd interpretations.

The attitude, however, does not go unnoticed; the natives consider it bad form indeed for a foreigner to stand on a rooftop and drive golf balls into their midst. Perhaps they lack sporting blood, or maybe a sense of humour, but the fact is that they resent it, and it is easy to see why they might go to the polls at the next opportunity and vote for the man who promises to rid the nation of 'arrogant gringo imperialists'.

Whether the candidate in question is a fool, a thief, a Communist, or even all three does not matter much when emotions run high – and few elections south of the Rio Grande are won on the basis of anything but blatant appeals to popular emotion.

The North American presence in South America is one of the most emotional political questions on the continent. In most countries, especially Argentina and Chile, there is a considerable European presence as well. But with recent history as it is, when the winds of anti-gringo opinion begin to blow, they blow due north, towards the United States, which to the Latin American is more easily identifiable with capitalism and imperialism than any other country in the world.

With this in mind, a traveller in South America gets one shock after another at the stance generally taken by his fellow gringos – and sometimes a worse shock at the stance he takes himself. One young American put it this way: 'I came down here a real gung-ho liberal, I wanted to get close to these people and help them – but in six months I turned into a hardnose conservative. These people don't know what I'm talking about, they won't help themselves, and all they want is my money. All I want to do now is get out.'

It is a sad fact that living for any length of time in a Latin American country has a tendency to do this to many Americans. To avoid it takes tremendous adaptability, idealism, and faith in the common future.

Take the example of a young man named John, a representative in a Latin American country for an international relief organization. His work consists mainly in distributing surplus food to the poor. He works hard, often going out on field trips, for three or four days of rough driving, bad food, primitive living, and dysentery.

But the people he has to work with bother him. He can't understand why the principal of a back-country school will steal food earmarked for the pupils and sell it to speculators. He can't understand why his warehouse – lying in the middle of a district where food is distributed regularly – is constantly being looted by the very people who were standing in line the week before to get their regular share.

He broods on these things and wonders if he is really accomplishing anything, or just being taken for a sucker. Then, one day when he is in a particularly bad mood over some new evidence of callousness or corruption, he hears below his window the shouting of a mob. A man is standing on the steps of a fountain, shouting hoarsely about 'the rights of the people' and what should be done to secure them. And the crowd happily roars an answer – 'Down with the capitalist swine!'

Our man, standing at his window, suddenly loses his temper and shakes his fist. *Abajo del pueblos!* he yells. Meaning, 'Down with the people.' Then he quickly ducks back inside.

But the Latin family next door, standing at their window, hears the gringo abusing the crowd. Word gets around, and several days later our man is insulted as he walks to the corner *cantina* for a pack of *cigarillos*. He speaks good Spanish, and curses back, not understanding why his neighbours are no longer friendly. But it makes him even more bitter, and once the tide starts running in that direction, it is hard to reverse.

One day a new American appears in town, a trainee for one of the United States banks that have branches in South America. Our man John meets him at the Anglo-American Club and, in the course of conversation, tell him what to expect from the nationals – 'a bunch of rotten ingrates, stupid and corrupt to the last man'.

The newcomer hears other gringos say the same kind of thing. At night, in his new and unfamiliar apartment, he begins to think the neighbours are making noise on purpose, to wear on his nerves. Soon he is as bitter as most of the others.

When the inevitable bank strike comes along – as it does at regular intervals in most Latin American countries – our newcomer takes the advice of an older gringo employee and shows up at work with a pistol, which he puts on his desk like a paperweight to show the employees he means business.

The reaction of the nationals hardly needs to be catalogued. Our trainee is chalked up as one more bit of two-legged evidence that gringos are vicious fools. The net result – as far as both John and the young banker are concerned – is a grievous setback for the hope that North and South America will come to understand each other, and thus avoid a split-up that would wreck the Western Hemisphere.

The young American in a Latin American country faces other hazards. For one thing, he has to contend with the American colony that blooms in every city of any size.

Americans living in Latin American countries are often more snobbish than the Latins themselves. The typical American has quite a bit of money by Latin American standards, and he rarely sees a countryman who doesn't. An American businessman who would think nothing of being seen in a sport shirt on the streets of his home town will be shocked and offended at a suggestion that he appear in Rio de Janeiro, for instance, in anything but a coat and tie. The same man – often no more than thirty years old – might have been living in a prefabricated tract house in the States, but in Rio he will live on Copacabana beach with two maids, servants' quarters, and a balcony overlooking the sea.

Some people say that the American is fouling his own image in South America – that instead of being a showpiece for 'democracy', he not only tends to ape the wealthy, anti-democratic Latins, but sometimes beats them at their own game. Suddenly finding himself among the élite, the nervous American is determined to hold his own – and, unlike the genuine aristocrat who never doubts his own worth, the newcomer to status seeks to prove it at every turn.

Others, though, repeat the old, familiar, 'When in Rome, do as the Romans do.' In South America, so the thinking goes, the lower classes have no grasp of equality and take informality for weakness. So the only alternative is to make them respect you. 'I know it's silly to shout at the maid every time she makes a mistake,' said one American housewife in Brazil. 'But she's lazy and I want her to know I'm watching her. With these people, it's either discipline or anarchy.'

Another problem that plagues the gringo is drink. Because he never really feels at home in a foreign language; because his income is usually embarrassingly large by local standards; because he worries continually about being cheated whenever he buys anything; because he never gets over the feeling that most upper-class Latins consider him a boob from a country where even the boobs are rich; and because he can never understand why people don't seem to like him for what he is – just a good guy who feels a bit out of place among these strange surroundings and customs – because of all these tensions and many more of the same kind, he tends to drink far more than he does at home.

'To relax' is the usual excuse, but sometimes there is almost no choice. In Rio, for instance, the evening traffic jams are so bad that getting from the business district out to Copacabana – where 'everybody' lives – is almost impossible between the hours of five and eight. One of the first things a new arrival is told is: 'If you can't get out of town by five, forget about it and settle down to serious drinking until eight.' This hiatus in the day is termed 'the drinking hour'.

With many people, the 'drinking hour' soon becomes a necessary habit. Sometimes it leads to disaster. Often an American will arrive home broke and bleary-eyed at three or four in the morning, still lugging his briefcase and cursing the long-gone traffic.

Because of things like the drinking hour and other, purely local, situations, a man returning to the States after a stay in Latin America is often struck dumb by the question, 'What can we do about that place?'

He has no idea, because he has never had time enough to relax and give it much thought. His concern has been survival. Objectivity is one of the first casualties of 'culture shock' – a term for the malady that appears when a North American, with his heritage of Puritan pragmatism, suddenly finds himself in a world with different traditions and a different outlook on life.

It is an odd feeling to return from a year in South America and read a book by some expense-account politician who toured the continent in six weeks and spoke only with presidents, cabinet ministers, and other 'leading figures' like himself. The problems and the issues suddenly become quite clear – as they never were when you were right there in the midst of them.

Now, looking back on that man with the golf club, it is easy to see him as a fool and a beast. But I recall quite well how normal it seemed at the time, and how surprised I would have been if any of the dozen people on the terrace had jumped up to protest.

National Observer, 19 August 1963

DEMOCRACY DIES IN PERU, BUT FEW SEEM TO MOURN ITS PASSING

The 'death of democracy' has not left much of a vacuum in Peru. It was more like the death of somebody's old uncle, whose name had been familiar in the household for many years, but who died, where he had always lived, in some far-off town the family never quite got around to visiting – although they had always meant to, or at least that's what they said.

If there is one profound reality in Peruvian politics it is the fact that this country has absolutely no democratic tradition, and any attempt to introduce one is going to meet violent opposition. The people who need democracy don't even know what the word means; the people who know what it means don't need it and they don't mind saying so. If the Alliance for Progress requires that democracy in Peru become a fact instead of just a pleasant word, then the Alliance is in for rough sledding too.

This is the basis of the current 'misunderstanding' between Washington and Lima. If the Peruvian people were as concerned about democracy as is President Kennedy, this country would right now be in the throes of a violent civil war. What happened in Lima on 18 July was more than enough to touch off armed conflict in many countries of the world, but democracy has never been a reality in Peru, and for that reason it goes largely unmourned; especially in Lima, which voted heavily for the return of an ex-dictator.

On 24 July, the un-elected government of Peru issued a decree-law, assuming all executive and legislative powers, and the third largest country in South America passed officially into the hands of the military.

The second largest, Argentina, had provided an easy-to-follow example some five months before. Next on the list, according to current speculation in Washington and other hemisphere capitals, will be Venezuela – and what might be precipitated by Brazil's congressional elections in October is anybody's guess.

It requires little guesswork, however, to see what this trend means for the Alliance for Progress, and also for the future of democracy in South America. The outlook is dreary at best, and as the pressure from Washington mounts, the reaction will mount just as fast. Peru was a good example.

Even so, after all these months of tension, all this talk and campaigning, all the space devoted in newspapers to the Peruvian elections, a visitor to Lima arrives with a feeling that there is bound to be some evidence that the whole thing was a bust – that it was all a put-up job, because the Armed Forces did exactly what they said they were going to do all along.

When the American Popular Revolutionary Alliance (APRA) won the recent elections, the military called it a 'fraud', took over the government, annulled what was undeniably the most honest and least fraudulent election in Peru's history, and installed a four-man junta that is a military dictatorship no matter which way you look at it.

Yet life goes on in Lima as if nothing had happened. The evening streets are full of pretty girls and slick-haired men in business suits, the opulent shops that flank the trolleys on Avenida Peirola are full of silver and alpaca and the soft rustle of money changing hands, and the all night *cantinas* still sound as if their frenzied, *pisco*-swilling patrons had abandoned all hope of ever seeing another dawn.

This is Lima, democracy or no democracy, dictators or no dictators. The city is full of people, in fact, who say that what happened is precisely nothing at all. They point out that the people in power now are those who have always been in power and that those faces on the outside, looking in, are the same faces that have been there for as long as anyone in Peru can remember. It is foolish, they say, to talk about the Junta 'seizing the reins', because the Junta is nothing more than a dress-uniform version of the same power bloc that has held the reins for centuries.

It is only in times of crisis that it puts on the jackboots and goes into the street with truncheons. In times of peace it wears mufti and busies itself with other, less militant pursuits – primarily that of maintaining itself in the style to which it has long been accustomed. It is as old as the Incas and every bit as ruthless wtih opposition. Its counterpart in the US has been labelled the Power Elite. In Peru it is called the Forty

Families, an all-powerful aristocracy that makes its North American cousin look weak and tame by comparison.

'That's what Kennedy doesn't understand,' explained one Lima-based American businessman. 'You just can't have democracy down here. The people don't understand it. Loeb was the same way: he went out to the futbol game and sat down in the grandstand with the common people – I saw him myself, with his feet propped up on the rail and the top of his hose showing – why, they thought he was crazy. It was absolutely incomprehensible, even to the people he was trying to make friends with. If you want to get anywhere down here, you have to make people respect you.'

However sad a commentary that may be on a lot of things – American businessmen included – it is sadder still because there is a lot of truth in it. From the beginning of their history the Peruvian people have been conditioned to understand that there are only two kinds of human beings in this world – the ins and outs, and a vast gulf in between. In a book called *The Ancient Civilizations of Peru* you read that 'The Inca state insured the people against hunger, exploitation, undue hardship and all kinds of want, but regimented them rigorously and left them no choice, independence or initiative ... There was a large class of nobles and priests, supported by the masses. Heavy tribute in the form of labour was demanded of the peasants, who profited very little from it.'

That was in 1438, and little has changed since then except that the peasants are no longer insured against hunger, exploitation, undue hardship and all kinds of want. There is ample evidence of all those conditions even in Lima, which differs from the rest of Peru much like Manhattan differs from the mountains of eastern Kentucky.

The strange assumption in Lima's business community – Americans and Peruvians alike – is that President Kennedy would join them in their endorsement of the system in Peru 'if he could only understand it, and stop paying so much attention to Loeb'.

US Ambassador James Isaac Loeb is undoubtedly the most second-guessed man in recent Peruvian history. There is not a man at the Bankers' Club, among other places, who cannot tell you where he went wrong and exactly what he should have done instead. The most common criticism is that he tried to force-feed democracy to a people who had not the faintest idea what he was talking about.

The nominal chief of the Junta, General Manuel Perez Godoy, has flatly called Loeb an '*aprista*', which is tantamount now to being called an enemy of the state. He is sure to be declared 'persona non grata' if he returns to Lima, and in business circles it is Loeb who draws most of the blame for the US refusal to recognize the Junta. The general sentiment is that Kennedy has been 'misled', Gen. Perez is of the same mind; in a recent statement on the US stand, he called the whole thing 'a misunderstanding'.

Gen. Perez has impressed foreign journalists in Lima with his unique feeling for words and their fundamental meanings. He is no mean orator, and in his first statement after the takeover he explained it this way: 'We have seen a fraudulent electoral process in which not even the most basic and elementary rights of the citizens have been respected. The Armed Forces have seen with pain, with anxiety, with tight lips and dry eyes, this sacrifice of our people, of our country, of our future.'

The fact that the Armed Forces had been able to dig up only seventy fraudulent ballots out of a total of some two million did not deter Gen. Perez from going on TV to amplify and reiterate his feelings.

'To the humble, to the forgotten worker, to the voter who has been deprived in many cases of the elementary social, economic and cultural benefits, it is now being attempted to take from him also his only hope – that of gaining the progress and social justice he deserves, to wipe out his liberty to vote with fraud.

'We will not consent to it. A military imperative forces on us the hard obligation of assuming the functions of government that normally should be in civilian hands, in order to establish peace, order and respect for the laws that rule the republic.

'We are stirred by a great ambition to save democracy.'

Earlier in the same speech Gen. Perez had talked of 'the great electoral fraud', said 'the people have been grossly cheated', accused the National Elections Board of an attempt 'to cover up this conduct', and explained that ex-President Prado – then languishing on a prison ship – had showed a 'lack of objectivity' for not having annulled the elections himself.

This was a little hard for some people to take, notably those 600,000 or so humbled and forgotten voters who had cast their ballots for APRA and Dr Victor Raul Haya de la Torre. Gen. Perez drew praise, however, from those quarters where it had not been previously understood that democracy is best preserved by installing a military dictatorship. He was also admired for his eloquent attack on those who would tamper with the people's right to express themselves by means of the ballot.

What is more than obvious in Lima is that the biggest fraud in the whole affair was the military's attempt to explain and justify the *coup*. It is hard to find anyone who seriously believes they took over because of 'a great electoral fraud'. The National Elections Board, a group of respected jurists with no ties to APRA, investigated the charges and found that, although there had been isolated cases of false registration and multiple voting, the sum of the infractions was far too small to have any effect on the outcome. President Prado agreed – and was exiled to Paris for his efforts when the military decided to back its charges with a Sherman tank and a US-trained ranger battalion.

The Junta has scheduled new elections for 9 June 1963, but the only people in Lima who seem to believe it are taxi drivers, hotel clerks and a varied assortment of small jobholders who voted for Gen. Manuel Odria, dictator from 1948 to 1956. In the circle most heartily in agreement with the takeover – namely, the business and finance community – the betting is against elections next year. 'These boys are in to stay,' said the president of a US businessmen's society. 'Once they get the taste of sugar on their tongues they're not going to give it up.'

Nor was he much alarmed by the prospect. 'These people are like children,' he explained. 'They'll complain all day about discipline, but deep down they like it. They need it.

'Let's be smart about it,' he added. 'The rich people are running this country. They're running the country back home. Why not face facts and be thankful for what stability we have? These people are anti-Communist. Let's recognize the Junta, keep the aid flowing, and get on with it.' He smiled indulgently. 'We think young Kennedy up there just flew off the handle. Now he's out on a limb and he doesn't know how to get back.'

Nearly everybody who wears a tie in Lima feels the same way. Business is good in Peru – it is the only South American country without a balance of payments deficit – and the vested interests want to keep it that way. Even the taxi driver, who is making a good living because there are enough people on the streets with money in their pockets, does not particularly care who sits in the Presidential Palace as long as they don't upset the apple cart.

This is what almost happened. APRA is more than just another political party; it is a genuine threat to a way of life that was 500 years old when the US was born. To say that the takeover came simply because of the military's long-standing feud with APRA is to gloss over the fact that the entire ruling class in Peru regards APRA as more dangerous than communism. APRA has an ally in the Alliance for Progress and therefore an ally in the US. Communism has never been more than a minor threat in Peru and is more a convenient whipping boy than anything else.

If anyone has carried the battle to the Communists, it is Haya de la Torre. One of his most popular campaign slogans was 'APRA, si! Communismo, no!' Fernando Belaunde Terry, who finished second in the presidential race, was not noted for any savage tirades against the red menace. Nor was Gen. Odria. Local Communists, however, have given the Junta their full-fledged support, although the party is still illegal and will undoubtedly remain that way.

APRA, primarily because of its appeal to the millions of voteless, illiterate Indians, is by long odds the main threat to Peru's *status quo*. At the moment, the party is still reeling from the jolt of having its hard-fought election victory annulled. When the soldiers pulled out of the Casa del Pueblos (House of the People) which is APRA's headquarters, the place was a total wreck. On 7 August, after two weeks of occupation, it was returned to the party, and a vast, silent crowd was on hand to view the remains. There were bullet holes in the walls and ceiling, doors and windows had been smashed and party records destroyed, and the entire building – nearly a city block of offices and facilities – was a shambles of glass, broken furniture and water-soaked paper. Among the smashed or stolen items were: the only dentist drill, all medicine from the clinic and drugs from the pharmacy, typewriters, a radio transmitter, all phonograph records, sculpture in the art workshop, instruments for the children's band, food and plates from the dining hall, records from the credit union, and just about everything else that human beings could put to any use at all.

Those who passed through the Casa del Pueblos that night, in what seemed like a huge funeral procession, could not be numbered in that alleged 'vast majority' of Peruvians who 'fully support the Junta'. The air was heavy with bitterness and defeat. They were anxious to know what the US was going to do about the takeover, and the only American there could only shake his head and say that it was too early to tell, although it seemed inevitable that the hue and cry for recognition would sooner or later have its effect.

This is the other side of the 'misunderstanding'. APRA represents some 600,000 of Peru's 2,000,000 voters, plus a vast majority of the fifty-three per cent of the population which neither reads, writes nor votes. Haya de la Torre got 14,000 more votes than any other candidate, and in a democratic country a man who did that well could expect to have at least some say in the government.

In Peru, however, the figures don't necessarily add up to the score. The will of the people is subject to the veto of that class for which armies have been the strong right arm ever since armies were invented. To these people, democracy means chaos. It will loosen their grip on the national purse strings, shatter the foundations of society, and send the rabble pouring into the vaults. A whole way of life would collapse if democracy became a reality in Peru. The military takeover was no accidental treading on Washington's toes. It was a step taken with full deliberation and plenty of warning beforehand. The military – and the oligarchy which supports the military – were, and still are, bound and determined not to let APRA get its hands on the throttle.

It follows then, that if the US reaction to the takeover is a misunderstanding, the whole Alliance for Progress is a misunderstanding, because the alliance is based rather firmly on the assumption that progress will not come at the expense of democracy. Mr Kennedy has said this over and over again, but it is a concept that has not gained wide acceptance in Peru. Not among the people who count, anyway.

National Observer, 27 August 1962

THE INCA OF THE ANDES: HE HAUNTS THE RUINS OF HIS ONCE-GREAT EMPIRE

Cuzco, Peru.

When the cold Andean dusk comes down on Cuzco, the waiters hurry to shut the venetian blinds in the lounge of the big hotel in the middle of town. They do it because the Indians come up on the stone porch and stare at the people inside. It tends to make tourists uncomfortable, so the blinds are pulled. The tall, oak-panelled room immediately seems more cheerful.

The Indians press their faces between the iron bars that protect the windows. They tap on the glass, hiss, hold up strange gimcracks for sale, plead for 'moneys', and generally ruin the tourist's appetite for his inevitable pisco sour.

It wasn't always this way. Until 1532 this city of crisp air and cold nights in the Andes Mountains served as the gold-rich capital of the Inca empire, the Indian society that South American expert Harold Osborne has called 'the only civilization which has succeeded in making the Andes genuinely habitable to man'. Many of Cuzco's buildings still rest on Inca foundations – massive walls of stone that have lasted through 400 years of wars, looting, erosion, earthquakes, and general neglect.

Today, the Indian is as sad and hopeless a specimen as ever walked in misery. Sick, dirty, barefoot, wrapped in rags, and chewing narcotic coca leaves to dull the pain of reality, he limps through the narrow cobblestone streets of the city that once was the capital of his civilization.

379

His culture has been reduced to a pile of stones. Archaeologists point out it's an interesting pile, but the Indian doesn't have much stomach for poking around in his own ruins. In fact, there's something pathetic about an Indian child leading you across a field to see what he calls *ruinas*. For this service he wants 'moneys', and then he'll be quiet unless you aim a camera at him, which will cost you about ten cents a shot.

Probably one Indian in a thousand has any idea why people come to Cuzco to look at *ruinas*. The rest have other things to think about, like getting enough to eat, and this has made Cuzco one of the continent's liveliest hotbeds of Communist agitation.

Communist-inspired 'peasant uprisings' are old-hat in Cuzco, dating back to the early 1940s. Indeed, they're familiar all over Peru. At one point during World War II, Communists took over Cuzco and built a giant hammer and sickle out of whitewashed stones on a hill overlooking the city.

The pattern hasn't changed too much since then. Last winter peasant leader Hugo Blanco organized an Indian militia in the Convención Valley near here and carried out a series of hit-and-run harassments. At about the same time, there were strikes and fighting at the United States-owned Cerro de Pasco mines.

But the phenomenon is restricted neither to the cities nor to Peru alone. It's also seen in the countryside and in the other two Andean countries, Ecuador and Bolivia. Of the three nations, only Bolivia has made any attempts to bring the Indians into the national life. Peru has taken some nervous and tentative steps, and Ecuador has done almost nothing.

Yet the combined populations of the three countries total some 18,500,000, of which about ten per cent are white. About forty per cent are pure Indian, and the rest are mixed-blood *cholos*, or *mestizos*. If the Indians and *cholos* join and develop their full power, the shape of northern South America may never be the same.

Communism, though, isn't the only persuasion that can rouse the normally placid Indians to violence. Another is the powerful *chicha* beer, the Andes' answer to home brew, which they drink in heavy amounts. In 1953 an anthropological field survey in Bolivia reported 979 bottles were consumed in one province for every adult man and woman, an average of two-and-a-half bottles a day.

Another agitating influence is extreme conservatism. One example: Last fall in Ecuador, a sanitation unit from the UN-sponsored Andean Indian Mission was attacked by Indians who'd been told the men were 'Communist agents'. A doctor and his assistant were killed, and the doctor's body was burned. The Ecuadorian press, pointing out the Communists certainly didn't tell the Indians the UN officials were 'Communist agents', called the incident 'a tragic consequence of the rivalry between the extreme left and the extreme right to win Indian support'.

This incident and many others like it were blamed on conservative elements opposed to land reform or any other change in the *status quo*. The example of Bolivia has shown that once the Indian begins voting, he has little common cause with large landowning or industrial interests. Thus the best hope for the *status quo* is to keep the Indian ignorant, sick, poverty-stricken, and politically impotent.

And the Indians, living mainly on a barren plateau that ranges from 10,000 feet above sea level in Ecuador to 15,000 in Bolivia (Denver, by contrast, is 5,280 feet above), are curiously receptive to this conservatism. Ever since the Spaniards' destruction of his empire in the mid-sixteenth century, the Indian has viewed all change as for the worse – except, sometimes, the changes advocated by his Communist-inspired 'peasant leaders'. The word 'government', for him, has been synonymous with 'exploitation'.

A fine old Indian tradition, now on the wane, was to greet all strangers with a hail of stones, because they invariably meant trouble. Until very recently any man arriving on 'official business' might have meant an entire village was being sent into the mines to labour for the rest of their lives.

Even when convinced somebody is trying to help him, the Indian is loath to change his ways. Arnaldo Sanjines, a Bolivian working for the Inter-American Agricultural Service in La Paz, tells of stopping at a tiny farm to demonstrate a steel plough to an Indian using the same primitive plough his ancestors used 500 years ago. The old man tried the new plough and was obviously convinced of its superiority, but finally handed it back.

'Ah, señor,' he said, 'this is a wonderful plough, but I like my old wooden one and I think I will die with it.'

Mr Sanjines shakes his head sadly as he talks of the twelve years he has spent with the service, trying to convince the Indians to give up their ancient methods of farming. One of the main stumbling blocks, he says, is that the Indian lives almost entirely outside the money economy; he exists, as he always has, on a system of barter. One Indian, after walking for miles to a village market, returned home to say he'd been cheated out of all his produce because all he got for it was money.

There is a sharp distinction, however, between 'city Indians' and those who stay in the mountains. From Bogotá south, the Andean cities are overrun with Indian beggars, who have no qualms about lying on a downtown sidewalk and grabbing at the legs of any passers-by who look prosperous.

One of the most effective groups now working with the Indians in Bolivia is the Maryknoll Fathers, a Catholic order based in La Paz. Says one priest: 'Bolivia hasn't got a chance unless the Indians join the country. We're making some progress here – more than the others, anyway. In Peru and Ecuador all they do is make the necessary concessions.'

In 1957 Father Ryan, one of the Maryknoll veterans, started *Radio Penas*, which broadcasts lessons in Spanish to the millions of Indians who speak only Quechua or Aymara. With 3,000 fixed-frequency receivers, donated by Bloomingdale's in New York, the Maryknollers have taught about 7,000 Indians in the past five years to speak the language of the country. There is one class a day, but it is difficult to get the Indians to tune in at the right hour, because they tell time by the sun.

The focus of the 'Indian problem' is Peru – the golden magnet that brought the Spaniards to South America in the sixteenth century. (In the first six months of the conquest, Francisco Pizarro and his men looted Inca temples of over $20,000,000 in gold ornaments, which they melted and sent back to Spain.) Peru was the scene of most of the conquest's bloody battles. In Peru, Pizarro chose to build Lima, his 'city of kings' from which the Spanish Viceroys ruled the Andes until they were driven out in 1821.

Today the 'wealth of the Andes' is no longer gold, but the political power lying dormant in the Indian population. This explains the long and bitter struggle for Indian support between Peru's Communists and the American Popular Revolutionary Alliance (APRA), the country's broadest-based political party.

Bolivia's 1952 revolution against dictatorial interests took the Indian pressure off that country; it gave the Indian land, a vote, and at least the beginnings of a say in the government. Nor does Ecuador seem immediately menacing; the boiling point there probably is still several years away.

But in Peru the pressure is on as it never has been before, and the main pressure point is here in Cuzco. And whoever consolidates Indian support in this nation will not only rule Peru but will influence events in Bolivia and Ecuador.

Today in Cuzco, though, tourists still wander about town and pay ragged Indians to pose for photos. They still take the little train to Machu Picchu to look at the fabled *ruinas*. They still sit in the comfortable old hotel and drink pisco sours while the waiters pull the blinds.

But the Indians are still outside the windows, and if recent events are any indication, they are getting tired of having the blinds pulled on them.

National Observer, 10 June 1963

BRAZILSHOOTING

Rio de Janeiro

Brazilian police have a reputation for extreme leniency, and the Brazilian army is said to be the most stable and democratically inclined in all of Latin America, but in recent weeks the administration of 'justice' has taken on a new look in Brazil, and many people are beginning to wonder just what the army and the police exist for.

On a recent night, with the temperature at its normal ninety-five and air conditioners humming all over the city, an American journalist was awakened by a telephone call at 4:30 in the morning. It was a friend, calling from the nightclub district of Copacabana.

'Get down here as fast as you can!' the voice shouted. 'Bring your camera! The army is all over the streets with machine guns! They've blown the Domino all to pieces and they're killing people right outside the bar where I'm sitting – we've locked the door, but they may break it down!'

Ten minutes later the half-dressed journalist jumped out of a cab a block away from the action. He walked quickly, but very casually, towards the Domino Club, with his camera and flashgun cradled in one arm like a football. In a Latin American country nervous with talk of revolution, no man with good sense runs headlong into a shooting party, because he is likely to get stitched across the chest with Czech machine gun slugs.

But at 4:45 the Domino Club was quiet. It is – or was – a well-known clip joint, catering mainly to American tourists and wealthy Brazilians. The lure was girls – some young and pretty, others slightly piggy and painted after long years of service.

Now the Domino is a shell, a dark room full of broken glass and bullet holes. The doorman is dead; he was cut down by gunfire as he fled towards a nearby corner. The bartender is in the hospital with a bullet-crease down the side of his skull, and several patrons are wounded. Most observers say another man is dead, but the bodies were taken away so quickly that nobody can be sure.

What happened? The *Correio de Manhã*, one of Rio's best papers, explained it this way: In an editorial entitled, 'Battlefield Copacabana', the paper said: 'Copacabana was the scene of a military operation on Friday. A detachment of paratroopers under the command of two lieutenants sealed off a street in order to assault a nightclub with machine guns, hand grenades and tear gas ...'

Correio went on to say: 'These arms have been acquired by the nation with the money of taxpayers and put at the disposal of the armed forces for the defence of the country, protection of the constitutional powers, and maintenance of the legal order ... in the Copacabana case, they were not used for these purposes ...'

That was not all of it. The attack on the Domino, carried out by uniformed paratroopers wearing black greasepaint on their faces, was a case of pure and simple vengeance. Several weeks ago an army sergeant was beaten to death as a result of a dispute over the size of his bill in the Domino. A few days later an army captain stopped in the club to say that the army intended to even the score. He was severely beaten by the doorman and several others. About ten days passed without incident, then the army evened the score.

When the journalist arrived, the street was cordoned off at both ends by soldiers with fixed bayonets and machine guns. Several bodies – some dead, others still alive – were being put into trucks. There was a large crowd around the entrance to the Domino. The journalist took a few photos, then slipped through the cordon – only to be nailed immediately by a captain, who escorted him out.

'But the Brazilian press is in there,' the American protested.

'Maybe so,' the captain replied, 'but you're not Brazilian.'

The journalist went around the block and slipped in from the other end, but by this time it was all over. The sky was getting light, and several blocks away a few early risers were out on Copacabana beach. In the middle of Rua Carvalho de Mendonça, where the body of the doorman had lain, was a large smear of blood and trampled flowers. Several cars were riddled with bullet holes. Near one corner, the cracks in the mosaic sidewalk were filled with blood, and there was a long smear across the sidewalk where a body had been dragged to a truck in the street. A drugstore had bullet holes in its windows, merchandise and glass counters inside. Concrete and marble walls on both sides of the street were pocked with bullet chips. On the sidewalk in front of the Domino lay a hand grenade that had failed to explode.

Had the grenade gone off inside the club, it could hardly have helped but kill at least one American – the Domino was always full of them – and the resulting *furor* would have been hard for Brazil to handle.

Even without the grenade, it is a wonder more people weren't killed in the attack. The soldiers burst through the door, ordered everybody to lie down on the floor, and sprayed the entire room with machine gun fire. The owner of the Domino, who was the main target of the raid, escaped into another nightclub. One patron grabbed a soldier's weapon and shot him with it. Another patron fled, then pulled a pistol and wounded one of the pursuing soldiers. Several witnesses say this man was the other dead body hauled off with that of the luckless doorman. But nobody knows for sure – except the army, and the flow of information from that quarter has all but ceased.

The Rio police were not in on the Domino attack. They have problems of their own. In recent weeks the newspapers have reported a half-dozen cases of police killing vagrants and beggars, then dumping the bodies into nearby rivers that flow into Guanabara Bay. So far two policemen have been arrested. One confessed, and officials assured the press that both would be dismissed from the force.

A columnist on the *Brazil Herald*, Rio's English-language daily, observed that, 'The method adopted by several members of the police to tackle the social problem and do away with misery by dumping beggars into a river ... is not meeting with general approval, despite undeniable efficacy.'

The *Jornal do Brasil* called for an immediate investigation, saying that policemen are suspected of 'summarily applying the death penalty to individuals considered bad elements ...' And, 'The people [of Rio] imagine the terror used in some police departments to be normal treatment not only for dangerous criminals, but mere suspects and possibly even personal enemies of policemen.'

One man voiced the opinion that 'Dismissal from the force cannot in any way be considered cruel or unusual punishment for policemen who kill beggars and vagrants who bother them and get in their way while they are trying to do their job – which mainly consists of making the rounds to collect payoffs.'

It was also pointed out that policemen dismissed from the force often go to work as doormen or bouncers for clubs like the Domino. Brazilian nightclubs, in fact, are not known for an excess of patience or generosity. A 'ballerina' named Maria, recently fired from a club in a small town near Rio, made a complaint to the police, accusing the owner of the place of 'transforming the backyard of his joint into a cemetery'. The girl reported that 'Customers who cannot pay the bill, or protest the amount, are invited to have a talk with him in the backyard, where they are shot and buried.' The police promised to investigate.

Meanwhile, there is a lot of talk in Rio over the Domino incident. It was not the first time that the army has taken commando-style vengeance on an unfriendly nightclub, but this was the first time anyone was machine-gunned. The question in most people's minds is, 'What next?'

Said one Copacabana club-owner: 'What am I supposed to do the next time a soldier causes trouble in here? I have to treat him with kid gloves or they'll come in here and shoot me like an animal.'

An American wondered what the reaction would be if soldiers from Ft Knox, Kentucky, shot up a bar in Louisville where a soldier had been cheated, beaten or even killed some weeks before. 'I can't even conceive of it,' he said, 'but if it ever happened I bet they'd all hang.'

Another American said, 'Hell, when I was a lieutenant [in the US Army] I could probably have requisitioned two trucks from the motor pool if I wanted to get back at some clip-joint, but I know damn well I could never have got two platoons of armed men to follow me.'

There is the nut of the problem, and one of the biggest differences between the United States and not only Brazil, but all Latin American countries. Where civil authority is weak and corrupt, the army is king by default. Even the words 'justice' and 'authority' take on different meanings. After the Domino attack, the *Jornal do Brasil* ran a follow-up story, headlined: 'Army Sees No Crime in Its Action'.

Or, as George Orwell observed, 'In the kingdom of the blind, the one-eyed man is king.'

National Observer, 11 February 1963

CHATTY LETTERS DURING A JOURNEY FROM ARUBA TO RIO

During the past seven months, journalist Hunter S. Thompson has been roaming through South America. His informative dispatches on social, economic, and political conditions there have been appearing in the *National Observer*.

But there's another side to reporting that seldom shows up in formal dispatches – the personal experiences of the digging, inquisitive newsman. These often give fascinating insights on the land and the people. Witness these excerpts from Mr Thompson's personal letters to his editor in Washington.

Aruba

I am leaving by smuggling boat for Colombia in a few hours and am rushing to get this off before I go. [Article on Aruba, the *National Ob-*

server, 16 July.] It is probably too late and too long for you, but I hope not, because I think it is a good and valid look at island politics, personalities, etc.

In about three days I plan to be in Barranquilla, Colombia. After Barran, I plan to go up the Magdalena River to Bogotá, thence to Peru in time for the 10 June elections. But this is tentative.

Bogotá, Colombia

Here is a sort of offbeat travel piece that might interest you [article on Guajira, the *National Observer*, 6 Aug.]. In Aruba, they are probably announcing the election results right about now and I imagine there are a lot of people digging holes in the bleak Aruba landscape.

If you can think of anything else you might want, let me know. By the time I get to Ecuador I will have seen most of Colombia at close range. If nothing else, I will have a lot of photos and, hopefully, an immunity to dysentery, which is now on me in full force.

The Valencia piece [article on Colombia, the *National Observer*, 24 June] will be in the mail tomorrow if they will stop ringing these bells – a mad clanging every five or ten minutes. Sometimes it goes on for twenty, and bounces me around the hotel room the whole while. Between the dysentery, the bells, and the unceasing loudspeakers in the street I am half-mad. (Ah, here go the bells again.) Ten minutes of it now; a lunatic in the belfry and worms in the stomach. What a town!

Cali, Colombia

My figures sent earlier on the price of Colombian coffee on the world market are correct, but not nearly as dramatic as the following: ninety cents a pound in 1954, thirty-nine cents a pound in 1962. As I said, Colombia depends on coffee for seventy-seven per cent of its export earnings.

Incidentally, Colombia gets another fifteen per cent of its export earnings from petroleum. That leaves eight per cent as a base to begin 'diversifying' with. Not much, eh? Some good minds are just about at the end of their tether with the problem.

While I'm talking here, the Alliance for Progress thing is a toughie, because most of the hard-nose opposition to it is sulky and silent. In a lot of cases, the Alliance faces a problem not unlike that of trying to convince Jay Gould that he is not acting in the best interests of his country.

Incidentally, Rojas Pinilla is without doubt the only dictator whose name is in the phone book in the capital city over which he once held sway. He lives in the best section of Bogota.

*

There is an alarming tendency (in Colombia, anyway) to view the problems of the local economies as essentially a thing for the Alliance to deal with. Almost like, 'Thank God, Big Brother finally come to the rescue – let him handle it.' This is, of course, a generalization, but there is a lot of truth in it.

Another ominous note is the attitude of a lot of American businessmen I have talked to – 'Sure, we'd like to help, but business is business, you know ...' And everything they say makes sense on at least one level: fears of arbitrary government price controls, expropriation, mounting labour difficulties, and the risks of long-term investments vs. the near-certainty of the short.

Quito, Ecuador

The sun is shining in Quito, the mountains are green and sparkling around the town, and my mind is running in high gear.

Most everything I have to say, however, revolves in one way or another around questions of money. There seems to be a universal impression that I am on some sort of divine dole, and the theory that I often require money in order to make money has not gained wide acceptance. I trust you have sufficient background in personal economics to grasp the full meaning of this.

I could toss in a few hair-raising stories about what happens to poor *Yanquis* who eat cheap food, or the fact that I caught a bad cold in Bogotá because my hotel didn't have hot water, but that would only depress us both. As it is, I am travelling at least half on gall. But in the course of these travels I have discovered that gall is not always the best currency, and there are times when I would be far better off with the other kind.

I am throwing this thing in your lap though I don't expect anyone to agree – at a distance of several thousand miles – with my certain knowledge that I am a paragon of wisdom, courage, decency, and visionary talent. On the other hand, I am working on my fourth case of dysentery, my stomach feels like a tree is growing in it, and I am medically forbidden to touch so much as a single beer.

Well, this is the longest letter I've written since I was in the Air Force and was sending love letters to a girl in Tallahassee. I don't expect you to be altogether happy with this one, but then the girl wasn't always happy with hers, either, and we both survived.

Ah, it is noon now, check-out time, and I can hear the clang of the cash register across the patio as they rack up another $7 to Señor Thompson, the gringo with the messy room.

*

Things are not going well here, my man. I limped in Saturday night after
a spine-cracking train ride, and on Sunday discovered to my horror that
the president and all the Guayaquil money men are leaving Wednesday
for Washington. For this reason I am having a time seeing anyone —
or at least the right people.

Aside from that problem, I am beset by other forms of plague. One, I
have not had any word from my New York secretary in two weeks so I
have no idea how I stand at the bank. Thus I am afraid to cash a cheque.
The first time I bounce down here I might as well give up and go back
to the States.

The moneyed community on this continent, which is what you have to
deal with when you want to cash cheques, is like Melville's circle of
genius – which 'all over the world stands hand in hand, and one shock
of recognition runs the whole circle round'. Which means, in my case,
that if I bounce a cheque in Cali my reputation as a crook will precede
me to Buenos Aires. So I have to be careful.

Optimism is a rare commodity here, and the daily harassments of life
in Guayaquil are just about as much as a man should have to bear.

Guayaquil, Ecuador
This is to confirm my not particularly pointed observations during yesterday's phone call, which I appreciated a whale of a lot and all the more
because I suspect you did it primarily to keep me from feeding myself
to the giant turtles.

Now I feel better in the head, if not in the stomach. On Monday I will
fly to Lima. I could go before that but Saturday and Sunday are holidays and we just finished a five-day lull having to do with Ecuadorian
history. These holidays are maddening; every time you turn around they
are rolling down the store fronts and locking the offices. That, in addition to a noon to four p.m. lunch hour, makes work just about impossible.

I understand that while I was in Quito my secretary told you I was
in Talara, Peru. I think the New York summer has affected her reason.
Just for the record, I have never been near Talara and will do everything
in my power to avoid it in the future.

Lima, Peru
I have a good peg on Peru. It may seem like heresy in Washington, but
it is a fact that democracy is just about as popular here as eating live
goldfish. I tell you now so you'll have time to ponder. (Some —— has
been throwing rocks at my window all night and if I hadn't sold my
pistol I'd whip up the blinds and crank off a few rounds at his feet. As it

is, all I can do is gripe to the desk.) The street outside is full of thugs, all drunk on pisco. In my weakened condition I am not about to go out there and tackle them like Joe Palooka.

It is all I can do to swing out of bed in the mornings and stumble to the shower, which has come to be my only pleasure. I am beginning to look like the portrait of Dorian Gray; pretty soon I am going to have the mirrors taken out.

Lima, Peru

First, I want to assure you that I exist. There is at present 171 pounds of me – down from 189 in Aruba – and just about the same weight in luggage spread out around this room. I am barred once again from touching even a single beer, any fried foods, spices, pepper, and just about everything else except broiled meat and mineral water.

(Now this hotel doesn't have any more mineral water – How long, O Lord, how long?)

La Paz, Bolivia

I blew in yesterday in unholy shape. This awful spate of pain and sickness puts the fear of God in a man. The latest was the sting of a poison insect in Cuzco, paralysing my leg as if I'd been hit by a fifty-pound sting ray. Anyway, after two visits to the clinic, much cortisone, many infrared lamps, and the inevitable drink-prohibiting antibiotics I was at least able to walk with a cane fashioned out of one of the legs of my camera tripod. That is the state I am in now. I hobble around La Paz like a vet from the Indian wars, averaging about 100 yards an hour on the flats and more like a turtle on the hills.

At the end of this week there will be no electricity in La Paz. Now it is rationed to the point where the United States embassy, for one, has elevator service only every other day. This means I have to go up five flights of stairs on one leg, so I have been impressed with the gravity of the situation.

They work it so that every section of the city gets a turn at having electricity. So on some days you have hot water, elevators, lights, etc., and on some days you don't. If the electricity goes off completely, however, I may have to flee. It is bad enough having to walk up the stairs on the cane, without having no lights or hot water when I get here. Or heat, I might add, and La Paz is cold as Christmas.

Rio de Janeiro, Brazil

I've been trying to get off a letter for about a week now, but have been hopping across jungle and Matto Grosso, touring oil camps, and spending all my money on antibiotics.

I figure, though, that every week I've spent in these countries is a week I won't have to spend the next time I go back. An investment, as it were, and now that I've survived this much of the thing I think I'd be kicking myself right now if I'd just skimmed through.

I definitely mean to base here – for a while, anyway. It is about time I lived like a human being for a change.

National Observer, 31 December 1962

WHAT LURED HEMINGWAY TO KETCHUM?

Ketchum, Idaho

'That poor old man. He used to walk out there on the road in the evenings. He was so frail and thin and old-looking that it was embarrassing to see him. I was always afraid a car would hit him, and that would have been an awful way for him to go. I was tempted to go out and tell him to be careful, and I would have if it had been anyone else. But with Hemingway it was different.'

The neighbour shrugged and glanced at Ernest Hemingway's empty house, a comfortable looking chalet with a big pair of elk horns over the front door. It is built on a hillside looking down on the Big Wood River, and out across the valley at the Sawtooth Mountains.

A mile or so away, in a small graveyard at the north end of town, is Hemingway's simple grave, lying in the afternoon shadow of Baldy Mountain and the Sun Valley ski runs.

Beyond Baldy are the high pastures of the Wood River National Forest, where thousands of sheep graze in the summer, tended by Basque sheepherders from the Pyrenees. All winter long the grave is covered with deep snow, but in the summer tourists come out and take pictures of each other standing beside it. Last summer there was a problem with people taking chunks of earth for souvenirs.

When news of his death made headlines in 1961 there must have been other people besides myself who were not as surprised by the suicide as by the fact that the story was datelined Ketchum, Idaho. What was he doing living there? When had he left Cuba, where most people assumed he was working, against what he knew was his last deadline, on the long-promised big novel?

The newspapers never answered those questions – not for me, at any rate – so it was with a feeling of long-restless curiosity that I came, last week, up the long bleak road to Ketchum, over the drainage divide between the Magic and the Wood River valleys, through Shoshone and Bellevue and Hailey – Ezra Pound's hometown – past Jack's Rock Shop on US 93, and into Ketchum itself, population 783.

Anybody who considers himself a writer or even a serious reader cannot help but wonder just what it was about this outback little Idaho village that struck such a responsive chord in America's most famous writer. He had been coming here off and on since 1938, until finally, in 1960, he bought a home just outside of town and, not incidentally, a ten-minute drive from Sun Valley, which is so much a part of Ketchum that they are really one and the same.

The answers might be instructive – not only as a key to Hemingway, but to a question he often pondered, even in print. 'We do not have great writers,' he explains to the Austrian in *Green Hills of Africa*. 'Something happens to our good writers at a certain age ... You see we make our writers into something very strange ... We destroy them in many ways.' But Hemingway himself never seemed to discover in what way he was being 'destroyed', and so he never understood how to avoid it.

Even so, he knew something had gone wrong with both himself and his writing, and after a few days in Ketchum you get a feeling that he came here for exactly that reason. Because it was here, in the years just before and after World War II, that he came to hunt and ski and raise hell in the local pubs with Gary Cooper and Robert Taylor and all the other celebrities who came to Sun Valley when it still loomed large on café society's map of diversions.

Those were 'the good years', and Hemingway never got over the fact that they couldn't last. He was here with his third wife in 1947, but then he settled in Cuba and twelve years went by before he came again – a different man this time, with yet another wife, Mary, and a different view of the world he had once been able 'to see clear and as a whole'.

Ketchum was perhaps the only place in his world that had not changed radically since the good years. Europe had been completely transformed, Africa was in the process of drastic upheaval, and finally even Cuba blew up around him like a volcano. Castro's educators taught the people that 'Mr Way' had been exploiting them, and he was in no mood in his old age to live with any more hostility than was necessary.

Only Ketchum seemed unchanged, and it was here that he decided to dig in. But there were changes here, too; Sun Valley was no longer a glittering, celebrity-filled winter retreat for the rich and famous, but just another good ski resort in a tough league. 'People were used to him here,' says Chuck Atkinson, owner of a Ketchum motel. 'They didn't bother him and he was grateful for it. His favourite time was the fall. We would go down to Shoshone for the pheasant shooting, or over on the river for some ducks. He was a fine shot, even towards the end, when he was sick.'

Hemingway didn't have many friends in Ketchum. Chuck Atkinson was one of them, and when I saw him one morning in his house on a peak overlooking the town, he had just received a copy of *A Moveable Feast*. 'Mary sent it from New York,' he explained. 'I read part of it after breakfast; it's good, it sounds more like him than some of the other stuff.'

Another friend was Taylor 'Beartracks' Williams, a veteran guide who died last year and was buried near the man who gave him the original manuscript of *For Whom the Bell Tolls*. It was 'Beartracks' who took Hemingway into the mountains after elk, bear, antelope, and sheep in the days when 'Papa' was still a meat-hunter.

Not surprisingly, Hemingway has acquired quite a few friends since his death. 'You're writing a story on Ketchum?' asked a bartender. 'Why don't you do one on all the people who knew Hemingway? Sometimes I get the feeling I'm the only person in town who didn't.'

Charley Mason, a wandering pianist, is one of the few people who spent much time with him, mainly listening, because 'When Ernie had a few drinks he could carry on for hours with all kinds of stories. It was better than reading his books.'

I met Mason in the Sawtooth Club on Main Street, when he came in to order coffee over the bar. He is off the booze these days and people who know him say he looks ten years younger. As he talked, I had an odd feeling that he was somehow a creation of Hemingway's, that he had escaped from one of the earlier short stories.

'He was a hell of a drinker,' Mason said with a chuckle. 'I remember one time over at the Tram [a local pub] just a few years ago; he was with two Cubans – one was a great big Negro, a gun-runner he knew from the Spanish Civil War, and the other was a delicate little guy, a neurosurgeon from Havana with fine hands like a musician. That was a three-day session. They were blasted on wine the whole time and jabbering in Spanish like revolutionaries. One afternoon when I was there, Hemingway jerked the chequered cloth off the table and he and the other big guy took turns making the little doctor play the bull. They'd whirl and jerk the cloth around – it was a hell of a sight.'

On another evening, out at Sun Valley, Mason took a break on the stand and sat down for a while at Hemingway's table. In the course of the conversation Mason asked him what it took 'to break in on the literary life, or anything else creative, for that matter'.

'Well,' said Hemingway, 'there's only one thing I live by – that's having the power of conviction and knowing what to leave out.' He had said the same thing before, but whether he still believed it in the winter of his years is another matter. There is good evidence that he was not always sure what to leave out, and very little evidence to show that his power of conviction survived the war.

That power of conviction is a hard thing for any writer to sustain, and especially so once he becomes conscious of it. Fitzgerald fell apart when the world no longer danced to his music; Faulkner's conviction faltered when he had to confront twentieth-century Negroes instead of the black symbols in his books; and when Dos Passos tried to change his convictions he lost all his power.

Today we have Mailer, Jones, and Styron, three potentially great writers bogged down in what seems to be a crisis of convictions brought on, like Hemingway's, by the mean nature of a world that will not stand still long enough for them to see it clear as a whole.

It is not just a writer's crisis, but they are the most obvious victims because the function of art is supposedly to bring order out of chaos, a tall order even when the chaos is static, and a superhuman task in a time when chaos is multiplying.

Hemingway was not a political man. He did not care for movements, but dealt in his fiction with the stresses and strains on individuals in a world that seemed far less complex, prior to World War II, than it has since. Rightly or wrongly, his taste ran to large and simple (but not easy) concepts – to blacks and whites, as it were, and he was not comfortable with the multitude of grey shadings that seem to be the wave of the future.

It was not Hemingway's wave, and in the end he came back to Ketchum, never ceasing to wonder, says Mason, why he hadn't been killed years earlier in the midst of violent action on some other part of the globe. Here, at least, he had mountains and a good river below his house; he could live among rugged, non-political people and visit, when he chose to, with a few of his famous friends who still came up to Sun Valley. He could sit in the Tram or the Alpine or the Sawtooth Club and talk with men who felt the same way he did about life, even if they were not so articulate. In this congenial atmosphere he felt he could get away from the pressures of a world gone mad, and 'write truly' about life as he had in the past.

Ketchum was Hemingway's Big Two Hearted River, and he wrote his own epitaph in the story of the same name, just as Scott Fitzgerald had written his epitaph in a book called *The Great Gatsby*. Neither man understood the vibrations of a world that had shaken them off their thrones, but of the two, Fitzgerald showed more resilience. His half-finished *Last Tycoon* was a sincere effort to catch up and come to grips with reality, no matter how distasteful it might have seemed to him.

Hemingway never made such an effort. The strength of his youth became rigidity as he grew older, and his last book was about Paris in the twenties.

Standing on a corner in the middle of Ketchum it is easy to see the connection Hemingway must have made between this place and those he had known in the good years. Aside from the brute beauty of the mountains, he must have recognized an atavistic distinctness in the people that piqued his sense of dramatic possibilities. It is a raw and peaceful little village, especially in the off season with neither winter skiers nor summer fishermen to dilute the image. Only the main street is paved; most of the others are no more than dirt and gravel tracks that seem at times to run right through front yards.

From such a vantage point a man tends to feel it is not so difficult, after all, to see the world clear and as a whole. Like many another writer, Hemingway did his best work when he felt he was standing on something solid – like an Idaho mountainside, or a sense of conviction.

Perhaps he found what he came here for, but the odds are huge that he didn't. He was an old, sick, and very troubled man, and the illusion of peace and contentment was not enough for him – not even when his friends came up from Cuba and played bullfight with him in the Tram. So finally, and for what he must have thought the best of reasons, he ended it with a shotgun.

National Observer, 25 May 1964

LIVING IN THE TIME OF ALGER, GREELEY, DEBS

OLD-TIME BOOMERS STILL STOMP THE WEST, BUT AIR CONDITIONING'S BETTER

Pierre, SD

I had met the tramp digger the night before. And because he was broke and I wasn't, I bought him a hotel room so he wouldn't have to sleep in the grass beside the road to Spokane. But instead of travelling the next day, he took what was left of his cash and sat by himself on a stool at the Thunderbird Bar in downtown Missoula, sullenly nursing his drinks as he had the night before, and putting his change in the juke box, which can be a very expensive machine for those who need steady noise to keep from thinking.

It was four in the morning when he knocked on the door of my hotel room. 'Sorry to bother you, pard,' he said. 'I heard your typewriter going, but I just got lonely, you know – I had to talk to somebody.'

'Well,' I said, not really surprised to find him still in town, 'I guess we could both use some coffee. Let's go to the Oxford, it's open all night.' We went down the stairs of the silent hotel and through the lobby where a sleepy desk clerk looked up and wondered, with that bailiff's leer that desk clerks have been cultivating since the beginning of time, just what sort of a journalist I was if it was necessary to have vagrants calling on me at this rude hour on a chill Montana morning.

Which may be a valid question. But then somebody else might ask what sort of a journalist would spend six weeks travelling around the West and not write about Bobby Cleary, the tramp digger with no home and a downhill run to a guaranteed early grave; Bob Barnes, the half-deaf wildcat trucker who never understood that his life was a desperate game of musical chairs; or the lean, stuttering redhead from Pennsylvania who said his name was Ray and had hitchhiked West to find a place 'where a man can still make an honest living'.

You will find them along the highways, in the all-night diners, and in the old brass-rail bars that still serve ten-cent beer – a motley, varied, and always talkative legion of men who fit no pattern except that they all seem like holdovers from the days of the Great Depression. You will not find them any place where men wear suits and ties or work at steady jobs. These are the boomers, the drifters, the hard travellers, and the tramp diggers who roam the long highways of the West as regularly and as stoically as other men ride the subways of New York City. Their work is where they find it, their luggage is rarely more than one small suitcase or a paper sack, and their view of the future is every bit as grim as it is limited.

These are the people who never got the message that rugged individualism has made some drastic adjustments in these hyper-organized times. They are still living in the era of Horace Greeley, Horatio Alger and, in some cases, Eugene Debs. They want no part of 'city living', but they have neither the education nor the interest to understand why it is ever more difficult for them to make a living 'out here in the open'. The demise of the easy-living, independent West has made them bitter and sometimes desperate. In the old days a man with a normal variety of skills could roll into any Western hamlet or junction and find an odd job or two that would pay his way and usually provide a little margin to spend with the local sports.

Today it takes a union card before you can talk turkey with most construction foremen, and many of the big companies have a hard core of regulars who move from one project to another. You see them on the highways in Wyoming, Colorado, and the Dakotas, caravans of pickups pulling house trailers, flat-beds hauling bulldozers, and hard-faced men from California and Texas with their families in the cab and their automobiles riding high in the beds of big dump trucks *en route* from an interstate highway job in Montana, for instance, to a dam-building project in Colorado.

This is the well-paid élite of the transient construction industry that is getting fat on Federal projects that more and more Western states are coming to view as economic necessities.

Some people accuse Western governors, senators, and representatives of dipping into the 'pork barrel', but others say these projects are no more than prudent allocations of the taxpayers' money for necessary construction that Western states either cannot or will not afford. At any rate it is a big industry in the West, a money tree for a lot of people including the foremen and the skilled heavy-equipment operators who make up the construction élite – and a massive source of both hope and frustration to the boomers, drifters, and other freelance labourers who go high on the hog when they get hired, and live like hobos when they don't.

'Bud', the broad-shouldered, pot-bellied cat driver, was not unhappy with life when I met him in a big dance hall in Jackson, Wyo. He was wearing an expensive grey stetson and a pair of fancy cowboy boots that had not made much of a dent in his $200-a-week salary on the road-building job outside of town. In the course of an hour he asked about thirty girls to dance, got turned down by at least twenty-five, and spent the rest of his time posing regally at the bar, dispensing wisdom and humour in every direction. At one point he let his gaze flash over the crowd and pronounced in the manner of a man long-skilled in the squandering of vast sums: 'These damn silly tourists think they're big spenders! Ha! We'll see.' At last, he swept his change off the bar and disappeared.

The tramp digger in Missoula had not been so lucky. He wore a cheap, frayed windbreaker that was all but useless in the bitter nights of a late Rocky Mountain spring. He was tall, with the thick neck and sloping shoulders of a man who works with his back, but his eyes were dull in a slack face, and he walked with a weary shuffle that made him seem like an old man at twenty-six.

As we walked along the deserted sidewalks of Higgins Avenue I asked him what plans he had. 'I don't know, pard,' he said with a shrug and a half smile, 'maybe California, maybe Utah, it's all the same. I'll just hit the road when it gets light. There's always work for a good hard-rock digger.'

Bobby Cleary was a specialist of sorts; as a tramp digger he is a body for hire in any kind of dangerous, underground work. He had come over from Butte where he said he was black-listed in the mines because he had quit too often. There was no work in Missoula, he was stone broke, and his prospects for the immediate future were not real bright. Now he looked up at the sky that was already getting grey, took the butt of an old cigarette from behind his ear, lit it, and recited what seemed to be his motto:

'That's the way it goes – first your money, then your clothes.'

He had said it several times the night before, when we had struck up a conversation in the Thunderbird after he had frightened everybody else at the bar with a loud diatribe on 'justice for the working man, by Jesus. My old man fought for the union and one of these days I'm gonna write it all down like Jack London. By Jesus he cared. He knew what it was like, and how about another whisky here, fella, for a no-count tramp digger!'

In the Oxford Café – or 'The Ox', as it is called by its generally unemployed and often homeless habitués – I ordered coffee, and Cleary asked for 'a bowl of beans'. He looked at me and grinned: 'I figure you're buyin', pard. Otherwise I'd have ordered a glass of water and crackers,' he nodded. 'Starch and water, it fills the belly.'

I reached in the pocket of my leather sheepherder's jacket, pulled out a black, passport-sized wallet, and put two dollars on the counter. In the dreary dawn of a hobo's breakfast at the Oxford Café, that wallet seemed as out of place as a diplomatic pouch or a pair of cashmere Levi's.

It was a week or so later when the wallet embarrassed me again. I had picked up an elderly hitchhiker named Bob Barnes on Interstate 90 near the cattle town of Miles City, Mont. We stopped for gas at the North Dakota line, and I left the wallet on the dashboard while I wired up a defective muffler. When I got back in the car he said very quietly: 'That's a real nice wallet; where did you get it?'

'Buenos Aires,' I said, then immediately added, 'things are cheap down there.' But I had not been quick enough and it showed in his face; here was a young punk with a fat black wallet, idly pulling rank on an old man who felt himself going down and out, for some reason that was either senseless or cruel, or both.

Bob Barnes was an ex-truck driver, who looked like an ageing schoolteacher. He was too old now for any chance of a job with the big hauling companies, but still able to work as a 'wildcatter', which is like saying a pitcher cut loose by the Yankees might still catch on with the Mets. He had borrowed some money to come out from Minneapolis to Great Falls, Mont., where he had an old friend who owned a small trucking firm and would give him a job. But the friend had moved to California and nothing else was available – at least not before his money ran out, and when that happened he began riding his thumb back to Minneapolis with not even a toothbrush or a pack of cigarettes for luggage, and not a dime in his pocket.

When I picked him up around noon on Saturday, he had not eaten since Friday morning. 'Every time I walked past one of those highway restaurants I thought about going in and asking if I could wash dishes for a meal,' he said, 'but I just couldn't do it. I'm not a bum and I don't know how to act like one.'

We were together all afternoon, a long hot drive across the plains and the badlands to Bismarck, but it was late in the day before he finally got around to admitting that his trip was not a lark of some kind.

When he finally began talking about himself, I wished he hadn't. His wife had been killed two years earlier in an automobile accident. Since then he had been a drifter, but it was a hard dollar for a man in his fifties, and this wild stab at a job in Montana was his last real idea what to do with himself. When he got back to Minneapolis he thought he could 'arrange a loan until things get better'.

Unlike the other boomers I met, Bob Barnes has gone the whole route and found it pretty barren in the homestretch. He has pushed big timber trucks through blizzards in northern Minnesota and driven straight through from Florida to Chicago with a load of tomatoes that would spoil if he stopped to sleep. He has driven every kind of rig on every major highway in the nation. He knows the names of waitresses in truck stops in Virginia and Texas and Oregon. And he can tell you how to get from New York to Los Angeles with a heavyweight load by taking back roads and avoiding the truck scales; there is only one route left, and only a few veteran wildcatters know it.

I dropped him at the Salvation Army in Bismarck, where he would get a bowl of soup and a cot for the night before striking out again in the morning for Minneapolis. We shook hands and wished each other good luck. I felt like a pious hypocrite and drove off rapidly, without looking back.

Several days later, on the flat back ribbon that runs from Bismarck down the prairie to Pierre, I picked up a young, happy-go-lucky type from Pennsylvania. He had just quit a hay-hauling job in North Dakota and was on his way to Los Angeles, where he felt sure of getting a job.

Maybe so, I thought, but I hope I don't have to pick you up in ten years when they've really tightened the screws, because the day of the boomer is rapidly coming to an end. In the age of automation and job security, a touch of the wanderlust is the kiss of death. In any count of the chronically unemployed the boomers will be very prominent; they have never sought security, but only work; they have never saved, but only earned and spent – participating, as it were, in an increasingly technological economy that has less and less room for their sort with every passing year.

When we got to Pierre I dropped the young optimist and his blue plastic suitcase on the south side of town. He got out in the middle of a small dust storm and pointed his thumb towards Los Angeles.

I returned to the Holiday Inn – where they have a swimming pool and air-conditioned rooms – to consider the paradox of a nation that has given so much to those who preach the glories of rugged individualism from the security of countless corporate sinecures, and so little to that diminishing band of yesterday's refugees who still practise it, day by day, in a tough, rootless and sometimes witless style that most of us have long since been weaned away from.

National Observer, 13 July 1964

MARLON BRANDO AND THE INDIAN FISH-IN

Olympia, Wash.
'As an actor, he's not much of a field general.' That was the consensus here last week after Marlon Brando's well-publicized but futile and disorganized attempt to help local Indians 'regain' fishing rights granted them more than 100 years ago under treaties with the US Government.

The old Governor Hotel, just down the street from the State Capitol, was almost taken over by Indians who came from every corner of the nation to protest 'encroachment' on their historic treaty rights. The show was billed as the turning point for the American Indian in this century. Said one of the leaders: 'Up to now we've always been on the defensive, but now we've reached a point where it's life or death for the Indian culture, and we've decided to take the offensive.'

Early rumours had it that not only Mr Brando, but Paul Newman, James Baldwin, and Eugene Burdick would be on hand to offer moral support and draw publicity. But of the four only Mr Brando showed up, along with writers Kay Boyle and Paul Jacobs from San Francisco, and the Rev. John J. Yaryan, canon precentor of San Francisco Grace Cathedral. The canon arrived with a white bucket marked 'bait', and the blessing of his bishop, James A. Pike. The idea was to stage a 'fish-in' for the Indian cause.

More than fifty tribes were represented by some 500 Indians at the gathering, and one of the leaders said happily that it was the first time Indians had demonstrated any unity since the battle of Little Big Horn.

This time, though, things didn't go so well for the red man. Mr Brando led the Indians in three separate assaults against 'the forces of injustice', and they lost all three. By week's end, the show had fizzled out and Mr Brando was off in the wilderness of the northwest Olympic Peninsula, trying to get himself arrested again and prove some point that had long since been lost in the chaos that characterized the affair from beginning to end.

Even so, the thing was a qualified success almost in spite of itself. Among the important results were:

√ A new feeling of unity among Indians, where previously there had been none.

√ Plenty of publicity for the Indian cause, thanks largely to Mr Brando's presence.

√ The emergence of a new, dynamic leadership in the form of the National Indian Youth Council.

√ Emergence of the fact that the Indian wants no part of the Negro civil-rights cause and will make every effort to detach himself from it.

√ The inescapable conclusion that the Indians still have a long way to go before they can speak with one voice, or even make themselves heard effectively without the help of people like Mr Brando.

The aim of the whole affair was to protest the state of Washington's forbidding the Indians to fish with nets on certain areas outside their tiny reservations.

The Indians point out that the Treaty of Medicine Creek, signed in 1854 by representatives of Washington state Indians and the US Government, deprived them of their reservations but permitted them to fish in 'usual and accustomed places'. So, they claim, did other treaties of similar vintage.

The most 'usual' place for these Indians – mostly members of the Nisqually and Puyallup tribes – has been the Nisqually River, fed by a Mt Rainier glacier and cutting sixty miles to enter Puget Sound a few miles south of Tacoma.

In recent years they have used nylon gill nets and other increasingly effective gear of the white man – to the discomfiture of sportsmen restricted to rod and reel, commercial fishermen banned from the river entirely, and fisheries officials who fear complete loss of salmon and steelhead trout runs.

So last month the state supreme court ruled that the state can restrict off-reservation Indian net-fishing in areas it deems the more necessary to protect salmon and steelhead runs. The state did so, and the Indians promptly claimed this action violated the Treaty of Medicine Creek.

Says Janet McCloud, Tulalip Indian whose husband fishes the Nisqually: 'They [the original treaty-makers] promised us we could fish for eternity – as long as the mountain stands, the grass grows green, and the sun shines ...' The state game department, she said, thinks the steelhead belongs to the white man. 'They must think the steelhead swam over behind the *Mayflower*.'

Since the state restricted their fishing, the Indians have been organizing in protest. The state, by way of defence of its action, points to the majority decision of the supreme court, which said, 'None of the signatories to the original treaty contemplated fishing with a 600-foot nylon gill net, which could prevent the escapement of any fish up the river for spawning purposes.'

The Indians deny this. They say such factors as pollution and dam-building are contributing heavily to depletion of Washington's fish, and add that only thirty per cent of fish caught in Washington are caught by Indians – the rest going to sportsmen and white commercial fishermen.

That was the background to last week's developments. For the Indians, the week began well and became progressively worse. On Monday Mr Brando and Canon Yaryan got themselves arrested for using a drift net to catch two steelheads in the Puyallup River near Tacoma, where a recently issued injunction forbids net-fishing by Indians or anyone else. They also got a lot of half-serious publicity, but to Mr Brando's chagrin the charges were quickly dropped. Said Pierce County Prosecutor John McCutcheon: 'Brando is no fisherman. He was here to make a point. There's no use prolonging this thing.'

And so, reluctantly, the rest of the day was taken up with a series of strategy meetings dominated by Mr Brando and a bevy of lawyers, one of whom gave a nearly superhuman performance by managing to appear in almost as many news photographs as did Mr Brando.

So the 'fish-in' proved nothing except that a Hollywood actor and an Episcopal minister can fish illegally in Washington and get away with it. The Indians were no better off, and the only one who took the risk of fishing with Mr Brando and the canon now faces a contempt-of-court charge for defying an injunction.

Nor did a mass demonstration at the State Capitol on Tuesday help the cause. Gov. Albert D. Rosellini, along with about 1500 others, listened to several fiery speeches and a 'proclamation of protest' concerning 'harassment' of Indians, then gave a flat 'no' to proposals that Indians be given greater freedom to fish in 'the usual and accustomed places'. To do so, said the governor, would be to condone a 'hazard' to state fish resources.

Mr Brando called the governor's stand 'unsatisfactory' and said he would step up his efforts on behalf of the Indians. 'We're prepared to go all the way to the wall with this thing,' he told reporters. 'I'll keep on fishing, and if it means going to jail, I'll go to jail.'

All of which made good copy for the local press, but nobody seemed to know what good would come of it. At one point, a lynx-eyed young lady in a very tight dress asked the actor if it was true that some of the Indians resented his new role as 'the Indian spokesman'.

Her question was merely the public echo of a feeling that quite a few people had expressed in private. There was no doubt that Mr Brando's presence at the affair drew a lot of public attention, but much of it was irrelevant and led to speculation – some in print – that he was 'doing the whole thing for personal publicity'.

He wasn't, but he so completely dominated the scene that many of the Indians felt lucky when anyone noticed them at all. The issue came to a head when a television network scheduled an interview with several leaders of the youth council. It was a chance for the Indians to present their point of view to a nationwide audience that is largely ignorant of their problems. But Mr Brando vetoed the interview because he had plans for another 'fish-in' on the same day, and wanted all the Indians with him.

Unfortunately, he couldn't convince the press to drive four hours through a rainstorm to cover an event that seemed to have no news value. Contrary to his expectations, the publicity effort was a flop.

•

In all, the whole affair suffered badly from lack of organization. Mr Brando was undoubtedly sincere in his effort; he talked persuasively and at great length about Indian problems, but he seemed to have no strategy except to get himself arrested.

Only three or four people among the several hundred involved seemed to have any idea what was happening from one hour to the next. An air of mystery and intrigue pervaded the whole affair. Mr Brando explained it as being necessary to keep the authorities in the dark, but the authorities were several jumps ahead of him at every turn, and the only people really in the dark were the reporters, who were generally sympathetic at first; the Indians, many of whom had taken time off from their jobs to come to Olympia and accomplish something; and the lawyers, whose laboriously contrived strategy proved ineffective at every showdown.

Aside from lack of organization, another root problem was the Indians' fear of getting their 'cause' identified in the public mind with the Negro civil-rights movement. 'We're happy to have Marlon on our side,' said one Indian leader. 'But he's one of our big problems, too, because he keeps making statements comparing Indians and Negroes; the two movements are entirely different. The Negroes don't have the law on their side yet and they have a lot of popular prejudice against them, while the Indians' problem is the Federal bureaucracy; we almost have the law on our side in the form of treaties, and all we ask the white man to do is live up to those treaties.'

A press statement explaining why a proclamation of protest was being presented to the governor was very explicit on this subject: 'The presentation shall be conducted in such a manner as to ensure that the great pride and dignity of the Indian people will be upheld.' Many Indians are very touchy about their pride, and regard the Negro effort as crude and undignified.

Here in Washington state, in fact, a 'splinter group' of Indians has caused a schism in Indian ranks by retaining Jack Tanner, president of the Tacoma branch of the National Association for the Advancement of Colored People (NAACP), to represent them. Mr Tanner, a Negro, called the Olympia protest 'ridiculous', and on Wednesday had five clients stage a separate 'fish-in' of their own, for which they were immediately arrested.

As the Indians press their fight, the youth council probably will do much of the fighting, and its emergence here was a major event. Up to now the relation between these 'young turks' and the Indians' traditional tribal councils has been roughly the same as once existed between young Negroes and the NAACP – the youths often felt they were 'on the outside'. But last week they were clearly running the Indian show.

*

'Sure, we made a lot of mistakes,' says Clyde Warrior, one of the most aggressive of the young turks, 'so now we know what not to do next time. This was just a beginning. Wait until we get rolling.'

Which will take a bit of time. The youth council operates on a financial shoestring, and its members hold down full-time jobs to support themselves. Most are college graduates, more articulate than their elders, and much more willing to 'offend a few people', as Mr Warrior says, in order to get things done.

The significant thing about last week's events here, in fact, was just that: The Indians, young and old, were willing 'to offend a few people'. Throughout the country, Indians are doing battle with Federal and state governments over a variety of causes. And even though last week's 'fish-in' and assorted protests have resulted only in a stand-off, the attitudes they represented could have wide-ranging repercussions.

National Observer, 9 March 1964

THE 'HASHBURY' IS THE CAPITAL OF THE HIPPIES

San Francisco

In 1965 Berkeley was the axis of what was just beginning to be called the 'new left'. Its leaders were radical, but they were also deeply committed to the society they wanted to change. A prestigious faculty committee said the Berkeley activists were the vanguard of 'a moral revolution among the young', and many professors approved.

Now, in 1967, there is not much doubt that Berkeley has gone through a revolution of some kind, but the end result is not exactly what the original leaders had in mind. Many one-time activists have forsaken politics entirely and turned to drugs. Others have even forsaken Berkeley. During 1966, the hot centre of revolutionary action on the coast began moving across the bay to San Francisco's Haight-Ashbury district, a run-down Victorian neighbourhood of about forty square blocks between the Negro/Fillmore district and Golden Gate Park.

The 'Hashbury' is the new capital of what is rapidly becoming a drug culture. Its denizens are not called radicals or beatniks, but 'hippies' – and perhaps as many as half are refugees from Berkeley and the old North Beach scene, the cradle and the casket of the so-called beat generation.

The other half of the hippy population is too young to identify with Jack Kerouac, or even with Mario Savio. Their average age is about twenty, and most are native Californians. The North Beach types of the late nineteen-fifties were not nearly as provincial as the Haight-Ashbury types are today. The majority of beatniks who flocked into San Francisco ten years ago were transients from the East and Midwest. The literary-artistic nucleus – Kerouac, Ginsberg, et al – was a package deal from New York. San Francisco was only a stop on the big circuit: Tangier, Paris, Greenwich Village, Tokyo and India. The senior beats had a pretty good idea what was going on in the world; they read newspapers, travelled constantly and had friends all over the globe.

The word 'hip' translates roughly as 'wise' or 'tuned-in'. A hippy is somebody who 'knows' what's really happening, and who adjusts or grooves with it. Hippies despise phoniness; they want to be open, honest, loving, free. They reject the plastic pretence of twentieth-century America, preferring to go back to the 'natural life', like Adam and Eve. They reject any kinship with the Beat Generation on the ground that 'those cats were negative, but our thing is positive'. They also reject politics, which is 'just another game'. They don't like money, either, or any kind of aggressiveness.

A serious problem in writing about the Haight-Ashbury is that most of the people you have to talk to are involved, one way or another, in the drug traffic. They have good reason to be leery of strangers who ask questions. A twenty-two-year-old student was recently sentenced to two years in prison for telling an undercover narcotics agent where to buy some marijuana. 'Love' is the password in the Haight-Ashbury, but paranoia is the style. Nobody wants to go to jail.

At the same time, marijuana is everywhere. People smoke it on the sidewalks, in doughnut shops, sitting in parked cars or lounging on the grass in Golden Gate Park. Nearly everyone on the streets between twenty and thirty is a 'head', a user, either of marijuana, LSD, or both. To refuse a proffered 'joint' is to risk being labelled a 'nark' – narcotics agent – a threat and a menace to almost everybody.

With a few loud exceptions, it is only the younger hippies who see themselves as a new breed. 'A completely new thing in this world, man.' The ex-beatniks among them, many of whom are now making money off the new scene, incline to the view that hippies are, in fact, second-generation beatniks and that everything genuine in the Haight-Ashbury is about to be swallowed – like North Beach and the Village – in a wave of publicity and commercialism.

Haight Street, the great white way of what the local papers call 'hippieland', is already dotted with stores catering mainly to the tourist trade. Few hippies can afford a pair of $20 sandals or a 'mod outfit' for $67.50. Nor can they afford the $3.50 door charge at the Fillmore Auditorium and the Avalon Ballroom, the twin wombs of the 'psychedelic, San Francisco, acid-rock sound'. Both the Fillmore and the Avalon are jammed every weekend with borderline hippies who don't mind paying for the music and the light shows. There is always a sprinkling of genuine, barefoot, freaked-out types on the dance floor, but few of them pay to get in. They arrive with the musicians or have other good connections.

Neither of the dance palaces is within walking distance of the Hashbury, especially if you're stoned, and since only a few of the hippies have contacts in the psychedelic power structure, most of them spend their weekend nights either drifting around on Haight Street or loading up on acid – LSD – in somebody's pad. Some of the rock bands play free concerts in Golden Gate Park for the benefit of those brethren who can't afford the dances. But beyond an occasional Happening in the park, the Haight-Ashbury scene is almost devoid of anything 'to do' – at least by conventional standards. An at-home entertainment is nude parties at which celebrants paint designs on each other.

There are no hippy bars, for instance, and only one restaurant above the level of a diner or a lunch counter. This is a reflection of the drug culture, which has no use for booze and regards food as a necessity to be acquired at the least possible expense. A 'family' of hippies will work for hours over an exotic stew or curry in a communal kitchen, but the idea of paying $3 for a meal in a restaurant is out of the question.

Some hippies work, others live on money from home and many are full-time beggars. The post office is a major source of hippy income. Jobs like sorting mail don't require much thought or effort. A hippy named Admiral Love of the Psychedelic Rangers delivers special-delivery letters at night. The admiral is in his mid-twenties and makes enough money to support an apartmentful of younger hippies who depend on him for their daily bread.

There is also a hippy-run employment agency on Haight Street and anyone needing part-time labour or some kind of specialized work can call and order as many freaks as he needs; they might look a bit weird, but many are far more capable than most 'temporary help', and vastly more interesting to have around.

Those hippies who don't work can easily pick up a few dollars a day panhandling along Haight Street. The fresh influx of curiosity-seekers has proved a great boon to the legion of psychedelic beggars. During several days of roaming around the area, I was touched so often that I began to keep a supply of quarters in my pocket so I wouldn't have to haggle over change. The panhandlers are usually barefoot, always young and never apologetic. They'll share what they collect anyway, so it seems entirely reasonable that strangers should share with them.

The best show on Haight Street is usually on the sidewalk in front of the Drog Store, a new coffee bar at the corner of Masonic Street. The Drog Store features an all-hippy revue that runs day and night. The acts change sporadically, but nobody cares. There will always be at least one man with long hair and sunglasses playing a wooden pipe of some kind. He will be wearing either a Dracula cape, a long Buddhist robe, or a Sioux Indian costume. There will also be a hairy blond fellow wearing a Black Bart cowboy hat and a spangled jacket that originally belonged to a drum major in the 1949 Rose Bowl parade. He will be playing the bongo drums. Next to the drummer will be a dazed-looking girl wearing a blouse (but no bra) and a plastic mini-skirt, slapping her thighs to the rhythm of it all.

These three will be the nucleus of the show. Backing them up will be an all-star cast of freaks, every one of them stoned. They will be stretched out on the sidewalk, twitching and babbling in time to the music. Now and then somebody will fall out of the audience and join the revue; perhaps a Hell's Angel or some grubby, chain-draped impostor who never owned a motorcycle in his life. Or maybe a girl wrapped in gauze or a thin man with wild eyes who took an overdose of acid nine days ago and changed himself into a raven. For those on a quick tour of the Hashbury, the Drog Store revue is a must.

Most of the local action is beyond the reach of anyone without access to drugs. There are four or five bars a nervous square might relax in, but one is a Lesbian place, another is a hangout for brutal-looking leather fetishists and the others are old neighbourhood taverns full of brooding middle-aged drunks. Prior to the hippy era there were three good Negro-run jazz bars on Haight Street, but they soon went out of style. Who needs jazz, or even beer, when you can sit down on a public kerbstone, drop a pill on your mouth, and hear fantastic music for hours at a time in your own head? A cap of good acid costs $5, and for that you can hear the Universal Symphony, with God singing solo and the Holy Ghost on drums.

Drugs have made formal entertainment obsolete in the Hashbury, but only until somebody comes up with something appropriate to the new style of the neighbourhood. This summer will see the opening of the new Straight Theater, formerly the Haight Theater, featuring homosexual movies for the trade, meetings, concerts, dances. 'It's going to be a kind of hippy community centre,' said Brent Dangerfield, a young radio engineer from Salt Lake City who stopped off in San Francisco on his way to a job in Hawaii and now is a partner in the Straight. When I asked

Dangerfield how old he was he had to think for a minute. 'I'm twenty-two,' he said finally, 'but I used to be much older.'

Another new divertissement, maybe, will be a hippy bus line running up and down Haight Street, housed in a 1930 Fagol bus – a huge, lumbering vehicle that might have been the world's first house trailer. I rode in it one afternoon with the driver, a young hippy named Tim Thibeau who proudly displayed a bathtub under one of the rear seats. The bus was a spectacle even on Haight Street: people stopped, stared and cheered as we rumbled by, going nowhere at all. Thibeau honked the horn and waved. He was from Chicago, he said, but when he got out of the Army he stopped in San Francisco and decided to stay. He was living, for the moment, on unemployment insurance, and his plans for the future were hazy. 'I'm in no hurry,' he said. 'Right now I'm just taking it easy, just floating along.' He smiled and reached for a beer can in the Fagol's icebox.

Dangerfield and Thibeau reflect the blind optimism of the younger hippy element. They see themselves as the vanguard of a new way of life in America – the psychedelic way – where love abounds and work is fun and people help each other. The young hippies are confident that things are going their way.

The older hippies are not so sure. They've been waiting a long time for the world to go their way, and those most involved in the hip scene are hedging their bets this time. 'That back to nature scene is okay when you're twenty,' said one. 'But when you're looking at thirty-five you want to know something's happening to you.'

Ed Denson, at twenty-seven, is an ex-beatnik, ex-Goldwaterite, ex-Berkeley radical and currently the manager of a successful rock band called Country Joe and the Fish. His home and headquarters is a complex of rooms above a liquor store in Berkeley. One room is an art studio, another is an office; there is also a kitchen, a bedroom and several sparsely furnished areas without definition.

Denson is deeply involved in the hippy music scene, but insists he's not a hippy. 'I'm very pessimistic about where this thing is going,' he said. 'Right now it's good for a lot of people. It's still very open. But I have to look back at the Berkeley scene. There was a tremendous optimism there, too, but look where all that went. The beat generation? Where are they now? What about hula-hoops? Maybe this hippy thing is more than a fad; maybe the whole world is turning on but I'm not optimistic. Most of the hippies I know don't really understand what kind of a world they're living in. I get tired of hearing about what beautiful people we all are. If the hippies were more realistic they'd stand a better chance of surviving.'

•

Most hippies take the question of survival for granted, but it's becoming increasingly obvious as the neighbourhood fills with penniless heads, that there is simply not enough food and lodging to go around. A partial solution may come from a group called the Diggers, who have been called the 'worker-priests' of the hippy movement and the 'invisible government' of the Hashbury. The Diggers are young and aggressively pragmatic; they have set up free lodging centres, free soup kitchens and free clothing distribution centres. They comb the neighbourhood soliciting donations of everything from money to stale bread to camping equipment. Diggers' signs are posted in local stores, asking for donations of hammers, saws, shovels, shoes and anything else that vagrant hippies might use to make themselves at least partially self-supporting.

The name and spirit derive from small groups of seventeenth-century English rural revolutionaries, called both Diggers and True Levellers, who had socialist ideas. Money should be abolished, communal farms could support all those willing to work them, and individual ownership of land would be outlawed. The Diggers were severely harassed and the movement eventually caved in under the weight of public opprobrium.

The Hashbury Diggers have fared a bit better, but the demand for food and lodging is beginning to exceed the supply. For a while, the Diggers were able to serve three meals, however meagre, each afternoon in Golden Gate Park. But as the word got around, more and more hippies showed up to eat, and the Diggers were forced to roam far afield to get food. Occasionally there were problems, as when Digger chieftain Emmett Grogan, twenty-three, called a local butcher a 'fascist pig and a coward' when he refused to donate meat scraps. The butcher whacked Grogan with the flat side of his meat cleaver.

The Digger ethic of mass sharing goes along with the American Indian motif that is basic to the Hashbury scene. The cult of 'tribalism' is regarded by many of the older hippies as the key to survival. Poet Gary Snyder, a hippy guru, sees a 'back to the land' movement as the answer to the food and lodging problem. He urges hippies to move out of the cities, form tribes, purchase land and live communally in remote areas. He cites a hippy 'clan' calling itself the Mama-Lila as a model (though the clan still dwells in the Hashbury):

'Well, now,' Snyder says, 'like, you are asking how it's going to work. Well, the Maha-Lila is a group of about three different families who have sort of pooled their resources, which are not very great. But they have decided to pay together and to work together and to take care of each other and that means all of them have ways of getting a small amount of bread, which they share. And other people contribute a little money when it comes in. And then they work together on creative projects, like they're working together on a light-show right now for a poetry reading that we're going to give. And they consider themselves a kind of extended family or clan.

'That's the model. They relate it to a larger sense of the tribe, which is loose, but for the time being everybody has to be able – from time to time – to do some little job. The thing that makes it different is that you don't have a very tight monogamous family unit, but a slightly larger unit where the sharing is greater.'

The tribal concept makes a lot better sense than simply depending on the Diggers. There are indications, however, that the youthful provincialism of the Haight-Ashbury is due for a forced consciousness-expansion. For the past few months, the scene has been filling up with would-be hippies from other parts of the country, primarily Los Angeles and New York. The real influx is expected this summer. The city is rife with rumours, reliable and otherwise, that anywhere from 50,000 to 200,000 'indigent young people' will descend on San Francisco as soon as the school year ends.

The Diggers are appalled at the prospect. 'Where are they going to stay?' says one. 'What are they going to do?' A girl who works in one of the Digger kitchens shrugs and says: 'The Diggers will continue to receive the casualties of the love generation.' Local officials, from the Mayor down, are beginning to panic. Civic leaders in the Haight-Ashbury have suggested that sleeping facilities be provided in Golden Gate Park or in nearby Kezar Stadium but Police Chief Tom Cahill said no.

'Law and order will prevail,' he insisted. 'There will be no sleeping in the park. There are no sanitation facilities and if we let them camp there we would have a tremendous health problem. Hippies are no asset to the community. These people do not have the courage to face the reality of life. They are trying to escape. Nobody should let their young children take part in this hippy thing.'

In March, the city's health director, Dr Ellis Sox, sent a task force of inspectors on a door-to-door sweep of the Haight-Ashbury. Reports of as many as 200 people living in one house or fifty in one apartment had stirred rumours of impending epidemics in the neighbourhood. In a two-day blitz, eight teams of inspectors checked roughly 1400 buildings and issued a total of sixty-five deadline notices to repair sanitation faults. But only sixteen of the sixty-five notices, according to the *San Francisco Chronicle*, were issued to occupants 'whose bizarre dress and communal living habits could class them as hippies'.

Dr Sox had no choice but to back off. 'The situation is not as bad as we thought,' he said. 'There has been a deterioration [of sanitation] in the Haight-Ashbury, but the hippies did not contribute much more to it than other members of the neighbourhood.' Dr Sox went on to deny that his mass inspection was part of a general campaign against weirdos, but nobody seemed to believe him.

The Haight-Ashbury Neighbourhood Council, a nonhippy group of permanent residents, denounced Dr Sox for his 'gratuitous criticism of our community'. The council accused city officials of 'creating an artificial problem' and harassing the hippies out of 'personal and official' prejudice.

As recently as 1962, the Haight-Ashbury was a drab, working-class district, slowly filling with Negroes and so plagued by crime and violence that residents formed vigilante patrols. Housewives were mugged on the way to the grocery store, teenagers were slashed and stomped in gang rumbles, and every drunk on Haight Street was fair game for local jack-rollers.

Now, with the coming of the drug culture, even the squarest of the neighbourhood old-timers say the streets are safer than they have been for years. Burglaries are still a problem but violence is increasingly rare. It is hard to find anyone outside the hippy community who will say that psychedelic drugs have made the neighbourhood a better place to live. But it's even harder to find a person who wouldn't rather step over a giggling freak on the sidewalk than worry about hoodlums with switchblades. The fact that the hippies and the squares have worked out such a peaceful coexistence seems to baffle the powers at City Hall.

A lot of cheap labels describe what is happening in the Hashbury, but none of them make much sense: the love generation, the happening generation, the combine generation and even the LSD generation. The last is the best of the lot, but in the interest of accuracy it should probably be amended to the head generation.

A 'head', in the language of hip, is a user of psychedelic drugs: LSD, marijuana ('grass'), mescaline, peyote, methedrine, benzedrine, and a half-dozen others that are classified in the trade as mind-stimulating, consciousness-expanding, or 'head' drugs. At the other end of the spectrum are 'body' drugs: opium, heroin, barbiturates and even alcohol. These are basically depressants, while head drugs are stimulants. But neither type comes with a manufacturer's guarantee, and the Hashbury is full of people whose minds have been jerked around savagely by drugs that were supposed to induce peaceful euphoria.

Another hazard is the widespread tendency to mix two or three drugs at one time. Acid and alcohol can be a lethal combination, causing fits of violence, suicidal depression and a general freak-out that ends in jail or a hospital.

There is widespread concern, at least in San Francisco, about the dangers of so many people using so much LSD. A doctor at San Francisco General Hospital says there are at least 10,000 hippies in the Haight-Ashbury, and that about four of them a day wind up in a psychiatric ward on bad trips. He estimates that acidheads make up only one-and-a-half per cent of the city's population, but that the figure for the Haight-Ashbury is more like 100 per cent.

The estimate is absurd; if every hippy in the Hashbury took acid every day, the percentage of users in the neighbourhood would still be less than fifty per cent. Many of the local squares try grass from time to time, but few have worked up an appetite for LSD; the difference in potency is roughly the same as the difference between beer and grain alcohol. Even among hippies, anything more than one dose of acid a week is considered excessive.

Most heads are relatively careful about their drug diets, but in recent months the area has attracted so many young, inexperienced hippies that public freak-outs are a fairly routine thing. Neighbourhood cops complain that acidheads throw themselves in front of moving cars, strip naked in grocery stores and run through plate-glass windows. On week-days, the action is about on a par with Macdougal Street in Greenwich Village, but weekend hippies and nervous *voyeurs* from the suburbs make Saturdays and Sundays a nightmarish traffic jam. The sidewalks are so crowded that even a mild freak-out is likely to cause a riot.

Municipal buses no longer use Haight Street on weekends; they were rerouted after mobs of hippies staged sit-down strikes in the street, called mill-ins, which brought all traffic to a standstill. The only buses still running regularly along Haight Street are those from the Gray Line, which recently added 'hippieland' to its daytime sightseeing tour of San Francisco. It was billed as 'the only foreign tour within the continental limits of the United States' and was an immediate hit with tourists who thought the Haight-Ashbury was a human zoo. The only sour note on the tour was struck by the occasional hippy who would run alongside the bus, holding up a mirror.

Last year in Berkeley, hard-core political radicals who had always viewed hippies as spiritual allies began to worry about the long-range implications of the Haight-Ashbury scene. Students who once were angry activists were content to lie back in their pads and smile at the world through a fog of marijuana smoke – or, worse, to dress like clowns or American Indians and stay zonked for days at a time on LSD.

Even in Berkeley, political rallies during 1966 had overtones of music, madness and absurdity. Instead of picket signs and revolutionary slogans, more and more demonstrators carried flowers, balloons and colourful posters featuring slogans from Dr Timothy Leary, the high priest of acid. The drug culture was spreading faster than political activists realized. Unlike the dedicated radicals who emerged from the Free Speech Movement, the hippies were more interested in dropping out of society than they were in changing it. They were generally younger than the political types, and the press dismissed them as the 'pot left', a frivolous gang of druggies and sex kooks who were only along for the ride.

Then Ronald Reagan was elected Governor by almost a million-vote plurality. Shortly afterwards, Clark Kerr was fired as president of the University of California – a direct result of Reagan's victory. In that same November, the GOP gained fifty seats in Congress and served a clear warning on the Johnson Administration that despite all the headlines about Berkeley and the new left, most of the electorate was a lot more hawkish, hard-nosed and conservative than the White House antennae had indicated.

The lesson was not lost on the hippies, many of whom still considered themselves at least part-time political activists. One of the most obvious casualties of the 1966 elections was the new left's illusion of its own leverage. The radical-hippy alliance had been counting on the voters to repudiate the 'right-wing, warmonger' elements in Congress, but instead it was the 'liberal' Democrats who got stomped.

So it is no coincidence that the Haight-Ashbury scene developed very suddenly in the winter of 1966–7 from the quiet, neo-Bohemian enclave that it had been for four or five years to the crowded, defiant dope fortress that it is today. The hippies, who had never really believed they were the wave of the future anyway, saw the election returns as brutal confirmation of the futility of fighting the establishment on its own terms.

There had to be a whole new scene, they said, and the only way to do it was to make the big move – either figuratively or literally – from Berkeley to the Haight-Ashbury, from pragmatism to mysticism, from politics to dope, from the hang-ups of protest to the peaceful disengagement of love, nature and spontaneity.

The credo of the Haight-Ashbury was expressed, about as well as it can be, by Joyce Francisco, twenty-three-year-old advertising manager of the new hippy newspaper, the *San Francisco Oracle*. She was talking a few months ago to a columnist from the establishment press, trying to explain what the hippy phenomenon meant: 'I love the whole world,' she said. 'I am the divine mother, part of Buddha, part of God, part of everything.'

'How do you live?' the columnist asked.

'From meal to meal. I have no money, no possessions. Money is beautiful only when it's flowing; when it piles up it's a hang-up. We take care of each other. There's always something to buy beans and rice for the group, and someone always sees that I get grass or acid. I was in a mental hospital once because I tried to conform and play the game. But now I'm free and happy.'

Next question: 'Do you use drugs often?'

'Fairly. When I find myself becoming confused I drop out and take a dose of acid. It's a short cut to reality; it throws you right into it. Everyone should take it, even children. Why shouldn't they be enlightened early, instead of waiting till they're old? Human beings need total freedom. That's where God is at. We need to shed hypocrisy, dishonesty, phoniness and go back to the purity of our childhood values.'

The columnist then asked if Miss Francisco ever prayed.

'Oh, yes,' she said. 'I pray in the morning sun. It nourishes me with its energy so I can spread my love and beauty and nourish others. I never pray *for* anything; I don't need anything. Whatever turns me on is a sacrament: LSD, sex, my bells, my colours ... that is the holy communion, you dig?'

The columnist wasn't sure if she did or not, but she passed on the interview for the benefit of those readers who might. Many did. Anyone who thinks all the hippies in the Bay Area are living in the Hashbury might just as well leave his head in the sand.

In normal circumstances, the mushrooming popularity of psychedelics would be a main factor in any article on hippies. But the vicious excesses of our drug laws make it impossible, or at least inhuman, to document the larger story. A journalist dealing with heads is caught in a strange dilemma. The only way to write honestly about the scene is to be part of it. If there is one quick truism about psychedelic drugs, it is that anyone who tries to write about them without firsthand experience is a fool and a fraud.

Yet to write from experience is an admission of felonious guilt; it is also a potential betrayal of people whose only 'crime' is the smoking of a weed that grows wild all over the world but the possession of which, in California, carries a minimum sentence of two years in prison for a second offence and a minimum of five years for a third. So, despite the fact that the whole journalism industry is full of unregenerate heads – just as many journalists were hard drinkers during Prohibition – it is not very likely that the frank, documented truth about the psychedelic underworld, for good or ill, will be illuminated at any time soon in the public prints.

If I were to write, for instance, that I recently spent ten days in San Francisco and was stoned almost constantly ... that in fact I was stoned for nine nights out of ten and that nearly everyone I dealt with smoked marijuana as casually as they drank beer ... and if I said many of the people I talked to were not freaks and dropouts, but competent professionals with bank accounts and spotless reputations ... and that I was amazed to find psychedelic drugs in homes where I would never have mentioned them two years ago – if all this were true, I could write an ominous screed to the effect that the hippy phenomenon in the Haight-Ashbury is little more than a freak show and a soft-sell advertisement for what is happening all around them ... that drugs, orgies and freak-outs are almost as common to a much larger and more discreet cross section of the Bay Area's respectable, upward-mobile society as they are to the colourful drop-outs of San Francisco's new Bohemia.

There is no shortage of documentation for the thesis that the current Haight-Ashbury scene is only the orgiastic tip of a great psychedelic iceberg that is already drifting in the sea lanes of the great society. Submerged and uncountable is the mass of intelligent, capable heads who want nothing so much as peaceful anonymity. In a nervous society where a man's image is frequently more important than his reality, the only people who can afford to advertise their drug menus are those with nothing to lose.

And these – for the moment, at least – are the young lotus-eaters, the barefoot mystics and hairy freaks of the Haight-Ashbury – all the primitive Christians, peaceful nay-sayers and half-deluded 'flower children' who refuse to participate in a society which looks to them like a mean, calculated and soul-destroying hoax.

As recently as two years ago, many of the best and brightest of them were passionately involved in the realities of political, social and economic life in America. But the scene has changed since then and political activism is going out of style. The thrust is no longer for 'change' or 'progress' or 'revolution', but merely to escape, to live on the far perimeter of a world that might have been – perhaps should have been – and strike a bargain for survival on purely personal terms.

The flourishing hippy scene is a matter of desperate concern to the political activists. They see a whole generation of rebels drifting off to a drugged limbo, ready to accept almost anything as long as it comes with enough 'soma'.

Steve DeCanio, an ex-Berkeley activist now doing graduate work at MIT, is a good example of a legion of young radicals who know they have lost their influence but have no clear idea how to get it back again. 'This alliance between hippies and political radicals is bound to break up,' he said in a recent letter. 'There's just too big a jump from the slogan of "flower power" to the deadly realm of politics. Something has to give, and drugs are too ready-made as opiates of the people for the bastards (the police) to fail to take advantage of it.'

DeCanio spent three months in various Bay Area jails as a result of his civil rights activities and now he is lying low for a while, waiting for an opening. 'I'm spending an amazing amount of time studying,' he wrote. 'It's mainly because I'm scared; three months on the bottom of humanity's trash heap got to me worse than it's healthy to admit. The country is going to hell, the left is going to pot, but not me. I still want to figure out a way to win.'

Meanwhile, like most other disappointed radicals, he is grimly amused at the impact the hippies are having on the establishment. The panic among San Francisco officialdom at the prospect of 200,000 hippies flocking into the Hashbury this summer is one of the few things that ex-Berkeley radicals can still laugh at. DeCanio's vision of the crisis was not written as prophecy, but considering the hidden reality of the situation, it may turn out that way: 'I can see Mayor Shelley standing on the steps of the Civic Center and shouting into TV microphones, "The people cry bread! Bread! Let them turn on!"'

New York Times Magazine, 14 May 1967

WHEN THE BEATNIKS WERE SOCIAL LIONS

San Francisco

What ever happened to the beat generation? The question wouldn't mean much in Detroit or Salt Lake City, perhaps, but here it brings back a lot of memories. As recently as 1960, San Francisco was the capital of the beat generation, and the corner of Grant and Columbus in the section known as North Beach was the crossroads of the 'beat' world.

It was a good time to be in San Francisco. Anybody with half a talent could wander around North Beach and pass himself off as a 'comer' in the new era. I know, because I was doing it, and so was a fellow we'll have to call Willard, the hulking, bearded son of a New Jersey minister. It was a time for breaking loose from the old codes, for digging new sounds and new ideas, and for doing everything possible to unnerve the establishment.

Since then, things have died down. The 'beatnik' is no longer a social lion in San Francisco, but a social leper; as a matter of fact, it looked for a while as if they had all left. But the city was recently startled by a 'rent strike' in North Beach and as it turned out, lo and behold, the strikers were 'beatniks'. The local papers, which once played beat generation stories as if the foundations of the system were crumbling before their very eyes, seized on the rent strike with strange affection – like a man encountering an old friend who owes him money, but whom he is glad to see anyway.

The rent strike lasted only about two days, but it got people talking again about the beat generation and its sudden demise from the American scene – or at least from the San Francisco scene, because it is still very extant in New York. But in New York it goes by a different name, and all the humour has gone out of it.

One of the most surprising things about the rent strike was the fact that so few people in San Francisco had any idea what the beat generation was. An interviewer from a radio station went into the streets seeking controversy on 'the return of the beatniks', but drew a blank. People remembered the term, and not much more.

But the beat generation was very real in its day, and it has a definite place in our history. There is a mountain of material explaining the sociological aspects of the thing, but most of it is dated and irrelevant. What remains are the people who were involved; most of them are still around, looking back with humour and affection on the uproar they caused, and drifting by a variety of routes towards debt, parenthood, and middle age.

My involvement was tangential at best. But Willard was in there at the axis of things, and in retrospect he stands out as one of the great 'beatniks' of his time. Certainly San Francisco has good cause to remember him; his one and only encounter with the forces of law and order provided one of the wildest beat generation stories of the era.

Before San Francisco he had been in Germany, teaching English and cultivating an oriental-type beard. On his way out to the coast he stopped in New York and picked up a mistress with a new Ford. It was *de rigueur*, in those days, to avoid marriage at all costs. He came to me through the recommendation of a friend then working in Europe for a British newspaper. 'Willard is a great man,' said the letter. 'He is an artist and a man of taste.'

As it turned out, he also was a prodigious drinker in the tradition of Brendan Behan, who was said to have had 'a thirst so great it would throw a shadow'. I was making my own beer at the time and Willard put a great strain on the ageing process; I had to lock the stuff up to keep him from getting at it before the appointed moment.

Sadly enough, my beer and Willard's impact on San Francisco were firmly linked. The story is a classic, and if you travel in the right circles out here you will still hear it told, although not always accurately. The truth, however, goes like this:

Willard arrived shortly before I packed up and left for the East; we had a convivial few weeks, and, as a parting gesture, I left him a five-gallon jug of beer that I did not feel qualified to transport across the nation. It still had a week or so to go in the jug, then another few weeks of ageing in quart bottles, after which it would have had a flavour to rival the nectar of the gods. Willard's only task was to bottle it and leave it alone until it was ready to drink.

Unfortunately, his thirst threw a heavy shadow on the schedule. He was living on a hill overlooking the southern section of the city, and among his neighbours were several others of the breed, mad drinkers and men of strange arts. Shortly after my departure he entertained one of these gentlemen, who, like my man Willard, was long on art and energy, but very short of funds.

The question of drink arose, as it will in the world of art, but the presence of poverty cast a bleak light on the scene. There was, however, the five-gallon jug of raw, unaged home brew in the kitchen. Of course, it was a crude drink and might produce beastly and undesired effects, but ... well ...

The rest is history. After drinking half the jug, the two artists laid hands on several gallons of blue paint and proceeded to refinish the front of the house Willard was living in. The landlord, who lived across the street, witnessed this horror and called the police. They arrived to find the front of the house looking like a Jackson Pollack canvas, and the sidewalk rapidly disappearing under a layer of sensual crimson. At this point, something of an argument ensued, but Willard is six feet four, and 230 pounds, and he prevailed. For a while.

Some moments later the police came back with reinforcements, but by this time Willard and his helper had drunk the rest of the jug and were eager for any kind of action, be it painting or friendly violence. The intrusion of the police had caused several mottos to be painted on the front of the house, and they were not without antisocial connotations. The landlord was weeping and gnashing his teeth, loud music emanated from the interior of the desecrated house, and the atmosphere in general was one of hypertension.

The scene that followed can only be likened to the rounding up of wild beasts escaped from a zoo. Willard says he attempted to flee, but floundered on a picket fence, which collapsed with his weight and that of a pursuing officer. His friend climbed to a roof and rained curses and shingles on the unfriendly world below. But the police worked methodically, and by the time the sun set over the Pacific the two artists were sealed in jail.

At this point the gentlemen of the press showed up for the usual photos. They tried to coax Willard up to the front of his cell to pose, but the other artist had undertaken to rip the toilet bowl out of the floor and smash it into small pieces. For the next hour, the press was held at bay with chunks of porcelain, hurled by the two men in the cell. 'We used up the toilet,' Willard recalls, 'then we got the sink. I don't remember much of it, but I can't understand why the cops didn't shoot us. We were out of our heads.'

The papers had a field day with the case. Nearly all the photos of the 'animal men' were taken with what is known among press photographers as 'the Frankenstein flash'. This technique produces somewhat the same impression of the subject as a flashlight held under his chin, but instead of a flashlight, the photographer simply holds his flash unit low, so that sinister shadows appear on the face of a subject, and a huge shadow looms on the wall behind him. It is a technique that could make Casper Milquetoast look like the Phantom of the Opera, but the effect, with Willard, was nothing short of devastating; he looked like King Kong.

Despite all the violence, the story has a happy ending. Willard and his friends were sentenced to six months in jail, but were quickly released for good behaviour, and neither lost any time in fleeing to New York. Willard now lives in Brooklyn, where he moves from one apartment to another as the walls fill up with paintings. His artistic method is to affix tin cans to a wall with tenpenny nails, then cover the wall with lumpy plaster and paint. Some say he has a great talent, but so far he goes unrecognized – except by the long-suffering San Francisco police, who were called upon to judge what was perhaps his most majestic effort.

Willard was as hard to define then as he is now; probably it is most accurate to say he had artistic inclinations and a superabundance of excess energy. At one point in his life he got the message that others of his type were gathering in San Francisco, and he came all the way from Germany to join the party.

Since then, things have never been the same. Life is more peaceful in San Francisco, but infinitely duller. That was pretty obvious when the rent strike cropped up; for a day or so it looked like the action was back in town, but it was no dice.

One of the 'strikers', an unemployed cartoonist with a wife and a child and a rundown apartment for which he refuses to pay rent, summed up the situation. His landlady had declined to make repairs on the apartment, and instead got an eviction order. In the old days, the fellow would have stayed in the place and gotten tough. But the cartoonist is taking the path of least resistance. 'It takes a long time to get people evicted,' he says with a shrug, 'and we're thinking of splitting to New York on a freight train anyway.'

That's the way it is these days in the erstwhile capital of the beat generation. The action has gone East, and the only people who really seem to mourn it are the reporters, who never lacked a good story, and a small handful of those who lived with it and had a few good laughs for a while. If Willard returned to San Francisco today, he probably would have to settle for a job as a house painter.

National Observer, 20 April 1964

THE NONSTUDENT LEFT

Berkeley

At the height of the 'Berkeley insurrection' press reports were loaded with mentions of outsiders, nonstudents and professional troublemakers. Terms like 'Cal's shadow college' and 'Berkeley's hidden community' became part of the journalistic lexicon. These people, it was said, were whipping the campus into a frenzy, goading the students to revolt, harassing the administration, and all the while working for their own fiendish ends. You could almost see them loping along the midnight streets with bags of seditious leaflets, strike orders, red banners of protest and cablegrams from Moscow, Peking or Havana. As in Mississippi and South Vietnam, outside agitators were said to be stirring up the locals, who wanted only to be left alone.

Something closer to the truth is beginning to emerge now, but down around the roots of the affair the fog is still pretty thick. The Sproul Hall sit-in trials ended in a series of unexpectedly harsh convictions, the Free Speech Movement has disbanded, four students have been expelled and sentenced to jail terms as a result of the 'dirty word' controversy, and the principal leader, Mario Savio, has gone to England, where he'll study and wait for word on the appeal of his four-month jail term – a procedure which may take as long as eighteen months.

As the new semester begins – with a new and inscrutable chancellor – the mood on the Berkeley campus is one of watchful waiting. The basic issues of last year are still unresolved, and a big new one has been added: Vietnam. A massive nationwide sit-in, with Berkeley as a focal point, is scheduled for 15-16 October, and if that doesn't open all the old wounds, then presumably nothing will.

For a time it looked as though Governor Edmund Brown had side-tracked any legislative investigation of the university, but late in August Assembly Speaker Jesse Unruh, an anti-Brown Democrat, named himself and four colleagues to a joint legislative committee that will investigate higher education in California. Mr Unruh told the press that 'there will be no isolated investigation of student-faculty problems at Berkeley', but in the same period he stated before a national conference of more than 1000 state legislators, meeting in Portland, that the academic community is 'probably the greatest enemy' of a state legislature.

Mr Unruh is a sign of the times. For a while last spring he appeared to be in conflict with the normally atavistic Board of Regents, which runs the university, but somewhere along the line a blue-chip compromise was reached, and whatever progressive ideas the Regents might have flirted with were lost in the summer lull. Governor Brown's role in these negotiations has not yet been made public.

One of the realities to come out of last semester's action is the new 'anti-outsider law', designed to keep 'nonstudents' off the campus in any hour of turmoil. It was sponsored by Assemblyman Don Mulford, a Republican from Oakland, who looks and talks quite a bit like the 'old' Richard Nixon. Mr Mulford is much concerned about 'subversive infiltration' on the Berkeley campus, which lies in his district. He thinks he knows that the outburst last fall was caused by New York Communists, beatnik perverts and other godless elements beyond his ken. The students themselves, he tells himself, would never have caused such a ruckus. Others in Sacramento apparently shared this view: the bill passed the Assembly by a vote of 54 to 11 and the Senate by 27 to 8. Governor Brown signed it on 2 June. The Mulford proposal got a good boost, while it was still pending, when J. Edgar Hoover testified in Washington that forty-three reds of one stripe or another were involved in the Free Speech Movement.

On hearing of this, one student grinned and said: 'Well I guess that means they'll send about 10,000 Marines out here this fall. Hell, they sent 20,000 after those fifty-eight reds in Santo Domingo. Man, that Lyndon is nothing but *hip*!'

Where Mr Hoover got his figure is a matter of speculation, but the guess in Berkeley is that it came from the San Francisco *Examiner*, a Hearst paper calling itself the 'monarch of the dailies'. The *Examiner* is particularly influential among those who fear King George III might still be alive in Argentina.

•

The significance of the Mulford law lies not in what it says but in the darkness it sheds on the whole situation in Berkeley, especially on the role of nonstudents and outsiders. Who are these thugs? What manner of man would lurk on a campus for no reason but to twist student minds? As anyone who lives or works around an urban campus knows, vast numbers of students are already more radical than any red Mr Hoover could name. Beyond that, the nonstudents and outsiders California has legislated against are in the main ex-students, graduates, would-be transfers, and other young activist types who differ from radical students only in that they don't carry university registration cards. On any urban campus the nonstudent is an old and dishonoured tradition. Every big city school has its fringe element: Harvard, New York University, Chicago, the Sorbonne, Berkeley, the University of Caracas. A dynamic university in a modern population centre simply can't be isolated from the realities, human or otherwise, that surround it. Mr Mulford would make an island of the Berkeley campus but, alas, there are too many guerrillas.

In 1958, I drifted north from Kentucky and became a nonstudent at Columbia. I signed up for two courses and am still getting bills for the tuition. My home was a $12-a-week room in an off-campus building full of jazz musicians, shoplifters, mainliners, screaming poets and sex addicts of every description. It was a good life. I used the university facilities and at one point was hired to stand in a booth all day for two days, collecting registration fees. Twice I walked almost the length of the campus at night with a big wooden box containing nearly $15,000. It was a wild feeling and I'm still not sure why I took the money to the bursar.

Being a 'non' or 'nco' student on an urban campus is not only simple but natural for anyone who is young, bright and convinced that the major he's after is not on the list. Any list. A serious nonstudent is his own guidance counsellor. The surprising thing is that so few people beyond the campus know this is going on.

The nonstudent tradition seems to date from the end of World War II. Before that it was a more individual thing. A professor at Columbia told me that the late R. P. Blackmur, one of the most academic and scholarly of literary critics, got most of his education by sitting in on classes at Harvard.

In the age of Eisenhower and Kerouac, the nonstudent went about stealing his education as quietly as possible. It never occurred to him to jump into campus politics; that was part of the game he had already quit. But then the decade ended. Nixon went down, and the civil rights struggle broke out. With this, a whole army of guilt-crippled Eisenhower deserters found the war they had almost given up hoping for. With Kennedy at the helm, politics became respectable for a change, and students who had sneered at the idea of voting found themselves joining the Peace Corps or standing on picket lines. Student radicals today may call Kennedy a phony liberal and a glamorous sellout, but only the very young will deny that it was Kennedy who got them excited enough to want to change the American reality, instead of just quitting it. Today's activist student or nonstudent talks about Kerouac as the hipsters of the fifties talked of Hemingway. He was a quitter, they say; he had good instincts and a good ear for the sadness of his time, but his talent soured instead of growing. The new campus radical has a cause, a multi-pronged attack on as many fronts as necessary : if not civil rights, then foreign policy or structural deprivation in domestic poverty pockets. Injustice is the demon, and the idea is to bust it.

What Mulford's law will do to change this situation is not clear. The language of the bill leaves no doubt that it shall henceforth be a mis-demeanour for any nonstudent or nonemployee to remain on a state university or state college campus after he or she has been ordered to leave, if it 'reasonably appears' to the chief administrative officer or the person designated by him to keep order on the campus 'that such person is committing an act likely to interfere with the peaceful conduct of the campus'.

In anything short of riot conditions, the real victims of Mulford's law will be the luckless flunkies appointed to enforce it. The mind of man could devise few tasks more helpless than rushing around this 1000-acre, 27,000-student campus in the midst of some crowded action, trying to apprehend and remove – on sight and before he can flee – any person who is not a Cal student and is not eligible for readmission. It would be a nightmare of lies, false seizures, double entries and certain provoca-tion. Meanwhile, most of those responsible for the action would be go-ing about their business in legal peace. If pure justice prevailed in this world, Don Mulford would be appointed to keep order and bag sub-versives at the next campus demonstrations.

There are those who seem surprised that a defective rat-trap like the Mulford law could be endorsed by the legislature of a supposedly pro-gressive, enlightened state. But these same people were surprised when Proposition14, which reopened the door to racial discrimination in housing, was endorsed by the electorate last November by a margin of nearly two to one.

Meanwhile, the nonstudent in Berkeley is part of the scene, a fact of life. The university estimates that about 3000 nonstudents use the cam-pus in various ways : working in the library with borrowed registration cards; attending lectures, concerts and student films; finding jobs and apartments via secondhand access to university listings; eating in the cafeteria, and monitoring classes. In appearance they are indistinguishable from students. Berkeley is full of wild-looking graduate students, bearded professors and long-haired English majors who look like Joan Baez.

Until recently there was no mention of nonstudents in campus politics, but at the beginning of the Free Speech rebellion President Kerr said 'nonstudent elements were partly responsible for the demonstration'. Since then, he has backed away from that stand, leaving it to the lawmakers. Even its goats and enemies now admit that the FSM revolt was the work of actual students. It has been a difficult fact for some people to accept, but a reliable poll of student attitudes at the time showed that roughly 18,000 of them supported the goals of the FSM, and about half that number supported its 'illegal' tactics. More than 800 were willing to defy the administration, the governor and the police, rather than back down. The faculty supported the FSM by close to 8 to 1. The nonstudents nearly all sided with the FSM. The percentage of radicals among them is much higher than among students. It is invariably the radicals, not the conservatives, who drop out of school and become activist nonstudents. But against this background, their attitude hardly matters.

'We don't play a big role politically,' says one. 'But philosophically we're a hell of a threat to the establishment. Just the fact that we exist proves that dropping out of school isn't the end of the world. Another important thing is that we're not looked down on by students. We're respectable. A lot of students I know are thinking of becoming nonstudents.'

'As a nonstudent I have nothing to lose,' said another. 'I can work full time on whatever I want, study what interests me, and figure out what's really happening in the world. That student routine is a drag. Until I quit the grind I didn't realize how many groovy things there are to do around Berkeley: concerts, films, good speakers, parties, pot, politics, women – I can't think of a better way to live, can you?'

Not all nonstudents worry the lawmakers and administrators. Some are fraternity bums who flunked out of the university, but don't want to leave the parties and the good atmosphere. Others are quiet squares or technical types, earning money between enrollments and meanwhile living nearby. But there is no longer the sharp division that used to exist between the beatnik and the square: too many radicals wear ties and sport coats; too many engineering students wear boots and levis. Some of the most bohemian-looking girls around the campus are left puritans, while some of the sweetest-looking sorority types are confirmed pot smokers and wear diaphragms on all occasions.

*

Nonstudents lump one another – and many students – into two very broad groups: 'political radicals' and 'social radicals'. Again, the division is not sharp, but in general, and with a few bizarre exceptions, a political radical is a left activist in one or more causes. His views are revolutionary in the sense that his idea of 'democratic solutions' alarms even the liberals. He may be a Young Trotskyist, a Du Bois Club organizer or merely an ex-Young Democrat, who despairs of President Johnson and is now looking for action with some friends in the Progressive Labor Party.

Social radicals tend to be 'arty'. Their gigs are poetry and folk music, rather than politics, although many are fervently committed to the civil rights movement. Their political bent is Left, but their real interests are writing, painting, good sex, good sounds and free marijuana. The realities of politics put them off, although they don't mind lending their talents to a demonstration here and there, or even getting arrested for a good cause. They have quit one system and they don't want to be organized into another; they feel they have more important things to do.

A report last spring by the faculty's Select Committee on Education tried to put it all in a nutshell: 'A significant and growing minority of students is simply not propelled by what we have come to regard as conventional motivation. Rather than aiming to be successful men in an achievement-oriented society, they want to be moral men in a moral society. They want to lead lives less tied to financial return than to social awareness and responsibility.'

The committee was severely critical of the whole university structure, saying: 'The atmosphere of the campus now suggests too much an intricate system of compulsions, rewards and punishments; too much of our attention is given to score keeping.' Among other failures, the university was accused of ignoring 'the moral revolution of the young'.

Talk like this strikes the radicals among 'the young' as paternalistic jargon, but they appreciate the old folks' sympathy. To them, anyone who takes part in 'the system' is a hypocrite. This is especially true among the Marxist, Mao-Castro element – the hipsters of the left.

One of these is Steve DeCanio, a twenty-two-year-old Berkeley radical and Cal graduate in math, now facing a two-month jail term as a result of the Sproul Hall sit-ins. He is doing graduate work, and therefore immune to the Mulford law. 'I became a radical after the 1962 auto row (civil rights) demonstrations in San Francisco,' he says. 'That's when I saw the power structure and understood the hopelessness of trying to be a liberal. After I got arrested I dropped the pre-med course I'd started at San Francisco State. The worst of it, though, was being screwed time and again in the courts. I'm out on appeal now with four and a half months of jail hanging over me.'

DeCanio is an editor of *Spider*, a wild-eyed new magazine with a circulation of about 2000 on and around the Berkeley campus. Once banned, it thrived on the publicity and is now officially ignored by the protest-weary administration. The eight-man editorial board is comprised of four students and four nonstudents. The magazine is dedicated, they say, to 'sex, politics, international communism, drugs, extremism and rock'n'roll'. Hence, S-P-I-D-E-R.

DeCanio is about two-thirds political radical and one-third social. He is bright, small, with dark hair and glasses, clean-shaven, and casually but not sloppily dressed. He listens carefully to questions, uses his hands for emphasis when he talks, and quietly says things like: 'What this country needs is a revolution; the society is so sick, so reactionary, that it just doesn't make sense to take part in it.'

He lives, with three other nonstudents and two students, in a comfortable house on College Avenue, a few blocks from campus. The $120-a-month rent is split six ways. There are three bedrooms, a kitchen and a big living room with a fireplace. Papers litter the floor, the phone rings continually, and people stop by to borrow things: a pretty blonde wants a Soviet army chorus record, a Tony Perkins type from the Oakland Du Bois Club wants a film projector; Art Goldberg – the arch-activist who also lives here – comes storming in, shouting for help on the 'Vietnam Days' teach-in arrangements.

It is all very friendly and collegiate. People wear plaid shirts and khaki pants, white socks and moccasins. There are books on the shelves, cans of beer and cokes in the refrigerator, and a manually operated light bulb in the bathroom. In the midst of all this it is weird to hear people talking about 'bringing the ruling class to their knees', or 'finding acceptable synonyms for Marxist terms'.

Political conversation in this house would drive Don Mulford right over the wall. There are riffs of absurdity and mad humour in it, but the base line remains a dead-serious alienation from the 'repugnant society' of twentieth-century America. You hear the same talk on the streets, in bars, on the walk near Ludwig's Fountain in front of Sproul Hall, and in other houses where activists live and gather. And why not? This is Berkeley, which DeCanio calls 'the centre of West Coast radicalism'. It has a long history of erratic politics, both on and off the campus. From 1911 to 1913, its Mayor was a Socialist named Stitt Wilson. It has more psychiatrists and fewer bars than any other city of comparable size in California. And there are 249 churches for 120,300 people, of which 25 per cent are Negroes – one of the highest percentages of any city outside the South.

Culturally, Berkeley is dominated by two factors: the campus and San Francisco across the Bay. The campus is so much a part of the community that the employment and housing markets have long since adjusted to student patterns. A $100-a-month apartment or cottage is no problem when four or five people split the rent, and there are plenty of ill-paid, minimum-strain jobs for those without money from home. Tutoring, typing, clerking, car washing, hash slinging and baby sitting are all easy ways to make a subsistence income; one of the favourites among nonstudents is computer programming, which pays well.

Therefore, Berkeley's nonstudents have no trouble getting by. The climate is easy, the people are congenial, and the action never dies. Jim Prickett, who quit the University of Oklahoma and flunked out of San Francisco State, is another of *Spider*'s nonstudent editors. 'State has no community,' he says, 'and the only nonstudent I know of at Oklahoma is now in jail.' Prickett came to Berkeley because 'things are happening here'. At twenty-three, he is about as far left as a man can get in these times, but his revolutionary zeal is gimped by pessimism. 'If we have a revolution in this country it will be a fascist takeover,' he says with a shrug. Meanwhile he earns $25 a week as *Spider*'s star writer, smiting the establishment hip and thigh at every opportunity. Prickett looks as much like a red menace as Will Rogers looked like a Bantu. He is tall, thin, blond, and shuffles. 'Hell, I'll probably sell out,' he says with a faint smile. 'Be a history teacher or something. But not for a while.'

Yet there is something about Prickett that suggests he won't sell out so easily. Unlike many nonstudent activists, he has no degree, and in the society that appalls him even a sellout needs credentials. That is one of the most tangible realities of the nonstudent; by quitting school he has taken a physical step outside the system – a move that more and more students seem to find admirable. It is not an easy thing to repudiate – not now, at any rate, while the tide is running that way. And 'the system' cannot be rejoined without some painful self-realization. Many a man has whipped up a hell of a broth of reasons to justify his sellout, but few recommend the taste of it.

The problem is not like that of high school dropouts. They are supposedly inadequate, but the activist nonstudent is generally said to be superior. 'A lot of these kids are top students,' says Dr David Powellson, chief of Cal's student psychiatric clinic, 'but no university is set up to handle them.'

How, then, are these bright mavericks to fit into the superbureaucracies of government and big business? Cal takes it undergraduates from the top eighth of the state's high school graduates, and those accepted from out of state are no less 'promising'. The ones who migrate to Berkeley after quitting other schools are usually the same type. They are seekers

– disturbed, perhaps, and perhaps for good reason. Many drift from one university to another, looking for the right programme, the right professor, the right atmosphere, and right way to deal with the deplorable world they have suddenly grown into. It is like an army of Holden Caulfields, looking for a home and beginning to suspect they may never find one.

These are the outsiders, the nonstudents, and the potential – if not professional – troublemakers. There is something primitive and tragic in California's effort to make a law against them. The law itself is relatively unimportant, but the thinking that conceived it is a strutting example of what the crisis is all about. A society that will legislate in ignorance against its unfulfilled children and its angry, half-desperate truth seekers is bound to be shaken as it goes about making a reality of mass education.

It is a race against time, complacency and vested interests. For the left-activist nonstudent the race is very personal. Whether he is right, wrong, ignorant, vicious, super-intelligent or simply bored, once he has committed himself to the extent of dropping out of school, he has also committed himself to 'making it' outside the framework of whatever he has quit. A social radical presumably has his talent, his private madness or some other insulated gimmick, but for the political radical the only true hope is somehow to bust the system that drove him into limbo. In this new era many believe they can do it, but most of those I talked to at Berkeley seemed a bit nervous. There was a singular vagueness as to the mechanics of the act, no real sense of the openings.

'What are you going to be doing ten years from now?' I asked a visiting radical in the house where *Spider* is put together. 'What if there's no revolution by then, and no prospects of one?'

'Hell,' he said. 'I don't think about that. Too much is happening right now. If the revolution's coming, it had better come damn quick.'

The Nation, vol. 201, 27 September 1965

THOSE DARING YOUNG MEN IN THEIR FLYING MACHINES . . . AIN'T WHAT THEY USED TO BE!

Myths and legends die hard in America. We love them for the extra dimension they provide, the illusion of near-infinite possibility to erase the narrow confines of most men's reality. Weird heroes and mould-breaking champions exist as living proof to those who need it that the tyranny of 'the rat race' is not yet final. Look at Joe Namath, they say; he broke all the rules and still beat the system like a gong. Or Hugh Hefner, the Horatio Alger of our time. And Cassius Clay – Muhammed Ali – who flew so high, like the U-2, that he couldn't quite believe it when the drone bees shot him down.

Gary Powers, the U-2 pilot shot down over Russia, is now a test pilot for Lockheed Aircraft, testing newer, more 'invincible' planes in the cool, bright skies above the Mojave Desert, in the Antelope Valley just north of Los Angeles. The valley is alive with aviation projects, particularly at Edwards Air Force Base, near Lancaster, where the Air Force tests its new planes and breeds a new, computerized version of the legendary, hell-for-leather test pilot. Air Force brass at Edwards is appalled at the persistence of the old 'kick the tyre, light the fire, and away we go' image. The key word in today's Air Force, they insist, is 'professionalism'.

This made my visit to the base a bit tricky. It was painfully obvious, even after an hour or so of casual talk, that the hard-nosed pros on the flight line resented the drift of my conversation – particularly when I asked about things like 'duelling societies'. The Air Force has never valued a sense of humour in its career men, and in high-risk fields like flight testing, a sense of the absurd will cripple a man's future just as surely as an LSD habit.

Test pilots are very straight people. They are totally dedicated to their work and not accustomed to dealing with slipshod civilians who seem even faintly disorganized – especially writers. My image was further queered by a painfully cracked bone in my right hand, which forced me to use my left in all formal introductions.

At one point, while talking to two colonels, I lamely explained that I break my hand about once a year. 'Last time,' I said, 'it was a motorcycle wreck on a rainy night; I missed a shift between second and third, doing about seventy on a bad curve.'

Zang! That did it. They were horrified. 'Why would anybody do a thing like that?' asked Lieutenant Colonel Ted Sturmthal, who had just come back from flying the huge XB-70 across the country at the speed of sound. Lieutenant Colonel Dean Godwin, who is rated, along with Sturmthal, as one of the top test pilots in the Air Force, stared at me as if I'd just produced a Vietcong watch fob.

We were sitting in a sort of grey-plastic office near the flight line. Outside, on the cold, grey runway, sat a plane called the SR-71, capable of flying 2000 mph – or about 3100 feet per second – in the thin air on the edge of the earth's atmosphere, nearly twenty miles up. The SR-71 has already made the U-2 obsolete; the thrust of its two engines equals the power of forty-five diesel locomotives and it cruises at an altitude just inside the realm of space flight. Yet neither Sturmthal nor Godwin would have balked for an instant at the prospect of climbing into the cockpit of the thing and pushing it as high and hard as it could possibly go.

The Air Force has been trying for twenty years to croak the image of the wild-eyed, full-force, 'aim it at the ground and see if it crashes' kind of test pilot, and they have finally succeeded. The vintage-69 test pilot is a supercautious, supertrained, superintelligent monument to the computer age. He is a perfect specimen, on paper, and so confident of his natural edge on other kinds of men that you begin to wonder – after spending a bit of time in the company of test pilots – if perhaps we might not all be better off if the White House could be moved, tomorrow morning, to this dreary wasteland called Edwards Air Force Base. If nothing else, my own visit to the base convinced me that Air Force test pilots see the rest of us, perhaps accurately, as either physical, mental, or moral rejects.

I came away from Edwards with a sense of having been to IBM's version of Olympus. Why had I ever left that perfect world? I had been in the Air Force once, and it had struck me then as being a clumsy experiment in mass lobotomy, using rules instead of scalpels. Now, ten years later, the Air Force still benefits from the romantic pilot myth that its personnel managers have long since destroyed.

Back in the good old days, when men were men and might was right and the devil took the hindmost, the peaceful desert highways in Antelope Valley were raceways for off-duty pilots on big motorcycles. Slow-moving travellers were frequently blown off the road by wildmen in leather jackets and white scarves, two-wheeled human torpedoes defying all speed limits and heedless of their own safety. Motorcycles were very popular toys with the pilots of that other, older era, and many an outraged citizen was jerked out of his bed at night by the awful roar of a huge four-cylinder Indian beneath his daughter's window. The image of the daredevil, speedball pilot is preserved in song and story, as it were, and in films like the Howard Hughes classic, *Hell's Angels*.

Prior to World War II, pilots were seen as doomed, half-mythical figures, much admired for their daring, but not quite sane when judged by normal standards. While other men rode trains or chugged around the earth in Model-Ts, barnstorming pilots toured the nation with spectacular 'aviation shows', dazzling the yokels at a million county fairs. When their stunts went wrong, they crashed – and often died. The survivors pushed on, treating death like a churlish, harping creditor, toasting their own legend with beakers of gin and wild parties to ward off the chill. 'Live fast, die young, and make a good-looking corpse.' That gag got a lot of laughs at debutante parties, but in aviation circles it seemed a bit raw, a little too close to the bone.

It was especially pertinent to test pilots, whose job it was to find out which planes would fly and which ones were natural death-traps. If the others took lunatic risks, at least they took them in proved planes. Test pilots, then and now, put the products of engineers' theories to the ultimate test. No experimental plane is 'safe' to fly. Some work beautifully, others have fatal flaws. The Mojave Desert is pockmarked with the scars of failure. Only the new ones are visible; the older scars have been covered over by drifting sand and mesquite brush.

Each funeral means more donations, from friends and survivors, to the 'window fund'. The Test Pilots' Memorial Window in the chapel is a wall of colourful stained-glass mosaics, paid for with donations that otherwise might have gone into the purchase of short-lived flowers. The original idea was to have only one memorial window, but each year invariably brought more donations, so that now there are only a few plain windows. All the others have been replaced by stained-glass memorials to the 100 names on the plaque in the chapel hallway.

Two or three new names are added each year, on the average, but some years are worse than others. There were no flight-test fatalities in either 1963 or 1964. Then, in 1965, there were eight. In 1966, the death count dropped to four, but two of these occurred on a single day, 8 June, in a mid-air crash between a single-seat fighter and one of the only two XB-70 bombers ever built.

That was a very bad day on Edwards. Test pilots are very close: They live and work together like a professional football team; their wives are good friends, and their children are part of the same small world. So a double fatality shatters everybody. Today's test pilots and their families live nearly as close to death as the old-time pilots ever did – but the new breed fears it more. With rare exceptions, they are married, with at least two children, and in their off-duty hours they live as carefully and quietly as any physics professor. A few ride little Hondas, Suzukis, and other midget motorcycles, but strictly for transportation – or, as one of the pilots explained, 'So Mama can use the family car.' The flight-line parking lot, where working pilots leave their cars, looks no different from any supermarket lot in San Bernardino. Here again, with rare exceptions, the test pilot's earthbound vehicle is modest – probably a five-year-old Ford or Chevy, perhaps a Volkswagen, Datsun, or other low-priced import. At the other end of the flight line, in front of the test pilots' school, the mix is a bit livelier. Of the forty-six cars I counted there one afternoon, there was one Jaguar XKE, one IK-150, one old Mercedes with a V-8 Chevy engine, one Stingray; all the rest were clunkers. A cluster of motorcycles stood near the door, but the hottest one in the lot was a mild-mannered 250 Yamaha.

The midnight roads around Antelope Valley are quiet these days, except for an occasional teenage drag race. Today's test pilots go to bed early, and they regard big motorcycles with the same analytical disdain they have for hippies, winos, and other failure symbols. They take their risks, on assignment, between dawn and 4:30 p.m. But when their time is their own, they prefer to hunker down in the wall-to-wall anonymity of their one-storey, flat-roofed, Levittown-style homes between the base golf course and the officers' club, there to relax in front of the tube with a succulent TV dinner. Their music is Mantovani, and their idea of an 'artist' is Norman Rockwell. On Friday afternoons, from four-thirty to seven, they crowd into the officers' club bar for the weekly 'happy hour', where most of the talk is about planes and current test projects. Then, just before seven, they go home to pick up their wives and dress for dinner, again at 'the club'. After dinner there will be a bit of dancing to the jukebox or maybe a small combo. Heavy drinking is out of the question; a drunken test pilot is viewed with genuine alarm by the others, who see any form of social excess – drink, wenching, late hours, any 'unusual' behaviour – as an indication of some deeper problem, an emotional cancer of some kind. Tonight's juicer is tomorrow's – or Monday's – hangover risk, a pair of slow-focusing eyes or an uncertain hand at the controls of a $100 million aircraft. The Air Force has trained three generations of élite-level pilots to abhor any hint of foreseeable human risk in the flight-test programme. The planes, after all, are risky enough, they are the necessary unknown factor in the equation that every test project ideally boils down to. (Test pilots are very hip to equations; they can describe a plane and all its characteristics, using nothing but numbers.) And a cool waterhead knows that an equation with only one unknown factor is a hell of a lot simpler to cope with than an equation with two. The idea, then, is to minimize the chance of a second unknown factor – such as an unpredictable pilot – that might turn a simple flight-test equation into a scorched crater on the desert and another wave of donations to the 'window fund'.

Civilian test pilots, working on contract for companies like Boeing or Lockheed, are just as carefully screened as their soul brothers in the Air Force. The men who run the 'military-industrial complex' are not about to entrust the fruits of their billion-dollar projects to the kind of pilot who might be tempted to zoom a new plane under the Golden Gate Bridge at rush hour. The whole philosophy of research testing is to *minimize the risk*. Test pilots are sent up with specific instructions. Their job is to perform a set of finely plotted manoeuvres with the plane, to assess its performance in specific circumstances – stability at high speeds, rate of acceleration at certain climb angles, etc. – and then to bring it down safely and write a detailed report for the engineers. There are plenty of fine pilots around, but only a handful can communicate in the language of superadvanced aerodynamics. The best pilot in the world – even if he could land a B-52 on the number eight green at Pebble Beach without taking a divot – would be useless on a test-flight project unless he could explain, in a written report, just how and why the landing could be made.

The Air Force is very keen on people who 'go by the book', and there *is*, in fact, a book – called a technical order – on every piece of equipment in use, including planes. Test pilots can't go by 'the book', however, because for all practical purposes, they are the people who write it. 'We push a plane to its absolute limits,' said a young major at Edwards. 'We want to know exactly how it performs under every conceivable circumstance. And then we explain it, on paper, so other pilots will know what to expect of it.'

He was standing on the flight line in a bright-orange flying suit, a baggy one-piece thing full of special pockets and zippers and flaps. These pilots are sporty-looking people, vaguely resembling a bunch of pro-football quarterbacks. The age bracket is early thirties to late forties, with a median around 37 or 38. The average age in the USAF Aerospace Research Pilot School at Edwards is 30. Nobody over 32 is accepted; few pilots younger than 29 have logged enough air time to qualify. From a list of 600 to 1000 applicants each year, the school picks two classes of sixteen men each. Washouts are rare; the screening process is so thorough that no candidate who appears to be even faintly questionable survives the final cut. Forty-one of the nation's sixty-three astronauts are graduates of the test pilots' school – a military version of Cal Tech and MIT – the ultimate in aviation academics.

A sense of élitism is pervasive among test pilots. There are less than 100 of them on Edwards, with several hundred more spread out on testing projects from coast to coast. But Edwards is the capital of their world. 'It's like the White House,' says recently retired Colonel Joseph Cotton. 'After Edwards, the only direction a test pilot can go is down; any other assignment is practically a demotion.'

Colonel Cotton is the man who saved one of the $350 million experimental XB-70s by short-circuiting a computer with a paper clip. The huge plane's landing gear had jammed, making it impossible to land. 'You can't argue with a black box,' said the colonel, 'so we had to fool it.' While the plane circled the base and engineers on the ground radioed careful instructions, Joe Cotton took a flashlight and a paper clip and crawled into the dark landing-gear bay to perform critical surgery in a maze of wires and relays.

Incredibly, it worked. He managed to short the faulty circuit out of the chain of command, as it were, and trick the computer into lowering the landing gear. The plane landed with locked brakes and flaming tyres, but no serious damage – and 'Joe Cotton's paper clip' was an instant legend.

I found Colonel Cotton at his new home in Lancaster, pacing around his living room while his wife tried to place a call to a fellow pilot whose teenage son had been killed the day before in a motorcycle accident. The funeral was set for the next afternoon, and the whole Cotton family was going. (The flight line was empty the next day. The only pilot in the test-operations building was a visiting Britisher. All the others had gone to the funeral.)

Joe Cotton is forty-seven, one of the last of the precomputer genera-tion. By today's standards, he wouldn't even qualify for test-pilot train-ing. He is not a college graduate, much less a master of advanced calculus with an honours degree in math or science. But the young pilots at Edwards speak of Joe Cotton as if he were already a myth. He is not quite real, in their terms: a shade too complex, not entirely predictable. At a recent symposium for the Society of Experimental Test Pilots, Colonel Cotton showed up wearing a Mickey Mouse wristwatch. All the other pilots thought it was 'great' – but none of them rushed out to buy one for themselves.

Joe Cotton is a very gentle, small-boned man with an obsessive in-terest in amost everything. We talked for nearly five hours. In an age of stereotypes, he manages to sound like a patriotic hippie and a Christian anarchist all at once.

'The greatest quality you can build into a plane,' he says, 'is the quality of forgiveness.' Or: 'Having control of that airplane is like hav-ing control of your life; you don't want it wandering around up there, trying to get into a spin and crash ...

'Flight testing is a beautiful racket ... Being a test pilot on the Mojave Desert in America is the greatest expression of freedom I can think of ...' And suddenly: 'Retiring from the Air Force is like getting out of a cage ...'

It is always a bit of a shock to meet an original, unfettered mind, and this was precisely the difference between Colonel Joe Cotton and the young pilots I met on the base. The Air Force computers have done their work well: They have screened out all but the near-perfect speci-mens. And the science of aviation will benefit, no doubt, from the ultimate perfection of the flight-test equation. Our planes will be safer and more efficient, and eventually we will breed all our pilots in test tubes.

Perhaps it will be for the best. Or maybe not. The last question I asked

Joe Cotton was how he felt about the war in Vietnam, and particularly the antiwar protests. 'Well,' he said, 'anytime you can get people emotionally disturbed about war, that's good. I've been an Air Force pilot most of my life, but I've never thought I was put on earth to kill people. The most important thing in life is concern for one another. When we've lost that, we've lost the right to live. If more people in Germany had been concerned about what Hitler was doing, well ...' He paused, half-aware – and only half-caring, it seemed – that he was no longer talking like a colonel just retired from the US Air Force.

'You know,' he said finally. 'When I fly over Los Angeles at night, I look down at all those lights ... six million people down there ... and that's how many Hitler killed ...' He shook his head.

We walked outside, and when Joe Cotton said good night, he smiled and extended his left hand – remembering, somehow, after all that rambling talk, that I couldn't use my right.

The next afternoon, in the officers' club bar, I decided to broach the same question about the war in a friendly conversation with a young test pilot from Virginia, who had spent some time in Vietnam before his assignment to Edwards. 'Well, I've changed my mind about the war,' he said. 'I used to be all for it, but now I don't give a damn. It's no fun any more, now that we can't go up north. You could see your targets up there, you could see what you hit. But hell, down south all you do is fly a pattern and drop a bunch of bombs through the clouds. There's no sense of accomplishment.' He shrugged and sipped his drink, dismissing the war as a sort of pointless equation, an irrelevant problem no longer deserving of his talents.

An hour or so later, driving back to Los Angeles, I picked up a news-cast on the radio: student riots at Duke, Wisconsin, and Berkeley; oil slick in the Santa Barbara Channel; Kennedy murder trials in New Orleans and Los Angeles. And suddenly Edwards Air Force Base and that young pilot from Virginia seemed a million miles away. Who would ever have thought, for instance, that the war in Vietnam could be solved by taking the fun out of bombing?

Pageant, September 1969

THE POLICE CHIEF

THE PROFESSIONAL VOICE OF LAW ENFORCEMENT

Weapons are my business. You *name* it and I *know* it: guns, bombs, gas, fire, knives and everything else. Damn few people in the world know more about weaponry than I do. I'm an expert on demolition, ballistics, blades, motors, animals – anything capable of causing damage to man, beast or structure. This is my *profession*, my bag, my trade, my thing ... my evil speciality. And for this reason the editors of *Scanlan's* have asked me to comment on a periodical called the *Police Chief*.

At first I refused ... but various pressures soon caused me to change my mind. Money was not a factor in my decision. What finally spurred me to action was a sense of duty, even urgency, to make my voice heard. I am, as I said, a pro – and in this foul and desperate hour in our history I think even pros should speak up.

Frankly, I love this country. And also, quite frankly, I despise being put in this position – for a lot of reasons, which I don't mind listing:

1 For one thing, the press used to have a good rule about not talking about each other – no matter what they thought, or even what they *knew*. In the good old days a newspaperman would always protect his own kind. There was no way to get those bastards to testify against each other. It was worse than trying to make doctors testify in a malpractice suit, or making a beat cop squeal on his buddy in a 'police brutality' case.

2 The reason I know about things like 'malpractice' and 'police brutality' is that I used to be a cop – a police chief, for that matter, in a small city just east of Los Angeles. And before that I was a boss detective in Nevada – and before that a beat cop in Oakland. So I know what I'm talking about when I say most journalists are lying shitheads. I never knew a reporter who could even *say* the word 'corrupt' without pissing in his pants from pure guilt.

3 The third reason for the bad way I feel about this 'article' is that I used to have tremendous faith in this magazine called the *Police Chief*. I read it cover-to-cover every month, like some people read the Bible, and *the city paid for my subscription*. Because they knew I was valuable to them, and the *Police Chief* was valuable to me. I *loved* that goddamn magazine. It *taught* me things. It kept me ahead of the game.

But no more. Things are different now – and not just for me either. As a respected law enforcement official for twenty years in the West, and now as a weapons consultant to a political candidate in Colorado, I can say from long and tremendous experience that the *Police Chief* has turned to cheap jelly. As a publication it no longer excites me, and as a phoney Voice of the Brotherhood it makes me sick with rage. One night in Oakland, about a dozen years ago, I actually got my rocks off from reading the advertisements ... I hate to admit such a thing, but it's true.

I remember one ad from Smith & Wesson when they first came out with their double-action .44 Magnum revolver: 240 grains of hot lead, exploding out of a big pipe in your hand at 1200 feet per second ... and super-accurate, even on a running target.

Up until that time we'd all thought the .357 Magnum was just about the bee's nuts. FBI-filed tests had proved what the .357 could do: in one case, with FBI agents giving fire-pursuit to a carload of fleeing subjects, an agent in the pursuing car brought the whole chase to an end with a single shot from his .357 revolver. His slug penetrated the trunk of the fleeing car, then the back seat, then the upper torso of a back seat passenger, then the front seat, then the neck of the driver, then the dashboard, and finally imbedded itself in the engine block. Indeed, the .357 was such a terrifying weapon that for ten years only qualified marksmen were allowed to carry them.

So it just about drove me crazy when – just after I'd qualified to carry a .357 – I picked up a new issue of the *Police Chief* and saw an ad for the .44 Magnum, a brand-new revolver with *twice* the velocity and *twice* the striking power of the 'old' .357.

One of the first real-life stories I heard about the .44 Magnum was from a Tennessee sheriff whom I met one spring at a law enforcement conference in St Louis. 'Most men can't handle the goddamn thing,' he said. 'It kicks worse than a goddamn bazooka, and it hits like a goddamn A-bomb. Last week I had to chase a nigger downtown, and when he got so far away that he couldn't even hear my warning yell, I just pulled down on the bastard with this .44 Magnum and blew the head clean off his body with one shot. All we found were some teeth and one eyeball. The rest was all mush and bone splinters.'

Well ... let's face it; that man was a bigot. We've learned a lot about racial problems since then ... but even a nigger could read the *Police Chief* in 1970 and see that we haven't learned much about weapons. Today's beat cop in any large city is a sitting duck for snipers, rapers, dope addicts, bomb-throwers and communist fruits. These scum are well-armed – with US Army weapons – and that's why I finally quit official police work.

As a weapons specialist I saw clearly – in the years between 1960 and 1969 – that the Army's weapons-testing programme on the Indo-Chinese peninsula was making huge strides. In that active decade the basic military cartridge developed from the ancient 30.06 to the neuter .308 to a rapid-fire .223. That lame old chestnut about 'sharpshooters' was finally muscled aside by the proven value of sustained-firescreens. The hand-thrown grenade was replaced, at long last, by the portable grenade launcher, the Claymore mine and the fiery missile-cluster. In the simplest of technical terms, the kill-potential of the individual soldier was in-creased from 1.6 per second to 26.4 per second – or nearly five KP points higher than Pentagon figures indicate we would need to prevail in a land war with China.

So the reason for this nation's dismal failure on the Indo-Chinese peninsula lies *not* in our weapons technology, but in a *failure of will*. Yes. Our GIs are doomed in Vietnam, Cambodia, Laos, Thailand, Burma, etc. for the same insane reason that our law enforcement agents are doomed in Los Angeles, New York and Chicago. They have been *shackled*, for years, by cowardly faggots and spies. Not all were con-scious traitors; some were morally weak, others were victims of drugs, and many were simply crazy ...

Let's face it. The majority of people in this country are mentally ill ... and this illness unfortunately extends into all walks of life, including law enforcement. The illness is manifest in our national stance from Bangkok to Bangor, to coin a phrase, but to those of us still dying on our feet in the dry rot of middle America there is no worse pain – and no more hideous proof of the plague that afflicts us all – than the know-ledge of what has happened to the *Police Chief*, a magazine we once loved because it was *great*.

But let's take a look at it now. The editor-in-chief is an FBI dropout by the name of Quinn Tamm, a middle-aged career cop who ruined his whole life one day by accidentally walking on the fighting side of J. Edgar Hoover's wiretrap fetish. Tamm is legally sane – by 'liberal' standards – but in grass-roots police circles he is primarily known as the model for Mitch Greenhill's famous song 'Pig in the Stash'. The real editor of the magazine is a woman named Pitcher. I knew her in the old days, but Tamm's son does most of the work, anyway ...

One of the most frightening things about the *Police Chief* is that it calls itself the 'professional voice of law enforcement'. But all it really is, is a house-organ for a gang of high-salaried pansies who call them-selves the 'International Association of Chiefs of Police, Inc.'

How about that? Here's a crowd of suck-asses putting out this maga-zine that says it's the voice of cops. Which is bullshit. All you have to do is look at the goddamn thing to see what it is. Look at the advertis-ing; fag tools! Breathalysers, 'paralysers', gas masks, sirens, funny little car radios with voice scramblers so the scum can't listen in ... but no ATTACK WEAPONS!!! Not one! The last really functional weapon that got mentioned in the *Police Chief* was the 'Nutcracker Flail', a combination club and pincers about three feet long that can cripple almost anybody. It works like a huge pair of pliers: the officers first flails the living shit out of anybody he can reach ... and then, when a suspect falls, he swiftly applies the 'nutcracker' action, gripping the victim's neck, extremities or genitals with the powerful pincers at the 'reaching' end of the tool, then squeezing until all resistance ceases.

Believe me, our city streets would be a lot safer if every beat cop in the nation carried a Nutcracker Flail ... So why is this fine weapon no longer advertised in *PC*? I'll tell you why: for the same reason they no longer advertise the .44 Magnum or the fantastically efficient Stoner rifle they can shoot through brick walls and make hash of the rabble inside. Yes ... and also for the same reason they won't advertise the Growler, a mobile sound unit that emits such unholy shrieks and roars that every human being within a radius of ten city blocks is paralysed with unbearable pain: they collapse in their tracks and curl up like worms, losing all control of their bowels and bleeding from the ears.

Every PD in the country should have a Growler, but the *PC* won't advertise it because they're afraid of *hurting their image*. They want to be *LOVED*. In this critical hour we don't need love, we need WEAPONS – the newest and best and most efficient weapons we can get our hands on. This is a time of extreme *peril*. The rising tide is almost on us ... but you'd never know it from reading the *Police Chief*. Let's look at the June 1970 issue.

The first thing we get is a bunch of gibberish written by the police chief of Miami, Florida, saying 'the law enforcement system [in the USA] is doomed to failure'. Facing this is a full-page ad for the Smith & Wesson 'Street Cleaner', described as a 'Pepper Fog tear smoke generator ... loaded with a new Super Strength Type CS [gas] just developed by Gen. Ordnance'. The 'Street Cleaner' with Super CS 'not only sends the meanest troublemakers running. It convinces them not to come back ... You can trigger anything from a 1-second puff to a 10-minute deluge ... Do *you* have a Street Cleaner yet?'

In all fairness, the Pepper Fogger is not a bad *tool*, but it's hardly a weapon. It may convince trouble-makers not to come back in ten minutes, but wait a few *hours* and the scum will be back in your face like wild rats. The obvious solution to this problem is to abandon our obsession with tear gas and fill the Street Cleaner with a nerve agent. CS only slaps at the problem: nerve gas solves it.

Yet the bulk of all advertising in the *PC* is devoted to tear gas weapons: Federal Laboratories offers the 201-Z gun, along with the Fed 233 Emergency Kit, featuring 'Speedheat' grenades and gas projectiles guaranteed to 'pierce barricades'. The AAI Corporation offers a 'multi-purpose grenade that can't be thrown back'. And, from Lake Erie Chemical, we have a new kind of gas mask that 'protects against CS'. (This difference is crucial; the ad explains that Army surplus gas masks do well enough against the now-obsolete CN gas, but they're virtually useless against CS – 'the powerful irritant agent that more and more departments are turning to and that's now "standard" with the National Guard'.

Unfortunately, this is about as far as the *Police Chief* goes, in terms of weapons (or tools) information. One of the few interesting items in the non-weapons category is a 'scrambler' for 'police-band' car radios – so 'the enemy' can't listen in. With the 'scrambler', everything will sound like Donald Duck.

The only consistently useful function of the *PC* is the old faithful 'positions open' section. For instance: Charlotte, NC, needs a 'firearms identification expert' for the new city-county crime lab. Ellenville, NY, is looking for a new chief of police, salary '$10,500 with liberal fringe benefits'. Indeed. And the US Department of Justice is 'now recruiting Special Agents for the Bureau of Narcotics and Dangerous Drugs'. The ad says they need 'a sizeable number' of new agents, to start at $8098 per annum, 'with opportunity for premium overtime pay to gross up to $10,000'.

(In my opinion, only a lunatic or a dope addict would do narc-work for that kind of money. The hours are brutal and the risks are worse: I once had a friend who went to work as a drug agent for the feds and lost both of his legs. A girl he was trusting put LSD in his beer, then took him to a party where a gang of vicious freaks snapped his femurs with a meat-axe.)

Let's face it: we live in savage times. Not only are cops called pigs – they are treated like swine and eat worse than hogs. Yet the *PC* still carries advertising for 'PIG' tie-clasps! What kind of two-legged scumsucker would wear a thing like that?

WHY ARE WE GROVELLING? This is the rootnut question! Why has the once great *Police Chief* turned on its rank and file?

Are we *dupes*? Do the red pansies want to *destroy* us? If not, why do they mock all we believe in?

So it should come as no surprise – to the self-proclaimed pigs who put out the *Police Chief* – that most of us no longer turn to that soggy-pink magazine when we're looking for serious information. Personally, I prefer the *Shooting Times*, or *Guns & Ammo*. Their editorials on 'gun control' are pure balls of fire, and their classified ads offer every conceivable kind of beastly weapon from brass knuckles and blowguns to 20 mm cannons.

Another fine source of weapons info – particularly for the private citizen – is a little-known book titled, *How to Defend Yourself, Your Family, and Your Home – a Complete Guide to Self-Protection.* Now here is a book with real class! It explains, in 307 pages of fine detail, how to set booby traps in your home so that 'midnight intruders' will destroy themselves upon entry; it tells which type of shotgun is best for rapid-fire work in narrow hallways (a sawed-off double-barrelled 12-gauge; one barrel loaded with a huge tear gas slug, the other with Double-O buckshot). This book is invaluable to anyone who fears that his home might be invaded, at any moment, by rioters, rapers, looters, dope addicts, niggers, reds or any other group. No detail has been spared: dogs, alarm wiring, screens, bars, poisons, knives, guns ... ah yes, this is a wonderful book, and highly recommended by the National Police Officers Association of America. This is a very different group from the police chiefs. Very different.

But why grapple now with a book of such massive stature? I need time to ponder it and to run tests on the many weapons and devices that appear in the text. No professional would attempt to deal lightly with this book. It is a rare combination of sociology and stone craziness, laced with weapons technology on a level that is rarely encountered.

You will *want* this book. But I want you to *know* it first. And for that, I need *time* ... to deal smartly with the bugger on its own terms. No pro would settle for less.

– Raoul Duke (Master of Weaponry)

Scanlan's Monthly, vol. 1, no. 7, June 1970

PART FOUR

THE GREAT SHARK HUNT

Four-thirty in Cozumel now; dawn is coming up on these gentle white beaches looking west at the Yucatán Channel. Thirty yards from my patio here at Cabañas del Caribe, the surf is rolling up, very softly, on the beach out there in the darkness beyond the palm trees.

Many vicious mosquitoes and sand fleas out here tonight. There are sixty units in this rambling beach-front hotel, but my room – number 129 – is the only one full of light and music and movement.

I have both my doors and all four windows propped open – a huge bright magnet for every bug on the island ... But I am not being bitten. Every inch of my body – from the soles of my bleeding bandaged feet to the top of my sun-scorched head – is covered with 6-12 Insect Repellent, a cheap foul-smelling oil with no redeeming social or aesthetic characteristics except that it works.

These goddamn bugs are all around – settling on the notebook, my wrists, my arms, circling the rim of my tall glass of Bacardi Añejo and ice ... but no bites. It has taken about six days to solve this hellish bug problem ... which is excellent news on the one level, but, as always, the solution to one problem just peels back another layer and exposes some new and more sensitive area.

At this stage of the gig, things like mosquitoes and sand fleas are the least of our worries ... because in about two hours and twenty-two minutes I have to get out of this hotel without paying an unnaturally massive bill, drive about three miles down the coast in a rented VW Safari that can't be paid for, either, and which may not even make it into town, due to serious mechanical problems – and then get my technical adviser Yail Bloor out of the Mesón San Miguel without paying his bill, either, and then drive us both out to the airport in that goddamn junk Safari to catch the 7:50 Aeromexico flight to Mérida and Monterrey, where we'll change planes for San Antonio and Denver.

So we are looking at a very heavy day ... 2000 miles between here and home, no cash at all, ten brutally expensive days in three hotels on the Striker Aluminum Yachts credit tab, which just got jerked out from under us when the local PR team decided we were acting too weird to be what we claim to be – and so now we are down to about $44 extra between us – with my bill at the Cabañas hovering around $650 and Bloor's at the San Miguel not much less – plus eleven days for that wretched car from the local Avis dealer who already hit me for $40 cash for a broken windshield, and God only knows how much he'll demand

when he sees what condition his car is in now ... plus about $400
worth of black coral that we ordered up from Chino: double-thumbed
fist, coke spoons, sharks' teeth, etc. ... and that $120 18-kt-gold chain at
the market ... also Sandy's black-coral necklace. We will need all avail-
able cash for the black-coral deal – so things like hotel bills and car
rentals will have to be put off and paid by cheque, if anybody will take
one ... or charged to Striker Aluminum Yachts, which got me into this
goddamn twisted scene in the first place. But the Striker people are no
longer with us; extreme out-front hostility. Bruce, Joyce – even the
bogus Lcher Eduardo. How did we blow the image?

'Dear Mr Thompson ... Here's some background information on the
Cozumel cruise and international fishing tournament ... Regarding the
cruise schedule, about fourteen Strikers will leave Fort Lauderdale on
23 April, arriving in Key West that night, leaving Key West midday on
the 25th, to assure skirting the Cuban coast in the daytime, and arriving
in Cozumel midafternoon on the 27th or 28th. In addition to the proven
sailfishing, there will be a Marlin Only Day on Saturday sixth May, in
the initial attempt on any volume basis to determine how good the blue-
marlin fishing is ... Each night during the tournament, there are cocktail
parties with over 250 people attending, mariachi and island music,
etc. ... We are happy you can make the trip ... Flights leave Miami
daily for Cozumel at 2:45 p.m. You will need a Mexican tourist card,
which you can pick up at the Mexican Tourism Department, 100 Biscayne Boulevard, Room 612 Miami. There are no shots required.

> Sincerely,
> Terence J. Byrne
> Public Relations Representative
> Striker Aluminum Yachts
> Fort Lauderdale, Florida

Indeed ... no shots: just a tourist card, plenty of Coppertone, a new
pair of Top-siders and a fine gringo smile for the customs officers. The
letter called up visions of heavy sport on the high seas, *mano a mano*
with giant sailfish and world-record marlin ... Reeling the bastards in,
fighting off sharks with big gaffs, strapped into a soft white-Naugahyde
fighting chair in the cockpit of a big power cruiser ... then back to the
harbour at dusk for a brace of gin and tonics, tall drinks in the sunset,
lounging around in cool deck chairs while the crew chops up bait and a
strolling mariachi band roams on the pier, wailing mournful Olmec love
songs ...
    Ah, yes, I was definitely ready for it. Sixteen months of straight poli-
tics had left me reeling around on the brink of a nervous breakdown. I

needed a change, something totally different from my normal line of work. Covering politics a vicious, health-ripping ordeal that often requires eight or nine shots at once – twice or three times a week in the peak season – so this unexpected assignment to 'cover' a deep-sea-fishing tournament off the Yucatán coast of Mexico was a welcome relief from the horrors of the campaign trail in 1972.

Right. Things would be different now: hot sun, salt air, early to bed and early to rise ... This one had all the signs of a high-style bag job: fly off to the Caribbean as a guest of the idle rich, hang around on their boats for a week or so, then crank out a left-handed story to cover expenses and pay for a new motorcycle back in the Rockies. The story itself was a bit on the hazy side, but the editor at *Playboy* said not to worry. Almost everybody unfortunate enough to have had any dealings with me since the campaign ended seemed convinced that I was in serious need of a vacation – a cooling-out period, a chance to back off – and this fishing tournament in Cozumel looked just about perfect. It would prise my head out of politics, they said, and force me off in a new direction – out of the valley of death and back towards the land of the living.

There was, however, a kink: I had just come *back* from 'vacation'. It was the first one I'd ever attempted, or at least the first one I'd tried since I was fired from my last regular job on Christmas Day in 1958, when the production manager at *Time* magazine ripped up my punch card in a stuttering rage and told me to get the fuck out of the building. Since then I had been unemployed – in the formal sense of that word – and when you've been out of work for fourteen years, it's almost impossible to relate to a word like vacation.

So I was extremely nervous when circumstances compelled me, in the late winter of 72, to fly to Cozumel with my wife, Sandy, in order to do nothing at all.

Three days later I ran out of air in a rip tide, ninety feet down on Palancar Reef, and I came so close to drowning that they said, later, I was lucky to get off with a serious case of the bends. The nearest decompression chamber was in Miami, so they chartered a plane and flew me there that same night.

I spent the next nineteen days in a pressurized sphere somewhere in downtown Miami, and when I finally came out, the bill was $3000. My wife finally located my attorney in a drug commune on the outskirts of Mazatlán. He flew immediately to Florida and had the courts declare me a pauper so I was able to leave without legal problems.

I went back to Colorado with the idea of resting for at least six months. But three days after I got home, this assignment came in to cover the fishing tournament. It was a natural, they said, because I was already familiar with the island. And besides, I needed a change from politics.

Which was true, in a way – but I had my own reasons for wanting to go back to Cozumel. On the evening before my near-fatal scuba dive on Palancar Reef, I had stashed fifty units of pure MDA in the adobe wall of the shark pool at the local aquarium next to the Hotel Barracuda – and this stash had been much on my mind while I was recovering from the bends in the Miami hospital.

So when the Cozumel assignment came through, I drove immediately into town to consult with my old friend and drug crony Yail Bloor. I explained the circumstances in detail, then asked his advice.

'It's clear as a fucking bell,' he snapped. 'We'll have to go down there at once. You'll handle the fishermen while I get the drugs.'

These were the circumstances that sent me back to Cozumel in late April. Neither the editor nor the high-powered sport-fishing crowd we'd be dealing with had any notion of my real reason for making the trip. Bloor knew, but he had a vested interest in maintaining the cover because I was passing him off, on the tab, as my 'technical adviser'. It made perfect sense, I felt: In order to cover a highly competitive situation, you need plenty of trustworthy help.

When I got to Cozumel, on Monday afternoon, everybody on the island with any clout in the tourism business was half-mad with excitement at the idea of having a genuwine, real-life *'Playboy* writer' in their midst for a week or ten days. When I slumped off the plane from Miami, I was greeted like Buffalo Bill on his first trip to Chicago – a whole gaggle of public-relations specialists met the plane, and at least three of them were waiting for *me*: What could they do for me? What did I *want*? How could they make my life pleasant?

Carry my bags?

Well ... why not?

To where?

Well ... I paused, sensing an unexpected opening that could lead almost anywhere ... 'I think I'm supposed to go to the Cabañas,' I said. 'But—'

'No,' said one of the handlers, 'you have a press suite at Cozumeleño.'

I shrugged. 'Whatever's right,' I muttered. 'Let's roll.'

I'd asked the travel agent in Colorado to get me one of those VW Safari jeeps – the same kind I'd had on my last trip to Cozumel – but the PR crowd at the airport insisted on taking me straight to the hotel. My jeep, they said, would be delivered within the hour, and in the meantime, I was treated like some kind of high-style dignitary: A few people actually addressed me as 'Mr Playboy' and the others kept calling me 'sir'. I was hustled into a waiting car and whisked off along the two-lane blacktop highway through the palm jungle and out in the general direction of the American Strip, a cluster of beach-front hotels on the northeast end of the island.

Despite my lame protests, they took me to the newest, biggest and most expensive hotel on the island – a huge, stark-white concrete hulk that reminded me of the Oakland city jail. We were met at the desk by the manager, the owner and several hired heavies who explained that the terrible hammering noise I heard was merely the workmen putting the finishing touches on the third floor of what would eventually be a five-storey colossus. 'We have just ninety rooms now,' the manager explained, 'but by Christmas we will have three hundred.'

'Jesus God!' I muttered.

'What?'

'Never mind,' I said. 'This is a hell of a thing you're building here: No doubt about that – it's extremely impressive in every way – but the odd fact is that I thought I had reservations down the beach at the Cabañas.' I flashed a nice shrug and a smile, ignoring the awkward chill that was already settling on us.

The manager coughed up a brittle laugh. 'The Cabañas? No, *Señor* Playboy. The Cozumeleño is *very different* from the Cabañas.'

'Yeah,' I said. 'I can see that right off.' The Mayan bellboy had already disappeared with my bags. 'We saved a junior suite for you,' said the manager. 'I think you'll be satisfied.' His English was very precise, his smile was unnaturally thick ... and it was clear, from a glance at my high-powered welcoming committee, that I was going to be their guest for at least one night ... And as soon as they forgot about me, I would flee this huge concrete morgue and sneak off to the comfortably rundown palm-shaded peace of the Cabañas, where I felt more at home.

On the drive out from the airport, the PR man, who was wearing a blue baseball cap and a stylish blue-and-white T-shirt, both emblazoned with the lightning-flash STRIKER logo, had told me that the owner of this new, huge Cozumeleño hotel was a member of the island's ruling family. 'They own about half of it,' he said with a grin, 'and what they don't own they control absolutely, with their fuel licence.'

'Fuel licence?'

'Yeah,' said the PR man. 'They control every gallon of fuel that's sold here – from the gasoline we're driving on right now in this jeep to the gas in every stove in all the hotel restaurants and even the goddamn jet fuel at the airport.'

449

I didn't pay much attention to that talk, at the time. It seemed like the same kind of sleazy, power-worshipping bullshit you'd expect to hear from *any* PR man, anywhere, on any subject in any situation ...

My problem was clear from the start. I had come down to Cozumel – officially, at least – to cover not just a fishing tournament but a *scene*: I'd explained to the editor that big-time sport fishing attracts a certain kind of people and it was the behaviour of these people – not the fishing – that interested me. On my first visit to Cozumel, I'd discovered the fishing harbour completely by accident one night when Sandy and I were driving around the island more or less naked, finely twisted on MDA, and the only reason we located the yacht basin was that I took a wrong turn around midnight and tried – without realizing where I was going – to run a roadblock manned by three Mexican soldiers with sub-machine guns at the entrance to the island's only airport.

It was a hard scene to cope with, as I recall, and now that I look back on it, I suspect that mouldy white powder we'd eaten was probably some kind of animal tranquillizer instead of true MDA. There is a lot of PCP on the drug market these days; anybody who wants to put a horse into a coma can buy it pretty easily from ... well ... why blow that, eh?

In any case, we were bent – and after being driven away from the airport by armed guards, I took the next available open road and we wound up in the yacht basin, where there was a party going on. I could hear it about a half mile off, so I homed in on the music and drove across the highway and about 200 yards down a steep grassy embankment to get to the dock. Sandy refused to get out of the jeep, saying that these weren't the kind of people she felt ready to mix with, under the circumstances ... so I left her huddled under a blanket on the front seat and walked out on to the dock by myself. It was exactly the kind of scene I'd been looking for – about thirty-five stone-drunk rich honkies from places like Jacksonville and Pompano Beach, reeling around in this midnight Mexican port on their $200,000 power cruisers and cursing the natives for not providing enough teenage whores to go with the mariachi music. It was a scene of total decadence and I felt right at home in it. I began mixing with the crowd and trying to hire a boat for the next morning – which proved to be very difficult, because nobody could understand what I was saying.

What's wrong here? I wondered. Is there speed in this drug? Why can't these people understand me?

One of the people I was talking to was the owner of a sixty-foot Chris-Craft from Milwaukee. He'd just arrived from Key West that afternoon, he said, and all he seemed to have any real interest in at the moment was the 'Argentine maid' he was grappling with in the cockpit of his boat. She was about fifteen years old, had dark-blonde hair and red eyes, but it was hard to get a good look at her, because 'Cap'n Tom' – as he introduced himself – was bending her over a Styrofoam bait box full of dolphin heads and trying to suck on her collarbone while he talked to me.

Finally I gave up on him and found a local fishing merchant called Fernando Murphy, whose drunkenness was so crude and extreme that we were able to communicate perfectly, even though he spoke little English. 'No fishing at night,' he said. 'Come to my shop downtown by the plaza tomorrow and I rent you a nice boat.'

'Wonderful,' I said. 'How much?'

He laughed and fell against a pasty blonde woman from New Orleans who was too drunk to talk. 'For you,' he said, 'a hundred and forty dollars a day – and I *guarantee* fish.'

'Why not?' I said. 'I'll be there at dawn. Have the boat ready.'

'*¡Chingado!*' he screamed. He dropped his drink on the dock and began grappling with his own shoulder blades. I was taken aback at his outburst, not understanding for a moment … until I saw that a laughing 300-pound man wearing Levis and a red baseball hat in the cockpit of a nearby boat called *Black Snapper* had hooked the back of Murphy's shirt with a thirty-pound marlin rod and was trying to reel him in.

Murphy staggered backwards, screaming '*¡Chingado!*' once again as he fell sideways on the dock and ripped his shirt open. Well, I thought, no point trying to do business with this crowd tonight and, in fact, I never fished on that trip. But the general low tone of that party had stayed with me – a living caricature of white trash run amuck on foreign shores; an appalling kind of story, but not without a certain human-interest quotient.

On the first day of the tournament, I spent eight hours at sea aboard the eventual winner – a fifty-four-foot Striker called *Sun Dancer*, owned by a wealthy middle-aged industrialist named Frank Oliver from Palatka, Florida.

Oliver ran a fleet of barges on the inland waterway out of Jacksonville, he said, and *Sun Dancer* was the only boat in the Cozumel Harbor flying a Confederate flag. He had 'about three hundred and twenty-five thousand in it' – including a network of built-in vacuum-cleaner wall plugs for the deep-pile carpets – and although he said he spent 'maybe five weeks out of the year' on the boat, he was a very serious angler and he meant to win this tournament.

To this end, he had hired one of the world's top fishing captains – a speedy little cracker named Cliff North – and turned *Sun Dancer* over to him on a year-round basis. North is a living legend in the sport-fishing world and the idea that Oliver would hire him as his personal captain was not entirely acceptable to the other anglers. One of them explained that it was like some rich weekend duffer hiring Arnold Palmer to shoot the final round of the Greater Cleveland Elks golf tourney for him. North lives on the boat, with his wife and two young 'mates', who do all the menial work, and during the ten months of the year when Oliver's not around, he charters *Sun Dancer* out to anybody who can pay the rate. All Cliff has to do – in return for this sinecure – is make sure Oliver wins the three or four fishing tournaments he finds time to enter each year.

Thanks to North and his expert boat handling, Frank Oliver is now listed in the sport-fishing record books as one of the world's top anglers. Whether or not Oliver would win any tournaments without North and *Sun Dancer* is a subject of widespread disagreement and occasional rude opinion among sport-fishing pros. Not even the most egotistical anglers will deny that a good boat and a hot-rod captain to handle it are crucial factors in ocean fishing – but there is a definite division of opinion between anglers (who are mainly rich amateurs) and pros (the boat captains and the crews) about the relative value of skills.

Most of the pros I talked to in Cozumel were reluctant, at first, to speak on this subject – at least for the record – but after the third or fourth drink, they would invariably come around to suggesting that anglers were more of a hazard than a help and, as a general rule of thumb, you could catch more fish by just jamming the rod into a holder on the rear end of the boat and letting the fish do the work. After two or three days on the boats, the most generous consensus I could get from the pros was that even the best angler is worth about a ten per cent advantage in a tournament, and that most are seen as handicaps.

'Jesus God Almighty,' said a veteran captain from Fort Lauderdale one night in a local hotel bar, 'you wouldn't believe the things I've seen these fools do!' He laughed, but the sound was nervous and his body seemed to shudder as the memories came back to him. 'One of the people I work for,' he said, 'has a wife who's just flat-out crazy.' He shook his head wearily. 'I don't want you to get me wrong, now – I love her dearly, as a person – but when it comes to fishing, goddamn it, I'd like to chop her up and toss her out for the sharks.' He took a long hit on his rum and coke. 'Yeah, I hate to say it, but that's all she's good for – shark bait and nothin' else. Jesus, the other day she almost killed herself! We hooked a big sailfish, and when that happens, you have to move pretty fast, you know – but all of a sudden, I heard her screaming like crazy, and when I looked down from the bridge, she had her hair all tangled up in the reel!' He laughed. 'Goddamn! Can you believe that! She almost got scalped! I had to *jump* down, about fifteen feet

452

on to a wet deck in a bad sea, we were wallowing all around – and cut the whole line loose with my knife. She came within about ten seconds of having all her hair pulled out!'

Few anglers – and especially winners like Frank Oliver – agree with the pros' 90-10 split. 'It's basically a *teamwork* situation,' says Oliver, 'like a chain with no weak links. The angler, the captain, the mates, the boat – they're all critical, they work like gears with each other.'

Well … maybe so. Oliver won the tournament with twenty-eight sailfish in the three days that counted. But he was fishing *alone* on *Sun Dancer* – a boat so lavishly outfitted it could have passed for the nautical den in Nelson Rockefeller's Fifth Avenue apartment – and with the Arnold Palmer of sport fishing up on the bridge. Most of his competition was fishing in twos and threes on charter boats they were assigned to at random, with wild-tempered, contemptuous captains they'd never even met before yesterday morning.

'Fishing against Cliff North is bad enough,' said Jerry Haugen, captain of a stripped-down hulk of a boat called *Lucky Striker*, 'but when you have to go against North and only *one* angler, with everything set up exactly the way *he* wants it, that's just about impossible.'

Which is neither here nor there, in the rules of big-time sport fishing. If Bebe Rebozo decided to borrow a half-million dollars from the Pentagon at no interest and enter the Cozumel tournament with the best boat he could buy and a crew of specially trained US Marines, he would compete on the same basis with *me*, if I entered the thing with a 110-year-old Colorado River J-boat and a crew of drug-crazed politicos from the Meat Possum Athletic Club. According to the rules, we'd be equal … And while Bebe could fish alone on his boat, the tournament directors could assign me a nightmarish trio of anglers like Sam Brown, John Mitchell and Baby Huey.

Could we win? Never in hell. But nobody connected with that tournament would ever forget the experience … which is almost what happened anyway, for different reasons. By the third day of the tournament, or maybe it was the fourth, I had lost all control of my coverage. At one point, when Bloor ran amuck and disappeared for thirty hours, I was forced to jerk a dope addict out of the island's only night club and press him into service as a 'special observer' for *Playboy*. He spent the final day of the tournament aboard *Sun Dancer*, snorting coke in the head and jabbering wildly at North while poor Oliver struggled desperately to maintain his one-fish lead over Haugen's manic crew on *Lucky Striker*.

Thursday night was definitely the turning point. Whatever rapport Bloor and I had developed with the Striker people was wearing very thin after three days of increasingly strange behaviour and the antisocial attitude we apparently manifested at the big Striker cocktail party at the Punta Moreña beach bar was clearly unacceptable. Almost everybody there was staggering drunk by nightfall and the ugliness threshold was low. Here were all these heavy anglers – prosperous Florida business-men, for the most part – snarling and snapping at one another like East Harlem street fighters on the eve of a long-awaited rumble:

'You potbellied asshole! You couldn't catch a fish in a goddamn barrel!'

'Watch your stupid lip, fella: That's my *wife* you just stepped on!'

'*Whose* wife, fatface? Keep your fuckin' hands to yourself.'

'Where's the goddamn waiter? Boy! *Boy!* Over here! Get me another drink, will ya?'

'Let me just put it to you this way, my friend. How 'bout a goddamn *fish-off*? Just *you* and *me* – for a thousand bucks, eh? Yeah, how 'bout it?'

People were lurching around in the sand with plates full of cold macaroni and shrimp sauce. Every now and then, somebody would jerk one of the giant turtles out of the tank on the patio and thrust it in the face of some bleary-eyed bystander, laughing wildly and struggling to hang on to the thing, big green flippers clawing frantically at the air and lashing a spray of stale turtle water on everybody within a radius of ten feet ... 'Here: I wantcha to meet my friend! She'll do a real job on yer pecker. How horny are ya?'

It was not a good scene to confront with a head full of acid. We drank heavily, trying to act natural, but the drug set us clearly apart. Bloor become obsessed with the notion that we'd stumbled into a gathering of drunken greedheads who were planning to turn Cozumel into 'a Mexi-can Miami Beach' – which was true, to a certain extent, but he pursued it with a zeal that churned up angry resentment in every conversation he wandered into. At one point, I found him shouting at the manager of the hotel he was staying in: 'You're just a bunch of goddamn money-grubbing creeps! All this bullshit about *tourism* and *development* – what the hell do you want here, another Aspen?'

The hotel man was baffled. 'What *is* Aspen?' he asked. 'What are you talking about?'

'You know goddamn well what I'm talking about, you sleazy bastard!' Bloor shouted. 'These dirty concrete hotels you're building all over the beach, these dirty little hot-dog stands and—'

I hurried across the patio and grabbed him by the shoulder. 'Never mind Yail,' I said, trying to focus at least one of my eyes on whoever he was talking to. 'He's still not adjusted to this altitude.' I tried to smile at them, but I could sense it wasn't working ... a drugged grimace, wild eyes and very jerky movements. I could hear myself talking, but the words made no sense: 'These goddamned iguanas all over the road ... we did a one-eighty back there at the U-turn ... Yail grabbed the emergency brake when he saw all those lizards, jerked it right out by the root ... Thank Christ we had those snow tyres. We live at five thousand feet, you know, damn little air pressure up there, but down here at sea level you feel it squeezing your brain like a vice ... No way to escape it, you can't even think straight ...'

Nobody smiled; I was babbling out of control and Bloor was still yelling about 'land rapers'. I left him and went to the bar. 'We're leaving,' I said, 'but I want some ice for the road.'

The bartender gave me a Pepsi-Cola cup full of melting shavings. 'We'll need more than that,' I said – so he filled up another cup. He spoke no English, but I could grasp what he was trying to tell me: There was no container available for the amount of ice I wanted and they were almost out of ice anyway.

My head was beginning to pulsate violently at this point. I could barely keep a focus on his face. Rather than argue, I went out to the parking lot and drove the Safari through a screen of small beach trees and up on to the patio, parking it right in front of the bar and indicating to the stunned bartender that I wanted the back seat filled with ice.

The Striker crowd was appalled. 'You crazy son of a bitch!' someone yelled. 'You mashed about fifteen trees!'

I nodded, but the words didn't register. All I could think about was ice – throwing one cupload after another into the back seat. The acid, by this time, had fucked up my vision to the point where I was seeing square out of one eye and round out of the other. It was impossible to focus on anything; I seemed to have four hands ...

The bartender had not been lying: The Punta Moreña ice vat was virtually empty. I scraped a few more cuploads out of the bottom – hearing Bloor's angry cursing somewhere above and behind me – then I jumped over the counter and into the front seat of the jeep.

Nobody seemed to notice, so I gunned the engine violently and leaned on the horn as I crept very slowly in first gear through the mashed trees and shrubbery. Loud voices seemed to be looming down on me from the rear and suddenly Bloor was climbing over the back, yelling, 'Get moving, goddamn it, get moving!' I stomped on the accelerator and we fishtailed out of the deep-sand parking lot.

Thirty minutes later, after a top-speed, bug-spattered run all the way to the other side of the island, we rolled into the parking lot of what appeared to be a night club. Bloor had calmed down a bit, but he was still in a high, wild condition as we lurched to a stop about five feet from the front door. I could hear loud music inside.

'We need a few drinks,' I muttered. 'My tongue feels like an iguana's been chewing on it.'

Bloor stepped out. 'Keep the engine running,' he said. 'I'll check the place out.'

He disappeared inside and I leaned back on the seat to stare straight up at the star-crazed sky. It seemed about six feet above my eyes. Or maybe 60 feet, or 600. I couldn't be sure, and it didn't matter, anyway, because by that time I was convinced I was in the cockpit of a 727 coming into LA at midnight. Jesus, I thought, I am ripped right straight to the tits. Where am I? Are we going up or down? Somewhere in the back of my brain, I knew I was sitting in a jeep in the parking lot of a night club on an island off the Mexican coast – but how could I really be sure, with another part of my brain apparently convinced that I was looking down on the huge glittering bowl of Los Angeles from the cockpit of a 727? Was that the Milky Way? Or Sunset Boulevard? Orion, or the Beverly Hills Hotel?

Who gives a fuck? I thought. It's a fine thing to just lie back and stare up or down at. My eyeballs felt cool, my body felt rested ...

Then Bloor was yelling at me again. 'Wake up, goddamn it! Park the car and let's go inside. I've met some wonderful people.'

The rest of that night is very hazy in my memory. The inside of the club was loud and almost empty – except for the people Bloor had met, who turned out to be two half-mad coke runners with a big silver can full of white powder. When I sat down at the table, one of them introduced himself as Frank and said, 'Here, I think you need something for your nose.'

'Why not?' I said, accepting the can he tossed into my lap, 'and I also need some rum.' I yelled at the waiter and then opened the can, despite a rustle of protests around the table.

I looked down at my lap, ignoring Frank's nervous behaviour, and thought, Zang! This is definitely *not* Los Angeles. We must be somewhere else.

I was staring down at what looked like a whole ounce of pure, glittering white cocaine. My first instinct was to jerk a 100-peso note out of my pocket and quickly roll it up for snorting purposes, but by this time Frank had his hand on my arm. 'For Christ's sake,' he was whispering, 'don't do that shit *here*. Take it into the bathroom.'

Which I did. It was a difficult trip, through all those chairs and tables, but I finally managed to lock myself in the toilet stall and start lashing the stuff up my nose with no thought at all of the ominous noise I was making. It was like kneeling down on a beach and sticking a straw into the sand; after five minutes or so, both my nostrils were locked up like epoxy and I hadn't even made a visible depression in the dune right in front of my eyes.

Good God, I thought. This can't be true. I must be hallucinating!

By the time I staggered back to the table, the others had calmed down. It was obvious that Bloor had already been into the can, so I handed it back to Frank with a twisted smile. 'Be careful with this stuff,' I mumbled. 'It'll turn your brain to jelly.'

He smiled. 'What are you people doing here?'

'You'd never believe it,' I replied, accepting a tall glass of rum from the waiter. The band was taking a break now and two of the musicians had wandered over to our table. Frank was saying something about a party later on. I shrugged, still fighting to clear my nasal passages with quick sniffs of rum. I sensed that this latest development might have serious consequences for the future of my story, but I was no longer especially concerned about that ...

From somewhere down deep in my memory, I heard a snatch of some half-remembered conversation between a construction worker and a bartender at a bar in Colorado. The construction man was explaining why he shouldn't have another drink: 'You can't wallow with the pigs at night and then soar with the eagles in the morning,' he said.

I thought briefly on this, then shrugged it off. My own situation was totally different, I felt. In about three hours, I was supposed to be down on the docks with my camera and tape recorder to spend another day on one of those goddamn boats.

No, I thought, that geek in Colorado had it all wrong. The real problem is how to wallow with the eagles at night and then soar with the pigs in the morning.

In any case, it made no difference. For a variety of good reasons, I missed my boat the next morning and spent the afternoon passed out in the sand on an empty beach about ten miles out of town.

By Friday night, it was clear that the story was not only a dry hole but maybe even a dry socket. Our most serious problem had to do with the rat-bastard tedium of spending eight hours a day out at sea in the boiling sun, being tossed around on the bridge of a high-powered motorboat and watching middle-aged businessmen reeling sailfish up to the side of the boat every once in a while. Both Bloor and I had spent a full day at sea – on the only boats in the tournament getting any real action, *Sun Dancer* and *Lucky Striker* – and by dusk on Friday, we had pretty well come to the conclusion that deep-sea fishing is not one of your king-hell spectator sports. I have watched a lot of bad acts in my time, from tag-team pro wrestling in Flomaton, Alabama, to the Roller Derby on Oakland TV and intramural softball tournaments at Scott Air Force Base in Illinois – but I'm damned if I can remember anything as insanely fucking dull as that Third Annual International Cozumel Fishing Tournament. The only thing that comes close to it, in recent memory, is an afternoon I spent last March in a traffic jam on the San Diego freeway ... but even *that* had a certain adrenalin factor; by the end of the second hour, I was so crazy with rage that I cracked the top half of the steering wheel off my rented Mustang, then exploded the water pump by racing the engine at top speed and finally abandoned the mess altogether in the outside lane about two miles north of the Newport Beach exit.

It was Saturday afternoon, I think, when the brain fog had cleared enough for a long, clean focus on our situation – which had been drastically altered, at that point, by three nights of no sleep and a handful of spastic confrontations with the Striker crowd. I had been thrown out of one hotel and moved to another and Bloor had been threatened with jail or deportation by the manager of his hotel on the midtown square.

I had managed another zombielike day at sea, with massive aid from Frank's can, but our relationship with the Striker people was apparently beyond redemption. Nobody connected with the tournament would have anything to do with us. We were treated like lepers. The only people we felt easy with, at that point, were a motley collection of local freaks, boozers, hustlers and black-coral divers who seemed to collect each afternoon on the porch of the Bal-Hai, the town's main bar.

They quickly befriended us – a sudden shift in old relationships with the island that caused me to begin signing all the tabs, splitting them about half and half between Striker and *Playboy*. Nobody seemed to care, especially the ever-growing crowd of new friends who came to drink with us. These people understood and were vaguely amused at the idea that we'd fallen into serious disfavour with the Strikers and the local power structure. For the past three sleepless days, we'd been gathering at the Bal-Hai to brood publicly on the likelihood of massive retaliation by local *jefes*, incensed by our rotten behaviour.

It was sometime around dusk on Saturday, hunkered down at a big round table on the Bal-Hai porch, that I noticed the pea-green Mustang making its second pass in less than ten minutes. There is only one pea-green Mustang on the island, and one of the divers had told me it belonged to the 'mayor' – a heavy-set young pol and an appointed, not elected, official who looked like a beer-bellied lifeguard on some beach at Acapulco. We had seen him often in the past few days, usually in the late afternoon and always cruising up and down the seaside *frontera*.

'That son of a bitch is beginning to make me nervous,' Bloor muttered.

'Don't worry,' I said. 'They won't shoot – not as long as we're here in a crowd.'

'What?' A grey-haired woman from Miami sitting next to us had caught the word shoot.

'It's the Striker crowd,' I explained. 'We hear they've decided to get heavy with us.'

'Jesus Christ!' said a retired airline pilot who'd been living off his boat and the Bal-Hai porch for the past few months. 'You don't think they'll start *shooting*, do you? Not on a peaceful island like this!'

I shrugged. 'Not here. They wouldn't shoot into a crowd. But we can't let them catch us alone.'

The woman from Miami started to say something, but Bloor cut her off with an outburst that spun heads the length of the porch:

'They're in for the shock of their goddamn lives, tomorrow,' he snarled. 'Wait till they see what gets off that goddamn ferry from Playa del Carmen in the morning.'

'What the hell are you talking about?' the ex-pilot asked.

Bloor said nothing, staring blankly out to sea. I hesitated a moment, then instinctively picked up the thread: 'Heavies,' I said. 'We made some calls last night. Tomorrow morning they'll come off that boat like a pack of goddamn wolverines.'

Our friends at the table were glancing nervously at one another. Violent crime is almost unheard of on Cozumel; the native oligarchy is into far more subtle varieties ... and the idea that the Bal-Hai might be the scene of a Chicago-style shoot-out was a hard thing to grasp, even for me.

Bloor cut in again, still staring off towards the mainland. 'You can hire just about anything you want in Mérida,' he said. 'We got these thugs for ten bucks a head, plus expenses. They'll crack every skull on the island if they have to – then burn every one of those goddamned redneck boats right down to the waterline.'

Nobody spoke for a moment, then the woman from Miami and the retired airline pilot got up to leave. 'See you later,' the man said stiffly. 'We have to get back to the boat and check things out.'

Moments later, the two divers who'd been sitting with us also left, saying they'd probably see us tomorrow at the Striker party.

'Don't count on it,' Bloor muttered. They grinned nervously and sped off down the *frontera* on their tiny Hondas. We were left alone at the big round table, sipping margaritas and staring out at the sunset over the Yucatán Peninsula, twelve miles across the channel. After a few long moments of silence, Bloor reached into his pocket and came up with a hollowed-out glass eye he had bought from one of the street peddlers. There was a silver cap on the back and he flipped it up, then jammed the straw from his margarita into the hole and snorted heavily before handing it over to me. 'Here,' he said. 'Try some of Frank's best.'

The waiter was hovering over us, but I ignored him – until I realized I was having problems, then I looked up from the eyeball in my hand and asked for two more drinks and a dry straw. '*¿Como no?*' he hissed, moving quickly away from the table.

'This thing's all jammed up from the moisture,' I said to Bloor, showing him the powder-packed straw. 'We'll have to slice it open.'

'Never mind,' he said. 'There's plenty more where that came from.'

I nodded, accepting a fresh drink and about six dry straws from the waiter. 'You notice how fast our friends left,' I said, bearing down on the eyeball again. 'I suspect they believed all that gibberish.'

He sipped his own new drink and stared at the glass eye in my hand. 'Why shouldn't they?' he mumbled. 'I'm beginning to believe it myself.'

I felt a great numbness in the back of my mouth and my throat as I snapped the cap shut and handed the eyeball back to him. 'Don't worry,' I said. 'We're professionals – keep that in mind.'

'I am,' he said. 'But I'm afraid they might figure that out.'

It was late Saturday night, as I recall, when we learned that Frank Oliver had officially won the tournament – by one fish, ahead of the balls-out poor-boy crew on *Lucky Striker*. I wrote this down in my notebook as we roamed round the dock where the boats were tied up. Nobody urged us to come aboard for 'a friendly drink' – as I heard some of the anglers put it to others on the dock – and, in fact, there were only a few people who spoke to us at all. Frank and his friends were sipping beers at the open-air bar nearby, but his kind of hospitality was not in tune with this scene. Jack Daniel's and heavy petting on the foredeck is about as heavy as the Striker crowd gets ... and after a week of mounting isolation from this scene I was supposed to be 'covering', I was hung on the dark and ugly truth that 'my story' was fucked. Not only did the boat people view me with gross disapproval but most of them no longer even believed I was working for *Playboy*. All they knew, for sure, was that there was something very strange and off-centre, to say the least, about me and all my 'assistants'.

Which was true, in a sense, and this feeling of alienation on both sides was compounded, on ours, by a galloping drug-induced paranoia that honed each small incident, with every passing day, to a grim and fearful edge. The paranoid sense of isolation was bad enough – along with trying to live in two entirely different worlds at the same time – but the worst problem of all was the fact that I'd spent a week on this goddamn wretched story and I still didn't have the flimsiest notion of what deep-sea fishing *felt like*. I had no idea what it was like to actually catch a big fish. All I'd seen was a gang of frantic redneck businessmen occasionally hauling dark shadows up to the side of various boats, just close enough to where some dollar-an-hour mate could cut the leader and score a point for 'the angler'. During the whole week, I'd never seen a fish out of the water – except on the rare occasions when a hooked sailfish had jumped for an instant, 100 or so yards from the boat, before going under again for the long reeling-in trip that usually took ten or fifteen minutes of silent struggle and always ended with the fish either slipping the hook or being dragged close enough to the boat to be 'tagged' and then cut loose.

The anglers assured me it was all a great thrill, but on the evidence, I couldn't believe it. The whole idea of fishing, it seemed to me, was to hook a thrashing sea monster of some kind and actually *boat* the bastard. And then eat it.

All the rest seemed like dilettante bullshit – like hunting wild boar with a can of spray paint, from the safety of a pickup truck ... and it was this half-crazed sense of frustration that led me finally to start wandering around the docks and trying to hire somebody to take me and Bloor out at night to fish for man-eating sharks. It seemed like the only way to get a real feel for this sport – to fish (or hunt) for something genuinely dangerous, a beast that would tear your leg off in an instant if you made the slightest mistake.

This concept was not widely understood on the dock in Cozumel. The businessmen-anglers saw no point in getting the cockpits of their expensive tubs messed up with real blood, and especially not theirs ... but I finally found two takers: Jerry Haugen on *Lucky Striker* and a local Mayan captain who worked for Fernando Murphy.

Both of these efforts ended in disaster – for entirely different reasons and also at different times; but for the record, I feel a powerful obligation to record at least a brief observation about our shark-hunting expeditions off the coast of Cozumel. The first is that I saw more sharks by accident while scuba-diving during the daylight hours than I did during either of our elaborate, big-money night-time 'hunts' off the fishing boats; and the second is that anybody who buys anything more complex or expensive than a bottle of beer on the waterfront of Cozumel is opting for serious trouble.

Cerveza Superior, at seventy-five cents a bottle on the porch of the Bal-Hai, is a genuine bargain – if only because you know what you're getting – compared with the insanely and even fatally inept 'deep-sea-fishing and scuba-diving tours' offered at dockside shacks like El Timon or Fernando Murphy's. These people rent boats to dumb gringos for

$140 a day (or night) and then take you out to sea and dump you over the side with faulty diving gear in shark-filled waters during the day, or run you around in circles during the night – a Fernando Murphy speciality -- while allegedly trolling for sharks about 500 yards offshore. There are plenty of bologna sandwiches while you wait for a strike, unable to communicate verbally with the guilt-stricken Mayan mate or the Mayan captain up top, who both understand what kind of a shuck they are running but who are only following Fernando Murphy's orders. Meanwhile Murphy is back in town playing *maître de* at his Tijuana-style night club, La Piñata.

We found Murphy at his night club after spending six useless hours 'at sea' on one of his boats, and came close to getting beaten and jailed when we noisily ruined the atmosphere of the place by accusing him of 'outright thievery' on the grounds of what his hired fisherman had already admitted he'd done to us – and the only thing that kept us from getting stomped by Murphy's heavies was the timely popping-off of flash-bulbs by an American photographer. There is nothing quite like the sudden white flash of a professional gringo camera to paralyse the brain of a Mexican punk long enough for the potential victims to make a quick, nonviolent exit.

We were counting on this and it worked; a sorry end to the only attempt we ever made to hire *local* fishermen for a shark hunt. Murphy had his $140 cash in advance, we had our harsh object lesson in commercial dealings on the Cozumel dock -- and with the photos in the can, we understood the wisdom of leaving the island at once.

Our other night-time shark hunt – with Jerry Haugen on *Lucky Striker* – was a totally different kind of experience. It was at least an honest value. Haugen and his two-man crew were the 'hippies' of the Striker fleet, and they took me and Bloor out one night for a *serious* shark hunt – a strange adventure that nearly sunk their boat when they hooked a reef in pitch-darkness about a mile out at sea and which ended with all of us up on the bridge while a four-foot nurse shark flopped crazily around in the cockpit, even after Haugen had shot it four times in the head with a .45 automatic.

Looking back on all that, my only feeling for deep-sea fishing is one of absolute and visceral aversion. Hemingway had the right idea when he decided that a .45-calibre submachine gun was the proper tool for shark fishing, but he was wrong about his targets. Why shoot innocent fish, when the guilty walk free along the docks, renting boats for $140 a day to drunken dupes who call themselves 'sport fishermen'?

Our departure from the island was not placid. The rough skeleton of the plan – as I conceived it with a head full of MDA on the night before

– was to wait until about an hour before the first early-morning flight to Mérida on Aeromexico, then jump both our hotel bills by checking out in a raving frenzy at dawn, at the end of the night clerk's shift – and signing '*Playboy*/Striker Aluminum Yachts' on both bills. I felt this bogus dual imprimatur would be heavy enough to confuse both desk clerks long enough for us to reach the airport and make the escape.

Our only other problem – except for connecting with the black-coral wizard who was expecting at least $300 *cash* for the work we'd assigned him – was dumping the Avis rental jeep at the airport no more than three minutes before boarding time. I knew that the local Avis people would have me under observation by the same shadowy observer who'd nailed me on the broken-windshield charge, but I also knew he'd been watching us long enough to know we were both late risers. He would set his psychic work clock, I felt, to coincide with our traditional noon-to-dawn working hours. I also knew that the hours he'd been keeping for the past week were so far off his normal wake-sleep schedule that by now he was probably a nervous, jabbering mess from trying to keep up with a gang of wild gringos fuelled from an apparently bottomless satchel full of speed, acid, MDA and cocaine.

It boiled down to a question of armaments – or lack of them – and their long-term effects in the crunch. Looking back on my experience over the years, I was confident of being able to function at peak-performance level, at least briefly, after eighty or ninety hours without sleep. There were negative factors, of course: eighty or ninety hours of continuous boozing, along with sporadic energy/adrenalin sappers like frantic, rock-dodging swims in the high surf at night and sudden, potentially disastrous confrontations with hotel managers – but on balance, I felt, the drug factor gave us a clear-cut advantage. In any twenty-four-hour period, a determined private eye can muster the energy to keep pace with veteran drug users ... but after forty-eight straight hours, and especially after seventy-two, fatigue symptoms begin manifesting drastically – hallucinations, hysteria, massive nerve failure. After seventy-two hours, both the body and the brain are so badly depleted that only sleep will make the nut ... while your habitual drug user, long accustomed to this weird and frenzied pace, is still hoarding at least three hours of high-speed reserve.

There was no question in my mind – once the plane was finally airborne out of Cozumel – about what to do with the drugs. I had eaten three of the remaining five caps of MDA during the night and Bloor had given our hash and all but six of his purple pills to the black-coral wizard as a bonus for his all-night efforts. As we zoomed over the Yucatán Channel at 8000 feet, we took stock of what we had left:

Two bits of MDA, six tabs of acid, about a gram and a half of raw cocaine, four reds and a random handful of speed. That – plus $44 and a desperate hope that Sandy had made and paid for our reservations beyond Monterrey, Mexico – was all we had between Cozumel and our refuge/destination at Sam Brown's house in Denver. We were airborne out of Cozumel at 8:13 a.m., Mountain Daylight Time – and if everything went right, we would arrive at Denver's Stapleton International Airport before seven.

We'd been airborne for about eight minutes when I looked over at Bloor and told him what I'd been thinking: 'We don't have enough drugs here to risk carrying them through Customs,' I said.

He nodded thoughtfully: 'Well ... we're pretty well fixed, for poor boys.'

'Yeah,' I replied. 'But I have my professional reputation to uphold. And there's only two things I've never done with drugs: sell them or take them through Customs – especially when we can replace everything we're holding for about ninety-nine dollars just as soon as we get off the plane.'

He hunkered down in his seat, saying nothing. Then he stared across at me. 'What are you saying? That we should just throw all this shit away?'

I thought for a moment. 'No. I think we should eat it.'

'What?'

'Yeah, why not? They can't bust you for what's already dissolved in your belly – no matter *how* weird you're acting.'

'Jesus Christ!' he muttered. 'We'll go stark raving nuts if we eat all this shit!'

I shrugged. 'Keep in mind where we'll be when we hit Customs,' I said. 'San Antonio, *Texas*. Are you ready to get busted in Texas?'

He stared down at his fingernails.

'Remember Tim Leary?' I said. 'Ten years for three ounces of grass in his daughter's panties ...'

He nodded. 'Jesus ... Texas! I'd forgotten about that.'

'Not me,' I said. 'When Sandy went through Customs in San Antonio about three weeks ago, they tore everything she was carrying apart. It took her two hours to put it back together.'

I could see him thinking. 'Well ...' he said finally, 'what if we eat this stuff and go crazy – and they nail us?'

'Nothing,' I said. 'We'll drink heavily. If we're seized, the stewardesses will testify we were drunk.'

He thought for a moment, then laughed. 'Yeah ... just a couple of good ole boys OD'd on booze. Nasty drunks, staggering back into the country after a shameful vacation in Mexico – totally fucked up.'

'Right,' I said. 'They can strip us down to the skin. It's no crime to enter the country helplessly drunk.'

He laughed. 'You're right. What do we start with? We shouldn't eat it all at once – that's too heavy.'

I nodded, reaching into my pocket for the MDA and offering him one as I tossed the other into my mouth. 'Let's eat some of the acid now, too,' I said. 'That way, we'll be adjusted to it by the time we have to eat the rest – and we can save the coke for emergencies.'

'Along with the speed,' he said. 'How much do you have left?'

'Ten hits,' I said. 'Pure-white amphetamine powder. It'll straighten us right out, if things get tense.'

'You should save that for the end,' he said. 'We can use this coke if we start getting messy.'

I swallowed the purple pill, ignoring the Mexican stewardess with her tray of *sangria*.

'I'll have two,' said Bloor, reaching across me.

'Same here,' I said, lifting two more off the tray.

Bloor grinned at her. 'Pay no attention. We're just tourists – down here making fools of ourselves.'

Moments later we hit down on the runway at Mérida. But it was a quick and painless stop. By nine a.m., we were cruising over central Mexico at 20,000 feet, headed for Monterrey. The plane was half empty and we could have moved around if we'd wanted to – but I glanced across at Bloor, trying to use him as a mirror for my own condition, and decided that wandering around in the aisles would not be wise. Making yourself noticeable is one thing – but causing innocent passengers to shrink off with feelings of shock and repugnance is a different game entirely. One of the few things that can't be controlled about acid is the glitter it puts in the eyes. No amount of booze will cause the same kind of laughing, that fine predatory glow that comes with the first rush of acid up the spine.

But Bloor felt like moving. 'Where's the goddamn head?' he muttered.

'Never mind,' I said. 'We're almost to Monterrey. Don't attract attention. We have to check through Immigration there.'

He straightened up in his seat. 'Immigration?'

'Nothing serious,' I said. 'Just turn in our tourist cards and see about the tickets to Denver ... But we'll have to act straight ...'

'Why?' he asked.

I gave it some thought. Why, indeed? We were clean. Or *almost* clean, anyway. About an hour out of Mérida we'd eaten another round of acid – which left us with two more of those, plus four reds and the coke and the speed. The luck of the split had left me with the speed and the acid; Bloor had the coke and the reds ... and by the time the ABROCHE SU CINTURON (FASTEN SEAT BELTS) sign flashed on above Monterrey, we'd agreed, more or less, that anything we hadn't eaten by the time we got to Texas would have to be flushed down the stainless-steel john in the plane's lavatory.

It had taken about forty-five tortured minutes to reach this agreement, because by that time, neither one of us could speak clearly. I tried to whisper, through gritted teeth, but each time I succeeded in uttering a coherent sentence my voice seemed to echo around the cabin like I was mumbling into a bullhorn. At one point, I leaned over as close as possible to Bloor's ear and hissed: 'Reds ... how many?' But the sound of my own voice was such a shock that I recoiled in horror and tried to pretend I'd said nothing.

Was the stewardess staring? I couldn't be sure. Bloor had seemed not to notice – but suddenly he was thrashing around in his seat and clawing frantically underneath himself with both hands. 'What the fuck?' he was screaming.

'Quiet!' I snapped. 'What's *wrong* with you?'

He was jerking at his seat belt, still shouting. The stewardess ran down the aisle and unbuckled it for him. There was fear in her face as she backed off and watched him spring out of his seat. 'Goddamn you clumsy bastard!' he yelled.

I stared straight ahead. Jesus, I thought, he's blowing it, he can't handle the acid, I should have abandoned this crazy bastard in Cozumel. I felt my teeth grinding as I tried to ignore his noise ... then I glanced across and saw him groping between the seats and coming up with a smouldering cigarette butt. 'Look at this!' he shouted at me. He was holding the butt in one hand and fondling the back of his thigh with the other ...

'Burned a big hole in my pants,' he was saying. 'He just spit this dirty thing right down in my seat!'

'What?' I said, feeling in front of my mouth for the cigarette in my filter ... but the filter was empty, and I suddenly understood. The fog in my brain suddenly cleared and I heard myself laughing. 'I warned you about these goddamn Bonanzas!' I said. 'They'll never stick in the filter!'

The stewardess was pushing him back down into his seat. 'Fasten belts,' she kept saying, 'fasten belts.'

I grabbed his arm and jerked downwards, pulling him off balance and causing him to fall heavily on to the back of the seat. It gave way and collapsed on the legs of whoever was sitting behind us. The stewardess jerked it quickly back to the upright position, then reached down to

466

fasten Bloor's seat belt. I saw his left arm snake out and settle affectionately around her shoulders.

Good God! I thought. This is it. I could see the headlines in tomorrow's *News*: 'DRUG FRACAS ON AIRLINER NEAR MONTERREY: GRINGOS JAILED ON ARSON, ASSAULT CHARGES.'

But the stewardess only smiled and backed off a few steps, dismissing Bloor's crude advance with a slap at his arm and an icy professional smile. I tried to return it, but my face was not working properly. Her eyes narrowed. She was clearly more insulted by the demented grin I was trying now to fix on her than she was by Bloor's attempt to push her head down into his lap.

He smiled happily as she stalked away. 'That'll teach you,' he said. 'You're a goddamn nightmare to travel with.'

The acid was levelling out now. I could tell by the tone of his voice that he was into the manic stage. No more of that jerky, paranoid whispering. He was feeling confident now; his face had settled into that glaze of brittle serenity you invariably see on the face of a veteran acid eater who knows that the first rush is past and now he can settle down for about six hours of real fun.

I was not quite there myself, but I knew it was coming – and we still had about seven more hours and two plane changes between now and Denver. I knew the Immigration scene at Monterrey was only a formality – just stand in line for a while with all the other gringos and not get hysterical when the cop at the gate asks for your tourist card.

We could ease through that one, I felt – on the strength of long experience. Anybody who's still on the street after seven or eight years of public acid eating has learned to trust his adrenalin gland for getting through routine confrontations with officialdom – traffic citations, bridge tolls, airline ticket counters ...

And we had one of these coming up: getting our baggage off this plane and not losing it in the airport until we found out which flight would take us to San Antonio and Denver. Bloor was travelling light, with only two bags. But I had my normal heavy load: two huge leather suitcases, a canvas seabag and tape recorder with two portable speakers. If we were going to lose anything, I wanted to lose it *north* of the border.

The Monterrey airport is a cool, bright little building, so immaculately clean and efficient that we were almost immediately lulled into a condition of grinning euphoria. Everything seemed to be working perfectly. No lost baggage, no sudden outbursts of wild jabbering at the Immigration desk, no cause for panic or fits of despair at the ticket counter ... Our first-class reservations had already been made and confirmed all the way to Denver. Bloor had been reluctant to blow thirty-two extra dollars 'just to sit up front with the businessmen', but I felt it was necessary. 'There's a lot more latitude for weird behaviour in first class.' I told him. 'The stewardesses back in the tourist section don't have as much experience, so they're more likely to freak out if they think they have a dangerous nut on their hands.'

He glared at me. 'Do I look like a dangerous nut?'

I shrugged. It was hard to focus on his face. We were standing in a corridor outside the souvenir shop. 'You look like a serious dope addict,' I said, finally. 'Your hair's all wild, your eyes are glittering, your nose is all red and—' I suddenly noticed white powder on the top edge of his moustache. 'You swine! You've been into the coke!'

He grinned blankly. 'Why not? Just a little pick-me-up.'

I nodded. 'Yeah. Just wait till you start explaining yourself to the Customs agent in San Antonio with white powder drooling out of your nose.' I laughed. 'Have you ever seen those big bullet-nosed flashlights they use for rectal searches?'

He was rubbing his nostrils vigorously. 'Where's the drugstore? I'll get some of that Dristan nasal spray.' He reached into his back pocket and I saw his face turn grey. 'Jesus,' he hissed. 'I've lost my wallet!' He kept fumbling in his pockets but no wallet turned up. 'Good God!' he moaned. 'It's still on the plane!' His eyes flashed wildly around the airport. 'Where's the gate?' he snapped. 'The wallet must be under the seat.'

I shook my head. 'No, it's too late.'

'What?'

'The plane. I saw it take off while you were in the rest room, snorting up the coke.'

He thought for a moment, then uttered a loud, wavering howl. 'My passport! All my money! I have *nothing*! They'll never let me back into the country, with no ID.'

I smiled. 'Ridiculous. I'll vouch for you.'

'Shit!' he said. 'You're crazy! You *look* crazy!'

'Let's go find the bar,' I said. 'We have forty-five minutes.'

'*What?*'

'The drunker you get, the less it'll bother you,' I said. 'The best thing, right now, is for you to get weeping, falling-down drunk. I'll swear you staggered in front of a moving plane on the runway in Mérida and a jet engine sucked the coat right off your back and into its turbine.' The whole thing seemed absurd. 'Your wallet was in the coat, right? I was a witness. It was all I could do to keep your *whole body* from being sucked into the turbine.'

I was laughing wildly now; the scene was very vivid. I could almost *feel* the terrible drag of the suction as we struggled to dig our heels into the hot asphalt runway. Somewhere in the distance, I could hear the wail of a mariachi band above the roar of the engines, sucking us ever closer to the whirling blades. I could hear the wild screech of a stewardess as she watched helplessly. A Mexican soldier with a machine gun was trying to help us, but suddenly he was sucked away like a leaf in the wind ... wild screams all around us, then a sickening *thump* as he disappeared feetfirst into the black maw of the turbine ... The engine seemed to stall momentarily, then spit a nasty shower of hamburger and bone splinters all over the runway ... more screaming from behind us as Bloor's coat ripped away; I was holding him by one arm when another soldier with a machine gun began firing at the plane, first at the cockpit and then at the murderous engine ... which suddenly exploded, like a bomb going off right in front of us; the blast hurled us 200 feet across the tarmac and through a wire-mesh fence ...

Jesus! What a scene! A fantastic tale to lay on the Customs agent in San Antonio: 'And then, officer, while we were lying there on the grass, too stunned to move, *another* engine exploded! And then another! Huge balls of fire! It was a miracle that we escaped with our lives ... Yes, so you'll have to make some allowance for Mr Bloor's unsteady condition right now. He was badly shaken, half-hysterical most of the afternoon ... I want to get him back to Denver and put him under sedation ...'

I was so caught up in this terrible vision that I'd failed to notice Bloor down on his knees until I heard him shout. He'd spread the contents of his kit bag all over the floor of the corridor rummaging through the mess, and now he was smiling happily at the wallet in his hand.

'You found it,' I said.

He nodded – clutching it with both hands, as if it might leap out of his grip with the strength of a half-captured lizard and disappear across the crowded lobby. I looked around and saw that people were stopping to watch us. My mind was still whirling from the fiery hallucination that had seized me, but I was able to kneel down and help Bloor stuff his belongings back into the kit bag. 'We're attracting a crowd.' I muttered. 'Let's get to the bar, where it's safe.'

Moments later we were sitting at a table overlooking the runway, sipping margaritas and watching the ground crew load the 727 that would take us to San Antonio. My plan was to stay hunkered down in the bar until the last moment, then dash for the plane. Our luck had been excellent, so far, but that scene in the lobby had triggered a wave of paranoia in my head. I felt very conspicuous. Bloor's mannerisms were becoming more and more psychotic. He took one sip of his drink, then whacked it down on to the table and stared at me. 'What *is* this?' he snarled.

'A double margarita,' I said, glancing over at the waitress to see if she had her eye on us.

She did, and Bloor waved at her.

'What do you want?' I whispered.

'Glaucoma,' he said.

The waitress was on us before I could argue. Glaucoma is an extremely complicated mix of about nine unlikely ingredients that Bloor had learned from some randy old woman he met on the porch of the Bal-Hai. She'd taught the bartender there how to make it: very precise measurements of gin, tequila, Kahlua, crushed ice, fruit juices, lime rinds, spices – all mixed to perfection in a tall frosted glass.

It is not the kind of drink you want to order in an airport bar with a head full of acid and a noticeable speech impediment; especially when you can't speak the local language and you just spilled the first drink you ordered all over the table.

But Bloor persisted. When the waitress abandoned all hope, he walked over to speak with the bartender. I slumped in my chair, keeping an eye on the plane and hoping it was almost ready to go. But they hadn't even loaded the baggage yet: departure time was still twenty minutes away – plenty of time for some minor incident to mushroom into serious trouble. I watched Bloor talking to the bartender, pointing to various bottles behind the bar and occasionally using his fingers to indicate measurements. The bartender was nodding his head patiently.

Finally, Bloor came back to the table. 'He's making it,' he said. 'I'll be back on a minute. I have business.'

I ignored him. My mind was drifting again. Two days and nights without sleep plus a steady diet of mind-altering drugs and double margaritas were beginning to affect my alertness. I ordered another drink and stared out at the hot brown hills beyond the runway. The bar was comfortably air conditioned, but I could feel the warm sun through the window.

Why worry? I thought. We've survived the worst. All we have to do now is not miss that plane out there. Once we're across the border, the worst that can happen is a nightmarish fuck-around at Customs in San Antonio. Maybe even a night in jail, but what the hell? A few misdemeanour charges – public drunkenness, disturbing the peace, resisting arrest – but nothing serious, no felony. All the evidence for *that* would be eaten by the time we landed in Texas.

My only real worry was the chance that there might already be grand-larceny charges filed against us in Cozumel. We had, after all, jumped two hotel bills totalling about 15,000 pesos, in addition to leaving that half-destroyed Avis jeep in the airport parking lot – another 15,000 pesos

– and we had spent the past four or five days in the constant company of a flagrant, big-volume drug runner whose every movement and contact, for all we knew, might have been watched or even photographed by Interpol agents.

Where was Frank now? Safe at home in California? Or jailed in Mexico City, swearing desperate ignorance about how all those cans of white powder got into his luggage? I could almost hear it: 'You've *got* to believe me, Captain! I went down to Cozumel to check on a land investment. I was sitting in a bar one night, minding my own business, when all of a sudden these two drunken acid freaks sat down next to me and said they worked for *Playboy*. One of them had a handful of purple pills and I was stupid enough to eat one. The next thing I knew, they were using my hotel room as their headquarters. They never slept. I tried to keep an eye on them, but there were plenty of times while I was sleeping when they could have put almost anything in my luggage ... What? Where are they now? Well ... I can't say for sure, but I can give you the names of the hotels they were using.'

Jesus! These terrible hallucinations! I tried to put them out of my mind as I finished my drink and called for another. A paranoid shudder jerked me out of my slump in the chair. I sat up and looked around. Where was that bastard Bloor? How long had he been gone? I glanced out at the plane and saw the fuel truck still parked under the wing. But they were loading baggage now. Ten more minutes.

I relaxed again, shoving a handful of pesos at the waitress to pay for our drinks, trying to smile at her ... when suddenly the whole airport seemed to echo with the sound of my name being shouted over a thousand loud-speakers ... then I heard Bloor's name ... a harsh, heavily accented voice, bellowing along the corridors like the scream of a banshee ... 'PASSENGERS HUNTER THOMPSON AND YAIL BLOOR. REPORT IMMEDIATELY TO THE IMMIGRATION DESK ...'

I was too stunned to move. 'Mother of twelve bastards!' I whispered. 'Did I actually *hear* that?' I gripped both arms of my chair and tried to concentrate. Was I hallucinating again? There was no way to be sure ...

Then I heard the voice again, booming all over the airport: 'WILL PASSENGERS HUNTER THOMPSON AND YAIL BLOOR RE-PORT IMMEDIATELY TO THE IMMIGRATION DESK ...'

No! I thought. This is impossible! It had to be paranoid dementia. My fear of being nailed at the last moment had become so intense that I was hearing voices! The sun through the window had caused the acid to boil in my brain; a huge bubble of drugs had burst a weak vein in my frontal lobes.

Then I saw Bloor rushing into the bar. His eyes were wild, his hands were flapping crazily. 'Did you hear *that*?' he shouted.

I stared at him. Well ... I thought, we're fucked. He heard it, too ... or even if he hadn't, even if we're *both* hallucinating, it means we've OD'd ... totally out of control for the next six hours, crazed with fear and confusion, feeling our bodies disappear and our heads swell up like balloons, unable to even recognize each other ...

'Wake up! Goddamn it!' he yelled. 'We have to make a run for the plane!'

I shrugged. 'It's no use. They'll grab us at the gate.'

He was frantically trying to zip up his kit bag. 'Are you sure those were *our* names they called? Are you *positive*?'

I nodded, still not moving. Somewhere in the middle of my half-numb brain, the truth was beginning to stir. I was *not* hallucinating; the nightmare was real ... and I suddenly remembered the Striker PR man's talk about that all-powerful *jefe* in Cozumel who had the fuel licence.

Of course. A man with that kind of leverage would have connections all over Mexico: police, airlines, Immigration. It was madness to think we could cross him and get away with it. No doubt he controlled the Avis franchise, too ... and he'd gone into action the minute his henchmen found that crippled jeep in the airport parking lot, with its windshield shattered and an eleven-day bill unpaid. The phone lines had been humming 20,000 feet beneath us all the way to Monterrey. And now, with less than ten minutes to spare, they had ambushed us.

I stood up and slung the seabag over my shoulder just as the waitress brought Bloor's glaucoma. He looked at her, then lifted it off the tray and drank the whole thing in one gulp. '*Gracias, gracias,*' he mumbled, handing her a 50-peso note. She started to make change, but he shook his head. '*Nada, nada,* keep the goddamn change.' Then he pointed towards the kitchen. 'Back door?' he said eagerly. '*¡Exito!*' He nodded at the plane about fifty feet below us on the runway. I could see a few passengers beginning to board. 'Big hurry!' Bloor told her. '*¡Importante!*'

She looked puzzled, then pointed to the main entrance to the bar.

He stuttered helplessly for a moment, then began shouting: 'Where's the goddamn *back door* to this place? We have to catch that plane *now*!'

A long-delayed rush of adrenalin was beginning to clear my head. I grabbed his arm and lurched towards the main door. 'Let's go,' I said. 'We'll run right past the bastards.' My brain was still foggy, but the adrenalin had triggered a basic survival instinct. Our only hope was to run like doomed rats for the only available opening and hope for a miracle.

As we hurried down the corridor, I jerked one of the PRESS tags off my seabag and gave it to Bloor. 'Start waving this at them when we hit the gate,' I said, leaping sideways to avoid a covey of nuns in our way. *'Pardonez!'* I shouted. *'¡Prensa! ¡Prensa! ¡Mucho importante!'*

Bloor picked up the cry as we approached the gate, running at full speed and shouting incoherently in garbled Spanish. The Immigration booth was just beyond the glass doors leading out to the runway. The stairway up to the plane was still full of passengers, but the clock above the gate said exactly 11:20 – departure time. Our only hope was to burst past the cops at the desk and dash aboard the plane just as the stewardess pulled the big silver door closed . . .

We had to slow down as we approached the glass doors, waving our tickets at the cops and yelling *'¡Prensa! ¡Prensa!'* at everybody in front of us. I was pouring sweat by this time and we were both gasping for breath.

A small, muscular-looking cop in a white shirt and dark glasses moved out to head us off as we stumbled through the doors. *'Señor* Bloor? *Señor* Thompson?' he asked sharply.

The voice of doom.

I staggered to a halt and sagged against the desk, but Bloor's leather-soled Mod boots wouldn't hold on the marble floor and he skidded past me at full speed and crashed into a ten-foot potted palm, dropping his kit bag and mangling several branches that he grabbed to keep from falling.

'Señor Thompson? *Señor* Bloor?' Our accuser had a one-track mind. One of his assistants had run over to help Bloor keep his feet. Another cop picked his kit bag off the floor and handed it to him.

I was too exhausted to do anything but nod my head meekly. The cop who'd called our names took the ticket out of my hand and glanced at it – then quickly handed it back to me. 'Ah-ha!' he said with a grin. *'Señor* Thompson!' Then he looked at Bloor: 'You are *Señor* Bloor?'

'You're goddamn right I am!' Bloor snapped. 'What the hell's going on here? This is a goddamn outrage -- all this wax on these floors! I almost got killed!'

The little cop grinned again. Was there something sadistic in his smile? I couldn't be sure. But it didn't matter now. They had us on the gaff. I flashed on all the people I knew who'd been busted in Mexico; dopers who'd pushed their luck too far, gotten careless. No doubt we would find friends in prison; I could almost hear them hooting their cheerful greetings as we were led into the yard and turned loose.

This scene passed through my head in milliseconds. Bloor's wild yells were still floating in the air as the cop began pushing me out the door towards the plane. 'Hurry! Hurry!' he was saying . . . and behind me I heard his assistant prodding Bloor. 'We were afraid you would miss the plane,' he was saying. 'We called on the PA system.' He was grinning broadly now. 'You almost missed the plane.'

We were almost to San Antonio before I got a grip on myself. The adrenalin was still pumping violently through my head; the acid and booze and fatigue had been totally neutralized by that scene at the gate. My nerves were so jangled as the plane took off that I had to beg the stewardess for two Scotch and waters, which I used to down two of our four reds.

Bloor ate the other two, with the help of two bloody marys. His hands were trembling badly, his eyes were filled with blood ... but as he came back to life, he began cursing 'those dirty bastards on the PA system' who had caused him to panic and get rid of all the coke.

'Jesus!' he said quietly, 'you can't imagine what a horror that was! I was standing there at the urinal, with my joint in one hand and a coke spoon in the other – jamming the stuff up my nose and trying to piss at the same time – when all of a fucking sudden it just exploded all around me! They have a speaker up there in the corner of that bathroom, and the whole place is *tile!*' He took a long hit on the drink. 'Shit, I almost went crazy! It was like somebody had snuck up behind me and dropped a cherry bomb down the back of my shirt. All I could think of was getting rid of the coke. I threw it into one of the urinals and ran like a bastard for the bar.' He laughed nervously. 'Hell, I didn't even zip up my pants; I was running down the hall with my joint hanging out.'

I smiled, remembering the sense of almost apocalyptic despair that seized me when I heard the first announcement. 'That's odd,' I said. 'It never even occurred to me to get rid of the drugs. I was thinking about all those hotel bills and that goddamn jeep. If they'd nailed us for that stuff, a few pills wouldn't make much difference.'

He seemed to brood for a while ... then he spoke, staring fixedly at the seat in front of him. 'Well ... I don't know about you ... but I don't think I could *stand* another shock like that one. I had just about ninety seconds of pure terror. I felt like my whole life had ended. Jesus! Standing at that urinal with a coke spoon up my nose and suddenly hearing my name on the speaker ...' He moaned softly. 'Now I know how Liddy must have felt when he saw those cops running into the Watergate ... seeing his whole life fall apart, from a hot rod in the White House to a twenty-year jailbird in sixty seconds.'

'Fuck Liddy,' I said. 'It couldn't have happened to a nicer guy.' I laughed out loud. 'Liddy was the bastard who ran Operation Intercept – remember that?'

Bloor nodded.

'What do you think would have happened if Gordon Liddy had been standing at the gate when we came crashing through?'

He smiled, sipping his drink.

'We'd be sitting in a Mexican jail right now,' I said. 'Just *one* of these pills' – I held up a purple acid tab – 'would have been enough to drive Liddy into a hate frenzy. He'd have had us locked up on suspicion of everything from hijacking to dope smuggling.'

He looked at the pill I was holding, then reached for it. 'Let's finish these off,' he said. 'I can't stand this nervousness.'

'You're right,' I said, reaching into my pocket for the other one. 'We're almost to San Antonio.' I tossed the pill down my throat and called the stewardess for another drink.

'Is that it?' he asked. 'Are we clean?'

I nodded. 'Except for the speed.'

'Get rid of it,' he said. 'We're almost there.'

'Don't worry,' I replied. 'The acid will take hold just about the time we land. We should order more drinks.' I unbuckled my seat belt and walked up the aisle to the lavatory, fully intending to flush the speed down the toilet ... but when I got inside, with the door locked behind me, I stared down at the little buggers resting so peacefully there in my palm ... ten caps of pure-white amphetamine powder ... and I thought: No, we might *need* these, in case of another emergency. I remembered the dangerous lethargy that had gripped me in Monterrey ... Then I looked down at my white-canvas basketball shoes and noticed how snugly the tongues fit under the laces ... plenty of pressure down there, I thought, and plenty of room for ten pills ... so I put all the speed in my shoes and went back to the seat. No point mentioning it to Bloor, I thought. *He's* clean, and therefore totally innocent. It would only inhibit his capacity for righteous anger, I felt, if I told him about the speed I was still carrying ... until we were safely through Customs and reeling blindly around the San Antonio airport; then he would thank me for it.

San Antonio was a cakewalk; no trouble at all – despite the fact that we virtually fell off the plane, badly twisted again, and by the time we got our bags on to the conveyor belt leading up to the tall black Customs agent, we were both laughing like fools at the trail of orange amphetamine pills strung out behind us on the floor of the tin-roofed Customs shed. I was arguing with the agent about how much import tax I would have to pay on the two bottles of *prima* tequila I was carrying when I noticed Bloor was almost doubled over with laughter right beside me. He had juts paid a tax of $5.88 on his own tequila, and now he was cracking up while the agent fussed over *my* tax.

'What the hell's wrong with you?' I snapped, glancing back at him ... Then I noticed he was looking down at my feet, fighting so hard to control his laughter that he was having trouble keeping his balance.

I looked down . . . and there, about six inches from my right shoe, was a bright-orange spansule. Another one was sitting on the black-rubber floor mat about two feet behind me . . . and two feet farther back was another one. They looked as big as footballs.

Insane, I thought. I've left a trail of speed all the way from the plane to this beetle-browed Customs agent – who was now handing me the official receipt for my liquor tax. I accepted it with a smile that was already disintegrating into hysteria as I took it out of his hand. He was staring grimly at Bloor, who was out of control now, still laughing at the floor. The Customs man couldn't see what Yail was laughing at because of the conveyor belt between us . . . but *I* could: it was another one of those goddamn orange balls, resting on the white-canvas toe of my shoe. I reached down as casually as I could and put the thing in my pocket. The Customs man watched us with a look of total disgust on his face and we hauled our bags through the swinging wooden doors and into the lobby of the San Antonio airport.

'Can you believe that?' Bloor said. 'He never even looked inside these damn things! For all he knows, we just came across the border with two hundred pounds of pure scag!'

I stopped laughing. It was true. My big suitcase – the elephantskin Abercrombie & Fitch job with brass corners – was still securely locked. Not one of our bags had been opened for even the laziest inspection. We had listed the five quarts of tequila on our declaration forms – and that was all that seemed to interest him.

'Jesus Christ!' Bloor was saying. 'If we'd only *known*.'

I smiled, but I was still feeling nervous about it. There was something almost eerie about two laughing, staggering dopers checking through one of the heaviest drug check points on the Customs map without even opening their bags. It was almost insulting. The more I thought about it, the angrier I felt . . . because that cold-eyed nigger had been absolutely *right*. He had sized us up perfectly with one glance. I could almost hear him thinking: '*Goddamn!* Look at these two slobbering honkies. Anybody *this* fucked up can't be serious.'

Which was true. The only thing we slipped past him was a single cap of speed, and even that was an accident. So, in truth, he had saved himself a lot of unnecessary work by ignoring our baggage. I would have preferred not to understand this embarrassment so keenly, because it plunged me into a fit of depression – despite the acid, or maybe because of it.

The rest of that trip was a nightmare of paranoid blunders and the kind of small humiliations that haunt you for many weeks afterwards. About halfway between San Antonio and Denver, Bloor reached out into the aisle and grabbed a stewardess by the leg, causing her to drop a tray of twenty-one wineglasses, which crashed in a heap at her feet and ignited rumblings of bad discontent from the other first-class passengers who had ordered wine with their lunch.

'You stinking, dope-addict bastard!' I muttered, trying to ignore him in the burst of ugliness that surrounded us.

He grinned stupidly, ignoring the howls of the stewardess and fixing me with a dazed, uncomprehending stare that confirmed, forever, my convictions that nobody with even latent inclinations to *use* drugs should ever try to smuggle them. We were virtually shovelled off the plane in Denver, laughing and staggering in such a rotten condition that we were barely able to claim our luggage.

Months later, I received a letter from a friend in Cozumel, asking if I were still interested in buying an interest in some beach acres on the Caribbean shores. It arrived just as I was preparing to leave for Washington to cover the impeachment of Richard Nixon, the final act in a drama that began, for me, almost exactly a year earlier when I had bought a *News* from a newsboy hustling the porch of the Bal-Hai in Cozumel and read John Dean's original outcry about refusing to be the 'scapegoat'.

Well ... a lot of madness has flowed under our various bridges since then, and we have all presumably learned a lot of things. John Dean is in prison, Richard Nixon has quit and been pardoned by his hand-picked successor, and my feeling for national politics is about the same as my feeling for deep-sea fishing, buying land in Cozumel or anything else where the losers end up thrashing around in the water on a barbed hook.

Playboy, December 1974

JIMMY CARTER AND THE GREAT LEAP OF FAITH

FEAR & LOATHING ON THE CAMPAIGN TRAIL 76
THIRD-RATE ROMANCE, LOW-RENT RENDEZVOUS

The View from Key West: Ninety Miles North of Havana and Nine
Hundred Years on the Campaign Trail ... Farewell to the Boys on the
Bus: Or, Johnny, I Never Knew Ye ... Another Rude and Wistful Tale
from the Bowels of the American Dream, With Notes, Nightmares
and Other Strange Memories from Manchester, Boston, Miami and
Plains, Georgia ... And 440 Volts from Castrato, the Demon Lover of
Coconut Grove

---

*A lot of people will tell you that horses get spooked because they're just
naturally nervous and jittery, but that ain't right. What you have to
remember is that a horse sees things maybe six or seven times bigger
than we do.*

  Billy Herman, a harness-racing trainer at Pompano Park in Miami

This news just came over the radio, followed by a song about 'faster
horses, younger women, older whisky and more money ...' and then
came a news item about a Polish gentleman who was arrested earlier
today for throwing 'more than two dozen bowling balls into the sea off
a pier in Fort Lauderdale' because, he told arresting officers, 'he thought
they were nigger eggs'.

 ... We are living in very strange times, and they are likely to get a lot
stranger before we bottom out. Which could happen a lot sooner than
even Henry Kissinger thinks ... Because this is, after all, another election year, and almost everybody I talk to seems to feel we are headed
for strangeness ... of one sort or another. And some people say we are
already deep in the midst of it. Which may be true. The evidence points
both ways ... But from my perch in this plastic catbird seat out here on
the southernmost rim of Key West, the barometer looks to be falling so
fast on all fronts that it no longer matters. And now comes this filthy
news in the latest Gallup Poll that Hubert Humphrey will be our next
president ... Or, failing that, he will foul the national air for the next
six months and drive us all to smack with his poison gibberish.

 Jesus, no wonder that poor bastard up in Fort Lauderdale ran amok
and decided that all bowling balls were actually nigger eggs that would
have to be hurled, at once, into shark-infested waters. He was probably

a desperate political activist of some kind trying to send a message to Washington.

Last night, on this same radio station, I heard a warning about 'a new outbreak of dog mutilations in Coconut Grove'. The disc jockey reading the news sounded angry and agitated. 'Three more mongrel dogs were found castrated and barely alive tonight,' he said, 'and investigating officers said there was no doubt that all three animals were victims of the same bloodthirsty psychotic – a stocky middle-aged Cuban known as "Castrato" – who has terrorized dog owners in Coconut Grove for the past three months.

'Today's mutilations, police said, were executed with the same sadistic precision as all the others. According to the owner of one victim, a half-breed chow watchdog named Willie, the dog was "minding his own business, just lying out there in the driveway, when all of a sudden I heard him start yelping and I looked out the front door just in time to see this dirty little spic shoot him again with one of those electric flash-light guns. Then the sonofabitch grabbed Willie by the hind legs and threw him into the back of an old red pickup. I yelled at him, but by the time I got hold of my shotgun and ran out on the porch, he was gone. It all happened so fast that I didn't even get the licence number off the truck." '

The voice on the radio paused for a long moment, then dipped a few octaves and went on with the story: 'Several hours later, police said, Willie and two other dogs – both mongrels – were found in a vacant lot near the Dinner Key yacht marina. All three had been expertly castrated ...'

Another long pause, followed by a moaning sound as the radio voice seemed to crack and stutter momentarily ... And then it continued, very slowly: 'The nature of the wounds, police said, left no room for doubt that today's mutilations were the work of the same fiendish hand responsible for all but two of the forty-nine previous dog castrations in Coconut Grove this year.

' "This is definitely the work of Castrato," said Senior Dog Warden Lionel Olay at a hastily called press conference late this afternoon. "Look at the razor work on this mongrel chow," Olay told reporters. "These cuts are surgically perfect, and so is this cauterization. This man you call 'Castrato' is no amateur, gentlemen. This is a very artistic surgery – maybe fifty or fifty-five seconds from start to finish, assuming he works with a whip-steel straight razor and a 220-volt soldering iron."

'Olay ended the press conference on a humorous note, urging reporters to "work like dogs" until this case is cracked. "And if any of you people own mongrels," he added, "either keep them out of Coconut Grove or have them put to sleep."

'Meanwhile,' said the newscaster, 'South Miami police have warned all dog owners in the area to be on the lookout for a red pickup truck cruising slowly in residential neighbourhoods. The driver, a small but muscular Cuban between forty and fifty years old, is known to be armed with an extremely dangerous, high-voltage electric weapon called a "Taser" and is also criminally insane.'

Jesus Christ! I'm not sure I can handle this kind of news and frantic stimulus at four o'clock in the morning – especially with a head full of speed, booze and percodan. It is extremely difficult to concentrate on the cheap realities of Campaign 76 under these circumstances. The idea of covering even the early stages of this cynical and increasingly retrograde campaign has already plunged me into a condition bordering on terminal despair, and if I thought I might have to stay with these people all the way to November I would change my name and seek work as a professional alligator poacher in the swamps around Lake Okeechobee. My frame of mind is not right for another long and maddening year of total involvement in a presidential campaign ... and somewhere in the back of my brain lurks a growing suspicion that this campaign is not right either; but that is not the kind of judgement any journalist should make at this point. At least not in print.

So for the moment I will try to suspend both the despair and the final judgement. Both will be massively justified in the next few months, I think – and until then I can fall back on the firmly held but rarely quoted conviction of most big-time Washington pols that *nobody* can function at top form on a full-time basis in more than one presidential campaign. This rule of thumb has never been applied to journalists, to my knowledge, but there is ample evidence to suggest it should be. There is no reason to think that even the best and brightest of journalists, as it were, can repeatedly or even more than once crank themselves up to the level of genuinely fanatical energy, commitment and total concentration it takes to live in the speeding vortex of a presidential campaign from start to finish. There is not enough room on that hell-bound train for anybody who wants to relax and act human now and then. It is a gig for ambitious zealots and terminal action-junkies ... and this is especially true of a campaign like this one, which so far lacks any central, overriding issue like the war in Vietnam that brought so many talented and totally dedicated nonpoliticians into the 68 and 72 campaigns.

The issues this time are too varied and far too complex for the instant polarization of a Which side are you on? crusade. There will not be many ideologues seriously involved in the 76 campaign; this one is a technician's trip, run by and for politicians ... Which is not really a hell of a lot different from any other campaign, except that this time it is going to be painfully obvious. This time, on the 200th anniversary of what used to be called the American Dream, we are going to have our noses rubbed, day after day – on the tube and in the headlines – in this mess we have made for ourselves.

Today, wherever in this world I meet a man or woman who fought for Spanish liberty, I meet a kindred soul. In those years we lived our best, and what has come after and what there is to come can never carry us to those heights again.

> Herbert Matthews, *The Education of a Correspondent*

My problem with this campaign began not quite two years ago, in May of 1974, when I flew down to Georgia with Teddy Kennedy and ran into Jimmy Carter. The meeting was not so much accidental as inevitable: I knew almost nothing about Carter at the time, and that was all I wanted to know. He was the lame duck governor of Georgia who had nominated 'Scoop' Jackson at the 1972 Democratic Convention in Miami, and in the course of that year I had written some ugly things about him.

... Or at least that's what he told me when I showed up at the governor's mansion for breakfast at eight o'clock in the morning. I had been up all night, in the company of serious degenerates ... ah, but let's not get into that, at least not quite yet. I just reread that Castrato business, and it strikes me that I am probably just one or two twisted tangents away from terminal fusing of the brain circuits.

Yes, the point: my feeling for Southern politicians is not especially warm, even now. Ever since the first cannonballs fell on Fort Sumter in 1861, Southern politics has been dominated by thieves, bigots, warmongers and buffoons. There were governors like Earl Long in Louisiana, 'Kissin' Jim' Folsom in Alabama and Orval Faubus in Arkansas ... and senators like Bilbo and Eastland from Mississippi, Smathers and Gurney from Florida ... and Lyndon Johnson from Texas.

Towards the end of the Civil Rights movement in the 1960s, the governor of Georgia was a white trash dingbat named Lester Maddox – who is still with us, in one crude form or another – and when the curtain finally falls on George Wallace, he will probably go down in history as the greatest thief of them all. Wallace was the first Southern politician to understand that there are just as many mean, stupid bigots above the Mason-Dixon Line as there are below it, and when he made the shrewd decision to 'go national' in 1968, he created an Alabama-based industry that has since made very rich men of himself and a handful of cronies. For more than a decade, George Wallace has bamboozled the national press and terrified the ranking fixers in both major parties. In 1968, he took enough Democratic votes from Hubert Humphrey to elect Richard Nixon, and if he had bothered to understand the delegate selection process in 1972, he could have prevented McGovern's nomination and muscled himself into the number two spot on a Humphrey-Wallace ticket.

McGovern could not have survived a second-ballot shortfall in Miami that year, and anybody who thinks the Happy Warrior would not have made that trade with Wallace is a fool. Hubert Humphrey would have traded *anything*, with *anybody*, to get the Democratic nomination for himself in 1972 ... and he'll be ready to trade again, this year, if he sees the slightest chance.

And he does. He saw it on the morning after the New Hampshire primary, when five per cent of the vote came in as 'uncommitted'. That rotten, truthless old freak was on national TV at the crack of dawn, cackling like a hen full of amyls at the 'wonderful news' from New Hampshire. After almost four years of relatively statesmanlike restraint and infrequent TV appearances that showed his grey hair and haggard jowls – four long and frantic years that saw the fall of Richard Nixon, the end of the war in Vietnam and a neo-collapse of the US economy – after all that time and all those sober denials that he would never run for president, all it took to jerk Hubert out of his closet was the news from New Hampshire that five per cent of the Democratic voters, less than 4000 people, in that strange little state had cast their ballots for 'uncommitted' delegates.

To Humphrey, who was not even entered in the New Hampshire primary, this meant *five per cent for him*. Never mind that a completely unknown ex-governor of Georgia had *won* the New Hampshire with more than 30 per cent of the vote; or that liberal Congressman Morris Udall had finished a solid but disappointing second with 24 per cent; or that liberal Senator Birch Bayh ran third with 16 per cent ... None of that mattered to Hubert, because he was privy to various rumours and force-fed press reports that many of the 'uncommitted' delegates in New Hampshire were secret Humphrey supporters. There was no way to be sure, of course – but no reason to doubt it, either; at least not in the mushy mind of the Happy Warrior.

His first TV appearance of the 76 campaign was a nasty shock to me. I had been up all night, tapping the glass and nursing my bets along (I had bet the quinella, taking Carter and Reagan against Udall and Ford) and when the sun came up on Wednesday I was slumped in front of a TV set in an ancient New England farmhouse on a hilltop near a hamlet called Contoocook. I had won early on Carter, but I had to wait for

Hughes Rudd and the *Morning News* to learn that Ford had finally overtaken Reagan. The margin at dawn was less than one per cent, but it was enough to blow my quinella and put Reagan back on Cheap Street, where he's been ever since ... and I was brooding on this unexpected loss, sipping my coffee and tapping the glass once again, when all of a sudden I was smacked right straight in the eyes with the wild-eyed babbling spectacle of Hubert Horatio Humphrey. His hair was bright orange, his cheeks were rouged, his forehead was caked with Mantan, and his mouth was moving so fast that the words poured out in a high-pitched chattering whine ... 'O my goodness, my gracious ... isn't it wonderful? Yes, yes indeed ... O yes, it just goes to show ... I just can't say enough ...'

No! I thought. This can't be true! Not *now*! Not so soon! Here was this *monster*, this shameful electrified corpse – giggling and raving and flapping his hands at the camera like he'd just been elected president. He looked like three iguanas in a feeding frenzy. I stood up and backed off from the TV set, but the view was no different from the other side of the room. I was seeing the real thing, and it stunned me ... Because I knew, in my heart, that he *was* real: that even with a five per cent shadow vote in the year's first primary, where his name was not on the ballot, and despite Jimmy Carter's surprising victory and four other nationally known candidates finishing higher than 'uncommitted', that Hubert Humphrey had somehow emerged from the chaos of New Hampshire with yet another new life, and another serious shot at the presidency of the United States.

This was more than a visceral feeling, or some painful flash of dread instinct. It was, in fact, a thing I'd predicted myself at least six months earlier ... It was a summer night in Washington and I was having dinner at an outdoor restaurant near the Capitol with what the *Wall Street Journal* later described as 'a half-dozen top operatives from the 1972 McGovern campaign'. And at that point there were already three certain candidates for 76 – Jimmy Carter, Mo Udall and Fred Harris. We had just come from a brief and feisty little session with Carter, and on the way to the restaurant we had run into Udall on the street, so the talk at the table was understandably 'deep politics'. Only one person in the group had even a tentative commitment to a candidate in 76, and after an hour or two of cruel judgements and bitter comment, Alan Baron – McGovern's press secretary and a prime mover in the 'new politics' wing of the Democratic party – proposed a secret ballot to find out which candidate those of us at the table actually believed would be the party nominee in 1976. 'Not who we want, or who we like,' Baron stressed, 'but who we really think is gonna get it.'

I tore a page out of my notebook and sliced it up to make ballots. We each took one, wrote a name on it, then folded it up and passed the ballots to Baron, a Farouk-like personage with a carnivorous sense of humour and the build of a sumo wrestler.

(Alan and I have not always been friends. He was Muskie's campaign manager for Florida in 72, and he had never entirely recovered from his encounter with the gin-crazed boohoo on Big Ed's 'Sunshine Special' ... and even now, after all this time, I will occasionally catch him staring at me with a feral glint in his eyes.)

Indeed, and so much for that – just another bucket of bad blood gone under the bridge, so to speak, and in presidential politics you learn to love the bridges and never look down.

Which gets us back to the vote count, and the leer on Baron's face when he unfolded the first ballot. 'I knew it,' he said. 'That's two already, counting mine ... yeah, here's another one.' He looked up and laughed. 'It's a landslide for Hubert.'

And it was. The final count was Humphrey four, Muskie two and one vote for Udall from Rick Stearns, who was already involved in the planning and organizing stages of Udall's campaign. Nobody else at the table was committed to anything except gloom, pessimism and a sort of aggressive neutrality.

So much for the idea of a sequel to *Fear and Loathing: On the Campaign Trail '72*. Barring some totally unexpected development, I will leave the dreary task of chronicling this low-rent trip to Teddy White, who is already trapped in a place I don't want to be.

But there is no way to escape without wallowing deep in the first few primaries and getting a feel, more or less, for the evidence ... And in order to properly depress and degrade myself for the ordeal to come, I decided in early January to resurrect the National Affairs Desk and set up, once again, in the place where I spent so much time in 1972 and then again in 1974. These were the boom-and-bust years of Richard Milhous Nixon, who was criminally insane and also president of the United States for five years.

Marching through Georgia with Ted Kennedy ... Deep, Down and Dirty; on the Darkest Side of Shame ... The Politics of Mystery and Blood on the Hands of Dean Rusk ... Jimmy Carter's Law Day Speech, and Why It Was Shrouded in Secrecy by Persons Unknown ... Derby Day in the Governor's Mansion and the Strangling of the Sloat Diamond

If any person shall carnally know in any manner any brute animal, or carnally know any male or female person by the anus or by and with the mouth, or voluntarily submit to such carnal knowledge, he or she shall be guilty of a felony and shall be confined in the penitentiary not less than one year nor more than three years.

Commonwealth of Virginia anti-sodomy statute, 1792

One of the most difficult problems for a journalist covering a presidential campaign is getting to know the candidates well enough to make confident judgements about them, because it is just about impossible for a journalist to establish a personal relationship with any candidate who has already made the big leap from 'long shot' to 'serious contender'. The problem becomes more and more serious as the stakes get higher, and by the time a candidate has survived enough primaries to convince himself and his staff that they will all be eating their lunches in the White House Mess for the next four years, he is long past the point of having either the time or the inclination to treat any journalist who doesn't already know him personally as anything but just another face in the campaign 'press corps'.

There are many complex theories about the progressive stages of a presidential campaign, but for the moment let's say there are three: stage one is the period between the decision to run for president and the morning after the New Hampshire primary when the field is still crowded, the staff organizations are still loose and relaxed, and most candidates are still hungry for all the help they can get – especially media exposure, so they can get their names in the Gallup Poll; stage two is the 'winnowing out', the separating of the sheep from the goats, when the two or three survivors of the early primaries begin looking like long-distance runners with a realistic shot at the party nomination; and stage three begins whenever the national media, the public opinion polls and Mayor Daley of Chicago decide that a candidate has picked up enough irreversible momentum to begin looking like at least a *probable* nominee, and a *possible* next president.

This three-stage breakdown is not rooted in any special wisdom or scientific analysis, but it fits both the 1972 and 1976 Democratic campaigns well enough to make the point that any journalist who doesn't get a pretty personal fix on a candidate while he's still in stage one might just as well go with his or her instincts all the way to election day in November, because once a candidate gets to stage two his whole lifestyle changes drastically.

At that point he becomes a public figure, a serious contender, and the demands on his time and energy begin escalating to the level of madness. He wakes up every morning to face a split-second, eighteen-hour-a-day schedule of meetings, airports, speeches, press conferences, motorcades and handshaking. Instead of rambling, off-the-cuff talks over a drink or two with reporters from small-town newspapers, he is suddenly flying all over the country in his own chartered jet full of syndicated columnists and network TV stars ... Cameras and microphones follow him everywhere he goes, and instead of pleading long and earnestly for the support of fifteen amateur political activists gathered in some English professor's living room in Keene, New Hampshire, he is reading the same cliché-riddled speech – often three or four times in a single day – to vast auditoriums full of people who either laugh or applaud at all the wrong times and who may or may not be supporters ... And all the fat cats, labour leaders and big-time pols who couldn't find the time to return his phone calls when he was desperately looking for help a few months ago are now ringing his phone off the hook within minutes after his arrival in whatever Boston, Miami or Milwaukee hotel his managers have booked him into that night. But they are not calling to offer their help and support, they just want to make sure he understands that they don't plan to help or support anybody else, until they get to know *him* a little better.

It is a very mean game that these high-rolling, coldhearted hustlers play. The president of the United States may no longer be 'the most powerful man in the world', but he is still close enough to be sure that nobody else in the world is going to cross him by accident. And anybody who starts looking like he might get his hands on that kind of power had better get comfortable, right from the start, with the certain knowledge that he is going to have to lean on some very mean and merciless people just to get himself elected.

The power of the presidency is so vast that it is probably a good thing, in retrospect, that only a very few people in this country understood the gravity of Richard Nixon's mental condition during his last year in the White House. There were moments in that year when even his closest friends and advisers were convinced that the president of the United States was so crazy with rage and booze and suicidal despair that he was only two martinis away from losing his grip entirely and suddenly locking himself in his office long enough to make that single telephone call that would have launched enough missiles and bombers to blow the whole world off its axis or at least kill 100 million people.

The sudden, hellish reality of a nuclear war with either Russia or China or both was probably the only thing that could have salvaged Nixon's presidency after the Supreme Court ruled that he had to yield up the incriminating tapes that he *knew* would finish him off. Would the action-starved generals at the Strategic Air Command Headquarters have ignored an emergency order from their commander-in-chief? And how long would it have taken Pat Buchanan or General Haig to realize that 'the boss' had finally flipped? Nixon spent so much time alone that nobody else in the White House would have given his absence a second thought until he failed to show up for dinner, and by that time he could have made enough phone calls to start wars all over the world.

A four-star general commandant of the US Marine Corps with three wars and thirty-five years of fanatical devotion to duty, honour and country in his system would hack off his own feet and eat them rather than refuse to obey a direct order from the president of the United State – even if he thought the president was crazy.

The key to all military thinking is a concept that nobody who ever wore a uniform with even one stripe on it will ever forget: 'You don't salute the man, you salute the uniform.' Once you've learned that, you're a soldier – and soldiers don't disobey orders from people they have to salute. If Nixon's tortured mind had bent far enough to let him think he could save himself by ordering a full-bore Marine/Airborne invasion of Cuba, he would not have given the boom-boom order to some closet-pacifist general who might be inclined to delay the invasion long enough to call Henry Kissinger for official reassurance that the president was not insane.

No West Pointer with four stars on his hat would take that kind of risk anyway. By the time word got back to the White House, or to Kissinger, that Nixon had given the order to invade Cuba, the whole Caribbean would be a sea of fire; Fidel Castro would be in a submarine on his way to Russia, and the sky above the Atlantic would be streaked from one horizon to the other with the vapour trails of a hundred panic-launched missiles.

Right. But it was mainly a matter of luck that Nixon's mental disintegration was so obvious and so crippling that by the time he came face to face with his final option, he was no longer able to even recognize it. When the going got tough, the politician who worshipped toughness above all else turned into a whimpering, gin-soaked vegetable ... But it is still worth wondering how long it would have taken Haig and

Kissinger to convince all those SAC generals out in Omaha to disregard a doomsday phone call from the president of the United States because a handful of civilians in the White House said he was crazy.

Ah ... but we are wandering off into wild speculation again, so let's chop it off right here. We were talking about the vast powers of the presidency and all the treacherous currents surrounding it ... Not to mention all the riptides, ambushes, Judas goats, fools and ruthless, dehumanized thugs that will sooner or later have to be dealt with by any presidential candidate who still feels strong on his feet when he comes to that magic moment for the leap from stage two to stage three.

But there will be plenty of time for that later on. And plenty of other journalists to write out it ... But not me. The most active and interesting phase of a presidential campaign is stage one, which is as totally different from the *Sturm und Drang* of stage three as a guerilla-style war among six or eight Gypsy nations is totally different from the bloody, hunkered down trench warfare that paralysed and destroyed half of Europe during World War I.

ATHENS, Ala. (AP) – Iladean Tribble, who had said she would marry entertainer Elvis Presley on Saturday, confirmed Sunday that the ceremony did not take place. Mrs Tribble, a forty-two-year-old widow with four children, was asked in a telephone interview why the wedding did not take place. She replied: 'This is the Sabbath day and I don't talk about things like this on the Lord's day.'

Well ... that's fair enough, I guess. Jimmy Carter had said that he won't talk about his foreign policy until the day he delivers his inaugural address. Everybody had a right to their own quirks and personal convictions – as long as they don't try to lay them on me – but just for the pure, meanspirited hell of it, I am going to call Iladean Tribble when the sun comes up in about three hours and ask her the same question the AP reporter insulted her faith by asking on the sabbath.

By Mrs Tribble's own logic, I should get a perfectly straight answer from her on Tuesday, which according to my calendar is not a religious holiday of any kind ... So in just a few hours I should have the answer, from Iladean herself, to the question regarding her mysterious nonmarriage to Elvis Presley.

And after I talk to Iladean, I am going to call my old friend Pat Caddell, who is Jimmy Carter's pollster and one of the two or three main wizards in Carter's brain trust, and we will have another one of our daily philosophical chats ...

When I read Mrs Tribble's quote to Pat earlier tonight, in the course of a more or less bare-knuckled telephone talk, he said he didn't know any woman named Iladean in Athens, Alabama – and besides that he didn't see any connection between her and the main topic of our conversation tonight, which was Jimmy Carter – who is always the main topic when I talk to Caddell, and we've been talking, arguing, plotting, haggling and generally whipping on each other almost constantly, ever since this third-rate, low-rent campaign circus hit the public roads about four months ago.

That was *before* Pat went to work for Jimmy, but long after I'd been cited in about thirty-three dozen journals all over the country as one of Carter's earliest and most fervent supporters. Everywhere I went for at least the past year, from Los Angeles to Austin, Nashville, Washington, Boston, Chicago and Key West, I've been publicly hammered by friends and strangers alike for saying that I 'like Jimmy Carter'. I have been jeered by large crowds for saying this; I have been mocked in print by liberal pundits and other Gucci people; I have been called a brain-damaged geek by some of my best and oldest friends; my own wife threw a knife at me on the night of the Wisconsin primary when the midnight radio stunned us both with a news bulletin from a CBS station in Los Angeles, saying that earlier announcements by NBC and ABC regarding Mo Udall's narrow victory over Carter in Wisconsin were not true, and that late returns from the rural districts were running so heavily in Carter's favour that CBS was now calling him the winner.

Sandy likes Mo Udall; and so do I, for that matter . . . I also like Jerry Jeff Walker, the scofflaw king of New Orleans and a lot of other people I don't necessarily believe should be president of the United States. The immense concentration of power in that office is just too goddamn heavy for anybody with good sense to turn his back on. Or *her* back. Or *its* back . . . At least not as long as whatever lives in the White House has the power to fill vacancies on the US Supreme Court; because anybody with that kind of power can use it – like Nixon did – to pack-crowd the court of final appeal in this country with the same kind of lame, vindictive yo-yos who recently voted to sustain the commonwealth of Virginia's anti-sodomy statutes . . . And anybody who thinks that 6–3 vote against 'sodomy' is some kind of abstract legal gibberish that doesn't really affect *them* had better hope they never get busted for anything the Bible or any local vice-squad cop calls an 'unnatural sex act'. Because 'unnatural' is defined by the laws of almost every state in the union as anything but a quick and dutiful hump in the classic missionary position, for purposes of procreation only. Anything else is a *felony crime*, and people who commit felony crimes *go to prison*.

Which won't make much difference to me. I took that fatal dive off the straight and narrow path so long ago that I can't remember when I first become a felon – but I have been one ever since, and it's way too late to change now. In the eyes of the law, my whole life has been one long and sinful felony. I have sinned repeatedly, as often as possible, and just as soon as I can get away from this goddamn Calvinist typewriter I am going to get right after it again ... God knows, I hate it, but I can't help myself after all these criminal years. Like Waylon Jennings says, 'The devil made me do it the first time. The second time, I done it on my own.'

Right. And the third time, I did it because of brain damage ... And after that: well, I figured that anybody who was already doomed to a life of crime and sin might as well learn to love it.

Anything worth all that risk and energy almost has to be beyond the reach of any kind of redemption except the power of pure love ... and this flesh of twisted wisdom brings us back, strangely enough, to *politics*, Pat Caddell, and the 1976 presidential campaign ... And, not incidentally, to the fact that any journal on any side of Wall Street that ever quoted me as saying 'I like Jimmy Carter' was absolutely accurate. I have said it many times, to many people, and I will keep on saying it until Jimmy Carter gives me some good reason to change my mind – which might happen about two minutes after he finishes reading this article: But I doubt it.

I have known Carter for more than two years and I have probably spent more private, human time with him than any other journalist on the 76 campaign trail. The first time I met him – at about eight o'clock on a Saturday morning in 1974 at the back door of the governor's mansion in Atlanta – I was about two degrees on the safe side of berserk, raving and babbling at Carter and his whole bemused family about some hostile bastard wearing a Georgia State Police uniform who had tried to prevent me from coming through the gate at the foot of the long, tree-shaded driveway leading up to the mansion.

I had been up all night, in the company of serious degenerates, and when I rolled up to the gatehouse in the back seat of a taxi I'd hailed in downtown Atlanta, the trooper was not amused by the sight and sound of my presence. I was trying to act calm but after about thirty seconds I realized it wasn't working; the look on his face told me I was not getting through to the man. He stared at me, saying nothing, while I explained from my crouch in the back seat of the cab that I was late for breakfast with 'the governor and Ted Kennedy' ... Then he suddenly stiffened and began shouting at the cabdriver: 'What kind of dumb shit are you trying to *pull*, buddy? Don't you know where you *are*?'

Before the cabbie could answer, the trooper smacked the flat of his hand down on the hood so hard that the whole cab rattled. 'You! Shut this engine!' Then he pointed at me: 'You! Out of the cab. Let's see some identification.' He reached out for my wallet and motioned for me to follow him into the gatehouse. The cabbie started to follow, but the trooper waved him back. 'Stay right where you are, good buddy. I'll *get* to you.' The look on my driver's face said we were both going to jail and it was my fault. 'It wasn't *my* idea to come out here,' he whined. 'This guy told me he was invited for breakfast with the governor.'

The trooper was looking at the press cards in my wallet. I was already pouring sweat, and just as he looked over at me I realized I was holding a can of beer in my hand. 'You always bring your own beer when you have breakfast with the governor?' he asked.

I shrugged and dropped it in a nearby wastebasket.

'You!' he shouted. 'What do you think you're doing?'

The scene went on for another twenty minutes. There were many phone calls, a lot of yelling, and finally the trooper reached somebody in the mansion who agreed to locate Senator Kennedy and ask if he knew 'some guy name of Thompson, I got him down here, he's all beered up and wants to come up there for breakfast ...'

Jesus, I thought, that's all Kennedy needs to hear. Right in the middle of breakfast with the governor of Georgia, some nervous old darky shuffles in from the kitchen to announce that the trooper down at the gatehouse is holding some drunkard who says he's a friend of Senator Kennedy's and he wants to come in and have breakfast ...

Which was, in fact, a lie. I had not been invited for breakfast with the governor, and up to that point I had done everything in my power to avoid it. Breakfast is the only meal of the day that I tend to view with the same kind of traditionalized reverence that most people associate with lunch and dinner.

I like to eat breakfast alone, and almost never before noon; anybody with a terminally jangled lifestyle needs at least one psychic anchor every twenty-four hours, and mine is breakfast. In Hong Kong, Dallas or at home – and regardless of whether or not I have been to bed – breakfast is a personal ritual that can only be properly observed alone, and in a spirit of genuine excess. The food factor should always be massive: four bloody marys, two grapefruits, a pot of coffee, Rangoon *crêpes*, a half-pound of either sausage, bacon or corned beef hash with diced chillies, a Spanish omelette or eggs Benedict, a quart of milk, a chopped lemon for random seasoning, and something like a slice of key lime pie, two margaritas and six lines of the best cocaine for dessert ... Right, and there should also be two or three newspapers, all mail and messages, a telephone, a notebook for planning the next twenty-four hours, and at least one source of good music ... All of which should be dealt with *outside*, in the warmth of a hot sun, and preferably stone naked.

It is not going to be easy for those poor bastards out in San Francisco who have been waiting all day in a condition of extreme fear and anxiety for my long and finely reasoned analysis of the 'meaning of Jimmy Carter' to come roaring out of my faithful mojo wire and across 2000 miles of telephone line to understand why I am sitting here in a Texas motel full of hookers and writing at length on the meaning of breakfast ... But like almost everything else worth understanding, the explanation for this is deceptively quick and basic.

After more than ten years of trying to deal with politics and politicians in a professional manner, I have finally come to the harsh understanding that there is no way at all – not even for a doctor of chemotherapy with total access to the whole spectrum of legal and illegal drugs, the physical constitution of a mule shark and a brain as rare and sharp and original as the Sloat diamond – to function as a political journalist without abandoning the whole concept of a decent breakfast. I have worked like twelve bastards for more than a decade to be able to have it both ways, but the conflict is too basic and too deeply rooted in the nature of both politics and breakfast to ever be reconciled. It is one of those very few great forks in the road of life that cannot be avoided: like a Jesuit priest who is also a practising nudist with a $200-a-day smack habit wanting to be the first naked pope (or Pope Naked the First, if we want to use the language of the church) ... Or a vegetarian pacifist with a .44 magnum fetish who wants to run for president without giving up his membership in the National Rifle Association or his New York City pistol permit that allows him to wear twin six-guns on *Meet the Press*, *Face the Nation* and all of his press conferences.

There are some combinations that *nobody* can handle: shooting bats on the wing with a double-barrelled .410 and a head full of jimson weed is one of them, and another is the idea that it is possible for a freelance writer with at least four close friends named Jones to cover a hopelessly scrambled presidential campaign better than any six-man team of career political journalists on the *New York Times* or the *Washington Post* and still eat a three-hour breakfast in the sun every morning.

But I had not made the final decision on that morning when I rolled up to the gatehouse of the governor's mansion in Atlanta to have breakfast with Jimmy Carter and Ted Kennedy. My reason for being there at that hour was simply to get my professional schedule back in phase with Kennedy's political obligations for that day. He was scheduled to address a crowd of establishment heavies who would convene at the University of Georgia Law School at 10:30 in the morning to officially witness the unveiling of a huge and prestigious oil portrait of former secretary of state Dean Rusk, and his tentative schedule for Saturday called for him to leave the governor's mansion after breakfast and make the sixty-mile trip to Athens by means of the governor's official air-plane ... So in order to hook up with Kennedy and make the trip with him, I had no choice but to meet him for breakfast at the mansion, where he had spent the previous night at Carter's invitation.

Oddly enough, I had also been invited to spend Friday night in a bed-room at the governor's mansion. I had come down from Washington with Kennedy on Friday afternoon, and since I was the only journalist travelling with him that weekend, Governor Carter had seen fit to in-clude me when he invited 'the Kennedy party' to overnight at the man-sion instead of a downtown motel.

But I am rarely in the right frame of mind to spend the night in the house of a politician – at least not if I can spend it anywhere else, and on the previous night I figured I would be a lot happier in a room at the Regency Hyatt House than I would in the Georgia governor's mansion. Which may or may not have been true, but regardless of all that, I still had to be at the mansion for breakfast if I wanted to get any work done that weekend, and my work was to stay with Ted Kennedy.

The scene at the gate had unhinged me so thoroughly that I couldn't find the door I'd been told to knock on when I finally got out of my cab at the mansion ... and by the time I finally got inside I was in no shape at all to deal with Jimmy Carter and his whole family. I didn't even recognize Carter when he met me at the door. All I knew was that a middle-aged man wearing Levi's was taking me into the dining room, where I insisted on sitting down for a while, until the tremors passed.

One of the first things I noticed about Carter, after I'd calmed down a bit, was the relaxed and confident way he handled himself with Ted Kennedy. The contrast between the two was so stark that I am still sur-prised whenever I hear somebody talking about the 'eerie resemblance' between Carter and John F. Kennedy. I have never noticed it, except every once in a while in some carefully staged photograph – and if there was ever a time when it seems like any such resemblance should have been impossible to miss, it was that morning in Atlanta when I walked into the dining room and saw Jimmy Carter and Ted Kennedy sitting about six feet apart at the same table.

Kennedy, whose presence usually dominates any room he walks into, was sitting there looking stiff and vaguely uncomfortable in his dark blue suit and black shoes. He glanced up as I entered and smiled faintly, then went back to staring at a portrait on the wall on the other side of the room. Paul Kirk, his executive wizard, was sitting next to him, wear-ing the same blue suit and black shoes – and Jimmy King, his executive advance man, was off in a distant corner yelling into a telephone. There were about fifteen other people in the room, most of them laughing and talking, and it took me a while to notice that nobody was talking to

Kennedy – which is a very rare thing to see, particularly in any situation involving other politicians or even politically conscious people.

Kennedy was obviously not in a very gregarious mood that morning, and I didn't learn why until an hour or so later when I found myself in one of the Secret Service cars with King, Kirk and Kennedy, running at top speed on the highway to Athens. The mood in the car was ugly. Kennedy was yelling at the SS driver for missing a turnoff that meant we'd be late for the unveiling. When we finally got there and I had a chance to talk privately with Jimmy King, he said Carter had waited until the last minute – just before I got to the mansion – to advise Kennedy that a sudden change in his own plans made it impossible for him to lend Teddy his plane for the trip to Athens. That was the reason for the tension I half-noticed when I got to the mansion. King had been forced to get on the phone immediately and locate the Secret Service detail and get two cars out to the mansion immediately. By the time they arrived it was obvious that we would not get to Athens in time for the unveiling of Rusk's portrait – which was fine with me, but Kennedy was scheduled to speak and he was very unhappy.

I refused to participate in any ceremony honouring a warmonger like Rusk, so I told King I would look around on the edge of the campus for a bar, and then meet them for lunch at the cafeteria for the Law Day luncheon ... He was happy enough to see me go, because in the space of three or four minutes I had insulted a half-dozen people. There was a beer parlour about ten minutes away, and I stayed there in relative peace until it was time for the luncheon.

There was no way to miss the campus cafeteria. There was a curious crowd of about 200 students waiting to catch a glimpse of Ted Kennedy, who was signing autographs and moving slowly up the concrete steps towards the door as I approached. Jimmy King saw me coming and waited by the door. 'Well, you missed the unveiling,' he said with a smile. 'You feel better?'

'Not much,' I replied. 'They should have run the bloodthirsty bastard up a flagpole by his heels.'

King started to smile again, but his mouth suddenly froze and I looked to my right just in time to see Dean Rusk's swollen face about eighteen inches away from my own. King reached out to shake his hand. 'Congratulations, sir,' he said. 'We're all very proud of you.'

'Balls,' I muttered.

After Rusk had gone inside, King stared at me and shook his head sadly. 'Why can't you give the old man some peace?' he said. 'He's harmless now. Jesus, you'll get us in trouble yet.'

'Don't worry,' I said. 'He's deaf as a rock.'

'Maybe so,' King replied. 'But some of those people with him can hear okay. One of the women over there at the ceremony asked me who you were and I said you were an undercover agent, but she was still pissed off about what you said. "You should have Senator Kennedy teach him some manners," she told me. "Not even a government agent should be allowed to talk like that in public." '

'Like what?' I said. 'That stuff about the blood on his hands?'

King laughed. 'Yeah, that really jolted her. Jesus, Hunter, you gotta remember, these are genteel people.' He nodded solemnly. 'And this is their turf. Dean Rusk is a goddamn national hero down here. What are his friends supposed to think when the senator comes down from Washington to deliver the eulogy at the unveiling of Rusk's portrait, and he brings some guy with him who starts asking people why the artist didn't paint any blood on the hands?'

'Don't worry,' I said. 'Just tell 'em it's part of my deep cover. Hell, nobody connects me with Kennedy anyway. I've been careful to stay a safe distance away from you bastards. You think I want to be seen at a ceremony honouring Dean Rusk?'

'Don't kid yourself,' he said as we walked inside. 'They know you're with us. You wouldn't be here if they didn't. This is a very exclusive gathering, my boy. We're the only ones on the guest list without some kind of *very* serious title: they're all either judges or state senators or the Right Honourable this, the Right Honourable that ...'

I looked around the room, and indeed there was no mistaking the nature of the crowd. This was not just a bunch of good ol' boys who all happened to be alumni of the University of Georgia Law School; these were the *honoured* alumni, the ranking 150 or so who had earned, stolen or inherited distinction to be culled from the lists and invited to the unveiling of Rusk's portrait, followed by a luncheon with Senator Kennedy, Governor Carter, Judge Crater and numerous other hyperdistinguished guests whose names I forget ... And Jimmy King was right: this was not a natural habitat for anybody wearing dirty white basketball shoes, no tie and nothing except *Rolling Stone* to follow his name on the guest list in that space reserved for titles. If it had been a gathering of distinguished alumni from the University of Georgia Medical School, the title space on the guest list would have been in front of the names, and I would have fit right in. Hell, I could even have joined a few conversations and nobody would have given a second thought to any talk about 'blood on the hands'.

Right. But this was law day in Georgia, and I was the only Doctor in the room ... So I had to be passed off as some kind of undercover agent, travelling for unknown reasons with Senator Kennedy. Not even the Secret Service agents understand my role in the entourage. All they knew was that I had walked off the plane from Washington with Teddy, and I had been with them ever since. Nobody gets introduced to a Secret Service agent; they are expected to *know* who everybody is – and if they don't know, they act like they do and hope for the best.

It is not my wont to take undue advantage of the Secret Service. We have gone through some heavy times together, as it were, and ever since I wandered into a room in the Baltimore Hotel in New York one night during the 1972 campaign and found three SS agents smoking a joint, I have felt pretty much at ease around them ... So it seemed only natural, down in Georgia, to ask one of the four agents in our detail for the keys to the trunk of his car so I could lock my leather satchel in a safe place, instead of carrying it around with me.

Actually, the agent had put the bag in the trunk on his own, rather than give me the key ... But when I sat down at our table in the cafeteria and saw that the only available beverage was iced tea, I remembered that one of the things in my satchel was a quart of Wild Turkey, and I wanted it. On the table in front of me – and everyone else – was a tall glass of iced tea that looked to be the same colour as bourbon. Each glass had a split slice of lemon on its rim: so I removed the lemon, poured the tea into Paul Kirk's water glass, and asked one of the agents at the next table for the key to the trunk. He hesitated for a moment, but one of the law school deans or maybe Judge Crater was already talking into the mike up there at the speakers' table, so the path of least disturbance was to give me the key, which he did ...

And I thought nothing of it until I got outside and opened the trunk ...

Cazart!

If your life ever gets dull, check out the trunk of the next SS car you happen to see. You won't need a key; they open just as easily as any other trunk when a six-foot whipsteel is properly applied ... But open the bugger *carefully*, because those gentlemen keep about sixty-nine varieties of instant death inside. Jesus, I was literally staggered by the mass of weaponry in the back of that car: there were machine guns, gas masks, hand grenades, cartridge belts, tear gas canisters, ammo boxes, bulletproof vests, chains, saws and probably a lot of other things ... But all of a sudden I realized that two passing students had stopped right next to me on the sidewalk and I heard one of them say, 'God almighty! Lo k at *that* stuff!'

So I quickly filled my glass with Wild Turkey, put the bottle back in the trunk and slammed it shut just like you'd slam any other trunk ... and that was when I turned around to see Jimmy Carter coming at me with his head down, his teeth bared and his eyes so wildly dilated that he looked like a springtime bat ...

What? No. That was later in the day, on my third or fourth trip to the trunk with the iced-tea glass. I have been sitting here in a frozen, bewildered stupor for fifty or fifty-five minutes trying to figure out where that last image came from. My memories of that day are extremely vivid, for the most part, and the more I think back on it now, the more certain I am that whatever I might have seen coming at me in that kind of bent-over, fast-swooping style of the springtime bat was *not* Governor Carter. Probably it was a hunchbacked student on his way to final exams in the school of landscaping, or maybe just trying to walk fast and tie his shoes at the same time ... Or it could have been nothing at all; there is no mention in my notebook about anything trying to sneak up on me in a high-speed crouch while I was standing out there in the street.

According to my notes, in fact, Jimmy Carter had arrived at the cafeteria not long after Kennedy – and if he attracted any attention from the crowd that had come to see Teddy I would probably have noticed it and made at least a small note to emphasize the contrast in style – something like: '12:09, Carter suddenly appears in slow-moving crowd behind TK. No autographs, no bodyguards & now a blue plastic suit instead of Levi's///No recognition, no greetings, just a small sandy-haired man looking for somebody to shake hands with ...'

That is the kind of note I would have made if I'd noticed his arrival at all, which I didn't. Because it was not until around ten o'clock on the night of the New Hampshire primary, almost two years later, that there was any real reason for a journalist to make a note on the time and style of Jimmy Carter's arrival for any occasion at all, and especially not in a crowd that had come to rub shoulders with big-time heavies like Ted Kennedy and Dean Rusk. He is not an imposing figure in any way: and even now, with his face on every TV screen in the country at least five nights a week, I'd be tempted to bet $100 to anybody else's $500 that Jimmy Carter could walk – by himself and in a normal noonday crowd – from one end of Chicago's huge O'Hare Airport to the other, without being recognized by anybody ...

Or at least not by anybody who had never met him personally, or who had not seen him anywhere except on TV. Because there is nothing about Carter that would make him any more noticeable than anyone else you might pass in one of those long and crowded corridors in O'Hare. He could pass for a Fuller Brush man on any street in America ... But if Jimmy Carter had decided, fifteen years ago, to sign on as a brush and gimcrack salesman for the Fuller people, he would be president of the Fuller Brush Company today and every medicine chest in the country would be loaded with Carter-Fuller brushes ... And if he had gone into the heroin business, every respectable household between Long Island and Los Angeles would have at least one resident junkie.

Ah ... but that is not what we need to be talking about right now, is it?

The only thing I remember about the first hour or so of that luncheon was a powerful sense of depression with the life I was drifting into. According to the programme, we were in for a long run of speeches, remarks, comments, etc., on matters connected with the law school. Carter and Kennedy were the last two names on the list of speakers, which meant there was no hope of leaving early. I thought about going back to the beer parlour and watching a baseball game on TV, but King warned me against it. 'We don't know how long this goddamn thing is gonna last,' he said, 'and that's a hell of a long walk from here, isn't it?'

I knew what he was getting at. Just as soon as the programme was over, the SS caravan would rush us out to the Athens airport, where Carter's plane was waiting to fly us back to Atlanta. Another big dinner banquet was scheduled for 6:30 that night, and immediately after that, a long flight back to Washington. Nobody would miss me if I wanted to go to the beer parlour, King said; but nobody would miss me when the time came to leave for the airport, either.

One of the constant nightmares of travelling with politicians is the need to keep them in sight at all times. Every presidential campaign has its own fearful litany of horror stories about reporters – and, occasionally, even a key staff member – who thought they had plenty of time to 'run across the street for a quick beer' instead of hanging around in the rear of some grim auditorium half-listening to the drone of a long-familiar speech, only to come back in twenty minutes to find the auditorium empty and no sign of the press bus, the candidate or anybody who can tell him where they went. These stories are invariably set in places like Butte, Buffalo, or Icepick, Minnesota, on a night in the middle of March. The temperature is always below zero, there is usually a raging blizzard to keep cabs off the street, and just as the victim remembers that he has left his wallet in his overcoat on the press bus, his stomach erupts with a sudden attack of ptomaine poisoning. And then, while crawling around on his knees in some ice-covered alley and racked with fits of projectile vomiting, he is grabbed by vicious cops and whipped on the shins with a night stick, then locked in the drunk tank of the local jail and buggered all night by winos.

These stories abound, and there is just enough truth in them to make most campaign journalists so fearful of a sudden change in the schedule that they will not even go looking for a bathroom until the pain becomes unendurable and at least three reliable people have promised to fetch them back to the fold at the first sign of any movement that could signal an early departure. The closest I ever came to getting left behind was during the California primary in 1972, when I emerged from a bathroom in the Salinas railroad depot and realized that the caboose car of McGovern's 'victory train' was about 100 yards further down the tracks than it had been only three minutes earlier. George was still standing outside the platform, waving to the crowd, but the train was moving – and as I started my sprint through the crowd, running over women, children, cripples and anything else that couldn't get out of my way, I thought I saw a big grin on McGovern's face as the train began picking up speed ... I am still amazed that I caught up with the goddamn thing without blowing every valve in my heart, or even missing the iron ladder when I made my last-second leap and being swept under the train and chopped in half by the wheels.

Ever since then I have not been inclined to take many risks while travelling in strange territory with politicians. Even the very few who might feel a bit guilty about leaving me behind would have to do it anyway, because they are all enslaved by their schedules, and when it comes to a choice between getting to the airport on time or waiting for a journalist who has wandered off to seek booze, they will shrug and race off to the airport.

This is particularly true when you travel with Kennedy, who moves at all times with a speedy, split-second precision on a schedule that nobody except a perfectly organized presidential candidate would even try to keep pace with. When he is travelling with a detail of Secret Service agents, the caravan stops for nothing and waits for nobody ... The SS agents assigned to Kennedy are hypersensitive about anything that might jack up the risk factor, and they move on the theory that safety increases with speed.

There was no need for King and Kirk to warn me that the SS detail would have a collective nervous breakdown at the prospect of taking Senator Kennedy and the governor of Georgia through the streets of downtown Athens – or any other city, for that matter – to search for some notoriously criminal journalist who might be in any one of the half-dozen bars and beer parlours on the edge of the campus.

So there was nothing to do except sit there in the university cafeteria, slumped in my chair at a table right next to Dean Rusk's, and drink one tall glass after another of straight Wild Turkey until the Law Day luncheon ceremonies were finished. After my third trip out to the trunk, the SS driver apparently decided that it was easier to just let me keep the car keys instead of causing a disturbance every fifteen or twenty minutes by passing them back and forth ... Which made a certain kind of fatalistic sense, because I'd already had plenty of time to do just about anything I wanted to with the savage contents of his trunk, so why start worrying now? We had, after all, been together for the better part of two days, and the agents were beginning to understand that there was no need to reach for their weapons every time I started talking about the blood on Dean Rusk's hands, or how easily I could reach over and cut off his ears with my steak knife. Most Secret Service agents have led a sheltered life, and they tend to get edgy when they hear that kind of talk from a large stranger in their midst who has managed to stash an apparently endless supply of powerful whisky right in the middle of their trunk arsenal. That is not one of your normal, everyday situations in the SS life; and especially not when this drunkard who keeps talking about taking a steak knife to the head of a former secretary of state has a red flag on his file in the Washington SS headquarters in addition to having the keys to the SS car in his pocket.

Carter was already speaking when I came back from my fourth or fifth trip out to the car. I had been careful all along to keep the slice of lemon on the rim of the glass, so it looked like all the other iced-tea glasses in the room. But Jimmy King was beginning to get nervous about the smell. 'Goddamnit Hunter, this whole end of the room smells like a distillery,' he said.

'Balls,' I said. 'That's blood you're smelling.'

King winced and I thought I saw Rusk's head start to swing around on me, but apparently he thought better of it. For at least two hours he'd been hearing all this ugly talk about blood coming over his shoulder from what he knew was 'the Kennedy table' right behind him. But why would a group of Secret Service agents and Senator Kennedy's personal staff be talking about him like that? And why was this powerful stench of whisky hanging around his head? Were they all drunk?

Not all – but I was rapidly closing the gap and the others had been subjected to the fumes for so long that I could tell by the sound of their laughter that even the SS agents were acting a little weird. Maybe it was a contact drunk of some kind, acting in combination with the fumes and fiendish drone of the speeches. We were trapped in that place, and nobody else at the table liked it any better than I did.

I am still not sure when I began listening to what Carter was saying, but at some point about ten minutes into his remarks I noticed a marked difference in the style and tone of the noise coming from the speakers' table and I found myself listening, for the first time all day. Carter had started off with a few quiet jokes about people feeling honoured to pay ten or twelve dollars a head to hear Kennedy speak, but the only way he could get people to listen to him was to toss in a free lunch along with his remarks. The audience laughed politely a few times, but after he'd been talking for about fifteen minutes I noticed a general uneasiness in the atmosphere of the room, and nobody was laughing any more. At that point we were all still under the impression that Carter's 'remarks' would consist of a few minutes of friendly talk about the law school, a bit of praise for Rusk, an introduction to Kennedy, and that would be it . . .

But we were wrong, and the tension in the room kept increasing as more and more people realized it. Very few if any of them had supported Carter when he won the governorship, and now that he was just about finished with his four-year term and barred by law from running again, they expected him to bow out gracefully and go back to raising peanuts. If he had chosen that occasion to announce that he'd decided to run for president in 1976, the reaction would almost certainly have been a ripple of polite laughter, because they would know he was kidding. Carter had not been a bad governor, but so what? We were, after all, in Georgia; and, besides that, the South already had one governor running for president . . . Back in the spring of 1974 George Wallace was a national power; he had rattled the hell out of that big cage called the Democratic National Committee in 72, and when he said he planned to do it again in 76 he was taken very seriously.

So I would probably have chuckled along with the others if Carter had said something about running for president at the *beginning* of his 'remarks' that day, but I would not have chuckled if he'd said it at the end . . . Because it was a king-hell bastard of a speech, and by the time it was over he had rung every bell in the room. Nobody seemed to know exactly what to make of it, but they knew it was sure as hell not what they'd come there to hear.

I have heard hundreds of speeches by all kinds of candidates and politicians – usually against my will and for generally the same reasons I got trapped into hearing this one – but I have never heard a sustained piece of political oratory that impressed me any more than the speech Jimmy Carter made on that Saturday afternoon in May 1974. It ran about forty-five minutes, climbing through five very distinct gear changes while the audience muttered uneasily and raised their eyebrows at each other, and one of the most remarkable things about the speech is that it is such a rare piece of oratorical artwork that it remains vastly impressive, even if you don't necessarily believe Carter was sincere and truthful in all the things he said. Viewed purely in the context of rhetorical drama and political theatre, it ranks with General Douglas MacArthur's 'old soldiers never die' address to the Congress in 1951 – which still stands as a masterpiece of insane bullshit, if nothing else.

There were, however, a lot of people who believed every word and sigh of MacArthur's speech, and they wanted to make him president – just as a lot of people who are still uncertain about Jimmy Carter would want to make him president if he could figure out some way to deliver a contemporary version of his 1974 Law Day speech on network TV . . . Or, hell, even the same identical speech; a national audience might be slightly puzzled by some of the references to obscure judges, grade-school teachers and backwoods Georgia courthouses, but I think the totality of the speech would have the same impact today as it did two years ago.

But there is not much chance of it happening ... And that brings up another remarkable aspect of the Law Day speech: it had virtually no impact at all when he delivered it, except on the people who heard it, and most of them were more stunned and puzzled by it than impressed. They had not come there to hear lawyers denounced as running dogs of the *status quo*, and there is still some question in my own mind – and in Carter's too, I suspect – about what he came there to say. There was no written text of the speech, no press to report it, no audience hungry to hear it, and no real reason for giving it – except that Jimmy Carter had a few serious things on his mind that day, and he figured it was about time to unload them, whether the audience liked it or not ...

Which gets to another interesting point of the speech: although Carter himself now says, 'That was probably the best speech I ever made,' he has yet to make another one like it – not even to the extent of lifting some of the best images and ideas for incorporation into his current speeches – and his campaign staff attached so little importance to it that Carter's only tape recording of his Law Day remarks got lost somewhere in the files and, until about two months ago, the only existing tape of the speech was the one I'd had copied off the original, before it was lost. I've been carrying the bastard around with me for two years, playing it in some extremely unlikely situations for people who would look at me like I was finally over the hump into terminal brain damage when I'd say they were going to have to spend the next forty-five minutes listening to a political speech by some ex-governor of Georgia.

It was not until I showed up in New Hampshire and Massachusetts for the 76 primaries and started playing my tape for the Law Day speech for a few friends, journalists and even some of Carter's top staff people who'd never heard it that Pat Caddell noticed that almost everybody who heard the speech was as impressed by it as I was ... But even now, after Caddell arranged to dub fifty tape copies off of my copy, nobody in Carter's brain trust has figured out what to do with them.

I am not quite sure what I would do with them, myself, if I were Carter, because it is entirely possible that the very qualities that made the Law Day speech so impressive for me would have exactly the opposite effect on Carter's new national constituency. The voice I hear on my tape is the same one all those good conservative folk out there on the campaign trail have found so appealing, but very few of them would find anything familiar in what the voice is saying. The Jimmy Carter who waltzed so triumphantly down the middle of the road through one Democratic primary after another is a cautious, conservative and vaguely ethereal Baptist Sunday school teacher who seems to promise, above all else, a return to normalcy, a resurrection of the national self-esteem, and a painless redemption from all the horrors and disillusion of Watergate. With President Carter's firm hand on the helm, the ship of state will once again sail a true and steady course, all the crooks and liars and thieves who somehow got control of the government during the turmoil of the sixties will be driven out of the temple once and for all, and the White House will be so overflowing with honesty, decency, justice, love and compassion that it might even glow in the dark.

It is a very alluring vision, and nobody understands this better than Jimmy Carter. The electorate feels a need to be cleansed, reassured and revitalized. The underdogs of yesteryear have had their day, and they blew it. The radicals and reformers of the sixties promised peace, but they turned out to be nothing but incompetent trouble-makers. Their plans that had looked so fine on paper led to chaos and disaster when hack politicians tried to implement them. The promise of civil rights turned into the nightmare of busing. The call for law and order led straight to Watergate. And the long struggle between the hawks and the doves caused violence in the streets and a military disaster in Vietnam. Nobody won, in the end, and when the dust finally settled, 'extremists' at both ends of the political spectrum were thoroughly discredited. And by the time the 1976 presidential campaign got under way, the high ground was all in the middle of the road.

Jimmy Carter understands this, and he has tailored his campaign image to fit the new mood almost perfectly ... But back in May of 74 when he flew up to Athens to make his 'remarks' at the Law Day ceremonies, he was not as concerned with preserving his moderate image as he is now. He was thinking more about all the trouble he'd had with judges, lawyers, lobbyists and other minions of the Georgia establishment while he was governor – and now, with only six more months in the office, he wanted to have a few words with these people.

There was not much anger in his voice when he started talking. But halfway through the speech it was too obvious for anybody in the room to ignore. But there was no way to cut him short, and he knew it. It was the anger in his voice that first caught my attention, I think, but what sent me back out to the trunk to get my tape recorder instead of another drink was the spectacle of a Southern politician telling a crowd of Southern judges and lawyers that 'I'm not qualified to talk to you about law, because in addition to being a peanut farmer, I'm an engineer and nuclear physicist, not a lawyer ... But I read a lot and I listen a lot. One of the sources for my understanding about the proper application of criminal justice and the system of equities is from Reinhold Niebuhr. The other source of my understanding about what's right and wrong in this society is from a friend of mine, a poet named Bob Dylan. Listening to his records about "The Lonesome Death of Hattie Carroll" and "Like a Rolling Stone" and "The Times They Are A-Changing", I've learned to appreciate the dynamism of change in a modern society.'

At first I wasn't sure I was hearing him right and I looked over at Jimmy King. 'What the hell did I just hear?' I asked.

King smiled and looked at Paul Kirk, who leaned across the table and whispered, 'He said his top two advisers are Bob Dylan and Reinhold Niebuhr.'

I nodded and got up to go outside for my tape recorder. I could tell by the rising anger in Carter's voice that we were in for an interesting ride ... And by the time I got back he was whipping on the crowd about judges who took bribes in return for reduced prison sentences, lawyers who deliberately cheated illiterate blacks, and cops who abused people's rights with something they called a 'consent warrant'.

'I had lunch this week with the members of the Judicial Selection Committee and they were talking about a "consent search warrant",' he said. 'I didn't know what a consent search warrant was. They said, "Well, that's when two policemen go to a house. One of them goes to the front door and knocks on it and the other one runs around to the back door and yells 'come in' ".'

The crowd got a laugh out of that one, but Carter was just warming up and for the next twenty or thirty minutes his voice was the only sound in the room. Kennedy was sitting just a few feet to Carter's left, listening carefully but never changing the thoughtful expression on his face as Carter railed and bitched about a system of criminal justice that allows the rich and the privileged to escape punishment for their crimes and sends poor people to prison because they can't afford to bribe the judge ...

(Jesus Babbling Christ! The phone is ringing again, and this time I know what it is for sure. Last time it was the Land Commissioner of Texas, threatening to have my legs broken because of something I wrote about him ... But now it is the grim reaper; he has come for my final page and in exactly thirteen minutes that goddamn mojo wire across the room will erupt in a frenzy of beeping and I will have to feed it again ... But before I leave this filthy sweatbox that is costing me $39 a day I am going to deal with that rotten mojo machine. I have dreamed of smashing that fucker for five long years, but ... Okay, okay, twelve more minutes and ... yes ...)

So this will have to be it ... I would need a lot more time and space than I have to properly describe either the reality or the reaction to

Jimmy Carter's Law Day speech, which was and still is the heaviest and most eloquent thing I have ever heard from the mouth of a politician. It was the voice of an angry agrarian populist, extremely precise in its judgements and laced with some of the most original, brilliant and occasionally bizarre political metaphors anybody in that room will ever be likely to hear.

The final turn of the screw was another ugly example of crime and degradation in the legal profession, and this time Carter went right to the top. Nixon had just released his own, self-serving version of the White House tapes, and Carter was shocked when he read the transcripts. 'The Constitution charges us with a direct responsibility for determining what our government is and ought to be,' he said. And then, after a long pause, he went on: 'Well ... I have read parts of the embarrassing transcripts, and I've seen the proud statement of a former attorney general who protected his boss, and now brags of the fact that he tiptoed through a minefield and came out ... quote, clean, unquote.' Another pause, and then: 'You know, I can't imagine somebody like Thomas Jefferson tiptoeing through a minefield on the technicalities of the law, and then bragging about being *clean* afterwards ...'

Forty-five minutes later, on our way back to Atlanta in the governor's small plane, I told Carter I wanted a transcript of his speech.

'There is no transcript,' he said.

I smiled, thinking he was putting me on. The speech had sounded like a product of five or six tortured drafts ... But he showed a page and a half of scrawled notes in his legal pad and said that was all he had.

'Jesus Christ,' I said. 'That was one of the damnedest things I've ever heard. You mean you just winged it all the way through?'

He shrugged and smiled faintly. 'Well,' he said, 'I had a pretty good idea what I was going to say, before I came up here – but I guess I was a little surprised at how it came out.'

Kennedy didn't have much to say about the speech. He said he'd 'enjoyed it', but he still seemed uncomfortable and preoccupied for some reason. Carter and I talked about the time he invited Dylan and some of his friends out to the governor's mansion after a concert in Atlanta. 'I really enjoyed it,' he said with a big grin. 'It was a real honour to have him visit my home.'

I had already decided, by then, that I liked Jimmy Carter – but I had no idea that he'd made up his mind, a few months earlier, to run for the presidency in 1976. And if he had told me his little secret that day on the plane back to Atlanta, I'm not sure I'd have taken him seriously ... But if he had told me and if I had taken him seriously, I would probably have said that he could have my vote, for no other reason except the speech I'd just heard.

Which hardly matters, because Jimmy Carter didn't mention the presidency to me that day, and I had other things on my mind. It was the first Saturday in May – Derby Day in Louisville – and I'd been harassing Jimmy King since early morning about getting us back to Atlanta in time to watch the race on TV. According to the schedule we were due back at the governor's mansion around three in the afternoon, and post time for the Derby was 4:30 ... But I have learned to be leery of politicians' schedules; they are about as reliable as campaign promises, and when I'd mentioned to Kennedy that I felt it was very important to get ourselves back to Atlanta in time for the Derby, I could tell by the look on his face that the only thing that might cause him to go out of his way to watch the Kentucky Derby was a written guarantee from the Churchill Downs management that I would be staked down on the track at the finish line when the horses came thundering down the stretch.

But Carter was definitely up for it, and he assured me that we would be back at the mansion in plenty of time for me to make all the bets I wanted before post time. 'We'll even try to find a mint julep for you,' he said. 'Rosalynn has some mint in the garden, and I notice you already have the main ingredient.'

When we got to the mansion I found a big TV set in one of the basement guest rooms. The mint juleps were no problem, but the only bet I could get was a $5 gig with Jody Powell, Carter's press secretary – which I won, and then compounded the insult by insisting that Powell pay off immediately. He had to wander around the mansion, borrowing dollars and even quarters from anybody who would lend him money, until he could scrape up five dollars.

Later that night we endured another banquet, and immediately afterwards I flew back to Washington with Kennedy, King and Kirk. Kennedy was still in a funk about something, and I thought it was probably me ... And while it was true that I had not brought any great distinction to the entourage, I had made enough of an effort to know that it could have been worse, and just to make sure he understood that – or maybe for reasons of sheer perversity – I waited until we were all strapped into our seats and I heard the stewardess asking Teddy if she could bring him a drink. He refused, as he always does in public, and just as the stewardess finished her spiel I leaned over the seat and said, 'How about some heroin?'

His face went stiff and for a moment I thought it was all over for me. But then I noticed that King and Kirk were smiling ... So I strangled the sloat and walked back to my hotel in the rain.

The Last Crazed Charge of the Liberal Brigade: The Shrewdness of
Richard Nixon, the Deep and Abiding Courage of Hubert Humphrey
and All of His New Found Friends ... Jimmy Carter at Home in Plains,
One Year Later the Leap of Faith

SPECIAL BULLETIN
BEAUMONT, TEXAS (29 Apr) – Anarchist presidential candidate Hunter
S. Thompson announced yesterday during opening ceremonies at the
Beaumont Annual Stock Auction that Democratic front-runner
Jimmy Carter was 'the only candidate who ever lied to me twice in
one day'. Thompson's harsh denunciation of Carter – who was also
at the auction, for purposes of wrestling his own bull – came as a
nasty shock to the crowd of celebrities, bull wranglers and other
politicos who were gathered to participate in ceremonies honouring
Texas Land Commissioner Bob Armstrong, who followed Thompson's attack on Carter with an unexpected statement of his own, saying he would be the number two man on a dark-horse(s) Demo ticket
with Colorado Senator Gary Hart. Armstrong also denounced Carter
for 'consciously lying to me, about the price of his bull'. The Carter-
owned animal, a two-year-old peanut-fed Brahman, had been advertised at a price of $2200 – but when the front-runner showed up in
Beaumont to ride his own bull, the price suddenly escalated to $7750.
And it was at this point that both Thompson and Armstrong stunned
the crowd with their back-to-back assaults on Carter, long considered
a personal friend of both men ... Carter, who seemed shocked by the
attacks, lied to newsmen who questioned him about the reasons, saying, 'I didn't hear what they said.'

The Law Day speech is not the kind of thing that would have much
appeal to the mind of a skilled technician, and that kind of mind is perhaps the only common denominator among the strategists, organizers
and advisers at the staff-command level of Carter's campaign. Very few
of them seem to have much interest in *why* Jimmy wants to be president,
or even in what he might do after he wins: their job and their meal
ticket is to put Jimmy Carter in the White House, that is all they know
and all they need to know – and so far they are doing their job pretty
well. According to political odds-maker Billy the Geek, Carter is now a
solid 3–2 bet to win the November election – up from 50–1 less than six
months ago.

This is another likely reason why Carter's brain trust is not especially
concerned with how to put the Law Day speech to good use: the people

507

most likely to be impressed or even converted by it are mainly the ones who make up the left/liberal, humanist/intellectual wing of the Democratic party and the national press – and in the wake of Carter's genuinely awesome blitzkrieg in Pennsylvania and Texas, destroying *all* of his remaining opposition in less than a week, it is hard to argue with the feeling among his staff-command technicians that he no longer *needs* any converts from the left/liberal wing of the party. He got where he is without the help he repeatedly asked them for during most of 1975 and early 76, and now the problem is *theirs*. The train has left the station, as it were, and anybody who wants to catch up with it now is going to come up with the air fare ...

But I have just been reminded by a terrible screeching on the telephone that the presses will roll in a few hours and that means there is no more time at *Rolling Stone* than there is in the Carter campaign for wondering *why* about anything. Idle speculation is a luxury reserved for people who are too rich, too poor or too crazy to get seriously concerned about anything outside their own private realities ... and just as soon as I finish this goddamn wretched piece of gibberish I am going to flee like a rat down a pipe into one of those categories. I have maintained a wild and serious flirtation with all three of them for so long that the flirtation itself was beginning to look like reality ... But I see it now for the madness it was from the start: there is no way to maintain four parallel states of being at the same time. I know from long experience that it is possible to be rich, poor and crazy all at once – but to be rich, poor, crazy and also a functioning political journalist at the same time is flatout impossible, so the time has come to make a terminal choice ...

But not quite yet. We still have to finish this twisted saga of vengeance and revelation in the shade of the Georgia pines ... So, what the hell? Let's get after it. There is plenty of room at the top in this bountiful nation of ours for a rich, poor and crazy political journalist who can sit down at a rented typewriter in a Texas motel with a heart full of hate and a head full of speed and Wild Turkey and lash out a capsule/narrative between midnight and dawn that will explain the whole meaning and tell the whole tale of the 1976 presidential campaign ...

Hell yes! Let's *whip* on this thing! Until I got that phone call a few minutes ago I would have said it was absolutely impossible, but now I know better ... If only because I have just been reminded that until I saw Hubert Humphrey 'quit the race' a few days ago I was telling anybody who would listen that there was no way to cure an egg-sucking dog ... So now is the time to finish this rotten job that I somehow got myself into, and also to congratulate my old buddy Hubert for having enough sense to ignore his advisers and keep the last faint glimmer of his presidential hopes alive by crouching in the weeds and praying for a brokered convention, instead of shooting his whole wad by entering the New Jersey primary and getting pushed off the wall and cracked like Humpty Dumpty by Jimmy Carter's technicians.

I am beginning to sense a distinctly pejorative drift in this emphasis on the word 'technician', but it is only half-intentional. There is nothing wrong with technicians, in politics or anywhere else. Any presidential campaign without a full complement of first-class political technicians – or with a drastic imbalance between technicians and ideologues – will meet the same fate that doomed the Fred Harris campaign in New Hampshire and Massachusetts. But the question of balance is critical, and there is something a little scary about a presidential campaign run almost entirely by technicians that can be as successful as Carter's.

'Awesome' is the mildest word I can think of to describe a campaign that can take an almost totally unknown ex-governor of Georgia with no national reputation, no power base in the Democratic party and not the slightest reluctance to tell Walter Cronkite, John Chancellor and anyone else who asks that 'the most important thing in my life is Jesus Christ' and to have him securely positioned, after only nine of thirty-two primaries, as an almost prohibitive favourite to win the presidential nomination of the nation's majority political party, and an even bet to win the November election against a relatively popular GOP president who has managed somehow to convince both big labour and big business that he has just rescued the country from economic disaster. If the presidential election were held tomorrow I would not bet more than three empty beer cans on Gerald Ford's chances of beating Jimmy Carter in November.

... What? No, cancel that bet. The screech on the telephone just informed me that *Time* has just released a poll – on the day after the Texas primary – saying Carter would beat Ford by 48 per cent to 38 per cent if the election were held now. Seven weeks ago, according to *Time* via the screech, the current figures were almost exactly reversed ... I have never been much with math, but a quick shuffling of these figures seems to mean that Carter has picked up twenty points in seven weeks, and Ford has lost twenty.

If this is true, then it is definitely time to call Billy the Geek and get something like ten cases of sixty-six-proof Sloat Ale down on Carter, and forget those three empty beer cans.

In other words, the panic is on and the last survivors of the ill-fated Stop Carter Movement are out in the streets shedding their uniforms and stacking their weapons on street corners all over Washington ... And now another phone call from CBS correspondent Ed Bradley – who is covering Carter now after starting the 76 campaign with Birch Bayh – saying Bayh will announce at a press conference in Washington tomorrow that he has decided to endorse Jimmy Carter.

Well ... how about that, eh? Never let it be said that a wharf rat can get off a sinking ship any faster than an eighty-seven per cent ADA liberal.

But this is no time for cruel jokes about liberals and wharf rats. Neither species has ever been known for blind courage or stubborn devotion to principle, so let the rotters go wherever they feel even temporarily comfortable ... Meanwhile, it is beginning to look like the time has come for the rest of us to get our business straight, because the only man who is going to keep Jimmy Carter out of the White House now is Jimmy Carter.

Which might happen, but it is a hard kind of thing to bet on, because there is no precedent in the annals of presidential politics for a situation like this: with more than half the primaries still ahead of him, Carter is now running virtually unopposed for the Democratic nomination, and – barring some queer and unlikely development – he is going to have to spend the next two months in a holding action until he can go to New York in July and pick up the nomination.

Just as soon as I can get some sleep and recover from this grim and useless ordeal I will call him and find out what he plans to do with all that time ... And if I were in that nervous position I think I would call a press conference and announce that I was off to a secret think tank on the Zondo Peninsula to finalize my plans for curing all the ills of society; because a lot of strange things can happen to a long-shot front-runner in two months of forced idleness, and a lot of idle minds are going to have plenty of time for brooding on all the things that still worry them about living for at least the next four years with a president who prays twenty-five times a day and reads the Bible in Spanish every night. Even the people who plan to vote for Jimmy Carter if he can hang on between now and November are going to have more time than they need to nurse any lingering doubts they might have about him.

I will probably nurse a few doubts of my own between now and July, for that matter, but unless something happens to convince me that I should waste any more time than I already have brooding on the evil potential that lurks, invariably, in the mind of just about *anybody* whose ego has become so dangerously swollen that he really wants to be president of the United States, I don't plan to spend much time worrying about the prospect of seeing Jimmy Carter in the White House. There is not a hell of a lot I can do about it, for one thing; and for another, I have spent enough time with Carter in the past two years to feel I have a pretty good sense of his candidacy. I went down to Plains, Georgia, to spend a few days with him on his own turf and to hopefully find out who Jimmy Carter really was before the campaign shroud came down on him and he started talking like a candidate instead of a human being. Once a presidential aspirant gets out on the campaign trail and starts seeing visions of himself hunkered down behind that big desk in the Oval Office, the idea of sitting down in his own living room and talking openly with some foul-mouthed, argumentative journalist carrying a tape recorder in one hand and a bottle of Wild Turkey in the other is totally out of the question.

But it was almost a year before the 76 New Hampshire primary when I talked to Carter at his home in Plains, and I came away from that weekend with six hours of taped conversation with him on subjects ranging all the way from the Allman Brothers, stock car racing and our strongly conflicting views on the use of undercover agents in law enforcement, to nuclear submarines, the war in Vietnam and the treachery of Richard Nixon. When I listened to the tapes again last week I noticed a lot of things that I had not paid much attention to at the time, and the most obvious of these was the extremely detailed precision of his answers to some of the questions that he is now accused of being either unable or unwilling to answer. There is no question in my mind, after hearing him talk on the tapes, that I was dealing with a candidate who had already done a massive amount of research on things like tax reform, national defence and the structure of the American political system by the time he announced his decision to run for president.

Nor is there any question that there are a lot of things Jimmy Carter and I will never agree on. I had warned him, before we sat down with the tape recorder for the first time, that – although I appreciated his hospitality and felt surprisingly relaxed and comfortable in his home – I was also a journalist and that some of the questions I knew I was going to ask him might seem unfriendly or even downright hostile. Because of this, I said, I wanted him to be able to stop the tape recorder by means of a remote-pause button if the talk got too heavy. But he said he would just as soon not have to bother turning the tape on and off; which surprised me at the time, but now that I listen to the tapes I realize that loose talk and bent humour are not among Jimmy Carter's vices.

They are definitely among mine, however, and since I had stayed up most of the night, drinking and talking in the living room with his sons Jack and Chip Carter and their wives – and then by myself in the guest room over the garage – I was still feeling weird around noon, when we started talking 'seriously', and the tape of that first conversation is liberally sprinkled with my own twisted comments about 'rotten fascist bastards', 'thieving cocksuckers who peddle their asses all over Washington', and 'these goddamn brainless fools who refuse to serve liquor in the Atlanta airport on Sunday'.

It was nothing more than my normal way of talking, and Carter was already familiar with it, but there are strange and awkward pauses here and there on the tape where I can almost hear Carter gritting his teeth and wondering whether to laugh or get angry at things I wasn't even conscious of saying at the time, but which sound on the tape like random outbursts of hostility or pure madness from the throat of a paranoid psychotic. Most of the conversation is intensely rational, but every once in a while it slips over the line and all I can hear is the sound of my own voice yelling something like 'Jesus Christ! What's that filthy smell?'

Both Carter and his wife have always been amazingly tolerant of my behaviour, and on one or two occasions they have had to deal with me in a noticeably bent condition. I have always been careful not to commit any felonies right in front of them, but other than that I have never made much of an effort to adjust my behaviour around Jimmy Carter or anyone else in his family – including his seventy-eight-year-old mother, Miss Lillian, who is the only member of the Carter family I could comfortably endorse for the presidency, right now, with no reservations at all.

Whoops! Well ... we will get to that in a moment. Right now I have other things to deal with and ... No, what the hell? Let's get to it now, because time is running out and so is that goddamn sloat; so now is the time to come to grips with my own 'Carter question'.

It has taken me almost a year to reach this point, and I am still not sure how to cope with it ... But I am getting there fast, thanks mainly to all the help I've been getting from my friends in the liberal community. I took more abuse from these petulant linthead bastards during the New Hampshire and Massachusetts primaries than I have ever taken from my friends on any political question since the first days of the Free Speech Movement in Berkeley, and that was nearly twelve years ago ... I felt the same way about the first wild violent days of the FSM as I still feel about Jimmy Carter. In both cases my initial reaction was positive, and I have lived too long on my instincts to start questioning them now. At least not until I get a good reason, and so far nobody has been able to give me any good reason for junking my first instinctive reaction to Jimmy Carter, which was that I liked him ... And if the editors of *Time* magazine and the friends of Hubert Humphrey consider that 'bizarre', fuck them. I liked Jimmy Carter the first time I met him, and in the two years that have passed since that Derby Day in Georgia I have come to know him a hell of a lot better than I knew George McGovern at this point in the 72 campaign, and I still like Jimmy Carter. He is one of the most intelligent politicians I've ever met, and also one of the strangest.

I have never felt comfortable around people who talk about their feeling for Jesus, or any other deity for that matter, because they are usually none too bright ... Or maybe 'stupid' is a better way of saying it; but I have never seen much point in getting heavy with either stupid people or Jesus freaks, just as long as they don't bother me. In a world as weird and cruel as this one we have made for ourselves, I figure anybody who can find peace and personal happiness without ripping off somebody else deserves to be left alone. They will not inherit the earth, but then neither will I ... And I have learned to live, as it were, with the idea that I will never find peace and happiness, either. But as long as I know there's a pretty good chance I can get my hands on either one of them every once in a while, I do the best I can between high spots.

And so much for all that gibberish. The bastards are taking the whole thing away from me now, and anything else I might have wanted to say about Jimmy Carter will have to wait for another time and place. At the moment, failing any new evidence that would cause me to change my mind, I would rather see Jimmy Carter in the White House than anybody else we are likely to be given a chance to vote for. And that narrows the field right down, for now, to Ford, Reagan and Humphrey.

Carter is the only unknown quantity of the four, and that fact alone says all I need to know. Admittedly, a vote for Carter requires a certain leap of faith, but on the evidence I don't mind taking it. I think he is enough of an ego maniac to bring the same kind of intensity to the task of doing the job in a way that will allow him to stay as happy with his own mirror in the White House as he is now with his mirror in Plains.

There is also the fact that I have that Law Day speech to fall back on, which is a lot better reason to vote for him than anything I've seen or heard on the campaign trail. I have never thought the problem with Carter is that he is two-faced in the sense of a two-headed coin ... But he is definitely a politician above all else right now, and that is the only way *anybody* gets into the White House. If Carter has two faces, my own feeling is that they are mounted one behind the other, but both looking in the same direction, instead of both ways at once, as the friends of Hubert Humphrey keep saying.

It also occurs to me now and then that many of the people who feel so strongly about keeping Jimmy Carter out of the White House don't know him at all. And a lot of the people who accuse him of lying, dissembling, waffling and being 'hazy' have never bothered to listen very carefully to what he says, or to try reading between the lines now when Carter comes out with some mawkish statement like the one he has used to end so many speeches: 'I just want to see us once again with a government that is as honest and truthful and fair and idealistic and compassionate and filled with love as are the American people.'

The first time I heard him say that up in New Hampshire I was
stunned. It sounded like he had eaten some of the acid I've been saving
up to offer him the first time he mentions anything to me about bringing
Jesus into my life ... But after I'd heard him say the same thing five or
six more times, it began to sound like something I'd heard long before
I'd ever heard Jimmy Carter's name ...

It took me a while to dig it out of my memory, but when it finally
surfaced I recognized the words of the late, great liberal, Adlai Stevenson, who once lashed it all together in one small and perfect capsule
when he said '... in a democracy, people usually get the kind of government they deserve'.

Rolling Stone no. 214, 3 June 1976

ADDRESS BY JIMMY CARTER ON LAW DAY: UNIVERSITY OF GEORGIA, ATHENS, GA

4 May 1974

Senator Kennedy, distinguished fellow Georgians, friends of the Law
School of Georgia and personal friends of mine:

Sometimes even a distinguished jurist on the Supreme Court doesn't
know all of the background on acceptances of invitations. As a matter
of fact, my wife was influential in this particular acceptance, but my son
was even more influential. This was really an acceptance to repair my
ego. There was established in 1969 the LQC Lamar Society. I was involved in the establishment of it, and I think a lot of it. As Governor of
Georgia I was invited this year, along with two distinguished Americans,
to make a speech at the annual meeting which is going on now.

I found out when the programme was prepared that Senator Kennedy
was to speak last night. They charged $10 to attend the occasion.
Senator William Brock from Tennessee is speaking to the Lamar Society
at noon today. I found out that they charged $7.50 for this occasion. I
spoke yesterday at noon, and I asked the Lamar Society officials, at the
last moment, how much they were charging to come to the luncheon
yesterday. They said they weren't charging anything. I said, 'You mean
they don't even have to pay for the lunch?' They said, 'No, we're
providing the lunch free.'

So, when my son Jack came and said, 'Daddy, I think more of you
than you thought I did; I'm paying $7.00 for two tickets to the lun-

514

cheon,' I figured that a $3.50 lunch ticket would salvage part of my ego and that's why I'm here today.

I'm not qualified to talk to you about law, because in addition to being a peanut farmer, I'm an engineer and a nuclear physicist, not a lawyer. I was planning, really, to talk to you more today about politics and the interrelationship of political affairs and law, than about what I'm actually going to speak on. But after Senator Kennedy's delightful and very fine response to political questions during his speech, and after his analysis of the Watergate problems, I stopped at a room on the way, while he had his press conference, and I changed my speech notes.

My own interest in the criminal justice system is very deep and heartfelt. Not having studied law, I've had to learn the hard way. I read a lot and listen a lot. One of the sources for my understanding about the proper application of criminal justice and the system of equity is from reading Reinhold Niebuhr, one of his books that Bill Gunter gave me quite a number of years ago. The other source of my understanding about what's right and wrong in this society is from a friend of mine, a poet named Bob Dylan. After listening to his records about 'The Ballad of Hattie Carol' and 'Like a Rolling Stone' and 'The Times, They Are A-Changing', I've learned to appreciate the dynamism of change in a modern society.

I grew up as a landowner's son. But, I don't think I ever realized the proper interrelationship between the landowner and those who worked on a farm until I heard Dylan's record, 'I Ain't Gonna Work on Maggie's Farm No More'. So I come here speaking to you today about your subject with a base for my information founded on Reinhold Niebuhr and Bob Dylan.

One of the things that Niebuhr says is that the sad duty of the political system is to establish justice in a sinful world. He goes on to say that there's no way to establish or maintain justice without law; that the laws are constantly changing to stabilize the social equilibrium of the forces and counterforces of a dynamic society, and that the law in its totality is an expression of the structure of government.

Well, as a farmer who has now been in office for three years, I've seen firsthand the inadequacy of my own comprehension of what government ought to do for its people. I've had a constant learning process, sometimes from lawyers, sometimes from practical experience, sometimes from failures and mistakes that have been pointed out to me after they were made.

I had lunch this week with the members of the Judicial Selection Committee, and they were talking about a consent search warrant. I said I didn't know what a consent search warrant was. They said, 'Well, that's when two policemen go to a house. One of them goes to the front door and knocks on it, and the other one runs around to the back door and yells "come in".' I have to admit that as Governor, quite often I search for ways to bring about my own hopes; not quite so stringently testing the law as that, but with a similar motivation.

I would like to talk to you for a few moments about some of the practical aspects of being a governor who is still deeply concerned about the inadequacies of a system of which it is obvious that you're so patently proud.

I have refrained completely from making any judicial appointments on the basis of political support or other factors, and have chosen, in every instance, Superior Court judges, quite often State judges, Appellate Court judges, on the basis of merit analysis by a highly competent, open, qualified group of distinguished Georgians. I'm proud of this.

We've now established in the Georgia Constitution a qualifications commission, which for the first time can hear complaints from average citizens about the performance in office of judges and can investigate those complaints and with the status and the force of the Georgia Constitution behind them can remove a judge from office or take other corrective steps.

We've now passed a constitutional amendment, which is waiting for the citizenry to approve, that establishes a uniform Criminal Justice Court System in this state so that the affairs of the judiciary can be more orderly structured, so that work loads can be balanced and so that over a period of time there might be an additional factor of equity, which quite often does not exist now because of the wide disparity among the different courts of Georgia.

We passed this year a judge sentencing bill for noncapital cases with a review procedure. I've had presented to me, by members of the Pardons and Paroles Board, an analysis of some of the sentences given to people by the Superior Court judges of this state, which grieved me deeply and shocked me as a layman. I believe that over a period of time, the fact that a group of other judges can review and comment on the sentences meted out in the different portions of Georgia will bring some more equity to the system.

We have finally eliminated the unsworn statement law in Georgia – the last state to do it.

This year, we analysed in depth the structure of the drug penalties in this state. I do believe in the future there will be a clear understanding of the seriousness of different crimes relating to drugs. We've finally been able to get through the legislature a law that removes alcoholism or drunkenness as a criminal offence. When this law goes into effect next year, I think it will create a new sense of compassion and concern and justice for the roughly 150,000 alcoholics in Georgia, many of whom escape the consequences of what has been a crime because of some social or economic prominence, and will remove a very heavy load from the criminal justice system.

In our prisons, which in the past have been a disgrace to Georgia, we've tried to make substantive changes in the quality of those who administer them and to put a new realm of understanding and hope and compassion into the administration of that portion of the system of justice. Ninety-five per cent of those who are presently incarcerated in prisons will be returned to be our neighbours. And now the thrust of the entire programme, as initiated under Ellis MacDougall and now continued under Dr Ault, is to try to discern in the soul of each convicted and sentenced person redeeming features that can be enhanced. We plan a career for that person to be pursued while he is in prison. I believe that the early data that we have on recidivism rates indicates the efficacy of what we've done.

The GBI, which was formerly a matter of great concern to all those who were interested in law enforcement, has now been substantially changed – for the better. I would put it up now in quality against the FBI, the Secret Service or any other crime control organization in this nation.

Well, does that mean that everything is all right?

It doesn't to me.

I don't know exactly how to say this, but I was thinking just a few moments ago about some of the things that are of deep concern to me as Governor. As a scientist, I was working constantly, along with almost everyone who professes that dedication of life, to probe, probe every day of my life for constant change for the better. It's completely anachronistic in the make-up of a nuclear physicist or an engineer or scientist to be satisfied with what we've got, or to rest on the laurels of past accomplishments. It's the nature of the profession.

As a farmer, the same motivation persists. Every farmer that I know of, who is worth his salt or who's just average, is ahead of the experiment stations and the research agronomist in finding better ways, changing ways to plant, cultivate, utilize herbicides, gather, cure, sell farm products. The competition for innovation is tremendous, equivalent to the realm of nuclear physics even.

In my opinion, it's different in the case of lawyers. And maybe this is a circumstance that is so inherently true that it can't be changed.

I'm a Sunday-school teacher, and I've always known that the structure of law is founded on the Christian ethic that you shall love the Lord your God and your neighbour as yourself – a very high and perfect standard. We all know the fallibility of man, and the contentions in society, as described by Reinhold Niebuhr and many others, don't permit us to achieve perfection. We do strive for equality, but not with a fervent and daily commitment. In general, the powerful and the influential in our society shape the laws and have a great influence on the legislature or the Congress. This creates a reluctance to change because the powerful and the influential have carved out for themselves or have inherited a privileged position in society, of wealth or social prominence or higher education or opportunity for the future. Quite often, those circumstances are circumvented at a very early age because college students, particularly undergraduates, don't have any commitment to the preservation of the way things are. But later, as their interrelationship with the present circumstances grows, they also become committed to approaching change very, very slowly and very, very cautiously, and there's a commitment to the *status quo*.

I remember when I was a child, I lived on a farm about three miles from Plains, and we didn't have electricity or running water. We lived on the railroad – Seaboard Coastline railroad. Like all farm boys I had a flip, a sling shot. They had stabilized the railroad bed with little white round rocks, which I used for ammunition. I would go out frequently to the railroad and gather the most perfectly shaped rocks of proper size. I always had a few in my pockets, and I had others cached away around the farm, so that they would be convenient if I ran out of my pocket supply.

One day I was leaving the railroad track with my pockets full of rocks and hands full of rocks, and my mother came out on the front porch – this is not a very interesting story but it illustrates a point – and she had in her hands a plate full of cookies that she had just baked for me. She called me, I am sure with love in her heart, and said, 'Jimmy, I've baked some cookies for you.' I remember very distinctly walking up to her and standing there for fifteen or twenty seconds, in honest doubt about whether I should drop those rocks which were worthless and take the cookies that my mother had prepared for me, which between her and me were very valuable.

Quite often, we have the same inclination in our everyday lives. We don't recognize that change can sometimes be very beneficial, although we fear it. Anyone who lives in the South looks back on the last fifteen to twenty years with some degree of embarrassment, including myself. To think about going back to a county unit system, which deliberately cheated for generations certain white voters of this state, is almost inconceivable. To revert back or to forgo the one man, one vote principle, we would now consider to be a horrible violation of the basic principles of justice and equality and fairness and equity.

The first speech I ever made in the Georgia Senate, representing the most conservative district in Georgia, was concerning the abolition of thirty questions that we had so proudly evolved as a subterfuge to keep black citizens from voting and which we used with a great deal of smirking and pride for decades or generations ever since the War between the States – questions that nobody could answer in this room, but which were applied to every black citizen that came to the Sumter County Courthouse or Webster County Courthouse and said, 'I want to vote.' I spoke in that chamber, fearful of the news media reporting it back home, but overwhelmed with a commitment to the abolition of that artificial barrier to the rights of an American citizen. I remember the thing that I used in my speech, that a black pencil salesman on the outer door of the Sumter County Courthouse could make a better judgement about who ought to be sheriff than two highly educated professors at Georgia Southwestern College.

Dr Martin Luther King Jr, who was perhaps despised by many in this room because he shook up our social structure that benefited us, and demanded simply that black citizens be treated the same as white citizens, wasn't greeted with approbation and accolades by the Georgia Bar Association or the Alabama Bar Association. He was greeted with horror. Still, once that change was made, a very simple but difficult change, no one in his right mind would want to go back to circumstances prior to that juncture in the development of our nation's society.

I don't want to go on and on, I'm part of it. But, the point I want to make to you is that we still have a long way to go. In every age or every year, we have a tendency to believe that we've come so far now, that there's no way to improve the present system. I'm sure when the Wright Brothers flew at Kitty Hawk, they felt that was the ultimate in transportation. When the first atomic bomb was exploded, that was the ultimate development in nuclear physics, and so forth.

Well, we haven't reached the ultimate. But who's going to search the heart and the soul of an organization like yours or a law school or state or nation and say, 'What can we still do to restore equity and justice or to preserve it or to enhance it in this society?'

You know, I'm not afraid to make the change. I don't have anything to lose. But, as a farmer I'm not qualified to assess the characteristics of the ninety-one hundred inmates in the Georgia prisons, fifty per cent of whom ought not to be there. They ought to be on probation or under some other supervision and assess what the results of previous court rulings might bring to bear on their lives.

I was in the Governor's Mansion for two years, enjoying the services of a very fine cook, who was a prisoner – a woman. One day she came to me, after she got over her two years of timidity, and said, 'Governor, I would like to borrow $250.00 from you.'

I said, 'I'm not sure that a lawyer would be worth that much.'

She said, 'I don't want to hire a lawyer, I want to pay the judge.'

I thought it was a ridiculous statement for her; I felt that she was ignorant. But I found out she wasn't. She had been sentenced by a Superior Court judge in the state, who still serves, to seven years or $750. She had raised, early in her prison career, $500. I didn't lend her the money, but I had Bill Harper, my legal aide, look into it. He found the circumstances were true. She was quickly released under a recent court ruling that had come down in the last few years.

I was down on the coast this weekend. I was approached by a woman who asked me to come by her home. I went by, and she showed me documents that indicated that her illiterate mother, who had a son in jail, had gone to the County Surveyor in that region and had borrowed $225 to get her son out of jail. She had a letter from the Justice of the Peace that showed that her mother had made a mark on the blank sheet of paper. They paid off the $225, and she has the receipts to show it. Then they started a five-year programme trying to get back the paper she signed, without success. They went to court. The lawyer that had originally advised her to sign the paper showed up as the attorney for the surveyor. She had put up fifty acres of land near the county seat as security. When she got to court she found that instead of signing a security deed, she had signed a warranty deed. That case has already been appealed to the Supreme Court, and she lost.

Well, I know that the technicalities of the law that would permit that are probably justifiable. She didn't have a good lawyer. My heart feels and cries out that something ought to be analysed, not just about the structure of government, judicial qualification councils and judicial appointment committees and eliminating the unsworn statement – those things are important. But they don't reach the crux of the point – that now we assign punishment to fit the criminal and not the crime.

You can go in the prisons of Georgia, and I don't know, it may be that poor people are the only ones who commit crimes, but I do know they are the only ones who serve prison sentences. When Ellis Mac-Dougall first went to Reidsville, he found people that had been in solitary confinement for ten years. We now have 500 misdemeanants in the Georgia prison system.

Well, I don't know the theory of law, but there is one other point I want to make, just for your own consideration. I think we've made great progress in the Pardons and Paroles Board since I've been in office and since we've reorganized the government. We have five very enlightened people there now. And on occasion they go out to the prison system to interview the inmates, to decide whether or not they are worthy to be released after they serve one-third of their sentence. I think most jurors and most judges feel that, when they give the sentence, they know that after a third of the sentence has gone by, they will be eligible for careful consideration. Just think for a moment about your own son or your own father or your own daughter being in prison, having served seven years of a lifetime term and being considered for a release. Don't you think that they ought to be examined and that the Pardons and Paroles Board ought to look them in the eye and ask them a question and if they are turned down, ought to give them some substantive reason why they are not released and what they can do to correct their defect?

I do.

I think it's just as important at their time for consideration of early release as it is even when they are sentenced. But, I don't know how to bring about that change.

We had an ethics bill in the state legislature this year. Half of it passed – to require an accounting for contributions during a campaign – but the part that applied to people after the campaign failed. We couldn't get through a requirement for revelation of payments or gifts to office-holders after they are in office.

The largest force against that ethics bill was the lawyers.

Some of you here tried to help get a consumer protection package passed without success.

The regulatory agencies in Washington are made up, not of people to regulate industries, but of representatives of the industries that are regulated. Is that fair and right and equitable? I don't think so.

I'm only going to serve four years as governor, as you know. I think that's enough. I enjoy it, but I think I've done all I can in the Governor's office. I see the lobbyists in the State Capitol filling the halls on occasions. Good people, competent people, the most pleasant, personable, extroverted citizens of Georgia. Those are the characteristics that are required for a lobbyist. They represent good folks. But I tell you that when a lobbyist goes to represent the Peanut Warehousemen's Association of the Southeast, which I belong to, which I helped to organize, they go there to represent the peanut warehouseman. They don't go there to represent the customers of the peanut warehouseman.

When the State Chamber of Commerce lobbyists go there, they go there to represent the businessman of Georgia. They don't go there to represent the customers of the businessman of Georgia.

When your own organization is interested in some legislation there in the Capitol, they're interested in the welfare or prerogatives or authority of the lawyers. They are not there to represent in any sort of exclusive way the client of the lawyers.

The American Medical Association and its Georgia equivalent – they represent the doctors, who are fine people. But they certainly don't represent the patients of a doctor.

As an elected governor, I feel that responsibility; but I also know that my qualifications are slight compared to the doctors or the lawyers or the teachers, to determine what's best for the client or the patient or the school child.

This bothers me; and I know that if there was a commitment on the part of the cumulative group of attorneys in this State, to search with a degree of commitment and fervency, to eliminate many of the inequities that I've just described that I thought of this morning, our state could be transformed in the attitude of its people towards the government.

Senator Kennedy described the malaise that exists in this nation, and it does.

In closing, I'd like to just illustrate the point by something that came to mind this morning when I was talking to Senator Kennedy about his trip to Russia.

When I was about twelve years old, I liked to read, and I had a school principal, named Miss Julia Coleman, Judge Marshall knows her. She forced me pretty much to read, read, read, classical books. She would give me a gold star when I read ten and a silver star when I read five.

One day, she called me in and she said, 'Jimmy, I think it's time for you to read *War and Peace*.' I was completely relieved because I thought it was a book about cowboys and Indians.

Well, I went to the library and checked it out, and it was 1415 pages thick, I think, written by Tolstoy, as you know, about Napoleon's entry into Russia in the 1812–1815 era. He had never been defeated and he was sure he could win, but he underestimated the severity of the Russian winter and the peasants' love for their land.

To make a long story short, the next spring he retreated in defeat. The course of history was changed; it probably affected our own lives.

The point of the book is, and what Tolstoy points out in the epilogue is, that he didn't write the book about Napoleon or the Czar of Russia or even the generals, except in a rare occasion. He wrote it about the students and the housewives and the barbers and the farmers and the privates in the army. And the point of the book is that the course of human events, even the greatest historical events, is not determined by the leaders of a nation or a state, like presidents or governors or senators. They are controlled by the combined wisdom and courage and commitment and discernment and unselfishness and compassion and love and idealism of the common ordinary people. If that was true in the case of Russia where they had a czar or France where they had an emperor, how much more true is it in our own case where the Constitution charges us with a direct responsibility for determining what our government is and ought to be?

Well, I've read parts of the embarrassing transcripts, and I've seen the proud statement of a former attorney general, who protected his boss, and now brags on the fact that he tiptoed through a mine field and came out 'clean'. I can't imagine somebody like Thomas Jefferson tiptoeing through a mine field on the technicalities of the law, and then bragging about being clean afterwards.

I think our people demand more than that. I believe that everyone in this room who is in a position of responsibility as a preserver of the law in its purest form ought to remember the oath that Thomas Jefferson and others took when they practically signed their own death warrant, writing the Declaration of Independence – to preserve justice and equity and freedom and fairness, they pledged their lives, their fortunes and their sacred honour.

Thank you very much.

THE BANSHEE SCREAMS FOR BUFFALO MEAT

Requiem for a Crazed Heavyweight . . . An Unfinished Memoir on the Life and Doom of Oscar Zeta Acosta, First & Last of the Savage Brown Buffalos . . . He Crawled with Lepers and Lawyers, but He Was Tall on His Own Hind Legs When He Walked at Night with the King . . .

The following memoir by Dr Thompson is the painful result of a nine-week struggle (between the management and the author) regarding the style, tone, length, payment, etc. – but mainly the subject matter of the National Affairs Desk's contribution to this star-crossed tenth anniversary issue . . .

And in at least momentary fairness to the management, we should note that the term 'star-crossed' is Dr Thompson's – as are all other harsh judgements he was finally compelled to submit . . .

'We work in the dark, we do what we can.' Some poet who never met Werner Erhard said that, but so what?

What began as a sort of riptide commentary on 'the meaning of the sixties' soon turned into a wild and hydra-headed screed on truth, vengeance, journalism and the meaning, such as it is, of Jimmy Carter.

But none of these things could be made to fit in the space we had available – so we were finally forced to compromise with the Doc and his people, who had all along favoured a long, dangerous and very costly piece titled: 'The Search for the Brown Buffalo'.

It was Dr Thompson's idea to have *Rolling Stone* finance this open-ended search for one of his friends who disappeared under mean and mysterious circumstances in the late months of 1974, or perhaps the early months of 1975. The Brown Buffalo was the nom de plume of the Chicano attorney from East Los Angeles who gained international notoriety as the brutal and relentless '300-pound Samoan attorney' in Thompson's book, *Fear and Loathing in Las Vegas*.

The Editors

Nobody knows the weirdness I've seen
On the trail of the brown buffalo
Old Black Joe

I walk in the night rain until the dawn of the new day. I have devised the plan, straightened out the philosophy and set up the organization. When I have the one million Brown Buffalos on my side I will present the demands for a new nation to both the US Government and the United Nations ... and then I'll split and write the book. I have no desire to be a politician. I don't want to lead anyone. I have no practical ego. I am not ambitious. I merely want to do what is right. Once in every century there comes a man who is chosen to speak for his people. Moses, Mao and Martin [Luther King Jr] are examples. Who's to say that I am not such a man? In this day and age the man for all seasons needs many voices. Perhaps that is why the gods have sent me into Riverbank, Panama, San Francisco, Alpine and Juarez. Perhaps that is why I've been taught so many trades. Who will deny that I am unique?
Oscar Acosta, *The Autobiography of a Brown Buffalo*

Well ... not me, old sport. Wherever you are and in whatever shape – dead or alive or even *both*, eh? That's one thing they can't take away from you ... Which is lucky, I think, for the rest of us: because (and, yeah – let's face it, Oscar) you were not real light on your feet in this world, and you were too goddamn heavy for most of the boats you jumped into. One of the great regrets of my life is that I was never able to introduce you to my old football buddy, Richard Nixon. The main thing he feared in this life – even worse than queers and Jews and mutants – was people who might run amuk; he called them 'loose cannons on the deck', and he wanted them all put to sleep.

That's one graveyard we never even checked, Oscar, but why not? If your classic 'doomed nigger' style of paranoia had any validity at all, you *must* understand that it was not just Richard Nixon who was out to

524

get you – but all the people who thought like Nixon and all the judges and US attorneys he appointed in those weird years. Were there any of Nixon's friends among all those Superior Court judges you subpoenaed and mocked and humiliated when you were trying to bust the grand jury selection system in LA? How many of those Brown Beret 'body-guards' you called 'brothers' were deep-cover cops or informants? I recall being seriously worried about that when we were working on that story about the killing of Chicano journalist Ruben Salazar by an LA County sheriffs' deputy. How many of those bomb-throwing, trigger-happy freaks who slept on mattresses in your apartment were talking to the sheriff on a chili-hall pay phone every morning? Or maybe to the judges who kept jailing you for contempt of court, when they didn't have anything else?

Yeah, and so much for the 'paranoid sixties'. It's time to end this bent seance – or *almost* closing time, anyway – but before we get back to raw facts and rude lawyer's humour, I want to make sure that at least one record will show that I tried and totally failed, for at least five years, to convince my allegedly erstwhile Samoan attorney, Oscar Zeta Acosta, that *there was no such thing as paranoia* : at least not in the cultural and political war zone called East LA in the late 1960s and especially not for an aggressively radical Chicano lawyer who thought he could stay up all night, *every* night, eating acid and throwing Molotov cock-tails with the same people he was going to have to represent in a downtown courtroom the next morning.

There were times – all too often, I felt – when Oscar would show up in front of the courthouse at nine in the morning with a stench of fresh gasoline on his hands and a green crust of charred soap-flakes on the toes of his $300 snakeskin cowboy boots. He would pause outside the courtroom just long enough to give the TV press five minutes of crazed rhetoric for the evening news, then he would shepherd his equally crazed 'clients' into the courtroom for their daily war-circus with the Judge. When you get into bear baiting on that level, paranoia is just another word for ignorance ... They really *are* out to get you.

The odds on his being dragged off to jail for 'contempt' were about fifty-fifty on any given day – which meant he was always in danger of being seized and booked with a pocket full of 'bennies' or 'black beauties' at the property desk. After several narrow escapes he decided that it was necessary to work in the courtroom as part of a three-man 'defence team'.

One of his 'associates' was usually a well-dressed, well-mannered young Chicano whose only job was to cary at least 100 milligrams of pure speed at all times and feed Oscar whenever he signalled; the other was not so well-dressed or mannered; his job was to stay alert and be one step ahead of the bailiffs when they made a move on Oscar – at which point he would reach out and grab any pills, powders, shivs or other evidence he was handed, then sprint like a human bazooka for the nearest exit.

This strategy worked so well for almost two years that Oscar and his people finally got careless. They had survived another long day in court – on felony arson charges, this time, for trying to burn down the Biltmore Hotel during a speech by then Governor Ronald Reagan – and they were driving back home to Oscar's headquarters pad in the *barrio* (and maybe running sixty or sixty-five in a fifty mph speed zone, Oscar later admitted) when they were suddenly jammed to a stop by two LAPD cruisers. 'They acted like we'd just robbed a bank,' said Frank, looking right down the barrel of a shotgun. 'They made us all lie face down on the street and then they searched the car, and—'

Yes. That's when they found the drugs: twenty or thirty white pills that the police quickly identified as 'illegal amphetamine tablets, belonging to Attorney Oscar Acosta'.

The fat spic for all seasons was jailed once again, this time on what the press called a 'high speed drug bust'. Oscar called a press conference in jail and accused the cops of 'planting' him – but not even his bodyguards believed him until long after the attendant publicity had done them all so much damage that the whole 'Brown Power Movement' was effectively stalled, splintered and discredited by the time *all* charges, both arson and drugs, were either dropped or reduced to small print on the back of the blotter.

I am not even sure, myself, how the cases were finally disposed of. Not long after the 'high speed drug bust', as I recall, two of his friends were charged with murder one for allegedly killing a smack dealer in the *barrio*, and I think Oscar finally copped on the drug charge and pleaded guilty to something like 'possession of ugly pills in a public place'.

But by that time his deal had already gone down. None of the respectable Chicano pols in East LA had ever liked him anyway, and that 'high speed drug bust' was all they needed to publicly denounce everything Left of *huevos rancheros* and start calling themselves Mexican-American again. The trial of the Biltmore Five was no longer a do-or-die cause for *la raza*, but a shameful crime that a handful of radical dope fiends had brought down on the whole community. The mood on Whittier Boulevard turned sour overnight, and the sight of a Brown Beret was suddenly as rare as a cash-client for Oscar Zeta Acosta – the ex-Chicano lawyer.

The entire ex-Chicano political community went as public as possible to make sure that the rest of the city understood that they had known all along that this dope addict *rata* who had somehow been one of their most articulate and certainly their most radical, popular and politically aggressive spokesman for almost two years was really just a self-seeking publicity dope freak who couldn't even run a bar tab at the Silver Dollar Café, much less rally friends or a following. There was no mention in the Mexican-American press about Acosta's surprisingly popular campaign for sheriff of LA County a year earlier, which had made him a minor hero among politically hip Chicanos all over the city.

No more of that dilly-dong bullshit on Whittier Boulevard. Oscar's drug bust was still alive on the evening news when he was evicted from his apartment on three days' notice and his car was either stolen or towed away from its customary parking place on the street in front of his driveway. His offer to defend his two friends on what he later assured me were absolutely valid charges of first degree murder were publicly rejected. Not even for free, they said. A dope-addled clown was worse than no lawyer at all.

It was dumb gunsel thinking, but Oscar was in no mood to offer his help more than once. So he beat a strategic retreat to Mazatlán, which he called his 'other home', to lick his wounds and start writing the great Chicano novel. It was the end of an era! The fireball Chicano lawyer was on his way to becoming a half-successful writer, a cult figure of sorts – then a fugitive, a freak, and finally either a permanently missing person or an undiscovered corpse.

Oscar's fate is still a mystery, but every time his case seems to be finally closed, something happens to bring him back to life . . . And one of them just happened again, but it came in a blizzard of chaos that caused a serious time warp in my thinking: my nerves are still too jangled for the moment to do anything but lay back and let it blow over.

The Flash Man Cometh . . . Queer News from Coconut Grove . . . Murder, Madness & The Battle of Biscayne Bay . . . The Death of a Cigarette Boat & A $48,000 Misunderstanding . . . *Res Ipsa Loquitur* . . .

A screech owl the size of a chow killed two of my peacocks on the front porch. The county attorney called the cops on me for interfering with the work of a labour crew painting yellow stripes on the Woody Creek Road. The antique winch-powered crossbow that Steadman sent over from England was seized and destroyed by sheriff's deputies and a man named Drake from Miami spent all afternoon at the Hotel Jerome, demanding my phone number from the bartenders because he claimed to have a bizarre message for me.

Then Sandy came back from the store with the mail and the latest issue of *Newsweek*, the one with the photo of Caroline Kennedy rolling Jann through the door of Elaine's on that custom-built, cut-glass dolly from Neiman-Marcus. Sandy didn't even recognize him at first; she thought it was a photo of Caroline and Bella Abzug on the campaign trail.

We went out on the porch, where there was plenty of light, to get a better look at the photos – but the sun made me blind for a moment, and just then Tom Benton came howling into the driveway on his 880 Husquavarna, and when he saw that story in *Newsweek* (you know Tom, with that fine artist's eye that he has), he said, 'Well I'll be fucked, that's Jann! And look at the wonderful *smile* on him. Wow! And look what he's done to his *hair* ... and those *teeth*. No wonder he moved to New York.'

Benton was taking off his leathers as he talked. He'd been riding up on the logging roads in the high pastures behind his house, looking for a rogue bear that tore the top off his jeep and killed his mule last week.

'I just want to hit him with this Taser, then chain him to a tree until we can go up and get him.'

'Get him?'

He nodded. 'It's that grizzly pup that Noonan turned loose before he left town. He's about a year and a half old by now, and he's starting to act crazy.'

'Fuck the Taser,' I said. 'It's no good beyond fifteen feet. We'll need the M-79, with CS grenades, then drag him down with a jeep.'

'No,' he said. 'I want to get the bugger in a van, then drive him into town and back the van right up to the side door of that restaurant where all the lawyers eat lunch. They'll love him.'

'Wonderful,' I said. 'Shoot him right into that private dining room where they have those Bar Association luncheons – feed him a whole bucket full of acid and raw meat, then take him into town for the meeting.'

Benton started to laugh, then stopped and reached into one of his pockets and handed me a small envelope. 'Speaking of lawyers,' he said, 'I almost forgot – there's a guy from Miami in town who says he has a message for you, from Oscar.'

I flinched and stepped back. 'What?' I said. 'Who?'

'Yeah,' Benton said. 'Oscar Acosta, the Brown Buffalo.'

He shook his head. 'This guy has a very *very* strange story. It's so strange that I wasn't even sure I should come out here and tell you.'

'I know all those stories,' I said. 'Hell I wrote most of them – and besides, Oscar's dead.'

Tom opened two more beers and handed me one.

'Not according to this guy Drake,' he said quietly. 'He says Oscar almost got killed about two months ago in Florida. They took a midnight ride out to Bimini in Drake's boat, and on the way back they got ambushed at sea and a friend of Oscar's got killed – and Drake's $48,000 cigarette boat was a total wreck; he says it was so full of bullet holes that they almost sunk in midocean.'

'Bullshit,' I said. 'That's impossible.'

He shrugged. 'Well, that's what Solheim said. But he talked to Drake for a long time last night and he says the guy is absolutely positive. He even had a photo.' I suddenly remembered the envelope I'd been holding. 'Let's see what this is,' I said, tearing off the end. Inside was a paperback book cover, folded lengthwise – the cover of Oscar's *Autobiography of a Brown Buffalo*, with a picture of the author on the front and a message scrawled on the blank side. 'Dear Thompson,' it said. 'Please call me as soon as you can. Very urgent. Acosta might be in bad trouble. HEAT! Not much time. Call me in no. 353 Hotel Jerome. Thanks. Drake.'

'Jesus,' I muttered. 'Why the hell does he want to talk to *me*?'

'He's looking for Oscar,' Benton replied. 'And so is the Coast Guard – and the DEA and the FBI and half the cops in Miami.'

'So what?' I said. 'He's been dead for two years.'

Tom shook his head. 'No, Drake says he's still working in and out of Florida, running a *lot* of white powder.'

'I doubt it,' I said.

'Well Drake doesn't,' he replied, 'and he's about to turn him over, unless Oscar pays for his boat. He wants forty grand and he says he knows Oscar has the money.'

'Balls,' I said. 'We should have this bastard locked up for blackmail.'

He shrugged again. 'Hang on. You haven't heard the rest of it. Drake's talking about *murder*, not drugs.'

'Murder?'

'Yeah. Drake says the Coast Guard came up with *three* bodies after that ambush, and two of them didn't have heads. Oscar ran that cigarette boat right over the top of a Boston whaler with at least two guy in it.'

I stared at him for a moment, then went over to the couch and sat down. 'Jesus Christ!' I said. 'Let's go back and run the whole story again. I must have missed something.'

＊

You are better lost than found.
Clement Robinson

Which was true. The story I got from Benton was from Mike Solheim, who got it in spades from a total stranger who said his name was Drake and who showed up in Aspen one afternoon, looking for me because he thought I could put him in touch with Oscar Acosta – a 'dead man' who somehow showed up at Drake's home in Coconut Grove one night last summer and offered $5000 in cash for a midnight ride out to Bimini and back in Drake's new $48,000 ocean racer, with no questions asked.

It was not the kind of business proposition that a veteran dope smuggler like Drake would have been likely to misunderstand. There are only two possible reasons for even *owning* a thirty-five-foot-long bullet-shaped fibreglass hull with *two* 370 horsepower engines on the back: one is to win races in the open sea at speeds up to 90.555 miles an hour (the current world record, set by the 'World Champion Cigarette Racing Team' in 1976) and the other has to do with the virtually priceless peace of mind that comes with doing business in a boat that will outrun anything the US Coast Guard can put in the water.

So there was no need for Drake to ask *why* these two cash-heavy Mexicans needed his boat, or even why one of them came aboard with a Uzi submachine gun. He had made this run before, and even on moonless nights he felt he knew every bump in the water, even at sixty miles an hour.

But he was not ready for what happened on the way back from Bimini *this* time: They were almost home, slowing down to half-speed or less about a mile off the south tip of Key Biscayne, when he was suddenly blinded by spotlights coming into his face from the front and both sides and the whole night erupted with gunfire. The Mexican with the Uzi was dead on his feet before Drake even heard the first shots; the Uzi bounced into the water and the Mexican sat down in the cockpit with at least ten big holes in his chest. Drake felt his boat shuddering in the water as the hull started coming apart in the crossfire. 'We're surrounded!' he screamed. 'They're killing us!' Then he fell down and tried to hide himself under the dead man just as Oscar got his hands on both the wheel and the throttle at the same time. The big speedboat lunged forwards with a roar and the next thing Drake felt was an airborne jolt as his boat ran straight over the top of a twenty-foot Boston whaler . . . and suddenly there was no more shooting as he felt the boat moving towards Miami at sixty miles an hour with the cockpit six inches deep in blood-coloured water and Oscar screaming in Spanish as they started coming up, too fast, on the lights of Dinner Key.

Drake stood up and took the wheel. The boat felt like it was coming apart in his hands as he aimed for a clump of trees on the dark end of the marina. By the time he felt the jolt of a sandbar under his feet, Oscar was already going over the side with the small suitcase they had picked up in Bimini, and that was the last time Drake saw him.

The boat stayed miraculously afloat long enough for him to hump the dead man and dump his $48,000 wreck about a half-mile down the beach in a place where he could drive it up under some branches and watch it sink out of sight in five feet of dark water. Drake covered the hulk as well as he could, then slogged out to Biscayne Boulevard and hitchhiked back to Coconut Grove where he spent the next forty-eight hours locked in his bedroom and trembling with a fear worse than anything he'd ever felt in his life.

This wild and puzzling story out of Coconut Grove was only the latest of a dozen or so 'Brown Buffalo sightings' in the past two years. Everybody who knew him as even a casual friend has heard stories about Oscar's 'secret life' and his high-speed criminal adventures all over the world. Ever since his alleged death/disappearance in 1973, 74 or even 1975, he's turned up all over the world – selling guns in Addis Ababa, buying orphans in Cambodia, smoking weed with Henry Kissinger in Acapulco, hanging around the airport bar in Lima with two or three overstuffed Pan Am flight bags on both shoulders or hunched impatiently on the steering wheel of a silver 450 Mercedes in the 'nothing to declare' lane on the Mexican side of US Customs checkpoint between San Diego and Tijuana.

There are not many gypsies on file at the Missing Persons Bureau – and if Oscar was not quite the classic gypsy, in his own eyes or mine, it was only because he was never able to cut that high-tension cord that kept him forever attached to his childhood home and hatchery. By the time he was twenty years old, Oscar was working overtime eight days a week at learning to live and even think like a gypsy, but he never quite jumped the gap.

Although I was born in El Paso, Texas, I am actually a small town kid. A hick from the sticks, a Mexican boy from the other side of the tracks. I grew up in Riverbank, California; Post Office Box 303; population 3969. It's the only town in the entire state whose essential numbers have remained unchanged. The sign that welcomes you as you round the curve coming in from Modesto says THE CITY OF ACTION.

We lived in a two-room shack without a floor. We had to pump our water and use kerosene if we wanted to read at night. But we never went hungry. My old man always bought the pinto beans and the white flour for the tortillas in one-hundred-pound sacks which my mother used to make dresses, sheets and curtains. We had two acres of land

531

which we planted every year with corn, tomatoes and yellow chiles for the hot sauce. Even before my father woke us, my old ma was busy at work making the tortillas at five a.m. while he chopped the logs we'd hauled up from the river at the weekends.

Riverbank is divided into three parts, and in my corner of the world there were only three kinds of people: Mexicans, Okies and Americans. Catholics, Holy Rollers and Protestants. Peach pickers, cannery workers and clerks.

We lived on the West Side, within smelling distance of the world's largest tomato paste cannery.

The West Side is still enclosed by the Santa Fé Railroad tracks to the east, the Modesto-Oakdale Highway to the north and the irrigation canal to the south. Within that concentration only Mexicans were safe from the neighbourhood dogs, who responded only to Spanish commands. Except for Bob Whitt and Emitt Brown, both friends of mine who could cuss in better Spanish than I, I never saw a white person walking the dirt roads of our neighbourhood.

Oscar Acosta, *The Autobiography of a Brown Buffalo*, 1972

The Lawn of Fire and Another Icepick for Richard Nixon for Old Times' Sake ... Slow Fadeout for Brown Power & a Salute to Crazy Ed ... Poison Fat Goes to Mazatlán; Libel Lawyers Go to the Mattresses ... Fear of the Plastic Fork & a Twisted Compromise ...

Oscar Zeta Acosta – despite any claims to the contrary – was a dangerous thug who lived every day of his life as a stalking monument to the notion that a man with a greed for the truth should expect no mercy and give none ...

... and that was the difference between Oscar and a lot of the merciless geeks he liked to tell strangers he admired: class acts like Benito Mussolini and Fatty Arbuckle.

When the great scorer comes to write against Oscar's name, one of the first few lines in the ledger will note that he usually lacked the courage of his consistently monstrous convictions. There was more mercy, madness, dignity and generosity in that overweight, overworked and always overindulged brown cannonball of a body than most of us will meet in any human package even three times Oscar's size for the rest of our lives – which are all running noticeably leaner on the high side, since that rotten fat spic disappeared.

He was a drug-addled brute and a genuinely fiendish adversary in court or on the street – but it was none of *these* things that finally pressured him into death or a disappearance so finely plotted that it amounts to the same thing.

What finally cracked the Brown Buffalo was the bridge he refused to build between the self-serving elegance of his instincts and the self-destructive carnival of his reality. He was a Baptist missionary at a leper colony in Panama before he was a lawyer in Oakland and East LA, or a radical-chic author in San Francisco and Beverly Hills ... But whenever things got tense or when he had to work close to the bone, he was always a missionary. And that was the governing instinct that ruined him for anything else. He was a preacher in the courtroom, a preacher at the typewriter and a flat-out awesome preacher when he cranked his head full of acid.

That's LSD-25, folks – a certified 'dangerous drug' that is no longer fashionable, due to reasons of extreme and unnatural heaviness. The CIA was right about acid: Some of their best and brightest operatives went over the side in the name of top secret research on a drug that was finally abandoned as a far too dangerous and unmanageable thing to be used as a public weapon. Not even the sacred minnock of 'national security' could justify the hazards of playing with a thing too small to be seen and too big to control. The professional spook mentality was far more comfortable with things like nerve gas and neutron bombs.

But not the Brown Buffalo – he ate LSD-25 with a relish that bordered on worship. When his brain felt bogged down in the mundane nuts and bolts horror of the law or some dead-end manuscript, he would simply take off in his hotrod Mustang for a week on the road and a few days of what he called 'walking with the king'. Oscar used acid like other lawyers use valium – a distinctly unprofessional and occasionally nasty habit that shocked even the most liberal of his colleagues and frequently panicked his clients.

I was with him one night in LA, when he decided that the only way to meaningfully communicate with a judge who'd been leaning on him in the courtroom was to drive out to the man's home in Santa Monica and set his whole front lawn on fire after soaking it down with ten gallons of gasoline ... and then, instead of fleeing into the night like some common lunatic vandal, Oscar stood in the street and howled through the flames at a face peering out from a shattered upstairs window, delivering one of his Billy Sunday style sermons on morality and justice.

The nut of his flame-enraged text, as I recall, was the mind-bending chunk of eternal damnation from Luke xi, 46 – a direct quote from Jesus Christ:

'And he said, Woe unto you also, ye lawyers, for ye lade men with burdens grievous to be borne, and ye yourselves touch not the burdens with one of your fingers.'

The lawn of fire was Oscar's answer to the Ku Klux Klan's burning cross, and he derived the same demonic satisfaction from doing it.

'Did you see his face?' he shouted as we screeched off at top speed towards Hollywood. 'That corrupt old fool! I *know* he recognized me but he'll never admit it! No officer of the court would set a judge's front yard on fire – the whole system would break down if lawyers could get away with crazy shit like this.'

I agreed. It is not my wont to disagree with even a criminally insane attorney on questions of basic law. But in truth it never occurred to me that Oscar was either insane or a criminal, given the generally fascist, Nixonian context of those angry years.

In an era when the Vice-President of the United States held court in Washington to accept payoffs from his former vassals in the form of big wads of one hundred dollar bills – and when the President himself routinely held secretly tape-recorded meetings with his top aides in the Oval Office to plot illegal wiretaps, political burglaries and other gross felonies in the name of a 'silent majority', it was hard to feel anything more than a flash of high, nervous humour at the sight of some acid-bent lawyer setting fire to a judge's front yard at four o'clock in the morning.

I might even be tempted to justify a thing like that – but of course *it would be wrong* ... And my attorney was not a crook and to the best of my knowledge, his mother was just as much 'a saint' as Richard Nixon's.

Indeed. And now – as an almost perfect tribute to every icepick ever wielded in the name of justice – I want to enter into the permanent record, at this point, as a strange but unchallenged fact that Oscar Z. Acosta was never disbarred from the practice of law in the state of California – and ex-President Richard Nixon *was*.

There are *some* things, apparently, that not even lawyers will tolerate; and in a naturally unjust world where the image of 'justice' is honoured for being blind, even a blind pig will find an acorn once in a while.

Or maybe not – because Oscar was eventually hurt far worse by professional ostracism than Nixon was hurt by disbarment. The great banshee screamed for them both at almost the same time – for entirely different reasons, but with ominously similar results.

Except that Richard Nixon got rich from his crimes, and Oscar Acosta got killed. The wheels of justice grind small and queer in this life and if they seem occasionally unbalanced or even stupid and capricious in their grinding, my own midnight guess is that they were probably fixed from the start. And any judge who can safely slide into full pension retirement without having to look back on anything worse in the way of criminal vengeance than a few scorched lawns is a man who got off easy.

There is, after all, considerable work and risk – and even a certain art – to the torching of a half-acre lawn without also destroying the house or exploding every car in the driveway. It would be a lot easier to simply make a funeral pyre of the whole place and leave the law for dilettantes.

That's how Oscar viewed arson – anything worth doing is worth doing well – and I'd watched enough of his fiery work to know he was right. If he was a king-hell pyromaniac, he was also a gut politician and occasionally a very skilled artist in the style and tone of his torchings.

Like most lawyers with an IQ higher than sixty, Oscar learned one definition of justice in law school, and a very different one in the courtroom. He got his degree at some night school on Post Street in San Francisco, while working as a copy boy for the Hearst *Examiner*. And for a while he was very proud to be a lawyer – for the same reasons he'd felt proud to be a missionary and lead clarinet man in the leper colony band.

But by the time I first met him in the summer of 1967, he was long past what he called his 'puppy love trip with the law'. It had gone the same way of his earlier missionary zeal, and after one year of casework at an East Oakland 'poverty law centre' he was ready to dump Holmes and Brandeis for Huey Newton and a Black Panther style of dealing wth the laws and courts of America.

When he came booming into a bar called Daisy Duck in Aspen and announced that he was the trouble we'd all been waiting for, he was definitely into the politics of confrontation – and on all fronts: in the bars or the courts or even the streets, if necessary.

Oscar was not into serious street-fighting, but he was hell on wheels in a bar brawl. Any combination of a 250-pound Mexican and LSD-25 is a potentially terminal menace for anything it can reach – but when the alleged Mexican is in fact a profoundly angry Chicano lawyer with no fear at all of anything that walks on less than three legs and a *de facto* suicidal conviction that he *will* die at the age of thirty-three – just like Jesus Christ – you have a serious piece of work on your hands. Specially if the bastard is *already* thirty-three and a half years old with a head full of Sandoz acid, a loaded .357 Magnum in his belt, a hatchet-wielding Chicano bodyguard on his elbow at all times, and a disconcerting habit of projectile-vomiting geysers of pure red blood off the front porch every thirty or forty minutes, or whenever his malignant ulcer can't handle any more raw tequila.

This was the Brown Buffalo in the full crazed flower of his prime – a man, indeed, for all seasons. And it was somewhere in the middle of his thirty-third year, in fact, when he came out to Colorado – with his faithful bodyguard, Frank – to rest for a while after his gruelling campaign for Sheriff of Los Angeles County, which he lost by a million or so votes. But in defeat, Oscar had managed to create an instant political base for himself in the vast Chicano *barrio* of East Los Angeles – where even the most conservative of the old-line 'Mexican-Americans' were suddenly calling themselves 'Chicanos' and getting their first taste of tear gas at *la raza* demonstrations, which Oscar was quickly learning to use as a fire and brimstone forum to feature himself as the main spokesman for a mushrooming 'brown power' movement that the LAPD called more dangerous than the Black Panthers.

Which was probably true, at the time – but in retrospect it sounds a bit different than it did back in 1969 when the sheriff was sending out fifteen or twenty helicopter sorties a night to scan the rooftops and backyards of the *barrio* with huge sweeping searchlights that drove Oscar and his people into fits of blind rage every time they got nailed in a pool of blazing white light with a joint in one hand and a machete in the other.

But that is another and very long story – and since I've already written it once ('Strange Rumblings in Aztlan', *RS* 81) and came close to getting my throat slit in the process, I think we'll just ease off and pass on it for right now.

The sad tale of Oscar's fall from grace in the *barrio* is still rife with bad blood and ugly paranoia. He was too stunned to fight back in the time-honoured style of a professional politician. He was also broke, divorced, depressed and so deep in public disgrace in the wake of his 'high speed drug bust' that not even junkies would have him for an attorney.

In a word, he and his dream of 'one million brown buffalos' were *finished* in East LA ... and everywhere else where it counted, for that matter, so Oscar 'took off' once again, and once again with a head full of acid.

But ...

Peacocks Can't Live at This Altitude ... New Home for Ebb Tide, False
Dawn in Atzlán and a Chain of Bull Maggots on the Neck of the Flat
Spic from Riverbank ... May Leeches Crawl on his Soul until the
Rivers Flow Up from the Sea and the Grass Grows Down into Hell ...
Beware of 300-Pound Samoan Attorneys Bearing Gifts of LSD-25

Follow not truth too near the heels, lest it dash out thy teeth.
George Herbert, *Jacula Prudentum*

Well ... it is not an easy thing to sit here and keep a straight face while
even considering the notion that there is any connection at all between
Oscar's sorry fate and his lifelong devotion to defending the truth at all
costs. There are a lot of people still wandering around, especially in
places like San Francisco and East LA, who would like nothing better
than to dash out Oscar's teeth with a ball-peen hammer for all the weird
and costly lies he laid on them at one point or another *in his frenzied
assaults* on the way to his place in the sun. He never denied he was a
lying pig who would use any means to justify his better end. Even his
friends felt the sting. Yet there were times when he took himself as seriously as any other bush league Mao or Moses, and in moments like
these he was capable of rare insights and a naive sort of grace in his
dealings with people that often touched on nobility. At its best, the
Brown Buffalo shuffle was a match for Muhammad Ali's.

After I'd known him for only three days he made me a solemn gift of
a crude wooden idol that I am still not sure he didn't occasionally worship in secret when not in the presence of the dreaded 'white ass
gabancos'. In a paragraph near the end of his autobiography, he describes that strangely touching transfer far better than I can.

'I opened my beat-up suitcase and took out my wooden idol. I had
him wrapped in a bright red and yellow cloth. A San Blas Indian had
given him to me when I left Panama. I called him Ebb Tide. He was
made of hard mahogany. An eighteen-inch god without eyes, without
a mouth and without a sexual organ. Perhaps the sculptor had the
same hang-up about drawing the body from the waist down as I'd had
in Miss Rollins' fourth-grade class. Ebb Tide was my oldest possession. A string of small, yellowed wild pig's fangs hung from its neck.'

Ebb Tide still hangs on a nail just above my living room window. I can
see him from where I sit now, scrawling these goddamn final desperate
lines before my head can explode like a ball of magnesium tossed into
a bucket of water. I have never been sure exactly what kind of luck Ebb

Tide was bringing down on me, over the years – but I've never taken the little bastard down or even thought about it, so he must be paying his way. He is perched just in front of the peacock perch outside, and right now there are two high-blue reptilian heads peering over his narrow wooden shoulders.

Does anybody out there believe that?

No?

Well ... peacocks can't live at this altitude anyway, like Doberman pinschers, sea snakes and gun-toting Chicano missionaries with bad-acid breath.

Why does a hearse horse snicker, hauling a lawyer away?
                                                          Carl Sandburg

Things were not going well in San Francisco or LA at that grim point in Oscar's time, either. To him, it must have seemed like open season on every Brown Buffalo west of the continental divide.

The only place he felt safe was down south on the warm foreign soil of the old country. But when he fled back to Mazatlán this time, it was not just to rest but to brood – and to plot what would be his final crazed leap for the great skyhook.

It would also turn out to be an act of such monumental perversity not even that gentle presence of Ebb Tide could change my sudden and savage decision that the treacherous bastard should have his nuts ripped off with a plastic fork – and then fed like big meat grapes to my peacocks.

The move he made this time was straight out of Jekyll and Hyde – the Brown Buffalo suddenly transmogrified into the form of a rabid hyena. And the bastard compounded his madness by hiding out in the low-rent bowels of Mazatlán like some half-mad leper gone over the brink after yet another debilitating attack of string warts and herpes simplex lesions.

This ugly moment came just as my second book, *Fear and Loathing in Las Vegas*, was only a week or so away from going to press. We were in the countdown stage and there is no way anybody who hasn't been there can understand the tension of having a new book *almost* on the presses, but not quite there. The only thing that stood between me and publication was a last minute assault on the very essence of the story by the publishers' libel lawyers. The book was malignant from start to finish, they said, with grievous libels that were totally indefensible. No publisher in his right mind would risk the nightmare of doomed litigation that a book like this was certain to drag us all into.

Which was true, on one level, but on another it seemed like a harmless joke – because almost every one of the most devastating libels they cited involved my old buddy, O. Z. Acosta; a fellow author, prominent Los Angeles attorney and an officer of many courts. Specifically they advised:

> We have read the above manuscript as requested. Our principal legal objection is to the description of the author's attorney as using and offering for sale dangerous drugs as well as indulging in other criminal acts while under the influence of such drugs. Although this attorney is not named, he is identified with some detail. Consequently, this material should be deleted as libellous.
>
> In addition, we have the following specific comments:
> Page 3: The author's attorney's attempt to break and enter and threats (sic) to bomb a salesman's residence is libellous and should be deleted. Page 4: This page suggests that the author's attorney was driving at an excessive speed while drunk all of which is libellous and should be deleted.
> Page 6: The incident in which the author's attorney advised the author to drive at top speed is libellous and should be deleted. The same applies to the attorney's being party to a fraud at the hotel. Page 31: The statement that the author's attorney will be disbarred is libellous and should be deleted. Page 40: The incident in which the author and his attorney impersonated police officers is libellous and should be deleted. Page 41: The reference to the attorney's ———* being a 'junkie' and shooting people is libellous and should be deleted unless it may be proven true. Page 48: The incident in which the author's attorney offers heroin for sale is libellous and should be deleted.
> We do not advise ——— to allow any material in this manuscript noted above as libellous to remain based upon expectancy of proving that it is true by the author's testimony. Inasmuch as the author admits being under the influence of illegal drugs at most if not all times, proof of truth would be extremely difficult through him.

'Balls,' I told them. 'We'll just have Oscar sign a release. He's no more concerned about this "libel" bullshit than I am.

'And besides, truth is an absolute defence against libel, anyway ... Jesus, you don't understand what kind of a monster we're dealing with. You should read the parts I left out ...'

But the libel wizards were not impressed – especially since we were heaping all this libellous abuse on a fellow attorney. Unless we got a signed release from Oscar, the book would not go to press.

* Deleted at the insistence of *Rolling Stone*'s attorney.

Okay, I said. But let's do it quick. He's down in Mazatlán now. Send the goddamn thing by air express and he'll sign it and ship it right back.

I think we are in Rats Alley where the dead men lost their bones.
T. S. Eliot, *The Waste Land*

Indeed. So they sent the release off at once ... and Oscar refused to sign it – but not for any reason a New York libel lawyer could possibly understand. He was, as I'd said, not concerned at all by the libels. Of course they were all true, he said when I finally reached him by telephone at his room in the Hotel Synaloa.

The only thing that bothered him – bothered him very badly – was the fact that I'd repeatedly described him as a 300-pound Samoan.

'What kind of journalist are you?' he screamed at me. 'Don't you have any respect for the truth? I can sink that whole publishing house for *defaming me*, trying to pass me off as one of those waterhead South Sea mongrels.'

The libel lawyers were stunned into paranoid silence. 'Was it either some kind of arcane legal trick,' they wondered, 'or was this dope-addled freak really crazy enough to insist on having hmself formally identified for all time, with one of the most depraved and degenerate figures in American literature?'

Should his angry threats and demands conceivably be taken seriously? Was it possible that a well-known practising attorney might not only freely admit to all these heinous crimes, but insist that every foul detail be documented as the absolute truth?

'Why not?' Oscar answered. And the only way he'd sign the release, he added, was in exchange for a firm guarantee from the lawyers that both his name and a suitable photograph of himself be prominently displayed on the book's dust cover.

They had never had to cope with a thing like this – a presumably sane attorney who flatly refused to release any other version of his clearly criminal behaviour, except the abysmal naked truth. The concession he was willing to make had to do with his identity throughout the entire book as a '300-pound Samoan'. But he could grit his teeth and tolerate that, he said, only because he understood that there was no way to make that many changes at that stage of the deadline without tearing up half the book. In exchange, however, he wanted a formal letter guaranteeing that he would be properly identified on the book jacket.

The lawyers would have no part of it. There was no precedent anywhere in the law for a bizarre situation like this ... but as the deadline pressures mounted and Oscar refused to bend, it became more and more obvious that the only choice except compromise was to scuttle the book entirely ... and if *that* happened, I warned them, I had enough plastic forks to mutilate every libel lawyer in New York.

That seemed to settle the issue in favour of a last-minute compromise, and *Fear and Loathing in Las Vegas* was finally sent to the printer with Oscar clearly identified on the back as the certified living model for the monstrous '300-pound Samoan attorney' who would soon be a far more public figure than any of us would have guessed at the time.

Alcohol, hashish, prussic acid, strychnine are weak dilutions. The surest poison is time.

Emerson, *Society and Solitude*

The libel lawyers have never understood what Oscar had in mind – and, at the time, I didn't understand it myself – one of the darker skills involved in the kind of journalism I normally get involved with has to do with ability to write the truth about 'criminals' without getting them busted – and, in the eyes of the law, *any* person committing a crime is criminal: whether it's a Hell's Angel laying an oil slick, on a freeway exit to send a pursuing motorcycle cop crashing over the high side, a presidential candidate smoking a joint in his hotel room, or a good friend who happens to be a lawyer, an arsonist and a serious drug abuser.

The line between writing truth and providing evidence is very, very thin – but for a journalist working constantly among highly paranoid criminals, it is also the line between trust and suspicion. And that is the difference between having free access to the truth and being treated like a spy. There is no such thing as 'forgiveness' on that level; one fuck-up will send you straight back to sportswriting – if you're lucky.

In Oscar's case, my only reason for describing him in the book as a 300-pound Samoan instead of a 250-pound Chicano lawyer was to protect him from the wrath of the LA cops and the whole California legal establishment he was constantly at war with. It would not serve either one of our interests, I felt, for Oscar to get busted or disbarred because of something I wrote about him. I had my reputation to protect.

The libel lawyers understood that much; what worried them was that I hadn't protected 'my attorney' well enough to protect also the book publisher from a libel suit – just in case my attorney was as crazy as he appeared to be in the manuscript they'd just vetoed ... or maybe he was crazy like a fox, they hinted; he was, after all, an *attorney* – who'd presumably worked just as hard and for just as many long years as *they* had – to earn his licence to steal – and it was inconceivable to them that one of their own kind, as it were, would give all that up on what appeared to be a whim. No, they said, it *must* be a trap; not even a 'brown power' *lawyer* could afford to laugh at the risk of almost certain disbarment.

Indeed. And they were at least half right – which is not a bad average for lawyers – because Oscar Z. Acosta, Chicano lawyer, very definitely could *not* afford the shitrain of suicidal publicity that he was doing everything possible to bring down on himself. There are a lot of *nice* ways to behave like a criminal – but hiring a camera to have yourself photographed doing it in the road is not one of them. It would have taken a reputation as formidable as Melvin Belli's to survive the kind of grossly illegal behaviour that Oscar was effectively admitting by signing that libel release. He might as well have burned his lawyer's licence on the steps of the Superior Court building in downtown LA.

That is what the Ivy League libel lawyers in New York could not accept. They *knew* what that licence was worth – at least to them; it averaged out to about $150 an hour – even for a borderline psychotic, as long as he had the credentials.

And Oscar had them – not because his father and grandfather had gone to Yale or Harvard Law; he'd paid his dues at night school, the only Chicano in his class, and his record in the courtroom was better than that of most colleagues who called him a disgrace to their venal profession.

Which may have been true, for whatever it's worth ... but what none of us knew at the time of the great madness that came so close to making *Fear and Loathing in Las Vegas* incurably unfit for publication was that we were no longer dealing with O. Z. Acosta, Attorney-at-Law – but with Zeta, the King of Brown Buffalos.

Last Train for the Top of the Mountain, Last Leap for the Great Skyhook ... Good Riddance to Bad Rubbish ... He Was Ugly & Vicious and He Sold Little Babies to Sand-Niggers ... Mutant Rumours on the Weird Grapevine, Wild Ghosts on the Bimini Run, Lights in Fat City ... No End to the Story and No Grave for the Brown Buffalo

---

In retrospect it is hard to know exactly when Oscar decided to quit the law just as finally as he'd once quit being a Baptist missionary – but it was obviously a lot earlier than even his few close friends realized, until long after he'd already made the move in his mind, to a new and higher place. The crazy attorney whose 'suicidal behaviour' so baffled the NY libel lawyers was only the locustlike shell of a thirty-six-year-old neo-prophet who was already long overdue for his gig at the top of the mountain.

There was no more time to be wasted in the company of lepers and lawyers. The hour had finally struck for the fat spic from Riverbank to start acting like that one man in every century 'chosen to speak for his people'.

None of this terminal madness was easy to see at the time – not even for me, and I knew him as well as anyone ... But not well enough, apparently, to understand the almost desperate sense of failure and loss that he felt when he was suddenly confronted with the stark possibility that he had never *really* been chosen to speak for anybody, except maybe himself – and even that was beginning to look like a halfway impossible task, in the short time he felt he had left.

I had never taken his burning bush trip very seriously – and I still have moments of doubt about how seriously he took it himself ... They are very *long* moments, sometimes; and as a matter of fact I think I feel one coming on right now ... We should have castrated that brain-damaged thief! That shyster! That blasphemous freak! He was ugly and greasy and he still owes me thousands of dollars!

The truth was not in him, goddamnit! He was put on this earth for no reason at all except to shit in every nest he could con his way into – but only after robbing them first, and selling the babies to sand-niggers. If that treacherous fist-fucker ever comes back to life, he'll wish we'd had the good sense to nail him up on a frozen telephone pole for his thirty-third birthday present.

DO NOT COME BACK OSCAR! Wherever you are – stay there! There's no room for you here any more. Not after all this maudlin gibberish I've written about you ... And besides, we have Werner Erhard now. So BURROW DEEP, you bastard, and take all that poison fat with you!

Cazart! And how's that for a left-handed whipsong?

Nevermind. There is no more time for questions – or answers either, for that matter. And I was never much good at this kind of thing, anyway.

The first thing we do, let's kill all the lawyers.
    William Shakespeare, *King Henry VI*

Well ... so much for whipsongs. Nobody laughed when Big Bill sat down to play. He was not into filigree when it came to dealing with lawyers.

And neither am I, at this point. That last outburst was probably unnecessary, but what the hell? Let them drink Drano if they can't take a joke. I'm tired of wallowing around in this goddamn thing.

What began as a quick and stylish epitaph for my allegedly erstwhile 300-pound Samoan attorney has long since gone out of control. Not even Oscar would have wanted an obituary with no end, at least not until he was legally dead, and that will take four more years.

Until then – and probably for many years afterwards – the weird grapevine will not wither for lack of bulletins, warning and other twisted rumours of the latest Brown Buffalo sightings. He will be seen at least once in Calcutta, buying nine-year-old girls out of cages on the white slave market ... and also in Houston, tending bar at a roadhouse on South Main that was once the Blue Fox ... or perhaps once again on the midnight run to Bimini; standing tall on his own hind legs in the cockpit of a fifty-foot black cigarette boat with a silver Uzi in one hand and a magnum of smack in the other, always running ninety miles an hour with no lights and howling Old Testament gibberish at the top of his bleeding lungs ...

It might even come to pass that he will suddenly appear on my porch in Woody Creek on some moonless night when the peacocks are screeching with lust ... Maybe so, and that is one ghost who will always be welcome in this house, even with a head full of acid and a chain of bull-maggots around his neck.

Oscar was one of God's own prototypes – a high-powered mutant of some kind who was never even considered for mass production. He was too weird to live and too rare to die – and as far as I'm concerned, that's just about all that needs to be said about him right now. I was tempted for a while to call that poor bastard Drake, down in Coconut Grove, to check a little deeper into that savage tale about Oscar and the battle of Biscayne Bay – the one that ended with at least one murder and the total destruction of Drake's $48,000 cigarette boat – but I just don't think I need it right now ...

Nobody needs it, in fact – but then nobody really needed Oscar Zeta Acosta either. Or *Rolling Stone*. Or Jimmy Carter or the Hindenberg ... or even the Sloat diamond.

Jesus! Is there no respect in this world for the perfectly useless dead?

Apparently not ... and Oscar *was* a lawyer, however reluctant he might have been at the end to admit it. He had a lawyer's cynical view of the truth – which he felt was not nearly as important to other people as it was to him; and he was never more savage and dangerous than when he felt he was being lied to. He was never much interested in the *concept* of truth; he had no time for what he called 'dumb Anglo abstracts'.

*

*Condemn'd to drudge, the meanest of the mean, and furbish falsehoods
for a magazine.*

Lord Byron

The truth, to Oscar, was a tool and even a weapon that he was convinced he could not do without – if only because anybody who had more of it than he did would sooner or later try to beat on him with it. Truth was power – as tangible to Oscar as a fistful of $100 bills or an ounce of pure LSD-25. His formula for survival in a world full of rich *gabancho* fascists was a kind of circle that began at the top with the idea that truth would bring him power, which would buy freedom – to crank his head full of acid so he could properly walk with the king, which would naturally put him even closer to more and finer truths ... indeed, the full circle.

Oscar believed it, and that was what finally croaked him.

I tried to warn the greedy bastard, but he was too paranoid to pay any attention ... Because he was actually a stupid, vicious quack with no morals at all and the soul of a hammerhead shark.

We are better off without him. Sooner or later he would have had to be put to sleep anyway ... So the world is a better place, now that he's at least out of sight, if not certifiably dead.

He will not be missed – except perhaps in Fat City, where every light in the town went dim when he heard that he'd finally cashed his cheque.

One owes respect to the living: To the dead one owes only the truth.

Voltaire

Rolling Stone no. 254, 15 December 1977

THE HOODLUM CIRCUS AND THE STATUTORY RAPE OF BASS LAKE

*Man, when you were fifteen or sixteen years old did you ever think
you'd end up as a Hell's Angel? How did I get screwed up with you
guys anyway? ... Christ, I got out of the army and came back to
Richmond, started ridin' a bike around, wearin' my chinos and clean
sport shirts, even a crash helmet ... And then I met you guys. I started
gettin' grubbier and grubbier, dirtier and dirtier, I couldn't believe it ...*

*Then I lost my job, started spendin' all my time either goin' on a run
or gettin' ready for one – Christ, I still can't believe it.*
                                        Fat D., a Richmond Hell's Angel

*Whaddeyou mean by that word 'right'? The only thing we're concerned
about is what's right for us. We got our own definition of 'right'.*
                                        Hell's Angel sunk in philosophy

According to Frenchy, the run would take off at eight a.m. from the El
Adobe, a tavern on East Fourteenth Street in Oakland. (Until the
autumn of 1965 the El Adobe was the unofficial headquarters of the
Oakland chapter and a focal point for all Hell's Angels activity in
northern California – but in October it was demolished to make way for
a parking lot, and the Angels moved back to the Sinners Club.)

Early weather forecasts said the whole state would be blazing hot that
day, but dawn in San Francisco was typically foggy. I overslept, and in
the rush to get moving I forgot my camera. There was no time for
breakfast but I ate a peanut-butter sandwich while loading the car ...
sleeping bag and beer cooler in back, tape recorder in front, and under
the driver's seat an unloaded Luger. I kept the clip in my pocket, thinking it might be useful if things got out of hand. Press cards are nice
things to have, but in riot situations a pistol is the best kind of safe-
conduct pass.

By the time I left my apartment it was almost eight, and somewhere
on the fog-shrouded Bay Bridge between San Francisco and Oakland, I
heard the first radio bulletin:

> The Sierra community of Bass Lake is bracing this morning for a re-
> ported invasion of the notorious Hell's Angels motorcycle gang.
> Heavily armed police and sheriff's deputies are stationed on all roads
> leading to Bass Lake. Madera County sheriff, Marlin Young, reports
> helicopters and other emergency forces standing by. Neighbouring
> law enforcement agencies, including the Kern County sheriff's Canine
> Patrol, have been alerted and are ready to move. Recent reports say
> the Hell's Angels are massing in Oakland and San Bernardino. Stay
> tuned for further details.

Among those who made a point of staying tuned that morning were
several thousand unarmed taxpayers *en route* to spend the holiday in
the vicinity of Bass Lake and Yosemite. They had just got under way,
most of them still irritable and sleepy from last-minute packing and
hurrying the children through breakfast ... when their car radios
crackled a warning that they were headed right into the vortex of what
might soon be a combat zone. They had read about Laconia and other

Hell's Angels outbursts, but in print the menace had always seemed distant – terrifying, to be sure, and real in its way, but with none of that sour-stomach fright that comes with the realization that this time it's *you*. Tomorrow's newspapers won't be talking about people being beaten and terrorized three thousand miles away, but right exactly where you and your family are planning to spend the weekend.

The bridge was crowded with vacationers getting an early start. I was running late by twenty or thirty minutes, and when I got to the toll plaza at the Oakland end of the bridge I asked the gatekeeper if any Hell's Angels had passed through before me. 'The dirty sonsabitches are right over there,' he said with a wave of his hand. I didn't know what he was talking about until some two hundred yards past the gate, when I suddenly passed a large cluster of people and motorcycles grouped around a grey pickup truck with a swastika painted on the side. They seemed to materialize out of the fog, and the sight was having a bad effect on traffic. There are seventeen eastbound toll gates on the bridge, and traffic coming out of them is funnelled into only three exits, with everyone scrambling for position in a short, high-speed run between the toll plaza and the traffic dividers about a half mile away. This stretch is hazardous on a clear afternoon, but in the fog of a holiday morning and with a dread spectacle suddenly looming beside the road the scramble was worse than usual. Horns sounded all around me as cars swerved and slowed down; heads snapped to the right; it was the same kind of traffic disruption that occurs near a serious accident, and many a driver went off on the wrong ramp that morning after staring too long at the monster rally that – if he'd been listening to his radio – he'd been warned about just moments before. And now here it was, in the stinking, tattooed flesh ... the menace.

I was close enough to recognize the Gypsy Jokers, about twenty of them, milling around the truck while they waited for late-running stragglers. They were paying no attention to the traffic but their appearance alone was enough to give anyone pause. Except for the colours, they looked exactly like any band of Hell's Angels: long hair, beards, black sleeveless vests ... and the inevitable low-slung motorcycles, many with sleeping bags lashed to the handlebars and girls sitting lazily on the little pillion seats.

The outlaws are very comfortable with their inaccessibility. It saves them a lot of trouble with bill collectors, revenge seekers and routine police harassment. They are as insulated from society as they want to be, but they have no trouble locating each other. When Sonny flies down to Los Angeles, Otto meets him at the airport. When Terry goes to Fresno, he quickly locates the chapter president, Ray – who exists in some kind of mysterious limbo and can only be found by means of a secret phone number, which changes constantly. The Oakland Angels find it convenient to use Barger's number, checking now and then for messages. Some use various saloons where they are well known. An Angel who wants to be reached will make an appointment either to meet somewhere or to be at a certain phone at a designated time.

One night I tried to arrange a contact with a young Angel named Rodger, a one-time disc jockey. It proved to be impossible. He had no idea where he might be from one day to the next. 'They don't call me Rodger the Lodger for nothing,' he said. 'I just make it wherever I can. It's all the same. Once you start worrying about it, you get hung up – and that's the end, man, you're finished.' If he'd been killed that night he'd have left no footprints in life, no evidence and no personal effects but his bike – which the others would have raffled off immediately. Hell's Angels don't find it necessary to leave wills, and their deaths don't require much paperwork ... A driver's licence expires, a police record goes into the dead file, a motorcycle changes hands and usually a few 'personal cards' will be taken out of wallets and dropped into wastebaskets.

Because of their gypsy style of life, their network has to be functional. A lost message can lead to serious trouble. An Angel who might have fled will be arrested; a freshly stolen bike will never reach the buyer; a pound of marijuana might miss a crucial connection; or at the very least, a whole chapter will never get word of a run or a big party.

The destination of a run is kept secret as long as possible – hopefully, to keep the cops guessing. The chapter presidents will figure it out by long-distance telephone, then each will tell his people the night before the run, either at a meeting or by putting the word with a handful of bartenders, waitresses and plugged-in chicks who are known contacts. The system is highly efficient, but it has never been leakproof, and by 1966 the Angels had decided that the only hope was to keep the destination a secret until the run was actually under way. Barger tried it once, but the police were able to track the outlaws by radioing ahead from one point to another. Radio tracking is only a device to give the cops an edge, a sense of confidence and control. Which it does, as long as no lapses occur ... but it is safe to predict that on one of these crowded holidays a convoy of Angels is going to disappear like a blip shooting off the edge of a radar screen. All it will take is one of those rare gigs the outlaws are forever seeking: a ranch or big farm with a friendly owner, a piece of rural turf beyond the reach of the fuzz, where they can all get drunk and naked and fall on each other like goats in the rut, until they all pass out from exhaustion.

It would be worth buying a police radio, just to hear the panic:

'Group of eighty just passed through Sacramento, going north on US Fifty, no violence, thought to be headed for Lake Tahoe area ...' Fifty miles north, in Placerville, the police chief gives his men a pep talk and deploys them with shotguns on both sides of the highway, south of the city limits. Two hours later they are still waiting and the dispatcher in Sacramento relays an impatient demand for a report on Placerville's handling of the crisis. The chief nervously reports no contact and asks if his restless troops can go home and enjoy the holiday.

The dispatcher, sitting in the radio room at Highway Patrol headquarters in Sacramento, says to sit tight while he checks around ... and moments later his voice squawks out of the speaker: 'Schwein! You lie! Vere are dey?'

'Don't call me no swine,' says the Placerville chief. 'They never got here.'

The dispatcher checks all over northern California, with no result. Police cars scream up and down the highways, checking every bar. Nothing. Eighty of the state's most vicious hoodlums are roaming around drunk somewhere between Sacramento and Reno, hungry for rape and pillage. It will be another embarrassment for California law enforcement ... to simply lose the buggers, a whole convoy, right out on a main highway ... heads will surely roll.

By now, the outlaws are far up a private road, having left the highway at a sign saying: OWL FARM, NO VISITORS. They are beyond the reach of the law unless the owner complains. Meanwhile, another group of fifty disappears in the same vicinity. Police search parties stalk the highway, checking for traces of spittle, grime and blood. The dispatcher still rages over his mike; the duty officer's voice cracks as he answers urgent queries from radio newsmen in San Francisco and Los Angeles: 'I'm sorry, that's all I can say. They seem to have ... ah ... our information is that they ... they disappeared, yes, they're gone.'

The only reason it hasn't happened is that the Hell's Angels have no access to private property in the boondocks. One or two claim to have relatives with farms, but there are no stories of the others being invited out for a picnic. The Angels don't have much contact with people who own land. They are city boys, economically and emotionally as well as physically. For at least one generation and sometimes two they come from people who never owned anything at all, not even a car.

The Hell's Angels are very definitely a lower-class phenomenon, but their backgrounds are not necessarily poverty-stricken. Despite some grim moments, their parents seem to have had credit. Most of the outlaws are the sons of people who came to California either just before or during World War II. Many have lost contact with their families, and I have never met an Angel who claimed to have a home town in any sense that people who use that term might understand it. Terry the Tramp, for instance, is 'from' Detroit, Norfolk, Long Island, Los Angeles, Fresno and Sacramento. As a child, he lived all over the country, not in poverty but in total mobility. Like most of the others, he has no roots. He relates entirely to the present, the moment, the action.

His longest bout with stability was a three-year hitch in the Coast Guard after finishing high school. Since then he has worked half-heartedly as a tree-trimmer, mechanic, bit actor, labourer, and hustler of various commodities. He tried college for a few months but quit to get married. After two years, two children and numerous quarrels, the marriage ended in divorce. He had another child, by his second wife, but that union didn't last either. Now, after two hugely publicized rape arrests, he refers to himself as an 'eligible bachelor'.

Despite his spectacular rap sheet, he estimates his total jail time at about six months – ninety days for trespassing and the rest for traffic offences. Terry is one of the most arrest-prone of all the Angels; cops are offended by the very sight of him. In one stretch, covering 1964 and 65, he paid roughly $2500 to bail bondsmen, lawyers and traffic courts. Like most of the other Angels he blames 'the cops' for making him a full-time outlaw.

At least half the Hell's Angels are war babies, but that is a very broad term. There are also war babies in the Peace Corps, in corporate training programmes, and fighting in Vietnam. World War II had a lot to do with the Hell's Angels' origins, but you have to stretch the war theory pretty thin to cover both Dirty Ed, in his early forties, and Clean Cut from Oakland, who is twenty years younger. Dirty Ed is old enough to be Clean Cut's father – which is not likely, though he's planted more seeds than he cares to remember.

It is easy enough to trace the Hell's Angels' mystique – and even their names and their emblems – back to World War II and Hollywood. But their genes and real history go back a lot further. World War II was not the original California boom, but a rebirth of a thing that began in the thirties and was already tapering off when the war economy made California a new Valhalla. In 1937 Woody Guthrie wrote a song called 'Do-Re-Mi'. The chorus goes like this:

California is a garden of Eden
A paradise for you and for me,
But believe it or not,
You won't think it's so hot,
If you ain't got the do-re-mi.

The song expressed the frustrated sentiments of more than a million

Okies, Arkies and hillbillies who made a long trek to the Golden State and found it was just another hard dollar. By the time these gentlemen arrived, the westward movement was already beginning to solidify. The 'California way of life' was the same old game to musical chairs – but it took a while for this news to filter back East, and meanwhile the Gold Rush continued. Once here, the newcomers hung on for a few years, breeding prolifically – until the war started. Then they either joined up or had their pick of jobs on a booming labour market. Either way, they were Californians when the war ended. The old way of life was scattered back along Route 66, and their children grew up in a new world. The Linkhorns had finally found a home.

Nelson Algren wrote about them in *A Walk on the Wild Side*, but that story was told before they crossed the Rockies. Dove Linkhorn, son of crazy Fitz, went to hustle for his fortune in New Orleans. Ten years later he would have gone to Los Angeles.

Algren's book opens with one of the best historical descriptions of American white trash ever written.* He traces the Linkhorn ancestry back to the first wave of bonded servants to arrive on these shores. These were the dregs of society from all over the British Isles – misfits, criminals, debtors, social bankrupts of every type and description – all of them willing to sign oppressive work contracts with future employers in exchange for ocean passage to the New World. Once here, they endured a form of slavery for a year or two – during which they were fed and sheltered by the boss – and when their time of bondage ended, they were turned loose to make their own way.

In theory and in the context of history the setup was mutually advantageous. Any man desperate enough to sell himself into bondage in the first place had pretty well shot his wad in the old country, so a chance for a foothold on a new continent was not to be taken lightly. After a period of hard labour and wretchedness he would then be free to seize whatever he might in a land of seemingly infinite natural wealth. Thousands of bonded servants came over, but by the time they earned their freedom the coastal strip was already settled. The unclaimed land was west, across the Alleghenies. So they drifted into the new states – Kentucky and Tennessee; their sons drifted on to Missouri, Arkansas and Oklahoma.

Drifting became a habit; with dead roots in the Old World and none in the New, the Linkhorns were not of a mind to dig in and cultivate things. Bondage too became a habit, but it was only the temporary kind. They were not pioneers, but sleazy rearguard camp followers of the

* A story called 'Barn Burning', by William Faulkner, is another white-trash classic. It provides the dimensions of humanity that Algren's description lacks.

original westward movement. By the time the Linkhorns arrived anywhere the land was already taken – so they worked for a while and moved on. Their world was a violent, boozing limbo between the pits of despair and the big rock candy mountain. They kept drifting west, chasing jobs, rumours, homestead grabs or the luck of some front-running kin. They lived off the surface of the land, like armyworms, stripping it of whatever they could before moving on. It was a day-to-day existence, and there was always more land to the west.

Some stayed behind and their lineal descendants are still there – in the Carolinas, Kentucky, West Virginia and Tennessee. There were dropouts along the way: hillbillies, Okies, Arkies – they're all the same people. Texas is a living monument to the breed. So is southern California. Algren called them 'fierce craving boys' with 'a feeling of having been cheated'. Freebooters, armed and drunk – a legion of gamblers, brawlers and whorehoppers. Blowing into town in a junk Model-A with bald tyres, no muffler and one headlight ... looking for quick work, with no questions asked and preferably no tax deductions. Just get the cash, fill up at a cut-rate gas station and hit the road, with a pint on the seat and Eddy Arnold on the radio moaning good back-country tunes about home sweet home, that Bluegrass sweetheart still waitin', and roses on Mama's grave.

Algren left the Linkhorns in Texas, but anyone who drives the Western highways knows they didn't stay there either. They kept moving until one day in the late 1930s they stood on the spine of a scrub-oak California hill and looked down on the Pacific Ocean – the end of the road. Things were tough for a while, but no tougher than they were in a hundred other places. And then came the war – fat city, big money even for Linkhorns.

When the war ended, California was full of veterans looking for ways to spend their separation bonuses. Many decided to stay on the coast, and while their new radios played hillbilly music they went out and bought big motorcycles – not knowing exactly why, but in the booming, rootless atmosphere of those times, it seemed like the thing to do. They were not all Linkhorns, but the forced democracy of four war years had erased so many old distinctions that even Linkhorns were confused. Their pattern of intermarriage was shattered, their children mixed freely and without violence. By 1950 many Linkhorns were participating in the money economy; they owned decent cars, and even houses.

Others, however, broke down under the strain of respectability and answered the call of the genes. There is a story about a Linkhorn who became a wealthy car dealer in Los Angeles. He married a beautiful Spanish actress and bought a mansion in Beverly Hills. But after a decade of opulence he suffered from soaking sweats and was unable to sleep at night. He began to sneak out of the house through the servants' entrance and run a few blocks to a gas station where he kept a hopped-up 37 Ford with no fenders ... and spend the rest of the night hanging around honky-tonk bars and truck stops, dressed in dirty overalls and a crusty green T-shirt with a Bardahl emblem on the back. He enjoyed cadging beers and belting whores around when they spurned his crude propositions. One night, after long haggling, he bought several mason jars full of home whisky, which he drank while driving at high speed through the Beverly Hills area. When the old Ford finally threw a rod he abandoned it and called a taxi, which took him to his own automobile agency. He kicked down a side door, hot-wired a convertible waiting for tune-up and drove out to Highway 101, where he got in a drag race with some hoodlums from Pasadena. He lost, and it so enraged him that he followed the other car until it stopped for a traffic light – where he rammed it from the rear at seventy miles an hour.

The publicity ruined him, but influential friends kept him out of jail by paying a psychiatrist to call him insane. He spent a year in a rest home; and now, according to the stories, he has a motorcycle dealership near San Diego. People who know him say he's happy – although his driver's licence has been revoked for numerous violations, his business is verging on bankruptcy, and his new wife, a jaded ex-beauty queen from West Virginia, is a half-mad alcoholic.

It would not be fair to say that all motorcycle outlaws carry Linkhorn genes, but nobody who has ever spent time among the inbred Anglo-Saxon tribes of Appalachia would need more than a few hours with the Hell's Angels to work up a very strong sense of *déjà vu*. There is the same sulking hostility towards 'outsiders', the same extremes of temper and action, and even the same names, sharp faces and long-boned bodies that never look quite natural unless they are leaning on something.

Most of the Angels are obvious Anglo-Saxons, but the Linkhorn attitude is contagious. The few outlaws with Mexican or Italian names not only act like the others but somehow look like them. Even Chinese Mel from Frisco and Charley, a young Negro from Oakland, have the Linkhorn gait and mannerisms.

ASHES TO ASHES & DUST TO DUST:
THE FUNERAL OF MOTHER MILES

He who makes a beast of himself gets rid of the pain of being a man.
                                                                Dr Johnson

The neighbourhood suddenly exploded with excited, morbid crowds.
Hysterical women surged forwards in a frenzy, screeching in almost
sexual ecstasy, scratching and fighting the agents and police in their
attempt to reach the body. One fat-breasted woman with stringy red
hair broke through the cordon and dipped her handkerchief in the
blood, clutched it to her sweaty dress and waddled off down the
street ...
                                        Account of the death of John Dillinger

Towards Christmas the action slowed down and the Angels dropped out
of the headlines. Tiny lost his job, Sonny got involved in a long jury trial
on the attempted-murder charge, and the El Adobe was demolished by
the wrecker's ball. The Angels drifted from one bar to another, but they
found it harder to establish a hangout than to maintain one. In San
Francisco it was just as slow. Frenchy spent three months in General
Hospital when a can of gasoline blew up on him, and Puff went to jail
after a fracas with two cops who raided an Angel birthday party. Winter
is always slow for the outlaws. Many have to go to work to stay eligible
for next summer's unemployment insurance, it is too cold for big outdoor parties, and the constant rain makes riding an uncomfortable
hazard.

It seemed like a good time to get some work done, so I dropped off the
circuit. Terry came by now and then to keep me posted. One day he
showed up with a broken arm, saying he'd wrecked his bike, his old lady
had left him and the niggers had blown up his house. I'd heard about the
house from Barger's wife, Elsie, who was handling the communications
post at their home in Oakland. During one of the sporadic flare-ups between the Hell's Angels and the Oakland Negroes somebody had thrown
a homemade bomb through the window of the house that Terry was
renting in East Oakland. The fire destroyed the house and all of Mari-
lyn's paintings. She was a pretty little girl about nineteen, with long
blonde hair and a respectable family in one of the valley towns. She'd
been living with Terry for nearly six months, covering the walls with her
artwork, but she had no stomach for bombs. The divorce was effected

soon after they moved to another dwelling. 'I came back one night and she was gone,' said Terry. 'All she left was a note: "Dear Terry, Fuck it." ' And that was that.

Nothing else happened until January, when Mother Miles got snuffed. He was riding his bike through Berkeley when a truck came out of a side street and hit him head on, breaking both legs and fracturing his skull. He hung in a coma for six days, then died on a Sunday morning, less than twenty-four hours before his thirtieth birthday – leaving a wife, two children and his righteous girl friend, Ann.

Miles had been president of the Sacramento chapter. His influence was so great that in 1965 he moved the whole club down to Oakland, claiming the police had made life intolerable for them by constant harassment. The outlaws simply picked up and moved, not questioning Miles' wisdom. His real name was James, but the Angels called him Mother.

'I guess it was because he was kind of motherly,' said Gut. 'Miles was great, great people. He took care of everybody. He worried. You could always depend on him.'

I knew Miles in a distant kind of way. He didn't trust writers, but there was nothing mean about him, and once he decided I wasn't going to get him locked up somehow, he was friendly. He had the build of a pot-bellied stevedore, with a round face and a wide, flaring beard. I never thought of him as a hoodlum. He had the usual Hell's Angel police record: drunk, disorderly, fighting, vagrancy, loitering, petty larceny and a handful of ominous 'suspicion of' charges that had never gone to trial. But he wasn't plagued by the same demons that motivate some of the others. He wasn't happy with the world, but he didn't brood about it, and his appetite for revenge didn't extend beyond specific wrongs done to the Angels or to him personally. You could drink with Miles without wondering when he was going to swing on somebody or lift your money off the bar. He wasn't that way. Booze seemed to make him more genial. Like most of the Angels' leaders, he had a quick mind and a quality of self-control which the others relied on.

When I heard he'd been killed I called Sonny to ask about the funeral, but by the time I finally got hold of him the details were already on the radio and in the newspapers. Miles' mother was arranging for the funeral in Sacramento. The outlaw caravan would form at Barger's house at eleven on Thursday morning. The Angels have gone to plenty of funerals for their own people, but until this one they had never tried to run the procession for ninety miles along a major highway. There was also a chance that the Sacramento police would try to keep them out of town.

The word went out on Monday and Tuesday by telephone. This was not going to be any Jay Gatsby funeral; the Angels wanted a full-dress rally. Miles' status was not the point; the death of any Angel requires a show of strength by the others. It is a form of affirmation – not for the dead, but the living. There are no set penalties for not showing up, because none are necessary. In the cheap loneliness that is the overriding fact of every outlaw's life, a funeral is a bleak reminder that the tribe is smaller by one. The circle is one link shorter, the enemy jacks up the odds just a little bit more, and defenders of the faith need something to take off the chill. A funeral is a time for counting the loyal, for seeing how many are left. There is no question about skipping work, going without sleep or riding for hours in a cold wind to be there on time.

Early Thursday morning the bikes began arriving in Oakland. Most of the outlaws were already in the Bay Area, or at least within fifty or sixty miles, but a handful of Satan's Slaves rode all of Wednesday night, five hundred miles from Los Angeles, to join the main caravan. Others came from Fresno and San Jose and Santa Rosa. There were Hangmen, Misfits, Presidents, Nightriders, Crossmen and some with no colours at all. A hard-faced little man who nobody spoke to wore an olive-drab bombardier's jacket with just the word 'Loner' on the back, written in small, blue-inked letters that looked like a signature.

I was crossing the Bay Bridge when a dozen Gypsy Jokers came roaring past, ignoring the speed limit as they split up to go around me on both sides of the car. Seconds later they disappeared up ahead in the fog. The morning was cold and bridge traffic was slow except for motorcycles. Down in the bay there were freighters lined up, waiting for open piers.

The procession rolled at exactly eleven – a hundred and fifty bikes and about twenty cars. A few miles north of Oakland, at the Carquinez Bridge, the outlaws picked up a police escort assigned to keep them under control. A Highway Patrol car led the caravan all the way to Sacramento. The lead Angels rode two abreast in the right lane, holding a steady sixty-five miles an hour. At the head, with Barger, was the scruffy praetorian guard: Magoo, Tommy, Jimmy, Skip, Tiny, Zorro, Terry and Charger Charley the Child Molester. The spectacle disrupted traffic all along the way. It looked like something from another world. Here was 'the scum of the earth', the 'lowest form of animals', an army of unwashed gang rapists ... being escorted towards the state capital by a Highway Patrol car with a flashing yellow light. The steady pace of the procession made it unnaturally solemn. Not even Senator Murphy could have mistaken it for a dangerous run. There were the same bearded faces; the same earrings, emblems, swastikas and grinning death's-heads flapping in the wind – but this time there were no party clothes, no hamming it up for the squares. They were still playing the role, but all the humour was missing. The only trouble *en route* came when the procession was halted after a filling-station owner complained that somebody had stolen fourteen quarts of oil at the last gas stop. Barger quickly took up a collection to pay the man off, muttering that whoever stole the oil was due for a chain-whipping later on. The Angels assured each other that it must have been a punk in one of the cars at the rear of the caravan, some shithead without any class.

In Sacramento there was no sign of harassment. Hundreds of curious spectators lined the route between the funeral home and the cemetery. Inside the chapel a handful of Jim Miles' childhood friends and relatives waited with his body, a hired minister and three nervous attendants. They knew what was coming – Mother Miles' 'people', hundreds of thugs, wild brawlers and bizarre-looking girls in tight Levis, scarves and waist-length platinum-coloured wigs. Miles' mother, a heavy middle-aged woman in a black suit, wept quietly in a front pew, facing the open casket.

At one-thirty the outlaw caravan arrived. The slow rumble of motorcycle engines rattled glass in the mortuary windows. Police tried to keep traffic moving as TV cameras followed Barger and perhaps a hundred others towards the door of the chapel. Many outlaws waited outside during the service. They stood in quiet groups, leaning against the bikes and killing time with lazy conversation. There was hardly any talk about Miles. In one group a pint of whisky made the rounds. Some of the outlaws talked to bystanders, trying to explain what was happening. 'Yeah, the guy was one of our leaders,' said an Angel to an elderly man in a baseball cap. 'He was good people. Some punk ran a stop sign and snuffed him. We came to bury him with the colours.'

Inside the pine-panelled chapel the minister was telling his weird congregation that 'the wages of sin is death'. He looked like a Norman Rockwell druggist and was obviously repelled by the whole scene. Not all the pews were full, but standing room in the rear was crowded all the way back to the door. The minister talked about 'sin' and 'justification', pausing now and then as if he expected a rebuttal from the crowd. 'It's not my business to pass judgement on anybody,' he continued. 'Nor is it my business to eulogize anybody. But it *is* my business to speak out a warning that *it will happen to you*! I don't know what philosophy some of you have about death, but I know the Scriptures tell us that God takes no pleasure in the death of the wicked ... Jesus didn't die for an animal, he died for a man ... What I say about Jim won't change anything, but I can preach the gospel to you and I have a responsibility to warn you that you will all have to *answer to God*!'

The crowd was shifting and sweating. The chapel was so hot that it seemed like the Devil himself was waiting in one of the anterooms, ready to claim the wicked just as soon as the sermon was over.

'How many of you—' asked the minister, 'how many of you asked yourself on the way up here. *"Who is next?"* '

At this point several Angels in the pews rose and walked out, cursing quietly at a way of life they had long ago left behind. The minister ignored these mutinous signs and launched into a story about a Philippian jailer. 'Holy shit!' mumbled Tiny. He'd been standing quietly in the rear for about thirty minutes, pouring sweat and eyeing the minister as if he meant to hunt him down later in the day and extract all his teeth. Tiny's departure caused five or six others to leave. The minister sensed he was losing his audience, so he brought the Philippian story to a quick end.

There was no music as the crowd filed out. I passed by the casket and was shocked to see Mother Miles clean-shaven, lying peacefully on his back in a blue suit, white shirt and a wide maroon tie. His Hell's Angels jacket, covered with exotic emblems, was mounted on a stand at the foot of the casket. Behind it were thirteen wreaths, some bearing names of other outlaw clubs.

I barely recognized Miles. He looked younger than twenty-nine and very ordinary. But his face was calm, as though he were not at all surprised to find himself there in a box. He wouldn't have liked the clothes he was wearing, but since the Angels weren't paying for the funeral, the best they could do was make sure the colours went into the casket before it was sealed. Barger stayed behind with the pallbearers to make sure the thing was done right.

After the funeral more than two hundred motorcycles followed the hearse to the cemetery. Behind the Angels rode all the other clubs, including a half dozen East Bay Dragons – and, according to a radio commentator, 'dozens of teenage riders who looked so solemn that you'd think Robin Hood had just died'.

The Hell's Angels knew better. Not all of them had read about Robin Hood, but they understood that the parallel was complimentary. Perhaps the younger outlaws believed it, but there is room in their margin for one or two friendly illusions. Those who are almost thirty, or more than that, have been living too long with their own scurvy image to think of themselves as heroes. They understand that heroes are always 'good guys', and they have seen enough cowboy movies to know that good guys win in the end. The myth didn't seem to include Miles, who was 'one of the best'. But all he got in the end was two broken legs, a smashed head and a tongue-lashing from the preacher. Only his Hell's Angels identity kept him from going to the grave as anonymously as any ribbon clerk. As it was, his funeral got nationwide press coverage: *Life* had a picture of the procession entering the cemetery, TV newscasts gave the funeral a solemn priority, and the *Chronicle* headline said:

HELL'S ANGELS BURY THEIR OWN – BLACK JACKETS AND AN ODD DIGNITY. Mother Miles would have been pleased.

Moments after the burial the caravan was escorted out of town by a phalanx of police cars, with sirens howling. The brief truce was ended. At the city limits the Angels screwed it on and roared back to Richmond, across the bay from San Francisco, where they held an all-night wake that kept police on edge until long after dawn. On Sunday night there was a meeting in Oakland to confirm Miles' successor, Big Al. It was a quiet affair, but without the grimness of the funeral. The banshee's wail that had seemed so loud on Thursday was already fading away. After the meeting there was a beer party at the Sinners Club, and by the time the place closed they had already set the date for the next run. The Angels would gather in Bakersfield, on the first day of spring.

All my life my heart has sought
A thing I cannot name.
> Remembered line from
> a long-forgotten poem

Months later, when I rarely saw the Angels, I still had the legacy of the big machine – four hundred pounds of chrome and deep red noise to take out on the Coast Highway and cut loose at three in the morning, when all the cops were lurking over on 101. My first crash had wrecked the bike completely and it took several months to have it rebuilt. After that I decided to ride it differently: I would stop pushing my luck on curves, always wear a helmet and try to keep within range of the nearest speed limit ... my insurance had already been cancelled and my driver's licence was hanging by a thread.

So it was always at night, like a werewolf, that I would take the thing out for an honest run down the coast. I would start in Golden Gate Park, thinking only to run a few long curves to clear my head ... but in a matter of minutes I'd be out at the beach with the sound of the engine in my ears, the surf booming up on the sea wall and a fine empty road stretching all the way down to Santa Cruz ... not even a gas station in the whole seventy miles; the only public light along the way is an all-night diner down around Rockaway Beach.

There was no helmet on those nights, no speed limit, and no cooling it down on the curves. The momentary freedom of the park was like the one unlucky drink that shoves a wavering alcoholic off the wagon. I would come out of the park near the soccer field and pause for a moment at the stop sign, wondering if I knew anyone parked out there on the midnight humping strip.

Then into first gear, forgetting the cars and letting the beast wind out ... thirty-five, forty-five ... then into second and wailing through the light at Lincoln Way, not worried about green or red signals, but only some other werewolf loony who might be pulling out, too slowly, to start his own run. Not many of these ... and with three lanes on a wide curve, a bike coming hard has plenty of room to get around almost anything ... then into third, the boomer gear, pushing seventy-five and the beginning of a windscream in the ears, a pressure on the eyeballs like diving into water off a high board.

Bent forwards, far back on the seat, and a rigid grip on the handlebars as the bike starts jumping and wavering in the wind. Taillights far up ahead coming closer, faster, and suddenly – zaaapppp – going past and leaning down for a curve near the zoo, where the road swings out to sea.

The dunes are flatter here, and on windy nights sand blows across the highway, piling up in thick drifts as deadly as any oil-slick ... instant loss of control, a crashing, cartwheeling slide and maybe one of those two-inch notices in the paper the next day: 'An unidentified motorcyclist was killed last night when he failed to negotiate a turn on Highway 1.'

Indeed ... but no sand this time, so the lever goes up into fourth, and now there's no sound except wind. Screw it all the way over, reach through the handlebars to raise the headlight beam, the needle leans down on a hundred, and wind-burned eyeballs strain to see down the centreline, trying to provide a margin for the reflexes.

But with the throttle screwed on there is only the barest margin, and no room at all for mistakes. It has to be done right ... and that's when the strange music starts, when you stretch your luck so far that fear becomes exhilaration and vibrates along your arms. You can barely see at a hundred; the tears blow back so fast that they vaporize before they get to your ears. The only sounds are wind and a dull roar floating back from the mufflers. You watch the white line and try to lean with it ... howling through a turn to the right, then to the left and down the long hill to Pacifica ... letting off now, watching for cops, but only until the next dark stretch and another few seconds on the edge ... the edge ... There is no honest way to explain it because the only people who really know where it is are the ones who have gone over. The others – the living – are those who pushed their control as far as they felt they could handle it, and then pulled back, or slowed down, or did whatever they had to when it came time to choose between now and later.

But the edge is still out there. Or maybe it's in. The association of motorcycles with LSD is no accident of publicity. The are both a means to an end, to the place of definitions.

Hell's Angels: A Strange and Terrible Saga, Random House, 1966

WELCOME TO LAS VEGAS: WHEN THE GOING GETS WEIRD, THE WEIRD TURN PRO

We were somewhere around Barstow on the edge of the desert when the drugs began to take hold. I remember saying something like 'I feel a bit lightheaded; maybe you should drive ...' And suddenly there was a terrible roar all around us and the sky was full of what looked like huge bats, all swooping and screeching and diving around the car, which was going about a hundred miles an hour with the top down to Las Vegas. And a voice was screaming: 'Holy Jesus! What are these goddamn animals?'

Then it was quiet again. My attorney had taken his shirt off and was pouring beer on his chest, to facilitate the tanning process. 'What the hell are you yelling about?' he muttered, staring up at the sun with his eyes closed and covered with wraparound Spanish sunglasses. 'Never mind,' I said. 'It's your turn to drive.' I hit the brakes and aimed the Great Red Shark towards the shoulder of the highway. No point mentioning those bats, I thought. The poor bastard will see them soon enough.

It was almost noon, and we still had more than a hundred miles to go. They would be tough miles. Very soon, I knew, we would both be completely twisted. But there was no going back, and no time to rest. We would have to ride it out. Press registration for the fabulous Mint 400 was already underway, and we had to get there by four to claim our soundproof suite. A fashionable sporting magazine in New York had taken care of the reservations, along with this huge red Chevy convertible we'd just rented off a lot on the Sunset Strip ... and I was, after all, a professional journalist; so I had an obligation to *cover the story*, for good or ill.

The sporting editors had also given me $300 in cash, most of which was already spent on extremely dangerous drugs. The trunk of the car looked like a mobile police narcotics lab. We had two bags of grass, seventy-five pellets of mescaline, five sheets of high-powered blotter acid, a salt shaker half full of cocaine, and a whole galaxy of multi-coloured uppers, downers, screamers, laughers ... and also a quart of tequila, a quart of rum, a case of Budweiser, a pint of raw ether and two dozen amyls.

All this had been rounded up the night before, in a frenzy of high-speed driving all over Los Angeles County – from Topanga to Watts, we picked up everything we could get our hands on. Not that we *needed* all that for the trip, but once you get locked into a serious drug collection, the tendency is to push it as far as you can.

The only thing that really worried me was the ether. There is nothing in the world more helpless and irresponsible and depraved than a man in the depths of an ether binge. And I knew we'd get into that rotten stuff pretty soon. Probably at the next gas station. We had sampled almost everything else, and now – yes, it was time for a long snort of ether. And then do the next hundred miles in a horrible, slobbering sort of spastic stupor. The only way to keep alert on ether is to do up a lot of amyls – not all at once, but steadily, just enough to maintain the focus at ninety miles an hour through Barstow.

'Man, this is the way to travel,' said my attorney. He leaned over to turn the volume up on the radio, humming along with the rhythm section and kind of moaning the words: 'One toke over the line, Sweet Jesus ... One toke over the line ...'

One toke? You poor fool! Wait till you see those goddamn bats. I could barely hear the radio ... slumped over on the far side of the seat, grappling with a tape recorder turned all the way up on 'Sympathy for the Devil'. That was the only tape we had, so we played it constantly, over and over, as a kind of demented counterpoint to the radio. And also to maintain our rhythm on the road. A constant speed is good for gas mileage – and for some reason that seemed important at the time. Indeed. On a trip like this one *must* be careful about gas consumption. Avoid those quick bursts of acceleration that drag blood to the back of the brain.

My attorney saw the hitchhiker long before I did. 'Let's give this boy a lift,' he said, and before I could mount any argument he was stopped and this poor Okie kid was running up to the car with a big grin on his face, saying, 'Hot damn! I never rode in a convertible before!'

'Is that right?' I said. 'Well, I guess you're about ready, eh?'

The kid nodded eagerly as we roared off.

'We're your friends,' said my attorney. 'We're not like the others.'

O Christ, I thought, he's gone around the bend. 'No more of that talk,' I said sharply. 'Or I'll put the leeches on you.' He grinned, seemed to understand. Luckily, the noise in the car was so awful – between the wind and the radio and the tape machine – that the kid in the back seat couldn't hear a word we were saying. Or could he?

How long can we *maintain*? I wondered. How long before one of us starts raving and jabbering at this boy? What will he think then? This same lonely desert was the last known home of the Manson family. Will he make that grim connection when my attorney starts screaming about bats and huge manta rays coming down on the car? If so – well, we'll just have to cut his head off and bury him somewhere. Because it goes without saying that we can't turn him loose. He'll report us at once to some kind of outback nazi law enforcement agency, and they'll run us down like dogs.

Jesus! Did I *say* that? Or just think it? Was I talking? Did they hear me? I glanced over at my attorney, but he seemed oblivious – watching the road, driving our Great Red Shark along at a hundred and ten or so. There was no sound from the back seat.

Maybe I'd better have a chat with this boy, I thought. Perhaps if I *explain* things, he'll rest easy.

Of course. I leaned around in the seat and gave him a fine big smile .. admiring the shape of his skull.

'By the way,' I said. 'There's one thing you should probably understand.'

He stared at me, not blinking. Was he gritting his teeth?

'Can you *hear* me?' I yelled.

He nodded.

'That's good,' I said. 'Because I want you to know that we're on our way to Las Vegas to find the American Dream.' I smiled. 'That's why we rented this car. It was the only way to do it. Can you grasp that?'

He nodded again, but his eyes were nervous.

'I want you to have all the background,' I said. 'Because this is a very ominous assignment – with overtones of extreme personal danger ... Hell, I forgot all about this beer; you want one?'

He shook his head.

'How about some ether?' I said.

'What?'

'Never mind. Let's get right to the heart of this thing. You see, about twenty-four hours ago we were sitting in the Polo Lounge of the Beverly Hills Hotel – in the patio section, of course – and we were just sitting there under a palm tree when this uniformed dwarf came up to me with a pink telephone and said, "This must be the call you've been waiting for all this time, sir." '

I laughed and ripped open a beer can that foamed all over the back seat while I kept talking. 'And you know? He was right! I'd been *expecting* that call, but I didn't know who it would come from. Do you follow me?'

The boy's face was a mask of pure fear and bewilderment.

I blundered on: 'I want you to understand that this man at the wheel is my *attorney*! He's not just some dingbat I found on the Strip. Shit, *look* at him! He doesn't look like you or me, right? That's because he's a foreigner. I think he's probably Samoan. But it doesn't matter, does it? Are you prejudiced?'

'Oh, hell *no!*' he blurted.

'I didn't think so,' I said. 'Because in spite of his race, this man is extremely valuable to me.' I glanced over at my attorney, but his mind was somewhere else.

I whacked the back of the driver's seat with my fist. 'This is *important*, goddamnit! This is a *true story!*' The car swerved sickeningly, then straightened out. 'Keep your hands off my fucking neck!' my attorney screamed. The kid in the back looked like he was ready to jump right out of the car and take his chances.

Our vibrations were getting nasty – but why? I was puzzled, frustrated. Was there no communication in this car? Had we deteriorated to the level of *dumb beasts*?

Because my story *was* true. I was certain of that. And it was extremely important, I felt, for the *meaning* of our journey to be made absolutely clear. We had actually been sitting there in the Polo Lounge – for many hours – drinking Singapore Slings with mescal on the side and beer chasers. And when the call came, I was ready.

The dwarf approached our table cautiously, as I recall, and when he handed me the pink telephone I said nothing, merely listened. And then I hung up, turning to face my attorney. 'That was headquarters,' I said. 'They want me to go to Las Vegas at once, and make contact with a Portuguese photographer named Lacerda. He'll have the details. All I have to do is check my suite and he'll seek me out.'

My attorney said nothing for a moment, then he suddenly came alive in his chair. 'God *hell!*' he exclaimed. 'I think I see the *pattern*. This one sounds like real trouble!' He tucked his khaki undershirt into his white rayon bellbottoms and called for more drink. 'You're going to need plenty of legal advice before this thing is over,' he said. 'And my first advice is that you should rent a very fast car with no top and get the hell out of LA for at least forty-eight hours.' He shook his head sadly. 'This blows my weekend, because naturally I'll have to go with you – and we'll have to arm ourselves.'

'Why not?' I said. 'If a thing like this is worth doing at all, it's worth doing right. We'll need some decent equipment and plenty of cash on the line – if only for drugs and a super-sensitive tape recorder, for the sake of a permanent record.'

'What kind of story is this?' he asked.

'The Mint 400,' I said. 'It's the richest off-the-road race for motorcycles and dune-buggies in the history of organized sport – a fantastic spectacle in honour of some fatback *grossero* named Del Webb, who owns the luxurious Mint Hotel in the heart of downtown Las Vegas ... at least that's what the press release says; my man in New York just read it to me.'

'Well,' he said, 'as your attorney I advise you to buy a motorcycle. How else can you cover a thing like this righteously?'

'No way,' I said. 'Where can we get hold of a Vincent Black Shadow?'

'What's that?'

'A fantastic bike,' I said. 'The new model is something like two thousand cubic inches, developing two hundred brake-horsepower at four thousand revolutions per minute on a magnesium frame with two styrofoam seats and a total kerb weight of exactly two hundred pounds.'

'That sounds about right for this gig,' he said.

'It is,' I assured him. 'The fucker's not much for turning, but it's pure hell on the straightaway. It'll outrun the F-111 until takeoff.'

'Takeoff?' he said. 'Can we handle that much torque?'

'Absolutely,' I said. 'I'll call New York for some cash.'

STRANGE MEDICINE IN THE DESERT ... A CRISIS OF CONFIDENCE

I am still vaguely haunted by our hitchhiker's remark about how he'd 'never rode in a convertible before'. Here's this poor geek living in a world of convertibles zipping past him on the highways all the time, and he's never even *ridden* in one. It made me feel like King Farouk. I was tempted to have my attorney pull into the next airport and arrange some kind of simple, common-law contract whereby we could just *give* the car to this unfortunate bastard. Just say: 'Here, sign this and the car's yours.' Give him the keys and then use the credit card to zap off on a jet to some place like Miami and rent another huge fireapple-red convertible for a drug-addled, top-speed run across the water all the way out to the last stop in Key West ... and then trade the car off for a boat. Keep moving.

But this manic notion passed quickly. There was no point in getting this harmless kid locked up – and, besides, I had *plans* for this car. I was looking forward to flashing around Las Vegas in the bugger. Maybe do a bit of serious drag-racing on the Strip: Pull up to that big stoplight in front of the Flamingo and start screaming at the traffic:

'Alright, you chickenshit wimps! You pansies! When this goddamn light flips green, I'm gonna stomp down on this thing and blow every one of you gutless punks off the road!'

Right. Challenge the bastards on their own turf. Come screeching up to the crosswalk, bucking and skidding with a bottle of rum in one hand and jamming the horn to drown out the music ... glazed eyes insanely dilated behind tiny black, gold-rimmed greaser shades, screaming gibberish ... a genuinely *dangerous* drunk, reeking of ether and terminal psychosis. Revving the engine up to a terrible high-pitched chattering whine, waiting for the light to change ...

How often does a chance like that come around? To jangle the bastards right down to the core of their spleens. Old elephants limp off to the hills to die; old Americans go out to the highway and drive themselves to death with huge cars.

But our trip was different. It was a classic affirmation of everything right and true and decent in the national character. It was a gross, physical salute to the fantastic *possibilities* of life in this country – but only for those with true grit. And we were chock full of that.

My attorney understood this concept, despite his racial handicap, but our hitchhiker was not an easy person to reach. He *said* he understood, but I could see in his eyes that he didn't. He was lying to me.

The car suddenly veered off the road and we came to a sliding halt in the gravel. I was hurled against the dashboard. My attorney was slumped over the wheel. 'What's wrong?' I yelled. 'We can't stop *here*. This is bat country!'

'My heart,' he groaned. 'Where's the medicine?'

'Oh,' I said. 'The medicine, yes, it's right here.' I reached into the kitbag for the amyls. The kid seemed petrified. 'Don't worry,' I said. 'This man has a bad heart – angina pectoris. But we have the cure for it. Yes, here they are.' I picked four amyls out of the tin box and handed two of them to my attorney. He immediately cracked one under his nose, and I did likewise.

He took a long snort and fell back on the seat, staring straight up at the sun. 'Turn up the fucking music!' he screamed. 'My heart feels like an alligator!

'Volume! Clarity! Bass! We must have bass!' He flailed his naked arms at the sky. 'What's *wrong* with us? Are we goddamn *old ladies*?'

I turned both the radio and the tape machine up full bore. 'You scurvy shyster bastard,' I said. 'Watch your language! You're talking to a doctor of journalism!'

He was laughing out of control. 'What the fuck are we *doing* out here in this desert?' he shouted. 'Somebody call the police! We need help!'

'Pay no attention to this swine,' I said to the hitchhiker. 'He can't handle the medicine. Actually, we're *both* doctors of journalism, and we're on our way to Las Vegas to cover the main story of our generation.' And then I began laughing ...

My attorney hunched around to face the hitchhiker. 'The truth is,' he said, 'we're going to Vegas to croak a scag baron named Savage Henry. I've known him for years, but he ripped us off – and you know what that means, right?'

I wanted to shut him off, but we were both helpless with laughter. What the fuck *were* we doing out here in this desert, when we both had bad hearts?

'Savage Henry has cashed his cheque!' My attorney snarled at the kid in the back seat. 'We're going to rip his lungs out!'

'And eat them!' I blurted. 'That bastard won't get away with this! What's going on in this country when a scumsucker like that can get away with sandbagging a doctor of journalism?'

Nobody answered. My attorney was cracking another amyl and the kid was climbing out of the back seat, scrambling down the trunk lid. 'Thanks for the ride,' he yelled. 'Thanks a *lot*. I *like* you guys. Don't worry about *me*.' His feet hit the asphalt and he started running back towards Baker. Out in the middle of the desert, not a tree in sight.

'Wait a minute,' I yelled. 'Come back and get a beer.' But apparently he couldn't hear me. The music was very loud, and he was moving away from us at good speed.

'Good riddance,' said my attorney. 'We had a real freak on our hands. That boy made me nervous. Did you see his *eyes*?' He was still laughing. 'Jesus,' he said. 'This is good medicine!'

I opened the door and reeled around to the driver's side. 'Move over,' I said. 'I'll drive. We have to get out of California before that kid finds a cop.'

'Shit, that'll be hours,' said my attorney. 'He's a hundred miles from anywhere.'

'So are we,' I said.

'Let's turn around and drive back to the Polo Lounge,' he said. 'They'll never look for us there.'

I ignored him. 'Open the tequila,' I yelled as the windscream took over again; I stomped on the accelerator as we hurtled back on to the highway. Moments later he leaned over with a map. 'There's a place up ahead called Mescal Springs,' he said. 'As your attorney, I advise you to stop and take a swim.'

I shook my head. 'It's absolutely imperative that we get to the Mint Hotel before the deadline for press registration,' I said. 'Otherwise, we might have to pay for our suite.'

He nodded. 'But let's forget that bullshit about the American Dream,' he said. 'The *important* thing is the Great Samoan Dream.' He was rummaging around in the kit-bag. 'I think it's about time to chew up a blotter,' he said. 'That cheap mescaline wore off a long time ago, and I don't know if I can stand the smell of that goddamn ether any longer.'

'I *like* it,' I said. 'We should soak a towel with that stuff and then put it down on the floorboard by the accelerator, so the fumes will rise up in my face all the way to Las Vegas.'

He was turning the tape cassette over. The radio was screaming: 'Power to the People – Right On!' John Lennon's political song, ten years too late. 'That poor fool should have stayed where he was,' said my attorney. 'Punks like that just get in the way when they try to be serious.'

'Speaking of serious,' I said. 'I think it's about time to get into the ether and the cocaine.'

'Forget ether,' he said. 'Let's save it for soaking down the rug in the suite. But here's this. Your half of the sunshine blotter. Just chew it up like baseball gum.'

I took the blotter and ate it. My attorney was now fumbling with the salt shaker containing the cocaine. Opening it. Spilling it. Then screaming and grabbing at the air, as our fine white dust blew up and out across the desert highway. A very expensive little twister rising up from the Great Red Shark. 'Oh, *Jesus*!' he moaned. 'Did you see what God just did to us?'

'God didn't do that!' I shouted. '*You* did it. You're a fucking narcotics agent! I was on to your stinking act from the start, you pig!'

'You better be careful,' he said. And suddenly he was waving a fat black .357 magnum at me. One of those snub-nosed Colt Pythons with the bevelled cylinder. 'Plenty of vultures out here,' he said. 'They'll pick your bones clean before morning.'

'You whore,' I said. 'When we get to Las Vegas I'll have you chopped into hamburger. What do you think the drug bund will do when I show up with a Samoan narcotics agent?'

'They'll kill us both,' he said. 'Savage Henry knows who I am. Shit, I'm your *attorney*.' He burst into wild laughter. 'You're full of acid, you fool. It'll be a goddamn miracle if we can get to the hotel and check in before you turn into a wild animal. Are you ready for that? Checking into a Vegas hotel under a phoney name with intent to commit capital fraud and a head full of acid?' He was laughing again, then he jammed his nose down towards the salt shaker, aiming the thin green roll of a $20 bill straight into what was left of the powder.

'How long do we have?' I said.

'Maybe thirty more minutes,' he replied. 'As your attorney I advise you to drive at top speed.'

Las Vegas was just up ahead. I could see the strip/hotel skyline looming up through the blue desert ground-haze: the Sahara, the landmark, the Americana and the ominous Thunderbird – a cluster of grey rectangles in the distance, rising out of the cactus.

Thirty minutes. It was going to be very close. The objective was the big tower of the Mint Hotel, downtown – and if we didn't get there before we lost all control, there was also the Nevada State prison upstate in Carson City. I had been there once, but only for a talk with the prisoners – and I didn't want to go back, for any reason at all. So there was really no choice: We would have to run the gauntlet, and acid be damned. Go through all the official gibberish, get the car into the hotel garage, work out on the desk clerk, deal with the bellboy, sign in for the press passes – all of it bogus, totally illegal, a fraud on its face, but of course it would have to be done.

'KILL THE BODY AND THE HEAD WILL DIE'

This line appears in my notebook, for some reason. Perhaps some connection with Joe Frazier. Is he still alive? Still able to talk? I watched that fight in Seattle – horribly twisted about four seats down the aisle from the Governor. A very painful experience in every way, a proper end to the sixties: Tim Leary a prisoner of Eldridge Cleaver in Algeria, Bob Dylan clipping coupons in Greenwich Village, both Kennedys murdered by mutants, Owsley folding napkins on Terminal Island, and finally Cassius/Ali belted incredibly off his pedestal by a human hamburger, a man on the verge of death. Joe Frazier, like Nixon, had finally prevailed for reasons that people like me refused to understand – at least not out loud.

... But that was some other era, burned out and long gone from the brutish realities of this foul year of Our Lord, 1971. A lot of things had changed in those years. And now I was in Las Vegas as the motor sports editor of this fine slick magazine that had sent me out here in the Great Red Shark for some reason that nobody claimed to understand. 'Just check it out,' they said, 'and we'll take it from there ...'

Indeed. Check it out. But when we finally arrived at the Mint Hotel my attorney was unable to cope artfully with the registration procedure. We were forced to stand in line with all the others – which proved to be extremely difficult under the circumstances. I kept telling myself: 'Be quiet, be calm, say nothing ... speak only when spoken to: name, rank and press affiliation, nothing else, ignore this terrible drug, pretend it's not happening ...'

There is no way to explain the terror I felt when I finally lunged up to the clerk and began babbling. All my well-rehearsed lines fell apart under that woman's stony glare. 'Hi there,' I said. 'My name is ... ah, Raoul Duke ... yes, *on the list*, that's for sure. Free lunch, final wisdom, total coverage ... why not? I have my attorney with me and I realize of course that *his* name is not on the list, but we *must* have that suite, yes, this man is actually my *driver*. We brought this Red Shark all the way from the Strip and now it's time for the desert, right? Yes. Just check the list and you'll see. Don't worry. What's the score here? What's next?'

The woman never blinked. 'Your room's not ready yet,' she said. 'But there's somebody looking for you.'

'No!' I shouted. 'Why? We haven't *done* anything yet!' My legs felt rubbery. I gripped the desk and sagged towards her as she held out the envelope, but I refused to accept it. The woman's face was *changing*: swelling, pulsing ... horrible green jowls and fangs jutting out, the face of a moray eel! Deadly poison! I lunged backwards into my attorney, who gripped my arm as he reached out to take the note. 'I'll handle this,' he said to the Moray woman. 'This man has a bad heart, but I have plenty of medicine. My name is Doctor Gonzo. Prepare our suite at once. We'll be in the bar.'

The woman shrugged as he led me away. In a town full of bedrock crazies, nobody even *notices* an acid freak. We struggled through the crowded lobby and found two stools at the bar. My attorney ordered two *cuba libres* with beer and mescal on the side, then he opened the envelope. 'Who's Lacerda?' he asked. 'He's waiting for us in a room on the twelfth floor.'

I couldn't remember. Lacerda? The name rang a bell, but I couldn't concentrate. Terrible things were happening all around us. Right next to me a huge reptile was gnawing on a woman's neck, the carpet was a blood-soaked sponge – impossible to walk on it, no footing at all. 'Order some golf shoes,' I whispered. 'Otherwise, we'll never get out of this place alive. You notice these lizards don't have any trouble moving around in this muck – that's because they have *claws* on their feet.'

'Lizards?' he said. 'If you think we're in trouble now, wait till you see what's happening in the elevators.' He took off his Brazilian sunglasses and I could see he'd been crying. 'I just went upstairs to see this man Lacerda,' he said. 'I told him we knew what he was up to. He *says* he's a photographer, but when I mentioned Savage Henry – well, that did it; he freaked. I could see it in his eyes. He knows we're on to him.'

'Does he understand we have magnums?' I said.

'No. But I told him we had a Vincent Black Shadow. That scared the piss out of him.'

'Good,' I said. 'But what about our room? And the golf shoes? We're right in the middle of a fucking reptile zoo! And somebody's giving *booze* to these goddamn things! It won't be long before they tear us to shreds. Jesus, look at the floor! Have you ever *seen* so much blood? How many have they killed *already*?' I pointed across the room to a group that seemed to be staring at us. 'Holy shit, look at that bunch over there! They've spotted us!'

'That's the press table,' he said. 'That's where you have to sign in for our credentials. Shit, let's get it over with. You handle that, and I'll get the room.'

BACK DOOR BEAUTY ... & FINALLY A BIT OF SERIOUS DRAG RACING ON THE STRIP

Sometime around midnight my attorney wanted coffee. He had been vomiting fairly regularly as we drove around the Strip, and the right flank of the Whale was badly streaked. We were idling at a stoplight in front of the Silver Slipper beside a big blue Ford with Oklahoma plates ... two hoggish-looking couples in the car, probably cops from Muskogee using the Drug Conference to give their wives a look at Vegas. They looked like they'd just beaten Caesar's Palace for about $33 at the blackjack tables, and now they were headed for the Circus-Circus to whoop it up ...

... But suddenly, they found themselves next to a white Cadillac convertible all covered with vomit and a 300-pound Samoan in a yellow fishnet T-shirt yelling at them:

'Hey there! You folks want to buy some heroin?'

No reply. No sign of recognition. They'd been warned about this kind of crap: Just ignore it ...

'Hey, honkies!' my attorney screamed. 'Goddamnit, I'm serious! I want to sell you some pure fuckin' *smack*!' He was leaning out of the car, very close to them. But still nobody answered. I glanced over, very briefly, and saw four middle-American faces frozen with shock, staring straight ahead.

We were in the middle lane. A quick left turn would be illegal. We would have to go straight ahead when the light changed, then escape at the next corner. I waited, tapping the accelerator nervously ...

My attorney was losing control: 'Cheap heroin!' he was shouting. 'This is the real stuff! You won't get hooked! Goddamnit, I *know* what I have here!' He whacked on the side of the car, as if to get their attention ... but they wanted no part of us.

'You folks never talked to a *vet* before?' said my attorney. 'I just got back from Veet Naam. This is *scag*, folks! Pure scag!'

Suddenly the light changed and the Ford bolted off like a rocket. I stomped on the accelerator and stayed right next to them for about two hundred yards, watching for cops in the mirror while my attorney kept screaming at them: 'Shoot! Fuck! Scag! Blood! Heroin! Rape! Cheap! Communist! Jab it right into your fucking eyeballs!'

We were approaching the Circus-Circus at high speed and the Oklahoma car was veering left, trying to muscle into the turn lane. I stomped the Whale into passing gear and we ran fender to fender for a moment. He wasn't up to hitting me; there was horror in his eyes ...

The man in the back seat lost control of himself ... lunging across his wife and snarling wildly: 'You dirty bastards! Pull over and I'll kill you! God damn you! You bastards!' He seemed ready to leap out the window and into our car, crazy with rage. Luckily the Ford was a two-door. He couldn't get out.

We were coming up to the next stoplight and the Ford was still trying to move left. We were both running full bore. I glanced over my shoulder and saw that we'd left the other traffic far behind; there was a big opening to the right. So I mashed on the brake, hurling my attorney against the dashboard, and in the instant the Ford surged ahead I cut across his tail and zoomed into a side-street. A sharp right turn across three lanes of traffic. But it worked. We left the Ford stalled in the middle of the intersection, hung in the middle of a screeching left turn. With a little luck, he'd be arrested for reckless driving.

My attorney was laughing as we careened in low gear, with the lights out, through a dusty tangle of back streets behind the Desert Inn. 'Jesus Christ,' he said. 'Those Okies were getting excited. That guy in the back seat was trying to *bite* me! Shit, he was frothing at the mouth.' He nodded solemnly. 'I should have maced the fucker ... a criminal psychotic, total breakdown ... you never know when they're likely to explode.'

I swung the Whale into a turn that seemed to lead out of the maze – but instead of skidding, the bastard almost rolled.

'Holy shit!' my attorney screamed. 'Turn on the fucking lights!' He was clinging to the top of the windshield ... and suddenly he was doing the big spit again, leaning over the side.

I refused to slow down until I was sure nobody was following us – especially that Oklahoma Ford: those people were definitely dangerous, at least until they calmed down. Would they report that terrible quick encounter to the police? Probably not. It had happened too fast, with no witnesses, and the odds were pretty good that nobody would believe them anyway. The idea that two heroin pushers in a white Cadillac convertible would be dragging up and down the Strip, abusing total strangers at stoplights, was prima facie absurd. Not even Sonny Liston ever got that far out of control.

We made another turn and almost rolled again. The Coup de Ville is not your ideal machine for high speed cornering in residential neighbourhoods. The handling is very mushy ... unlike the Red Shark, which had responded very nicely to situations requiring the quick four-wheel drift. But the Whale – instead of cutting loose at the critical moment –

had a tendency to *dig in*, which accounted for that sickening 'here we go' sensation.

At first I thought it was only because the tyres were soft, so I took it into the Texaco station next to the Flamingo and had the tyres pumped up to fifty pounds each – which alarmed the attendant, until I explained that these were 'experimental' tyres.

But fifty pounds each didn't help the cornering, so I went back a few hours later and told him I wanted to try seventy-five. He shook his head nervously. 'Not me,' he said, handing me the air hose. 'Here. They're your tyres. *You* do it.'

'What's wrong?' I asked. 'You think they can't *take* seventy-five?'

He nodded, moving away as I stooped to deal with the left front. 'You're damn right,' he said. 'Those tyres want twenty-eight in the front and thirty-two in the rear. Hell, fifty's *dangerous*, but seventy-five is *crazy*. They'll explode!'

I shook my head and kept filling the left front. 'I told you,' I said. 'Sandoz laboratories designed these tyres. They're special. I could load them up to a hundred.'

'God almighty!' he groaned. 'Don't do that here.'

'Not today,' I replied. 'I want to see how they corner with seventy-five.'

He chuckled. 'You won't even *get* to the corner, Mister.'

'We'll see,' I said, moving around to the rear with the air hose. In truth, I was nervous. The two front ones were tighter than snare drums; they felt like teak wood when I tapped on them with the rod. But what the hell? I thought. If they explode, so what? It's not often that a man gets a chance to run terminal experiments on a virgin Cadillac and four brand-new $80 tyres. For all I knew, the thing might start cornering like a Lotus Elan. If not, all I had to do was call the VIP agency and have another one delivered ... maybe threaten them with a lawsuit because all four tyres had exploded on me, while driving in heavy traffic. Demand an Eldorado, next time, with four Michelin Xs. And put it all on the card ... charge it to the St Louis Browns.

As it turned out, the Whale behaved very nicely with the altered tyre pressures. The ride was a trifle rough; I could feel every pebble on the highway, like being on roller skates in a gravel pit ... but the thing began cornering in a very stylish manner, very much like driving a motorcycle at top speed in a hard rain: one slip and ZANG, over the high side, cartwheeling across the landscape with your head in your hands.

About thirty minutes after our brush with the Okies we pulled into an all-night diner on the Tonopah highway, on the outskirts of a mean/ scag ghetto called North Las Vegas. Which is actually outside the city limits of Vegas proper. North Vegas is where you go when you've fucked up once too often on the Strip, and when you're not even welcome in the cut-rate downtown places around Casino Center.

This is Nevada's answer to East St Louis – a slum and a graveyard, last stop before permanent exile to Ely or Winnemuca. North Vegas is where you go if you're a hooker turning forty and the syndicate men on the Strip decide you're no longer much good for business out there with the high rollers ... or if you're a pimp with bad credit at the Sands ... or what they still call, in Vegas, 'a hophead'. This can mean almost anything from a mean drunk to a junkie, but in terms of commercial acceptability, it means you're finished in all the right places.

The big hotels and casinos pay a lot of muscle to make sure the high rollers don't have even momentary hassles with 'undesirables'. Security in a place like Caesar's Palace is super tense and strict. Probably a third of the people on the floor at any given time are either shills or watchdogs. Public drunks and known pickpockets are dealt with instantly – hustled out to the parking lot by Secret Service-type thugs and given a quick, impersonal lecture about the cost of dental work and the difficulties of trying to make a living with two broken arms.

The 'high side' of Vegas is probably the most closed society west of Sicily – and it makes no difference, in terms of the day to day lifestyle of the place, whether the man at the top is Lucky Luciano or Howard Hughes. In an economy where Tom Jones can make $75,000 a week for two shows a night at Caesar's, the palace guard is indispensable, and they don't care who signs their paycheques. A gold mine like Vegas breeds its own army, like any other gold mine. Hired muscle tends to accumulate in fast layers around money/power poles ... and big money, in Vegas, is synonymous with the power to protect it.

So once you get blacklisted on the Strip, for any reason at all, you either get out of town or retire to nurse your act along, on the cheap, in the shoddy limbo of North Vegas ... out there with the gunsels, the hustlers, the drug cripples and all the other losers. North Vegas, for instance, is where you go if you need to score smack before midnight with no references.

But if you're looking for cocaine, and you're ready up front with some bills and the proper code words, you want to stay on the Strip and get next to a well-connected hooker, which will take at least one bill for starters.

And so much for all that. We didn't fit the mould. There is no formula for finding yourself in Vegas with a white Cadillac full of drugs and nothing to mix with properly. The Fillmore style never quite caught on here. People like Sinatra and Dean Martin are still considered 'far out' in Vegas. The 'underground newspaper' here – the Las Vegas *Free*

Press – is a cautious echo of the *People's World*, or maybe the *National Guardian*.

A week in Vegas is like stumbling into a time warp, a regression to the late fifties. Which is wholly understandable when you see the people who come here, the big spenders from places like Denver and Dallas. Along with National Elks Club conventions (no niggers allowed) and the All-West Volunteer Sheepherders' Rally. These are people who go absolutely crazy at the sight of an old hooker stripping down to her pasties and prancing out on the runway to the big-beat sound of a dozen fifty-year-old junkies kicking out the jams on 'September Song'.

It was some time around three when we pulled into the parking lot of the North Vegas diner. I was looking for a copy of the Los Angeles *Times*, for news of the outside world, but a quick glance at the newspaper racks made a bad joke of that notion. They don't need the *Times* in North Vegas. No news is good news.

'Fuck newspapers,' said my attorney. 'What we need right now is coffee.'

I agreed, but I stole a copy of the Vegas *Sun* anyway. It was yesterday's edition, but I didn't care. The idea of entering a coffee shop without a newspaper in my hands made me nervous. There was always the sports section; get wired on the baseball scores and pro-football rumours: 'Bart Starr Beaten by Thugs in Chicago Tavern; Packers Seek Trade' ... 'Namath Quits Jets to be Governor of Alabama' ... and a speculative piece on page forty-six about a rookie sensation named Harrison Fire, out of Grambling: runs the hundred in nine flat, 344 pounds and still growing.

'This man Fire has definite promise,' says the coach. 'Yesterday, before practice, he destroyed a Greyhound Bus with his bare hands, and last night he killed a subway. He's a natural for colour TV. I'm not one to play favourites, but it looks like we'll have to make room for him.'

Indeed. There is always room on TV for a man who can beat people to jelly in nine flat ... But not many of these were gathered, on this night, in the North Star Coffee Lounge. We had the place to ourselves – which proved to be fortunate, because we'd eaten two more pellets of mescaline on the way over, and the effects were beginning to manifest.

My attorney was no longer vomiting, or even acting sick. He ordered coffee with the authority of a man long accustomed to quick service. The waitress had the appearance of a very old hooker who had finally found her place in life. She was definitely *in charge* here, and she eyed us with obvious disapproval as we settled on to our stools.

I wasn't paying much attention. The North Star Coffee Lounge seemed like a fairly safe haven from our storms. There are some you go into –

in this line of work – that you know will be heavy. The details don't matter. All you know, for sure, is that your brain starts humming with brutal vibes as you approach the front door. Something wild and evil is about to happen; and it's going to involve *you*.

But there was nothing in the atmosphere of the North Star to put me on my guard. The waitress was passively hostile, but I was accustomed to that. She was a big woman. Not fat, but large in every way, long sinewy arms and a brawler's jawbone. A burned-out caricature of Jane Russell: a big head of dark hair, face slashed with lipstick and a 48 Double-E chest that was probably spectacular about twenty years ago when she might have been a Mama for the Hell's Angels chapter in Berdoo ... but now she was strapped up in a giant pink elastic brassiere that showed like a bandage through the sweaty white rayon of her uniform.

Probably she was married to somebody, but I didn't feel like speculating. All I wanted from her, tonight, was a cup of black coffee and a twenty-nine-cent hamburger with pickles and onions. No hassles, no talk – just a place to rest and re-group. I wasn't even hungry.

My attorney had no newspaper or anything else to compel his attention. So he focused, out of boredom, on the waitress. She was taking our orders like a robot when he punched through her crust with a demand for 'two glasses of ice water – with ice'.

My attorney drank his in one long gulp, then asked for another. I noticed that the waitress seemed tense.

Fuck it, I thought. I was reading the funnies.

About ten minutes later, when she brought the hamburgers, I saw my attorney hand her a napkin with something printed on it. He did it very casually, with no expression at all on his face. But I knew, from the vibes, that our peace was about to be shattered.

'What was that?' I asked him.

He shrugged, smiling vaguely at the waitress who was standing about ten feet away, at the end of the counter, keeping her back to us while she pondered the napkin. Finally she turned and stared ... then she stepped resolutely forwards and tossed the napkin at my attorney.

'What *is* this?' she snapped.

'A napkin,' said my attorney.

There was a moment of nasty silence, then she began screaming: 'Don't give me that bullshit! I *know* what it means! You goddamn fat pimp bastard!'

My attorney picked up the napkin, looked at what he'd written, then dropped it back on the counter. 'That's the name of a horse I used to own,' he said calmly. 'What's *wrong* with you?'

'You sonofabitch!' she screamed. 'I take a lot of shit in this space, but I sure as hell don't have to take it off a *spic pimp*!'

Jesus! I thought. What's happening? I was watching the woman's hands, hoping she wouldn't pick up anything sharp or heavy. I picked up the napkin and read what the bastard had printed on it, in careful red letters: 'Back Door Beauty?' The question mark was emphasized.

The woman was screaming again: 'Pay your bill and get the hell out! You want me to call the cops?'

I reached for my wallet, but my attorney was already on his feet, never taking his eyes off the woman ... then he reached under his shirt, not into his pocket, coming up suddenly with the Gerber Mini-Magnum, a nasty silver blade which the waitress seemed to understand instantly.

She froze: her eyes fixed about six feet down the aisle and lifted the receiver off the hook of the pay phone. He sliced it off, then brought the receiver back to his stool and sat down.

The waitress didn't move. I was stupid with shock, not knowing whether to run or start laughing.

'How much is that lemon meringue pie?' my attorney asked. His voice was casual, as if he had just wandered into the place and was debating what to order.

'Thirty-five cents!' the woman blurted. Her eyes were turgid with fear, but her brain was apparently functioning on some basic motor survival level.

My attorney laughed. 'I mean the *whole* pie,' he said.

She moaned.

My attorney put a bill on the counter. 'Let's say it's five dollars,' he said. 'OK?'

She nodded, still frozen, watching my attorney as he walked around the counter and got the pie out of the display case. I prepared to leave.

The waitress was clearly in shock. The sight of the blade, jerked out in the heat of an argument, had apparently triggered bad memories. The glazed look in her eyes said her throat had been cut. She was still in the grip of paralysis when we left.

Fear and Loathing in Las Vegas, Random House, 1972

LAST TANGO IN VEGAS: FEAR AND LOATHING IN THE NEAR ROOM

ONE

Muhammad Ali Bites the Bullet, Leon Spinks Croaks a Legend ... Sting Like a Butterfly, Float Like a Bee ... Wild Notes of a Weird Cornerman

When I'm gone, boxing will be nothing again. The fans with the cigars and the hats turned down'll be there, but no more housewives and little men in the street and foreign presidents. It's goin' to be back to the fighter who comes to town, smells a flower, visits a hospital, blows a horn and says he's in shape. Old hat. I was the onliest boxer in history people asked questions like a senator.

Muhammad Ali, 1967

Life had been good to Pat Patterson for so long that he'd almost forgotten what it was like to be anything but a free-riding, first-class passenger on a flight near the top of the world ...

It is a long, long way from the frostbitten midnight streets around Chicago's Clark and Division to the deep-rug hallways of the Park Lane Hotel on Central Park South in Manhattan ... But Patterson had made that trip in high style, with stops along the way in London, Paris, Manila, Kinshasa, Kuala Lumpur, Tokyo and almost everywhere else in the world on that circuit where the menus list no prices and you need at least three pairs of $100 sunglasses just to cope with the TV lights every time you touch down at an airport for another frenzied press conference and then a ticker-tape parade along the route to the presidential palace and another pricely reception.

That is Muhammad Ali's world, an orbit so high, a circuit so fast and strong and with rarefied air so thin that only 'the champ', 'the greatest', and a few close friends have unlimited breathing rights. Anybody who can sell his act for $5 million an hour all over the world is working a vein somewhere between magic and madness ... And now, on this warm winter night in Manhattan, Pat Patterson was not entirely sure which way the balance was tipping. The main shock had come three weeks ago in Las Vegas, when he'd been forced to sit passively at ringside and watch the man whose life he would gladly have given his own to protect, under any other circumstances, take a savage and wholly unexpected beating in front of 5000 screaming banshees at the Hilton Hotel and something like sixty million stunned spectators on national/ network TV. The Champ was no longer the Champ: a young brute named Leon Spinks had settled that matter, and not even Muhammad seemed to know just exactly what that awful defeat would mean – for himself or anyone else; not even for his new wife and children, or the handful of friends and advisers who'd been working that high white vein right beside him for so long that they acted and felt like his family.

It was definitely an odd lot, ranging from solemn Black Muslims like Herbert Muhammad, his manager – to shrewd white hipsters like Harold Conrad, his executive spokesman, and Irish Gene Kilroy, Ali's version of Hamilton Jordan: a sort of all-purpose administrative assistant, logistics manager and chief troubleshooter. Kilroy and Conrad are the Champ's answer to Ham and Jody – but mad dogs and wombats will roam the damp streets of Washington, babbling perfect Shakespearean English, before Jimmy Carter comes up with *his* version of Drew 'Bundini' Brown, Ali's *alter ego* and court wizard for so long now that he can't really remember being anything else. Carter's thin-ice sense of humour would not support the weight of a zany friend like Bundini. It would not even support the far more discreet weight of a court jester like J.F.K.'s Dave Powers, whose role in the White House was much closer to Bundini Brown's deeply personal friendship with Ali than Jordan's essentially political and deceptively hard-nosed relationship with Jimmy ... and even Hamilton seems to be gaining weight by geometric progressions these days, and the time may be just about ripe for him to have a chat with the Holy Ghost and come out as a 'born-again Christian'.

That might make the nut for a while – at least through the 1980 reelection campaign – but not even Jesus could save Jordan from a fate worse than any hell he'd ever imagined if Jimmy Carter woke up one morning and read in the *Washington Post* that Hamilton had pawned the great presidential seal for $500 in some fashionable Georgetown hockshop ... eye for collateral.

Indeed ... and this twisted vision would seem almost too bent for print if Bundini hadn't already raised at least the raw possibility of it by once pawning Muhammad Ali's 'Heavyweight Champion of the World' gold & jewel studded belt for $500 – just an overnight loan from a friend, he said later; but the word got out and Bundini was banished from the family and the whole entourage for eighteen months when the Champ was told what he'd done.

That heinous transgression is shrouded in a mix of jive-shame and *real* black humour at this point: the Champ, after all, had once hurled his Olympic gold medal into the Ohio River, in a fit of pique at some alleged racial insult in Louisville – and what was the difference between a gold medal and a jewel-studded belt? They were both symbols of a 'white devil's' world that Ali, if not Bundini, was already learning to treat with a very calculated measure of public disrespect ... What they shared, far beyond a very real friendship, was a shrewd kind of street-theatre sense of how far out on that limb they could go, without crashing. Bundini has always had a finer sense than anyone else in the Family about where the Champ *wanted* to go, the shifting winds of his instincts, and he has never been worried about things like limits or consequences. That was the province of others, like Conrad or Herbert. Drew B. has always known exactly which side he was on, and so has Cassius/Muhammad. Bundini is the man who came up with 'Float like a butterfly, sting like a bee', and ever since then he has been as close to both Cassius Clay and Muhammad Ali as anyone else in the world.

Pat Patterson, by contrast, was a virtual newcomer to the Family. A 200-pound, forty-year-old black cop, he was a veteran of the Chicago Vice Squad before he hired on as Ali's personal bodyguard. And, despite the total devotion and relentless zeal he brought to his responsibility for protecting the Champ at all times from *any* kind of danger, hassles or even minor inconvenience, six years on the job had caused him to understand, however reluctantly, that there were at least a few people who could come and go as they pleased through the wall of absolute security he was supposed to maintain around the Champ.

Bundini and Conrad were two of these. They have been around for so long that they had once called the boss 'Cassius', or even 'Cash' – while Patterson had never addressed him as anything but 'Muhammad', or 'Champ'. He had come aboard at high tide, as it were, and even though he was now in charge of everything from carrying Ali's money – in a big roll of $100 bills – to protecting his life with an ever-present chrome-plated revolver and the lethal fists and feet of a black belt with a licence to kill, it had always galled him a bit to know that Muhammad's capricious instincts and occasionally perverse sense of humour made it certifiably impossible for *any* one bodyguard, or even *four*, to protect him from danger in public. His moods were too unpredictable: one minute he would be in an almost catatonic funk, crouched in the back seat of a black Cadillac limousine with an overcoat over his head – and then, with no warning at all, he would suddenly be out of the car at a red light somewhere in the Bronx, playing stickball in the street with a gang of teenage junkies. Patterson had learned to deal with the Champ's moods but he also knew that in any crowd around the Greatest there would be at least a few who felt the same way about Ali as they had about Malcolm X or Martin Luther King.

There was a time, shortly after his conversion to the Black Muslim religion in the mid-sixties, when Ali seemed to emerge as a main spokesman for what the Muslims were then perfecting as the state of the art in racial paranoia – which seemed a bit heavy and not a little naive at the time, but which the white devils moved quickly to justify ...

Yes. But that is a very long story and we will get to it later. The only point we need to deal with right now is that Muhammad Ali somehow emerged from one of the meanest and most shameful ordeals any prominent American has ever endured as one of the few real martyrs of that goddamn wretched war in Vietnam and a sort of instant folk hero all over the world, except in the USA.

That would come later ...

The Spinks disaster in Vegas had been a terrible shock to the Family. They had all known it had to come *sometime*, but the scene had already been set and the papers already signed for that 'sometime' – a $16 million purse and a mind-boggling, damn-the-cost television spectacle with Ali's old nemesis Ken Norton as the bogeyman, and one last king-hell payday for *everybody*. They were prepared, in the back of their hearts, for that one – but not for the cheap torpedo that blew their whole ship out of the water in Vegas for no payday at all. Leon Spinks crippled a whole industry in one hour on that fateful Wednesday evening in Las Vegas – *the Muhammad Ali industry*, which has churned out roughly $56 million in over fifteen years and at least twice or three times that much for the people who kept the big engine running all this time. (It would take Bill Walton 112 years on an annual NBA salary of $500,000 to equal that figure.)

I knew it was too close for comfort. I told him to stop fooling around. He was giving up too many rounds. But I heard the decision and I thought, 'Well, what are you going to do? That's it. I've prepared myself for this day for a long time. I conditioned myself for it. I was young with him and now I feel old with him.'

Angelo Dundee, Ali's trainer

Dundee was not the only person who was feeling old with Muhammad Ali on that cold Wednesday night in Las Vegas. Somewhere around the middle of the fifteenth round a whole generation went over the hump as the last great prince of the sixties went out in a blizzard of pain, shock and angry confusion so total that it was hard to even know how to feel, much less what to say, when the thing was finally over. The last shot came just at the final bell, when 'Crazy Leon' whacked Ali with a savage overhand right that almost dropped the Champ in his tracks and killed the last glimmer of hope for the patented 'miracle finish' that Angelo Dundee knew was his fighter's only chance. As Muhammad wandered back to his corner about six feet in front of me, the deal had clearly gone down.

The decision was anticlimatic. Leon Spinks, a twenty-four-year-old brawler from St Louis with only seven professional fights on his record, was the new Heavyweight Boxing Champion of the World. And the roar of the pro-Spinks crowd was the clearest message of all: that uppity nigger from Louisville had finally got what was coming to him. For fifteen long years he had mocked everything they all thought they stood for: changing his name, dodging the draft, beating the best they could hurl at him ... But now, thank God, they were seeing him finally go down.

Six presidents have lived in the White House in the time of Muhammad Ali. Dwight Eisenhower was still rapping golf balls around the Oval Office when Cassius Clay Jr won a gold medal for the US as a light-heavyweight in the 1960 Olympics and then turned pro and won his first fight for money against a journeyman heavyweight named Tunney Hunsaker in Louisville on 29 October of that same year.

Less than four years later and almost three months to the day after John Fitzgerald Kennedy was murdered in Dallas, Cassius Clay – the 'Louisville Lip' by then – made a permanent enemy of every 'boxing expert' in the Western world by beating World Heavyweight Champion Sonny Liston, the meanest of the mean, so badly that Liston refused to come out of his corner for the seventh round.

That was fourteen years ago. Jesus! And it seems like fourteen months.

Why?

Brain damage.

THE REAL STORY: A MEMO WITH NAILS IN BOTH NOSTRILS ... BY RAOUL DUKE, SPORTS EDITOR

This story is badly bogged down, and I think I know the reason: Dr Thompson has been on it so long – in the belly of the beast, as it were – that he has lost all functional contact with his sense of humour; and where I come from they call that condition 'insanity'.

But there are a lot of high-powered fools where I come from, and it's been about fifteen years since I took any one of them seriously ... And in fact it was Thompson himself who originally made that connection between humour and sanity; which changes nothing, because we come from the same place – from the elm-shaded, white-frame 'highlands' of Louisville, Kentucky, about halfway between the Cassius Clay residence down on South Fourth Street and the homes of the men who originally launched Cassius Clay Jr on his long wild ride on the great roller-coaster of professional boxing and paraprofessional show business. They lived out in Indian Hills or on Mockingbird Valley Road near the Louisville Country Club, and they owned every bank in the city – along with both newspapers, all the radio stations that white folks took seriously, and at least half the major distilleries and tobacco companies that funded the municipal tax base.

They know a good thing when they saw one, and in the year of our Lord 1960 the good thing they saw was an eighteen-year-old local Negro boxer, a big, fast and impressively intelligent young light-heavyweight named Cassius Clay Jr, who had just won a gold medal for the USA in the 1960 Olympics ... So ten of these gents got together and made the boy an offer he couldn't refuse: they were willing to take a long risk on him, they said, just as soon as he gained a few pounds and decided to fight professionally as the new morning star among heavyweights.

They would finance his move for the title in a division that Floyd Patterson and his crafty manager, Cus D'Amato, had dominated for so long – by means of a new gimmick known as 'closed-circuit TV' – that a whole generation of what might have been promising young heavyweight challengers had died on the vine while they waited in line for a chance to fight Patterson, who didn't *really* want to fight anybody.

Floyd was 'the champ' and he used that fact as leverage as Richard Nixon would later learn to retreat behind the odious truth that 'I am, you know, the President.'

Indeed ... and they were both right for a while; but bad karma tends to generate its own kind of poison, which – like typhoid chickens and rotten bread cast out on the waters – will usually come home to either roost, fester or mutate very close to its own point of origin.

Richard Nixon abused karma, chickens and even bread for so long that they all came home at once and totally destroyed him ... And Floyd Patterson's neurotic, anal-compulsive reluctance to get in the ring with anything at all with two arms and legs under thirty was what eventually created the vacuum that hatched Sonny Liston, an ageing ex-con who twice turned poor Floyd to jelly, just by climbing into the ring.

... Hot damn! We may be approaching a heinous new record for mixed metaphors in this thing; the rats have swarmed into the belfry, and anything sane that survives will be hurled out to sea and stomped down like a dwarf in a shitrain ...

Why not?

It was never my intention to make any real sense in this memo. The Sports Desk has never loved logic; mainly because there is no money in it – and pro sports without money is like a Vincent Black Shadow with no gas. Dumb greed is the backbone of all sports, except maybe college wrestling – which may or may not be a good & healthy thing for some people, in places like Kansas and Idaho, but not *here*. Those knotty little monsters can write their own stories, and toss them in over the transom ... If we have enough room or maybe a bad cheque for a half-page ad from the *Shotgun News* or the 'Billy Beer' people, that's when we'll focus the whole twisted energy of the Sports Desk on a college wrestling feature:

UTAH CHAMP DROGO PINS THREE-ARMED COWBOY
FOR WEST SLOPE TITLE IN NINE-HOUR CLASSIC

How's that for a stylish headline?
Well ... shucks; let's try it again, from the other side of the fence:

CRIPPLED COWBOY CHALLENGER FALLS SHORT
IN MAT FINALS; ANGRY FANS MAUL REF AS
MATCH ENDS; HUGE DROGO GAINS SPLIT WIN

Jesus! I could get a job writing sports heads for the *Daily News* with that kind of feel for the word count ... Right, with a big salary too, in the core of the Big Apple ...

But that is not what we had in mind here, is it?

No. We were talking of sport, and big money. Which gets us back to pro boxing, the most shameless racket of all. It is more a spectacle than a sport, one of the purest forms of atavistic endeavour still extant in a world that only big-time politicians feel a need to call 'civilized'. Nobody who has ever sat in a front-row, ringside seat less than six feet just below and away from the sickening thumps and cracks and groans of two desperate, adrenalin-crazed giants who are whipping and pounding each other like two pit bulls in a death battle will ever forget what it felt like to be there.

No TV camera or any other kind will ever convey the almost four-dimensional reality of total, frenzied violence of seeing, hearing and almost *feeling* the sudden WHACK of Leon Spinks' thinly padded fist against Muhammad Ali's cheekbone so close in front of your own face that it is hard to keep from flinching and trying to duck backwards – while a whole row of $200-a-seat ringsiders right behind you are leaping and stomping and howling for *more* showers of flying sweat to fall down on them, *more* droplets of human blood to rain down on the sleeves and tailored shoulders of their tan cashmere sport coats ... and then, with Leon still pounding and the sweat and blood still flying, some fist-flailing geek screaming over your shoulder loses his balance and cracks you between the shoulder blades with a shot that sends you reeling into a cop hanging on to the ring apron – who reacts with a vicious elbow to your chest, and the next thing you see is shoes bouncing inches in front of your face on a concrete floor.

'The horror! The horror! ... Exterminate all the brutes!'

Mistah Kurtz said that but the smart money called him a joker ... Ho, ho, good ole Kurtz, that Prussian sense of humour will zing you every time.

I said that. We were sitting in a sauna at the health spa in the Las Vegas Hilton – me and my friend Bob Arum, the sinister promoter – when all of a sudden the redwood door swung open and in comes Leon Spinks.

'Hi there, Leon,' said Arum.

Leon grinned and tossed his towel across the room at the stove full of hot rocks. 'What's happenin', jewboy?' he replied. 'I heard you was too stoned to be foolin' around down here with us health freaks.'

Arum turned beet red and moved off towards the corner.

Leon laughed again, and reached for his teeth. 'These damn things get hot,' he snarled. 'Who needs these goddamn teeth, anyway.'

He turned to laugh at Arum again, and right then I saw my chance. I stood up in a sort of linebacker's crouch and hooked him hard in the ribs. He fell back on the hot rocks and I hooked him again.

'O my God!' Arum shrieked. 'I heard something break!'

Leon looked up from where he was sitting on the duckboard floor, his face warped with pain. 'Well,' he said slowly, 'now we know you ain't deaf, Bob.' He was leaning back on both hands, wincing with every breath as he slowly raised his eyes to glare at me.

'Real smart friends you got, Arum,' he whispered, 'but this one's *mine*, now.' He winced again: every breath was painful and he spoke very slowly. 'Call my brother Michael,' he said to Arum. 'Tell him to fix a hook on this honky bastard's head and hang him up alongside the big bag, for when I get well.'

Arum was kneeling beside him now, gently probing his rib cage ... And it was just about then that I felt myself waking up; but instead of lying down in a bed, I suddenly realized that something ugly had happened. My first thought was that I'd passed out from the heat of the sauna: indeed, a quick trip to the Near Room and some dim memory of violence, but only as part of a dream ...

Or ... well ... maybe not. As my head began to clear and Arum's face came into focus – his beady eyes, his trembling hands, the sweat squirting out of his pores – I realized that I was not lying down or coming out of a faint, but standing naked in the middle of a hot wooden cell and staring down like a zombie at – ye gods! – it was Leon Spinks!

And Bob Arum, his eyes bulged out like a frog's, was massaging Leon's chest. I stared for a moment, then recoiled with shock ... No, I thought, this can't be happening!

But it was. I was wide-awake now, and I knew this hideous thing was actually happening, right in front of my eyes. Arum was moaning and trembling, while his hands stroked the challenger's chest. Leon was leaning back with his eyes closed, his teeth clenched, and his whole body stiff as a corpse.

Neither one of them seemed to notice my recovery – from what was later diagnosed, by the nervous hotel doctor, as nothing more than a mild acid flashback ... But I didn't learn *that* until later.

High Risk on the Low Road, New Boy on Queer Street ... Five Million Dollars an Hour, Five Miles to the Terminal Hotel ... The Devil and Pat Patterson ... No Nigger Ever Called Me Hippie ...

THE NEAR ROOM

When he got in trouble in the ring, [Ali] imagined a door swung open and inside he could see neon, orange and green lights blinking, and bats blowing trumpets and alligators playing trombones, and he could hear snakes screaming. Weird masks and actors' clothes hung on the wall, and if he stepped across the sill and reached for them, he knew that he was committing himself to destruction.

George Plimpton, *Shadow Box*

It was almost midnight when Pat Patterson got off the elevator and headed down the corridor towards 905, his room right next door to the Champ's. They had flown in from Chicago a few hours earlier and Muhammad had said he was tired and felt like sleeping. No midnight strolls down the block to the Plaza fountain, he promised, no wandering around the hotel or causing a scene in the lobby.

Beautiful, thought Patterson. No worries tonight. With Muhammad in bed and Veronica there to watch over him, Pat felt things were under control and he might even have time for a bit of refreshment downstairs, and then get a decent night's sleep for himself. The only conceivable problem was the volatile presence of Bundini and a friend, who had dropped by around ten for a chat with the Champ about his run for the Triple Crown. The family had been in a state of collective shock for two weeks or so after Vegas, but now it was the first week in March and they were eager to get the big engine cranked up for the return bout with

Spinks in September. No contracts had been signed yet, and every sportswriter in New York seemed to be on the take from either Ken Norton or Don King or both ... But none of that mattered, said Ali, because he and Leon had already agreed on the rematch, and by the end of this year he would be the first man in history to win the Heavyweight Championship of the World THREE TIMES.

Patterson had left them whooping and laughing at each other, but only after securing a promise from Hal Conrad that he and Bundini leave early and let the Champ sleep. They were scheduled to tape a show with Dick Cavett the next day, then drive for three or four hours up into the mountains of eastern Pennsylvania to Ali's custom-built training camp at Deer Lake. Kilroy was getting the place ready for what Patterson and all the rest of the Family understood was going to be some very serious use. Ali had announced almost immediately after losing to Spinks in Vegas any talk of his 'retiring from the ring was nonsense', and that soon he'd begin training for his rematch with Leon.

So the fat was in the fire: a second loss to Spinks would be even worse than the first – the end of the line for Ali, the Family, and in fact the whole Ali industry. No more paydays, no more limousines, no more suites and crab cocktails from room service in the world's most expensive hotels. For Pat Patterson and a lot of other people, another defeat by Spinks would mean the end of a whole way of life ... And, worse yet, the first wave of public reaction to Ali's 'comeback' announcement had been anything but reassuring. An otherwise sympathetic story in the *Los Angeles Times* described the almost universal reaction of the sporting press:

'There were smiles and a shaking of hands all around when the thirty-six-year-old ex-champion said after the fight last Wednesday night: "I'll be back. I'll be the first man to win the heavyweight title three times." But no one laughed out loud.'

A touch of this doomsday thinking had even showed up in the Family. Dr Ferdie Pacheco, who had been in the Champ's corner for every fight since he first won the title from Liston – except the last one – had gone on the Tom Snyder show and said that Muhammad was finished as a fighter, that he was a shadow of his former self, and that he (Pacheco) had done everything but beg Ali to retire even *before* the Spinks fight.

Pacheco had already been expelled from the Family for his heresy, but it had planted a seed of doubt that was hard to ignore. The 'Doc' was no quack and he was also a personal friend; did he know something the others didn't? Was it even *possible* that the Champ was 'washed up'? There was no way to think that by looking at him, or listening to him either. He looked sharp, talked sharp, and there was a calmness, a kind of muted intensity, in his confidence that made it sound almost understated.

Pat Patterson believed – or if he didn't, there was no way that even the Champ could guess it. The loyalty of those close to Muhammad Ali is so profound that it sometimes clouds their own vision ... But Leon Spinks had swept those clouds away, and now it was time to get serious. No more show business, no more clowning. Now they had come to the crunch.

Pat Patterson had tried not to brood on these things, but every newspaper rack he'd come close to in Chicago, New York or anywhere else seemed to echo the baying of hounds on a blood scent. Every media voice in the country was poised for ultimate revenge on this uppity nigger who had laughed in their faces for so long that a whole generation of sportswriters had grown up in the shadow of a mocking, dancing presence that most of them had never half-understood until now, when it seemed almost gone.

Even the rematch with Spinks was bogged down in the arcane politics of big-money boxing – and Pat Patterson, like all the others who had geared their lives to the fortunes of Muhammad Ali, understood that the rematch would have to be *soon*. Very soon. And the Champ would have to be *ready* this time – as he had not been ready in Vegas. There was no avoiding the memory of Sonny Liston's grim fate, after losing *again* to Ali in a fight that convinced even the 'experts'.

But Muhammad Ali was no Liston. There was magic in his head, as well as his fists and his feet – but time was not on his side, this time, and the only thing more important than slashing the Gordian knot of boxing-industry politics that was already menacing the reality of a quick rematch with Spinks was the absolute necessity of making sure that the Champ would take this next fight as seriously as it was clearly going to be. A whole industry would be up for grabs – not to mention the fate of the Family – and the bizarre scenes of chaos and wild scrambling for position that had followed Spinks' first shocking upset would not be repeated if Ali lost the rematch.

Nobody was ready for Spinks' stunning victory in Vegas, but every power freak and leverage-monger with any real-life connection to boxing would be ready to go either way on this next one. There would be no more of this low-rent political bullshit about 'recognition' by the World Boxing Council (WBC) or the World Boxing Association (WBA) if Ali lost the rematch with Leon – and no more big-money fights for Muhammad Ali, either. They would all be pushed over the brink that was already just a few steps in front of them – and no 'comeback' would be likely, or even possible.

These things were among the dark shadows that Pat Patterson would rather not have been thinking about on that night in Manhattan as he walked down the corridor to his room in the Park Lane Hotel. The Champ had already convinced him that he would indeed be the first man in history to win the first Triple Crown in the history of heavyweight boxing – and Pat Patterson was far from alone in his conviction that Leon Spinks would be easy prey, next time, for a Muhammad Ali in top condition both mentally and physically. Spinks was vulnerable: the same crazy/mean style that made him dangerous also made him easy to hit. His hands were surprisingly fast, but his feet were as slow as Joe Frazier's and it was only the crafty coaching of his trainer, the ancient Sam Solomon, that had given him the early five-round edge in Las Vegas that Ali had refused to understand until he was so far behind that his only hope was a blazing last-minute assault and a knockout or at least a few knockdowns that he was too tired, in the end, to deliver.

Leon was dead on his feet in that savage fifteenth round – but so was Muhammad Ali, and that's why Spinks won the fight ...

Yes ... but that is no special secret and there will be plenty of time to deal with those questions of ego and strategy later on in this saga, if in fact we ever get there. The sun is up, the peacocks are screaming with lust, and this story is so far off the game plan that no hope of salvage exists at this time – or at least nothing less than a sweeping, all-points injunction by Judge Crater, who maintains an unlisted number so private that not even Bob Arum can reach him on short notice.

So we are left with the unhurried vision of Pat Patterson finally reaching the door of his room, number 905 in the Park Lane Hotel in Manhattan – and just as he pulls the room key out of his pocket on the way to a good night's sleep, his body goes suddenly stiff as he picks up the sound of raucous laughter and strange voices in room number 904.

Weird sounds from the Champ's suite ... Impossible, but Pat Patterson *knows* he's stone sober and nowhere near deaf, so he drops his key back in his pocket and moves one step down the hallway, listening carefully now to these sounds he hopes are not really there ... Hallucinations, bad nerves, almost anything but the sound of a totally unknown voice – and the voice of a 'white devil', no doubt about that – from the room where Ali and Veronica are supposed to be sleeping peacefully. Bundini and Conrad had both promised to be gone at least an hour ago ... But, no! Not this: not Bundini and Conrad and *the voice of some stranger, too*; along with the unmistakable sound of laughter from both the Champ and his wife ... Not *now*, just when things were getting close to intolerably serious.

What was the meaning?

Pat Patterson knew what he had to do: he planted both feet in the rug in front of 904 and *knocked*. Whatever was going on would have to be cut short at once, and it was his job to do the cutting – even if he had to get rude with Bundini and Conrad.

Well ... this next scene is so strange that not even the people who were part of it can recount exactly what happened ... but it went more or less like this: Bundini and I had just emerged from a strategy conference in the bathroom when we heard the sudden sound of knocking on the door. Bundini waved us all into silence as Conrad slouched nervously against the wall below the big window that looked out on the snow-covered wasteland of Central Park; Veronica was sitting fully clothed on the king-size bed right next to Ali, who was stretched out and relaxed with the covers pulled up to his waist, wearing nothing at all except ... Well, let's take it again from Pat Patterson's view from the doorway, when Bundini answered his knock:

The first thing he saw when the door opened was a white stranger with a can of beer in one hand and a lit cigarette in the other, sitting cross-legged on the bureau that faced the Champ's bed – a bad omen for sure and a thing to be dealt with at once at this ominous point in time; but the next thing Pat Patterson saw turned his face into spastic wax and caused his body to leap straight back towards the doorway like he'd just been struck by lightning.

His professional bodyguard's eyes had fixed on me just long enough to be sure I was passive and with both hands harmlessly occupied for at least the few seconds it would take him to sweep the rest of the room and see what was wrong with his five-million-dollars-an-hour responsibility ... and I could tell by the way he moved into the room and the look on his face that I was suddenly back at that point where any movement at all or even the blink of an eye could change my life for ever. But I also knew what was coming and I recall a split second of real fear as Pat Patterson's drop-forged glance swept past me and over to the bed to Veronica and the inert lump that lay under the sheets right beside her.

For an instant that frightened us all, the room was electric with absolute silence – and then the bed seemed to literally explode as the sheets flew away and a huge body with the hairy red face of the Devil himself leaped up like some jack-in-the-box out of hell and uttered a wild cry that jolted us all and sent such an obvious shock through Pat Patterson that he leaped backwards and shot out both elbows like Kareem coming down with a rebound ...

Rolling Stone no. 264, 4 May 1978

LAST TANGO IN VEGAS: FEAR AND LOATHING IN THE FAR ROOM

TWO

Wild Ravings of an Autograph Hound ... A Threat of Public Madness ... the Pantyhose Press Conference

I waited until I was sure the Muhammad Ali party was well off the plane and up the ramp before I finally stood and moved up the aisle, fixing the stewardess at the door with a blind stare from behind two mirror lenses so dark that I could barely see to walk – but not so dark that I failed to notice a touch of mockery in her smile as I nodded and stepped past her. 'Goodbye, sir,' she chirped. 'I hope you got an interesting story.'

You nasty little bitch! I hope your next flight crashes in a cannibal country ... But I kept this thought to myself as I laughed bitterly and stomped up the empty tunnel to a bank of pay phones in the concourse. It was New York's La Guardia airport, around eight-thirty on a warm Sunday night in the first week of March, and I had just flown in from Chicago – supposedly 'with the Muhammad Ali party'. But things had not worked out that way and my temper was hovering dangerously on the far edge of control as I listened to the sound of nobody answering the phone in Hal Conrad's West Side apartment ... *That swine! That treacherous lying bastard!*

We were almost to the ten-ring limit, that point where I knew I'd start pounding on things unless I hung up quickly before we got to eleven ... when suddenly a voice sounding almost as angry as I felt came booming over the line. 'Yeah, yeah, what *is* it?' Conrad snapped. 'I'm in a hell of a hurry. Jesus! I was just about into the elevator when I had to come back and answer this goddamn—'

'YOU CRAZY BASTARD!' I screamed, cutting into his gravelly mumbling as I slammed my hand down on the tin counter and saw a woman using the phone next to me jump like a rat had just run up her leg.

'It's *me*, Harold!' I shouted. 'I'm out here at La Guardia and my whole story's fucked and just as soon as I find all my baggage I'm going to get a cab and track you down and slit your goddamn throat!'

'*Wait* a minute!' he said. 'What the hell is wrong? Where's Ali? Not with *you*?'

'Are you kidding?' I snarled. 'That crazy bastard didn't even know who I *was* when I met him in Chicago. I made a GODDAMN FOOL OF MYSELF, Harold! He looked at me like I was some kind of *autograph hound*!'

'No!' said Conrad. 'I told him all about you – that you were a good friend of mine and you'd be on the flight with him from Chicago. He was *expecting* you.'

'Bullshit!' I yelled. 'You told me he'd be travelling alone, too ... So I stayed up all night and busted my ass to get a first-class seat on that Continental flight that I'd knew he'd be catching at O'Hare; then I got everything arranged with the flight crew between Denver and Chicago, making sure they blocked off the first two seats so we could sit together ... Jesus, Harold,' I muttered, suddenly feeling very tired, 'what kind of sick instinct would cause you to do a thing like this to me?'

'Where the hell is Ali?' Conrad shouted, ignoring my question. 'I sent a car out to pick you up, *both* of you!'

'You mean *all* of us,' I said. 'His wife was with him, along with Pat Patterson and maybe a few others – I couldn't tell, but it wouldn't have made any difference; they *all* looked at me like I was weird; some kind of psycho trying to muscle into the act, babbling about sitting in Veronica's seat ...'

'That's impossible,' Conrad snapped. 'He knew—'

'Well, I guess he *forgot*!' I shouted, feeling my temper roving out on the edge again. 'Are we talking about *brain damage*, Harold? Are you saying he *has no memory*?'

He hesitated just long enough to let me smile for the first time all day. 'This could be an *ugly* story, Harold,' I said. 'Ali is so punch-drunk that his memory's all scrambled? Maybe they should lift his licence, eh? "Yeah, let's croak all this talk about comebacks, Dumbo. Your memory's fucked, you're on queer street – and by the way, Champ, what are your job prospects?"'

'You son of a bitch,' Conrad muttered. 'Okay. To hell with all this bullshit. Just get a cab and meet us at the Plaza. I should have been there a half-hour ago.'

'I thought you had us all booked into the Park Lane,' I said.

'Get moving and don't worry about it,' he croaked. 'I'll meet you at the Plaza. Don't waste any time.'

'WHAT?' I screamed. 'What am I doing *right now*? I have a *Friday deadline*, Harold, and this is Sunday! You call me in the middle of the goddamn night in Colorado and tell me to get on the first plane to Chicago because Muhammad Ali has all of a sudden decided he wants to talk to me – after all that lame bullshit in Vegas – so I take the *insane* risk of dumping my whole story in a parachute bag and flying off on a 2000-mile freakout right in the middle of a deadline crunch to meet a

man in Chicago who treats me like a wino when I finally get there ...
And now you're talking to *me*, you pigfucker, about WASTING
TIME?'

I was raving at the top of my lungs, drawing stares from every direction – so I tried to calm down; no need to get busted for public madness
in the airport, I thought; but I was also in New York with no story and
no place to work and only five days away from a clearly impossible
deadline, and now Conrad was telling me that my long-overdue talk
with Ali had once again 'gone wrong'.

'Just get in a cab and meet me at the Plaza,' he was saying. 'I'll pull
this mess together, don't worry ...'

'Well ...' I said. 'I'm already here in New York and I definitely *want
to see you*, Harold – so yeah, I'll be there. But—' I paused for a moment,
fascinated by a scene that was suddenly running very vividly behind my
eyeballs as I stood there at the pay phone in the concourse '—let me *tell*
you what I'm going to do at noon tomorrow, if you *don't* pull this mess
together.'

'Not now,' he said. 'I have to get going—'

'Listen!' I yelled. 'I want you to *understand* this, Harold, because it
could do serious things to your image.'

Silence.

'What I plan to do when I wake up in the Plaza at exactly eleven
o'clock tomorrow morning,' I said calmly, 'is have a few bloody marys
and then go down to the hotel drugstore and buy some of those sheer
pantyhose, along with a black wig and some shades like yours,
Harold ... Then I'll go back up to my room and call the *Daily News* to
say they should have a photographer at the Plaza fountain exactly at
noon for a press conference with Ali and Bob Arum ... and, yes that my
name is Hal Conrad, the well-known boxing wizard and executive
spokesman for Muhammad Ali.

'And *then*, Harold,' I continued, 'exactly at noon I will leave my room
in the Plaza, wearing nothing but a pair of sheer pantyhose and a wig
and black shades ... and I will take the elevator down to the lobby and
stroll very casually outside and across the street and climb *into the
Plaza fountain*, waving a bottle of Fernet Branca in one hand and a joint
in the other ... And I'll be SCREAMING, Harold, at anybody who
gets in my way or even stops to stare.'

'Bullshit!' he snapped. 'You'll get yourself locked up.'

'No,' I said. 'I'll get *you* locked up. When they grab me I'll say I'm
Hal Conrad and all I wanted to do was get things organized for the upcoming Ali-Arum press conference – and then you'll have a new picture
for your scrapbook, a front-page shot in the *News* of "famous boxing
wizard Hal Conrad".'

I suddenly saw the whole scene in that movie behind my eyes. I would intimidate anybody in the elevator by raving and screeching at them about things like '*the broken spirit*' and '*fixers who steal clothes from the poor*'. That, followed by an outburst of deranged weeping, would get me down to the lobby where I would quickly get a grip and start introducing myself to everybody within reach and inviting them all to the press conference in the fountain ... and then, when I finally climbed into the water and took a real stance for the noon/lunch crowd, I could hear myself screeching, 'Cast out VANITY! Look at me – I'm not VAIN! My name is Hal Conrad and I feel *wonderful*! I'm *proud* to wear pantyhose in the streets of New York – *and so is Muhammad Ali.* Yes! He'll be here in just a few moments, and he'll be dressed *just like me. And Bob Arum too!*' I would shriek, 'He's not ashamed to wear pantyhose.'

The crowd would not be comfortable with this gig; there was not much doubt about that. A naked man in the streets is one thing, but the sight of the recently dethroned Heavyweight Champion of the World parading around in the fountain, wearing nothing but sheer pantyhose, was too weird to tolerate.

Boxing was bad enough as it was, and wrestling was worse: but not even a mob of New Yorkers could handle such a nasty spectacle as this. They would be ripping up the paving stones by the time the police arrived.

'Stop *threatening* me, you *drunken freak*!' Conrad shouted. 'Just get in a cab and meet me at the Plaza. I'll have everything under control by the time you get there – we'll go up to his room and talk *there.*'

I shrugged and hung up the phone. Why not? I thought. It was too late to catch a turnaround flight back to Colorado, so I might as well check into the Plaza and get rid of another credit card, along with another friend. Conrad was *trying*; I knew that – but I also knew that this time he was grasping at straws, because we both understood the deep and deceptively narrow-looking moat that eighteen years of celebrity forced Ali to dig between his 'public' and his 'private' personas.

It is more like a *ring* of moats than just one, and Ali has learned the subtler art of making each one seem like the last great leap between the intruder and himself ... But there is always *one more moat* to get across, and not many curious strangers have ever made it that far.

Some people will settle happily for a smile and joke in a hotel lobby, and others will insist on crossing two or even three of his moats before they feel comfortably 'private' with the Champ ... But very few people understand how many rings there really are:

My own quick guess would be nine; but Ali's quick mind and his instinct for public relations can easily make the third moat *seem* like the ninth; and this world is full of sporting journalists who never realized where they were until the same 'private thoughts' and 'spontaneous bits of eloquence' they had worked so desperately to glean from the Champ, in some rare flash of personal communication that none other would ever share, appeared word for word, in cold black type, under somebody else's byline.

This is not a man who *needs* hired pros and wizards to speak for him; but he has learned how to use them so skilfully that he can save himself for the rare moments of confrontation that *interest* him ... Which are few and far between, but anybody who has ever met Muhammad Ali on that level will never forget it. He has a very lonely sense of humour, and a sense of himself so firmly entrenched that it seems to hover, at times, in that nervous limbo between egomania and genuine invulnerability.

There is not much difference in his mind between a challenge *inside* the ring, with Joe Frazier, or in a TV studio with Dick Cavett. He honestly believes he can handle it all; and he has almost two decades of evidence to back him up, at this point; so it takes a rare sense of challenge to get him cranked up. He had coped with everything from the white heavies of Louisville to Sonny Liston and the war in Vietnam; from the hostility of old/white draft boards to the sullen enigma of the Black Muslims; from the genuine menace of Joe Frazier to the puzzling threat of Ken Norton ... and he has beaten every person or thing that God or even Allah ever put in his way – except perhaps Joe Frazier and the eternal mystery of women ...

And now, as my cab moved jerkily through the snow-black streets of Brooklyn towards the Plaza Hotel, I was brooding on Conrad's deranged plot that I felt would almost certainly cause me another nightmare of professional grief and personal humiliation. I felt like a rape victim on the way to a discussion with the rapist on the Johnny Carson show. Not even Hal Conrad's fine sense of reality could take me past moat number five – which would not be enough, because I'd made it clear from the start that I was not especially interested in anything short of at least number seven or eight.

Which struck me as far enough, for my purposes, because I understood number nine well enough to know that, if Muhammad was as smart as I thought he was, I would never see or even smell that last moat.

Wilfrid Sheed, an elegant writer who wrote a whole book titled *Muhammad Ali* without ever crossing the sixth or seventh moat, much less the ninth, has described that misty battlefield far better than I can ... but he was paid a lot better, too, which tends to bring a certain balance to situations that would otherwise be intolerable.

In any case, here is Sheed recounting the agonies of merely trying to talk to the subject of his twenty-dollar-per-copy book:

'... Ali moves so fast that he even outruns his own people, and no one seems to know for sure where he is. I am about to head for his training camp in the Poconos one more time when word arrives that he has broken camp for good. What? Where? Rumours of his comings and goings suddenly rival Patty Hearst's. His promoters say he's in Cleveland, and the *Times* says he's in New York, sparring at the Felt Forum, but he hasn't been seen at either place. It is a game he plays with the world: dancing out of range, then suddenly sticking out his face and pulling it back again ...

'Meanwhile, his elusiveness is abetted by one of the cagiest inner circles since Cardinal Richelieu. *Anyone* can see him publicly – I think it is his secret wish to be seen by every man, woman and child on the planet Earth – but to see him privately is harder than getting a visa from the Chinese Embassy.'

Well ... I have beat on both those doors in my time, meeting with failure and frustration on both fronts; but I have a feeling that Sheed never properly understood *the importance of speaking Chinese*. Or at least having the right interpreter; and not many of these are attached to either Muhammad Ali or the Chinese Embassy ... But in Ali's case, I did, after all, have my old buddy Hal Conrad, whose delicate function as Muhammad's not-quite-official interpreter with the world of white media I was just beginning to understand ...

I have known Conrad since 1962, when I met him in Las Vegas at the second Liston-Patterson fight. He was handling the press and publicity for that cruel oddity, and I was the youngest and most ignorant sportswriter ever accredited to cover a heavyweight championship fight ... But Conrad, who had total control of *all access to everything*, went out of his way to overlook my nervous ignorance and my total lack of expense money – including me along with all 'big names' for things like press parties, interviews with the fighters and, above all, the awesome spectacle of Sonny Liston working out on the big bag, to the tune of 'Night Train', at his crowded and carpeted base camp in the Thunderbird Hotel ... As the song moved louder and heavier towards a climax of big-band, rock and roll frenzy, Liston would step into the 200-pound bag and hook it *straight up in the air* – where it would hang for one long and terrifying instant, before it fell back into place at the end of a one-inch logging chain with a vicious CLANG and a jerk that would shake the whole room.

I watched Sonny work out on that bag every afternoon for a week or

so, or at least long enough to think he had to be at least nine feet tall ...
until one evening, a day or so prior to the fight when I literally bumped
into Liston, and his two huge bodyguards at the door of the Thunderbird Casino, and I didn't even recognize the Champ for a moment because he was only about six feet tall and with nothing but the dull, fixed
stare in his eyes to make him seem different from all the other rich/mean
niggers a man could bump into around the Thunderbird that week.

So now, on this jangled Sunday night in New York – more than fifteen
years and 55,000 olive-drab tombstones from Maine to California since
I first realized that Sonny Liston was three inches shorter than me – it
was all coming together, or maybe coming apart once again, as my cab
approached the Plaza and another wholly unpredictable but probably
doomed and dumb encounter with the world of big time boxing. I had
stopped for a six-pack of Ballantine Ale on the way in from the airport,
and I also had a quart of Old Fitzgerald that I'd brought with me from
home. My mood was ugly and cynical, tailored very carefully on the
long drive through Brooklyn to match my lack of expectations with
regard to anything Conrad might have tried to 'set up' with Ali.

*My way of joking is to tell the truth. That's the funniest joke in the
world.*

Muhammad Ali

Indeed ... And that is also as fine a definition of 'gonzo journalism'
as anything I've ever heard, for good or ill. But I was in no mood for
joking when my cab pulled up to the Plaza that night. I was half-drunk,
fully cranked, and pissed off at everything that moved. My only real plan
was to get past this ordeal that Conrad was supposedly organizing with
Ali, then retire in shame to my eighty-eight-dollar-a-night bed and deal
with Conrad tomorrow.

But this world does not work on 'real plans' – mine or anyone else's –
so I was not especially surprised when a total stranger wearing a *serious*
black overcoat laid a hand on my shoulder as I was having my bags
carried into the Plaza:

'Doctor Thompson?' he said.

'What?' I spun away and glared at him just long enough to know
there was no point in denying it ... He had the look of a rich undertaker
who had once been the light-heavyweight karate champion of the
Italian Navy; a *very quiet* presence that was far too heavy for a cop ...
He was on *my* side.

And he seemed to understand my bad nervous condition; before I
could ask anything, he was already picking up my bags and saying –

with a smile as uncomfortable as my own: 'We're going to the Park Lane; Mister Conrad is waiting for you ...'

I shrugged and followed him outside to the long black limo that was parked with the engine running so close to the front door of the Plaza that it was almost up on the sidewalk ... and about three minutes later I was face to face with Hal Conrad in the lobby of the Park Lane Hotel, more baffled than ever and not even allowed enough time to sign in and get my luggage up to the room ...

'What took you so goddamn long?'

'I was masturbating in the limo,' I said. 'We took a spin out around Sheepshead Bay and I—'

'Sober up!' he snapped. 'Ali's been *waiting* for you since ten o'clock.'

'Balls,' I said, as the door opened and he aimed me down the hall. 'I'm tired of your bullshit, Harold – and where the hell is my luggage?'

'Fuck your luggage,' he replied as we stopped in front of 904 and he knocked, saying, 'Open up, it's *me*.'

The door swung open and there was Bundini, with a dilated grin on his face, reaching out to shake hands. 'Welcome!' he said. 'Come right in, Doc – make yourself at home.'

I was still shaking hands with Bundini when I realized where I was – standing at the foot of a king-size bed where Muhammad Ali was laid back with the covers pulled up to his waist and his wife, Veronica, sitting next to him: they were both eyeing me with very different expressions than I'd seen on their faces in Chicago.

Muhammad leaned up to shake hands, grinning first at me and then at Conrad: 'Is this *him*?' he asked. 'You sure he's safe?'

Bundini and Conrad were laughing as I tried to hide my confusion at this sudden plunge into unreality by lighting two Dunhills at once, as I backed off and tried to get grounded ... but my head was still whirling from this hurricane of changes and I heard myself saying, 'What do you mean – *Is this him?* You bastard! I should have you *arrested* for what you did to me in Chicago!'

Ali fell back on the pillows and laughed. 'I'm sorry, boss, but I just couldn't *recognize* you. I knew I was supposed to meet *somebody*, but—'

'Yeah!' I said. 'That's what I was trying to *tell* you. What did you think I was *there* for – an autograph?'

Everybody in the room laughed this time, and I felt like I'd been shot out of a cannon and straight into somebody else's movie. I put my satchel down on the bureau across from the bed and reached in for a beer ... The pop-top came off with a hiss and a blast of brown foam that dripped on the rug as I tried to calm down.

'You *scared* me,' Ali was saying. 'You looked like some kind of a bum – or a hippie.'

'What?' I almost shouted. '*A bum? A hippie?*' I lit another cigarette or maybe two, not realizing or even thinking about the gross transgression I was committing by smoking *and* drinking in the presence of the Champ. (Conrad told me later that *nobody* smokes or drinks in the same room with Muhammad Ali – and Jesus Christ! Not – of all places – in the sacred privacy of *his own bedroom at midnight*, where I had no business being in the first place.) ... But I was mercifully and obviously ignorant of what I was doing. Smoking and drinking and tossing off crude bursts of language are not *second* nature to me, but *first* – and my mood, at that point, was still so mean and jangled that it took me about ten minutes of foulmouthed raving before I began to get a grip on myself.

Everybody else in the room was obviously relaxed and getting a wonderful boot out of this bizarre spectacle – which was *me*; and when the adrenalin finally burned off I realized that I'd backed so far away from the bed and into the bureau that I was actually *sitting* on the goddamn thing, with my legs crossed in front of me like some kind of wild-eyed, dope-addled budda (Bhuddah? Buddah? Budda? ... Ah, fuck these wretched idols with unspellable names – let's use *Budda*, and to hell with Edwin Newman) ... and suddenly I felt just fine.

And why not?

I was, after all, the undisputed heavyweight gonzo champion of the world – and this giggling yoyo in the bed across the room from me was no longer the champion of *anything*, or at least nothing he could get a notary public to vouch for ... So I sat back on the bureau with my head against the mirror and I thought, 'Well, shit – here I am, and it's definitely a weird place to be; but not *really*, and not half as weird as a lot of other places I've been ... Nice view, decent company, and no *real* worries at all in this tight group of friends who were obviously having a good time with each other as the conversation recovered from my flaky entrance and got back on the fast-break, bump-and-run track they were used to ...'

Conrad was sitting on the floor with his back to the big window that looks out on the savage, snow-covered wasteland of Central Park – and one look at his face told me that he was *finished working* for the night; he had worked a major miracle, smuggling a hyena into the house of mirrors, and now he was content to sit back and see what happened ...

Conrad was as happy as a serious smoker without a serious smoke could have been right then ... And so was I, for that matter, despite the crossfire of abuse and bent humour that I found myself caught in, between Bundini and the bed.

Ali was doing most of the talking: his mind seemed to be sort of wandering around and every once in a while taking a quick bite out of anything that caught his interest, like a good-humoured wolverine ... There was no talk about boxing, as I recall: we'd agreed to save that for the 'formal interview' tomorrow morning, so this midnight gig was a bit like a warm up for what Conrad described as 'the *serious* bullshit'.

There was a lot of talk about 'drunkards', the sacred nature of 'un-sweetened grapefruit' and the madness of handling money – a subject I told him I'd long since mastered: 'How many acres do you own?' I kept asking him whenever he started getting too high on his own riffs. 'Not as many as me,' I assured him. 'I'm richer than Midas, and nine times as shrewd – whole valleys and mountains of acres,' I continued, keeping a very straight face: 'Thousands of cattle, stallions, peacocks, wild boar, sloats ...' And then the final twist: 'You and Frazier never learned how to handle money – but for twenty per cent of the nut I can make you almost as rich as I am.'

I could see that he didn't believe me. Ali is a hard man to con – but when he got on the subject of his tragic loss of 'all privacy', I figured it was time for the frill.

'You really want a cure for your privacy problem?' I asked him, ripping the top out of another Ballantine Ale.

He smiled wickedly. 'Sure boss – what you got?'

I slid off the bureau and moved towards the door, 'Hang on,' I told him. 'I'll be right back.'

Conrad was suddenly alert. 'Where the hell are you going?' he snapped.

'To my room,' I said. 'I have the ultimate cure for Muhammad's privacy problem.'

'*What* room?' he asked. 'You don't even know where it is, do you?'

More laughter.

'It's 1011,' Conrad said, 'right upstairs – but hurry back,' he added. 'And if you run into Pat, we never heard of you.'

Pat Patterson, Ali's fearfully diligent bodyguard, was known to be prowling the halls and putting a swift arm on anything human or other-wise that might disturb Ali's sleep. The rematch with Spinks was already getting cranked up, and it was Patterson's job to make sure the Champ stayed deadly serious about his new training schedule.

'Don't worry,' I said. 'I just want to go up to the room and put on my pantyhose. I'll be a lot more comfortable.'

The sound of raucous laughter followed me down the hall as I sprinted off towards the fire exit, knowing I would have to be fast or I'd never get back in that room – tonight *or* tomorrow.

But I knew what I wanted, and I knew where it was in my parachute bag: yes, a spectacularly hideous full-head, real-hair, seventy-five-dollar movie-style red devil mask – a thing so fiendishly *real* and ugly that I still wonder, in moments like these, what sort of twisted impulse caused me to even pack the goddamn thing, much less wear it through the halls of the Park Lane Hotel and back into Muhammad Ali's suite at this unholy hour of the night.

Three minutes later I was back at the door, with the mask zipped over my head and the neck-flap tucked into my shirt. I knocked twice, then leaped into the room when Bundini opened the door, screaming some brainless slogan like 'DEATH TO THE WEIRD!'

For a second or two there was no sound at all in the room – then the whole place exploded in wild laughter as I pranced around, smoking and drinking through the moulded rubber mouth and raving about whatever came into my head.

The moment I saw the expression on Muhammad's face, I knew my mask would never get back to Woody Creek. His eyes lit up like he'd just seen the one toy he'd wanted all his life, and he almost came out of the bed after me ...

'Okay,' I said, lifting it off my head and tossing it across the room to the bed. 'It's yours, my man – but let me warn you that not *everybody* thinks this thing is real funny.'

('Especially *black* people,' Conrad told me later. 'Jesus,' he said, 'I just about flipped when you jumped into the room with that goddamn mask on your head. That *was* really pushing your luck.')

Ali put the mask on immediately and was just starting to enjoy himself in the mirror when ... ye gods, we all went stiff as the sound of harsh knocking came through the door, along with the voice of Pat Patterson. 'Open up,' he was shouting. 'What the hell is going on in there?'

I rushed for the bathroom, but Bundini was two steps ahead of me ... Ali, still wearing the hideous mask, ducked under the covers and Conrad went to open the door.

It all happened so fast that we all simply *froze* in position as Patterson came in like Dick Butkus on a blood scent ... and that was when Muhammad came out of the bed with a wild cry and a mushroom cloud of flying sheets, pointing one long brown arm and a finger like Satan's own cattle prod, straight into Pat Patterson's face.

And that, folks, was a moment that I'd just as soon not have to live through again. We were all lucky, I think, that Patterson didn't go for his gun and blow Muhammad away in that moment of madness before he recognized the body under the mask.

It was only a split second, but it could easily have been a hell of a lot longer for all of us if Ali hadn't dissolved in a fit of whooping laughter at the sight of Pat Patterson's face ... And although Pat recovered instantly, the smile he finally showed us was uncomfortably thin.

The problem, I think, was not so much the mask itself and the shock it had caused him but *why* the Champ was wearing the goddamn thing at all; where had it come from? And why? These were serious times, but a scene like this could have ominous implications for the future – particularly with Ali so pleased with his new toy that he kept it on his head for the next ten or fifteen minutes, staring around the room and saying with no hint of a smile in his voice that he would definitely wear it for his appearance on the Dick Cavett show the next day. 'This is the new *me*,' he told us. 'I'll wear it on TV tomorrow and tell Cavett that I promised Veronica that I won't take it off until I win my title back. I'm gonna wear this ugly thing everywhere I go – even when I get into the ring with Spinks next time.' He laughed wildly and jabbed at himself in the mirror. 'Yes indeed!' he chuckled. 'They thought I was crazy *before*, but they ain't seen *nothin'* yet.'

I was feeling a little on the crazy side myself, at that point – and Patterson's accusing presence soon told us it was time to go.

'Okay boss,' Ali said to me on the way out. 'Tomorrow we get serious, right? Nine o'clock in the morning. We'll have breakfast, and get *real* serious.'

I agreed, and went upstairs to my room for a bit of the good smoke.

Muhammad Speaks ... A Second Shot from Spinks ... The Hippie in the Wing Tips ... The Triple Greatest of All Times ...

I was up at eight-thirty the next day, but when I called Ali's suite, Veronica said he'd been up since seven and 'was wandering around downstairs somewhere'.

I found him in the restaurant, sitting at one end of a table full of cut glass and silver, dressed almost as formally as the *maître d'* in a dark blue pin-stripe suit and talking very seriously with a group of friends and very earnest black businessmen types who were all dressed the same way he was. It was a completely different man from the one I'd been sparring and laughing with the night before. The conversation around the table ranged from what to do about a just received invitation to visit some new country in Africa, to a bewildering variety of endorsement offers, to book contracts, real estate and the molecular structure of crabmeat.

It was midmorning before we finally went upstairs to his suite 'to get serious' ... And what follows is a ninety-nine per cent verbatim transcript of our conversation for almost the next two hours. Muhammad was stretched out on the bed, still wearing his 'senator's suit', and balancing my tape recorder on his stomach while he talked. I was sitting cross-legged right next to him on the bed, with a bottle of Heineken in one hand, a cigarette in the other and my shoes on the floor beside me.

The room was alive with the constant comings and goings of people bearing messages, luggage, warnings about getting to the Cavett show on time ... and also a very alert curiosity about *me* and what I was up to. The mask was nowhere in sight, but Pat Patterson *was*, along with three or four other very serious-looking black gentlemen who listened to every word we said. One of them actually kneeled on the floor right next to the bed, with his ear about thirteen inches away from the tape recorder, the whole time we talked.

Okay, we might as well get back to what we were talking about downstairs. You said you're definitely going to fight Spinks again, right?

I can't say I'm definitely going to fight Spinks again. I think we are. I'm sure we are – but I might die, he might die.

But as far as you're concerned, you want to, you're counting on it.

Yeah, he plans to fight me. I gave him a chance and he will give me a shot back at it. The people won't believe he's a true champion until he beats me twice. See, I had to beat Liston twice, Johansson had to beat Patterson twice, but he didn't. Randy Turpin had to beat Sugar Ray twice, but he didn't. If he can beat me twice, then people will really believe that he might possibly be the greatest.

Okay, let me ask you ... at what point, at what time – I was in Vegas for the fight – when did you realize that things were getting real serious?

Round twelve.

Up to then you still thought you had control.

I was told that I was probably losing, but maybe I was even. I had to win the last three and I was too *tired* to win the last three, then I knew I was in trouble.

But you figured you could pull it off ... up until round twelve.

Yeah, but I couldn't, 'cause he is confident, 'cause he is winning and I had to pull it off and he was 197 and I'm 228 and that's too heavy.

Didn't you tell me downstairs at breakfast that you're going to come in at 205 next time?

I don't know what I'm going to come in at, 205 is really impossible. If I get to 220 I'll be happy. Just to be eight pounds lighter ... I'll be happy. I did pretty good at that weight, to be in condition around 220, even if it's 225, 223, I could do better.

Well, on a scale of one hundred, what kind of condition were you in for Spinks?

Scale of one hundred? I was eighty.

Where should you have been?

Should have been ... ninety-eight.

Why didn't you know him better? You didn't seem ready ...

Why didn't anybody know him? He slipped up on the press, a ten to one underdog, they called him. He hadn't gone over ten rounds and only seven pro fights. What can you know about him?

Okay let's get to another point: I was down there in Vegas for two weeks and there wasn't much to do except talk and gossip, and there was a lot of talk about whether it would be better for you to come out and zing him right away, take charge – or do what I think you did, sort of lay back and ...

No, you couldn't have said it was better for me to take charge.

Well, there were two schools of thought: one was you come out zooming and cracking – and the other was the sort of slow start, rope-a-dope trip.

No, that wouldn't be wise at my age and my weight to come out zooming and wear myself out in case I didn't knock him out. When you don't know a man you got to feel him out ... but I know one thing, everybody tires, that's why I laid on the ropes for four, five or six rounds hoping he'd tire, but he didn't. We didn't know he had the stamina and I wasn't in shape so for me to come off *bing bing* bing real fast, I know for sure I'm going to tire but I don't know for sure I'm going to stop him. But after I tire then I'm in trouble.

How long could you have gone, if you came out zinging right from the start?

I could have zinged about six rounds.

So you would have died after six?

No, I wouldn't have died after six, I would have just slowed down and been on defence, but *nobody* can tell me how to come out, or how I should have come out, I did the best thing for my condition.

This may be an odd question but I want to ask you anyway, at the press conference after the fight I remember Leon saying, 'I just wanted to beat this nigger.' And it seems to me it was done with a smile, but when I heard that I felt the whole room get tense.

No, that's okay. I say the same things. We black people talk about each other that way, in a humorous way. 'Ah, niggah, be quiet.' 'Ah – ahh, I can whop that niggah.' 'Niggah, you crazy.' Those are our expressions. If you say it, I'll slap you. The white man can't call me nigger like they do.

So it was a joke? It struck me as a very raw note, but ...

I can't blame you. When I beat Sonny Liston, I didn't say those words, but I was glad to win, so I can't take nothing from Spinks – he's good, he's a lot better fighter than people thought he was.

Tell me a little about this tri-cornered thing between you and Norton and Spinks.

Well, Norton feels he deserves the next shot.

Do you think he does?

No, he deserves a shot at the winner between me and Spinks. I gave Spinks a shot, he owes me a shot for giving him a shot. The champion always gets a return. They used to have return clauses. We didn't have that, I don't have that. He's giving me a shot 'cause I gave him a break. I beat Norton twice. Foreman annihilated Norton, so therefore he's not better than me. I'm the number one contender, not him.

What did Leon tell you? When I talked to him in Vegas, I got the feeling he honestly wants to give you a return shot. I think he's ready for that.

Sure he will. By the time this article will come out the fight probably will have been signed and everything, the date set and we ready to fight. Don't say yet, but I'm sure it's getting pretty close and I'm the one they'll choose. He makes $5 million with me and $1.5 million with Norton. Who would you fight?

Anyway, what happens if it turns out that Leon is legally obligated to fight Norton first?

That's all right, I ain't tired. I got four or five more years of good fighting.

Four or five years?

[*Ali nods, grins*] Plenty of time, boss. All the time I need.

How do you think Spinks would do against Norton?

I think he'd beat Norton.

Did I hear you say that you were going up to the camp today?

I start training in about two weeks.

And that's going to be straight through five or six months? You've never done that before, have you?

Never in my life, never more than two months. But this time I'm going to be in there five months, chopping trees, running up hills, I'll be coming in dancing! Dancing! [*Sudden grin*] I'll be winning my title for the third time ... [*Shouting*] The greatest of all times! Of all times!! [*Laughing and jabbing*]

Come on now! We're not on TV! Let's get back to this Norton-Spinks thing. Why do you say Spinks will win?

'Cause he's too fast, he's aggressive, he's young, he takes a punch, the mere fact that he can beat me means he can beat Norton. I'm better than Norton. I pick him, it don't have to be that way, but I pick him.

*How about Frazier? Could Leon have beaten the Joe Frazier of four
or five years ago? Around the first or second time you fought him?
Who does Leon compare to?*

Leon, compare to, he compare to Frazier's style, always coming in,
Spinks ... Frazier.

Frazier at his best?

Frazier at his best, yeah.

How good is Leon? I don't really know myself.

Leon is unexplored, unknown – and after I beat him, he'll come back
and win the title and he'll hold it four or five years and he'll go down in
history as one of the great heavyweights. Not the greatest, but one of the
greatest.

*So if you fought him one more time, you think that'd be it? Is that
what you're saying?*

I'm not sure that'll be it for me ... I might take another fight – don't
know yet, according to how I feel when that time comes.

*Did you see Kallie Knoetze, that South African fighter? The one who
beat Bobick?*

I heard about him.

*Me and Conrad spent a lot of time talking to him before the fight. I
was trying to work up a really serious spectacle between you and him
down in South Africa.*

He seemed like a nice fellow.

*Oh yeah, he was really eager to have you come down there and fight.
Does that interest you, to fight a white cop in South Africa?*

On the basis that on that day there'd be equality in the arena where
I'm fighting.

*But would that interest you? With all the heavy political overtones?
How do you feel about something like that? Along with a million-dollar
gate?*

Yeah, I like it. With the approval of all the other African nations and
Moslem countries. I wouldn't go against their wishes, regardless of how
they made the arena that night, if the masses of the country and the
world were against it, I wouldn't go. I know that I have a lot of fans in
South Africa, and they want to see me. But I'm not going to crawl over
other nations to go. The world would have to say: 'Well, this case is
special, they've given the people justice. His going is helping the freedom.'

*There's a dramatic quality to that thing – I can't think of any other
fight that would have that kind of theatre. Actually it might even be too
much politics ...*

What worries me is gettin' whupped by a white man in South Africa.

Oh ho! Yeah! [Nervous chuckle]

[*Room breaks into laughter*]

[*Laughing*] That's what the world needs ... me getting whupped by a white man in South Africa! [*Still laughing*]

Oh yeah ...

Getting whupped by a white man *period*, but in South Africa? If a *white South African* fighter beat me ...?

Jesus.

Oh, Lord. [*Chuckles*]

Oh, you'd have to win ... You would definitely have to win. Did you see the film of his fight with Bobick? When he took him out in the third round?

Was he good?

He was a little slow, but he looked powerful ... He didn't look to me like you would have any trouble with him, but I'm not an expert. He looked like you'd have to watch it ...

Yeah, he took Bobick real hard. I don't think it would be wise for me to fight him in South Africa. If I beat him too bad and then leave the country, they might beat up some of the brothers. [*Laughter in the room*] Or if he whup me too bad then there might be riots ... People crazy. You know what I mean? If I whup him up too bad and look too good, then the brothers might get beat up after I leave. I wouldn't fool with it. I'm a representative of black people ... It'd be good if I don't go to nothing like that. It's too touchy – *it's more than a sport when I get involved.*

But it's the fact that he's white ...

[*Confidentially*] Did you know he called me a nigger?

What?

You didn't hear it? The South African ...

[*Aghast*] *No!*

You was in Vegas, right?

[*Confused*] *Yeah ... we talked to him ...*

He said, 'That cocky nigger, that's one nigger I want ...'

[*Laughing*] *Aw, c'mon. He didn't say that. That guy was on his best behaviour.*

He said: 'I want that nigger.'

C'mon ...

[*Deep laugh*] I was jokin' ...

He was on best behaviour ... The lawyers said, 'You don't understand our country. I mean, it's not like you've heard at all ...' And Conrad was saying, 'Bullshit! You got cages for those black people down there.' He was rude.

CONRAD: He gave me a big argument.

Did he slap you?

CONRAD: Slap *me*? [*Laughs*] I had *Hunter* with me!

I had a can of mace in my pocket ...

[*Ali, laughing and looking at his watch*] Okay, now you've got five minutes.

Let's see ... five minutes.

I'll give you ten minutes ... See, see the clock?

Yeah, don't worry, I've got my own clock – see this magnesium Rolex? Heavy, eh? ... And see these? After you called me a bum and a hippie last night, look what I wore for you this morning [*holding up perforated wing tips*].

You're getting a good interview, man.

Yeah [*reaches for one of the shoes*]*, look at that shine too.*

Those are some good shoes – those shoes must've cost about fifty dollars.

Yeah. They're about ten years old.

Are they? Same soles?

Yeah, these are my FBI shoes. I only wear them for special occasions – nobody's called me a bum and a hippie for a long time.

[*Laughs*] You're not going to drink your beer? You an alcoholic?

Alcoholic! Bum! Hippie! Remember I've got to write an article about you before Friday!

Heh, heh, heh. You've got the beer ... Heh, heh, heh. Bum and a hippie.

Where you going?

Right here, I'll talk louder so you can hear ... What else you want to ask me?

My head's, uh, I'm still on that South Africa trip, I guess there'd be no way you could go down there without beating Leon first, right?

No, I got to beat Leon first. I will defeat Leon first. I will go down as the triple greatest of all time.

Oh yeah, I think you might. If you train, if you get serious.

If I get serious? I'm as serious as cancer. Is cancer serious?

Well, yeah, I didn't realize, uh ... if you're going to start training now that is serious, that's five months, six months.

I'm going to be ready!

Would you call him a fast fighter ... Leon? It seems like a funny word to use for him.

Fast? Yeah he was fast. Faster than I was that night. He's fast period.

Fast hands? Fast feet?

Fast hands. Not as fast as reflexes because of his weight. When I'm down to my weight that I would like to be I know I'm faster.

I noticed in the third round the first time I smelled a little bit of trouble was when I saw you missing him with the jab ... it would be about six inches.

The one thing I did wrong, I didn't do no boxing hardly before this fight.

Why?

Well, my belief was at this age, too much pounding and getting hit and unnecessary training wasn't necessary.

Well, if too much training would have been bad for that fight, how about the next one, why would it be good for the next fight?

My timing was lost. Well, I'm going to have to box ... I'm not saying it would have been bad to box; better for me, see, I wasn't boxing nobody and, I was missing a lot of punches in that fight.

Yeah, I noticed that, that's when I first thought, 'Oh oh ... it'll be a long fight.'

That's 'cause I wasn't boxing, I was hitting bad.

You think you could knock Leon out? ... I thought you could have in the fifteenth round.

I couldn't follow him up, might knock him out and might not ...

Was there any time you thought maybe you might have ... did you ever think he was going to knock you out ... was there any time you thought, oh, oh, he might even put you down?

No, nothing like that.

Would it be more important next time to get faster?

No, next time it's to be in better shape, to take him more serious, to know him.

Why the hell didn't you this time?

Didn't know him.

You got some of the smartest people in the business working with you.

Didn't know him ... See all of my worst fights was when I fought nobodies. Jurgen Blin, Zurich, Switzerland, seven rounds with him, didn't look too good. Al Lewis, Dublin, Ireland, a nobody, went eleven rounds. Jean-Pierre Coopman, San Juan, Puerto Rico ... a nobody.

Bonavena?

He was pretty good. Alfredo Evangelista. A nobody, didn't look that hot.

Yeah, but Leon, you saw him fight several times, didn't you?

Amateurs, just seven ... what can this man do with seven pro fights, never been over ten rounds ...

But you had about fifteen or eighteen pro fights when you fought Liston the first time.

I don't know.

I think I counted them up the other day ... nineteen maybe.

I caught him off guard too, I was supposed to have been annihilated like this boy was. But my best fights were those fights where I was the underdog: George Foreman's comeback, two Liston fights, Frazier fights, Norton ...

Is that something in your head?

It makes you hungry, got something to work for. I'm doing good. Everything is going my way. I'm eating dinner. I'm living with my wife and my two children all up to the fight which ain't that good. Least six weeks before the fight I should get away from my children 'cause they make you soft. You hug 'em and you kiss them, you know, you 'round babies all day. Day before the fight, I'm babysitting 'cause my wife done some shopping. She didn't mean no harm.

You can't blame it on her, though.

No. I got to get away from the babies, I got to get evil. Got to chop trees, run up hills, get in my old log cabin.

You plan to go up there to stay, at the camp, live there until the fight? Where ... what fight ...?

You say you're to go up there and do a monk sort of trip?

No, my wife and babies would be with me, but my babies they cry at night and they'll be in another cabin ...

What about Leon's rib, do you think you broke his rib?

He got hurt in the fight some kind of way, and I was told after the fight he was hurt and some doctor was looking at him and that it wasn't that bad, and I guess when it looked like he was going to fight Norton they had to admit he was hurt 'cause Norton's a body puncher.

Well, speaking of that, I don't want to bring up any sore subject, but did you see Pacheco on the Tom Snyder show when he was talking about all athletes getting old...? He seemed to come down pretty hard. He said physically it would just be impossible for you to get back in shape to beat Leon.

I was fighting years before I knew Pacheco. He got famous hanging around me. They all got known ... popular. They'd never admit it ... and also Pacheco don't know me, he works in my corner, he's not my real physical doctor.

So you think you can get back in ninety-eight on a scale of a hundred?

Yeah. What I like, this is what I love ... to do the impossible, be the underdog. Pressure makes me go. I couldn't ... I didn't beat Frazier the first time, I didn't beat Norton the first time. I gotta beat the animal. I almost got to lose to keep going. It would be hard for me to keep getting the spirit up, what have I got to accomplish, who have I got to prove wrong?

Speaking of that, how did you ever get yourself in the situation where

*you had so much to lose and so little to gain by fighting Leon down
there? ...*

How did I get in what?

*You got yourself in an almost no-win situation there where you had
very little to win and a hell of a lot to lose. It struck me as strategically
bad ...*

That's the way it is, that's the way it's been ever since I held the crown,
I didn't have nothing to gain by fighting Bugner. I didn't have nothing to
gain by fighting Jean-Pierre Coopman. I didn't have nothing to gain by
fighting a lot of people.

*You sure as hell will next time by fighting Leon. That will be real
pressure.*

Oh yeah, I like the pressure, need the pressure ... the world likes ...
people like to see miracles ... people like to see ... people like to see
underdogs that do it ... people like to be there when history is made.

Raw Eggs and Beer in the Top Rank Suite ... A Sea of Noise and
Violence ... An Eeerie. Roaring Chant ... The Final Bell

---

*One thing that Ernest Hemingway had always told me was that it was a
bad idea to get to know an active fighter and become interested in his
career. Sooner or later he was going to get hurt in the ring, and beaten,
and it would be an almost unbearable thing to see if he were a friend.*
                                                George Plimpton, *Shadow Box*

Well ... I wondered why George never showed up in Las Vegas.
Muhammad Ali is a friend of Norman Mailer's, too, and also Budd
Schulberg's; along with most of the other big-time boxing writers who
skipped the Spinks fight. I was too strung out on the simple horror of
spending two weeks in the Las Vegas Hilton to understand anything
more complex than fear, hunger and daytime TV, at the time, to grasp
my own lack of sensitivity.

And at first I thought it was some kind of monumental botch on my
part. Sybil Arum tried to reassure me, but others said I was paranoid.
Day after endless day, I would check into top rank headquarters on
the fifth floor 'director's suite' and ask as casually as possible if George
or Norman had showed up yet – and the answer was always the same.

Or perhaps I was overcompensating, somehow, for my shameful
malaria freakout in Zaire by showing up for this one two weeks earlier
than anybody except Arum and Leon.

After a week or so of feeling so conspicuously alone in my role of 'behind the scenes fight writer' I finally began passing myself off as the official Top Rank bartender, instead. I began to get seriously paranoid about the situation. What was wrong, I wondered? Had I chosen the wrong hotel? Were all the heavies staying somewhere else like the Aladdin or Caesar's Palace, where the real action was?

Or maybe I was working too hard; doing unnatural things like waking up at ten o'clock in the morning to attend the daily promo/strategy meetings down in Arum's top rank 'director's suite' ... taking voluminous notes on such problems as the Ghanaian featherweight challenger's baffling refusal to wear Everlast gloves for his fight with Danny Lopez; and whether the public should be charged one or two dollars to attend Ali's daily workouts – if and when Ali finally showed up for any workouts at all; he was not taking the fight seriously, according to rumours out of Dundee's gym in Miami, and to make matters worse he was also refusing to talk to anybody except his wife.

There was also the matter of how to cope with a mind-set ranging from blank apathy to outright mockery on the part of the national boxing press. The only fight writers who could be counted on for daily ink were locals such as Tommy Lopez from the *Review Journal* and Mike Marley from the *Las Vegas Sun* – which was good for *me*, because they both knew a hell of a lot more about the 'fight game' than I did, and between the two of them I was getting a dose of education about the technical aspects of boxing that I have never known much about ... But the New York media continued to dismiss the fight as either a farce or a fraud – or perhaps even a *fix*, as frustrated challenger Ken Norton would suggest afterwards; and Arum's humour grew more and more foul as Leon absorbed more and more bum-of-the-month jokes from the national boxing press. Arum was shocked and genuinely outraged as the prefight coverage dwindled down to a one-line joke about 'this upcoming mystery match between *one fighter who won't talk, and another who can't*'.

Spinks wandered in and out of the suite from time to time, seeming totally oblivious to what anybody in the world – including me and Arum – had to say about the fight or anything else. He was not even disturbed when his mother arrived in Las Vegas and told the first reporter she met that she thought it was 'a shame' that her son was going to have to 'get beat up on TV' just to make a bundle of money for 'big business people from New York'.

Leon Spinks is not one of your chronic worriers. His mind moves in pretty straight lines, and the more I saw of him in Las Vegas, the more I became convinced that the idea of fighting his boyhood idol for the Heavyweight Championship of the World didn't bother him at all, win or lose. 'Sure he's the greatest,' he would say to the few reporters who managed to track him down and ask how he felt about Ali, 'but he has to give it up *sometime*, right?'

He was polite with the press, but it was clear that he had no interest at all in their questions – and even less in his own answers, which he passed off as casually as he dropped two raw eggs in every glass of beer he drank during interviews.

Nor did he have any interest in Arum's desperate scrambling for pre-fight publicity.

No half-bright presidential candidate, rock star or championship boxing promoter would do anything but fire any ranking adviser who arranged for him and his wife to spend two weeks in a small bedroom *adjoining* the main suite/bar/war room and the base for all serious business ... But this is what Bob Arum did in Las Vegas, and it was so entirely out of character for *anybody* dealing in power and leverage and money on that scale that it made me suspicious. Bob and I have been friends long enough for me to be relatively certain he wasn't either dumb *or* crazy. But I have a lot of strange friends and I still trust my instincts in this area about ninety-eight per cent, despite a few glaring exceptions in the area of Southern politicians and black drug dealers wearing Iron Boy overalls, and until Arum pulls that kind of switch on me I will still call him my friend and treat him the same way.

Indeed ... and now that we've settled that, let's get back to this twisted saga and my feelings in Las Vegas, as the day of the fight approached and my lonely perceptions with regard to its possible *meaning* and in fact my whole understanding of professional boxing as either a sport *or* a business came more and more into question ... Well, I began to feel very *isolated*, down there in the huge Vegas Hilton, and when even my good friends smiled indulgently when I said on the phone that I was having a hell of a hard time getting a bet on Leon Spinks at *ten* or even *eight to one*, I had a few nervous moments wondering if perhaps I really *was* as crazy as so much of the evidence suggested.

This was, however, *before* I'd read Plimpton's book and found out that I was the only writer in America so cold-hearted as to show up in Las Vegas to watch Muhammad Ali *get beaten*.

Whatever else I might or might not have been, I was clearly no friend of the Champ's ... Which was true on one level, because I not only showed for the fight, but wallowed so deep in the quicksands of human treachery as to *bet against him*.

At ten to one.

Let's not forget those numbers – especially not if the difference between ten and five is really the difference between a friend and an enemy.

When the bell rang to start number fifteen in Vegas, Leon Spinks was so tired and wasted that he could barely keep his balance for the next three minutes – and now, after watching that fight on videotape at least twenty times, I think that even World Lightweight Champ Roberto Duran could have taken Leon out with one quick and savage combination; a hard jab in the eyes to bring his hands up in front of his face just long enough to crack him under the heart with a right uppercut – then another left into the stomach to bring his head forwards again, to that target point in the cross hairs of Ali's brittle but still murderous bazooka right hand, at twenty or twenty-one inches ...

No fighter except Joe Frazier had ever survived one of Muhammad's frenzied killer-combinations in a round as late as the fifteenth; and, until those last, incredibly brutal three minutes in Las Vegas, Leon Spinks had never gone more than ten rounds in his life. When he shuffled half-blindly out of his corner for number fifteen against the Champ, who was obviously and terminally behind *on points* after fourteen, Leon Spinks was 'ready to go', as they say in that merciless, million-dollar-a-minute world of 'the squared circle'.

... But so was Muhammad Ali: fight films shot from a catwalk directly above the ring, looking straight down from the high ceiling of the Hilton Pavilion, show *both* fighters reeling off balance and virtually holding on to each other at times, just to keep from falling down in that vicious final round.

There was no more *strategy* at that point, and the bloodlust-howl of the small crowd of 5000 or so white-on-white pro-Spinks high rollers who had made the fight a cynical and almost reluctant sellout in a town where a shrewd promoter like Arum or Don King or even Raoul Duke could sell 5000 tickets to a world championship cock fight, told Muhammad Ali all he needed to know at that point in time. The same people who'd been chanting '*All-eee! All-eee!*' just a few minutes ago, when it looked like the Champ had once again known exactly what he was doing, all along, as Leon looked to be fading badly in the late rounds ... These *same people* were now chanting, as if led by some unseen cheerleader: but they were no longer saying '*All-eee!*'

As it became more and more obvious that Muhammad was just as dead on his feet as Spinks seemed to be, the hall slowly filled with a new sound. It began late in the fourteenth, as I recall, and I was by that time engulfed in the hell-on-earth chaos that had overtaken the fifty or so close friends and Family members in the Champ's corner where people like ex-Heavyweight Champ Jimmy Ellis and Ali's hot-tempered brother Rachaman had been clawing at the ring ropes and screaming doomed advice at Muhammad ever since Bundini had become sick and collapsed right next to Angelo Dundee in the corner at the end of round number twelve, causing Kilroy and Patterson to start yelling into the mob for a doctor. Patterson, right in front of me, was holding Bundini with one arm and waving at Kilroy with the other. 'Drew's had a heart attack,' he shouted. 'A heart attack.'

Ali's corner was a deafening mix of fear, madness and emotional disfunction at that point, a sea of noise and violence ...

Total chaos; and then came the eerie roaring chant from the crowd: '... *LEE-ONN! LEE-ONN!* ...' The chant grew louder and somehow malignant as the fifteenth round staggered on to its obvious end ... 'LEE-ONN! LEE-ONN! LEE-ONN!'

Muhammad Ali had never heard that chant before – and neither had Leon Spinks ...

Or me, either.

Or Angelo, or Bundini, or Kilroy, or Conrad, or Pat Patterson – or Kris Kristofferson either; who was hanging on to Rita Coolidge just a few feet away from me and looking very *stricken* while the last few seconds ticked off until the bell finally rang and made every one of us in that corner feel, suddenly, very *old*.

BILLY THE GEEK CALLS NEW ORLEANS: EVEN ODDS AND RANCID KARMA

The Ali-Spinks rematch on 15 September will not be dull. The early rumour line has Ali a two-to-one favourite, but these numbers will not hold up – or, if they do, Spinks as a two to one underdog will be a very tempting bet, even for me: and anything higher than that will be almost irresistible.

When I arrived in Las Vegas two weeks before the last fight I told Bob Arum that I figured Leon had a twenty per cent chance of winning. That translates into four to one odds, which even the nickel-and-dime 'experts' said was a bad joke. The fight was considered such a gross mismatch that every bookie in Vegas except one had it 'off the board', meaning no bets at all, because Ali was such a prohibitive favourite even ten to one was deemed a sure way to lose money. As late as the thirteenth round, in fact, freelance bookies at ringside were still laying eight to one on Muhammad. My friend Semmes Luckett, sitting in one of the $200 seats with a gaggle of high rollers, watched the round-by-round destruction of one poor bastard who lost *at least* $40,000 in forty-five minutes – betting on Ali first at ten to one, then down to eight to one after the first six or seven rounds – then four to one after eleven, and finally all the way down to two to one at the end of thirteen.

The man was in a blathering rage by the time the fight was over. 'I was betting on a goddamn legend,' he shouted. 'I must have been out of my mind.'

I have watched the videotape of that fight enough times to risk wondering out loud, at this point, on the subject of what may or may not have been wrong with Ali's right hand in that fight. It was totally ineffective. The jab was still there, even with five or six pounds of flab to slow it down ... and the right was getting through Leon's guard with a consistency that would have ended the fight in ten or eleven rounds if Muhammad had been able to land it with any power at all. Spinks must have taken twenty-five or thirty right-hand shots from Ali, and I doubt if he felt more than one or two of them.

That was the real key to the fight, and if Ali's right hand is as useless in New Orleans as it was in Las Vegas, Spinks will win by a TKO in eight or nine rounds. Both fighters understand, at this point, that Ali has already tried what he and his handlers felt was the *best strategy* for dealing with Leon: that was the time-tested rope-a-dope, which assumed that a frenzied, undisciplined fighter like Spinks would punch himself out in the early rounds, like George Foreman, and become a tired sitting duck for Ali by the time the bell rang for number ten.

That was a very bad mistake, because Leon did *not* punch himself out – and there is no reason to think he will in the rematch. Which means that Ali will have to fight a very different fight this time: he will have to risk punching *himself* out in the first five or six rounds in what Arum is calling 'the battle of New Orleans', and the odds on his getting away with it are no better than fifty-fifty. And he will have to be in miraculously top shape, even then – because if he can't come zooming out of his corner at the opening bell and whack Leon off balance real quick, Muhammad will not last ten rounds.

If I were a bookie I would make Leon a sixty-forty favourite, which is exactly the same way Bob Arum was seeing it, even before the fight finally found a home in New Orleans.

There are some people in the 'fight game' who will tell you that Arum doesn't know boxing from badminton – but not one of them went on the record last time with anything riskier than the idea that Leon 'might have a chance'.

Bob Arum called it sixty-forty Ali at least six weeks prior to the fight – which stunned me at first, because I thought my own twenty per cent figure was borderline madness, at best.

But Arum stuck with his forty per cent bet on Leon, all the way up to the fight ... and after watching Leon for two weeks in Vegas my own figure went up to thirty or thirty-five per cent; or perhaps even forty or forty-five per cent on the day of the fight when I heard Arum screaming at Spinks on the house phone at 2:30 in the afternoon, telling him to stop worrying about getting tickets for his friends and get ready to do battle against a man that a lot of people including me still call the best fighter who ever climbed into a ring ... and if I had known, before the fight, that Leon forced his handlers to get him a steak for lunch at 5:00, I would probably have called the fight even.

That's how the battle of New Orleans looks to me now: dead even – and if the numbers turn up that way on 15 September I will bet on Muhammad Ali, for reasons of my own. I hate to lose any *bet*, but losing on this one would not hurt that much. The last twenty years of my life would have been just a little bit cheaper and duller if Muhammad Ali had not been around to keep me cranked up, and there is no way I could bet against him this time, in what could well be his last fight. I figure I can afford to bet *on* him and lose; that is an acceptable risk ... But something very deep inside me curdles at the thought of what kind of rancid karma I could bring down on myself if I bet against him, and he won.

That is not an acceptable risk.

The Roving Tripod, the Experts at the Hilton Bar ... A Final Adventure in Fish-Wrap Journalism

---

Muhammad Ali has interested a lot of different people for a lot of very different reasons since he became a media superstar and a high-energy national presence almost two decades ago ... And he has interested me, too, for reasons that ranged from a sort of amused camaraderie in the beginning, to wary admiration, then sympathy and a new level of personal respect, followed by a dip into a different kind of wariness that was more exasperation than admiration ... and finally into a mix of all these things that never really surfaced and came together until I heard that he'd signed to fight Leon Spinks as a 'warm up' for his $16 million swan song against Ken Norton.

This was the point where my interest in Muhammad Ali moved almost subconsciously to a new and higher gear. I had seen all of Leon's fights in the 1976 Montreal Olympics, and I recall being impressed to the point of awe at the way he attacked and destroyed whatever they put in front of him. I had never seen a *young* fighter who could get away with planting *both* feet and leaning forwards when he hooked with either hand.

Archie Moore was probably the last *big* fighter with that rare combination of power, reflexes and high tactical instinct that a boxer *must* have to get away with risking moments of total commitment even occasionally ... But Leon did it *constantly*, and in most of his fights that was *all* he did.

It was a pure *kamikaze* style: the roving tripod, as it were – with Leon's legs forming two poles of the tripod, and the body of his opponent forming the third. Which is interesting for at least two reasons: 1) There *is no tripod* until a punch off that stance connects with the opponent's head or body, so the effect of a miss can range from fatal to unnerving, or at the very least it will cause raised eyebrows and even a faint smile or two among the ringside judges who are scoring the fight ... and, 2) If the punch connects solidly, then the tripod is formed and an almost preternatural blast of energy is delivered at the point of impact, especially if the hapless target is leaning as far back on the ropes as he can get with his head ducked in and forward in a cover-up stance – like Ali's rope-a-dope.

A boxer who plants both feet and then leans forward to lash out with a hook has his whole weight *and also his whole balance* behind it; he cannot pull back at that point, and if he fails to connect he will not only lose points for dumb awkwardness, but he'll plunge his head out front, low and wide open for one of those close-in jackhammer combinations that usually end with a knockdown.

That was Leon's style in the Olympics, and it was a terrifying thing to see. All he had to do was catch his opponent with no place to run, then land one or two of those brain-rattling tripod shots in the first round – and once you get stunned and intimidated like that in the first round of a three-round (Olympic) bout, there is not enough time to recover ...

... or even *want* to, for that matter, once you begin to think that this brute they pushed you into the ring with has no reverse gear and would just as soon attack a telephone pole as a human being.

Not many fighters can handle that style of all-out assault without having to back off and devise a new game plan. But there is no time for devising new plans in a three-round fight – and perhaps not in ten, twelve or fifteen rounds either, because Leon doesn't give you much time to think. He keeps coming, swarming, pounding; and he can land three or four shots from *both* directions once he gets braced and leans out to meet that third leg of the tripod.

On the other hand, those poor geeks that Leon beat silly in the Olympics were *amateurs* ... and we are all a bit poorer for the fact that he was a *light-heavyweight* when he won that gold medal; because if he'd been a few pounds heavier he would have had to go against the elegant Cuban heavyweight champion, Teofilo Stevenson, who would have beaten him like a gong for all three rounds.

But Stevenson, the Olympic heavyweight champ in both 1972 and 76, and the only modern heavyweight with the physical and mental equipment to compete with Muhammad Ali, has insisted for reasons of his own and Fidel Castro's on remaining the *amateur* heavyweight champion of the world, instead of taking that one final leap for the great ring that a fight against Muhammad Ali could have been for him.

Whatever reasons might have led Castro to decide that an Ali-Stevenson match – sometime in 1973 or 74 after Muhammad had won the hearts and minds of the whole world with his win over George Foreman in Zaire – was not in the interest of either Cuba, Castro or perhaps even Stevenson himself, will always be clouded in the dark fog of politics and the conviction of people like me that the same low-rent political priorities that heaped a legacy of failure and shame on every other main issue of this generation were also the real reason why the two great heavyweight artists of our time were never allowed in the ring with each other.

This is one of those private opinions of my own that even my friends in the 'boxing industry' still dismiss as the flaky gibberish of a half-smart writer who was doing okay with things like drugs, violence and presidential politics, but who couldn't quite cut the mustard in *their* world.

Boxing.

These were the same people who chuckled indulgently when I said, in Las Vegas, that I'd take every bet I could get on Leon Spinks against Muhammad Ali at ten to one, and with anybody who was seriously into numbers I was ready to haggle all the way down to five to one, or maybe even four ... but even at eight to one it was somewhere between hard and impossible to get a bet down on Spinks with anybody in Vegas who was even a fifty-fifty bet to pay off in real money.

One of the few consistent traits shared by 'experts' in any field is that they will almost never bet money or anything else that might turn up in public on whatever they call their convictions. That is why they are 'experts'. They have waltzed through that mine field of high-risk commitments that separates politicians from gamblers, and once you've reached that plateau where you can pass for an expert, the best way to stay there is to hedge all your bets, private and public, so artistically that nothing short of a thing so bizarre that it can pass for an 'act of God' can damage your high-priced reputation ...

I remember vividly, for instance, my frustration at Norman Mailer's refusal to bet money on his almost certain conviction that George Foreman was too powerful for Muhammad Ali to cope with in Zaire ... And I also recall being slapped on the chest by an Associated Press boxing writer in Las Vegas while we were talking about the fight one afternoon at the casino bar in the Hilton. 'Leon Spinks is a *dumb midget*,' he snarled in the teeth of all the other experts who'd gathered on that afternoon to get each other's fix on the fight. 'He has about as much chance of winning the heavyweight championship as *this guy*.'

This guy was me, and the AP writer emphasized his total conviction by giving me a swift backhand to the sternum ...

I have talked to him since, on this subject, and when I said I planned to quote him *absolutely verbatim* with regard to his prefight wisdom in Vegas, he seemed like a different man and said that, if I was going to quote him on his outburst of public stupidity, I should at least be fair enough to explain that he had 'been with Muhammad Ali for so long and through so many wild scenes that he *simply couldn't go against him on this one*'.

Well ... this is my final adventure in fish-wrap journalism and I frankly don't give a fuck whether or not it makes sense to the readers ... especially since you chintzy greedheads tried to put a double-page, full-colour H—* ad right in the middle of this story ...

Somewhere in my files I have a letter from Honda's US ad agency that says they would just as soon avoid any image identification with *Rolling Stone* ... and those lame/tin bastards have heaped enough abuse on me over the years to make me wonder what kind of mentality we're dealing with if they've come so far around the bend that they now want to put a gigantic Honda ad right in the middle of *my* article.

Fuck those people. I wouldn't ride a Honda to Richard Nixon's funeral ... and in fact the last person I knew who owned a Honda was Ron Ziegler; that was down in San Clemente, just before the resignation, and I recall that Ron was eager to lend the thing to me, for reasons I never quite understood ... but I remember a cocktail party down at Nixon's house, crazed on mescaline and bending the casual elbow with Ron, Henry Kissinger, General Haig and others of that stripe, who were all very friendly at that point in time. Even to me ... Annie Leibovitz was there and I was negotiating with Ziegler about trading me his Honda for my Z-Datsun for a few days, while Ziegler's deputy, Gerald Warren, was laughing with Annie about how Kissinger thought I was 'an Air Force colonel in mufti ...'

'Tell him he's right,' I whispered to Annie. 'Then let's trade for Ziegler's bike and run it straight off the Laguna Beach pier tomorrow morning. I'll take the bugger out over the water at top speed while you get a few good shots, then I'll get off in midair before it hits ... Right and we'll give Ron an autographed photo from "the colonel".'

* The name of this manufacturer was deleted at the last minute by the publisher after angry & greedy consultations with the *RS* advertising department.

Whoops ... here we go again, drifting back to the good old days, when men were men and fun was fun and a well-mannered Air Force doctor could still have cocktails with the President without causing a scandal.

That was 'before the circus left town', as Dick Goodwin put it so starkly as we sat in a Washington peg-house on the day of Nixon's resignation ... And, indeed, everything since then has been downhill. Hamilton Jordan is too fat to ride a motorcycle and Jody Powell is too slow.

Jesus! How low have we sunk! Was Ron Ziegler the last free spirit in the White House? Jimmy's sister, Gloria, rides a big Honda – but they won't let her north of Chattanooga and the rest of the family is laying low, working feverishly on a formula to convert peanuts into Swiss francs.

Ah ... mother of raving God! What are we into? How did we get down in this hole! And how can we get out?

Or – more on the point – how can this cross-eyed story be salvaged, now that I've spent a whole night babbling about Ron Ziegler and Hondas and that crowd of flabby clubfoots in the White House?

What about the rest of the story? What about serious journalism? And *decency* ... And truth? and beauty ... the eternal verities ... and Law Day in Georgia? Yes, that's almost on us again, and this time they want *me* to deliver the main address.

Why not?

For $100,000 I'll do *anything*, just as long as the cash comes up front ... What? Ye gods! What have I said? Should we *cut* that last outburst? Or maybe just print the bugger and get braced for a Spinks-like assault from the Secret Service?

No, this shit can't go on ... it could get me in serious trouble ... And what a tragedy it would be if I got locked up *now*, after ten years of abusing the White House for what were always good reasons. Ziegler said it was because I was crazy and Kissinger thought I was some kind of rogue Air Force colonel: but my old friend Pat Buchanan called it 'a character defect' ... which may or may not have been true; but if calling Richard Nixon a liar and a thief was evidence of a 'character defect', what in the hell kind of defect, disease or even brain damage would cause a man to spend ten years of his life writing angry, self-righteous speeches for Richard Nixon and Spiro Agnew?

'No Vietcong ever called me "nigger".'

Muhammad Ali said that, back in 1967, and he almost went to prison for it – which says all that needs to be said right now about justice and gibberish in the White House.

Some people write their novels and others roll high enough to live them and some fools try to do both – but Ali can barely read, much less write, so he came to that fork in the road a long time ago and he had the rare instinct to find that one seam in the defence that let him opt for a third choice: he would get rid of words altogether and live his own movie.

A brown Jay Gatsby – not black and with a head that would never be white: he moved from the very beginning with the same instinct that drove Gatsby – an endless fascination with that green light at the end of the pier. He had shirts for Daisy, magic leverage for Wolfsheim, a delicate and dangerously vulnerable Ali-Gatsby shuffle for Tom Buchanan and no answers at all for Nick Carraway, the word junkie.

There are two kinds of counter punchers in this world: one learns early to live by his reactions and quick reflexes, and the other – the one with a taste for high rolling – has the instinct to make an aggressor's art of what is essentially the defensive, survivor's style of the counter puncher.

Muhammad Ali decided one day a long time ago, not long after his twenty-first birthday that he was not only going to be king of the world on his own turf, but crown prince on everybody else's . . .

Which is very, very *high* thinking – even if you can't pull it off. Most people can't handle the action on whatever they chose or have to call their own turf; and the few who can usually have better sense than to push their luck any further.

That was always the difference between Muhammad Ali and the rest of us. He came, he saw, and if he didn't entirely conquer – he came as close as anybody we are likely to see in the lifetime of this doomed generation.

Res ipsa loquitur.

Rolling Stone no. 265, 18 May 1978

BIBLIOGRAPHY OF WORKS BY DR HUNTER S. THOMPSON, BY KIHM WINSHIP

'Renfro Valley',
Chicago (Sunday) *Tribune*, 18 February 1962:
' "Leary Optimism" at Home for Kennedy Visitor',
National Observer, 24 June 1962, p. 11.
   On President Valencia of Colombia.
'Nobody Is Neutral Under Aruba's Hot Sun',
NO,* 16 July 1962, p. 14.
   Bar chat and politics in Aruba, with phoιo of Thompson on the beach.
   'The author, Hunter S. Thompson, is a freelance writer reporting for
   the *National Observer* during a lengthy tour of S. America.'
'A Footloose American in a Smugglers' Den',
NO, 6 August 1962, p. 13.
   Smuggling from Aruba to Colombia, with photos by Thompson.
'Democracy Dies in Peru, But Few Seem to Mourn Its Passing',
NO, 27 August 1962, p. 16.
   Aftermath of Peruvian election and subsequent coup, with photos by
   Thompson.
'How Democracy is Nudged Ahead in Equador',
NO, 17 September 1962, p. 13.
   Role of USIS in Equador.
'Ballots in Brazil Will Measure the Allure of Leftist Nationalism',
NO, 1 October 1962, p. 4.
   Upcoming elections in Brazil.
'Operation Triangular: Bolivia's Fate Rides With It',
NO, 15 October 1962, p. 13.
   Tin-mining, strikes, etc.
'Uruguay Goes to Polls, With Economy Sagging',
NO, 19 November 1962, p. 14.
   Politics and economy in Uruguay.
'Chatty Letters During a Journey From Aruba to Rio',
NO, 31 December 1962, p. 14.
   Samples of correspondence between Thompson and his editor, with
   photo of Thompson.
'Troubled Brazil Holds Key Vote',

* *NO* is used here and below as an abbreviation for *National Observer*.

NO, 7 January 1963, pp. 1, 10.
'It's a Dictatorship, but Few Seem to Care Enough to Stay and Fight',
NO, 28 January 1963, p. 17.

Paraguay's upcoming election and current situation.

'Brazilian Soldiers Stage a Raid in Revenge',
NO, 11 February 1963, p. 13.

Army soldiers destroy a clip-joint after some difficulties the week before. 'Hunter S. Thompson, author of this account, is a *National Observer* special correspondent.'

'Leftist Trend and Empty Treasury Plague the Latin American Giant',
NO, 11 March 1963, p. 11.

Economic conditions in Brazil after election.

'A Never-Never Land High Above the Sea',
NO, 15 April 1963, p. 11.

Bolivia's political and economic problems.

'Election Watched as Barometer of Continent's Anti-Democratic Trend',
NO, 20 May 1963, p. 12.

Election in Peru.

'A Time for Sittin', Listenin', and Reverie',
NO, 3 June 1963, p. 16.

National Folk Festival in Covington, Ky. A contrast in the music and the following morning's newspapers.

'He Haunts the Ruins of His Once-Great Empire',
NO, 10 June 1963, p. 13.

Plight of the Inca Indians in Cuzco, Peru.

'Kelso Looks Just Like Any $1,307,000 Horse ... A Day With a Champion',
NO, 15 July 1963, p. 1, 7.

Visit with Kelso at Belmont Park.

'When the Thumb Was a Ticket to Adventures on the Highway ... The Extinct Hitchhiker',
NO, 22 July 1963, p. 12.

A super article. 'At age twenty-two I set what I insist is the all-time record for distance hitchhiking in Bermuda shorts; 3,700 miles in three weeks.'

'Where Are the Writing Talents of Yesteryear?'
NO, 5 August 1963, p. 17.

A review of then current novelists; Thompson as literary critic.

'Why Anti-Gringo Winds Often Blow South of the Border',
NO, 19 August 1963, p. 18.

Thompson's comments on Americans he observed while in South America; the 'ugly American' syndrome and its causes.

'An Aussie Paul Bunyan Shows Our Loggers How',

NO, 2 September 1963, p. 12.

Pacific Coast loggers championship in Quincey, California.

'Executives Crank Open Philosophy's Windows',

NO, 9 September 1963, p. 13.

On Aspen Institute for Humanistic Studies in Aspen, Colorado.

'One of the Darkest Documents Ever Put Down is *The Red Lances*',

NO, 7 October 1963, p. 19.

Review of Latin American author Arturo Ulsar Pietri's *The Red Lances*.

'Can Brazil Hold Out Until the Next Election?'

NO, 28 October 1963, p. 13.

'Donleavy Proves His Lunatic Humour Is Original',

NO, 11 November 1963, p. 17.

Review of *A Singular Man* by J. P. Donleavy.

'The Crow, a Novelist, and a Hunt; Man in Search of His Primitive Self',

NO, 2 December 1963, p. 17.

Review of Vance Bourjaily's *The Unnatural Enemy*, a book on bird hunting.

'What Miners Lost in Taking an Irishman',

NO, 16 December 1963, p. 4.

Comment on kidnapping of USIS official Tom Martin by Bolivian tin-miners.

'When Buck Fever Hits Larkspur's Slopes',

NO, 16 December 1963, p. 13.

Deer and elk hunting in Colorado; amateurs vs. experienced hunters. Dateline: Woody Creek.

'Southern City with Northern Problems',

Reporter, 19 December 1963 (v. 29), pp. 26–9.

Study of integration in Louisville, Ky. (Thompson's hometown.)

'Mr Thompson is a freelance writer.'

'And Now a Proletariat on Aspen's Ski Slopes',

NO, 10 February 1964, p. 12.

A strike by Aspen's ski patrol brings on Federal arbitration.

'The Catch is Limited in Indians' "Fish-In" ',

NO, 9 March 1964, p. 13.

Marlon Brando's attempt to regain fishing rights for Indians in Washington (State); beginnings of current Indian rights campaign in US.

'Dr Pflaum Looks at the Latins, But His View is Tired and Foggy',

NO, 9 March 1964, p. 19.

Review of *Arena of Decision* by Irving P. Pflaum.

'When the Beatniks Were Social Lions',

NO, 20 April 1964, pp. 1, 14.

Memoir of beat scene in San Francisco.

'Brazilian's Fable of a Phoney Carries the Touch of Mark Twain',
NO, 20 April 1964, p. 17.

Review of Jorge Amado's *Home Is the Sailor*.

'Golding Tries *Lord of the Flies* Formula Again, But It Falls Short',,
NO, 27 April 1964, p. 16.

Review of William Golding's *The Spire*.

'What Lured Hemingway to Ketchum?'
NO, 25 May 1964, pp. 1, 13.

Haunting consideration of why Hemingway moved to Ketchum, Idaho, and his life there; discussion of writers in America, and the pressures of success.

'Whither the Old Copper Capital of the West? To Boom or Bust?'
NO, 1 June 1964, p. 13.

Thoughts on the future of Butte, Montana.

'The Atmosphere Has Never Been Quite the Same',
NO, 15 July 1964, pp. 1, 16.

Change and friction on campus in Missoula, Montana; awakening student movement in the US.

'Why Montana's "Shanty Irishman" Corrals Votes Year After Year',
NO, 22 June 1964, p. 12.

Mike Mansfield and his Montana supporters.

'Living in the Time of Alger, Greeley, Debs',
NO, 13 July 1964, pp. 1, 16.

Dateline: Pierre, South Dakota – stories of men he has met while on the road, 'boomers' who travel looking for work.

'Bagpipes Wail, Cabers Fly as the Clans Gather',
NO, 14 September 1964, p. 12.

Scottish Gathering and Games in Santa Rosa, California.

'You'd Be Fried Like a Piece of Lean Bacon',
NO, 28 September 1964, pp. 1, 19.

Forest fires in California in late summer of 1964.

'People Want Bad Taste ... In Everything',
NO, 2 November 1964, pp. 1, 15.

Influx of 'topless joints' in the North Beach neighbourhood of San Francisco.

'A Surgeon's Fingers Fashion a Literary Career',
NO, 21 December 1964, p. 17.

On Dr Robert Geiger, MD and novelist and his struggle to be both.

'Motorcycle Gangs: Losers and Outsiders',
Nation, 17 May 1965 (v.200), pp. 522–6.

Article that eventually turned into the book *Hell's Angels*; mainly concerned with distorted press coverage of the Angels.

Reprinted as: 'Losers And Outsiders' in *Violence in the Streets*, compiled by Shalom Endleman. Chicago: Quadrangle Books, 1968, pp. 259–69.

'Nonstudent Left',

Nation, 27 September 1965 (v.201), pp. 154–8.

Study of Berkeley campus, Free Speech Movement and California's response; the non-student population, its ethos and effects.

'Collect Telegram from a Mad Dog',

Spider Magazine, 13 October 1965.

Poem.

Hell's Angels: A Strange and Terrible Saga,

New York: Random House, 1966.

'Life Styles: the Cyclist',

Esquire, January 1967 (v.67), pp. 57–63.

Excerpt from *Hell's Angels*.

'Hell's Angels',

The New Journalism, Tom Wolfe, New York: Harper & Row, 1973, pp. 340–55.

Excerpt from *Hell's Angels*, with notes by Tom Wolfe.

'Strange Rumblings in Aztlán',

'The only way to write honestly about the scene is to be a part of it.' (p. 124)

'The Ultimate Free Lancer',

The Distant Drummer, v.1 no.1, November 1967.

'Presenting: The Richard Nixon Doll',

Pageant, July 1968, pp. 6–16.

'Memoirs of a Wretched Weekend in Washington',

Boston (Sunday) *Globe*, 23 February 1969, pp. 6–11.

'Those Daring Young Men in Their Flying Machines',

Pageant, September 1969, pp. 68–78.

'The Temptations of Jean-Claude Killy',

Scanlan's Monthly, March 1970, v.1 no.1, pp. 89–100.

Thompson observing the ski champ as he merchandizes himself.

'The Kentucky Derby Is Decadent and Depraved',

Scanlan's Monthly, June 1970, v.1 no.4, pp. 1–12.

Reputed to be the first piece of 'gonzo journalism'.

Reprinted in *The New Journalism* (see above) pp. 177–87.

'Police Chief – The Indispensable Magazine of Law Enforcement', by Raoul Duke,

Scanlan's Monthly, September 1970, v.1, no.7, pp. 63–6.

Thompson, writing as Duke, airing his weapons fetish.

'The Battle of Aspen',

Rolling Stone no. 67, 1 October 1970, pp. 30–37.

Thompson describes his run for sheriff.
'The Aspen Wallposter' (advertisement),
Scanlan's Monthly, January 1971, v.1 no.8, p. 96.

Mentions that issues 1–4 are already in print, no. 5 coming. Each poster contains graphics by Thomas W. Benton on one side, 'screed' by Thompson on the other. Eight wallposters were eventually published.
Rolling Stone no. 81, 29 April 1971, pp. 30–37.

Death/murder of Ruben Salazar and subsequent mood in LA *bariro*. Describes first meeting with Oscar Zeta Acosta in the Daisy Duck in Aspen – similar to the account in Acosta's book, *Autobiography of a Brown Buffalo*.

Liner notes for: *Travelin' Lady* by Rosalie Sorrels on Sire (Polydor) SI5902. Released August 1971.

Thompson's notes on back of album cover.
'Memo From the Sports Desk: The So-Called "Jesus-Freak" Scare', by Raoul Duke,
Rolling Stone no. 90, 2 September 1971, p. 24.
'Fear and Loathing in Las Vegas: A Savage Journey to the Heart of the American Dream', by Raoul Duke,
Rolling Stone no. 95, 11 November 1971, pp. 36–48; and no. 96, 25 November 1971, pp. 38–50.

Illustrated by Ralph Steadman.
Fear and Loathing in Las Vegas,
New York: Random House, 1972.
'The "Hashbury" Is the Capital of the Hippies',
New York Times Magazine, 14 May 1967, pp. 28–9+.
'Why Boys Will Be Girls',
Pageant, August 1967, pp. 94–101.

THOMPSON'S COVERAGE OF THE ELECTION CAMPAIGN FOR *Rolling Stone*

'Fear and Loathing in Washington: Is This Trip Necessary?'
no. 99, 6 January 1972, pp. 5–8.
'Fear and Loathing in Washington: The Million Pound Shithammer',
no. 101, 3 February 1972, pp. 6–10.

Contains his comments on 'objective journalism'.
'Fear and Loathing in New Hampshire',
no. 103, 2 March 1972, pp. 6–12.

Contains car-ride-with-Nixon-talking-football story from 1968 campaign.
'Fear and Loathing: The View from Key Biscayne',
no. 104, 16 March 1972, p. 14.

On Nixon.

'Fear and Loathing: The Banshee Screams in Florida',
no. 106, 13 April 1972, pp. 6–14.
   Florida primary.
'Fear and Loathing in Wisconsin',
no. 107, 27 April 1972, p. 12.
'Fear and Loathing: Late News from Bleak House',
no. 108, 11 May 1972, pp. 26–32.
'Fear and Loathing: Crank-Time on the Low Road',
no. 110, 8 June 1972, pp. 36–40.
   Nebraska primary.
'Fear and Loathing in California: Traditional Politics with a Vengeance',
no. 112, 6 July 1972, pp. 38–43.
'Fear and Loathing: In the Eye of the Hurricane',
no. 113, 20 July 1972, pp. 22–4.
'Fear and Loathing in Miami: Old Bulls Meet the Butcher',
no. 115, 17 August 1972, pp. 30–46.
   Democratic convention.
'Fear and Loathing in Miami: Nixon Bites the Bomb',
no. 118, 28 September 1972, pp. 30–46.
'Fear and Loathing: The Fat City Blues',
no. 120, 26 October 1972, pp. 28–30.
'Ask Not For Whom the Bell Tolls ...'
no. 121, 9 November 1972, p. 48.
   Final comment on election.
'Fear and Loathing at the Superbowl: No Rest for the Wretched ...'
Rolling Stone no. 128, 15 February 1973, p. 10.
   Discusses early career as sportswriter against Superbowl backdrop.
'Time Warp: Campaign 72',
Rolling Stone no. 138, 5 July 1973, pp. 48–62.
   Excerpts from forthcoming *Fear and Loathing: On the Campaign Trail.*
Fear and Loathing: On the Campaign Trail,
San Francisco: Straight Arrow Books, 1973.
   Collection of reports Thompson sent to *Rolling Stone* from 6 January
   1972 to 15 February 1973 with additions, corrections and introduction.
'Memo from the Sports Desk & Rude Notes from a Decompression
Chamber in Miami',
Rolling Stone no. 140, 2 August 1973, pp. 8–10.
   Thompson writing as Raoul Duke and himself.
'Fear and Loathing at the Watergate: Mr Nixon Has Cashed His
Cheque',
Rolling Stone no. 144, 27 September 1973, pp. 30–39, 73–92.

Numerous Steadman illustrations.
'Fear and Loathing in the Bunker',
New York Times, 1 January 1974, p. 19.

Thompson's comments on 1973 and fearful predictions for 1974.

America by Ralph Steadman,
San Francisco: Straight Arrow, 1974.

Introduction by Thompson.

'Fear and Loathing at the Superbowl',
Rolling Stone no. 155, 28 February 1974, pp. 28–38, 42–52.

Later excerpted in *Reporting: The Rolling Stone Style* edited by Paul Scanlon, Garden City, NY: Anchor Doubleday, 1977, pp'. 215–29, with an introduction. Refers to *North Dallas Forty* by Pete Gent, a book of some interest tc Thompson scholars.

'Fear and Loathing in Washington: It Was a Nice Place. They Were Principled People, Generally' (cover title: 'The Boys in the Bag'),
Rolling Stone no. 164, 4 July 1974, pp. 42–7.

'Fear and Loathing in Limbo: The Scum Also Rises',
Rolling Stone no. 171, 10 October 1974, pp. 28–36, 49–52.

Reaction to Ford's pardon of Nixon.

'The Great Shark Hunt',
Playboy, December 1974, p. 183+.

'Fear and Loathing in Saigon: Interdicted Dispatch from the Global Affairs Desk',
Rolling Stone no. 187, 22 May 1975, pp. 32–4.

Thompson in Saigon as the Vietcong close in.

'Fear and Loathing on the Campaign Trail 76: Third Rate Romance, Low Rent Rendezvous',
Rolling Stone no. 214, 3 June 1976, pp. 54–64, 84–8.

Refers to Jimmy Carter's Law Day speech. The speech itself is excerpted in *Rolling Stone* no. 228, 16 December 1976, p. 72.

'The Banshee Screams for Buffalo Meat: Fear and Loathing in the Graveyard of the Weird',
Rolling Stone no. 254, 15 December 1977, pp. 48–59.

On Oscar Zeta Acosta; his past, his disappearance.

'Last Tango in Vegas: Fear and Loathing in the Near Room',
Rolling Stone no. 264, 4 May 1978, pp. 40–46; no. 265, 18 May 1978, pp. 62–8, 98–101.

On the Ali-Spinks championship bout.

To be published in 1979:
The Great Shark Hunt
New York: Summit Books, 1979.

A collection of shorter pieces.

BIBLIOGRAPHY OF WORKS ON DR HUNTER S. THOMPSON, BY KIHM WINSHIP

'What *The Spire* Inspires Among Reviewers',
National Observer, 1 June 1964, p. 17.
   Mentions Thompson's review of *The Spire* (*NO* 27 April 1964, p. 16).
'In and Out of Books',
Lewis Nichols,
New York Times Book Review, 5 March 1967, p. 8.
   Brief discussion of Thompson's trip to NYC to promote *Hell's Angels*.
'Thompson, Hunter',
Contemporary Authors, Detroit: Gale, 1968, v.19–20, pp. 429–30.
   Standard bio.
The Electric Kool-Aid Acid Test,
Tom Wolfe,
New York: Bantam, 1969.
   Chapter 13: The Hell's Angels pp. 150–51
   Describes how Ken Kesey met the Angels through Thompson.
' "Freak Power" Candidate May Be the Next Sheriff in Placid Aspen, Colorado',
Anthony Ripley, photo by David Hiser,
New York Times, 19 October 1970, p. 44.
'Will Aspen's Hippies Elect a Sheriff?'
Edwin A. Roberts Jr,
National Observer, 2 November 1970, p. 6.
   Good photo of Thompson, shaved scalp, can of Bud and large poster of J. Edgar Hoover in background; excellent article.
'Aspen Rejects Bid of Hippie Candidate for Sheriff's Office',
New York Times, 5 November 1970, p. 32.
   Short AP news release.
'Catcher in the Wry',
Newsweek, 1 May 1972, p. 65.
   With photo.
'Covering Politics and Getting High',
Women's Wear Daily credit, in San Francisco *Chronicle*, 10 July 1972, p. 17.
   Good photo of Thompson with bottle of Ballantine Ale.
'For Hunter Thompson, Outrage Is the Only Way Out',
Henry Allen,

Book World (Washington *Post*), 23 July 1972, p. 4.
  Interview and article.
'The Prince of Gonzo',
J. Anthony Lukas,
More: A Journalism Review, November 1972, pp. 4–7.
  Includes photo.
The Autobiography of a Brown Buffalo,
Oscar Zeta Acosta,
San Francisco: Straight Arrow, 1972.
  Thompson may be seen in the character of Karl King, Ch. 12, 14–15,
  pp. 135–141, 157–181.
'A Political Disease',
Kurt Vonnegut Jr,
Harpers Magazine, July 1973, pp. 92, 94.
  A very fine review.
The Boys on the Bus,
Timothy Crouse,
New York: Random House, 1973, pp. 54, 91–2, 159, 260, 261, 311–19,
361.
  Based on writing for *Rolling Stone* no. 119, 12 October 1972; dis-
  cusses Thompson's coverage of 1972 presidential campaign.
Us and Them: How the Press Covered the 1972 Election,
James M. Perry,
New York: Clarkson N. Potter, 1973, pp. 7, 104, 117–18, 171.
  Brief references to Thompson's political reporting.
'Loathing and Ignorance on the Campaign Trail: 1972',
Wayne Booth,
Columbia Journalism Review, November 1973, pp. 7–12.
  Critical discussion of Theodore White's *The Making of the President
  1972* and Thompson's campaign coverage; sets forth standard con-
  servative objections to Thompson's style, methods, etc.
'Hunter S. Thompson: Commando Journalism',
In 'On the Scene', *Playboy*, November 1973, p. 188.
  Short paragraph with photo.
'Paranoia and Wild Turkey: Hunter Thompson in Buffalo',
Gene Goffin,
Buffalo New Times, 3 March 1974.
  Good, but hard to find, article in a new defunct Buffalo, NY, weekly
  paper.
'Playboy Interview: Hunter Thompson',
Craig Vetter,
Playboy, November 1974, p. 75+.
  The major biographical source.

'Trudeaumania',
Newsweek, 13 January 1975, p. 49.

On Garry Trudeau's *Doonesbury*: 'Last week he was parodying *Rolling Stone* writer Hunter Thompson.'

'The Apocalyptic Fact and the Eclipse of Fiction in Recent American Prose Narratives',
Mas'ud Zavarzadeh,
Journal of American Studies, April 1975, v.9 no.1, p. 69.

Truth outstripping fiction in work of Mailer, Thompson, Wolfe, etc.

From *The Journal of Popular Culture*, summer 1975:

'Gonzo',
James Green,
pp. 204–10.

'The Freaking New Journalism',
Kent Jacobson,
pp. 183–96.

Discusses Kentucky Derby article.

'There Shall Be No Night',
Elizabeth Landreth,
pp. 197–203.

Discusses Thompson's views of Las Vegas as seen in *Fear and Loathing in Las Vegas*.

'We've Been Had By the New Journalism: A Put Down',
Robert J. VanDellen,
p. 219.

Discusses Kentucky Derby article.

'Fear and Loathing at *Rolling Stone*',
Sandy Rovner,
Washington *Post*, 30 May 1975, B, p. 3.

Short article on Thompson's departure from *Rolling Stone*.

'Manifest Destiny in Pago Pago',
Nicholas von Hoffman and Garry Trudeau,
Rolling Stone no. 194, 28 August 1975, p. 32+.

Pictures and comment on Trudeau's 'Uncle Duke', a character in Doonesbury patterned after Thompson.

The Fight,
Norman Mailer,
Boston: Little, Brown, 1975, pp. 33, 118–21.

Mailer comments on Thompson in Zaire to cover Foreman-Ali bout for *Rolling Stone*.

'Doonesbury: Drawing and Quartering for Fun and Profit',
Time, 9 February 1976, pp. 57–66.

Cover drawing of characters with Uncle Duke in the centre; photo, drawing and famous comment by Thompson re Trudeau: 'If I ever catch the little bastard, I'll tear his lungs out.'

'Thompson, Hunter',
Contemporary Authors,
Detroit: Gale, 1976, v.17–20, first revision, p. 728.
Standard bio, updated from earlier *CA*.

'Travels Through America',
Harrison E. Salisbury,
Esquire, February 1976, p. 28+.
Thompson on pp. 43–4 comments on violence in American history and life.

'Dr Hunter S. Thompson and a New Psychiatry',
Arnold J. Mandell, MD,
Psychiatry Digest, v.37, pp. 12–17.
Reprint March 1976 by Medical Digest, Inc.
Discussion of Thompson's drug intake and its effects on his prose style.

'New Psychiatry',
William Stuckey,
Science Digest, March 1976, pp. 26–34.
Discusses Dr Mandell's article.

'TRB: What Carter's Not',
New Republic, 9 June 1976, p. 2.
Opinions on Jimmy Carter, including Thompson's, which is prefaced, 'And here is an unusual character witness ...'

'Fear and Loathing and Ripping Off',
T. Griffith,
Time, 19 July 1976, pp. 52–3.

'Checking in with Dr Gonzo',
Playboy, November 1976, p. 254.
Short article with photo.

'The Rolling Stone Saga, Part Two',
Robert Sam Anson,
New Times, 10 December 1976, p. 22+.
Longest article available on Thompson's time at *Rolling Stone*, numerous photos.

'Member of the Lynching',
Craig Vetter,
Aspen Anthology, Winter 1976, pp. 63–80.
A gonzo memoir by the author of the *Playboy* interview, concerning mutual adventures in Washington, DC, in the summer of 1974.

The Book of Lists,
David Wallechinsky,

New York: Morrow, 1977,
    'Twelve writers Who Ran (Unsuccessfully) for Public Office', p. 245.
    'Fifteen people Who Have Taken Peyote or Mescaline', p. 404.
'The Last Laugh',
George Plimpton.
New York Review of Books, 4 August 1977, p. 29.
    Plimpton's article is on death and death fantasies; mentions that
    Thompson has contributed one to a forthcoming book, *Shadow Box*.
Shadow Box,
George Plimpton,
New York: G. P. Putnam's Sons, 1977.
    Numerous Thompson stories; the book is indexed, but it's worth the
    time to read the whole thing.
'Hunter Thompson: The good doctor tells all ... about Carter, cocaine,
adrenalin and the birth of gonzo journalism',
Ron Rosenbaum,
High Times, September 1977, pp. 31–9.
'Literary Lasagna',
Charles T. Powers,
Rolling Stone, 6 October 1977, p. 47.
    Interview with Elaine Kaufman of 'Elaine's' in NYC; she describes
    cashing a cheque for Thompson as if it were a high-wire act.
'After Begelman: The Whiz Kids Take Over',
Maureen Orth,
New York, 12 June 1978, pp. 59–64.
    Mentions film in progress on Thompson.
'The Aspen Story',
Outside, September/October 1978, p. 25+.
    Three articles on Aspen, with mentions of Thompson's run for Sheriff;
    photo on p. 33.
'Notes from the Battle of New Orleans',
George Plimpton,
Rolling Stone no. 277, 2 November 1978, pp. 52–6.
    Article on the second Ali-Spinks heavyweight title fight; reference to
    HST as intended collaborator for this article on p. 55.

picador.com

blog
videos
interviews
extracts